Sustainable Civil Infrastructures

Sustainable Civil Infrastructures (SUCI) is a series of peer-reviewed books and proceedings based on the best studies on emerging research from all fields related to sustainable infrastructures and aiming at improving our well-being and day-to-day lives. The infrastructures we are building today will shape our lives tomorrow. The complex and diverse nature of the impacts due to weather extremes on transportation and civil infrastructures can be seen in our roadways, bridges, and buildings. Extreme summer temperatures, droughts, flash floods, and rising numbers of freeze-thaw cycles pose challenges for civil infrastructure and can endanger public safety. We constantly hear how civil infrastructures need constant attention, preservation, and upgrading. Such improvements and developments would obviously benefit from our desired book series that provide sustainable engineering materials and designs. The economic impact is huge and much research has been conducted worldwide. The future holds many opportunities, not only for researchers in a given country, but also for the worldwide field engineers who apply and implement these technologies. We believe that no approach can succeed if it does not unite the efforts of various engineering disciplines from all over the world under one umbrella to offer a beacon of modern solutions to the global infrastructure. Experts from the various engineering disciplines around the globe will participate in this series, including: Geotechnical, Geological, Geoscience, Petroleum, Structural, Transportation, Bridge, Infrastructure, Energy, Architectural, Chemical and Materials, and other related Engineering disciplines.

SUCI series is now indexed in SCOPUS

and EI Compendex.

Imad Aboudrar · Farhad Ilahi Bakhsh ·
Anand Nayyar · Ilias Ouachtouk
Editors

Innovative Technologies on Electrical Power Systems for Smart Cities Infrastructure

Proceedings of the 1st International Conference on Electrical Systems and Smart Technologies

Springer

Editors
Imad Aboudrar
Electrical Engineering
Université Ibn Zohr
Agadir, Morocco

Anand Nayyar
Faculty of Information Technology
Duy Tan University
Da Nang, Vietnam

Farhad Ilahi Bakhsh
National Institute of Technology
Srinagar, Jammu and Kashmir, India

Ilias Ouachtouk
ENSAM Casablanca
Hassan II University
Casablanca, Morocco

ISSN 2366-3405 ISSN 2366-3413 (electronic)
Sustainable Civil Infrastructures
ISBN 978-3-031-86704-0 ISBN 978-3-031-86705-7 (eBook)
https://doi.org/10.1007/978-3-031-86705-7

This Springer imprint is published by the registered company Springer Nature Switzerland AG
The registered company address is: Gewerbestrasse 11, 6330 Cham, Switzerland

This book is dedicated to the brilliant minds and relentless innovators who work tirelessly to advance technologies for a smarter, more sustainable future. To the researchers, engineers, and visionaries, your efforts illuminate the path toward better living, resilient cities, and a harmonious coexistence with our environment. We also honor the educators who nurture future generations of scientists and engineers and the dreamers who dare to envision a brighter tomorrow.

Foreword

The rapid evolution of technology is fundamentally transforming the way we live, work, and interact with our surroundings. At the heart of these transformations lies a growing need for intelligent, sustainable, and resilient infrastructure, especially in the realm of electrical power systems for smart cities.

This book, *Innovative Technologies on Electrical Power Systems for Smart Cities Infrastructure*, serves as a testament to the remarkable strides achieved in the field. It brings together contributions from esteemed researchers and practitioners who have explored cutting-edge solutions across a wide spectrum of topics, including artificial intelligence, cybersecurity, advanced manufacturing, and sustainable energy systems.

As we stand on the threshold of unprecedented urbanization and technological advancement, the concepts and solutions presented here are more critical than ever. These chapters delve into the integration of technology with infrastructure, aiming to address challenges such as energy efficiency, cybersecurity threats, and urban sustainability. The work presented is not only innovative but also actionable, providing a roadmap for both researchers and practitioners.

As you delve into these pages, you will encounter novel ideas, groundbreaking research, and practical applications that redefine the boundaries of technological innovation. These contributions underscore the importance of interdisciplinary collaboration and the collective pursuit of excellence to address the challenges of our time.

We are at the cusp of a technological renaissance. This book invites readers to explore and be inspired by the possibilities it unveils.

Preface

The book you hold in your hands is the culmination of years of research, collaboration, and dedication by a global community of scholars and professionals. It reflects the proceedings and innovative ideas presented at ICESST—the International Conference on Electrical Systems for Sustainable Technologies—hosted at the Higher School of Technology, Dakhla, Morocco, from December 11 to 13, 2024.

The overarching theme of this book, *Innovative Technologies on Electrical Power Systems for Smart Cities Infrastructure*, reflects the critical need for sustainable and intelligent solutions in our ever-evolving urban landscapes. Each chapter explores a unique facet of technological innovation, offering insights into how advanced systems can shape the future of smart cities.

This book is organized into six thematic sections: Artificial Intelligence and Smart Systems, Sustainable Energy and Infrastructure, Cybersecurity and IoT Solutions, Advanced Manufacturing, Optimization and Control Systems, and Smart City Applications. These themes reflect the diverse yet interconnected challenges and opportunities in building resilient and efficient urban ecosystems.

Special thanks go to the contributors who have not only enriched this volume with their work but also extended the frontiers of knowledge. This book serves as both a reference and a source of inspiration, capturing the spirit of innovation that drives progress in smart city infrastructure.

We hope that the ideas and knowledge shared within these pages will inspire further exploration, innovation, and collaboration.

Imad Aboudrar
Farhad Ilahi Bakhsh
Anand Nayyar
Ilias Ouachtouk

Acknowledgments

The successful completion of this book would not have been possible without the collective efforts of numerous individuals and organizations. We extend our heartfelt gratitude to the authors, whose exceptional contributions form the backbone of this volume. Their hard work and dedication are deeply appreciated. We also thank the reviewers and editorial board members for their invaluable feedback and guidance, which ensured the highest quality of the chapters.

Our sincere thanks go to the organizers of ICESST, particularly the general chairs, Pr. Imad Aboudrar and Pr. Ilias Ouachtouk, for providing a platform that fostered knowledge exchange and innovation. We are grateful to the Higher School of Technology in Dakhla, Morocco, for hosting the conference and supporting this publication.

We also acknowledge the unwavering support of the Presidents of Hassan II University and Ibn Zohr University. Special thanks to Pr. Abdelmajid Badri (Director of ENSAM-CASA) and Pr. Zouhir Mahani (Director of EST Dakhla) for their vision and inspiring leadership.

Our heartfelt gratitude goes to our sponsors and partners for their generous support. We also thank the speakers, industrial experts, and moderators for their insightful and impactful presentations.

The organizing committee deserves special recognition for their dedication, rigor, and efficiency. We are deeply appreciative of the participants and delegates whose enthusiasm and rich discussions added immense value to the event.

Lastly, we express our deepest gratitude to our families and loved ones for their unwavering encouragement and patience throughout this journey.

Finally, we would like to thank you, the readers, for your interest in this book. We hope it serves as a valuable resource and inspires future advancements in the field. May it ignite your curiosity and drive for innovation in building the smart cities of tomorrow.

Organization

General Chairs

Imad Aboudrar	EST Dakhla, IBN ZOHR University, Morocco
lias Ouachtouk	ENSAM Casablanca, Hassan II University, Morocco

Honorary Chairs

Abdelaziz Bendou	President of IBN ZOHR University, Morocco
Houssine Azeddoug	President of Hassan II University, Morocco
Zouhir Mahani	Director of EST Dakhla
Abdelmajid Badri	Director of ENSAM Casablanca

Program Committee

Khalid Dahi	Centrale casablanca, Morocco
Soumia El Hani	ENSAM Rabat, Mohammed V University, Morocco
Mourad Zegrari	ENSAM Casablanca, UH2C, Morocco
Sahar Saoud	Ibn Zohr University, EST Dakhla, Morocco
Fatih Barki	Ibn Zohr University, EST Dakhla, Morocco
Ayoub Bahnasse	ENSAM Casablanca, UH2C, Morocco
Anand Nayyar	School of Computer Science-Duy Tan University, Da Nang, Vietnam
Farhad Ilahi Bakhsh	National Institute of Technology, India
Abdelhafid Ait Elmahjoub	ENSAM Casablanca, UH2C, Morocco
Radouane Majdoul	ENSAM Casablanca, UH2C, Morocco
Ahmed El Moukhtari	Faculty of Sciences Ben M'sick, UH2C, CASABLANCA, Morocco
Said Idrissi	Mohammed V University, Rabat, Morocco
Nabil El Fezazi	Ibn Zohr University, EST Dakhla, Morocco.
Mohammed Bendaoued	Hassan I University, FST Settat, Morocco
Bouchra Bessas	ENSAM Casablanca, Hassan II University, Morocco
Khaoula Chaoui El Ghor	Ibn Zohr University, EST Dakhla, Morocco

Maha Annoukoubi	Centrale Casablanca, Morocco
Meriem Houmer	Ibn Zohr University, EST Dakhla, Morocco
Kaoutar Saidi Alaoui	Ibn Zohr University, EST Dakhla, Morocco
Nadia Machkour	ENSAM Casablanca, Hassan II University, Morocco
Meryem Khissi	Ibn Zohr University, EST Dakhla, Morocco
Ghita Zaz	ENSAM Casablanca, UH2C, Morocco
Wajih Rhalem	ENSAM Rabat, Mohammed V University, Morocco
Hammadi Laghridat	SUPTECH SANTE
Mouaad Mohy-Eddine	ENSAM Casablanca, Hassan II University , Morocco
Mounir Abid	Ibn Zohr University, EST Dakhla, Morocco
Lahssan Ben Tarla	ENSAM Casablanca, UH2C, Morocco
Hamza Ouachtouk	Faculty of Sciences Ben M'sick, UH2C, CASABLANCA, Morocco
Fatima Hassine	Ibn Zohr University, EST Dakhla, Morocco
El Mehdi Mellouli	Mohammed V University in Rabat
Elmehdi Benmalek	Mohammed V University in Rabat
Fouad Demami	Ibn Zohr University, EST Guelmim, Morocco
Mohamed Fahim	Ibn Tofail University, Kenitra, Morocco
Arjdal El Hanafi	Faculty of science, Ibn Zohr University, Morocco
Ahmed Sali	FSDEM, Sidi Mohamed Ben Abdellah University
Ishak Hbiak	Hassania School of Public Works
Azidine Guezzaz	EST Essaouira, Cadi Ayyad University
Moutchou Mohamed	ENSAM Casablanca, Hassan II University , Morocco
Nabila Rabbah	ENSAM Casablanca, Hassan II University , Morocco
Anas Had	Jean Monnet University Saint-Etienne
Ibtissam Kharchouf	Florida International University in Miami, USA
Marouane Rayyam	ENSAM Rabat, Mohammed V University, Morocco
Soufiane El Moumni	ENSAM Casablanca, Hassan II University, Morocco
Abdelwahed Touati	ENSAM Casablanca, Hassan II University, Morocco
Abdelilah Chalh	FST Mohammedia, Hassan II University, Morocco
Said Bahassine	ENSAM Casablanca, Hassan II University, Morocco
Loubna El Faquih	ENSAM Casablanca, UH2C, Morocco

Mohamed Azmi	ENSAM Casablanca, Hassan II University, Morocco
Mustapha Elyaqouti	Faculty of science, Ibn Zohr University, Morocco
Sara Rabiai	Ibn Zohr University, EST Dakhla, Morocco
Zahra Saad	Ibn Zohr University, EST Dakhla, Morocco
Samira El Hafid Allah	Ibn Zohr University, EST Dakhla, Morocco
Baba Youssef	ENSAM Casablanca, Hassan II University, Morocco
Baghouri Mustapha	ENSAM Casablanca, Hassan II University, Morocco
Bounouar Said	ENSAM Casablanca, Hassan II University, Morocco
EL Afia Aziz	ENSAM Casablanca, Hassan II University, Morocco
El Hansali Hasnaa	Abdelmalek Essaâdi University, Faculty of Sciences and Techniques
Elbouchikhi Elhoussine	ISEN Yncréa Ouest, ISEN Nantes, France
Essaadaoui Alami	ENSAM Casablanca Hassan II University, Morocco
Hamdoun Ouafae	Sultane Moulay Slimane University, Beni Mellal, Morocco
Hamlich Mohamed	ENSAM Casablanca Hassan II University, Morocco
HISSOU Hasna	Chouaib Doukkali University, Morocco
Mottahir Saad	University of sidi Mohammed Ben Abdellah, Fez, Morocco
Qabouche Hicham	ENSAM Casablanca, UH2C, Morocco

Contents

AI for Predictive and Sustainable Infrastructure

AI for Smart Urban Development and Sustainability

Smart Manufacturing and Urban Infrastructure Innovations

Electrical Power Systems, Sustainable Technologies and Smart City Infrastructure

Novel Metamaterials Based Patch Antenna for 6G and Biomedical Applications

Siraj Younes[1(✉)], Saidi Alaoui Kaoutar[2], and Foshi Jaouad[1]

[1] ISMSE Laboratory, Faculty of Sciences and Technology Errachidia, Moulay Ismail University, Meknes, Morocco
sirajyounes95@gmail.com

[2] EST DAKHLA, Ibn Zohr University, Agadir, Morocco

Abstract. This paper introduces an innovative approach to enhance the performance of a terahertz (THz) patch antenna through the integration of metamaterials (MTM). The proposed design features a rectangular slotted patch antenna with a partial ground plane operating at 3.64 THz. Positioned on a silicon dioxide (SiO_2) substrate with a dielectric constant of 4 and thickness of 2 μm, the antenna is complemented by a 6 × 5 MTM array placed on an FR4 substrate (dielectric constant of 4.2, thickness 2 μm) beneath it. This strategic integration significantly improves the antenna's performance by enhancing impedance matching and directivity. The results show a notable reduction in return loss from −16.21 dB to −30.01 dB, a gain increase from 2.25 dB to 4.45 dB, and an improvement in directivity from 3.76 dB to 5.88 dB. All simulations were conducted using HFSS software. These enhancements demonstrate the potential of metamaterials to address the performance limitations of THz antennas, offering a promising solution for high-frequency applications.

Keywords: Patch Antenna · Metamaterials · Biomedical applications · 6G

1 Introduction

The terahertz (THz) frequency range, spanning from 0.1 to 10 THz, is increasingly recognized for its potential in transformative applications such as high-resolution biomedical imaging [1, 2], advanced communication systems [3], and non-destructive testing [4]. THz patch antennas are particularly advantageous for these applications due to their compact size, ease of integration with electronic systems, and potential for high-resolution sensing [5, 6].In other hands, the advent of 6G technology is set to revolutionize communication systems with unprecedented data rates, ultra-reliable low-latency communications, and massive connectivity. THz frequencies are anticipated to play a critical role in achieving these goals, providing the bandwidth necessary for 6G networks [7–9]. Despite these advantages, THz patch antennas are plagued by significant performance challenges, including low radiation efficiency, narrow bandwidth, and reduced gain. These issues are largely attributed to high material losses and inefficient wave propagation characteristics inherent at THz frequencies. Traditional approaches, such as optimizing antenna geometry or using advanced materials, have yielded only incremental improvements and have not fully addressed these performance constraints.

I. Aboudrar et al. (Eds.): ICESST 2024, SUCI, pp. 3–12, 2025.
https://doi.org/10.1007/978-3-031-86705-7_1

Metamaterials, artificially engineered materials designed to exhibit unique electromagnetic properties, offer a promising solution to these challenges. By incorporating metamaterials with engineered responses such as negative refractive indices and tailored dispersion characteristics, it is possible to manipulate electromagnetic waves in ways that conventional materials cannot achieve. Incorporating metamaterials into antenna designs results in significantly enhanced performance. The enhancement of patch antenna gain using MTM is discussed in [10], while the strategy for bandwidth improvement with MTM is outlined in [11, 12]. Further, [13] provides a detailed analysis of how negative permeability MTM can be employed to boost both gain and directivity, enhancing the antenna's overall efficiency and focusing its radiation pattern more effectively. In [14], A gain enhancement of 4.42 dB is achieved with the help of a 3-layer HRI-based Lens superstrate. These studies collectively highlight the versatile applications of MTM in advancing antenna design.

This paper investigates the enhancement of THz patch antennas through the innovative integration of metamaterials to address critical performance requirements in 6G communication systems and biomedical applications. We present a novel metamaterial design optimized for THz frequencies, specifically developed to overcome prevalent challenges like narrow bandwidth, low radiation efficiency, and inadequate impedance matching. Our study involves detailed simulations and theoretical analyses to assess the metamaterials' impact on key antenna performance metrics, including radiation efficiency, gain, directivity, and bandwidth. Furthermore, we provide a comprehensive examination of how these metamaterials interact with THz electromagnetic fields, offering insights into their effects on wave propagation, resonance behavior, and impedance matching.

This paper is organized as follows: The first section presents the designs of the antenna and metamaterials, outlining their configurations and theoretical principles. The second section offers a detailed analysis of the results obtained from the simulations. The paper concludes with a summary of findings, discusses the limitations of the study, and outlines potential directions for future research.

2 Design of the Proposed Metamaterials Based Antenna

2.1 Design of the Patch Antenna

The suggested antenna is a patch with a partial ground, placed on a silicon dioxide (SiO_2) substrate with a dielectric of 4 and a thickness of 2 μm. The complete design is shown in Fig. 1, while Table 1 provides the dimensions of the antenna. With an operating frequency of 3.64 THz, the antenna has overall dimensions of W $\times$ L. To improve the impedance matching, the radiating element includes three rectangular slots, and the ground plane is partially reduced to dimensions of W $\times$ Lg. Figure 2 illustrates the step-by-step design process used to reach the final configuration. This design strategy, which involves selecting a specific substrate and incorporating slots into the patch, guarantees optimal performance at the targeted frequency.

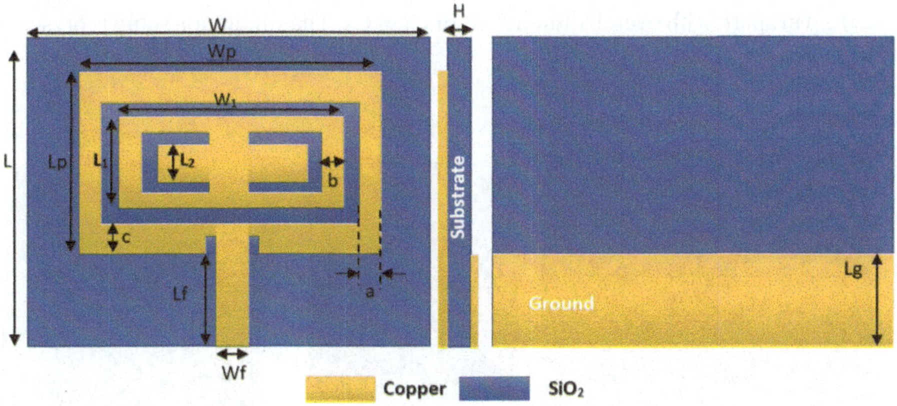

Fig. 1. Design of the proposed Patch antenna.

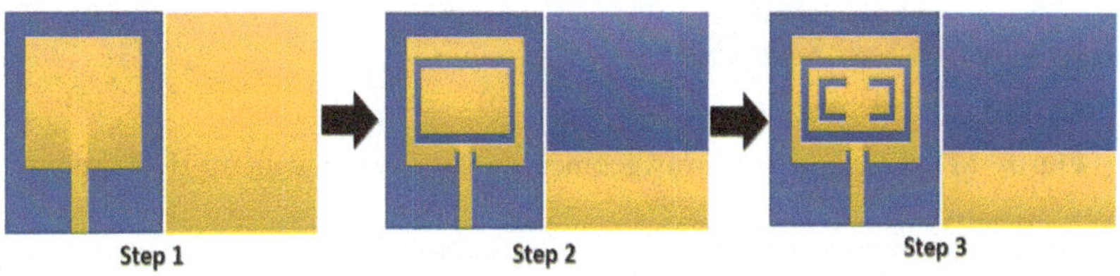

Fig. 2. Design process.

Table 1. The proposed antenna dimensions.

Variable	Value(μm)	Variable	Value(μm)
W	69	L2	11
L	54	Wf	4.8
Lp	35	Lf	15
Wp	46	a	3.5
W1	35	b	3
L1	21	c	5
H	2	Lg	18.7

2.2 Design of the Metamaterials

The suggested metamaterials features a 6 × 5 array of elements positioned on an FR4 substrate, which has a dielectric of 4.2, a loss tangent of 0.02, and a thickness of 2 μm. The total dimensions of the metamaterials are $W_{MTM} \times L_{MTM}$, as presented in Fig. 3(a) and detailed in Table 2. Figure 3(b) shows the structure and configuration of the split-ring resonator unit cells. Each unit cell in the array contains periodic split-ring resonators, spaced 2 μm apart, with overall dimensions of $C_1 \times C_4$. The simulation setup is presented in Fig. 3(c).

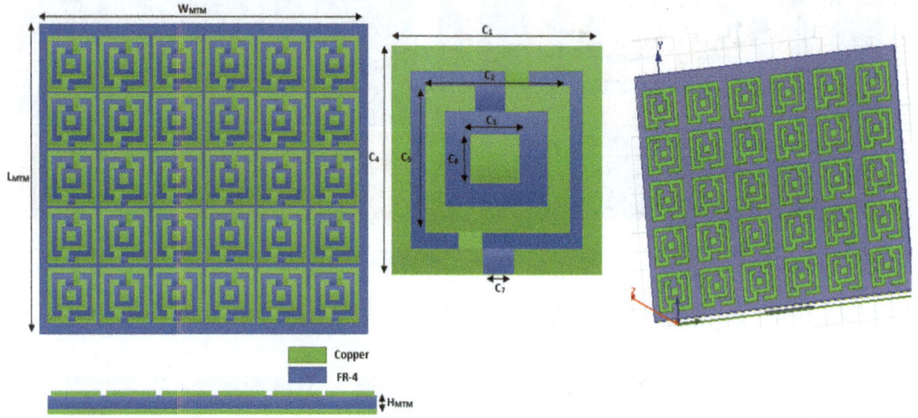

Fig. 3. MTM Design; (a) Array geometries, (b) The unit cell, (c) HFSS setup

Table 2. The proposed MTM dimensions.

Variable	Value(μm)	Variable	Value(μm)
W_{MTM}	79	C3	2
L_{MTM}	64	C4	10
H_{MTM}	2	C5	6
C1	10	C6	2
C2	6	C7	2

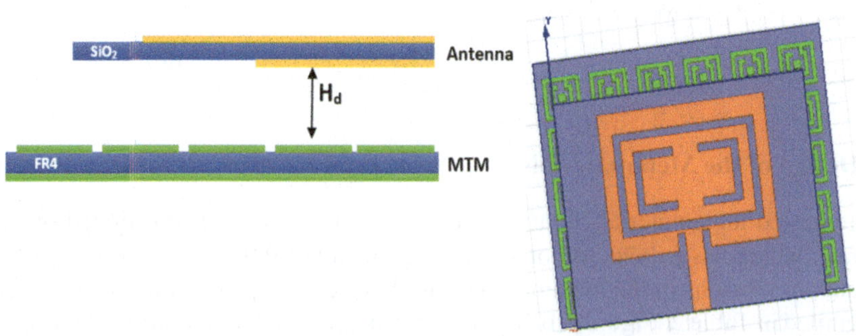

Fig. 4. Position of the antenna and MTM.

The MTM is situated under the antenna at a distance H_d of 20 μm as showed in Fig. 4. This strategic placement enhances the antenna impedance matching by optimizing the interaction between the antenna and the surrounding medium, leading to more efficient transmission and reception of signals. Additionally, the MTM reduces energy loss by minimizing unwanted radiation and surface waves, thereby improving overall antenna performance, including gain, directivity and bandwidth. This configuration is particularly beneficial for applications where compact size and high efficiency are critical.

3 Results and Discussion

3.1 Reflection Coefficient

The reflection coefficient of the proposed antenna is presented in Fig. 5, the inclusion of metamaterials in antenna design significantly improves its performance by enhancing impedance matching, as demonstrated by the sharp dip in the reflection coefficient S_{11} curve. With the MTM, the antenna achieves a much lower S_{11} value of −30.01 dB at 3.64 THz, compared to −16.21 dB without MTM, indicating a substantial reduction in reflected power and more efficient radiation. Furthermore, the MTM broaden the frequency range over which the antenna maintains an S_{11} below −10 dB, thereby extending the operational bandwidth from 210 GHz to 300 GHz, making the antenna more effective across a wider spectrum. This enhancement highlights the potential of metamaterials in optimizing antenna performance for various applications.

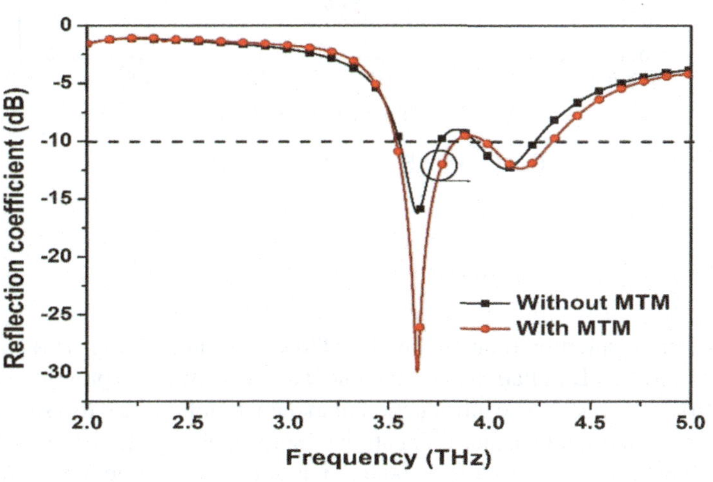

Fig. 5. Reflection coefficient of the proposed antenna.

3.2 VSWR

The Voltage Standing Wave Ratio (VSWR) of the proposed patch antenna with and without the inclusion of MTM is illustrated in Fig. 6. The VSWR is a measure of how efficiently radio-frequency power is transmitted from the power source, through a transmission line, into the load (antenna). A lower VSWR value, ideally close to 1, indicates better matching and less reflection of power. In our case, the VSWR without MTM has a minimum of 1.36 at 3.64THz, indicating relatively good matching. However, with the inclusion of MTM, the VSWR shows an even more pronounced dip, reaching a value of 1.06 at the same frequency, demonstrating significantly improved impedance matching. Additionally, the VSWR with MTM remains below 2 over a wider frequency range than without MTM, suggesting an extended operational bandwidth and overall better antenna performance. Thus, the incorporation of metamaterials enhances the antenna's efficiency by reducing the VSWR and optimizing power transmission over a broader frequency range.

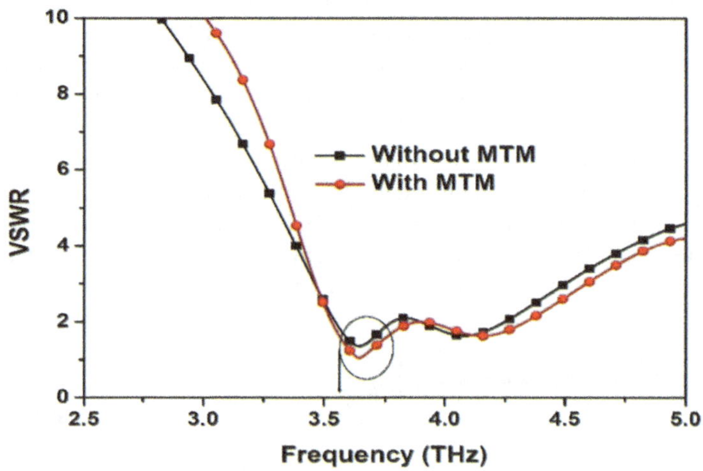

Fig. 6. VSWR of the proposed antenna.

3.3 Gain

The 2D radiation pattern without and with MTM is presented in Fig. 7(a) and Fig. 7(b) respectively and the 3D radiation pattern without and with MTM is presented in Fig. 8(a) and Fig. 8(b) respectively. The introduction of metamaterials has led to a substantial gain improvement for the antenna, increasing its maximum gain from 2.25 dB to 4.45 dB. This gain enhancement results from the metamaterials ability to manipulate electromagnetic waves through their unique properties, such as negative permeability and permittivity. These properties help to confine and guide electromagnetic waves more effectively, directing a greater portion of the radiated energy in the desired direction.

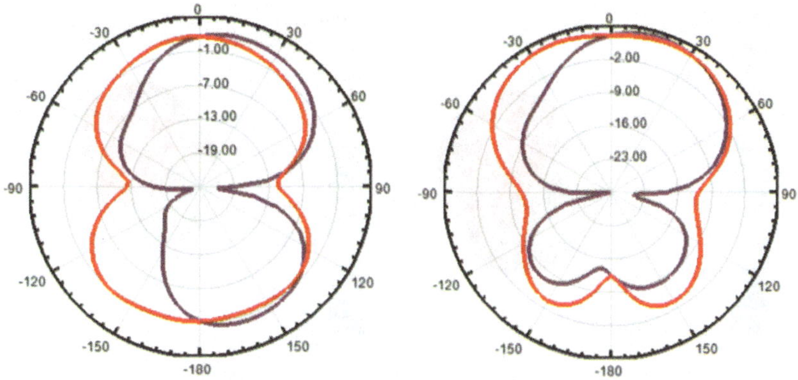

(a) (b)

Fig. 7. 2D radiation pattern; (a) without MTM (b) with MTM.

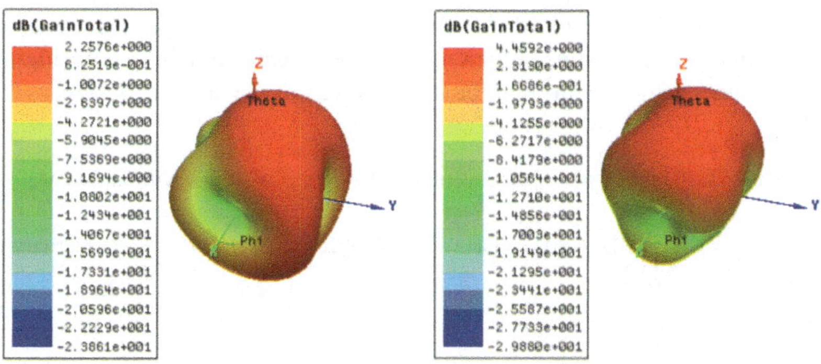

(a) (b)

Fig. 8. 3D radiation pattern; (a) without MTM (b) with MTM.

3.4 Directivity

The directivity of proposed antenna is disputed in Fig. 9. The results reveal that the use of metamaterials has significantly enhanced the antenna performance. Figure 9(a), illustrates the antenna directivity without metamaterials, the maximum directivity reaches 3.76 dB. In comparison, Fig. 9(b), shows the antenna operating with metamaterials, where the maximum directivity increases to 5.88 dB. This increase in directivity indicates that the antenna with metamaterials is more effective at concentrating radiated power in the desired direction. The sharper, more focused radiation pattern with metamaterials suggests that the antenna is better able to transmit or receive signals in a specific direction, thereby improving its overall efficiency and reducing the power lost to side lobes and back radiation. The enhancement in directivity is due to the unique electromagnetic properties of metamaterials, which optimize wave propagation and reduce scattering, leading to a more directional radiation pattern.

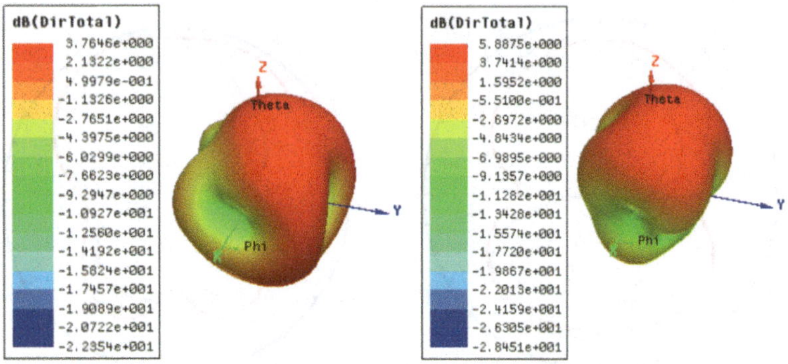

(a) (b)

Fig. 9. Directivity of the proposed antenna; (a) without MTM (b) with MTM.

Table 3, presents a comprehensive comparison of the antenna performance metrics with and without the integration MTM. The comparison includes key parameters such as operating frequency, reflection coefficient, bandwidth, gain, and directivity, highlighting the improvements achieved through the use of MTM in the antenna design.

Table 3. Comparison of the antenna performance with and without MTM.

	S_{11}(dB)	BW(GHz)	VSWR	Gain(dB)	Directivity(dB)
Without MTM	−16.21	210	1.36	2.25	3.76
With MTM	−30.01	300	1.06	4.45	5.88

Table 4 offers a detailed analysis between our proposed antenna design and those reported in other studies, showcasing the effectiveness of our approach. The results indicate that our antenna achieves enhanced performance across several key parameters, such as gain, bandwidth, and directivity, demonstrating its advantages over existing designs.

Table 4. Comparison of our design with previous works.

Ref	Frequency(THz)	S_{11}(dB)	BW(GHz)	Gain(dB)	Directivity(dB)
[15]	3.26	−12.26	260.26	-	4.26
[16]	3.65	−29	-	-	6.06
[17]	4.17	−34.74	180	6.8	6.42
This work	3.64	−30.01	300	4.45	5.88

4 Conclusion

This study demonstrates notable performance improvements in a terahertz patch antenna obtained through the strategic use of metamaterials. By integrating a 6×5 element metamaterials structure beneath a rectangular slotted patch antenna with a partial ground structure at an operating frequency of 3.64 THz, we achieved significant enhancements in critical antenna parameters. The MTM integration greatly improved impedance matching, reducing the reflection coefficient from −16.21 dB to −30.01 dB. Furthermore, the antenna's gain increased from 2.45 dB to 4.45 dB, while its directivity improved from 3.76 dB to 5.88 dB. These findings validate the success of incorporating metamaterials (MTM) in mitigating the inherent challenges of THz patch antennas.

References

1. Srinivasa Rao, V., Reddy, K.V.V.S., Prasad, A.M.: Bandwidth enhancement of metamaterial loaded microstrip antenna using double layered substrate. IJEECS **5**, 661 (2017). https://doi.org/10.11591/ijeecs.v5.i3.pp661-665
2. Wan, M., Healy, J.J., Sheridan, J.T.: Terahertz phase imaging and biomedical applications. Opt. Laser Technol. **122**, 105859 (2020). https://doi.org/10.1016/j.optlastec.2019.105859
3. Bergen, M.H., Lowry, S.N., Mitchell, M.E., Jenne, M.F., Collier, C.M., Holzman, J.F.: Terahertz wireless communication systems: challenges and solutions for realizations of effective bidirectional links. Opt. Continuum. **2**, 2154 (2023). https://doi.org/10.1364/OPTCON.500014
4. Besson, A., Minasyan, A.: Terahertz Imaging for Composite Non Destructive Testing
5. Islam, M.T., Islam, S.S., Rocky, A.S., Alam, A., Chy, M.H., Faruque, M.R.I.: Design of a microstrip patch sensor antenna for the measurement of permittivity. Mater. Today Proc. **42**, 1341–1344 (2021). https://doi.org/10.1016/j.matpr.2020.12.1192
6. Younes, S., Jaouad, F.: Enhancement of a THz patch antenna performance using metamaterials for biomedical applications. In: Mejdoub, Y., Elamri, A. (eds.) Proceeding of the International Conference on Connected Objects and Artificial Intelligence (COCIA2024), pp. 22–28. Springer, Cham (2024). https://doi.org/10.1007/978-3-031-70411-6_4
7. Hajiyat, Z.R.M., Ismail, A., Sali, A., Hamidon, Mohd.N.: Antenna in 6G wireless communication system: specifications, challenges, and research directions. Optik. **231**, 166415 (2021). https://doi.org/10.1016/j.ijleo.2021.166415
8. Asaad, N.S., Saleh, A.M., Alzubaidy, M.A.: Analyzing performance of THz band graphene-based MIMO antenna for 6G applications. JTIT (2024). https://doi.org/10.26636/jtit.2024.3.1518
9. Saeed, M.A., Nwajana, A.: U-shaped terahertz microstrip patch antenna for 6G future communications. In: 2023 7th International Electromagnetic Compatibility Conference (EMC Turkiye), pp. 1–4. IEEE, İstanbul, Turkiye (2023). https://doi.org/10.1109/EMCTurkiye59424.2023.10287461
10. Khouser, G.H., Choukiker, Y.K., Bhowmick, A.: Gain enhancement in microstrip patch antenna with high negative refractive index 3D-metamaterial inspired superstrate for wireless applications. IEEE Access **12**, 7372–7381 (2024). https://doi.org/10.1109/ACCESS.2024.3352118
11. Dawar, P., De, A.: Bandwidth Enhancement of RMPA using ENG metamaterials at THz (2013)
12. Sansa, I., Nasri, A., Zairi, H.: Bandwidth enhancement of an anctenna based metamaterial using characteristic mode analysis for microwave applications. **18** (2023)

13. Gao, X.-J., Cai, T., Zhu, L.: Enhancement of gain and directivity for microstrip antenna using negative permeability metamaterial. AEU-Int. J. Electron. C. **70**, 880–885 (2016). https://doi.org/10.1016/j.aeue.2016.03.019
14. Reddy, G.B., Kumar, D.S.: Gain enhancement of patch antenna using high refractive index metamaterial-based bi-convex lens for base station applications. IETE J. Res. **69**, 1241–1248 (2023). https://doi.org/10.1080/03772063.2022.2091043
15. Mezache, Z.: Analysis of multiband graphene-based terahertz square-ring fractal antenna. Ukr. J. Phys. Opt. **21**, 93–102 (2020). https://doi.org/10.3116/16091833/21/2/93/2020
16. Zubair, M., Jabbar, A., Akinsolu, M.O., Ali Imran, M., Liu, B., Abbasi, Q.H.: Design of truncated microstrip square patch antenna for terahertz communication. In: 2022 IEEE International Symposium on Antennas and Propagation and USNC-URSI Radio Science Meeting (AP-S/URSI), pp. 1558–1559. IEEE, Denver, CO, USA (2022). https://doi.org/10.1109/AP-S/USNC-URSI47032.2022.9886809
17. Kalra, P., Sidhu, E.: Novel terahertz microstrip patch antenna design employing FR4 as substrate for detection of riboflavin. **8** (2017)

Feasibility of Industrial Marine Infrastructure for Zero-Energy Seawater Desalination: Harnessing Hydrostatic Pressure

Achraf El Allaoui[1,2](✉), Atae Semmar[2], Loubna El Ansari[2], Hammadi Laghridat[2], Hassan Gziri[1,2], Wafaa Dachry[1,2], and Hicham Medromi[2,3]

[1] Laboratory of Engineering, Industrial Management and Innovation, Hassan 1 University, Settat, Morocco
a.elallaoui.doc@uhp.ac.ma
[2] Research Foundation for Development and Innovation in Science and Engineering, Casablanca, Morocco
[3] The International Academy of Scientific Francophone (IASF), Rabat, Morocco

Abstract. This paper explores the feasibility of utilizing natural oceanic forces, particularly hydrostatic pressure, for zero-energy seawater desalination. As water scarcity becomes an increasing global challenge, innovative solutions are needed to reduce energy consumption and environmental impacts. Traditional desalination methods, such as reverse osmosis, require substantial energy input due to the need for high-pressure pumps. This study proposes an alternative approach by harnessing hydrostatic pressure at significant ocean depths to drive the desalination process without mechanical pumps. The research conducts a comprehensive feasibility study that examines various oceanic factors such as water density, salinity, temperature, marine currents, and local gravity effects. The study evaluates pressure variations at different depths, exploring how natural forces can be harnessed to reduce operational costs and improve sustainability. While challenges remain, such as harsh marine environments and the complexity of deep-sea installations, the findings suggest that using natural pressure forces has significant potential to transform seawater desalination into a more sustainable, cost-effective solution.

Keywords: Desalination · Hydrostatic · pressure · Seawater and Marine infrastructure

1 Introduction

Amidst the ever-growing global water crisis [1], the oceans present an untapped resource with immense potential [2]. Desalination, the process of converting saline water into potable freshwater, has garnered significant attention as a viable solution to address water scarcity [3]. While traditional land-based desalination plants have faced various challenges, such as high energy consumption and environmental impacts [4]. Various installations designed for underwater operations already exist in the oceans across different sectors, including petroleum, energy, and marine resource exploration [5]. However,

I. Aboudrar et al. (Eds.): ICESST 2024, SUCI, pp. 13–23, 2025.
https://doi.org/10.1007/978-3-031-86705-7_2

deploying these underwater installations remains challenging due to numerous technical and economic constraints, such as the harsh environmental conditions, remote locations, and the need for specialized equipment and expertise [6, 7].

This study aims to determine how hydrostatic pressure can be used to desalinate water without pumps, with the hypothesis that this pressure is sufficient for desalination, thereby reducing costs. The objectives include evaluating pressure at different depths, What specific technical challenges arise when adapting underwater infrastructure for desalination determining technical requirements, comparing costs with traditional methods, and analyzing environmental impacts (Fig. 1).

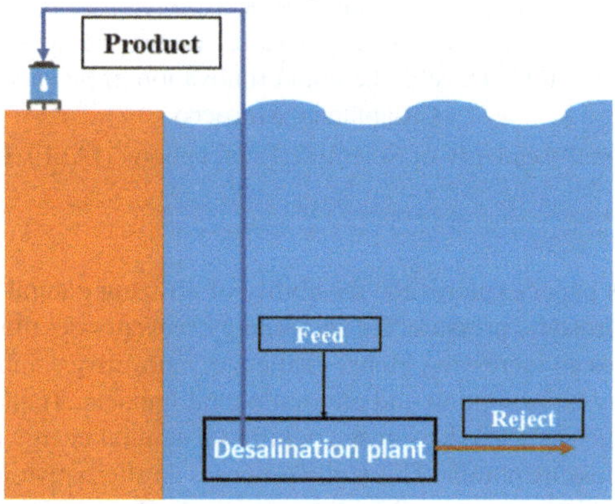

Fig. 1. Conceptual illustration of a sustainable seawater desalination system utilizing natural oceanic forces and hydrostatic pressure.

2 Water Composition: Seawater

Similar to classification schemes for continental water bodies, marine waters can also be categorized according to their salinity levels. Table 1 provides an overview of the various seawater classes and their corresponding Total Dissolved Solids concentrations. TDS encompasses the diverse minerals, salts, metals, cations, and anions dissolved within the water [7].

Table 1. Water classification based on salinity content.

Type	Total dissolved solids (TDS)
Freshwater	up to 1500 ppm
Brackish water	15000–10000 ppm
Salt water	>10000 ppm
Seawater	10000–45000 ppm
Standard seawater	35000 ppm

* TDS: Total dissolved solids

Table 2 outlines the chemical composition and corresponding concentrations of seawater, using the example of seawater from Casablanca, Morocco. The data reveals that ions such as chloride and sodium are present at notably high concentrations, along with a high total dissolved solids content [8].

Table 2. Physicochemical characteristics of the brackish water of Casablanca.

BW water (Casablanca WHO*)	
T (°C)	7,4
pH	7,4
TDS (mg/L)	2 652
Cl^- (mg/L)	1 204
NO_3^- (mg/L)	43
HCO_3^- (mg/L)	380
SO_4^{2-} (mg/L)	179
Ca^{2+} (mg/L)	260
Mg^{2+} (mg/L)	176
Na^+ (mg/L)	408
K^+ (mg/L)	2

* World Health organization, BW: Brackish water.

Regarding temperature, seawater is typically cold, but industrial applications often involve carefully controlling the temperature to enable the optimal operation of technologies like reverse osmosis membranes. Table 3 provides an example of a membrane and its operational parameters.

Table 3. Operational boundaries for various desalination technologies in the market.

	Product X High-rejection BW	Product Y High-rejection SW
Maximum feed water temperature °F (°C)	113(45)	113 (45)
Feed water chlorine concentration (ppm)	<0.1	Not detectable
Maximum operating pressure Psi (MPa, bar)	600 (4.1, 41.36)	1200 (8.3, 82.73)

* SW: Seawater, BW: Brackish water.

Analyzing the chemical composition of seawater is fundamental, as it directly shapes the needs of desalination technologies, particularly reverse osmosis. In the next section, we will investigate how these technologies are customized to address the unique properties of seawater.

3 Desalination Plant: Reverse Osmosis

In desalination facilities, the desalination process starts with water intake, succeeded by a critical pretreatment phase. Whether for wastewater purification or potable water production, the pretreatment stage is pivotal for forecasting and optimizing subsequent treatment steps, including determining the requisite dosage, duration, and pressure [9]. Within desalination plants, maintaining the Silt Density Index below 3 prior to the water's entry into the reverse osmosis membranes is vital for prolonging the lifespan of these sensitive membranes (see Fig. 2).

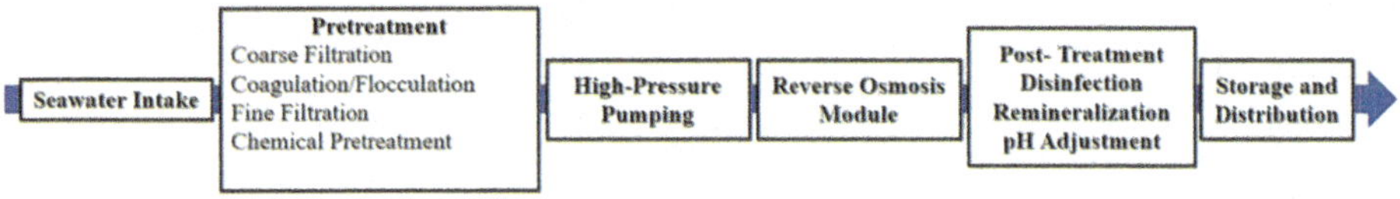

Fig. 2. Desalination process steps.

This parameter is key to effectively mitigating membrane fouling stemming from biofouling and scaling, which can significantly impair the desalination process. Following this critical pretreatment phase, the water is subjected to high pressure, up to 80 bars, facilitated by high-pressure pumps, and then enters the reverse osmosis membranes [10].

Seawater reverse osmosis has emerged as the predominant desalination technique, but it is associated with high energy demands due to the high-pressure forces required. In an effort to decrease the total energy consumption of the seawater reverse osmosis desalination unit, various energy recovery methods have been developed, Numerous advanced membranes have been developed to effectively minimize fouling and scaling,

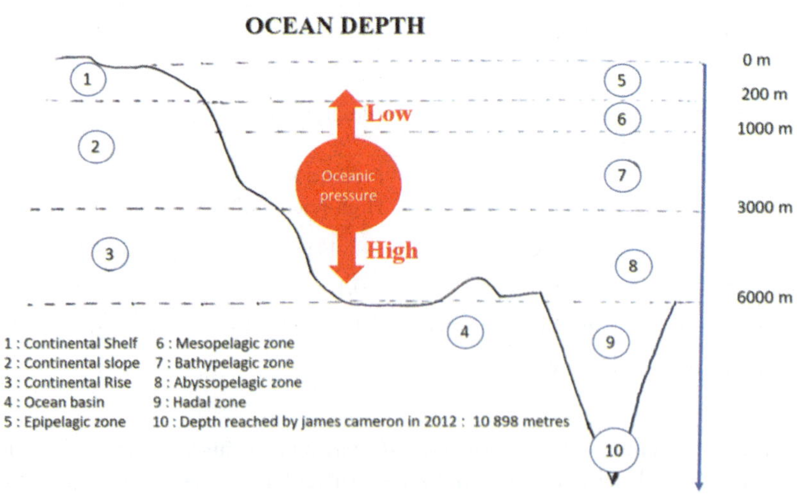

Fig. 3. Variation of pressure in the depth ocean.

thereby significantly reducing the high-pressure requirements typically associated with seawater reverse osmosis desalination processes [11] (Fig. 3).

An alternative approach leveraging natural oceanic hydrostatic pressure is proposed to replace the high-pressure pumps typically used in traditional desalination systems. The subsequent section outlines the mathematical frameworks and equations underpinning this innovative solution.

4 Mathematical Model and Equations

4.1 Basic Hydrostatic Pressure Equation

The hydrostatic pressure P at a depth h is given by [12]:

$$P = \rho \cdot g \cdot h_{(x,y)} \tag{1}$$

where, P is the hydrostatic pressure (in pascals, Pa), ρ is the density of seawater (in kilograms per cubic meter, kg/m^3), g is the acceleration due to gravity (in meters per second squared, m/s^2), $h_{(x,y)}$ is the depth (in meters, m).

4.2 Inclusion of Marine Currents

For a simplified model, we examine the influence of ocean currents on the distribution of pressure. For this reason, we use a simplified approach [13]:

$$P_{Current} = \rho\left(\frac{\vartheta v}{\vartheta t} + (v \cdot \nabla)v\right) \tag{2}$$

where v is the velocity vector of the current.

4.3 Density Variations

The seawater density is contingent upon various parameters, encompassing temperature, salinity, and pressure [14]. Elucidating the interrelationships amongst these factors is pivotal for the precise modeling of oceanographic phenomena. This dynamic can be represented mathematically through the following equation:

$$\rho = \rho(T, S, P) = \rho_0\left(1 - \beta(T - T_0) + \alpha S + \frac{P}{k}\right) \tag{3}$$

where ρ is the density, ρ_0 the reference density, β is the thermal expansion coefficient, α is the salinity coefficient, k is the compressibility factor and S is the salt factor.

4.4 Seafloor Topography

The topography of the seafloor, including features such as underwater mountains, valleys, and plateaus, influences local water depth and density variations. Variations in seafloor elevation can create significant local differences in pressure and density.

$$h = h_{(x,y)} \tag{4}$$

4.5 Atmospheric Pressure

Atmospheric pressure contributes to the overall pressure experienced at any given depth in the ocean. The process exerts pressure on the seawater surface, which affects the pressure measurements at depth.

$$P_{atm} \tag{5}$$

4.6 Local Gravity Effect

In the calculation of hydrostatic pressure, the effect of local gravity g_{Local} is considered to improve the accuracy based on geographic location [15]. Earth's gravity slightly varies with latitude due to the planet's slightly flattened shape. The formula used to adjust for local gravity is:

$$g_{Local} = g_0(1 - 0.0026373 \cdot cos(2 \cdot \varnothing) \tag{6}$$

where g_0 is the standard gravity (9.81 m/s^2) and Ø represents the latitude.

4.7 Final Integrated Mathematical Model

By combining these terms, we obtain:

$$\begin{aligned} P_{total(x,y,t)} = &\rho_0 \cdot \left(1 - \beta \cdot (T - T_0) + \alpha \cdot S + \frac{P}{k}\right) \cdot g_{Local} \cdot h_{(x,y)} \\ &+ \rho\left(\frac{\vartheta v}{\vartheta t} + (v \cdot \nabla)v\right) + \rho \cdot g \cdot h \cdot cos(\omega \cdot t) + P_{atm} \end{aligned} \tag{7}$$

5 OPEX and CAPEX in Desalination Plant Operations

The operational costs (OPEX) of desalination plants, especially those using reverse osmosis (RO) technology, are mainly driven by energy consumption, maintenance, and personnel expenses. Energy consumption is the largest cost factor, but implementing energy recovery systems and high-efficiency pumps can reduce these expenses. Maintenance costs are also significant, particularly for membrane replacement and pump upkeep. Capital expenditure (CAPEX), covering initial construction and infrastructure, is influenced by site choice, material selection, and technology complexity. Newer plants with advanced technology tend to have lower operating costs, highlighting the need to consider both OPEX and CAPEX for the long-term viability of desalination projects [16, 17].

Following the discussion on the factors influencing both OPEX and CAPEX in desalination plants, it is essential to analyze these elements across different studies to understand their broader impact on the feasibility of underwater desalination stations. The following table summarizes key insights from various articles, highlighting how these factors are addressed in different contexts and providing a comprehensive overview of the considerations necessary for successful desalination projects.

This section explores the practical performance and potential impact of leveraging hydrostatic pressure for zero-energy desalination. It presents the results of our model and discusses the feasibility, technical challenges, and benefits of this approach compared to conventional desalination methods.

6 Results and Discussion

We created a detailed mathematical model to simulate the hydrostatic pressure at the ocean floor, considering various influencing factors such as water density variations, marine currents, atmospheric pressure, and tidal effects. This research comprehensively examined the potential of leveraging marine infrastructure to enable zero-energy seawater desalination through the exploitation of natural hydrostatic pressure at diverse ocean depths. The primary aim was to mitigate the high energy consumption typically associated with conventional desalination technologies, such as reverse osmosis, by eliminating the requirement for high-pressure pumps.

The Fig. 4 demonstrates that hydrostatic pressure in the ocean increases with depth, and that this natural pressure can be leveraged to power desalination processes for seawater (80 bars) and brackish water (40 bars) without additional energy input.

The complex interactions of these factors provide a robust framework for understanding pressure distributions at depth, by neglecting the effects of these factors, we can obtain a simpler comprehension of the pressure distribution within the depths of seawater as shown in Fig. 4. However, the inclusion of these elements in future models remains a viable option. Regardless, the pressure will increase with the incorporation of additional parameters.

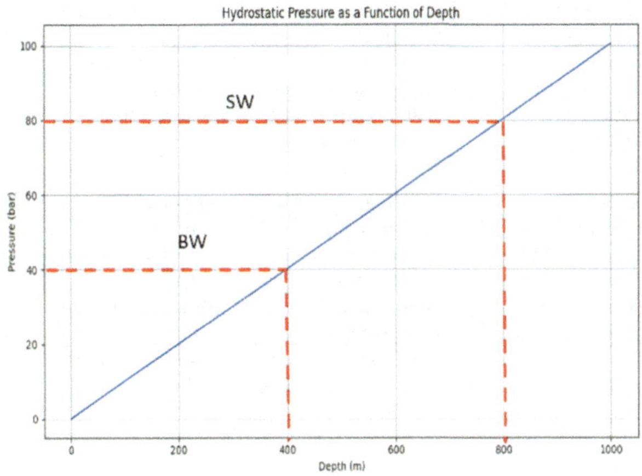

Fig. 4. Performance of desalination membranes as a function of pressure and ocean depth (SW: Seawater, BW: Brackish water).

The paper includes a Table 4 that provides an overview of current marine desalination installations. It examine the technical and economic considerations of different solutions, outlines ongoing projects and required infrastructure, and addresses environmental factors related to brine discharge and marine ecosystems.

Table 4. Overview of existing marine desalination installations: technical considerations, economic evaluation, and environmental impact.

Article Name	Analysis of Existing Underwater Infrastructure	Technical Considerations	Economic Evaluation	Environmental Impact
Edwards et al. (2023) [18]	Floating offshore platforms like Hywind and WindFloat offer adaptable infrastructure for deep-water environments	The integration of desalination systems on offshore platforms requires specific technical adaptations for stability under variable marine conditions	While initial costs are high, long-term savings can be achieved through optimization of existing structures	Floating platforms, such as Hywind, are designed to minimize environmental impact by reducing movements and optimizing mooring systems
Van Rij et al. (2017) [19]	Wave energy conversion systems offer a strong infrastructure for adapting to underwater desalination operations due to their robustness	Adjustments in pressure management and design optimization are needed for the integration of wave energy systems with desalination technology	Long-term economic benefits through the use of optimized wave energy systems	Wave energy systems are designed to minimize the impact on marine environments, which is critical for underwater desalination operations
Cradden et al. (2016) [20]	Infrastructures such as offshore jacket platforms can support underwater desalination systems, thereby enhancing their resilience and reliability	Integration of desalination technologies requires specific technical adjustments to ensure compatibility with high-pressure conditions and fatigue	High initial costs for installation and operation, but long-term savings through optimization of existing infrastructure	Offshore platforms can minimize environmental impact by effectively dispersing brine discharges into ocean currents
IFREMER (2016) [21]	Existing infrastructures such as those used for oceanographic research can be adapted to support underwater desalination stations	Existing underwater communication technologies can be adapted for the control and monitoring of desalination systems in harsh underwater conditions	Costs can be reduced by leveraging existing underwater infrastructure and technology developed for other applications	Continuous environmental monitoring and gliders can manage the impact of brine discharges

(continued)

Table 4. (*continued*)

Article Name	Analysis of Existing Underwater Infrastructure	Technical Considerations	Economic Evaluation	Environmental Impact
Ghaffour et al. (2013) [22]	Existing offshore installations and pipelines can be adapted for desalination, including the use of offshore wind farms	Desalination technologies such as RO and MED must be adapted to underwater conditions to take advantage of hydrostatic pressure	The integration of renewable energy sources with desalination systems can reduce operational costs	Effective brine management strategies are essential to minimize environmental impact

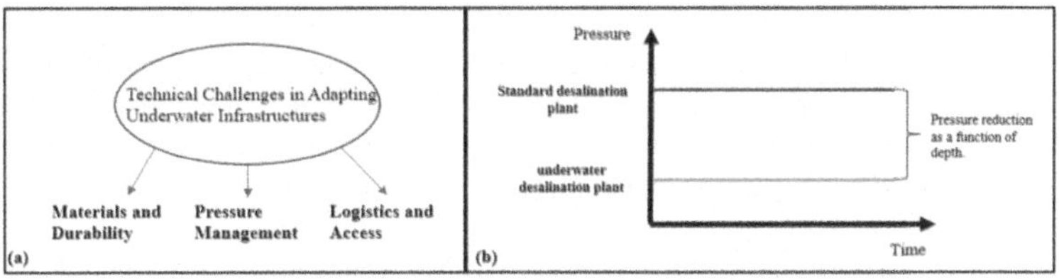

Fig. 5. (a) Challenges in Adapting Underwater Infrastructures for Desalination, (b) Comparative Pressure Requirements in Standard vs. Underwater Desalination Plants.

The Fig. 5(a) outlines the primary technical obstacles associated with adapting submerged infrastructures for desalination applications. Key factors include pressure regulation, and logistical accessibility, each presenting distinct challenges for the design and operation of underwater systems. Materials must endure the harsh subsea environment, pressure management is essential to harmonize natural underwater pressure with system needs, and logistical accessibility is complex due to the remote location.

The Fig. 5(b) shows that as the depth increases, the pressure needed for underwater desalination plants is lower than for standard plants. This pressure drop, from using underwater locations, can cut the energy used in desalination, suggesting underwater systems may be more efficient.

In conclusion, while this technology has enormous potential to lower costs and energy footprint of desalination, technical challenges related to the installation, maintenance, and durability of these underwater infrastructures must be addressed before large-scale applications can be realized.

7 Conclusion

This study explores the viability of harnessing natural oceanic forces, particularly hydrostatic pressure at significant depths, as an alternative to conventional energy-intensive desalination methods. By reducing dependence on high-energy pumps and optimizing the utilization of naturally available forces, this approach holds the potential to lower operational costs and mitigate environmental impacts. The mathematical models developed in this research confirm that seawater desalination employing hydrostatic pressure can lead to more sustainable and cost-effective solutions for freshwater production. As water scarcity continues to be a pressing global challenge, the adoption of such innovative techniques has the potential to transform the desalination industry, enhancing accessibility and environmental friendliness. More work is needed to look into overcoming the technical hurdles associated with deep-sea installations, improving the scalability of the system, and further refining the models for practical large-scale applications to maximize the impact of this innovative approach.

References

1. Mishra, A., Kumar, R.: Water resource management: an approach to sustainable water management. In: Advances in Water Management Under Climate Change, pp. 1–16. CRC Press (2024)
2. Thennakoon, T.M.T.N., et al.: Harnessing the power of ocean energy: a comprehensive review of power generation technologies and future perspectives. J. Res. Technol. Eng. **4**(3), 73–102 (2023)
3. Mechell, J.K., Lesikar, B.: Desalination methods for producing drinking water. J Res Technol Eng **4**(3), 73–102 (2023)
4. Ayaz, M., Namazi, M., Uddin, M.A., Ershath, M.M., Mansour, A., Aggoune, E.M.: Sustainable seawater desalination: current status, environmental implications and future expectations. Desalination **540**, 116022 (2022)
5. Ali, M.G., Hegazy, G.M., Atef, A., Ali, M.G.: Innovative submarine solution for overcoming challenges in offshore oil and gas operations. In: Abu Dhabi International Petroleum Exhibition and Conference, p. D021S045R003. SPE (2023)
6. Bruschi, R., Vitali, L., Marchionni, L., Parrella, A., Mancini, A.: Pipe technology and installation equipment for frontier deep water projects. Ocean Eng. **108**, 369–392 (2015)
7. Esteban, M., Leary, D.: Current developments and future prospects of offshore wind and ocean energy. Appl. Energy **90**(1), 128–136 (2012)
8. Pawlowicz, R.: Salinity in the ocean. Oceanography (2017)
9. Rizzuti, L., Micale, G., Cipollina, A.: Seawater Desalination: Conventional and Renewable Energy Processes. Springer, Berlin (2009)
10. Abushawish, A., et al.: Desalination pretreatment technologies: current status and future developments. Water **15**(8), 1572 (2023)
11. Lilane, A., Saifaoui, D., Hariss, S., Jenkal, H., Chouiekh, M.: Modeling and simulation of the performances of the reverse osmosis membrane. In: Materials Today: Proceedings, vol. 24, pp. 114–118 (2020)
12. Tansakul, C.: Procédés hybrides à membranes pour le prétraitement d'eau de mer avant dessalement par osmose inverse. Ph.D. dissertation. Institut National des Sciences Appliquées de Toulouse (2009)
13. Rahou, I., Korichi, K.: Comparative analysis of numerical solutions of 2D unsteady dambreak waves using FVM and SPH method. J. Hydrol. Hydromechanics **71**(3), 305–315 (2023)
14. Boittin, L., Bristeau, M.-O., Bouchut, F., Mangeney, A., Sainte-Marie, J., Souillé, F.: Low-Mach type approximation of the Navier-Stokes system with temperature and salinity for free surface flows. Commun. Math. Sci. **21**(1), 151–172 (2023)
15. Xian, P., Ji, B., Bian, S., Zong, J., Zhang, T.: Influence of differences in the density of seawater on the measurement of the underwater gravity gradient. Sensors **23**(2), 714 (2023)
16. Chu, P.C.: Horizontal gravity disturbance vector in atmospheric dynamics. Dyn. Atmos. Oceans **102**, 101369 (2023)

17. Ghaffour, N., Missimer, T.M., Amy, G.L.: Cost studies of reverse osmosis desalination plants. Desalination **309**, 197–207 (2013)
18. Al-Karaghouli, A., Renne, D., Kazmerski, L.L.: Solar and wind opportunities for water desalination in the Arab regions. Renew. Sustain. Energy Rev. **13**(9), 2397–2407 (2009)
19. Edwards, E.C., et al.: Evolution of floating offshore wind platforms: a review of at-sea devices. Renew. Sustain. Energy Rev. **183**, 113416 (2023)
20. Van Rij, J., et al.: Ocean power technology design optimization. Int. J. Marine Energy **20**, 97–108 (2017)
21. Cradden, L., et al.: Multi-criteria site selection for offshore renewable energy platforms. Renew. Energy **87**, 791–806 (2016)
22. CNRS: Inauguration of the Provence Mediterranean Underwater Laboratory. Press Release, France (2023)
23. Ghaffour, N., Missimer, T.M., Amy, G.L.: Desalination technologies and their environmental impacts: a review. Desalination **309**, 197–207 (2013)

Power Boost Converter Modeling, Design and MPPT Control Comparative Study for Photovoltaic Power Generation in Connected Smart Micro Grid

Hind Mouheddani(✉), Fatima Zahra Bourki, and LHoussine Abaali

ERTTI Laboratory, Engineering Science Department, Faculty of Sciences and Technics, Moulay Ismail University of Meknes, Errachidia, Morocco
hindmouheddani@gmail.com, fat.bourki@edu.umi.ac.ma, h.abaali@fste.umi.ac.ma

Abstract. This work proposes the modeling, design and a comparative study of P&O and incremental conductance MPPT control algorithms for power boost converter for photovoltaic power generation in connected smart micro grid. Under non-linear output of a photovoltaic module PV and different irradiance and temperature levels the proposed model and the comparative study are tested and evaluated with operating point changes and effect of restore inductance filter of power boost converter. A behavioral analysis of the proposed model and two maximum power point tracking algorithms in terms of speed, accuracy, and stability has been established through numerical simulation.

Keywords: Photovoltaic power generation · Power boost converter · MPPT Algorithms

1 Introduction

The demand for electrical energy has increased incredibly and explosively in recent years [1]. The potential alternative solution is to integrate photovoltaic system [2, 3] into the distribution electricity grid through an efficient and intelligent system called a smart micro-grid [4, 5]. The production of renewable energy is expected to grow and their share in the global electricity supply is also expected to increase. The smart micro-grid is a very advanced concept of the conventional electrical grid. A smart micro-grid is defined as a system consisting of i) Photovoltaic power generation, ii) Power boost converter based on MPPT control, iii) Grid-connected three phase inverter, iv) Electrical connected and controller loads, v) Storage equipment [6], and iv) Smart energy Management S = system [7, 8]. Power boost converters convert low level DC voltage signal to high level stabilized DC voltage signal. Due to its switching characteristics, the control problem poses a challenge for researchers. The objective of power converter control is to achieve power transfer efficiency and good output voltage tracking. Many control methods are used to control the power converter; those faster and low-cost are

I. Aboudrar et al. (Eds.): ICESST 2024, SUCI, pp. 24–33, 2025.
https://doi.org/10.1007/978-3-031-86705-7_3

always requested. Conventionally, the power boost converters have been controlled by using linear voltage mode and current mode controls such as proportional integral (PI) and proportional integral derivative (PID) controllers [8]. The power boost converters for photovoltaic power system and smart micro grid applications have received more and more an increasing deal of interest [9]. Recently, many Maximum Power Point Tracking (MPPT) algorithms control loop for this kind of application have been continuously developed and improved, such as, Perturbation and observation (P&O), Incremental conductance [10], Fractional open-circuit voltage, MPPT Genetic algorithm, MPPT fuzzy logic algorithm.

The objective of our study is modeling; design and comparative study the P&O and incremental conductance algorithms for power boost converters for photovoltaic generation in connected smart micro grid [11, 12]. Under non linear output of a photovoltaic module PV and with changing weather conditions (temperature and irradiance) [7] levels the proposed model and the comparative study are tested and evaluated with operating point changes and effect of restore inductance filter. A behavioral analysis of the proposed model and two maximum power point tracking algorithm in terms of speed, accuracy, and stability has been established through numerical simulation. The obtained simulation results show that the proposed algorithms are very efficient in terms of speed and tracking the maximum power of the PV module.

This paper is organized as following: after the introduction and short description of power boost converter circuit, we present in the second section the components design. The third section gives the non-ideal boost converter model. The fourth section gives the PV System Modeling. The fifth presents the MPPT perturb & observe and conductance algorithms. The sixth section presents the simulation results and discussion. Finally, the obtained results are commented in the last section.

2 Components Design and Waveforms Power Boost Converter

2.1 Power Boost Converter Circuit

The switch K is commonly realized using an Insulated Gate Bipolar Transistor (IGBT) and a power diode. However, other semiconductor switches such as Bipolar Transistor, power Gate Turn-Off Thyristor (GTO) and Metal–Oxide–Semiconductor Field-Effect Transistor, can be substituted if desired. To obtain the differential equations describing

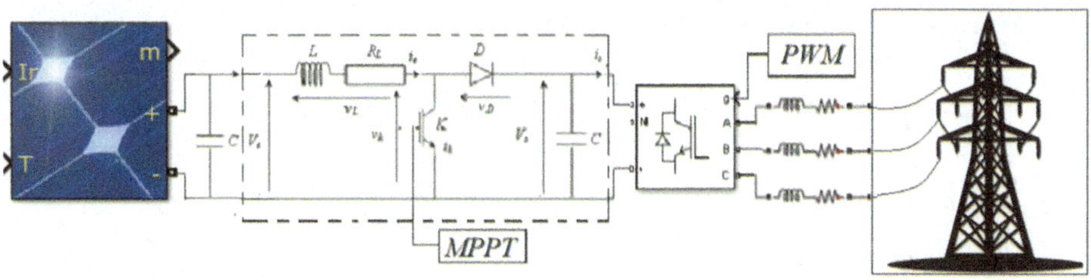

Fig. 1. Overall layout of photovoltaic power generation connected smart micro grid

the power boost converter, we consider the ideal topology shown. The differential equations describing the dynamics of the power boost converter are obtained by the direct application of Kirchoff's rules laws.

2.2 Current and Voltage Components

During t_{on}: $(0 < t < \alpha T)$ (K: on, D: off) $\alpha = t_{on}/T$

$$i_e(t) = i_L(t) = i_k(t), v_D(t) = v_k - V_s v_k(t) = 0 \text{ and } V_s(t) = 0$$

$$V_e = v_L(t) = L\frac{di_e(t)}{dt} \tag{1}$$

During t_{off} $(\alpha T < t < T$ (K:OFF, D: ON)

$$i_s(t) = i_e(t) = i_D(t), i_k(t) = 0, v_D(t) = 0 \text{ and } v_L = V_e - v_D - V_s = V_e - V_s$$

$$v_k = v_D + V_s = V_s \tag{2}$$

2.3 Differential Equations

During t_{on}:

$$V_e = v_L(t) = L\frac{di_e(t)}{dt} \tag{3}$$

The solution of (3) is given by:

$$i_e(t) = \frac{V_e}{L}t + i_e(0), i_e(0) = I_{e\,\min} \tag{4}$$

During t_{off}:

$$V_e = L\frac{di_e(t)}{dt} + V_s \tag{5}$$

The solution of (5) is given by:

$$i_e(t) = \frac{V_e - V_s}{L}(t - \alpha T) + i_e(\alpha T) \tag{6}$$

2.4 Average Value Output Voltage and Current

$$\overline{V}_L = \frac{1}{T}\int_0^{\alpha T} V_e dt + \frac{1}{T}\int_{\alpha T}^{T} (V_e - V_s)dt = \frac{V_e}{T}\alpha T + \frac{1}{T}(V_e - \overline{V}_s)(1-\alpha)T \tag{7}$$

In steady state, the average voltage across the inductance L is $\overline{V}_L = 0$:
From (7): $\alpha V_e + (V_e - \overline{V}_s)(1 - \alpha) = 0$

$$\overline{V}_s = \frac{V_e}{1-\alpha} \tag{8}$$

2.5 Output Current $i_s(t)$

We assume that the ripples of the input current $i_e(t)$ is negligible:

$$\overline{I}_s = \frac{1}{T}\int_0^T i_s(t)dt = \frac{1}{T}\int_{\alpha T}^T i_e(t)dt = (1-\alpha)\overline{I}_e \tag{9}$$

2.6 Output Voltage Ripple ΔV_s

The current flowing in the capacitor C is expressed as:

$$i_C(t) = C\frac{dv_C(t)}{dt} = C\frac{dV_s(t)}{dt} \tag{10}$$

since: $v_C(t) = V_s(t)$

If the switching frequency is high, the output current is composed of straight parts, then the capacitor voltage is composed of parabolic parts.

In fact:

$$V_s(t) = \frac{1}{C}\int_0^t i_C(\tau)d\tau \tag{11}$$

$i_c(t)$: AC component of the output current flows through the capacitor. If K is on:

$$\Delta V_s = V_{s\max} - V_{s\min} = \frac{1}{C}\int_0^{\alpha T} i_C(t)dt = \frac{1}{C}\int_0^{\alpha T} \overline{I}_s dt = \frac{1}{C}\overline{I}_s\alpha T \tag{12}$$

$$\overline{I}_s = \frac{\overline{V}_s}{R} = \frac{V_e}{R(1-\alpha)} \tag{13}$$

Finally:

$$\Delta V_s = \frac{V_e}{CRf}\frac{\alpha}{(1-\alpha)} \tag{14}$$

2.7 Output Current Ripple Δi_e

When $v_L > 0$: $v_L = V_e = L\frac{di_e(t)}{dt} \approx L\frac{\Delta i_e}{\alpha T}$

$$\Delta i_e = \frac{V_e}{Lf}\alpha \tag{15}$$

Δi_e is directly proportional to α. L is designed for α_{max} so that Δi_e never exceeds the prescribed value. We take into account the influence of f, which we choose as high as possible: this makes it possible to reduce the value of L making it possible to fix Δi_e.

- The voltage relationship obtained illustrates the nature of the power boost converter.
- The current relationship parallels the voltage relationship: The power boost converter functions as a current (variable-ratio transformer$1/(1-\alpha)$)
- α varies from 0 to 1, so the average value varies from V_e to ∞: a problem of sizing a diode and a transistor capable of withstanding an infinite voltage! In practice, a much higher output voltage can be obtained than input voltage.

2.8 Non-ideal Power Boost Converter Model

In solar power plants, the maximum power is extracted using the power boost converters. Figure 1 displays a power boost converter topology. In this study, all components of this power boost converter are ideal except the input inductance. The internal resistance is RL $\neq 0$ of (real inductance). In addition, this converter functions in continuous conduction mode.

Using the average value method, we can write:

$$V_e = \overline{V}_L + \overline{V}_K \tag{16}$$

In steady state, the average current through the inductor is constant and the average voltage across the inductor becomes:

$$\overline{V}_L = L\frac{d\overline{I}_L}{dt} + R_L\overline{I}_L = R_L\overline{I}_L \tag{17}$$

When K is on, $V_K = 0$. When K is off, D becomes conducting and $V_K = V_s$. Therefore, the average voltage across the K is:

$$\overline{V}_K = \alpha.0 + (1-\alpha)\overline{V}_s = (1-\alpha)\overline{V}_s$$

$$\overline{V}_L = V_e - \overline{V}_K = V_e - (1-\alpha)\overline{V}_s \tag{18}$$

The output current is equal to the current in the inductor during the off-state of K. The average current in the inductor is therefore written as:

$$\overline{I}_s = (1-\alpha)\overline{I}_e, \overline{I}_L = \overline{I}_e = \frac{\overline{I}_s}{1-\alpha} \tag{19}$$

If the output voltage and current ripples are negligible, the load can be considered resistive. By designating R as the load resistance, Eq. (19) becomes:

$\overline{I}_s = \frac{\overline{V}_s}{R}, \overline{I}_L = \frac{\overline{V}_s}{(1-\alpha)R}$ if $V_e = \overline{V}_L + \overline{V}_K$

$$V_e = \overline{I}_L R_L + (1-\alpha)\overline{V}_s = \frac{R_L}{R(1-\alpha)}\overline{V}_s + (1-\alpha)\overline{V}_s \tag{20}$$

This expression can be written in the form:

$$\frac{\overline{V}_s}{V_e} = \frac{1}{\frac{1}{\frac{R}{R_L}(1-\alpha)} + (1-\alpha)} \tag{21}$$

3 PV System Modeling

A PV module is a set of cells capable of producing high power and has a non-linear characteristic which depends on the load, cell temperature, solar radiation, spectral characteristics of sunlight, shaded condition, dirt, and output voltage. In this work, the SunPower SPR-305E-WHT-D photovoltaic module was chosen to analyze the effect of irradiance and temperature on the proposed method. The electrical characteristics of this module are given in Table 1 for $I_r = 1000\ W/m^2$ and T = 25 °C [13, 14].

Table 1. Electrical characteristics of SunPower SPR-305E-WHT-D

Description	SunPower SPR-305E-WHT-D
Maximum power (P_m)	305.226 W
Voltage P_{max} (V_m)	54.7 V
Current at P_{max} (I_m)	5.58 A
Short circuit current (I_{sc})	5.96 A
Open circuit voltage (V_{oc})	64.2 V
Temperature co-eff of V_{oc}	−0.27269
Temperature co-eff of I_{sc}	0.061745 °C
Temperature co-eff of power	−0.38 °C
Nominal operating cell temperature NOCT2	45 °C

4 Maximum Power Point Tracking Algorithms Description

4.1 MPPT Perturbation and Observation Algorithm

Perturb & Observe algorithm is widely applied in the MPPT controllers due to its simplicity and easy implementation [10]. The MPPT P&O algorithm is based on the disturbance of output voltage k of PV module and corresponding output power k. This power k is compared with the previous power (k − 1), if the power increases, the voltage change (k + 1) continues in the same direction.

4.2 Incremental Conductance Algorithm

The Incremental Conductance algorithm is used to maximize the power output of a solar module PV [10]. This algorithm is based on the variation of the conductance of PV cells and the operating point with respect to the voltage and current of the module calculates the slope of the power characteristics to determine the MPP as the peak of the curve.

5 Simulation Results

The Table 2 shows the Power boost converter simulation parameters.

Table 2. Power boost converter simulation parameters.

Heading level	Example	Font size and style
ΔV_s	voltage ripple	6% V_s
Δi_e	current ripple	5% Ie
α	Duty cycle	65%
L	Inductance	53.083 mH
C	Output filter capacitance	36.11 μF
V_e	Input voltage	125 V
V_s	Output voltage	357.14 V
P_n	Power load	17.88 kW
F	Switching frequency	30 kHz
R	Load	10 Ω

5.1 I = f(V) and P = f(V) Characteristics of SunPower SPR-305E-WHT-D for Various Irradiation and Temperature Levels

The I = f(V) and P = f(V) curves for various irradiation and temperature levels are shown in Fig. 2.

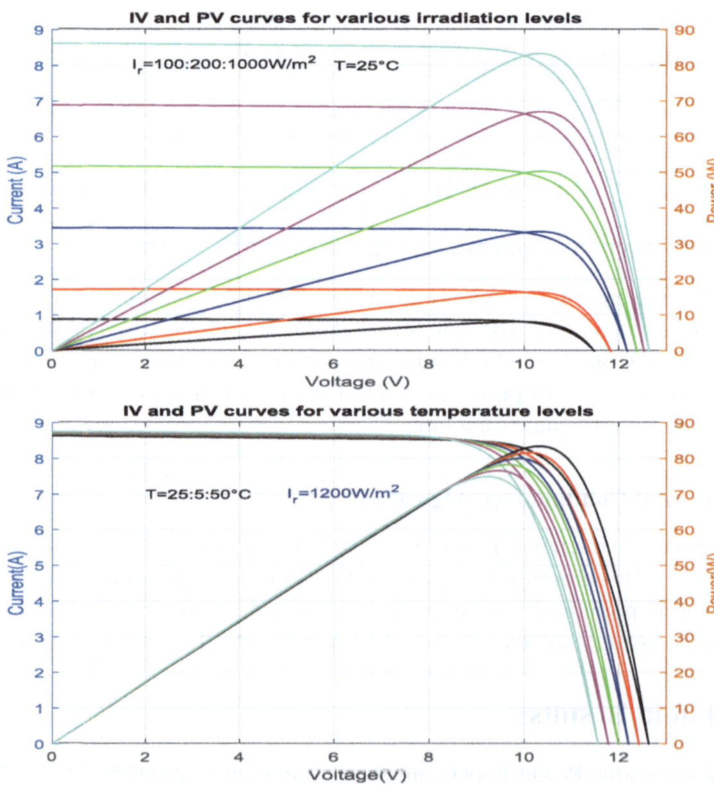

Fig. 2. I = f(V) and P = f(V) curves for various irradiation and temperature levels

- Different irradiation levels (100, 200, 400, 600, 800, 1000 W/m^2) at constant temperature T = 25 °C.
- Different temperature levels (25, 30, 35, 40, 45, 50 °C) at constant irradiance I_r = 1000 W/m^2.

5.2 Output Characteristics of Power Boost Converter According to the Different Irradiation and Temperature Levels

The irradiation and temperature levels can change rapidly due to weather conditions or cloud passage. In order to evaluate the performance of SunPower SPR-305E-WHT-D module with the MPPT perturb & observe and incremental conductance algorithm we used the MATLAB/Simulink software for different irradiation and temperature levels.

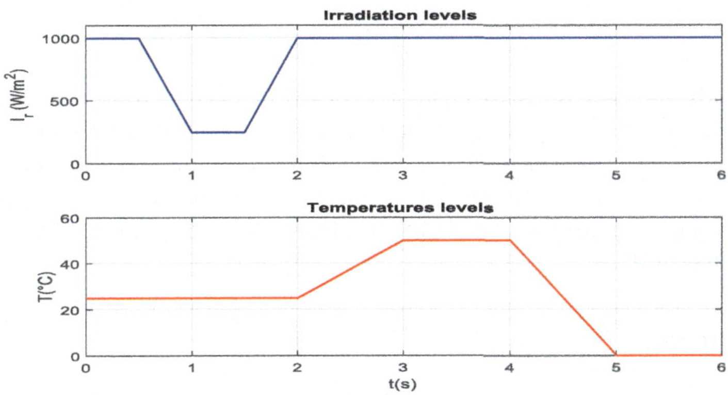

Fig. 3. Irradiation and temperature levels PV solar module

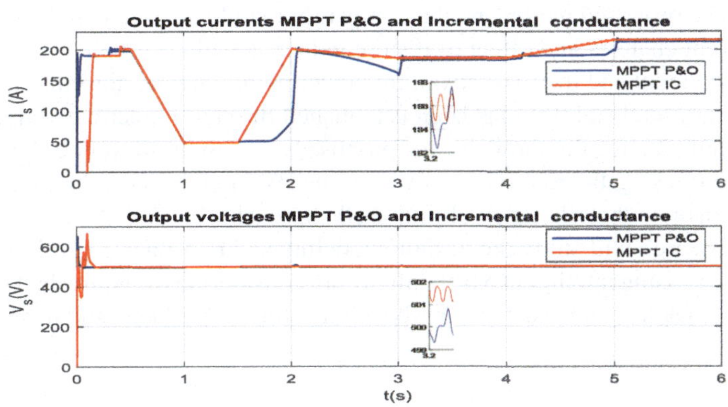

Fig. 4. Output voltage and current of power boost converter using MPPT P&O and IC

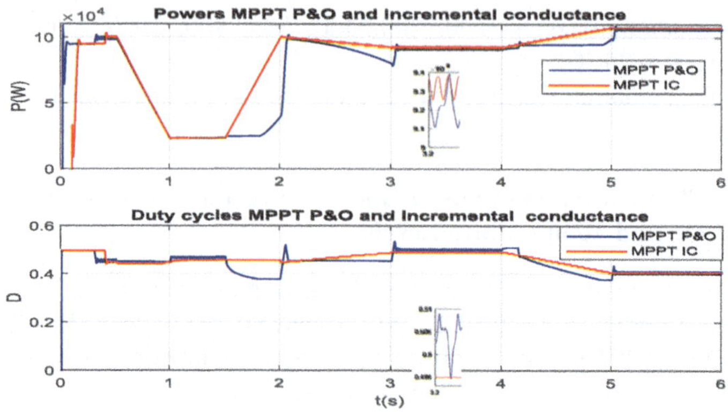

Fig. 5. Output power and duty cycle variations of power boost converter using MPPT P&O and IC algorithms

The steady-state and transient characteristics of the proposed control algorithms are analyzed. The Fig. 3, Fig. 4 and Fig. 5 show the simulation results of a comparative study of perturb & observe and incremental conductance algorithms power boost converter with photovoltaic power generation in connected smart micro grid. From Fig. 4 and Fig. 5 the IC algorithm is faster and provides better efficiency than the P&O algorithm in tracking the MPP.

6 Conclusion

This work proposes the modeling, design and a comparative study of perturb & observe and incremental conductance algorithms for power boost converter with photovoltaic power generation in connected smart micro grid. Under different irradiance and temperature levels the proposed model and the comparative study are tested and evaluated with operating point changes and effect of restore inductance filter. A behavioral analysis of the proposed model and the two maximum power point tracking algorithms in terms of speed, accuracy, and stability has been established through numerical simulation. The obtained simulation results show that the proposed algorithms are very efficient in terms of speed and tracking the maximum power of the PV module. The obtained simulation results demonstrate the efficiency of proposed approach.

Future research will study the design, modeling and non-liner control of real power boost converter using intelligent MPPT algorithm considering the equivalent series resistance of the capacitor, the resistance in the diode while it conducts, and the resistance in the inductor.

References

1. Jabir, H.J., Teh, J., Ishak, D., Abunima, H.: Impacts of demand-side management on electrical power systems: a review. Energies **11**(5), 1050 (2018)
2. Sarah, K.E., Roland, U., Okafor Ephraim, N.C.: A review of solar photovoltaic technologies. Int. J. Eng. Res. Technol. (IJERT) **9**(07) (2020). ISSN 2278-0181

3. Wan, C., Zhao, J., Song, Y., Xu, Z., Lin, J., Hu, Z.: Photovoltaic and solar power forecasting for smart grid energy management. CSEE J. Power Energy Syst. **1**(4), 38–46 (2016)
4. Tsang, K.F.: Smart grid, and renewable energy. In: 2022 IEEE International Conference on Power Electronics (2022). IEEE Ind. Electron. Mag. **16**(2), 79–80
5. Sivadharshini, B., Saxena, A., Saritha, G., Alawady, A., Lall, S., Dhabliya, D.: Solar energy forecasting models for grid integration and power balancing. In: E3S Web of Conferences, vol. 540, no. 6 (2024)
6. Abaali, H.: Design modeling control and simulation of DC/DC power buck converter. World Acad. Sci. Eng. Technol. Int. J. Electr. Comput. Energetic Electron. Commun. Eng. **9**(10), 1149–1155 (2015)
7. Ramos-Hernanz, J., Lopez-Guede, J.M., Barambones, O., Zulueta, E., Fernandez-Gamiz, U.: Novel control algorithm for MPPT with Boost converters in photovoltaic systems. Int. J. Hydrogen Energy **42**(28), 17831–17855 (2017)
8. Srinivasan, K.G., Sivalingam, R.: Design, analysis, and real-time validation of type-2 fractional order fuzzy PID controller for energy storage–based microgrid frequency regulation. Int. Trans. Electr. Energy Syst. **31**(4), (2020). ISBN 2050-7038
9. Yau, Y.-T.: Boost DC-DC converter with regenerative snubber. Energy Rep. **12**, 798–819 (2024)
10. Asoh, D.A., Noumsi, B.D., Mbinkar, E.N.: Maximum power point tracking using the incremental conductance algorithm for PV systems operating in rapidly changing environmental conditions. Smart Grid Renew. Energy **13**(5) (2022)
11. Khabou, H., Souissi, M., Aitouche, A.: MPPT implementation on boost converter by using T-S fuzzy method. Math. Comput. Simul **167**, 119–134 (2020)
12. SabanOzdemir, N., Sefa, I.: Fuzzy logic based MPPT controller for high conversion ratio quadratic boost converter. Int. J. Hydrogen Energy **42**, 17748–17759 (2017)
13. Guanghua, L., Siddiqu, F.A., Shaikh, S.: Improved maximum power point tracking algorithms by using numerical analysis techniques for photovoltaic systems. Results Eng. **21**, 101740 (2024)
14. Seyedmahmoudian, M., et al.: Renew. Sustain. Energy Rev. **64**, 435–455 (2016)

Numerical Investigation of the Relationship Between Environmental Parameters and the Operating Temperature of a Solar Panel

Mohamed Ahliouati[1](✉), Rabie El Otmani[1], Khalid Kandoussi[1], and M'Hamed Boutaous[2]

[1] Science Engineer Laboratory for Energy (LabSIPE) at National School of Applied Sciences, Chouaib Doukkali University, El Jadida, Morocco
ahliouati.m@ucd.ac.ma

[2] University of Lyon, CNRS, INSA Lyon, Claude Bernard University Lyon-1, CETHIL UMR 5008, Villeurbanne Cedex, France

Abstract. The operating temperature of solar panels is considered as an important factor influencing the performance of photovoltaic panels, directly impacted by external environmental conditions. The main focus of this paper is to examine the combined impact of solar irradiation and wind velocity on the operating temperature of a solar panel, in order to accurately assess their energy efficiency. This research is based on a mathematical relationship linking the temperature of the system studied to various climatic parameters, enabling us to identify the main elements characterizing the energy properties of the analyzed PV panel. The results show a significant correlation between variations in wind speed and solar radiation on solar panel performance. A 35.8% drop in operating temperature is observed when wind speed is increased from 1 m/s to 10 m/s, while a clear improvement for the convection coefficient is observed, rising from 9.53 to 44.27 $W \cdot m^{-2}.K^{-1}$ in the same range of wind velocity variation. In parallel, the effect of variations in solar irradiance received on the studied panel's performance is also examined. It is noted that an increase in solar radiation results in a direct improvement in electrical efficiency, provided that operating temperatures remain close to moderate values, near to normalized test parameters.

Keywords: Solar panel · Efficiency · Wind speed · Operating temperature · Solar radiation

1 Introduction

The temperature that characterizes the operation of photovoltaic modules is considered as a main element that can affect the energy efficiency of a solar system. A rise in the temperature of a PV system doesn't just reduce its generated power, but also increases the rapidity of its degradation [1–3]. Wind speed also regarded as key environmental factors that impacts the operating temperature of PV panels, which in turn has a direct impact on their performance; it contributes significantly to reducing the operating temperature

I. Aboudrar et al. (Eds.): ICESST 2024, SUCI, pp. 34–42, 2025.
https://doi.org/10.1007/978-3-031-86705-7_4

[4–6], leading to improved energy efficiency [7]. Numerous studies have been carried out in the literature to assess the temperature of photovoltaic modules. These studies aim to establish the dependence of solar panel temperature on various meteorological parameters including wind velocity, surrounding temperature and incoming irradiation. An experimental research conducted by Goossens et al. [8] focused on the effect of wind velocity on the cooling process of a photovoltaic panel, taking into account soiling and its influence on the energy yield provided by photovoltaic units. Gökmen et al. [9] have carried out a comparative analysis of annual energy production, including or excluding the impact of wind, in a Danish windy location in northern Europe, their findings underline the importance of not neglecting the wind speed factor when assessing the productivity of photovoltaic systems. In another research carried out by Koehl et al. [10], it has been proven that wind velocity has a direct influence on the difference between ambient and PV module temperatures, they observed that this difference is close to 32 °C in wind velocity of 2 m/s, while it is no more than 12 °C once the wind reaches a given value of around 10 m/s [10]. Another study by Kaldellis et al. [11] performed an experimental analysis to assess the effect of temperature variations on the performance of photovoltaic panels, and discovered that the working temperature had a significant influence in photoelectric conversion within a photovoltaic system.

It's fundamental to understand the major influence of wind speed and incoming irradiation on the energy efficiency of solar systems. For this reason, the primary aim of this research is to carry out an in-depth investigation to determine the operating temperature of a solar panel by varying the wind speed which is characteristic of the site where the solar panel is installed. In addition, this research will propose an energy efficiency assessment of the PV panel under investigation, taking into account the relationship between the various fundamental climatic parameters that significantly influence the operating temperature of a photovoltaic module.

The present paper is structured into key sections: "Introduction" which sets the context and research aims; "Description of the studied solar panel" detailing the specific examined photovoltaic system; "Research Method" outlining data collection and analysis procedures; "Results and Analysis" presenting the main findings supported by some statistical analyses; and "Conclusions" summarizing key results and emphasizing their significance.

2 PV Panel Description

The study is conducted on the basis of a monocrystalline PV panel offering a maximum output of 140 W, with geometric dimensions of 1.25 m in length and 0.668 m in width. As shown in Fig. 1, a glazing layer at the top of the panel ensures transmission of the irradiation received to the solar cells, which convert this received energy into electrical energy. The key intrinsic parameters characterizing the photovoltaic system under examination are detailed in Table 1.

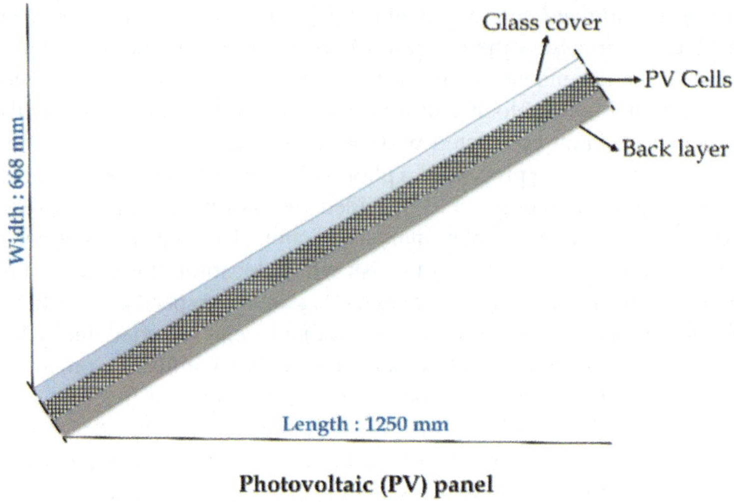

Fig. 1. A schematic view of the solar panel under examination.

Table 1. The main properties of the solar panel studied.

Characteristics	Value	Unit
Length, L	1.25	m
Module surface, S_m	0.835	m^2
Maximum power, P_{max}	140	W
Reference efficiency, η_r	16.76	%
Short-circuit current, I_{sc}	8.05	A
Packing factor, β	0.88	-
Cell number, N	36	-
Open-circuit voltage, V_{oc}	23.6	V
Temperature coefficient, β_p	0.0045	/°C
Solar radiation factor, δ	0.052	-
Glass transmissivity, τ_g	0.84	-
Solar cell absorptivity, α_c	0.85	-
Glass absorptivity, α_g	0.06	-
Tedlar absorptivity, α_t	0.8	-

3 Research Method

A linear formulation is established to calculate the working temperature of photovoltaic panels, taking into account key climatic variables, including the surrounding temperature, solar irradiation and wind velocity. Using this linear relationship, it becomes possible to estimate module temperature in a simplified way by referring to the following equation [3, 12]:

$$T_{PV} = aT_a + bG_T + cV_w + d \tag{1}$$

with:

c = −1.528 °C·s/m, a = 0.943, b = 0.028 °C·m^2/W correspond to coefficients for wind speed (V_w), surrounding temperature (T_a) and incoming irradiation (G_T) respectively, while d = 4.3 °C represents a constant [3].

The power absorbed fluctuates according to the optical properties specified by each component that constitutes the solar panel; the absorbed powers can be expressed by specific formulas for each component as follows;

For the PV cell [13, 14]:

$$P_c = \alpha_c \cdot \tau_g \cdot \beta \cdot G_T \tag{2}$$

For the glass [13]:

$$P_g = \alpha_g \cdot G_T \tag{3}$$

For the back layer [13, 14]:

$$P_t = \alpha_t \cdot \tau_g (1 - \beta) \cdot G_T \tag{4}$$

The heat transfer parameter by convective mode can be given by this formula [15–18]:

$$h_{cv} = 5.7 + 3.8V_w \tag{5}$$

The electrical yield is defined in terms of climatic parameters, as follows [19–22]:

$$\eta_{PV} = \eta_r \cdot (1 - \beta_p(T_{PV} - T_{c,r}) + \delta \ln(\frac{G_T}{G_r})) \tag{6}$$

where: $T_{c,r}$ = 25 °C and G_r = 1000 W/m^2 represent reference cell temperature and reference irradiance respectively.

4 Results and Analysis

4.1 Absorbed Powers

The power absorbed by the various layers that make up a solar panel depends on their specific properties and the intensity of the incoming irradiance captured by the photovoltaic panel, each layer assists in absorbing incoming solar radiation and the process of converting it into electricity, the absorption depends on the intrinsic characteristics of the layer, which are highly important and should be considered in the energy performance analysis of solar panels.

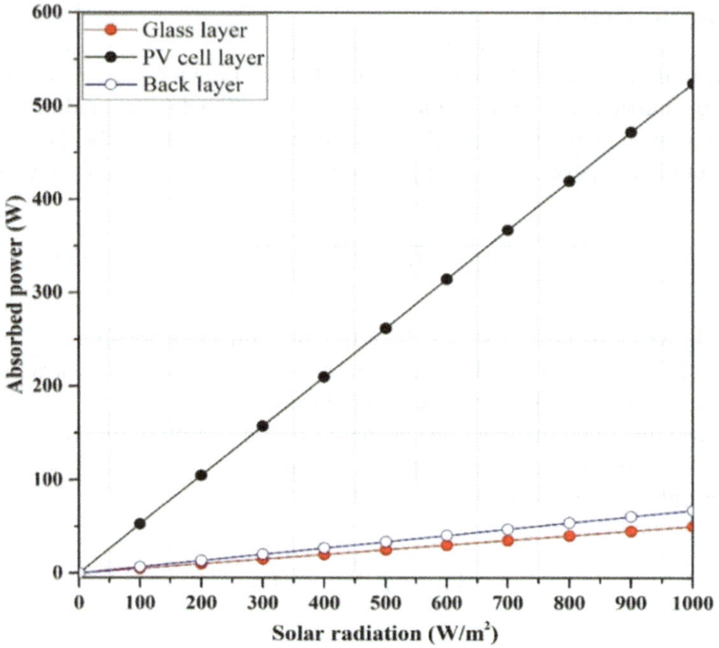

Fig. 2. The effect of variations in incoming irradiance on the absorbed power by various layers.

Referring to the variation in the intensity of incoming irradiance captured by the surface of the PV panel, as illustrated in Fig. 2, the use of Eqs. (2), (3) and (4) enable tracking of the absorbed power evolution by the various components of the photovoltaic system under examination.

It is important to mention that the power absorbed by the glazing and back layers is relatively small and consistently lower than the power absorbed by the photovoltaic cell layer, this can be attributed to the optical properties of the glass, characterized by a low absorption coefficient and high transmission coefficient. Conversely, the power absorbed by the solar cell layer is significant because their absorption coefficient is particularly high. It's important to note that the power absorbed increases as the irradiation received by the PV module surface rises. For an incoming irradiance of 800 $W \cdot m^{-2}$, the absorbed power by the glazing and back layers is 5 W and 54 W respectively, while the photovoltaic cell layer absorbs 420 W, highlighting the importance of the PV cell layer, which is responsible for photoelectric conversion.

4.2 Impact of Incoming Irradiance on Electrical Yield

Figure 3 illustrates the influence of variations in solar irradiance on the electrical efficiency of the examined PV system by varying operating temperature. As solar irradiation increases, it is observable that the yield of the examined solar system also increases, provided the operating temperature remains constant (see Fig. 3). It is also essential to observe that higher operating temperatures leads to a decrease in panel's electrical efficiency due to the effects of processes related to the photoelectric conversion of photovoltaic cells, such as the increased heat losses that occur between the different layers making up the PV system under study.

When the panel receives a constant irradiation of 800 W/m^2 and the operating temperature is increased from 25 °C to 50 °C, it is observed that the electrical efficiency decreases from 16.57% to 14.68% (see Fig. 3). This indicates that the PV module analyzed performs significantly when the irradiation received was high and the temperature remained moderate, approaching normalized test conditions (G_T = 1000 W·m^{-2}, T_{PV} = 25 °C).

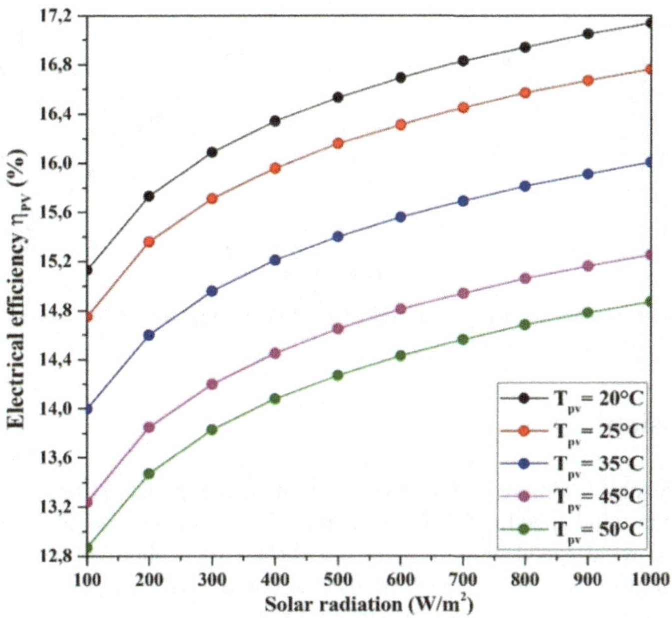

Fig. 3. The impact of variations in solar radiation on the on electrical efficiency.

4.3 Impact of Wind Velocity on Operating Temperature

Figure 4 illustrates the influence of fluctuating wind speed on the convection transfer coefficient and operating temperature that defines the solar panel; the findings show that significant wind velocities can cause an elevation in the convective transfer coefficient, thus helping to dissipate the heat generated during the panel's photoelectric process, resulting in a cooling effect on PV module.

It should be mentioned that the convective parameter due to wind grows linearly with wind speed, while the operating temperature tends to decrease progressively. When wind velocity rises from 1 to 10 m/s, the convective coefficient increases from 9.53 to 44.27 W·m^{-2}.K^{-1}, where as the operating temperature falls from 49.6 °C to 35.8 °C in the same range of wind speed variation.

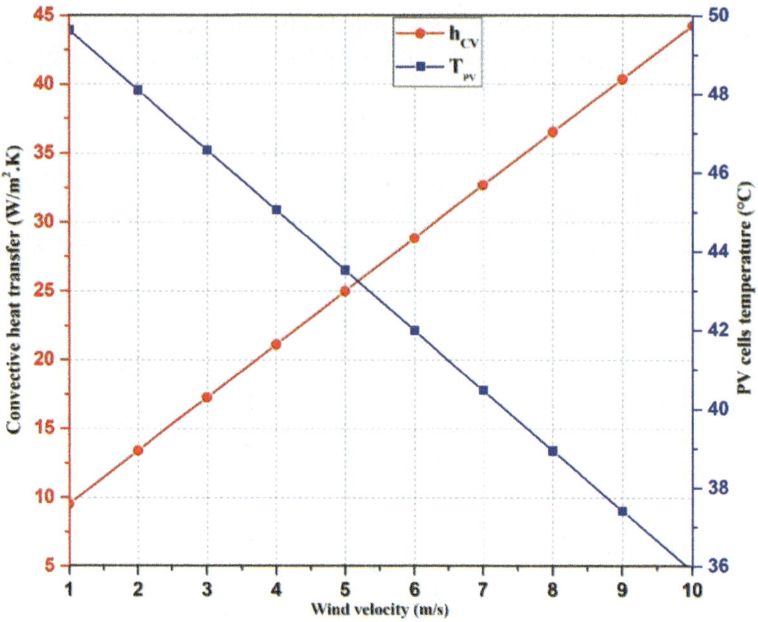

Fig. 4. The impact of variations in wind velocity on operating temperature (G_T = 1000 W/m^2, T_a = 20 °C).

5 Conclusion

This paper presents a comprehensive investigation of solar panel performance as affected by variations in wind speed and solar irradiance. The obtained results demonstrate that increasing the wind speed blowing over the surface of a photovoltaic panel leads to an improvement in its electrical performance, accompanied by a decrease in operating temperature. A solar panel exposed to strong wind can improve its convective transfer coefficient due to wind flow. However, a rise in wind speed from 1 to 10 m/s can reduce operating temperature by 35.8%.

The findings also highlight the significant impact of variations in solar irradiation received by the surface of the solar panel studied on its electrical efficiency, which also fluctuates as a function of the panel's working temperature. With a temperature of 25 °C, and when incoming irradiance varied from 100 W·m^{-2} to 1000 W·m^{-2}, it was found that the yield of the PV panel studied has grown from 14.57% to 16.76%, representing a 13.6% improvement in panel efficiency.

This study carried out a detailed assessment to precisely analyze the specific impact of variations in wind speed and irradiation intensity on the energy characteristics of a photovoltaic system, establishing a linear correlation between the various climatic parameters and the operating temperature of solar panels. In perspective, the present paper can be seen as a departure point for conducting parametric studies on the effect of other environmental factors for optimizing the energy yield of solar panels and define the optimum operating conditions for PV systems.

References

1. Ndiaye, A., Kébé, C.M.F., Charki, A., Ndiaye, P.A., Sambou, V., Kobi, A.: Degradation evaluation of crystalline-silicon photovoltaic modules after a few operation years in a tropical environment. Sol. Energy **103**, 70–77 (2014). https://doi.org/10.1016/j.solener.2014.02.006
2. Sinha, A., Sastry, O.S., Gupta, R.: Nondestructive characterization of encapsulant discoloration effects in crystalline-silicon PV modules. Sol. Energy Mater. Sol. Cells **155**, 234–242 (2016). https://doi.org/10.1016/j.solmat.2016.06.019
3. Magare, D., Sastry, O., Gupta, R., Bora, B., Singh, Y., Mohammed, H.: Wind effect modeling and analysis for estimation of photovoltaic module temperature. J. Sol. Energy Eng. **140**, 11008 (2017). https://doi.org/10.1115/1.4038590
4. Mani, M., Pillai, R.: Impact of dust on solar photovoltaic (PV) performance: research status, challenges and recommendations. Renew. Sustain. Energy Rev. **14**, 3124–3131 (2010). https://doi.org/10.1016/j.rser.2010.07.065
5. Skoplaki, E., Palyvos, J.A.: On the temperature dependence of photovoltaic module electrical performance: a review of efficiency/power correlations. Sol. Energy **83**, 614–624 (2009). https://doi.org/10.1016/j.solener.2008.10.008
6. Yuan, W., et al.: Comparison study of the performance of two kinds of photovoltaic/thermal(PV/T) systems and a PV module at high ambient temperature. Energy **148**, 1153–1161 (2018). https://doi.org/10.1016/j.energy.2018.01.121
7. Schwingshackl, C., et al.: Wind effect on PV module temperature: analysis of different techniques for an accurate estimation. Energy Procedia **40**, 77–86 (2013). https://doi.org/10.1016/j.egypro.2013.08.010
8. Goossens, D., Lundholm, R., Goverde, H., Govaerts, J.: Effect of soiling on wind-induced cooling of photovoltaic modules and consequences for electrical performance. Sustain. Energy Technol. Assess. **34**, 116–125 (2019). https://doi.org/10.1016/j.seta.2019.05.007
9. Gökmen, N., Hu, W., Hou, P., Chen, Z., Sera, D., Spataru, S.: Investigation of wind speed cooling effect on PV panels in windy locations. Renew. Energy **90**, 283–290 (2016). https://doi.org/10.1016/j.renene.2016.01.017
10. Koehl, M., Heck, M., Wiesmeier, S., Wirth, J.: Modeling of the nominal operating cell temperature based on outdoor weathering. Sol. Energy Mater. Sol. Cells **95**, 1638–1646 (2011). https://doi.org/10.1016/j.solmat.2011.01.020
11. Kaldellis, J.K., Kapsali, M., Kavadias, K.A.: Temperature and wind speed impact on the efficiency of PV installations. Experience obtained from outdoor measurements in Greece. Renew. Energy **66**, 612–624 (2014). https://doi.org/10.1016/j.renene.2013.12.041
12. Chenni, R., Makhlouf, M., Kerbache, T., Bouzid, A.: A detailed modeling method for photovoltaic cells. Energy **32**, 1724–1730 (2007). https://doi.org/10.1016/j.energy.2006.12.006
13. Ahliouati, M., El Otmani, R., Kandoussi, K.: Performance analysis of monocrystalline PV module under the effect of Moroccan arid climatic conditions. In: 2023 3rd International Conference on Innovative Research in Applied Science, Engineering and Technology (IRASET), pp. 1–6 (2023). https://doi.org/10.1109/IRASET57153.2023.10152959
14. Tiwari, G.N., Dubey, S.: Fundamentals of Photovoltaic Modules and Their Applications. Royal Society of Chemistry (2010)
15. Cetina-Quiñones, A.J., Polanco-Ortiz, I., Mijangos Alonzo, P., Hernandez-Perez, J.G., Bassam, A.: Innovative heat dissipation design incorporated into a solar photovoltaic thermal (PV/T) air collector: an optimization approach based on 9E analysis. Therm. Sci. Eng. Prog. **38**, 101635 (2023). https://doi.org/10.1016/j.tsep.2022.101635
16. Ji, J., Wang, Y., Yuan, W., Sun, W., He, W., Guo, C.: Experimental comparison of two PV direct-coupled solar water heating systems with the traditional system. Appl. Energy **136**, 110–118 (2014). https://doi.org/10.1016/j.apenergy.2014.09.037

17. Amori, K.E., Abd-AlRaheem, M.A.: Field study of various air based photovoltaic/thermal hybrid solar collectors. Renew. Energy **63**, 402–414 (2014). https://doi.org/10.1016/j.renene.2013.09.047
18. Ahliouati, M., et al.: Energetic and parametric studies of a basic hybrid collector (PV/T-Air) and a photovoltaic (PV) module for building applications: performance analysis under El Jadida weather conditions. Mater. Sci. Energy Technol. **6**, 267–281 (2023). https://doi.org/10.1016/j.mset.2023.02.001
19. Orioli, A., Di Gangi, A.: A procedure to calculate the five-parameter model of crystalline silicon photovoltaic modules on the basis of the tabular performance data. Appl. Energy **102**, 1160–1177 (2013). https://doi.org/10.1016/j.apenergy.2012.06.036
20. Asefi, G., Ma, T., Wang, R.: Parametric investigation of photovoltaic-thermal systems integrated with porous phase change material. Appl. Therm. Eng. **201**, 117727 (2022). https://doi.org/10.1016/j.applthermaleng.2021.117727
21. Evans, D.L.: Simplified method for predicting photovoltaic array output. Sol. Energy **27**, 555–560 (1981). https://doi.org/10.1016/0038-092X(81)90051-7
22. Slimani, M.E.A., Amirat, M., Kurucz, I., Bahria, S., Hamidat, A., Chaouch, W.B.: A detailed thermal-electrical model of three photovoltaic/thermal (PV/T) hybrid air collectors and photovoltaic (PV) module: comparative study under Algiers climatic conditions. Energy Convers. Manag. **133**, 458–476 (2017). https://doi.org/10.1016/j.enconman.2016.10.066

Hydrogen Production Prediction Model Based on an Artificial Neural Network for an EMS System in a Smart Grid: Case of the Dakhla Oued Ed-Dahab Region

Omar Chahir[1](✉), Imad Aboudrar[2], El Hanafi Arjdal[1], Mustapha Elyaqouti[1], El Mehdi Mellouli[3], Fouad demami[4], and Akram Sedki[5]

[1] Laboratory of Materials, Signals, Systems and Physical Modeling Faculty of Sciences of Agadir, Agadir, Morocco
omarchahir1994@gmail.com
[2] Engineering and Sustainable Development Research Team, EST of Dakhla Ibn Zohr University, Agadir, Morocco
[3] Laboratory of Engineering Systems and Applications (LISA), Sidi Mohamed Ben Abdellah University, Fez, Morocco
[4] Laboratory of Theoretical Physics and High Energy, Ibn Zohr University, Agadir, Morocco
[5] Mathematical and Computer Engineering, Ibn Zohr University, Agadir, Morocco

Abstract. This paper proposes an artificial neural network (ANN)-based prediction model to accurately estimate green hydrogen production in the Dakhla Oued Ed-Dahab region, using detailed data ex-extracted from HOMER Pro software. This model aims to optimize the management of renewable energy resources in a smart microgrid, particularly with regard to hydrogen production and storage, a key solution for sustainable development. The approach integrates crucial parameters from renewable sources such as solar and wind power, as well as operational data from the microgrid. The results obtained show a high degree of model robustness with reliable predictions.

This model can be directly integrated into an energy management system (EMS) to improve decisions related to hydrogen production and storage, contributing to better management of energy surpluses and reduced dependence on fossil fuels. Prospects include improving the model by integrating additional data and considering other environmental parameters.

Keywords: Energy management system · alkaline water electrolysis · Proton exchange membrane · artificial neural network · hydrogen production · smart grid · Matlab/Simulink · Hommer Pro

1 Introduction

The transition to renewable energy sources has become a global priority in response to current environmental and economic challenges. This image shows a modern smart microgrid system that incorporates solar and wind energy sources, an electolyzer for

I. Aboudrar et al. (Eds.): ICESST 2024, SUCI, pp. 43–53, 2025.
https://doi.org/10.1007/978-3-031-86705-7_5

hydrogen production, hydrogen storage, and an energy management system (EMS). In these new grids, hydrogen production and storage are essential considerations, supporting sectors like aviation, chemical industry, and electric vehicles, while also providing electrical energy to power loads and store in batteries. Green hydrogen, produced from the electrolysis of water using renewable energy sources (see Fig. 1) such as solar and wind power, represents a promising solution for meeting growing energy needs while reducing carbon emissions [1]. Hydrogen plays a crucial role, particularly in long-term energy storage, helping to smooth out the variations in production inherent in intermittent renewable energies such as solar and wind power [2]. However, efficient management of hydrogen production and storage in smart microgrids requires robust predictive tools [3]. Energy management systems (EMS) enable intelligent, optimized regulation of energy production and consumption within smart grids, enabling efficient use of available resources. Integrating a predictive model of hydrogen production into an EMS can significantly improve decisions linked to the storage and use of this hydrogen, thus helping to maximize the energy efficiency of systems [4].Within this framework, the main objective of this study is to develop a predictive model based on artificial intelligence (AI) capable of estimating hydrogen production in the Dakhla Oued Ed-Dahab region in real time. This model will be integrated into an EMS to optimize production and storage decisions, ensuring better exploitation of surplus renewable energy and sustainable management of energy resources.

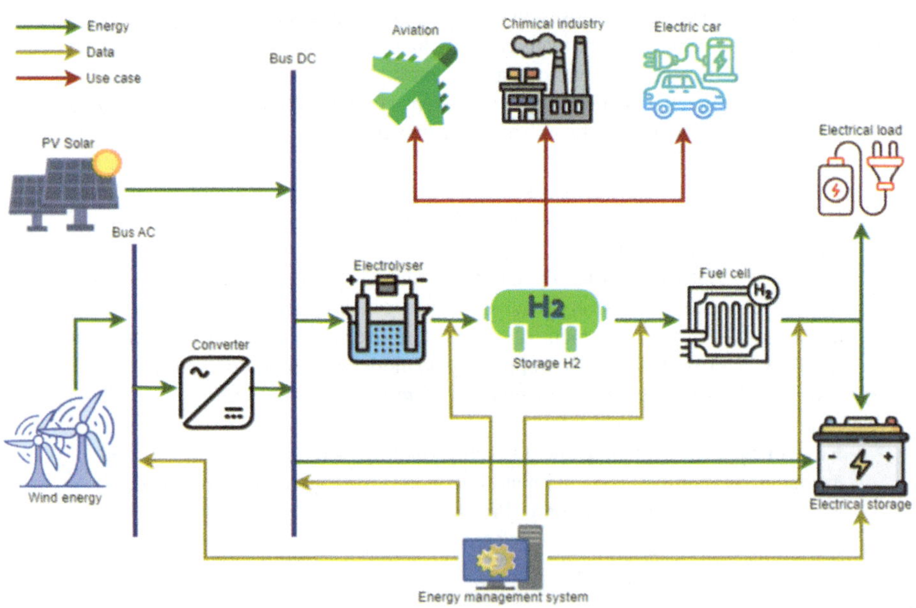

Fig. 1. Production process of hydrogen

Numerous studies have demonstrated the effectiveness of artificial neural networks (ANNs) in predicting and optimizing hydrogen production. **Bilgiç and Öztürk** used ANNs to model hydrogen production via water electrolysis, optimizing process variables and achieving high accuracy (93%) in predicting electrolysis parameters [5]. **Abiodun et al.** provided a broad overview of ANN applications across various fields, including energy, while highlighting combined ANN models to improve performance in complex systems such as hydrogen production [6]**. Zamaniyan et al**. showed that applying ANNs in an industrial hydrogen plant allowed better control of critical parameters such as temperature and pressure, thereby optimizing production [7]. **Abdelkareem et al.** reviewed the advancements of ANNs in hydrogen production technologies, emphasizing their potential to maximize productivity and reduce costs [8]. **Tawalbeh et al.** used ANNs with the Levenberg-Marquardt backpropagation algorithm to optimize hydrogen production in proton exchange membrane water electrolysis (PEMWE) systems, achieving better predictive performance than conventional models [9]. **Mensah et al**. developed an ANN model to predict hydrogen production from excess energy in a solar PV microgrid, demonstrating the efficiency of ANNs in harnessing this surplus energy [10]. Finally, **Tawalbeh et al**. also used ANNs to predict hydrogen production in electrolysis systems, outperforming methods such as linear regression and random forests in terms of accuracy [9]. These studies highlight the central role of ANNs in accurately predicting hydrogen production, contributing to efficiency improvements and cost reductions, which align with the goals of your own research on optimizing hydrogen production in smart microgrids.

The Dakhla Oued Ed-Dahab region was chosen due to ongoing megaprojects for green hydrogen production, but the model can be adapted to other regions, with precise localization in Homer Pro to obtain the corresponding meteorological parameters.

In our work, we employed a similar approach using artificial neural networks (ANNs); however, the analysis was conducted with a focus on performance metrics such as Mean Squared Error (MSE), histogram error data, and regression analysis. The curves were obtained using MATLAB SIMULINK. Additionally, we implemented a data division strategy where 70% of the dataset was used for training, 15% for validation, and 15% for testing, ensuring robust model evaluation. A key distinction in our research lies in the data sources, which include comprehensive simulations from **Homer Pro**. Furthermore, our model is designed for a smart grid system that integrates multiple components, such as photovoltaic (PV) panels, wind turbines, battery storage, electrical loads, and fuel cells. This generalist model aims to accurately reflect real-world smart grid scenarios, where various energy sources and storage systems interact dynamically an aspect not fully addressed in previous studies.

2 Data Sources and Methodology

2.1 Study Region: Dakhla Oued Ed-Dahab

Dakhla, located in southern Morocco, has a particularly favorable climate for renewable energy production, thanks in particular to its average sunshine of over 300 days per year and its favorable wind resources, with constant wind speeds regularly reaching 6 to 8 m/s. These conditions make the region an ideal setting in which to study the potential for producing green hydrogen via electrolysis, using abundant renewable resources.

Although we didn't carry out direct measurements in the region, simulations carried out using HOMER Pro software enabled us to reliably model the area's energy performance, considering its specific geographical and meteorological characteristics. By choosing this location for our simulations (see Fig. 2), we were able to exploit Dakhla Oued Ed-Dahab's strong potential as a strategic area for green hydrogen production, providing a solid basis for the prediction and optimization of hydrogen production systems.

Fig. 2. Dakhla location on HOMMER PRO

2.2 Data Extraction with HOMER Pro

HOMER Pro is an advanced simulation software package designed to model complex energy systems by integrating renewable resources and storage technologies. It enables energy configurations to be simulated and optimized according to local conditions and specific energy requirements. In this study, HOMER Pro was used to simulate solar and wind energy production in the Dakhla region, as well as the performance of hydrogen storage systems. These simulations consider meteorological variations in HOMER Pro about this region as it is presented (see Fig. 3), electrical loads and existing energy infrastructures to generate accurate data on energy flows.

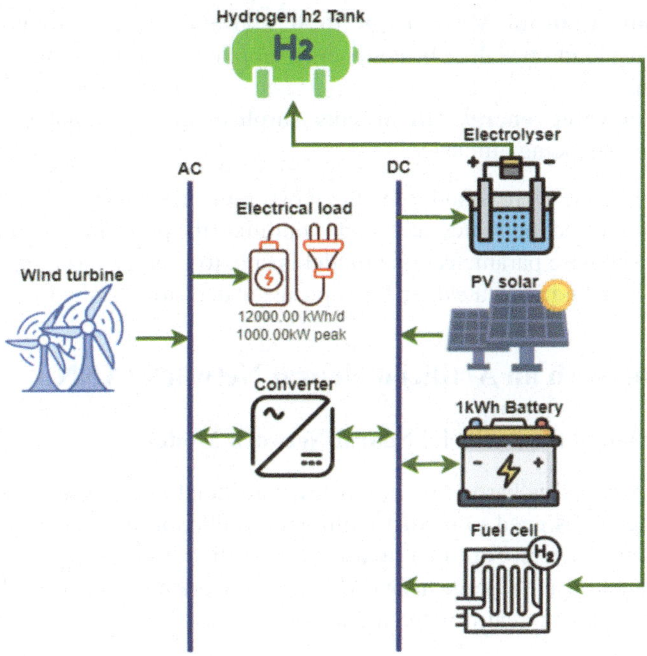

Fig. 3. Smart Grid installation employed

3 Choice of Relevance Parameters

3.1 Parameter Selection Criteria

Parameter selection criteria are based on their direct and measurable influence on hydrogen production. We have chosen to focus on parameters that directly affect the amount of energy available to feed the electolyzer, as well as those that influence energy management in the power system. Consequently, the model takes into account the energy produced by solar panels and wind turbines, the output power of the inverter, the AC electrical load served, as well as excess renewable energy. These factors are essential for understanding the dynamics of hydrogen production in a smart grid environment.

3.2 Parameters Used for Model Training

Here are the main parameters used, taken from simulations carried out with HOMER Pro:

- **Global solar radiation**: Indicates energy available for photovoltaic panels, affecting electricity production.
- **Wind speed**: Directly impacts wind energy production; higher speeds mean more hydrogen potential.
- **Solar panel power output**: Represents electricity produced for electrolysis.
- **Wind turbine power output**: Reflects wind energy available for the electolyzer, influenced by local weather.

- **Inverter power output**: Measures DC to AC conversion, crucial for powering loads.
- **AC electrical load served**: Indicates energy supplied to AC loads, key for optimizing distribution.
- **Excess renewable energy**: Represents surplus energy available for hydrogen production, enhancing efficiency.

These parameters were found to be the most influential on hydrogen production in the region studied, and their integration helps optimize the performance of the predictive model. Based on these parameters, the model is able to capture variations in renewable energy production and translate them into optimized decisions for hydrogen production.

4 Modeling with an Artificial Neural Network (ANN)

4.1 Description of the Artificial Neural Network Model

The model developed is based on a multi-layer artificial neural network (ANN). This network has been designed to predict hydrogen production in kg/day as a function of selected input parameters. The aim is to use these predictions to improve decisions about hydrogen production and storage in an EMS. The network has been trained on simulated data to provide accurate real-time predictions.

4.2 Network Architecture

The architecture of the ANN model (see Fig. 4) is composed of three main layers: an input layer, two hidden layers and an output layer. The input layer contains 7 neurons, each corresponding to one of the selected input parameters, such as solar radiation and wind speed. The two hidden layers, each comprising 40 neurons, model complex non-linear relationships between input parameters. The output layer produces a prediction of hydrogen production. The choice of using two hidden layers with 40 neurons each was based on preliminary tests which showed that this configuration offers a good balance between performance and computational complexity, while avoiding over-fitting.

4.3 Data Analysis

The data processing starts with an initial matrix of size 8760×36, representing a full year of hourly observations across 36 variables, and reduces it to a matrix of inputs with size 8760×7. This is achieved by selecting only the 7 most relevant variables for predicting hydrogen production, such as global solar energy, wind speed, inverter power output, and more. This reduction helps simplify the data, making the training of the neural network more efficient while preserving the key information needed for accurate predictions.

The input and output data are normalized to improve model performance. The data is then split into three sets: 70% for training, 15% for validation, and 15% for testing. This split allows the model to be trained on the majority of the data while using the validation and test sets to assess its generalization ability. The neural network used has two hidden layers with 40 neurons each, utilizing ReLU activation functions.

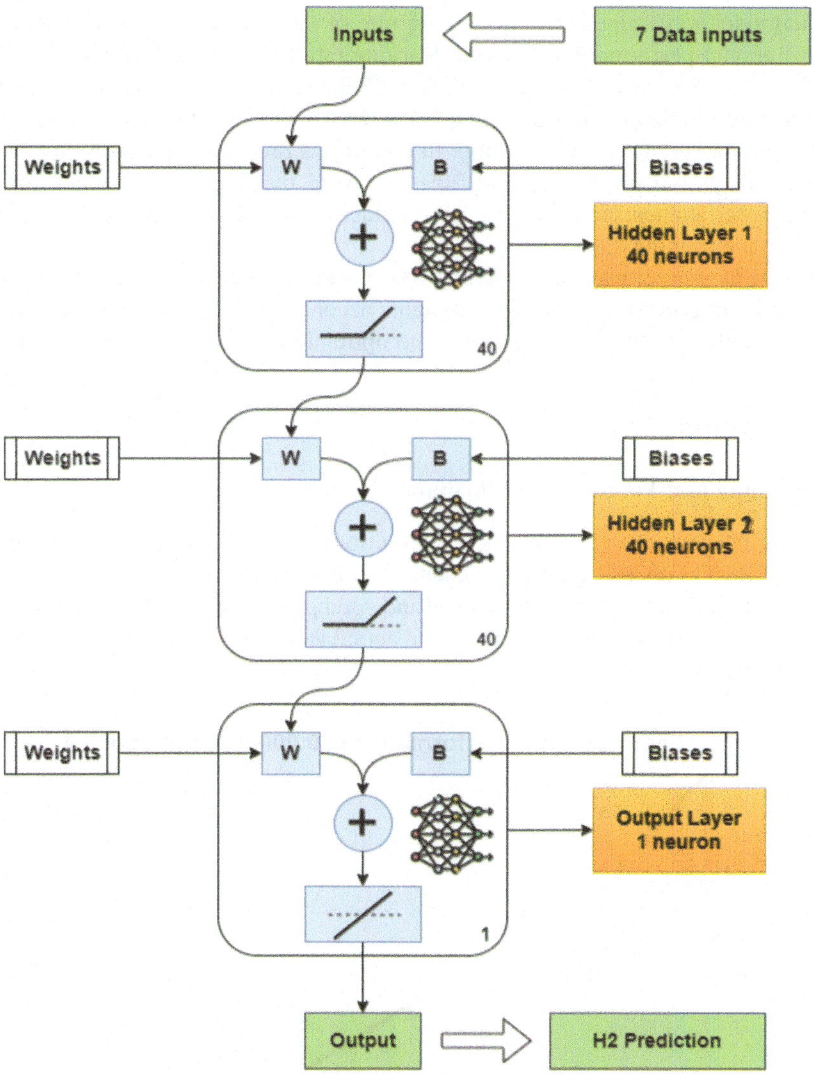

Fig. 4. Neural network architecture

4.4 Activation Function and Hyperparameter Settings

The activation function used in hidden layers is the ReLU (Rectified Linear Unit) function. The choice of ReLU is justified by its ability to introduce nonlinearity while avoiding certain problems encountered with functions such as sigmoid or tanh, notably gradient saturation. ReLU also enables faster convergence of the model during training. For the output layer, a linear activation function was chosen, as the prediction of hydrogen production is a continuous variable.

The model was trained with a learning rate of 0.01, after cross-validation tests to optimize model performance. A higher learning rate led to instability in convergence, while a lower rate slowed down training without significantly improving results. A stopping criterion based on mean square error (MSE) was used to evaluate performance during training and avoid overlearning. In addition, a dropout regularization technique was applied, with a dropout rate of 20%, to avoid overlearning. Dropout randomly deactivates certain neurons during training, reducing the risk of the model becoming too specific to the training data.

Finally, the model was trained over 1000 epochs, with periodic validation to assess performance at each stage and adjust weights accordingly. The total training time was reasonable, allowing stable convergence and optimal generalization to the test data.

5 Results and Analysis

5.1 Training and Validation Performance Curves

The figure below (see Fig. 5) shows the evolution of model performance during training. After just 4 epochs, the model reaches a minimum mean square error (MSE) of 0.00066794, indicating rapid convergence and good prediction accuracy. MSE measures the difference between model-predicted and actual values, with a lower value indicating a better model fit.

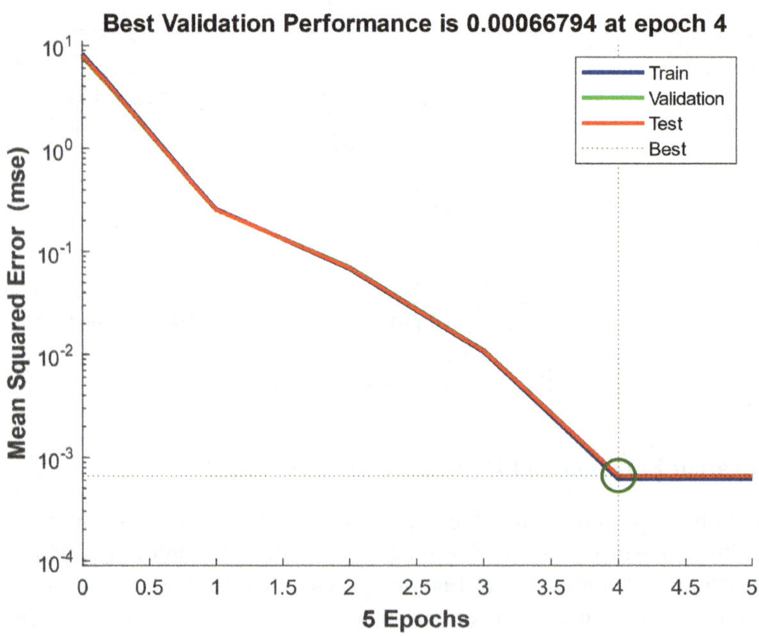

Fig. 5. Model performance

5.2 Analysis of Prediction Errors

The error histogram (see Fig. 6) shows that the majority of predictions are concentrated around the zero error, indicating high model accuracy. A very low number of significant errors is observed, reflecting good model generalization and an ability to minimize deviations between predicted and actual values.

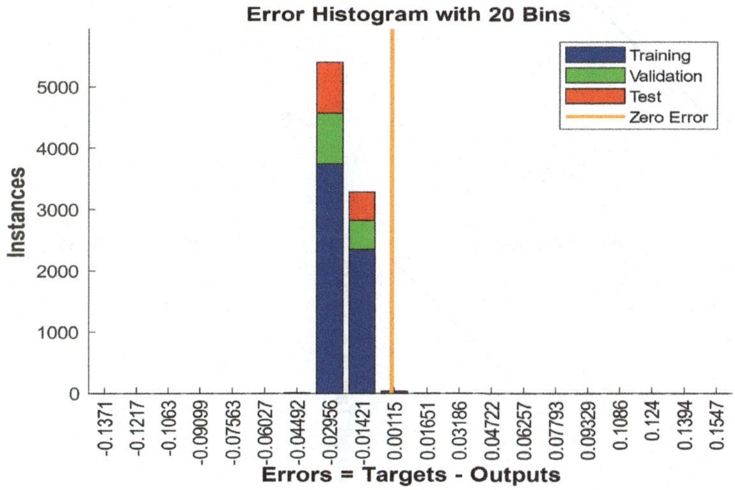

Fig. 6. Histogram of errors

5.3 Regression Analysis

The correlation coefficients (R) (see Fig. 7) show a strong correspondence between predicted and actual data, with values close to 0.99 for training, validation and test.

These results indicate that the model predicts with high accuracy and generalizes well across different data sets.

5.4 Assessment of Model Robustness

The results obtained show a high degree of model robustness, confirmed by a low prediction error and a high regression coefficient (R close to 0.999). These indicators show that the ANN model is capable of predicting hydrogen production from input data with a high degree of accuracy, while effectively generalizing the results to different data sets.

5.5 Justification of the Model's Robustness

The use of techniques such as dropout and hyperparameter optimization has minimized overlearning errors and improved model generalization. The careful choice of input parameters, based on their relevance to hydrogen production, also enhanced the model's robustness, as evidenced by the low prediction error and high correlation coefficient.

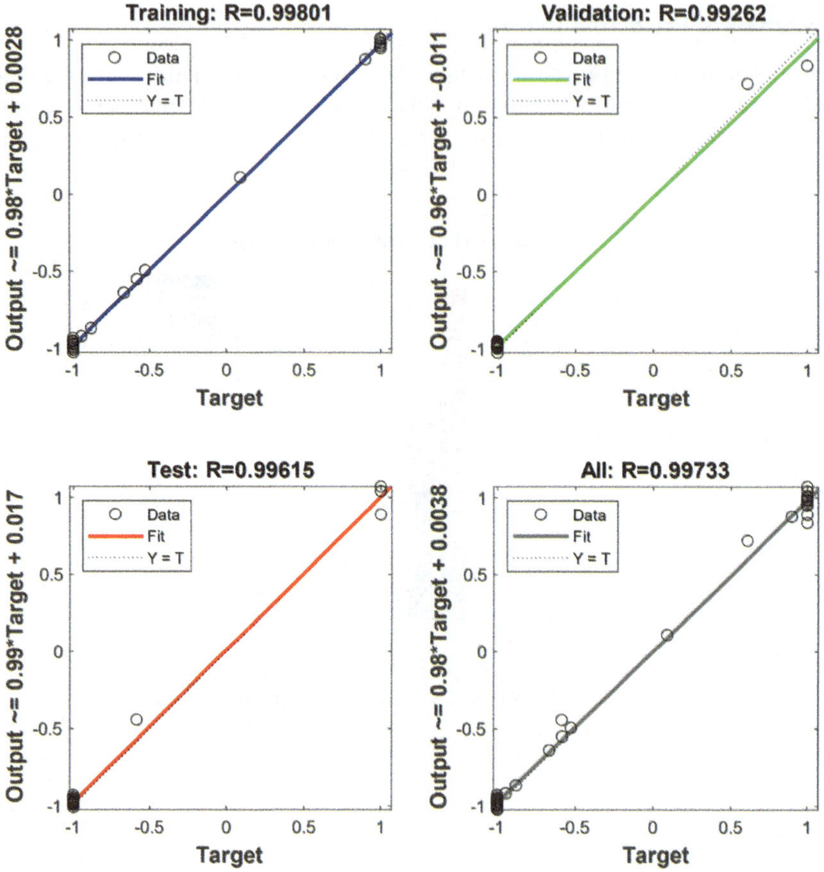

Fig. 7. Regression

5.6 Prospects and Possible Improvements

Improvements can be envisaged, such as the addition of historical weather data to capture seasonal variations, the integration of additional parameters such as ambient temperature to improve accuracy, and the use of deep neural networks (DNNs) which could enable better modeling of complex energy system dynamics, further increasing the accuracy of predictions.

6 Conclusion

The artificial neural network (ANN) model developed in this study proved highly effective in predicting hydrogen production within a smart grid. Based on relevant input parameters from HOMER Pro simulations, the model not only proved its robustness, but also its ability to provide accurate predictions, even in a context of energy complexity.

The potential impact of this model is considerable. Its integration into an energy management system (EMS) would optimize both hydrogen production and storage, while improving the management of renewable energies, particularly in resource-rich regions such as Dakhla Oued Ed-Dahab. This could make a significant contribution to the energy transition to sustainable sources.

To take this further, future research could focus on improving predictive models, notably by including additional parameters such as historical weather data or load dynamics. The application of the model to other geographical regions, as well as the integration of more complex neural networks into EMS systems, would offer new prospects for enhancing the management of renewable energies in smart grids.

References

1. Hassan, Q., Algburi, S.: Green hydrogen: a pathway to a sustainable energy future. Int. J. Hydrogen Energy **50**, 310–333 (2024)
2. Nnabuife, S.G., Hamzat, A.K.: Integration of renewable energy sources in tandem with electrolysis: a technology review for green hydrogen production. Int. J. Hydrogen Energy. Article in press
3. Jia, C., He, H.: Learning-based model predictive energy management for fuel cell hybrid electric bus with health-aware control. Appl. Energy **335**, 122228 (2024)
4. Valverde, L., Rosa, F.: Energy management strategies in hydrogen smart-grids: a laboratory experience. Int. J. Hydrogen Energy **41**, 13715–13725 (2016)
5. Bilgiç, G., Öztürk, B.: Modeling of artificial neural networks for hydrogen production via water electrolysis. Ecjse **10**, 137–146 (2023)
6. Abiodun, O.I., Jantan, A.: State of the art in artificial neural network applications: a survey. Heliyon Article no. e00938 (2018)
7. Zamaniyan, A., Joda, F.: Application of artificial neural networks (ANN) for modeling of industrial hydrogen plant. Inte. J. Hydrogen Energy **38**, 6289–6297 (2013)
8. Abdelkareem, M.A., Soudan, B.: Progress of artificial neural networks applications in hydrogen production. Chem. Eng. Res. Des. **182**, 66–86 (2022)
9. Tawalbeh, M., Shomope, I.: Prediction of hydrogen production in proton exchange membrane water electrolysis via neural networks. Int. J. Thermofluids **24**, 100849 (2024)
10. Mensah, G., Opoku, R.: Investigating green hydrogen production operated by redundant energy on a solar PV mini grid through matlab simulation and artificial neural network. Int. J. Hydrogen Energy. Article in press

Electric Vehicles and Charging Infrastructures in Morocco: Challenges and Recommendations

Mouaad Boulakhbar[1(✉)] and Youssef Oubail[2]

[1] Université de Pau et des Pays de L'Adour, E2S UPPA, SIAME, Pau, France
mouad.boulakhbar@gmail.com

[2] Laboratoire des Sciences de l'Ingénieur et Management de l'Energie, ENSA Agadur, Université Ibn Zohr, Agadir, Morocco

Abstract. The development of renewable energies will lead to more electric vehicles (EVs) to eventually replace a part of ICE (Internal Combustion Engine) vehicles in order to decarbonize the transport sector. This shift to electric vehicles necessitates anticipating potential storage requirements, as well as the services and users of vehicle batteries. This shift requires urgent restructuring of the transport sector to integrate electric vehicles as a core component of future energy systems. In this article, the development strategy of the electric vehicles is Morocco are outlined. The status of EVs and charging infrastructures in the country are reviewed. The paper addresses the challenges and proposes instructive recommendations to the Moroccan ecosystem towards a large-scale adoption of electric vehicles. To increase the development of electric mobility in Morocco, this research concludes that governmental policies for a local EV and battery industries in parallel with an organized installation of charging stations in public locations are required. This study also demonstrates the need of legislating charging requirements for electric vehicles to maximize their adoption in Morocco, with the objective of deploying electric vehicles on a wider scale.

Keywords: electric vehicles · charging infrastructures · road map · Morocco

1 Introduction

The world is currently experiencing a major energy revolution. Climate change and the massive exploitation of fossil fuel reserves are forcing policy makers to encourage the adoption of less polluting and more environmentally friendly solutions for producing and storing electrical energy [1]. In 2020, the transportation industry was responsible for more than 20% of worldwide CO2 emissions. Since 1960, global greenhouse gas (GHG) emissions from the transportation industry and sub-sectors have more than doubled and are growing faster than any other end-use sector to reach 15 Gt CO2 emissions in 2020 [2]. Road vehicles accounted for almost 21% of this expansion (See Fig. 1) [3].

Therefore, reducing emissions from the transportation sector has been a daunting task given the inevitable increase in demand, the slow turnover and salvageability of stock and infrastructure costs [4]. In this context, Electric Vehicles (EVs) have been

I. Aboudrar et al. (Eds.): ICESST 2024, SUCI, pp. 54–65, 2025.
https://doi.org/10.1007/978-3-031-86705-7_6

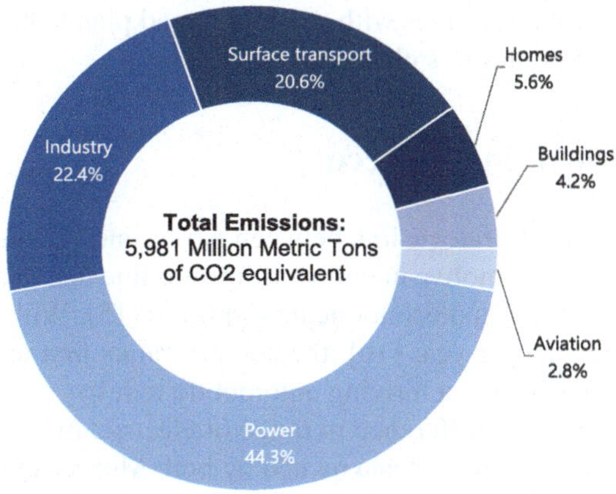

Fig. 1. Global greenhouse gas emissions by economic sector in 2020. Source

introduced as a sustainable alternative to conventional transport in terms of fossil fuel consumption and atmospheric pollution [5, 6].

Indeed, EVs have several advantages. First, they assist to reduce CO2 emissions, particularly when combined with renewable energy systems (RES), such as PVs in metropolitan settings [7]. The efficiency of EVs integration with renewable energy systems can be further increased by using demand-side management (DSM) methods [8] and smart charging [9]. Second, they could assist eliminate the "pick curve" issue produced by high PV (photovoltaic) penetration during noon [10], as well as reduce grid operating costs by smoothing the demand profile using smart charging schemes [11]. Third, EVs can play a key role in the power system stabilization while exchanging energy with the power grid upon the emerging concept of the smart grid [12]. While a single electric vehicle can play this role of power compensation between the home and grid or the building and grid [13], a fleet of electric vehicles can be the indispensable solution as adjustable generators to compensate the community-grid system [14].

The EVs market in Morocco is still in the very beginning stage. Despite certain advancements and efforts in recent years, the number of registered electric vehicles remains quite low. A dearth of legislative and political backing exists to enhance and encourage the electric car market. As a result, this article analyses Morocco's EV (Electric Vehicle) and charging infrastructure (EVCI). Local challenges and opportunities related to EVs in the Moroccan context are discussed. The study examines the country's uneven distribution of EVCI and makes recommendations to improve future EVCS system implementation in Morocco. A SWOT analysis of electric vehicles in Morocco is given, along with a set of recommendations and a detailed roadmap for the country's transition to electric vehicles.

This paper is organized as follows; Sect. 2 and present an overview of EVs development in Morocco. Section 3 discusses the variables impacting Morocco's EV market development and gives a series of recommendations to assesses the country's EVCI in light of renewable energy integration, development of a charging tariff system adapted to the Moroccan context. Section 4 includes a SWOT analysis to give a broad overview of all positive and negative variables with a detailed road plan to boost EVs adoption in the kingdom. Section 5 comes to a close.

2 EVs Development in Morocco

Morocco is currently a vital strategic link between Africa and Europe. Morocco is one of Africa's most important automotive manufacturing sites due to its geographical position and competitive, competent, and economical workforce [15]. With an ambitious target of 700,000 units produced per year [16], the country ranks first in Africa. Morocco is also one of the countries having a thriving automobile industry.

On the Moroccan roads a difference in range of electric, hybrid and plug-in hybrid cars can be distinguished between Tesla owned by both Moroccan immigrant and local Moroccan citizens, Range Rover plug-in hybrids, Toyota hybrids, and Renault ZOE.

Otherwise, many studies investigated the EVs in Morocco from different perspectives. For example, Chachdi et al. [17] looked at forecasting EV demand in Morocco. The results show that demand depends significantly on the age of potential EV buyers, their daily mileage, and the owners of conventional cars who will be the most in demand for this type of vehicle. Benabdelaziz et al. [18] addresses the adaptation of mid and low-cost vehicles to the excess temperatures, which would add a challenge on the life of batteries in southern Morocco. The results highlight how the high temperatures of the southern area may be impeding the development of this technology, as well as the recommended novel ways to ensure the safety and increase the cycle life of batteries in electric cars. Meanwhile, Boulakhbar et al. [19] focused on predicting the EVs charging duration in public charging duration in Morocco and [20] applied deep learning to predict the EVs arrival and departure times in Morocco in order to evaluate the grid impact of EVs integration in the Kingdom.

Meanwhile, a study on the potential of the sustainable transport market in Morocco was carried out by the energy federation. The calculation model used in this study was established based on the evolution of the world market of electric vehicles during the last 15 years, the projections of evolution of the market of electric vehicles to Horizon 2030 [21] (established by the International Energy Agency), the interviewed participants' visions of market evolution, the industrial projects for the manufacturing of electric vehicles in Morocco. Three scenarios were considered (see Table 1). They result in very different potentials, depending mainly on the involvement of the Moroccan government.

Table 1. EVs potential evolution scenarios

Scenario	Details
Optimistic scenario	425,704 vehicles in 2030 if the state is fully involved in implementing the policy recommendations
Moderate scenario	257,777 vehicles in 2030 if the State's involvement is average
Pessimistic scenario	11,391 vehicles if the Moroccan market follows the global growth of the sustainable vehicle stock without any government intervention

Hybrid electric vehicles (HEVs) sales in Morocco are greater than all electric cars due to their low cost, long market standing, long distance, and compliance with usage patterns in terms of fueling manner. In addition, there are still insufficient incentives for electric vehicles and electric vehicles are not widely used. HEV is more acceptable in social psychology because it is impossible to change user habits immediately [48].

3 Charging Infrastructure Development in Morocco

Meanwhile, the development of a robust charging infrastructure laid the basis for the introduction of electric cars [22]. With IRESEN (Institute of Research in Renewable and New Energies), Morocco has taken several initiatives to promote charging infrastructure development. As an example, the Green Miles project [23] focused on installing 74 charging stations to cover more than 600 km of highways. Also implemented two chargers connected to a solar panel in the city of Rabat. Total Morocco has completed the construction of 15 electric charging stations. These 50 kW and 22 kW charging stations located in the 10 TOTAL highway service stations on the Tangier-Agadir route, as well as in the main cities of the Kingdom (Agadir, Marrakech, Casablanca, Rabat, and Tangier). Customers who have chosen electric vehicles can now travel on these major routes without any problems of autonomy, by refueling in the TOTAL network. In November 2021, Afrimobility has announced the deployment of its first network of fast charging stations for cars, called "Fastvolt" throughout the Kingdom. The AKWA Group subsidiary has 50 kW charging stations located in Afriquia service stations on the Tangier-Agadir axis, for electric and plug-in hybrid vehicles. Figure 2 represent the distribution of plugs by charging speed [24].

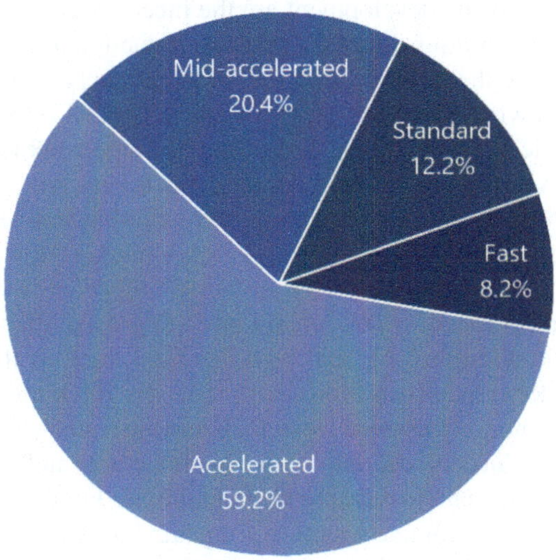

Fig. 2. Distribution of plugs by charging speed

The lack of a uniform distribution of EVCS infrastructure across the country is one of the reasons why EV use has not become widespread in Morocco. Currently, the

EVCS network is concentrated on the country's most populated cities, such as Rabat, Casablanca, Marrakech, and Tangier. The West, which is home to most industrial facilities and large firms, has a greater GDP (Gross Domestic Product) per capita (which makes electric cars cheaper). As a result, the majority of EVCSs are located in the same geographic area. The majority of provinces without EVCS are in the east and south. As a result, EV drivers will most certainly have difficulty charging their vehicles as they travel from west to east.

Morocco expects real growth in the sale of electric vehicles in the coming years. However, the government will have to encourage each region to establish a roadmap to facilitate and accelerate the deployment of charging infrastructures on a regional scale.

4 EVs Integration Challenges and Recommendations

This discussion section is divided into five subsections to help readers better comprehend Morocco's EV and EVCS areas. First, a list of proposals to support the proliferation of electric cars throughout the Kingdom is offered. The following section describes potential solutions to EVCS infrastructure challenges. Following that, an evaluation of the renewable energy integration of EVs and associated domains is made. Then, the importance of smart grid development and the establishment of a charging tariffs are respectively discussed.

4.1 Integration of EVs in Morocco

Electric vehicles market penetration is not uniform across countries and regions [25]. The most significant factors of its development are the incentives offered and the country's buying power [26]. Purchase subsidies, tax breaks, production incentives, and infrastructure incentive billing are the top EV incentives in the globe [26]. To date, Morocco has implemented the following measures, incorporated in the 2017 finance law, to develop the hybrid and electric vehicle market: Lowering the import tax to 2.5% from 17.5%, exemption from the vignette, and exemption from the luxury tax.

Even though the tax decrease is regarded a substantial incentive, Morocco's limited purchasing power need other steps to encourage the EV market. However, these measures have not yet led to a significant reduction in the selling prices of hybrid and electric vehicles marketed in Morocco, which remain more expensive than combustion engine vehicles. However, in addition to global considerations such as the difficulty of CO_2 emissions, there are local factors in Morocco that need a quick transition to EVs:

The country's reliance on imported fossil fuels and the country's high gasoline prices. Morocco's aim to introduce a local automotive manufacturer and capture a share of the new and growing electric vehicle market, which requires a large-scale domestic market. Morocco is currently an automotive manufacturing hub for many worldwide companies. High internal demand for EVs will be a factor in these companies' decision to relocate their EV manufacturing facilities to Morocco.

For these reasons, in addition some incentives can be implemented to increase the adoption of electric cars in the Kingdom: It would be necessary to create a commission including all the actors of the sector of the transport for a better implication cross-sectorial namely the ministry of the interior, the ministry of the transport and the associations as the AIVAM (Association of Vehicle Importers in Morocco), the users of EV, as well as the actors of the energy such as the ministry of the energy, MASEN (Moroccan Agency for Sustainable Energy), the ONEE (National Office of Electricity and Water), the federations of the energy and the sector of the car industry to its head the ministry of the industry and the CGEM (General Confederation of Moroccan Enterprises).

Public awareness is one of the important keys to accelerate the EVs adoption, this through different awareness campaigns in different cities and through high level events. The Moroccan authorities should integrate the technological uncertainties into formalized procurement plans. The procurement models that work for each entity and each city should be also carefully studied and analyzed.

4.2 EVs Charging Infrastructures in Morocco

With all efforts to promote electric mobility and EVs adoption, the deployment of an effective and adequate charging infrastructure still a key point to rise the EVs adoption. Drivers, on the other hand, are concerned about the lack of conveniently available charging infrastructure.

Sufficient charging infrastructure is critical to the successful deployment of massive electric vehicles. The transportation company and the EV operation company must arrange every detail. Furthermore, infrastructure investment must be properly scrutinized. Conducted a survey on the feasibility of constructing an electric car charging infrastructure. Infrastructure surveys should be carried out in states that do not have EVCS, largely with the assistance of local governments and with incentives and instructions created by appropriate private sector ministries. As well as installation of facilities dedicated to the recharging of electric vehicles in parking lots and new buildings and progressive deployment of normal and accelerated recharging infrastructure within local authorities for the urban network, using public lighting panels is big priority.

Electric vehicle batteries have a relatively large capacity and charging an electric vehicle can require a significant amount of grid electricity. Given the extensive use of electric cars, the detrimental impact on the power infrastructure must be carefully assessed. Charging an electric vehicle at home or in an EVCS can have a variety of consequences. Connected substations can experience problems such as overload, overheating, high losses, undervoltage, frequency regulation, tripping, and harmonics [28]. This can affect infrastructure, impede new investments and incur additional costs. At the same time, all charging operations in progress are free, and the creation of a charging system or institution is still mandatory.

Relevant ministries and agencies, as well as ONEE (National Office of Electricity and Water), must perform forecast surveys on the growth of electric cars, upgrade grid infrastructure in line with the prediction, invest in distant locations and support the integration of electric vehicles with renewables.

4.3 EVs Integration with Renewables and V2G

Morocco's high solar and wind energy potential is an advantage to encourage EV development. When compared to other countries, the installation of an intelligent charging infrastructure powered by renewable energy can minimize the cost of charging electric vehicles in Morocco. In addition, the storage capacity of the electric vehicle is "peak load" so that the surplus solar energy can be used to charge the electric vehicle at noon and the battery of the electric vehicle can stabilize its intermittent properties. It will be a solution to overcome the problem. Morocco's renewable energy source [29] is possible.

PV (Photovoltaic) parking lots are an excellent way to mitigate the negative impacts of EV charging on the grid. However, the present PV-equipped parking lots in Morocco are generally devoid of EVCS and are solely utilized to power the buildings. Additional feed-in tariff incentives [30] or subsidies can be provided for PV parking lots in Morocco, this can also provide lower grid infrastructure investments with lower capacity increase.

4.4 Smart Grid and Smart Charging

According to the European Technology Platform for Smart Grids [31], a smart grid (SG) is one that can successfully integrate all relevant users' activities and behaviors (distributed power generation, customers, and users who do both) to ensure low loss, high quality, and supply security in a sustainable and economical manner. It is possible to secure an efficient energy system [32]. In general, a SG is a system that enables two-way communication between power end users, such as private individuals or businesses, and electricity providers. The information gathered throughout this communication procedure improves the efficiency of the energy grid's operation. The investigations the prospects for smart grid development in Morocco are outlined in [33], an overview of recommendations and solutions to remove some obstacles to the deployment of the smart grid in Morocco are proposed by [34]. While opportunities and challenges of management and control of smart grid systems in the Kingdom were deeply detailed in [35]. The presentation of a comparative study of metaheuristic methods applied to the smart grid in Morocco was given in [36].

The usage of bidirectional charging is one of the known approaches to address the problem that Morocco's infrastructure cannot withstand large peak charges. Protocols such as Vehicle to Grid (V2G), Vehicle to Building (V2B), and Vehicle to Home (V2H) have been proposed for this purpose [37]. These protocols try to exploit the batteries of an electric car as an energy storage device for usage during peak loads by adopting a smart grid [38]. The three main differences are scope. This refers to the entire electrical network, vehicle fleet, or vehicle owner's home.

4.5 EV Charging Tariffs

Charging fees are one of the most powerful tools regulators have at their disposal for influencing EV-grid interactions, such as where, when, and how EV charging happens [39]. Reduction of capital and operating costs in large facilities requires careful management of charging [40]. Connecting many electric vehicles in the same area can reduce electricity quality and supply reliability because the distribution network is not designed for these moving loads [41]. To alleviate the damage, the charging price must be adjusted to change the spatial distribution of the PEV charging load. Many governments have introduced utility rates in their area [42].

Currently charging an EV in Morocco is free and the determination of a pricing model adapted to the Moroccan context is urgent. Generally, the cost of charging an electric vehicle (EV) is determined by the price of energy at various charging stations (home, work, public), vehicle usage, area, time of day, charging power and equipment, and installation cost. Morocco is a pure regulated electricity market where the ONEE holds a long-term contract with different distributers and all distributers have different electricity prices. For these reasons, Morocco needs a charging tariffs model applicable to regulated electricity markets which jointly optimizes the EV admission control, pricing, and charging scheduling to maximize the charging station's profit.

5 SWOT Analysis and EV Roadmap of Morocco

A SWOT (Strengths, Weaknesses, Opportunities and Threats) analysis was conducted (see Table 2) to summarize the strengths and weaknesses of the Moroccan government's strategy for the transition to electric mobility.

Table 2. SWOT analysis of EVs in Morocco

Strengths	Weaknesses
Morocco's highly developed automobile sector (ranked first in Africa in terms of exports), as well as its qualified and inexpensive labor force Voluntary government policy, as embodied in the National Strategy for Sustainable Development through 2030 State exemplarity (30% of new acquisitions by 2030) Increased possibilities for EV-RES integration (high solar and wind potential in Morocco)	The costs of EVs are higher than those of internal combustion automobiles Limited incentives that do not significantly decrease the price of EVs on the market A scarcity of fast charging facilities on the national highway system The country's non-homogeneous distribution of EVCSs (EVCSs are concentrated in the north part) Lack of a regulatory framework on sustainable mobility and energy sales by charging station operators
Opportunities	**Threats**
Orientations of manufacturers installed in Morocco (Renault, Peugeot) towards the electric vehicle Memorandum of Understanding on the development of an electric transport ecosystem in Morocco by the Chinese group "BYD Auto Industry" High compatibility with the area's development of renewable energies (particularly solar) High gasoline prices in Morocco Open and flexible to new business models	Treatment of sustainable mobility outside the energy transition Conservative ICEV users The lack of public knowledge and information regarding EVs The expense of EVCSs and the requirement for additional infrastructure Unexpected demand on the grid as a result of erratic consumer behavior

Based on this analysis, a roadmap for the development of EVs in Morocco can be drawn up for the short, medium, and long term, as shown in Table 3. Issues analyzed in Table 3 were identified based on different global strategies for integrating and developing EVs and improving their infrastructure. Our analysis is in line with the results presented by [43] which gives a Metrex barrier of EV adoption in Morocco.

Table 3. Proposed priority roadmap for EVs and EV subsectors in Morocco.

Period	EV	Battery technologies	EVCS
Short term (1–2 years)	- Increasing public awareness of e-mobility - Implementation of incentivizing or encouraging policies relating to electric mobility - Establishment of a framework on state exemplarity of and Local Authorities	- Designing an intelligent battery management system and encouraging researchers to work on it	- Setting up dedicated facilities for recharging electric vehicles in car parks and new buildings - Establishment of a framework for the sale of electrical energy by the operators of charging stations - Wide distribution of EVCS in the country - Setting of a charging tariff model - Common mobile Platform
Medium term (3–7 years)	- Increasing the public e-transportation (e-buses, e-taxis etc.)	- Domestic battery cell production and incentives for innovative technologies Assistance in the establishment of battery manufacturing factories in Morocco	- Improving fast charging facilities - Investment planning with detailed analysis of grid effects
Long term (7+ years)	- Being an EV production center	- Improving the second-life battery integration with renewables	- Implementation of a Pilot City project for the development of urban recharging infrastructure - Subsidies for charging station installation are being implemented

6 Conclusion and Policy Implications

This paper offers a comprehensive evaluation of the EV and EVCS markets in Morocco, and its conclusions are designed to assist decision-makers, industry stakeholders, and researchers in understanding the obstacles and potential for EVs in Morocco.

Importantly, the implementation of the roadmap requires cross-cutting governance at local, regional, and national levels. Beyond the political implementation of sustainable mobility, the continuous exchange and engagement of stakeholders could be ensured by a permanent and neutral platform, serving as a facilitator and focal point to create a real sustainable mobility community, deepen priorities, make common recommendations, and strengthen Morocco's international presence in international initiatives and coalitions.

References

1. Ağbulut, Ü., Sarıdemir, S.: A general view to converting fossil fuels to cleaner energy source by adding nanoparticles. Int. J. Ambient Energy **42**(13), 1569–1574 (2021). https://doi.org/10.1080/01430750.2018.1563822
2. Kang, J.N., Wei, Y.M., Liu, L.C., Han, R., Yu, B.Y., Wang, J.W.: Energy systems for climate change mitigation: a systematic review. Appl. Energy **263** (2020). https://doi.org/10.1016/j.apenergy.2020.114602

3. Huntingford, C., et al.: The link between a global 2 °C warming threshold and emissions in years 2020, 2050 and beyond. Environ. Res. Lett. **7**(1) (2012). https://doi.org/10.1088/1748-9326/7/1/014039
4. Transport Environment (2021)
5. Asdrubali, F., Carrese, S., Patella, S.M., Sabatini, L.: Development of electric urban mobility: comparative research and preliminary survey. Eur. J. Sustain. Dev. Res. **2**(3), 32 (2018). https://doi.org/10.20897/ejosdr/89694
6. Virta Global Report. https://www.virta.global/global-electric-vehicle-market. Accessed 11 June 2022
7. Sujitha, N., Krithiga, S.: RES based EV battery charging system: a review. Renew. Sustain. Energy Rev. **75**, 978–988 (2017). https://doi.org/10.1016/j.rser.2016.11.078
8. Mahmud, K., Town, G.E., Morsalin, S., Hossain, M.J.: Integration of electric vehicles and management in the internet of energy. Renew. Sustain. Energy Rev. **82**, 4179–4203 (2018). https://doi.org/10.1016/j.rser.2017.11.004
9. Shi, R., Li, S., Zhang, P., Lee, K.Y.: Integration of renewable energy sources and electric vehicles in V2G network with adjustable robust optimization. Renew. Energy **153**, 1067–1080 (2020). https://doi.org/10.1016/j.renene.2020.02.027
10. Salisbury, M., Toor, W.: How and why leading utilities are embracing electric vehicles. Electricity J. **29**(6), 22–27 (2016). https://doi.org/10.1016/j.tej.2016.07.004
11. Paterakis, N.G., Erdinç, O., Bakirtzis, A.G., Catalão, J.P.S.: Optimal household appliances scheduling under day-ahead pricing and load-shaping demand response strategies. IEEE Trans. Ind. Inf. **11**(6), 1509–1519 (2015). https://doi.org/10.1109/TII.2015.2438534
12. Barone, G., Buonomano, A., Calise, F., Forzano, C., Palombo, A.: Building to vehicle to building concept toward a novel zero energy paradigm: Modelling and case studies. Renew. Sustain. Energy Rev. **101**, 625–648 (2019). https://doi.org/10.1016/j.rser.2018.11.003
13. De, S., Electrique, G.: Couplage énergies renouvelables et électromobilité : Cas d'étude pour le Maroc (2018)
14. Benabdelhadi. Recent developments in the automobile industry in Morocco as part of the 2014–2020 industrial acceleration plan. CHERJAOUI & BENABDELHADI/Revue AME **3**(1), 481–497 (2021). https://revues.imist.ma/?journal=AME
15. Oxford Business Group Report. https://oxfordbusinessgroup.com/analysis/driver%E2%80%99s-seat-automotive-manufacturers-and-suppliers-flock-kingdom. Accessed 11 June 2022
16. Chachdi, Rahmouni, B., Zahi, J., Ikken, B.: Forecasting the demand for electric cars in morocco. Int. J. Smart Grid Clean Energy **8**(2), 191–200 (2019). https://doi.org/10.12720/sgce.8.2.191-200
17. Benabdelaziz, K., Maaroufi, M., Ikken, B.: Degradation of lithium-ion batteries in electric vehicles at high temperatures: a case study (2018). https://doi.org/10.1109/IRSEC.2018.8702871
18. Mouaad, B., Farag, M., Kawtar, B., Tarik, K., Malika, Z.: A deep learning approach for electric vehicle charging duration prediction at public charging stations: the case of Morocco. In: ITM Web of Conferences, vol. 43, p. 01024 (2022). https://doi.org/10.1051/itmconf/20224301024
19. Boulakhbar, M., et al.: Electric vehicles arrival and departure time prediction based on deep learning: the case of Morocco. In: 2nd International Conference on Innovative Research in Applied Science, Engineering and Technology (IRASET), pp. 1–8 (2022)
20. IEA Global Energy Review (2021). https://www.iea.org/reports/global-energy-review-2021. Accessed 11 June 2022
21. Chachdi, Rahmouni, B., Aniba, G.: Socio-economic analysis of electric vehicles in Morocco. Energy Procedia **141**, 644–653 (2017). https://doi.org/10.1016/j.egypro.2017.11.087
22. Illmann, U., Kluge, J.: Public charging infrastructure and the market diffusion of electric vehicles. Transp. Res. Part D: Transp. Environ. **86** (2020). https://doi.org/10.1016/j.trd.2020.102413

23. Hybrid and Electric Vehicles in Morocco (2019). https://www.voitureelectrique.ma/green-miles-mises-en-service-fin-juin/. Accessed 11 June 2022
24. Chargemap. https://chargemap.com/about/stats/morocco. Accessed 11 June 2022
25. Yabe, K., Shinoda, Y., Seki, T., Tanaka, H., Akisawa, A.: Market penetration speed and effects on CO2 reduction of electric vehicles and plug-in hybrid electric vehicles in Japan. Energy Policy **45**, 529–540 (2012). https://doi.org/10.1016/j.enpol.2012.02.068
26. Ma, S.C., Xu, J.H., Fan, Y.: Willingness to pay and preferences for alternative incentives to EV purchase subsidies: an empirical study in China. Energy Economics **81**, 197–215 (2019). https://doi.org/10.1016/j.eneco.2019.03.012
27. Fang, Y., Wei, W., Mei, S., Chen, L., Zhang, X., Huang, S.: Promoting electric vehicle charging infrastructure considering policy incentives and user preferences: an evolutionary game model in a small-world network. J. Cleaner Prod. **258** (2020). https://doi.org/10.1016/j.jclepro.2020.120753
28. Groupe-sunergia
29. Hua, Y., Liu, X., Zhou, S., Huang, Y., Ling, H., Yang, S.: Toward sustainable reuse of retired lithium-ion batteries from electric vehicles. Resour. Conserv. Recycling **168** (2021). https://doi.org/10.1016/j.resconrec.2020.105249
30. Sustainable Energy Advantage
31. SmartGrids
32. Clastres, C.: Smart grids: another step towards competition, energy security and climate change objectives. Energy Policy **39**(9), 5399–5408 (2011). https://doi.org/10.1016/j.enpol.2011.05.024
33. Sahbani, S., Mahmoudi, H., Hasnaoui, A., Kchikach, M.: Development prospect of smart grid in Morocco. Procedia Comput. Sci. **83**, 1313–1320 (2016). https://doi.org/10.1016/j.procs.2016.04.274
34. Habachi, R., Touil, A., Boulal, A., Charkaoui, A., Echchatbi, A.: Recommendations and solutions to remove some barriers to the deployment of smart grid in Morocco. Int. J. Power Electron. Drive Syst. (IJPEDS) **10**(2), 744 (2019). https://doi.org/10.11591/ijpeds.v10.i2.pp744-752
35. Habachi, R., Touil, A., Charkaoui, A., Echchatbi, A.: Management and control of smart grid systems: opportunities and challenges in Morocco. Int. J. Math. Comput. Sci. **3**(2), 6–14 (2017). http://www.aiscience.org/journal/ijmcs. http://creativecommons.org/licenses/by/4.0/
36. Habachi, R., Touil, A., Boulal, A., Charkaoui, A., Echchatbi, A.: Comparative study of meta-heuristics methods applied to smart grid network in Morocco. Int. J. Power Electron. Drive Syst. **11**(1), 487–495 (2020). https://doi.org/10.11591/ijpeds.v11.i1.pp487-495
37. Clement-Nyns, K., Haesen, E., Driesen, J.: The impact of vehicle-to-grid on the distribution grid. Electr. Power Syst. Res. **81**(1), 185–192 (2011). https://doi.org/10.1016/j.epsr.2010.08.007
38. Zio, E., Aven, T.: Uncertainties in smart grids behavior and modeling: what are the risks and vulnerabilities? How to analyze them? Energy Policy **39**(10), 6308–6320 (2011). https://doi.org/10.1016/j.enpol.2011.07.030
39. Aravinthan, V., Jewell, W.: Controlled electric vehicle charging for mitigating impacts on distribution assets. IEEE Trans. Smart Grid **6**(2), 999–1009 (2015). https://doi.org/10.1109/TSG.2015.2389875
40. Wang, Q., Liu, X., Du, J., Kong, F.: Smart charging for electric vehicles: a survey from the algorithmic perspective. IEEE Commun. Surv. Tutor. **18**(2), 1500–1517 (2016). https://doi.org/10.1109/COMST.2016.2518628
41. Green, R.C., Wang, L., Alam, M.: The impact of plug-in hybrid electric vehicles on distribution networks: a review and outlook. Renew. Sustain. Energy Rev. **15**(1), 544–553 (2011). https://doi.org/10.1016/j.rser.2010.08.015

42. King, C., Datta, B.: EV charging tariffs that work for EV owners, utilities and society. Electricity J. **31**(9), 24–27 (2018). https://doi.org/10.1016/j.tej.2018.10.010
43. Boulakhbar, M., et al.: Towards a large-scale integration of renewable energies in Morocco. J. Energy Storage **32** (2020). https://doi.org/10.1016/j.est.2020.101806

Study of Mechanical Effects in a Proton Exchange Membrane Fuel Cell

Ilham Sebbani[1(✉)], Mohammed Karim Ettouhami[1], and Hamid Mounir[2]

[1] Université Mohammed V, ENSAM, Rabat, Morocco
ilham.sebbani@gmail.com
[2] Mohammadia School of Engineers, Mohammed V University in Rabat, Rabat, Morocco

Abstract. Proton Exchange Membrane Fuel Cell (PEMFC) performance is highly dependent on key structural and operational parameters. Among these, the contact resistance between the bipolar plate (BPP) and the gas diffusion layer (GDL), as well as the porosity of the GDL, play critical roles in determining power density. This study aims to develop a comprehensive numerical model to analyze the mechanical interactions at the interfaces between these layers. The model focuses on quantifying contact behavior, including contact area and contact force, under varying conditions. By integrating these mechanical effects into the simulation, the work proposes an optimized interface structure to enhance fuel cell performance. The results provide valuable insights into PEMFC behavior, aiding in the design of more efficient and durable fuel cells. This research contributes to advancing fuel cell technology by addressing critical mechanical factors that influence overall efficiency and reliability.

Keywords: proton exchange membrane · fuel cell · contact · deformation

1 Introduction

The fuel cell is an efficient generator of electrical energy from chemical energy, utilizing the electrochemical redox reaction between hydrogen and oxygen to produce electricity. Research on fuel cells dates back over a century, with sustained interest since 1893 due to their advantages in efficiency, environmental protection, and modular construction. More recently, fuel cell technology has garnered significant attention as a clean and efficient energy source with potential for widespread applications.

Despite these advantages, durability, reliability, and performance remain critical challenges that limit the practical implementation of fuel cells. Among the factors affecting fuel cell behavior, the mechanical response of its components under various operating conditions plays a pivotal role in determining its longevity and efficiency. The mechanical interactions between layers influence durability, reliability, and safety, making a comprehensive understanding of these effects essential for improving performance and ensuring long-term operation.

This study addresses these challenges by proposing a numerical investigation of the mechanical behavior of fuel cells. Specifically, a finite element model is developed to

I. Aboudrar et al. (Eds.): ICESST 2024, SUCI, pp. 66–80, 2025.
https://doi.org/10.1007/978-3-031-86705-7_7

analyze the mechanical response of key components, such as the gas diffusion layer, bipolar plate, and membrane electrode assembly under various operating conditions. The model focuses on the critical contact regions between layers, examining stress distribution, contact pressure, contact area, and deformation. Furthermore, the study incorporates the effects of precompression loading, simulating the mechanical pressures experienced during operation.

The results of this work aim to provide:

- A deeper understanding of the mechanical behavior of PEMFCs and its implications for performance and durability.
- Optimization guidelines for design and operating conditions to enhance performance and reliability.
- Insights into the fundamental mechanics of fuel cells, contributing to their future development and widespread adoption.

This study represents a significant step forward in addressing the mechanical challenges of fuel cells, providing a foundation for optimized designs and operational strategies to improve their practical implementation.

2 Overview of the Fuel Cell

2.1 General Description of Fuel Cell

A fuel cell is an electrical energy generator. It converts the chemical energy of the fuel directly into electrical energy. It is a system that produces virtually no noise pollution, since it does not have any mechanical components in motion, such as turbines and motors. Moreover, the electric current is produced as long as the cell is supplied with fuel (hydrocarbons, alcohols, biomass, natural gas, hydrogen) and oxidizer (oxygen from the air). This is what differentiates it from batteries, accumulators and other cells, where a limited amount of electrical energy is stored in chemical form and which must either be recharged when possible (vehicle batteries) or replaced (radio batteries) [1, 2]. The following figure Fig. 1 represents a fuel cell system.

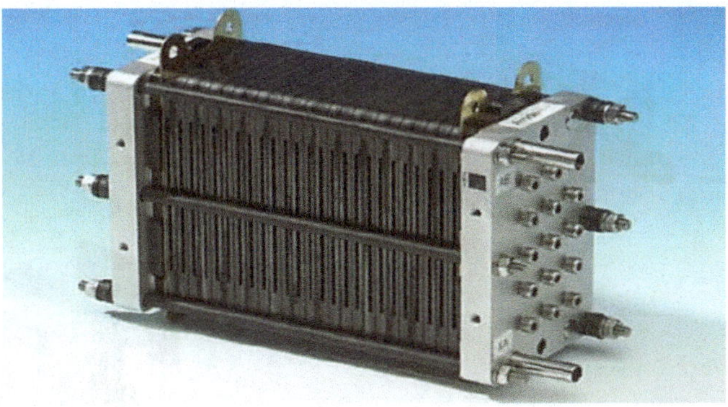

Fig. 1. Fuel Cell system [3]

2.2 Proton Exchange Membrane Fuel Cell

Among all the existing families, the Proton Exchange Membrane (PEM) fuel cell type has generated numerous research and development efforts worldwide. The technology is advancing rapidly, driven by the manufacturers' desire to offer economically viable and reliable products as quickly as possible [8].

We will focus solely on the PEM fuel cell because this technology appears to be the closest to commercialization in the transportation sector. In comparison to other fuel cell types, the PEM fuel cell has several attractive characteristics, such as [9]:

- Higher power density;
- High efficiency in converting chemical energy into electrical energy;
- Operates at low temperatures, enabling quick and easy start-up;
- Solid polymer construction reduces concerns related to construction, transportation, and reliability;
- More compact and lightweight, offering better volumetric power density;
- Modular design, making installation easy.

2.3 Fuel Cell Structure

The structure of fuel cells remains consistent across all types. Figure 2 illustrates a diagram the of a fuel cell structure. Each fuel cell comprises two electrodes, namely the anode and the cathode. The direction of current flow, whether in the form of negative electrons from the anode to the cathode or vice versa, depends on the specific fuel cell type. Situated between the anode and the cathode is the electrolyte, which varies according to the type of fuel cell. Apart from the electrodes and the electrolyte, a fuel cell incorporates two bipolar plates that play a crucial role. These plates not only ensure the uniform distribution of fuel to the cell but also regulate the efficient transfer of thermal and electrical energy. When multiple fuel cells are interconnected in a series, it is referred to as a fuel cell stack. By connecting the individual cells in this manner, the power output of the stack can be amplified. This characteristic offers a substantial advantage of fuel cell technology, as it enables a highly adaptable scalability of power [10].

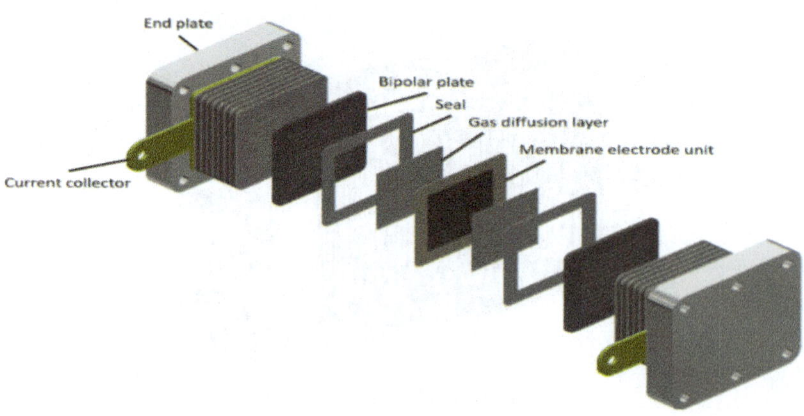

Fig. 2. Fuel cell stack [10]

The structure of the PEM fuel cell is relatively simple compared to other types of fuel cells because the components of the cell are solid and modular. Today, many developers have proposed their fuel cell designs.

PEM fuel cells are composed of multiple layers comprising various materials. These fuel cells encompass several essential components, such as membranes, catalyst layers (CL), gas diffusion layers (GDL), bipolar plates, and gaskets. The membrane electrode assembly (MEA) is a crucial part of the fuel cell, consisting of a polymer electrolyte membrane. Both sides of the membrane feature catalyst layers and gas distribution layers (anode and cathode). It is important to note that any degradation or malfunction of these individual components can lead to the deterioration or failure of the entire fuel cell system.

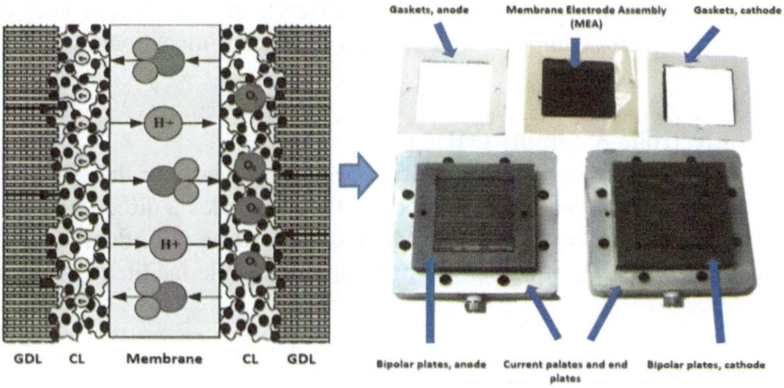

Fig. 3. PEM fuel cell components [11]

Below is a description of the construction of a typical proton exchange membrane (PEM) fuel cell, illustrated in Fig. 2 and Fig. 3, which is commonly used [12–17]:

Anode

The anode is the fuel electrode where the fuel, such as hydrogen gas (H2), is supplied. In hydrogen fuel cells, the anode typically consists of a catalyst, such as platinum, on a porous material that facilitates the electrochemical reaction.

Cathode

The cathode is the oxidant electrode where the oxidant, typically oxygen (O2) from the air, is supplied. The cathode also contains a catalyst, often platinum or another suitable material, to facilitate the electrochemical reaction [18].

Electrolyte

The electrolyte is a special material that allows the movement of ions between the anode and the cathode while preventing the mixing of the fuel and oxidant gases. It enables the transfer of ions and maintains electrical neutrality in the cell [19]. Different types of fuel cells employ various types of electrolytes, such as proton exchange membrane (PEM), solid oxide, molten carbonate, or alkaline electrolytes.

Catalyst Layers (CL)
In a PEM fuel cell, catalyst layers are applied on both sides of the membrane: the anode layer on one side and the cathode layer on the other. The conventional catalyst layers consist of tiny platinum particles dispersed on a carbon support with a high surface area. These platinum catalysts, supported by carbon, are combined with an ion-conducting polymer (ionomer) and positioned between the membrane and the gas diffusion layers (GDLs) [19]. The platinum catalyst on the anode side facilitates the splitting of hydrogen molecules into protons and electrons. On the cathode side, the platinum catalyst aids in the reduction of oxygen by reacting with the protons generated by the anode, resulting in the production of water. The ionomer mixed within the catalyst layers allows for the movement of protons through these layers. Catalyst degradation in PEM fuel cells during long-term operation under normal conditions is a complex process involving multiple simultaneous mechanisms. Various factors, such as fuel cell operating conditions, preparation conditions, and catalyst type, can impact catalyst degradation [20].

Membrane Electrode Assembly (MEA)
The MEA is a crucial component of the fuel cell that consists of the electrolyte layer sandwiched between the anode and cathode [21]. It provides a direct interface for the electrochemical reactions to occur. The MEA is typically a thin, flexible, and porous structure that allows the flow of fuel and oxidant gases while facilitating the transfer of ions [22].

Bipolar Plates (BP)
Bipolar plates are used to separate individual fuel cells within a stack and distribute fuel and oxidant gases uniformly across the electrodes. They also provide electrical conductivity between adjacent fuel cells and serve as current collectors for the generated electrical energy [22].

Gas Diffusion Layers (GDL)
Gas diffusion layers are typically carbon-based materials that are placed adjacent to the anode and cathode. They provide a porous and conductive structure to distribute the fuel and oxidant gases evenly over the electrode surfaces. GDLs also facilitate the removal of reaction byproducts, such as water vapor, from the electrodes [23].

Current Collectors
Current collectors are used to collect the electrical current generated by the fuel cell and deliver it to an external circuit. They are usually metallic plates or grids that make contact with the electrodes to capture the generated electrons [23].

Seals and Gaskets
Seals and gaskets are used to prevent gas leakage from the fuel cell and maintain the separation between the fuel and oxidant streams. They ensure the integrity and efficient operation of the fuel cell system [23].

These components are assembled together to form a fuel cell stack, which consists of multiple individual fuel cells connected in series or parallel configurations. The stack design and the arrangement of the cells depend on the specific application and power requirements.

2.4 Fuel Cell Assembly

For normal fuel cell operation, stacked components are assembled by screwing the stack together using tension bolts [19], as illustrated in Fig. 4.

Fig. 4. Fuel cell stack assembly [24]

These clamping forces are exerted from two ends of a stack towards the inside of the fuel cell stack. Fuel cell components are held in contact at the interfaces through which the electric current flows [25]. At the same time, these clamping forces compress the seals between bipolar plates and prevent the leakage of reactive gases [23]. In this way, the clamping force ensures:

- fuel cell tightness;
- mechanical strength of fuel cell components;
- contact generation at fuel cell interfaces.

The tightening process in the assembly of a PEM fuel cell is a critical step to ensure proper sealing and electrical contact between different components. Here's how the tightening is typically performed for key elements:

- Tightening of the Proton Exchange Membrane (PEM): During the Membrane Electrode Assembly (MEA) process, the PEM is placed between the anode and cathode catalyst layers. Careful tightening is applied to ensure uniform contact between the PEM and the catalyst layers. The tightening must be sufficient to hold the PEM in place without damaging it [25].
- Tightening of Bipolar Plates: Once the MEA is assembled, the bipolar plates are positioned on each side. Bipolar plates have gas flow channels and cooling channels. During assembly, uniform tightening is applied to hold the different layers together and ensure proper electrical connection between the bipolar plates and the catalyst layers [25].

- Tightening of End Plates: After the bipolar plates are assembled, the end plates are attached to the ends of the fuel cell stack. The tightening process is performed carefully to achieve a perfect seal between the end plates, bipolar plates, and other components [25].
- Tightening Control: Monitoring and controlling the tightening process are essential throughout the assembly. Over-tightening can lead to component damage or leaks, while under-tightening may result in poor electrical contact and fuel cell performance [25].
- Tightening Techniques: Various tightening techniques can be employed based on the design and size of the PEM fuel cell. Methods such as nuts and bolts, tightening screws, compression systems, or hydraulic presses may be used to achieve precise and uniform tightening [25].
- Sealing Tests: Upon completion of the tightening process, sealing tests are usually conducted to verify that the fuel cell is airtight, and there are no gas or coolant leaks [25].

Careful tightening in the assembly of a PEM fuel cell is crucial to ensure efficient and reliable fuel cell operation. Once the fuel cell is properly tightened and assembled, it is ready for performance testing and specific applications.

3 Failure Modes

PEM fuel cells experience heightened vulnerability due to mechanical failures, significantly diminishing their lifespan. These failures stem from localized stress concentration and varying mechanical stress imposed on the constrained membrane, prompted by alternating swelling and shrinking in response to fluctuations in water content and temperature. Consequently, this dynamic environment induces material fatigue, creep, and the development of structural issues such as wrinkles, delamination, pinholes, tears, or cracks, which can initiate and propagate across the membrane's surface or throughout its bulk. These inherent defects may be exacerbated during the fabrication process or improper assembly of fuel cell stacks.

Various factors, both internal and external, contribute to the mechanical failure of the membrane. These include the fabrication process of the membrane itself, the assembly of the fuel cell, the quality of the assembled components, and the operating conditions. Table 1 provides a comprehensive summary of the primary factors influencing mechanical failures in PEM fuel cells [26].

Table 1. Mechanical failure

Component	Failure modes	Causes
Membrane	Mechanical degradation	Mechanical stress due to non-uniform press pressure, inadequate humidify cation or penetration of the catalyst and seal material traces
	Thermal degradation	Thermal stress due to non-uniform temperature; thermal cycles
	Chemical/electrochemical degradation	Contamination; radical attack
Catalyst layer	Decrease in mass transport rate of reactants	Mechanical stress
	Conductivity loss	Corrosion of electrocatalyst support
	Loss of activation	Sintering or dealloying of electrocatalyst
	Loss of reformate tolerance	Contamination
	Decrease in water management ability	Change in hydrophobicity of materials due to Nafion or PTFE dissolution
Gas diffusion layer	Decrease in water management ability	Mechanical stress; change in the hydrophobicity of materials
	Decrease in mass transport	Degradation of backing material
	Conductivity loss	Corrosion
Bipolar plate	Fracture/deformation	Mechanical stress
	Conductivity loss	Corrosion; oxidation
Sealing gasket	Mechanical failure	Mechanical stress; corrosion

Table 2 provides a comprehensive breakdown of the principal failure modes associated with various PEM fuel cell components, including the membrane, catalyst layer, gas diffusion layer, bipolar plate, and sealing material (gasket) [27].

Table 2. Failure modes of PEM fuel cell components

Fabrication process	Assembly process	Short-time operation	Long-time operation
Membrane defects **-Thickness variation** **- Micro crack** **- Delamination** **- Catalyst orientation** **- Electrolyte cluster** **- Pt cluster**	**Assembly process** -Component structure -Endplate deformation -Assembly force **Manufacturing error** -Dimensional error -Shape error -Assembly error **Bonding by frame**	**Humidity & temperature** -Mechanical strength -In-plane stress -Plastic deformation **Freeze-thaw process** -Subfreezing condition - Strat-up **Failure along the frame**	**Cyclic physical loads** -RH and temperature -Gas flow -Cell vibration **Chemical acceleration** -Molecular structure - Pt dispersion - Degradation rate **Effect of CL**

4 Study of Mechanical Effects

Tightness plays an important role in the mechanical effects within the fuel cell assembly, in particular contact force, contact behavior, and GDL deformation, which influence fuel cell performance and lifespan [21, 22]. The tightening force can be considered as a static charge compared to the dynamic charge in the transport situation. Numerical modeling of precompression can identify contact force distribution, contact zone, and deformation at fuel cell interfaces. The mesh, boundary conditions, and precompression represent the real case.

4.1 Description and Hypotheses

During assembly of a PEM stack, structural components are brought into contact. The clamping force is transmitted through the stack via contact points at the interfaces. Contact in the multi-contact structure of the fuel cell exists mainly at the interfaces between the GDL plate and the BPP plate, and between the GDL plate and the MEA plate. Contact pressure distribution is not uniform at the interfaces due to small teeth present on the BPPs. The force applied externally and the configuration of the plates at the contacts are important for the contact zone. The contact problem in the fuel cell is impossible to solve analytically, but is achievable with the finite element method. In our studies, the materials of the cell components are linear and elastic, and the fuel cell model has been developed using the following assumptions:

1. All material properties are isotropic,
2. The applied precompression force is imposed by a displacement achieving the perfect sealing condition of the seals in the fuel cell,
3. Considering the symmetry of the structure and the boundary conditions, the modeling of the structure can be simplified,
4. The stress in the model does not reach the yield point, so this is a purely elastic study,
5. The study is limited to the mechanical behavior of the solid elements making up the fuel cell. Neither chemical reaction nor fluidic phenomena are considered.

4.2 Studied Model

In a PEM fuel cell stack, maintaining contact at the multi-layer interfaces (illustrated in Fig. 5) is essential for efficient electron flow. This contact supports the critical transfer of reactive gases and electrons across these interfaces, which plays a major role in the performance and longevity of PEM fuel cells. These interfaces include several key points of contact, such as the interface between the MEA and GDL, and the BPP and GDL interface. At the BPP/GDL interface, specifically, contact occurs between the ribs of the BPP and the GDL.

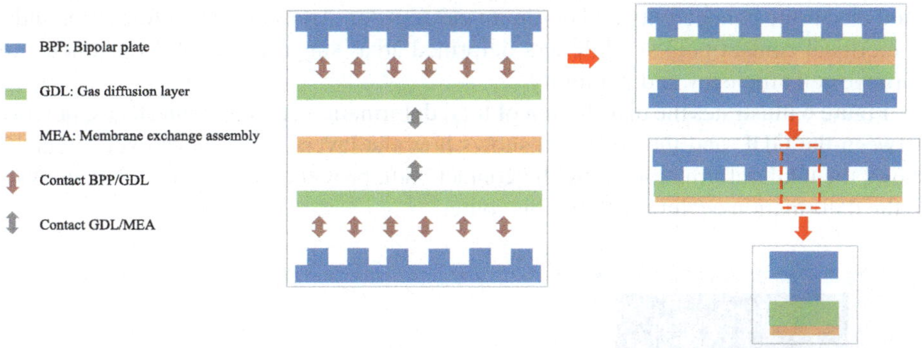

Fig. 5. Studied model

4.3 Model's Properties

The table below shows the mechanical properties of BPP plate, GDL plate and MEA plate [30–33] (Table 3).

Table 3. Model's Properties

Parameters	End plates	BPP	GDL	MEA
Thickness	$T_{EP} = 5$ **mm**	$T_{BPP} = 1.5$ **mm**	$T_{GDL} = 0.375$ **mm**	$T_{MEA} = 0.045$ **mm**
Width	$W_{EP} = 4.2$ **mm**	$W_{BPP} = 4.2$ **mm**	$W_{GDL} = 4.2$ **mm**	$W_{MEA} = 4.2$ **mm**
Young's modulus	$E_{EP} = 70$ **GPa**	$E_{BPP} = 200$ **GPa**	$E_{GDL} = 0.00613$ **GPa**	$E_{MEA} = 0.021$ **GPa**
Poisson's ratio	$\nu_{EP} = 0.3$	$\nu_{BPP} = 0.3$	$\nu_{GDL} = 0.3$	$\nu_{MEA} = 0.001$
Width of the channel	–	$W_{CN} = 0.1$ **mm**	---	–
Width of the rib	–	$W_{RIB} = 4$ **mm**	–	–
Depth of the channel	–	$T_{CN} = 1$ **mm**	–	–
Bending radius	–	$R_{RIB} = 0.04$ **mm**	–	
Diameters of the pores	–	–	$Ø_P = 0.053$ **mm**	–

4.4 Total Deformation Study

Total deformation represents the mechanical response of the fuel cell interfaces to the applied load. It enables us to assess the quality of contact, which is essential to ensure good electronic conductivity and optimum gas transfer. Areas of high deformation indicate critical contact points, while less deformed areas suggest possible adjustments to improve cell efficiency and durability.

Figure 6 illustrates the distribution of total deformation at critical interfaces, notably between the GDL and the BPP, and shows how the layers react under load. Figure 7 shows the total deformation along the contact path, providing a more detailed analysis of the deformation evolution along this route.

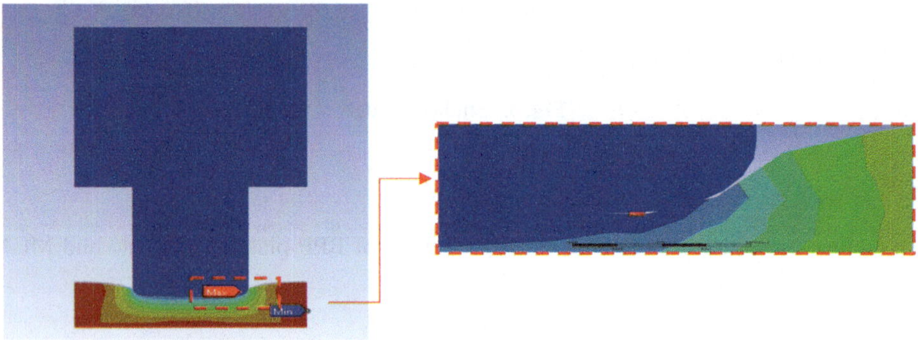

Fig. 6. Total deformation

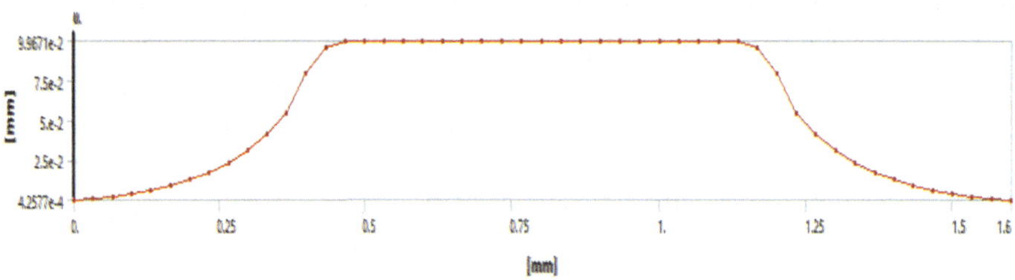

Fig. 7. Total deformation Path

4.5 Results

This study provides valuable insights into the mechanical behavior of a fuel cell through numerical modeling. The results highlight the deformation distribution, its uniformity, and its implications for contact quality and potential design optimizations:

Deformation Distribution

The simulation shows that total deformation is concentrated near the contact interfaces, with maximum deformation observed in regions of high load absorption (indicated in red) and minimum deformation in low-stress areas (indicated in blue).

- **Key Observation:** The concentration of deformation in the contact region suggests that these areas play a critical role in maintaining the structural integrity of the fuel cell under operational pressure.

- **Implication for Performance:** This deformation behavior enhances contact pressure, a key parameter for reducing contact resistance and improving conductivity. However, excessive deformation in these regions could lead to material fatigue or failure over time, underscoring the need for careful material selection and structural optimization.

Uniformity Along the Path
Deformation profiles along specific paths reveal a plateau in the central region, indicating uniform deformation. This region likely corresponds to the most effective mechanical contact. In contrast, deformation decreases towards the edges, signaling regions with reduced contact pressure.

- **Key Observation:** Uniform deformation in the central area is beneficial for consistent conductivity and gas transfer. However, the non-uniform deformation at the edges could limit overall fuel cell performance if these regions contribute to significant contact resistance.
- **Design Implications:** Addressing this non-uniformity through structural adjustments, such as modifying clamping force distribution or material stiffness, could improve overall contact quality and performance.

Implications for Contact Quality
The observed deformation patterns highlight the importance of ensuring optimal contact in the central region while mitigating potential losses due to lower pressure at the edges.

- **Enhancing Contact Quality:** Improvements in design, such as introducing materials with adaptive stiffness or optimized preloading mechanisms, may help achieve more uniform contact across the interface.
- **Minimizing Edge Effects:** Strategies such as tapering the edges or introducing reinforcing structures could prevent performance losses in these critical zones.

Potential for Optimization
The variations in deformation along the path emphasize opportunities for optimization:

- **Structural Adjustments:** Refining the geometric design of the fuel cell layers could help distribute deformation more evenly.
- **Operational Adjustments:** Tailoring the clamping force to align with the mechanical properties of the materials could reduce stress concentrations and enhance uniformity.
- **Material Enhancements:** Using materials with higher resilience or conductivity in high-stress regions could further mitigate the risks associated with excessive deformation while maintaining performance.

5 Conclusion

This study provides a comprehensive analysis of the mechanical behavior of Proton Exchange Membrane Fuel Cells (PEMFCs), emphasizing the critical role of deformation at the interfaces between the gas diffusion layer (GDL) and the bipolar plate (BPP).

The findings reveal that excessive deformation adversely impacts GDL porosity and permeability, leading to inefficient gas transport and reduced fuel cell performance. Furthermore, the non-uniform distribution of pressure and strain at the interface results in uneven porosity, which further compromises the fuel cell's efficiency and durability.

The numerical model developed in this study offers valuable insights into the deformation and stress distribution within the fuel cell layers under various operating conditions. By analyzing the interaction between mechanical deformation and performance, this work highlights the importance of maintaining uniform pressure and minimizing excessive deformation to optimize fuel cell functionality. These findings underscore the need for careful design and material selection to enhance the durability, reliability, and efficiency of PEMFCs.

In future work, we aim to focus on design optimization to address the challenges identified in this study. This includes developing optimized clamping mechanisms or preloading strategies to ensure uniform pressure distribution across the GDL-BPP interface. Additionally, we plan to explore novel structural designs, such as patterned or reinforced GDL configurations, to enhance uniformity and minimize deformation. These efforts will contribute to the development of more efficient and robust fuel cells, paving the way for their broader application and improved performance in real-world scenarios.

References

1. Pile à combustible : définition, fonctionnement, enjeux, histoire. https://www.connaissancedesenergies.org/fiche-pedagogique/pile-combustible. Accessed 27 May 2023
2. Pile à combustible : fonctionnement, avantages et inconvénients. https://www.h2-mobile.fr/dossiers/pile-combustible-fonctionnement-avantages-inconvenients/. Accessed 27 May 2023
3. Schneider, J., Klugman, J., Boyd, B., Ward, J.: The implementation of SAE J2601: hydrogen fuelling proto-col guideline for demonstration projects CORE view metadata, citation and similar papers at core.ac.uk provided by Juelich Shared Electronic Resources. Essen Schriften des Forschungszentrums Jülich/Energy Environ. **78**(1) (2010)
4. Types of Fuel Cells | Department of Energy. https://www.energy.gov/eere/fuelcells/types-fuel-cells. Accessed 01 July 2023
5. Sundén, B.: Fuel cell types – overview. Hydrogen, Batteries and Fuel Cells, pp. 123–144 (2019). https://doi.org/10.1016/b978-0-12-816950-6.00008-7
6. Carrette, L., Friedrich, K.A., Stimming, U.: Fuel cells: principles, types, fuels, and applications. ChemPhysChem **1**(4), 162–193 (2000). https://doi.org/10.1002/1439-7641(20001215)1:4%3c162::aid-cphc162%3e3.0.co;2-z
7. Lyonnard, S.: Membranes pour piles à combustible : structure et transport. apport de la diffusion neutronique. École thématique de la Société Française de la Neutronique **11**, 177–197 (2010). https://doi.org/10.1051/sfn/201011011
8. Tellez-Cruz, M.M., Escorihuela, J., Solorza-Feria, O., Compañ, V.: Proton exchange membrane fuel cells (Pemfcs): advances and challenges. Polymers **13**(18), 1–54 (2021). https://doi.org/10.3390/polym13183064
9. Fuel Cell Fundamentals - Ryan O'Hayre, Suk-Won Cha, Whitney Colella, Fritz B. Prinz - Google Livres. https://books.google.fr/books?id=O2JYCwAAQBAJ&printsec=copyright#v=onepage&q&f=false. Accessed 01 July 2023
10. Fuel cells: Function & application | DiLiCo. https://www.dilico.de/en/brennstoffzellen.php. Accessed 08 July 2023

11. Al-Baghdadi, M.A.R.S.: CFD models for analysis and design of PEM fuel cells, p. 201 (2008)
12. Al Baghdadi, M.: Mechanical durability of PEM fuel. Energy, no. Cl
13. Algerienne, L.A.R., et al.: Année Universitaire: 2021/2022 1 (2022)
14. HAMAZ. Outils de caractérisation et de diagnostic d'une pile à combustible de type PEM par mesure du champ électromagnétique externe (2014)
15. Martemianov, S., Gueguen, M., Grandidier, J.C., Bograchev, D.: Mechanical effects in PEM fuel cell: application to modeling of assembly procedure. J. Appl. Fluid Mech. **2**(2), 49–54 (2009). https://doi.org/10.36884/jafm.2.02.11869
16. Abdelhak, Y., Belkacem, T.: Modélisation d' une pile à combustible de type PEM (2017)
17. Pichonat, T.: Miniature pour applications portables (2005)
18. Cimen, F.M., Kumuk, B., Ilbas, M.: Simulation of hydrogen and coal gas fueled flat-tubular solid oxide fuel cell (FT-SOFC). Int. J. Hydrogen Energy **47**(5), 3429–3436 (2022). https://doi.org/10.1016/J.IJHYDENE.2021.07.231
19. Song, K., et al.: Assembly techniques for proton exchange membrane fuel cell stack: a literature review. Renew. Sustain. Energy Rev. **153**, 111777 (2022). https://doi.org/10.1016/J.RSER.2021.111777
20. Fuel cell technology. http://www.still.co.uk/fuel-cell-technology-uk.0.0.html. Accessed 26 Feb 2023
21. Noguer, N., Candusso, D., Kouta, R., Harel, F., Charon, W., Coquery, G.: A PEMFC multi-physical model to evaluate the consequences of parameter uncertainty on the fuel cell performance. Int. J. Hydrogen Energy **40**(10), 3968–3980 (2015). https://doi.org/10.1016/j.ijhydene.2015.01.050
22. Wang, H., et al.: Effect of binder and compression on the transport parameters of a multilayer gas diffusion layer. Energy Fuels **35**(18), 15058–15073 (2021). https://doi.org/10.1021/ACS.ENERGYFUELS.1C01598
23. Ouaidat, G., Cherouat, A., Kouta, R., Chamoret, D.: Numerical modeling of the mechanical behavior of proton exchange membrane fuel cell performance: design of experiment study and optimization. Int. J. Hydrogen Energy **45**(46), 25210–25226 (2020). https://doi.org/10.1016/J.IJHYDENE.2020.06.015
24. Considerations for Fuel Cell Design. https://www.fuelcellstore.com/blog-section/considerations-for-fuel-cell-design. Accessed 26 Nov 2023
25. Macdonald, C.S.: Effect of compressive force on PEM fuel cell performance (2009)
26. (PDF) Proton exchange membrane fuel cells modeling: A review of the last ten years results of the Fuel Cell Research Center-IEEF. https://www.researchgate.net/publication/324278379_Proton_exchange_membrane_fuel_cells_modeling_A_review_of_the_last_ten_years_results_of_the_Fuel_Cell_Research_Center-IEEF. Accessed 03 Dec 2023
27. Al-Baghdadi, M.: Advanced CFD technology for design and optimize future PEM fuel cells with a higher power density and long cell life: a comprehensive study. SSRN Electron. J. (2021). https://doi.org/10.2139/SSRN.3908743
28. (PDF) Mechanical Effects in PEM Fuel Cell: Application to Modeling of Assembly Procedure. https://www.researchgate.net/publication/228883397_Mechanical_Effects_in_PEM_Fuel_Cell_Application_to_Modeling_of_Assembly_Procedure. Accessed 03 Dec 2023
29. Martemianov, S., Gueguen, M., Grandidier, J.C., Bograchev, D.: Mechanical effects in PEM fuel cell: application to modeling of assembly procedure (2012). https://doi.org/10.36884/jafm.2.02.11869
30. Zhang, J., Hu, Y., Han, C., Zhang, H.: Stress response and contact behavior of PEMFC during the assembly and working condition. Int. J. Hydrogen Energy **46**(59), 30467–30478 (2021). https://doi.org/10.1016/j.ijhydene.2021.06.200

31. Xu, Q., Zhao, J., Chen, Y., Liu, S., Wang, Z.: Effects of gas permeation on the sealing performance of PEMFC stacks. Int. J. Hydrogen Energy **46**(73), 36424–36435 (2021). https://doi.org/10.1016/j.ijhydene.2021.08.137
32. Meng, L., Zhou, P., Yan, Y., Guo, D.: Compression properties of gas diffusion layers and its constitutive model under cyclic loading. Int. J. Hydrogen Energy **46**(29), 15965–15975 (2021). https://doi.org/10.1016/j.ijhydene.2021.02.083
33. Irmscher, P., Qui, D., Janßen, H., Lehnert, W., Stolten, D.: Impact of gas diffusion layer mechanics on PEM fuel cell performance. Int. J. Hydrogen Energy **44**(41), 23406–23415 (2019). https://doi.org/10.1016/j.ijhydene.2019.07.047

Hybrid Method for Stability Improvement of RDS

Chaymae Makri[1](✉), Said Guedira[2], Imad El Harraki[3], and Soumia El Hani[1]

[1] Energy Optimization, Diagnostics and Control Team, ENSAM Rabat, Mohammed V University in Rabat, Rabat, Morocco
chaymae.makri@gmail.com, s.elhani@um5r.ac.ma

[2] Laboratory of Control, Piloting and Monitoring of Electrical Energy, ENSMR, Rabat, Morocco
guedira@enim.ac.ma

[3] Laboratory of Applied Mathematics and Business Intelligence, ENSMR, Rabat, Morocco
elharraki@enim.ac.ma

Abstract. A new hybrid approach has been applied to determine the optimal location and size of shunt capacitors to improve the power factor (PF), enhance the voltage profile (VP), and consequently reduce total active and reactive power losses in the Radial Distribution System (RDS). This paper proposes a hybrid approach combining Reactive Power Flow Analysis (RPFA), Weak Bus Identification (WBI), and the Particle Swarm Optimizer (PSO) algorithm, the RPFA-WBI-PSO. Indeed, the RPFA-WBI index identifies the network nodes most sensitive to the addition of capacitors, while the PSO algorithm optimizes their sizes. The proposed approach was evaluated on 10- and 33-bus RDSs to assess its performance compared to other methods in the literature. The RPFA-WBI-PSO method presents a percentage reduction in active power loss of 14.09% for the 10-bus RDS and 34.95% in the case of the 33-bus RDS.

Keywords: RDS · Power loss · VP · Capacitors · Placement and size · RPFA · WBS

1 Introduction

Some of the negative effects of reactive power within an RDS are voltage distortion, deterioration of the PF, and increased power losses. These phenomena reduce the stability of the network. To minimize these problems, one of the best-known solutions is to install reactive power compensation sources, which can be shunt capacitors [1, 2].

Determining the optimal size and location of these capacitors within an RDS is a complex problem that has been the subject of numerous studies. The resolution methods generally adopted are divided into two steps: 1) Identification of optimal locations and 2) Calculation of optimal sizes. The first step involves analyzing the sensitivity of the different nodes of the network to determine the points where the installation of capacitors would have the most positive impact. Once the locations have been identified, the second step uses the optimization algorithms to calculate the exact capacities of the capacitors to be installed at each location, to minimize losses and improve the VP.

I. Aboudrar et al. (Eds.): ICESST 2024, SUCI, pp. 81–90, 2025.
https://doi.org/10.1007/978-3-031-86705-7_8

Previous research has explored various hybrid methods to optimize capacitor placement and sizing in RDS. For instance, in [3], the authors proposed a newly nature-inspired metaheuristic approach combining the Loss Sensitivity Factor (LSF) and the Beluga Whale Optimization (BWO) algorithm. LSF was used to identify sensitive buses, and BWO optimized capacitor locations and sizes. The method outperformed other metaheuristic algorithms like PSO, Whale Optimization (WO), Bacterial Foraging Optimization Algorithm (BFOA) Grey Wolf Optimization (GWO), And Improved Whale Optimization (IWO) on IEEE 34- and 85-bus systems. Similarly, in [4], a new analytical-metaheuristic approach was presented, combining the Bus Voltage Stability Index (BVSI) with a genetic algorithm (GA). BVSI identified potential capacitor locations, and GA optimized their sizes. This method demonstrated superior performance compared to Fuzzy-GA, LSF with Differential evolution (DE), LSF_PSO, and Power Loss index (PLI) with DE on the IEEE 69-bus system. [5] focused on improving VPs and reducing power losses using the Improved Binary Particle Swarm Optimization (IBPSO) algorithm. IBPSO was applied to both location and size optimization, achieving significant results on the IEEE 69-bus system compared to other algorithms. A non-linear mixed integer programming (MINLP) solver was employed in [6] to optimize capacitor placement and sizing. The modified Loss Sensitivity Index (MLSI) was used to identify candidate buses. The proposed method outperformed PSO and Multiverse Optimizer (MVO) on 10-, 33-, and 69-bus systems. While [7] employed the Least Squares Method (LSF) to identify potential locations and the Mine Blast Algorithm (MBA) as an optimization algorithm to determine the optimal capacitor size, MBA was compared to the Firefly Algorithm (FPA) on 10- and 85-bus systems. A novel meta-heuristic technique proposed in [8] aimed to minimize active power losses, average voltage deviation index, and maximize voltage stability index and annual energy loss cost savings. The Voltage Sensitivity Index (VSI) was used to select top 10 locations, and the Giant Trevally Optimizer (GTO) algorithm was employed for optimization. GTO outperformed PSO, Teaching-Learning-Based Optimization (TLBO), Cuckoo Search Algorithm (CSA), and FPA on IEEE 33- and 69-bus systems.

While each of these hybrid approaches offers unique advantages, their overall effectiveness and applicability can vary depending on system characteristics and specific optimization objectives.

This paper introduces a new combined approach that significantly improves the optimization of capacitor placement and sizing in RDSs. By combining the strong RPFA-WBI index and the effective PSO algorithm, our method efficiently identifies important network nodes and determines the best capacitor sizes. The Key contributions of this study:

- The RPFA-WBI index precisely identifies network locations that would benefit most from capacitor installation, optimizing resource allocation and maximizing system improvements.
- The PSO algorithm carefully determines the best capacitor sizes, considering factors such as power loss reduction, VP enhancement, and economic feasibility.

Through rigorous testing on standard IEEE 10 and 33-bus systems, our proposed approach demonstrates superior performance compared to existing methods in the literature, leading to substantial reductions in power losses, improved VPs, and increased system reliability.

This paper is structured into four key parts: problem formulation, description of the proposed methodology, presentation and analysis of results, and finally the conclusion.

2 Problem Formulation

The optimization problem of locating and sizing capacitors to be installed in an RDS can be formulated as a constrained non-linear problem. Our goal is to reduce the total cost of losses and capacitors installation [9], as expressed in the following equation:

$$\min F_1 + F_2 \tag{1}$$

$$F_1 = T * K_p * P_{loss} \tag{2}$$

$$F_2 = \sum_{i=1}^{N_c} K_{ci} * Q_{ci} \tag{3}$$

With:

- T: The total duration (h),
- K_p: The active power cost (\$/kW.year),
- P_{loss}: The total active power losses in the network (kW),
- N_c: Number of candidate buses,
- K_c: The reactive power cost (\$/kvar),
- Q_C: The shunt capacitor power (kvar).

This problem is subject to several equality and inequality constraints, such as:

- Active and reactive power balance:

$$\begin{cases} P_g = P_d + P_L \\ Q_g + Q_c = Q_d + Q_L \end{cases} \tag{4}$$

With P_g, P_d and P_L are the generator, charge and loss active power, and Q_g, Q_d and Q_L are the generator, charge and loss reactive power.

- Voltage limits:

$$V_{i_{min}} \leq V_i \leq V_{i_{max}} \tag{5}$$

- Capacitor limits:

$$Q_{c_{imin}} \leq Q_{c_i} \leq Q_{c_{imax}} \tag{6}$$

- PF limit:

$$PF_{min} \leq PF \leq PF_{max} \tag{7}$$

3 Methodology

3.1 Dataset

The 10-bus and 33-bus are the RDSs used to evaluate the capability and the efficacity of the proposed methodology. Detailed system information, including the number of buses and branches, loads, losses, and rated voltage, can be found in [6]. For the lines, loads, and generators data are presented in [10]. For other data, such as Kp = 168 $/kW, T = 24*368 h and capacitors cost is given in [6]. Figures 1 and 2 show the schematics of the 10- and 33-bus RDSs.

Fig. 1. 10-bus RDS.

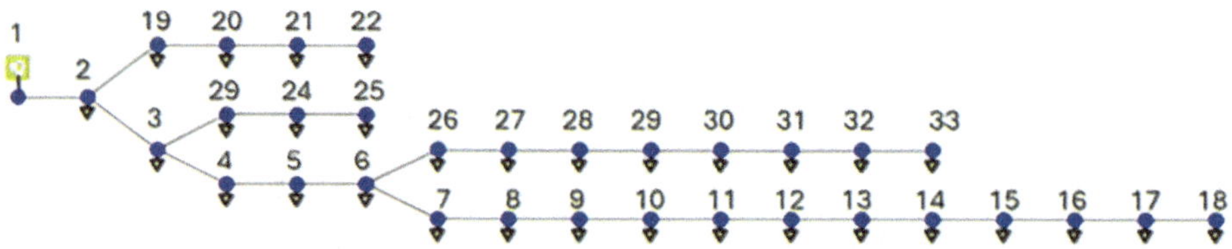

Fig. 2. 33-Bus RDS.

3.2 Power Flow

The power flow analysis calculates the network quantities in terms of the magnitude and phase angle of each bus voltage and active and reactive power flow through branches [11]. In this work, a load flow algorithm, known as the Backward/Forward Sweep method has been adopted and implemented in a Python package called Pandapower [12].

The active and reactive power flow through a branch k, interfacing the nodes "p" and "q", are calculated using expressions (8) and (9), respectively:

$$P_{loss_k} = R_{pq} * I_{pq}^2 = R_{pq} * \left(\frac{P_{pq}^2 + Q_{pq}^2}{|V_q|^2} \right) \tag{8}$$

$$Q_{loss_k} = X_{pq} * I_{pq}^2 = X_{pq} * \left(\frac{P_{pq}^2 + Q_{pq}^2}{|V_q|^2} \right) \tag{9}$$

Branch k has active and reactive power P_{pq} and Q_{pq}, resistance R_{pq}, reactance X_{pq}, and node q voltage magnitude V_q.

3.3 Candidate Buses

Discovering the candidate buses to solve the problem of finding the optimal location and size in RDS aims to reduce the calculation time of the optimization algorithm and improve the result of the optimization problem. Using the sensitivity analysis is the most common method employed to find the candidate buses. In literature, several sensitivity analyses are used, such as LSF and BVSI. In this study, a combination of Reactive Power Flow Analysis (RPFA) and Weak Bus Identification (WBI), named RPFA-WBI, is used for determining the capacitor placement of our RDS.

The process consists of four steps:

- **Step 1: Power flow calculation**
  We calculate the power flow to get the reactive power demand and VP for each bus.
- **Step 2: Identify buses with high reactive power demand**
  In this step, we start by setting a threshold based on mean and standard deviation. Then we plot the distribution of reactive power demand with the threshold to get it, such as in Figure 3 (the first for 10-bus and the second for 33-bus).

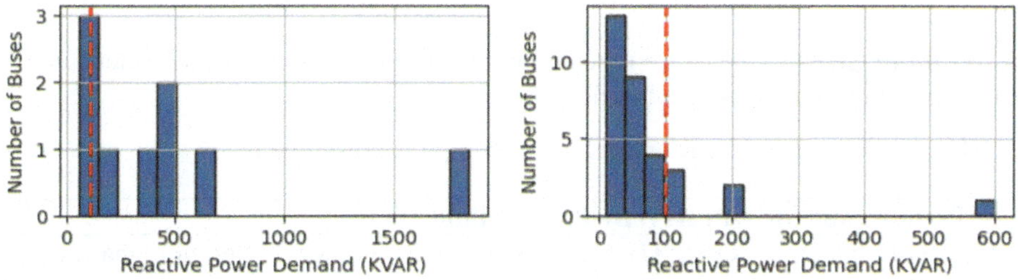

Fig. 3. Distribution of Reactive Power Demand with Threshold for 10- and 33-bus RDS.

  From the graph, we can interpret that the buses with reactive power demand above this threshold (around 100 kvar) are considered to have high demand, which is useful for determining capacitor placement to improve system performance.
- **Step 3: Identify buses with low voltage**
  In this step, the WBI method is used to identifying the buses with voltage < 0.95.
- **Step 4: Identify the optimal placement of capacitors**
  In this step, the high reactive power buses and low voltage buses are combined as candidate buses for capacitor placement.

3.4 Optimization Algorithm

In literature, several optimization algorithms are used to solve the problem of finding the optimal capacitor size in RDS. In this study, we are exploiting the simplicity, efficacy, and robustness of the PSO algorithm to find the optimal solution.

The PSO is a metaheuristic algorithm introduced by Kennedy and Eberhart in 1995 and inspired by the collective behavior of animal swarms [13]. It explores a solution space by iteratively adjusting the positions of virtual particles, each representing a potential solution [14].

The PSO algorithm operates in four stages:

1) Initialization: The algorithm randomly initializes a swarm of particles within the search space. Each particle is characterized by its position, velocity, personal best (pBest), and the global best (gBest) position of the swarm.
2) Evaluation: The quality of each particle's position is evaluated using an objective function.
3) Mise à jour: The position and velocity of each particle are updated iteratively according to the following equation:

$$V_i^{k+1} = wV_i^k + c_1 r_1 rand\left(pbest_i - X_i^k\right) + c_2 r_2 rand\left(Gbest_i - X_i^k\right) \quad (10)$$

- V_i: Velocity of particle i at the next iteration,
- w: Inertia weight,
- c_1 et c_2: Cognitive and social learning factors,
- r_1 et r_2: Random numbers the range [0,1],
- X_i: Current position of particle i.

4) Iteration: Steps 2 and 3 are repeated until a termination criterion is met, such as reaching a maximum number of iterations.

The pseudo-code of the proposed methodology is presented below:

Pseudo code for RPFA-WBI-PSO method
Inputs: R, P_g, Q_g, P_l, Q_l, P_d, Q_d, V, capacitors_size, K_c, K_e, T, Iteration_max **Outputs:** optimal_size & optimal_placement 1- Build network, 2- Run power flow, 3- Finding candidates buses placement of capacitors using RPFA-WBI method 4- Build objective function & constraints, 5- Generate the initial population from the capacitors_size list, 6- **While** i < iteration_max, Do: 7- Evaluate the quality of each particle's position 8- Update the position and velocity of each particle **9- End while** 10- Return the best solution (optimal_size & optimal_placement)

4 Results and Discussion

The implementation and the simulation has been made it in Python version 3.9.13 in a computer with Inter (R) Core (TM) i7-6600U CPU and 16 GB in RAM.

The outcomes of the initial step, the RPFA-WBI method, are presented below:

- The candidates buses for the 10-bus RDS:

[2, 3, 4, 5, 6, 7, 8, 9, 10]

- The candidates buses for the 33-bus RDS:

[5, 6, 7, 8, 9, 10, 11, 12, 13, 14, 15, 16, 17, 24, 25, 26, 27, 28, 29, 30, 31, 32]

The implementation for the second step, the PSO algorithm, is summarized in the following Table 1.

Table 1. The simulation parameters.

Parameters	Values
Maximum number of iterations	100
Population Size	50
Inertia Weight (w)	0.9
Cognitive Component (c1)	0.3
Social Component (c2)	0.3
Stopping Criteria	1000

Simulation Result for 10-Bus RDS. Table 2 presents the results obtained for the proposed method in the case of 10-bus DRS, compared to the previous hybrid methods, LSF-MBA [7] and MLSI-MINLP [6]. The results indicate the need to add 4050, 1350, 2100, 1200, and 450 kvar capacitors to buses 3, 4, 5, 6, and 9, respectively. This approach significantly reduces total active power losses, decreasing from 783.77 kW to 673.38 kW. Consequently, we observe a reduction in total cost and an improvement in the PF from 0.9542 to 0.9774.

Figure 4 illustrates the evolution of the VP for the base case and the case after compensation. A significant improvement in the VP is evident, particularly on all buses.

Simulation result for 33-bus RDS. Table 3 presents the results obtained for the proposed method in the case of 33-bus DRS, compared to the previous methods, VSI-GTO [8] and VSF-LSF-EA [15]. The results indicate the need to add 300, 300, 600, and 1050 kvar capacitors to buses 8, 13, 24, and 30, respectively. This implementation reduces total active power losses from 202.6783 kW to 132.046 kW. Consequently, we observe a reduction in total cost and an improvement in PF from 0.9131 to 0.9426.

Figure 5 illustrates the evolution of the VP for the base case and the case after compensation. A significant improvement in the VP is evident, particularly on buses 5 to 17 and 24 to 32.

As shown in Tables 2 and 3, adding a substantial amount of reactive power to the RDS doesn't guarantee a reduction in total active power loss or an improved VP. The strategic placement of capacitors is crucial. Table 3 highlights a significant improvement in minimum voltage and PF compared to the VSI-GTO, MLSI-MINLP and VSF-LSF-EA methods.

Table 2. Results of 10-bus RDS.

	Base	LSF-MBA [7]	MLSI-MINLP [6]	Proposed
Optimal placement & Optimal size	-	5 -> 1200 6 -> 1200 9 -> 600 10 -> 300	3 -> 4050 4 -> 2100 5 -> 2100 6 -> 1200 9 -> 450 10 -> 150	3 -> 4050 4 -> 1350 5 -> 2100 6 -> 1200 9 -> 450
Qc totale (kvar)	-	3300	10050	**9150**
P_{loss} (kw)	783.77	679.7	673.659	**673.382**
Q_{loss}(kvar)	1036.66	-	-	**908.108**
Total cost ($/years)	131673	-	115031	**114819**
V_{min}	0.8375	0.933	0.8961	**0.8856**
PF	0.9542	0.99	0.9725	**0.9774**
Ploss reduction (%)	-	13.28	14.05	**14.09**

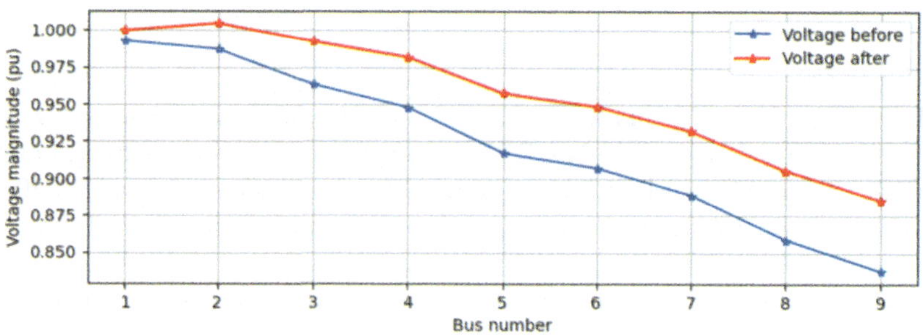

Fig. 4. VP before and after compensation for 10-bus RDS.

Conversely to the findings in Table 2, the LSF-MBA method yields significant improvements in minimum voltage and PF over the MLSI-MINLP and RPFA-WBI-PSO methods.

The RPFA-WBI method's effectiveness lies in its ability to identify buses with low voltage magnitudes and high reactive power demands. This selection enables the PSO algorithm to determine the appropriate size of shunt capacitors for these buses.

Moreover, the total cost is a sum of active power losses and capacitor installation costs. For the 10-bus RDS, we observe a decrease in total cost with a reduction in power losses and added reactive power, in contrast to the 33-bus system.

This indicates that the effectiveness of the optimization algorithm and the careful selection of capacitor locations significantly impact overall system performance.

Table 3. Results of 33-bus RDS

	Base	VSI-GTO [8]	VSF-LSF-EA [15]	Proposed
Optimal placement & Optimal size	-	14 -> 300 24 -> 600 30 -> 1050	13 -> 300 24 -> 300 26 -> 750 30 -> 750	8 -> 300 13 -> 300 24 -> 600 30 -> 1050
Qc totale (kvar)	-	1950	2100	**2250**
P_{loss} (kw)	202.6783	132.4256	132.19	**132.046**
Q_{loss}(kvar)	135.1558	88.5522	-	**88.06**
Total cost ($/years)	34049.95	22248	22593	**22765**
V_{min}	0.9131	0.9368	0.9388	**0.9426**
PF	0.8322	-	0. 9878	**0.9910**
Ploss reduction (%)	-	34.6618	34 .77	**34.84**

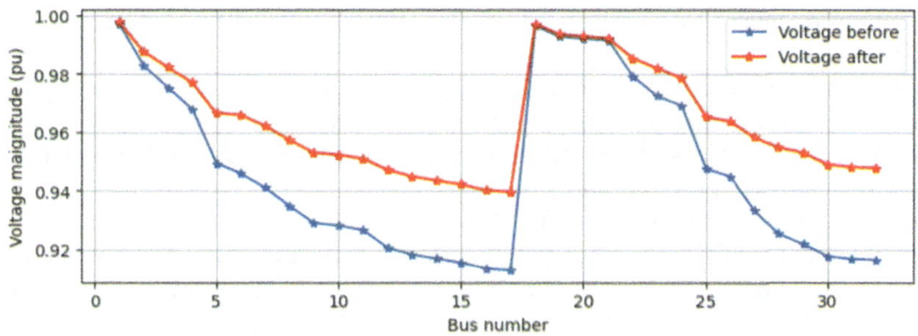

Fig. 5. VP before and after compensation for 33-bus RDS.

5 Conclusion

Identifying the optimal placement and size of shunt capacitors in RDS can significantly enhance network stability, minimize power losses, improve VPs, and correct the PF. The RPFA-WBI-PSO method has proven its effectiveness in solving this problem compared to other approaches found in the literature. This effectiveness stems from the sensitivity analysis used to identify optimal candidate buses and the PSO algorithm's ability to determine the optimal size for selected buses.

For future research, applying this proposed approach to real-world systems can contribute to increased efficiency and robustness. Additionally, modifying the method used to identify candidate buses can potentially streamline the optimization process.

References

1. Salimon, S.A., Omofuma, O.I., Akinrogunde, O.O., Thomas, T.G., Edwin, T.E.: Optimal allocation of shunt capacitors in radial distribution networks using Constriction-Factor Particle

Swarm Optimization and its techno-economic analysis. Frank. Open **7**, 100093 (2024). https://doi.org/10.1016/j.fraope.2024.100093
2. Bunch, J., Miller, R., Wheeler, J.: Distribution system integrated voltage and reactive power control. IEEE Trans. Power Apparatus Syst. **PAS-101**(2), 284–289 (1982). https://doi.org/10.1109/TPAS.1982.317104
3. Adal, S.M., Reda, E.T.: Optimal allocation and sizing of capacitor banks in distribution system to reduce the power loss using beluga whale optimization. Int. Trans. Electr. Energy Syst. **2024**(1), 7837832 (2024). https://doi.org/10.1155/2024/7837832
4. Ibrahim, H.O., Oloulade, A., Gonda, M., Fifatin, F.X.: Optimal location of capacitor in a radial distribution system using new hybrid method. Eng. Innov. **9**, 31–38 (2024). https://doi.org/10.4028/p-5yiHYg
5. Yaqoob, M.M., Hussain, A.N., Abed, W.R., Pereira, D.A.: power loss reduction and reliability improvement of radial distribution systems using optimal capacitor placement technique. J. Tech. **6**(1), Art. no. 1 (2024). https://doi.org/10.51173/jt.v6i1.1215
6. Makri, C., Guedira, S., Harraki, I.E., Hani, S.E.: Mixed integer nonlinear programming for optimal placement and size of capacitors in RDS. In: 2023 3rd International Conference on Innovative Research in Applied Science, Engineering and Technology (IRASET), pp. 01–06 (2023). https://doi.org/10.1109/IRASET57153.2023.10152896
7. Abd Elazim, S.M., Ali, E.S.: Optimal locations and sizing of capacitors in radial distribution systems using mine blast algorithm. Electr. Eng. **100**(1), 1–9 (2018). https://doi.org/10.1007/s00202-016-0475-1
8. Bhavana, K., Rajeswari, V., Rajan, V.R., Muthukumar, P.: An efficient hybrid approach for optimal integration of capacitors in radial distribution networks with realistic load models using giant trevally optimizer and voltage stability index. Int. J. Intell. Eng. Syst. (2024). https://openurl.ebsco.com/contentitem/10.22266%2Fijies2023.0831.15?sid=ebsco:plink:crawler&id=ebsco:10.22266%2Fijies2023.0831.15
9. Gnanasekaran, N., Chandramohan, S., Sudhakar, T.D., Kumar, P.S.: Maximum cost saving approach for optimal capacitor placement in radial distribution systems using modified ABC algorithm. IJEEI **7**(4), 665–678 (2015). https://doi.org/10.15676/ijeei.2015.7.4.10
10. Mtonga, T.P.M., Kaberere, K.K., Irungu, G.K.: Optimal shunt capacitors' placement and sizing in radial distribution systems using multiverse optimizer. IEEE Can. J. Electr. Comput. Eng. **44**(1), 10–21 (2021). https://doi.org/10.1109/ICJECE.2020.3012041
11. Rana, A.D., Darji, J.B., Pandya, M.: Backward/forward sweep load flow algorithm for radial distribution system, vol. 2, no. 01 (2014)
12. pandapower - pandapower. https://www.pandapower.org/. Accessed 23 Sept 2024
13. Kennedy, J., Eberhart, R.: Particle swarm optimization. In: Proceedings of ICNN 1995 - International Conference on Neural Networks, vol. 4, pp. 1942–1948 (1995). https://doi.org/10.1109/ICNN.1995.488968
14. Daghouri, A., Makri, C., El Hani, S.: Design of an electrical power system for a 1U nanosatellite using modified G3PCX. CEAS Space J. (2024). https://doi.org/10.1007/s12567-024-00565-9
15. Makri, C., Guedira, S., Harraki, I.E., Hani, S.E.: Combined approach for optimal placement and sizing capacitors in RDN. World J. Eng. (2024). https://doi.org/10.1108/WJE-02-2024-0068

AI for Predictive and Sustainable Infrastructure

Artificial Intelligence and Digital Infrastructure for Sustainable Industry and Enhanced Corporate Performance: A Bibliometric Analysis of Smart Optimization Technologies

Marwane Boussetta[1(✉)], Mariame Ababou[1,2], Sanae Faquir[3], and Sara Rabiai[4]

[1] Laboratory of Research in Entrepreneurship and Management of Organizations (REMO), Fez Business School, Private University of Fez, Fes, Morocco
marwane.boussetta@usmba.ac.ma, ABABOU@upf.ac.ma
[2] Higher School of Technology, Nador (ESTN), University Mohammed I, Oujda, Morocco
[3] Laboratory of Smart Systems, Energy and Sustainable Development (SIEDD), Faculty of Engineering Sciences, Private University of Fez, Fes, Morocco
faquir@upf.ac.ma
[4] Higher School of Technology, Dakhla (ESTD), Ibn Zohr University, Agadir, Morocco
s.rabiai@uiz.ac.ma

Abstract. This bibliometric review explores the transformative role of artificial intelligence (AI) in advancing sustainable industrial practices and boosting business performance through intelligent digital infrastructures. Focusing on the integration of AI with technologies such as the Internet of Things (IoT), big data analytics and blockchain, this study systematically examines research from the Web of Science (WoS) database to map trends and highlight emerging applications in resource optimization, predictive maintenance and real-time environmental monitoring.

The results demonstrate the potential of AI to improve operational efficiency, supply chain transparency and data-driven decision-making in industrial and corporate contexts. This supports growth, resilience and environmental responsibility. This analysis provides valuable insights into the intersection of AI, digital infrastructure and sustainability, charting paths for future research to deliver robust and effective solutions in line with corporate and environmental objectives.

Keywords: Artificial Intelligence · Corporate Performance · Digital Infrastructure · IoT · Predictive Maintenance · Resource Optimization

1 Introduction

In recent years, artificial intelligence (AI) has become central to advancing industrial efficiency and sustainability. The integration of machine learning (ML), digital infrastructure and the Internet of Things (IoT) has led to groundbreaking innovations in resource optimization, waste reduction and operational resilience. These advances are particularly relevant in industrial systems that aim to balance productivity and environmental

I. Aboudrar et al. (Eds.): ICESST 2024, SUCI, pp. 93–102, 2025.
https://doi.org/10.1007/978-3-031-86705-7_9

responsibility. Research by Abdar et al. (2021) highlights the critical role of AI in predictive maintenance and resource management, while Deng et al. (2020) emphasize the potential of edge intelligence for real-time decision-making and efficiency gains [1, 2].

However, significant challenges remain. As Venkatasubramanian (2019) and Ahmad et al. (2021) note, industries face data quality issues, limitations in terms of AI scalability and a lack of adaptability of AI models to complex industrial scenarios. These constraints often prevent industries from taking full advantage of AI's potential for sustainable resource management. Addressing these challenges requires AI models capable of handling diverse data sets and dynamically adapting to the changing conditions of industrial operations. Developing such models requires combining sophisticated digital infrastructures with adaptive data-driven algorithms that can both improve industrial productivity and sustainability [3, 4].

This report introduces a new framework comprising of ML algorithms and IoT-based systems to help achieve sustainable industrial improvements. The proposed model uses data analytics, both real-time and predictive analytics to address some of the key industrial challenges; such as energy inefficiency and variability in resource demand. Based on the pioneering work of Darko et al. (2020) regarding AI in architecture and engineering as well as the use of AI for sustainability conducted by Nishant et al. (2020), this study introduces a new unique solution, scalable to complex industrial settings. Leveraging explainable AI and adaptive algorithms, the framework intends to contribute towards a sustainable and resource-circularized industrial model in line with global environmental agendas [5, 6].

2 Methodology

2.1 Database

This bibliometric analysis is based exclusively on the Web of Science (WoS) database, a well-known source for high-quality peer-reviewed literature across multiple fields. The motivation for the decision to use only WoS is its strong and multidisciplinary primary characterization.

However, there is always a possibility of bias due to the use of a single database as WoS does not include all literature available from other specialist databases such as Scopus or IEEE Xplore. This may therefore lead to the exclusion of important studies related to specific niches or emergent applications of AI within certain industries. Future studies may be capable of overcoming the limitations and improving the accuracy level of research through bibliometric by considering other databases to provide a wider perspective regarding the role of AI in sustainable industrial practices.

2.2 Search String

A focused search strategy was then designed to identify works at the intersection of AI, industrial optimization and digital infrastructure. The keywords were based on the recent literature relating to AI and sustainability in smart systems, such as "Artificial Intelligence," "Machine Learning," "IoT," "Predictive Maintenance", "Digital Infrastructure" and "Optimization". The search string used was:

(TS = ("Artificial Intelligence" OR "AI") AND TS = ("Internet of Things" OR "Machine Learning" OR "Predictive Maintenance") AND TS = ("Digital Infrastructure" OR "Industrial Performance" OR "Optimization")).

2.3 Inclusion and Exclusion Criteria

Strict inclusion/exclusion criteria ensured that only relevant, high-quality research articles were included in the dataset. Priority was given to peer-reviewed articles written in English from the years 2019 to 2024. To focus on the empirical and review studies examined, we excluded document types such as editorials, proposals, conference papers, book chapters or non-academic publications. Additional filters decreased the dataset to only those articles that explain an AI solution for industrial optimization, resource management within sustainable environments, predictive maintenance and/or promoting efficiency practices within corporations, thus further refining the initial dataset by targeting the AI processes related to improvements of sustainability in industry or corporate settings.

We noticed that articles (Including Review Articles) made up 81% of all publications as shown in the Fig. 1.

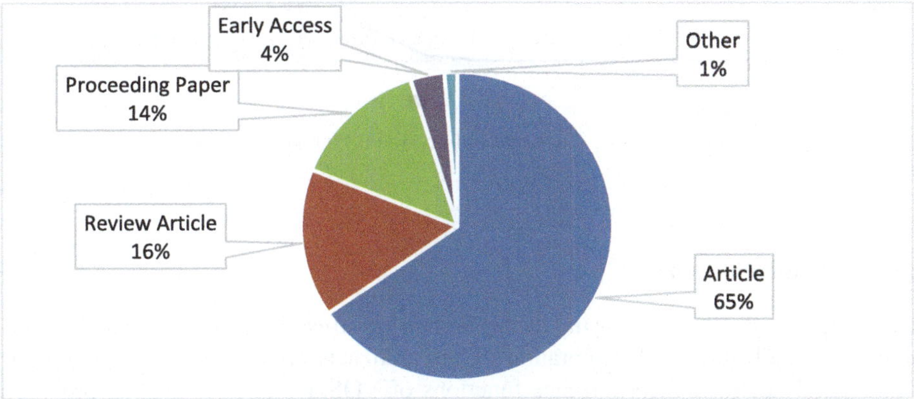

Fig. 1. Distribution of Publication Types

2.4 Data Processing

The initial search yielded 6,467 records in the Web of Science database. After applying the inclusion criteria, which entailed restricting the dataset to English-language peer-reviewed articles and review articles published between 2019 and 2024, the dataset was refined to 5,241 records. These records were exported in a format compatible with the bibliometric analysis software.

Figure 2 plots the distribution of these articles temporally (number of publications and their citations) to observe how the research on AI and sustainability has evolved through time. This sharp rise in the number of articles published and total citations between 2019 and 2024 highlights the increasing interest and research on these topics.

This trend evinces a mounting recognition of the significance of incorporating AI technologies into industrial settings as a means of confronting sustainability-related challenges and enhancing business performance. By mapping these temporal dynamics, the graph underscores the extent of AI-related knowledge and the mounting influence on sustainable practices, reflecting the sustained expansion and academic engagement in this interdisciplinary field.

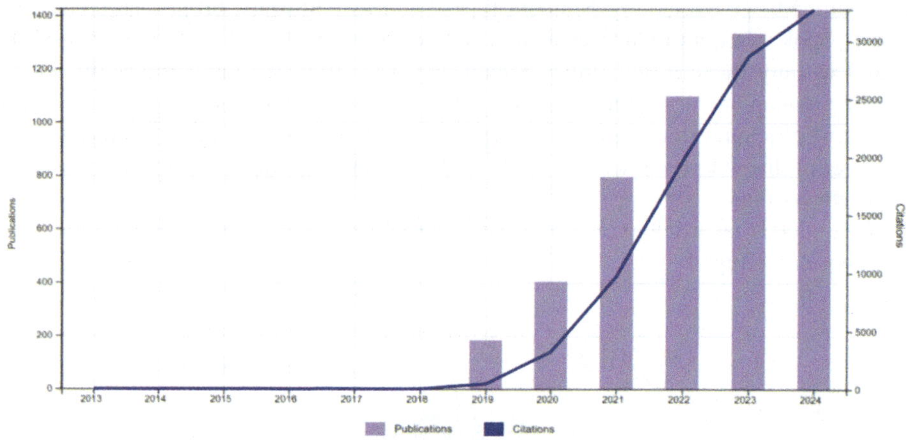

Fig. 2. Times Cited and Publications Over Time (WoS)

2.5 Bibliometric Tools

The analysis was carried out using the bibliometric software VOSviewer, which is suitable for visualization and exploration of research networks. The co-authorship, co-citation and keyword co-occurrence functions of VOSviewer were used to provide a clearer understanding of the research clusters by emphasizing relationships between central themes, key authors and main influential institutions. This approach facilitated a visualization as well as quantitative analysis of the research landscape that highlighted AI application in sustainable industrial practices and operational efficiencies at corporate-organizational level.

2.6 Analytical Methods

The bibliometric analysis incorporated two main components: performance analysis and science mapping. Performance analysis provides a quantitative examination of publication and citation metrics, identifying leading authors and countries contributing to the fields of AI, digital infrastructure, and industrial sustainability. Science mapping further explores the conceptual structure of the field, using citation and keyword co-occurrence analyses to visualize thematic clusters and highlight trending topics in AI-driven resource optimization, industrial efficiency, and corporate sustainability. Bibliometric maps were generated to reveal interconnections between these themes, allowing for a comprehensive understanding of the evolving research landscape.

Through this systematic methodology, the paper provides a comprehensive and systematic review of existing literature, from which key trends along with research gaps at the convergence of AI, sustainable industry and corporate efficiency are determined. It offers a valuable perspective on long-term development for academia, directing researchers to realms which arguably require investigation and highlighting the key role of digital infrastructure/smart technologies in facilitating sustainable/efficient practices in industrial/corporate settings.

3 Bibliometric Analysis

As shown in Table 1, this paper analyses the publication rate by country, and the results indicate that AI research in the field of sustainable industries is highly valued, led by strong countries such as China (1,300 papers) and the United States (927 papers). The large number of research outputs reflects the active support of these countries for initiatives to integrate AI and sustainable practices into industry and business. India published 689 papers, highlighting its increasingly important role in the development of these areas, followed by countries such as Saudi Arabia and the UK.

The number of papers published not only reflects the individual contributions made by these countries, but also highlights the importance of international collaboration as efforts from different regions come together to address global issues such as sustainability and industrial optimization through AI. The United States and China, in particular, have been leading the way in developing AI and investing in the Internet of Things and big data analytics to improve business performance and industrial resilience, which is critical for economic and environmental balance.

Table 1. Top 10 countries based on Number of articles Published

Countries/Regions	Record Count
Peoples R China	1300
USA	927
India	689
Saudi Arabia	518
England	336
South Korea	300
Canada	291
Iran	267
Germany	263
Australia	226

Table 2 shows that Amir Mosavi is the most active author in AI for sustainable industries with 34 publications and 155 citations. His research focuses on AI-based predictive modelling and optimization, applying advanced Machine Learning models to complex environmental and industrial challenges. Mosavi's work is central to the use of AI for climate resilience and resource management and supports sustainable development by improving decision-making capabilities.

Jianguo Liu and Ashit Kumar Dutta also feature prominently in Table 2 as they both make important contributions to the interface between AI and sustainability. Liu, with 11 publications and 375 citations, applies an ecological perspective and develops frameworks such as metacoupling to analyze global environmental impacts. Dutta, with 11 publications and 466 citations, focuses on neural network models, which are essential for predictive analyses in environmental and diagnostic applications. Together, these researchers highlight the diverse potential of artificial intelligence in sustainable development.

The impact of the research is in line with the article's most cited reference, 'Memory Devices and Applications for In-Memory Computing' by Sebastian et al. With more than 1,200 citations, this work shows how innovations in high-performance hardware support data-intensive AI applications and form a technological backbone that empowers AI applied to sustainable development [7].

Table 2. Top 15 authors based on Number of articles Published

Author	Documents	Citations
Mosavi, Amir	34	155
Bacanin, Nebojsa	17	144
Band, Shahab S	16	155
Zivkovic, Miodrag	15	21
Khan, Muhammad Attique	14	44
Khan, Muhammad Adnan	13	305
Moayedi, Hossein	13	75
Al Duhayyim, Mesfer	13	52
Chou, Jui-Sheng	12	120
Mirjalili, Seyedali	12	39
Hilal, Anwer Mustafa	12	34
Ragab, Mahmoud	12	28
Dutta, Ashit Kumar	11	466
Liu, Jianguo	11	375
Binh Thai Pham	11	137

4 Discussion

4.1 Keywords Co-occurrence

To cluster the pertinent literature, we created a keyword co-occurrence network using VOSviewer. "Author keywords" was selected as our unit of analysis, and we set a minimum of thirty occurrences. To further clean the data, we used a thesaurus file [8].

The resulting keyword co-occurrence network is shown in Fig. 3, where VOSviewer has classified the keywords into four different color-coded clusters.

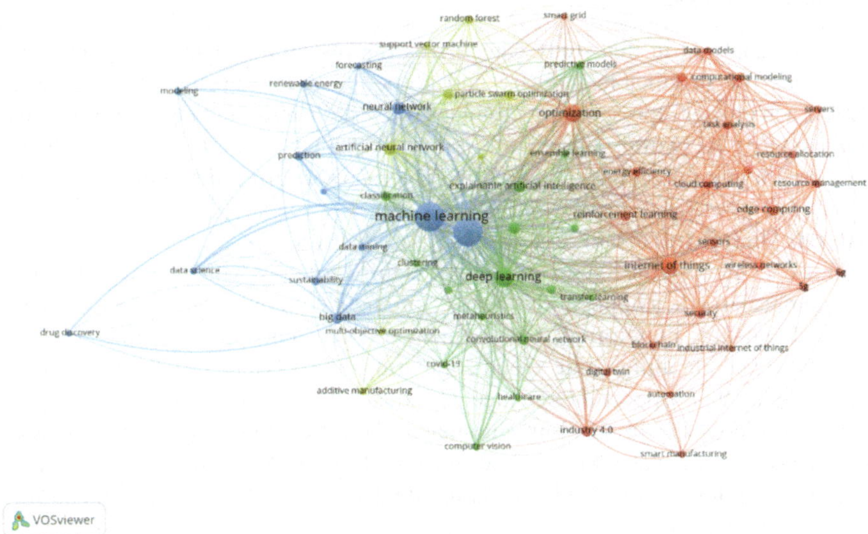

Fig. 3. Keywords Co-Occurrence Network

Figure 3 illustrates the network of overlapping keywords in the literature on AI-based sustainable production practices and highlights the dominant themes and trends in the field. The network is visualized using VOSviewer, which divides the keywords into four color-coded groups, each representing a thematic axis. Keywords such as 'machine learning' and 'artificial intelligence' highlight the fundamental role of these concepts in sustainable industrial applications. Key words such as 'deep learning', 'optimization' and 'Internet of Things' (IoT) reflect a strong focus on advanced data processing and integration technologies, which are in high demand.

Specific industries poised to take full advantage of AI-based resource optimization and predictive maintenance include manufacturing, energy and logistics. In manufacturing, AI enables real-time quality control and predictive maintenance, minimizing downtime and improving operational efficiency. In the energy sector, AI helps manage the renewable energy grid, predicting demand and optimizing resource allocation to support reliability and sustainability goals. The logistics industry benefits from AI by optimizing route planning, inventory management and demand forecasting, increasing operational transparency and reducing environmental impacts.

Practical case studies provide examples of how AI-based optimization techniques can make a difference in these industries. For example, Rolls-Royce uses digital twins and predictive maintenance in aerospace manufacturing to monitor engine performance and identify potential failures before they occur, improving efficiency and safety. Similarly, Siemens is using artificial intelligence-based optimization in smart grid management to balance renewable energy supply and demand in real-time to reduce energy waste.

Together, these teams highlight how AI and digital infrastructure are increasingly key to achieving operational and environmental goals in a sustainable industrial environment.

4.2 Cluster Analysis

The cluster analysis in this study categorizes the research landscape surrounding AI applications for sustainable industry and corporate efficiency into distinct thematic groups. Each cluster represents interconnected research areas and highlights the diverse applications of AI within sustainable industry frameworks. Below, we outline and examine each identified cluster based on keyword co-occurrence and thematic focus.

Cluster 1: Digital Infrastructure and IoT Integration
This cluster centers on the integration of digital infrastructure with the Internet of Things (IoT), emphasizing key applications such as predictive maintenance, resource management, and real-time monitoring. The frequent co-occurrence of terms like "Internet of Things," "edge computing," and "cloud computing" reflects a focus on creating resilient digital systems that support interconnected industrial networks. This cluster highlights the critical role of IoT in enabling automated, data-driven decision-making processes that enhance operational efficiency. Authors such as Fuller et al. have examined the convergence of digital twins and IoT to provide real-time insights in manufacturing and smart city contexts [9].

Cluster 2: Machine Learning and Optimization Techniques
The second cluster explores advancements in machine learning algorithms for optimizing industrial processes. Keywords like "deep learning," "feature extraction," and "explainable AI" indicate a thematic focus on enhancing the interpretability and accuracy of AI models for industrial applications. Researchers in this cluster address challenges in resource optimization, hyperparameter tuning, and explainability, which are crucial for operationalizing AI within corporate systems. Studies by Shrestha and Mahmood on deep learning architectures for complex, high-dimensional data exemplify the ongoing improvements in machine learning for industrial optimization [10].

Cluster 3: Sustainable and Renewable Energy Applications
This cluster of research is concerned with the application of artificial intelligence to the support of sustainable development and energy management. For example, the terms "renewable energy," "sustainability," and "forecasting" illustrate the application of AI in forecasting energy demand and managing renewable resources. AI-driven approaches in this domain address challenges associated with the variability of energy generated, enhancing power grid stability and reducing environmental harm. Wang et al. identified five key considerations for improving renewable energy forecasts using AI. This

finding underscores the significance of clustered methodologies in AI directed towards sustainability goals [11].

Cluster 4: Advanced Optimization and Intelligent Manufacturing
The fourth cluster is concerned with advanced optimization techniques and intelligent manufacturing. The use of terms like "genetic algorithm," "swarm intelligence," and "multi-objective optimization" underscores the emphasis on metaheuristic algorithms for complex, multivariable industrial challenges. To enable flexible and efficient production systems, these optimization techniques are critical for smart manufacturing. Yang et al.'s "Hunger Games Search" is an example of cutting-edge optimization methods that aim to balance exploration and exploitation in industrial applications, thereby improving the quality of solutions and the speed of convergence in manufacturing contexts [12].

These clusters are indicative of the large impact that AI is having on sustainable industry and corporate performance. Additionally, they highlight a range of interesting research subject matters in IoT enabled systems, machine learning, renewable energy, and intelligent manufacturing.

5 Conclusion and Future Directions

In this study, we analyzed research related to artificial intelligence (AI) and digital infrastructure in the sustainability sector, highlighting the role of intelligent optimization techniques in improving business outcomes. Looking at trends, key publications and influential authors in the field, our findings indicate a growing interest in AI-based approaches, such as machine learning, digital twins and IoT systems, to optimize resources, predictive maintenance and improve environmental sustainability.

Our analysis shows that leading researchers, including Sebastian et al. (2020) on in-memory computing, Rasheed et al. (2020) on digital twin applications, and Zhao et al. (2021) on AI in power electronics, are shaping the development of these technologies, with substantial contributions focused on industrial efficiency and resource management [7, 13, 14].

Additionally, Baryannis et al. (2019)'s work on supply chain risk management and Cuomo et al. (2022) on physics-informed neural networks indicate an increasing integration of AI across complex, multi-disciplinary areas critical to sustainable industrial practices [15, 16].

This helps us in formulating business strategies, especially in green technology and sustainability. For example, predictive analytics can be used for different sustainability measures; they use data to optimize energy consumption, reduces waste & enables more efficient resource allocation. Moreover, relevant AI technologies like digital twins for real time monitoring and machine learning for predictive maintenance are immediately deployable to yield substantially improved resource efficiency. Incorporating these tools enables organizations to more closely align their operational trench activities with corporate sustainability ambitions, resulting in better environmental and economic outcomes.

Potential future directions for research include the development of cross-industry AI models, advancing meta-heuristics and hybrid methods in robust optimization, as well as evaluation of the ethical impact of AI-led transformation of sustainable practices across industry.

References

1. Abdar, M., Pourpanah, F., Hussain, S., Rezazadegan, D., Liu, L., Ghavamzadeh, M., et al.: A review of uncertainty quantification in deep learning: techniques, applications and challenges. Inf. Fusion **76**, 243–97 (2021)
2. Deng, S., Zhao, H., Fang, W., Yin, J., Dustdar, S., Zomaya, A.: Edge intelligence: the confluence of edge computing and artificial intelligence. IEEE Internet Things J. **7**, 7457–69 (2020)
3. Venkatasubramanian, V.: The promise of artificial intelligence in chemical engineering: Is it here, finally? AICHE J. **65**, 466–78 (2019)
4. Ahmad, T., et al.: Artificial intelligence in sustainable energy industry: status Quo, challenges and opportunities. J. Clean. Prod. **289** (2021)
5. Darko, A., Chan, A., Adabre, M., Edwards, D., Hosseini, M., Ameyaw, E.: Artificial intelligence in the AEC industry: Scientometric analysis and visualization of research activities. Autom. Constr. **112** (2020)
6. Nishant, R., Kennedy, M., Corbett, J.: Artificial intelligence for sustainability: challenges, opportunities, and a research agenda. Int. J. Inf. Manag. **53**, 102104 (2020)
7. Sebastian, A., Le Gallo, M., Khaddam-Aljameh, R., Eleftheriou, E.: Memory devices and applications for in-memory computing. Nat. Nanotechnol. **15**, 529–44 (2020)
8. van Eck, N.J., Waltman, L.: VOSviewer Manual (2023)
9. Fuller, A., Fan, Z., Day, C., Barlow, C.: Digital twin: enabling technologies, challenges open research. IEEE Access **8**, 108952–71 (2020)
10. Shrestha, A., Mahmood, A.: Review of deep learning algorithms and architectures. IEEE Access **7**, 53040–65 (2019)
11. Wang, H., Lei, Z., Zhang, X., Zhou, B., Peng, J.: A review of deep learning for renewable energy forecasting. ENERGY Convers. Manag. **198** (2019)
12. Yang, Y., Chen, H., Heidari, A., Gandomi, A.: Hunger games search: visions, conception, implementation, deep analysis, perspectives, and towards performance shifts. EXPERT Syst. Appl. **177** (2021)
13. Rasheed, A., San, O., Kvamsdal, T.: Digital twin: values, challenges and enablers from a modeling perspective. IEEE Access **8**, 21980–2012 (2020)
14. Zhao, S., Blaabjerg, F., Wang, H.: An overview of artificial intelligence applications for power electronics. IEEE Trans. Power Electron. **36**, 4633–58 (2021)
15. Baryannis, G., Validi, S., Dani, S., Antoniou, G.: Supply chain risk management and artificial intelligence: state of the art and future research directions. Int. J. Prod. Res. **57**, 2179–202 (2019)
16. Cuomo, S., Di Cola, V., Giampaolo, F., Rozza, G., Raissi, M., Piccialli, F.: Scientific machine learning through physics-informed neural networks: where we are and what's next. J. Sci. Comput. **92** (2022)

The Future of Travel: A Review of Chatbot Recommender Systems in E-Tourism and Smart Tourism

Mohamed Badouch[1](✉), Mehdi Boutaounte[2], Omar Zioudi[1], and Hasna Mahmoud[1]

[1] Faculty of Sciences, Ibn Zohr University, Agadir, Morocco
mohamed.badouch@edu.uiz.ac.ma

[2] National School of Commerce and Management, Ibn Zohr University, Dakhla, Morocco

Abstract. This systematic review explores the implementation of AI-powered chatbots in the travel, tourism, and hospitality sectors, emphasizing their role in enhancing e-tourism and smart tourism strategies. It synthesizes key literature, highlighting the benefits of chatbots, such as improved efficiency and responsiveness in online customer service, while addressing challenges like managing complex queries and ensuring data privacy. The review examines various machine learning approaches, including natural language processing, sentiment analysis, and recommendation systems, which enhance chatbot functionalities. Despite their potential, chatbots face issues like handling complex queries and inherent biases in data. Continuous advancements in machine learning algorithms are crucial for further customization and improved customer experiences. The review concludes that while chatbots may not entirely replace human agents, their integration into the tourism industry holds significant potential for improving e-tourism processes and increasing customer satisfaction.

Keywords: Chatbots · Tourism · Machine Learning · E-tourism · Customer Service

1 Introduction

The travel industry is undergoing a significant transformation as customers increasingly use digital platforms for researching, booking, and managing travel itineraries. This shift has heightened the demand for efficient and personalized customer service, leading to the implementation of AI-powered chatbots in the travel and hospitality sectors. These chatbots, utilizing natural language processing (NLP) and machine learning (ML) algorithms, simulate human interaction, providing travelers with 24/7 support.

Several trends have integrated chatbots into the tourism industry. Tourists seek personalized travel recommendations based on unique interests, preferences, and budgets. The tourism industry aims to enhance operational efficiency and reduce costs, with chatbots handling high volumes of queries, allowing human agents to focus on complex tasks. Travelers also expect round-the-clock support, which chatbots can provide.

I. Aboudrar et al. (Eds.): ICESST 2024, SUCI, pp. 103–115, 2025.
https://doi.org/10.1007/978-3-031-86705-7_10

Chatbots offer numerous benefits for both tourists and tourism companies. They can answer questions quickly and accurately, improving the user experience and reducing waiting times. Chatbots can also analyze user preferences and past travel history to offer personalized recommendations, enhancing travel discovery and booking. Additionally, they provide valuable customer data to companies, aiding in marketing and product development. However, integrating chatbots into the travel industry presents challenges. While they promise enhanced efficiency and personalization, there are concerns about their ability to handle complex queries and complaints. Recommendations may be biased due to the data used by chatbots, and data privacy is a significant concern as chatbots collect user information.

This review addresses these challenges by systematically examining the literature on chatbot recommender systems in e-tourism and smart tourism. It aims to summarize key questions, methodologies, and findings from current studies on chatbot adoption in travel and hospitality contexts. The review also assesses the advantages and costs of implementing chatbot systems to extend online customer service in the tourism industry and maps the current research landscape to outline an agenda for future research.

The review is structured as follows: The Literature Review section provides an overview of existing research on chatbot recommender systems in the travel, tourism, and hospitality industries, discussing methodologies and key findings. The Methodology section outlines the systematic approach used to identify, evaluate, and synthesize relevant research. The Key Findings section synthesizes core findings, focusing on chatbot systems, their applications, and emerging trends. The Challenges and Limitations section discusses issues related to natural language understanding, algorithmic bias, data privacy, and system integration. The Discussion section evaluates the benefits and costs of chatbot adoption, exploring future research directions. The Implications for Tourism Businesses section offers practical recommendations for adopting chatbot systems. Finally, the Conclusion section summarizes key insights, emphasizing the potential of AI-driven chatbots to revolutionize customer interactions and improve business efficiency in the travel and tourism sector.

2 Literature Review

2.1 Methodology

This systematic review employed a rigorous methodology to identify, evaluate, and synthesize relevant research on chatbot recommender systems in the travel, tourism, and hospitality industries. A comprehensive search strategy was developed using a combination of relevant keywords related to chatbots, tourism, e-tourism, smart tourism, machine learning, and customer service. The following databases were searched: Scopus, Web of Science, Springer, ACM Digital Library, and Google Scholar. The search terms used were: ("Chatbot" OR "Conversational AI" OR "Dialogue System") AND ("Tourism" OR "Travel" OR "Hospitality" OR "E-tourism" OR "Smart Tourism"), ("Chatbot" OR "Conversational AI" OR "Dialogue System") AND ("Recommendation System" OR "Recommender System"), and ("Chatbot" OR "Conversational AI" OR "Dialogue System") AND ("Machine Learning" OR "AI").

These findings were then reviewed to find those that matched pre-defined inclusion and exclusion criteria. A review was needed on articles about research into chatbot recommender systems in the travel, tourism, and hospitality domains published in English in a peer-reviewed journal or conference proceeding using empirical research methods such as surveys, experiments, and case studies. Studies focusing solely on theoretical frameworks or general AI applications, without a clear context of tourism; not written in the English language; presented in non-peer-reviewed publications; or specifically targeted only chatbots in other industries (like healthcare or finance) were out of scope (Table 1).

Table 1. Summary of Studies on Chatbot Recommender Systems in Smart Tourism.

Year	Title	Methodology	Authors	Sub-theme
2021	Predicting the intentions to use chatbots for travel and tourism	Surveys, Experiments	Melián-González, S., Gutiérrez-Taño, D., Bulchand-Gidumal, J	Customer Service Automation
2022	Human-computer interaction in customer service: the experience with AI chatbots—a systematic literature review	Surveys, Experiments	Nicolescu, L., Tudorache, M.T	
2021	What makes you continuously use chatbot services? Evidence from Chinese online travel agencies	Surveys, Experiments, Case Studies	Li, L., Lee, K.Y., Emokpae, E., Yang, S.B	Personalized Travel Recommendation Engines
2023	Tourist interaction and satisfaction with the chatbot evokes pre-visit destination image formation? A case study	Surveys, Experiments, Case Studies	Orden-Mejía, M.A., Huertas, A	
2024	Unveiling the e-Servicescape of ChatGPT: Exploring User Psychology and Engagement in AI-Powered Chatbot Experiences	Surveys, Experiments, Case Studies	Kim, M	
2023	Leveraging inter-tourists interactions via chatbots to bridge academia, tourism industries and future societies	Case Studies	Calvaresi, D., Ibrahim, A., Calbimonte, J.P., Fragniere, E., Schegg, R., Schumacher, M.I	Providing Contextualized Travel Information

(continued)

Table 1. *(continued)*

Year	Title	Methodology	Authors	Sub-theme
2023	Application of AI Technology for the Development of Destination Tourism towards an Intelligent Information System	Case Studies	Mishra, D., Das, S., Patnaik, R	
2023	Artificial intelligence's impact on hospitality and tourism marketing: exploring key themes and addressing challenges	Experiments	Bulchand-Gidumal, J., William Secin, E., O'Connor, P., Buhalis, D	Addressing Limitations in Natural Language Understanding
2019	Technological disruptions in services: lessons from tourism and hospitality	Experiments	Buhalis, D., Harwood, T., Bogicevic, V., Viglia, G., Beldona, S., Hofacker, C	
2023	Assessing user satisfaction with information chatbots: a preliminary investigation	Experiments	Balaji, D	Enhancing NLU and Conversational AI
2024	Artificial Intelligence and the Great Transformation in the Tourism Industry Revolutionizing Travel Services	Experiments	Moghaddasnian, A.H	

2.2 Key Findings

This section synthesizes the core findings extracted from the reviewed literature on chatbot recommender systems within the e-tourism landscape. We analysed the types of chatbot systems employed, their applications within the tourism sector, assessments of their effectiveness, and the emerging trends shaping the future of chatbot integration. The aim is to provide a comprehensive overview of how artificial intelligence (AI), and more specifically, machine learning (ML), are influencing the development and deployment of chatbots within the evolving e-tourism ecosystem.

The literature reveals a shift in the architectural design of chatbots implemented in the tourism sector. Initially, rule-based systems were dominant, relying on pre-defined rules and decision trees to generate responses. However, the integration of AI, particularly ML algorithms, has led to a growing adoption of more sophisticated chatbot architectures [26]. ML-powered chatbots leverage large datasets of user interactions and travel information to refine their responses, personalize recommendations, and enhance their ability to understand and respond to diverse user queries. For instance, a study by [1] highlighted the effectiveness of ML-driven chatbot systems in providing personalized travel itineraries based on individual user preferences and historical data, a crucial feature for optimizing e-tourism experiences (Fig. 1).

Fig. 1. Percentage of studies that focused on each specific application of chatbots.

The integration of chatbots within the e-tourism ecosystem is evident across several applications:

- **Customer Service Automation:** Chatbots are increasingly being used to automate routine customer service interactions, handling FAQs, providing information on travel policies, and resolving simple issues 24/7. [2] showed that chatbot-powered customer service platforms can significantly reduce customer wait times and improve overall satisfaction levels, especially within online travel agencies.
- **Personalized Travel Recommendation Engines:** Personalization of travel recommendations has lately become one of the most decisive factors in the adoption of chatbots in the e-tourism domain. AI-driven chatbots can present recommended travel destinations, accommodations, activities, and packages tailored to each user by using data on previous travel history, user preferences, and browsing behaviour. This enhances user experiences and leads to higher conversion rates. [3] found that AI-powered personalized suggestions have a positive influence on increasing user engagement and intention to book.
- **Streamlining Booking Processes:** Chatbots are effectively simplifying the online booking process, offering automated booking assistance for flights, hotels, and other travel services. [4] found that chatbots can significantly accelerate booking times and improve the overall booking experience, particularly for users seeking quick and efficient solutions.
- **Providing Contextualized Travel Information:** Context-aware travel information delivery: chatbots serve as an intelligent travel assistant for providing destination or location-related knowledge, on tourist attractions, and events in the area, as well as available local transportation choices; it delivers real-time, context-aware information, thus supporting decision-making for the traveller's journey [5]. Showcased the promise of chatbots to provide timely access to destination-specific relevant information thus promotes pre-trip planning and overall satisfaction of travellers.

Research assessing the performance and effectiveness of chatbots within e-tourism reveals a mix of successes and challenges:

- **Enhanced User Engagement and Satisfaction:** Several studies indicate that users generally have a positive experience with chatbot interactions, particularly when chatbots can promptly address their inquiries and provide helpful information. [6] found that user satisfaction with chatbot-mediated interactions was higher when users perceived the chatbot as being helpful, efficient, and easy to use.
- **Addressing Limitations in Natural Language Understanding:** One of the major challenges encountered with chatbots is their ability to understand and respond appropriately to complex or ambiguous user queries. Emphasized the need for continued research and development in Natural language Understanding (NLU) to enhance chatbot capabilities and minimize errors in interpreting user requests [7].
- **Mitigation of Biases and Ensuring Fairness:** The training data used to develop chatbots can introduce biases into the system, potentially resulting in unfair or discriminatory recommendations. Highlights the importance of ensuring that the data used to train chatbots is diverse and representative to minimize the risk of algorithmic bias in travel recommendations [8].

The field of chatbot development for e-tourism is rapidly evolving, with advancements in AI and ML continuously shaping the future of these technologies:

- Enhancing NLU and Conversational AI: Ongoing research focuses on improving the ability of chatbots to understand and respond to complex, nuanced language, leading to more natural and human-like conversations. This focus on developing more sophisticated conversational AI technologies is critical for enabling chatbots to address a broader range of user needs and enhance the overall e-tourism experience [9].
- Personalization Through Advanced ML Techniques: The use of advanced ML techniques, such as deep learning [27] and reinforcement learning, is enabling more personalized and context-aware chatbot interactions within e-tourism platforms. Researchers are exploring how to leverage these techniques to deliver more tailored travel recommendations, dynamic pricing, and customized travel itineraries. [10].
- Integration with Emerging Technologies: Chatbots are increasingly being integrated with other emerging technologies within the e-tourism landscape, such as VR/AR, to create more immersive and interactive travel experiences. [11] investigated how VR/AR experiences enhanced by chatbot interactions can improve traveller engagement and satisfaction, leading to a shift in how travel services are consumed and delivered (Fig. 2).

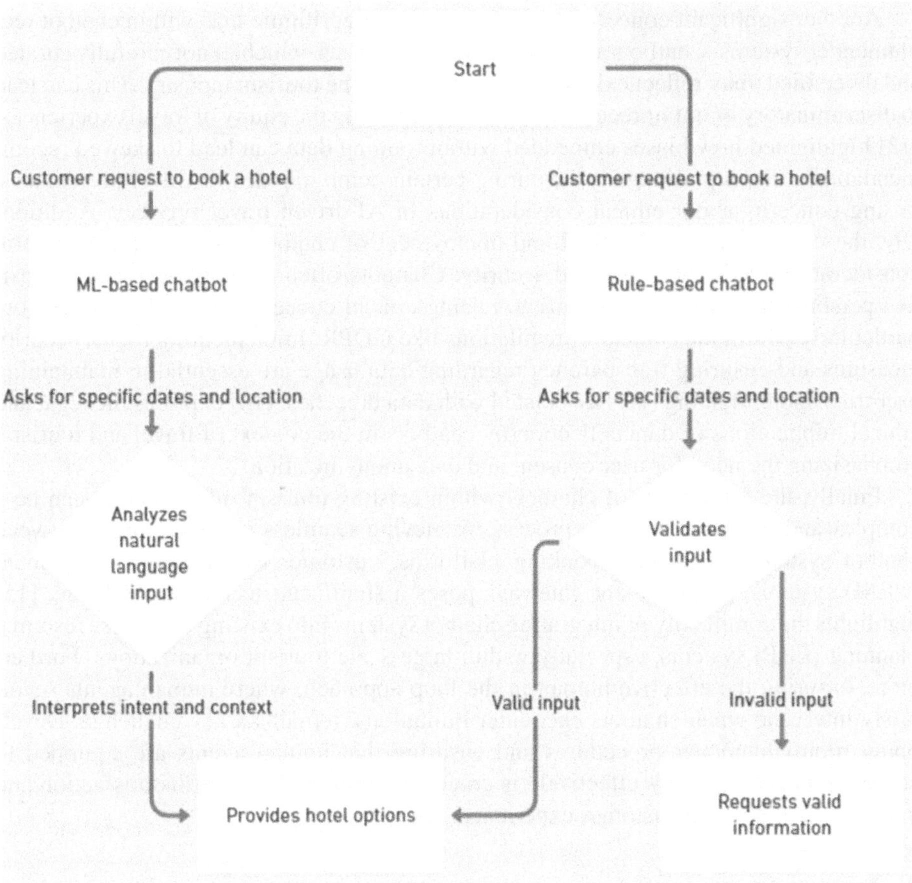

Fig. 2. The process of a customer interaction with a rule-based chatbot versus an ML-based chatbot for booking a hotel.

2.3 Challenges and Limitations

Despite the promise of AI-powered chatbots to enhance the e-tourism landscape, several challenges and limitations hinder their widespread adoption and full potential realization. One critical hurdle stem from the limitations of Natural Language Understanding (NLU) within current chatbot architectures. While advancements in NLP have improved chatbot capabilities, complex or nuanced user queries often prove challenging to interpret accurately. This can lead to misinterpretations, irrelevant responses, and ultimately, user frustration. [12] emphasizes that current chatbots often struggle to process intricate user requests, particularly those involving ambiguous language or multiple intents, resulting in a decline in user satisfaction. Furthermore, the lack of robust contextual awareness in many chatbot systems presents a barrier to providing truly personalized and relevant assistance.

Another significant concern is the potential for algorithmic bias within chatbot recommender systems. Chatbots are trained on large datasets, which, if not carefully curated and diversified, may reflect existing biases present in the tourism industry. This can lead to discriminatory or unfair recommendations, impacting the equity of travel experiences. [13] highlighted how biases embedded within training data can lead to skewed recommendations, disproportionately favouring certain demographics or travel preferences, raising concerns about ethical considerations in AI-driven travel services. Additionally, the continuous development and deployment of chatbot systems require careful consideration of data privacy and security. Chatbots often collect and process sensitive personal information about users, raising crucial concerns about data protection, particularly within the context of regulations like GDPR. Implementing robust security measures and ensuring transparency regarding data usage are essential to maintaining user trust and mitigating risks associated with data breaches. [14] explores the legal and ethical implications of data collection by chatbots in the context of travel and tourism, emphasizing the need for user consent and data anonymization.

Finally, the integration of chatbots within existing tourism infrastructure can be a complex and resource-intensive process. Achieving seamless interoperability between chatbot systems and legacy booking platforms, customer relationship management (CRM) systems, and payment gateways poses a significant technical challenge. [15] highlights the complexity of integrating chatbot systems into existing enterprise resource planning (ERP) systems, especially within large-scale tourism organizations. Furthermore, ensuring the effective human-in-the-loop approach, where human agents seamlessly intervene when chatbots encounter limitations, remains a key challenge. Developing robust handover procedures and ensuring that human agents are equipped to address unresolved issues effectively is crucial for minimizing user dissatisfaction and maintaining a positive customer experience.

3 Discussion

3.1 Benefits and Costs of Chatbot Adoption

In this paper, some of the benefits that the integration has brought forth are AI-powered conversational agents popularly known as chatbots within the tourism industry. Overall, benefits accruing from their core functionalities include NLP, ML, and dialogue management. The aspect of the ability to address customer inquiries on anything, for example-"Can you suggest a family-friendly hotel near the Eiffel Tower?"-in the most natural and intuitive way, increases the customer experience. Precisely, chatbots allow supporting customers 24/7, thus enabling tourism companies to support travellers at any time, from anywhere in the world. For example, a tourist in Tokyo changes flight plans because of changed plans.

A chatbot would swing into action right at that moment with little friction to satisfaction compared to calling customer service and sending emails. Advanced chatbots would make recommendations personalized as they learn about user preference and travel history. For instance, if a client usually inquiries about budget-friendly accommodations in resort zones, he will keep receiving further recommendations on the same for any other query that might arise later. Such chatbots use machine learning algorithms to intelligently compose responses to identify and cater to unique tastes and preferences of end-users in real-time, thereby driving up conversions and loyalty. That means chatbots make the automation of routine time-consuming actions performed by human agents quicker, reduce work, and thereby enhance efficiency in business operations, along with financial efficiency among tourism-related companies. In other words, if a human worker is answering basic questions like "What is the check-in time?" or "Where is a restaurant nearby?", chatbots release the human resources to deal with more complex problems and useful contacts.

However, the implementation of chatbot systems within the tourism industry also comes with a set of associated costs. The development of sophisticated chatbot systems necessitates significant investment in software development and AI model training. Building a chatbot that can understand travel-related language and answer nuanced questions requires extensive training data and development resources [16]. Furthermore, the ongoing maintenance and updates of chatbot systems require continuous investment in natural language processing (NLP) model refinement, machine learning model retraining, and dialogue management optimization. For example, a chatbot designed to provide information about local attractions would need continuous updates to reflect any changes in operating hours, ticket prices, or event schedules. The potential impact on human workforce requirements is another key cost factor. While chatbots can automate certain tasks, they may lead to a reduction in the need for human agents in certain roles, potentially impacting the roles of travel agents or customer service representatives.

3.2 Future Research Directions

Modern chatbot technologies very often face significant problems in answering complex questions and subtle requests. Subsequent research should aim to work on more complex frameworks of NLU, able to grasp an extended scope of the linguistic appearance and intentions of users. The development of chatbots capable of perceiving idiomatic phrases, sarcasm, or emotional sentoid would exponentially enhance the quality of contacts with the user. Further, high relevance comes in the studies of contextual awareness while interacting with chatbots. This will help the chatbots retain knowledge about the past interactions of users or their personal preferences, making the responses more personalized and relevant. Visualize a scenario where a chatbot remembers that a given user prefers accommodation options that are ecologically friendly and goes ahead to proactively suggest similar options when other travel requests come up. Further research in dialogue management systems could fine-tune dialog dynamics into more engaging and user-friendly interactions [17].

The use of AI-driven chatbots in the tourism industry raises some key ethical concerns and data privacy issues. Future research should focus on ways of ensuring equity and minimizing biases in chatbot recommendation systems. For example, researchers might explore a model of determining and rectifying potential biases in the training data so that chatbots' recommendations are fair and do not create undue harm for a certain demographic or travel preference. Second, research must be done to come up with mechanisms to protect user data with evolving privacy regulations, such as the GDPR [18]. For example, some federated learning techniques are being developed that could one day help a chatbot learn from user data without collecting sensitive information from users in one central store, hence improving privacy and security. The research of explainable methodologies in artificial intelligence (XAI) will further improve the transparency of the decision-making mechanism behind chatbots [19]; hence, users understand how recommendations have been made, thereby engendering trust.

Incorporating chatbots with other new technologies shows great potential for transforming the tourism experience. Future studies should investigate how chatbots can be smoothly incorporated with virtual reality (VR) and augmented reality (AR) technologies to offer immersive travel experiences [20]. For instance, picture a virtual reality tour of a historic location led by a chatbot offering background details and responding to inquiries instantly. Investigating the combination of chatbots and blockchain technology may lead to more secure travel booking platforms, decreasing the chance of fraud and improving trust between travelers and tourism providers. Additionally, examining how sentiment analysis can be incorporated into chatbot interactions can offer valuable information about user feelings and choices, helping tourism companies customize their services and products with greater efficiency.

3.3 Implications for Tourism Businesses

Tourism businesses considering chatbot adoption should prioritize a strategic approach that aligns with their specific operational goals and target audience. Firstly, selecting the appropriate chatbot platform is crucial. Businesses need to carefully evaluate the capabilities of different platforms, considering factors like NLP capabilities, ML-based learning, and integration with existing systems [21]. For instance, a small boutique hotel might benefit from a simpler, rule-based chatbot focused on answering basic FAQs, while a large international travel agency might require a more sophisticated platform with advanced ML capabilities for personalized recommendations and complex booking assistance.Secondly, the training data used to develop and refine the chatbot is of paramount importance. Chatbots should be trained on a comprehensive dataset that reflects the specific language, queries, and information needs of the target audience [22]. For instance, a chatbot designed for a luxury travel agency would require training data that includes vocabulary related to high-end accommodations, specialized travel services, and the preferences of affluent travelers. The process of knowledge engineering plays a crucial role in defining the knowledge base of the chatbot, ensuring it can accurately respond to a wide range of user inquiries.

Tourism businesses can also leverage emerging technologies to enhance the capabilities of their chatbot systems:

- **Integrating Conversational AI with VR/AR Experiences:** VR and AR technologies can provide immersive and interactive travel experiences and integrating them with chatbots can enhance the overall user experience [23]. Imagine a chatbot guiding a user through a VR tour of a historical site, providing contextual information about the location, and answering questions in real-time.
- **Utilizing Blockchain for Secure Transactions:** Blockchain technology can provide a secure and transparent platform for booking travel services [24], enhancing trust, and reducing the risk of fraudulent activities. Chatbots can be integrated into blockchain-based booking systems to provide secure and efficient booking experiences (Fig. 3).

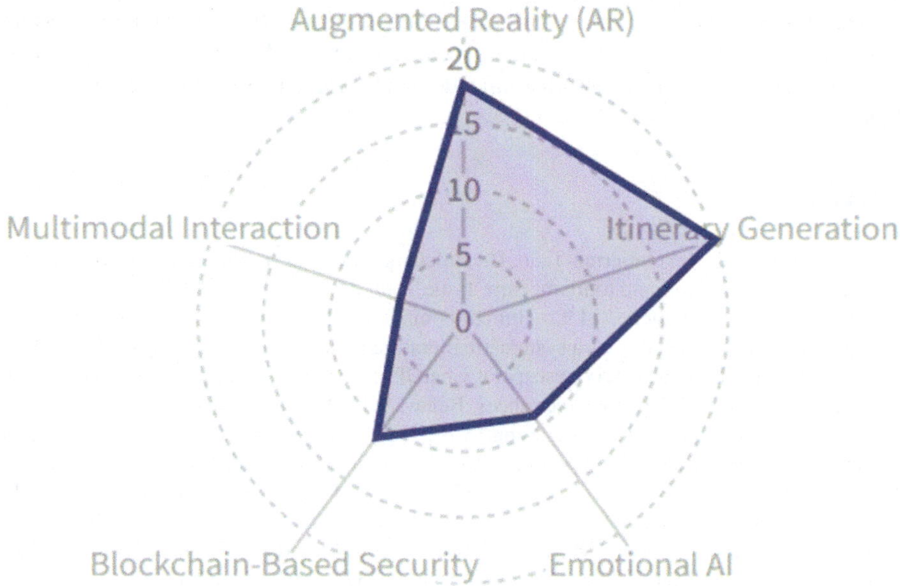

Fig. 3. Future Trends in Chatbot Recommender Systems for Smart Tourism.

- **Utilizing Sentiment Analysis to Improve Personalization:** Enhancing chatbot interactions through the integration of sentiment analysis [25]. This enables chatbots to assess the emotional tone of user interactions and adjust their replies, resulting in a more customized and empathetic user experience. If a chatbot senses that a user is upset in their question, it can transfer the conversation to a human representative.

4 Conclusion

This analysis has investigated the growing area of chatbot recommendation systems in the travel and tourism sector, emphasizing the possibility of AI-driven conversational agents to revolutionize customer interactions and improve business efficiency. Our examination shows big chances to improve customer service by offering around-the-clock support and automated task management, along with personalized travel experiences driven by machine learning (ML) algorithms. Nevertheless, we also recognized significant obstacles, such as constraints in comprehending natural language (NLU), the risk of algorithmic prejudice in suggestions, worries regarding data confidentiality and protection, and the difficulties of merging chatbots into current tourism systems.

The advancement of chatbot technology in the travel industry depends on ongoing research and development work. Overcoming restrictions in NLU, reducing prejudice in recommendations, and protecting data privacy are crucial for establishing trust and promoting ethical AI practices in the field. Moreover, combining chatbots with emerging technologies such as virtual reality (VR) and augmented reality (AR) offers thrilling chances to improve the travel journey. Tourism businesses need to take a strategic approach when implementing chatbots, which involves choosing platforms wisely, creating thorough training data, and giving priority to data security. By adopting new ideas and considering moral concerns, the tourism sector can utilize AI-driven chatbots to offer more immersive, effective, and customized travel experiences for people around the globe.

References

1. Melián-González, S., Gutiérrez-Taño, D., Bulchand-Gidumal, J.: Predicting the intentions to use chatbots for travel and tourism. Curr. Issue Tour. **24**(2), 192–210 (2021)
2. Nicolescu, L., Tudorache, M.T.: Human-computer interaction in customer service: the experience with AI chatbots—a systematic literature review. Electronics **11**(10), 1579 (2022)
3. Kim, M.: Unveiling the e-servicescape of ChatGPT: exploring user psychology and engagement in AI-powered Chatbot experiences. Behav. Sci. **14**(7), 558 (2024)
4. Li, L., Lee, K.Y., Emokpae, E., Yang, S.B.: What makes you continuously use chatbot services? Evidence from Chinese online travel agencies. Electron. Mark. 1–25 (2021)
5. Orden-Mejía, M.A., Huertas, A.: Tourist interaction and satisfaction with the chatbot evokes pre-visit destination image formation? A case study. Anatolia **34**(4), 509–523 (2023)
6. Brandtzaeg, P.B., Følstad, A.: Why people use chatbots. In: Internet Science: 4th International Conference, INSCI 2017, Thessaloniki, Greece, pp. 377–392. Springer (2017)
7. Lin, W.Y.: Prototyping a Chatbot for site managers using building information modeling (BIM) and natural language understanding (NLU) techniques. Sensors **23**(6), 2942 (2023)
8. Calvaresi, D., Ibrahim, A., Calbimonte, J.P., Fragniere, E., Schegg, R., Schumacher, M.I.: Leveraging inter-tourists interactions via chatbots to bridge academia, tourism industries and future societies. J. Tour. Futures **9**(3), 311–337 (2023)
9. Mishra, D., Das, S., Patnaik, R.: Application of AI technology for the development of destination tourism towards an intelligent information system. Econ. Aff. **69**(02), 1083–1095 (2024)
10. Bulchand-Gidumal, J., William Secin, E., O'Connor, P., Buhalis, D.: Artificial intelligence's impact on hospitality and tourism marketing: exploring key themes and addressing challenges. Curr. Issue Tour. **27**(14), 2345–2362 (2024)
11. Buhalis, D., Harwood, T., Bogicevic, V., Viglia, G., Beldona, S., Hofacker, C.: Technological disruptions in services: lessons from tourism and hospitality. J. Serv. Manag. **30**(4), 484–506 (2019)
12. Balaji, D.: Assessing user satisfaction with information chatbots: a preliminary investigation. Master's thesis, University of Twente (2019)
13. Moghaddasnian, A.H.: Artificial intelligence and the great transformation in the tourism industry revolutionizing travel services. J. Bus. Data Sci. Res. **3**(01), 36–47 (2024)
14. Masseno, M.D., Santos, C.: Personalization and profiling of tourists in smart tourism destinations–a data protection perspective. Rev. Argumentum-Argumentum J. Law **20**(3), 1–215 (2019)
15. Zhang, S., Le Duigou, J.: Implementing vocal natural language interface to enterprise resource planning system. In: International Joint Conference on Mechanics, Design Engineering & Advanced Manufacturing, pp. 399–409. Springer, Cham (2022)
16. Chaves, A.P., Egbert, J., Hocking, T., Doerry, E., Gerosa, M.A.: Chatbots language design: the influence of language variation on user experience with tourist assistant chatbots. ACM Trans. Comput.-Hum. Interact. **29**(2), 1–38 (2022)
17. Varitimiadis, S., Kotis, K., Pittou, D., Konstantakis, G.: Graph-based conversational AI: Towards a distributed and collaborative multi-chatbot approach for museums. Appl. Sci. **11**(19), 9160 (2021)

18. Hasal, M., Nowaková, J., Ahmed Saghair, K., Abdulla, H., Snášel, V., Ogiela, L.: Chatbots: security, privacy, data protection, and social aspects. Concurr. Comput.: Pract. Exp. **33**(19), e6426 (2021)
19. Jangoan, S., Krishnamoorthy, G., Muthusubramanian, M., Sharma, K.K.: Demystifying explainable AI: understanding, transparency, and trust. Int. J. Multidiscip. Res. **6**(2), 1–13 (2024)
20. Tsepapadakis, M., Gavalas, D., Koutsabasis, P.: 3D audio+ augmented reality+ AI chatbots+ IoT: an immersive conversational cultural guide. In: International Conference on Extended Reality, pp. 249–260. Springer, Cham (2022)
21. Chao, M.H., Trappey, A.J., Wu, C.T.: Emerging technologies of natural language-enabled chatbots: a review and trend forecast using intelligent ontology extraction and patent analytics. Complexity **2021**(1), 5511866 (2021)
22. Abdellatif, A., Badran, K., Costa, D.E., Shihab, E.: A comparison of natural language understanding platforms for chatbots in software engineering. IEEE Trans. Softw. Eng. **48**(8), 3087–3102 (2021)
23. Kannan, R.: Revolutionizing the tourism industry through artificial intelligence: a comprehensive review of ai integration, impact on customer experience, operational efficiency, and future trends. Int. J. Multidimensional Res. Perspect. **2**(2), 01–14 (2024)
24. Banerji, D., Rashideh, W., Arora, B., Pratihari, A.R.: Application potential of blockchain technologies in the travel and tourism industry. In: Blockchain Applications in IoT Ecosystem, pp. 289–299. Springer, Cham (2021)
25. El-Ansari, A., Beni-Hssane, A.: Sentiment analysis for personalized chatbots in e-commerce applications. Wirel. Pers. Commun. **129**(3), 1623–1644 (2023)
26. Cahn, J.: CHATBOT: architecture, design, & development. University of Pennsylvania School of Engineering and Applied Science Department of Computer and Information Science (2017)
27. Badouch, M., Boutaounte, M.: Design and implementation of a hotel recommendation system using deep learning. In: AI and Data Engineering Solutions for Effective Marketing, pp. 388–408. IGI Global (2024)

Precision Bearing Fault Diagnosis Using Advanced Machine Learning Models and Comprehensive Vibration Signal Feature Extraction

Soufiane Aychour[1(✉)], Ilias Ouachtouk[1], and Ahmed Mouchtachi[2]

[1] National School of Arts and Crafts (ENSAM) - Hassan II University of Casablanca, 150 Nile Blvd, 20670 Casablanca, Morocco
soufianeaychour@gmail.com

[2] Moulay Ismail University of Meknes, Marjane II, B.P 15290, Meknes, Morocco

Abstract. Bearing fault diagnosis is crucial for machine reliability and cost reduction. This project applies machine learning to classify bearing faults via vibration signal analysis. Data, prepared by Dr. Eric Bechhoefer for Machinery Failure Prevention Technology (MFPT), includes healthy bearings and those with inner and outer race faults under various loads. Key features like kurtosis, RMS frequency, and standard deviation were extracted, normalized, and ranked using a chi-squared test.

Machine learning models, including decision trees (DT), Support Vector Machine (SVMs), and neural networks, were trained to classify bearing conditions. Performance was evaluated by accuracy, with discriminant analysis (DA) and ensemble models (EN) achieving high accuracy. This study demonstrates the effectiveness of combining vibration feature extraction with machine learning for precise bearing fault diagnosis, advancing predictive maintenance.

Keywords: Bearing Fault Diagnosis · Vibration Analysis · Machine Learning · Feature Extraction · Predictive Maintenance · Time Domain Features · Frequency Domain Features

1 Introduction

Bearing fault diagnosis is critical for predictive maintenance, helping to prevent unexpected downtimes and reduce maintenance costs [1]. Bearings, essential components in rotating machinery, are prone to failures that can lead to costly interruptions [2]. This study presents an innovative approach to bearing fault diagnosis by applying advanced machine learning models to vibration signal analysis. Our approach stands out through comprehensive feature extraction and selection from both time and frequency domains, enabling precise classification of bearing conditions [3].

Using data from the Condition Based Maintenance Fault Database [4], our method leverages advanced signal analysis techniques and machine learning models, including

I. Aboudrar et al. (Eds.): ICESST 2024, SUCI, pp. 116–125, 2025.
https://doi.org/10.1007/978-3-031-86705-7_11

decision trees, SVMs, and neural networks, to classify bearing states. Unlike traditional methods, our work incorporates feature normalization and a chi-square test to select the most informative features, which enhances detection accuracy and reduces maintenance costs [5]. Our results demonstrate high classification accuracy, showcasing the effectiveness of the proposed approach in a predictive maintenance context [6].

2 MFPT Bearing Fault Dataset

2.1 Defects Generation

The objective of this study is to demonstrate the effectiveness of machine learning models in diagnosing bearing faults by using key vibration signal features, such as kurtosis, Root Mean Square RMS frequency, and standard deviation (SDT), to train classification models like decision trees, support vector machines, and neural networks [7]. The Condition Based Maintenance (CBM) paradigm is employed to enhance reliability and reduce costs by limiting unscheduled maintenance, despite CBM's limited adoption due to challenges in accurate condition reporting. The CBM Fault Database provides a comprehensive dataset to support research in bearing fault diagnosis [1].

The dataset includes a variety of known good and faulted conditions for bearings, collected using a specialized bearing test rig. This rig was equipped with a NICE bearing with the following parameters (Fig. 1 and Table 1):

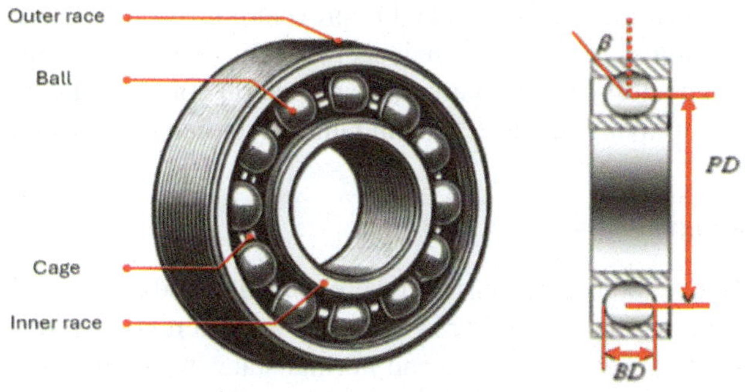

Fig. 1. Various failures of bearing

Table 1. Geometric parameters of the bearing.

Parameter	Value
Number of balls (N)	8
Contact angle (β)	0
Ball diameter (BD)	5.969 mm
Pitch diameter (PD)	31.623 mm

To facilitate research into bearing analysis, the dataset includes:

- Baseline Conditions: Data from bearings under normal operating conditions, collected with a load of 270 lbs, an input shaft rate of 25 Hz, and a sampling rate of 97,656 samples per second (sps) for a duration of 6 s.
- Outer Race Fault Conditions: Data from bearings with an outer race fault under the same operating conditions (270 lbs, 25 Hz, 97,656 sps) and a duration of 6 s.
- Variable Load Outer Race Fault Conditions: Data from outer race faults under varying loads of 25, 50, 100, 150, 200, 250, and 300 lbs, with an input shaft rate of 25 Hz and a sampling rate of 48,828 sps for 3 s. It was observed that bearing resonance occurred at frequencies below 20 kHz.
- Inner Race Fault Conditions: Data from inner race faults, also collected under varying loads (0, 50, 100, 150, 200, 250, and 300 lbs), with an input shaft rate of 25 Hz and a sampling rate of 48,828 sps for 3 s.

These conditions are crucial for developing and validating algorithms to accurately detect bearing faults, aiming to help CBM researchers and practitioners enhance their techniques and advance CBM systems.

3 Data Analysis

3.1 Introduction

Early detection of bearing faults is crucial to prevent unexpected failures and minimize downtime. This study uses vibration analysis to diagnose inner and outer race faults by examining key characteristics like kurtosis and spectral content. The goal is to identify fault signatures, improving the detection and understanding of bearing anomalies.

3.2 Vibration Signal Analysis

Signal Extraction. Vibration signals x(t) were collected and analyzed for each bearing condition, representing the dynamic responses under different operating states. Signals for inner race faults, outer race faults, and normal states were compared, with kurtosis K calculated to quantify anomalies, where high kurtosis indicates potential faults. The kurtosis is defined by the following equation:

$$\mathrm{K} = \frac{E[(x(t) - \mu)^4]}{\sigma^4}, \tag{1}$$

where:

- $E[\cdot]$ is the expected value,
- μ is the mean of the signal x(t),
- σ is the standard deviation of the signal.

High kurtosis indicates extreme values in the signal, which are often associated with the presence of faults.

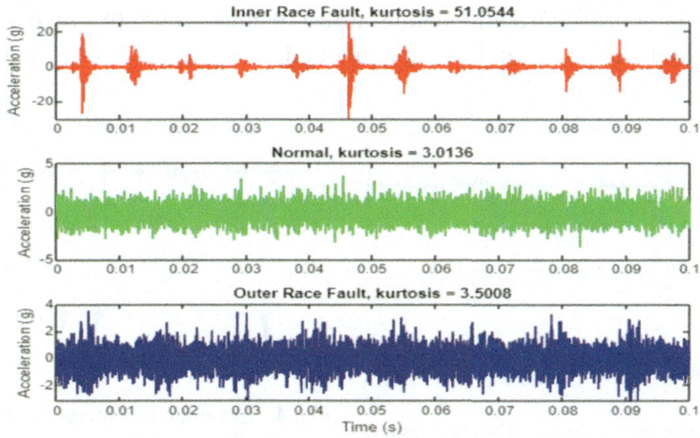

Fig. 2. Vibration Signals and Kurtosis Values for Different Bearing Conditions

The figure Fig. 2 The above displays the vibration signals for three bearing conditions: inner race fault, normal state, and outer race fault. The inner race fault shows a high kurtosis value of 51.0544, indicating significant peaks and potential faults. The normal state has a low kurtosis of 3.0136, reflecting stable behavior. The outer race fault, with a kurtosis of 3.5008, shows more variation than the normal state but is less extreme than the inner race fault.

Envelope Analysis and Fault Frequency Identification. This section analyzes vibration signals using the envelope spectrum to identify bearing faults, with characteristic fault frequencies from Table 2 essential for interpreting the results.

Table 2. Bearing fault frequencies

Fréquency name	Formula	Value (Hz)	References
Ball Spin Frequency	$BSF = \frac{P}{B} \times F \times \left[1 - \left(\frac{P}{B} \times \cos(\beta)\right)^2\right]$	63.91	[8]
Ball Pass Frequency Outer Race	$BPFO = \frac{N}{2} \times F \times \left[1 - \frac{P}{B} \times \cos(\beta)\right]$	81.125	[9]
Ball Pass Frequency Inner Race	$BPFI = \frac{N}{2} \times F \times \left[1 + \frac{P}{B} \times \cos(\beta)\right]$	118,875	[10]

Kurtosis rises sharply for the inner race fault (51.0544 raw, 97.5741 filtered) with distinct spectrum peaks, indicating a severe defect. The normal condition shows low kurtosis (3.0136 raw, 3.393 filtered) and no significant peaks, confirming a healthy bearing. The outer race fault has moderate kurtosis increases (3.5008 raw, 6.7228 filtered) with less pronounced peaks, indicating a milder defect (Figs. 3, 4, 5, 6, 7 and 8).

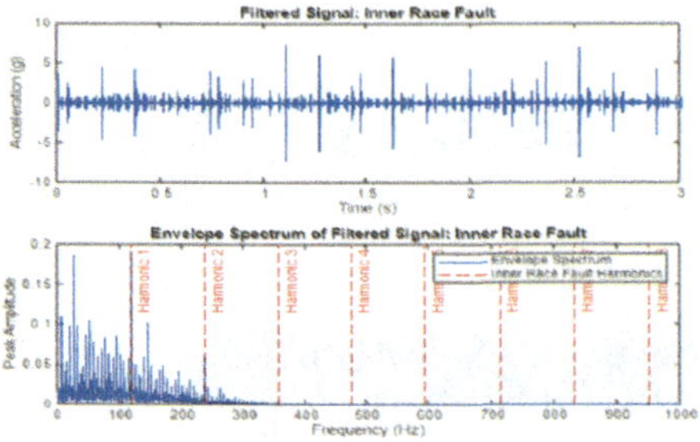

Fig. 3. Envelope spectrum of Filtered Signal for Inner Race Fault

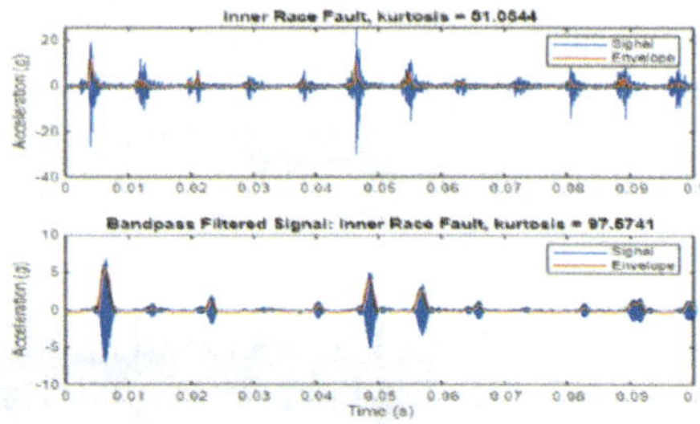

Fig. 4. Envelope of Filtered Signal for Inner Race Fault

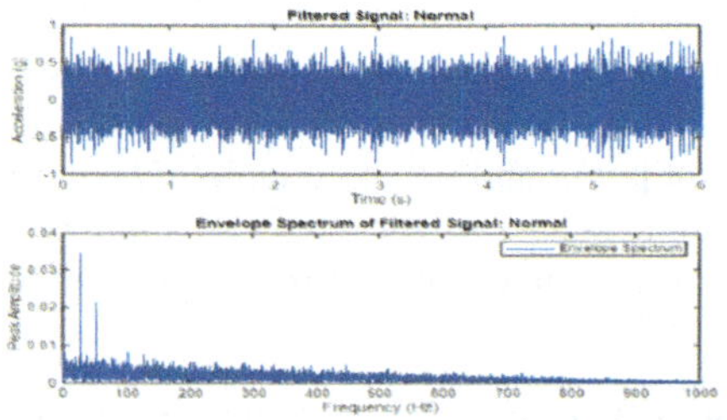

Fig. 5. Envelope spectrum of Filtered Signal for normal condition

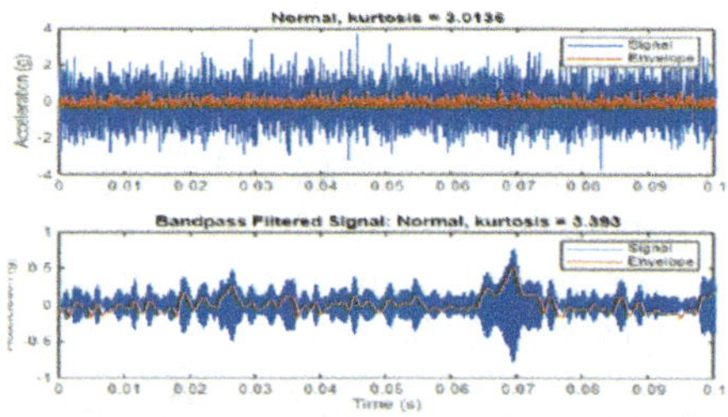

Fig. 6. Envelope of Filtered Signal for normal condition

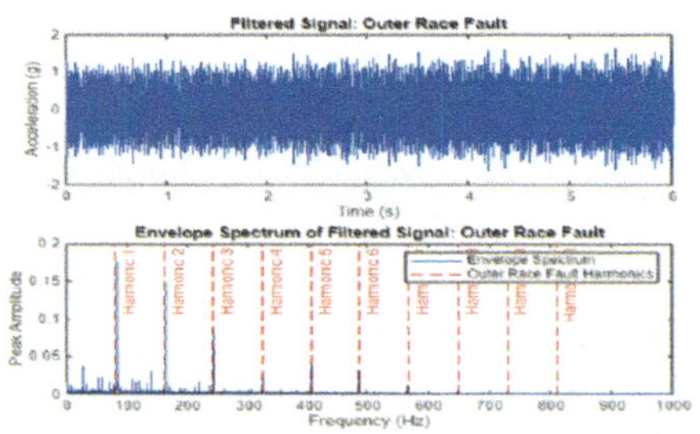

Fig. 7. Envelope spectrum of Filtered Signal for Outer Race Fault

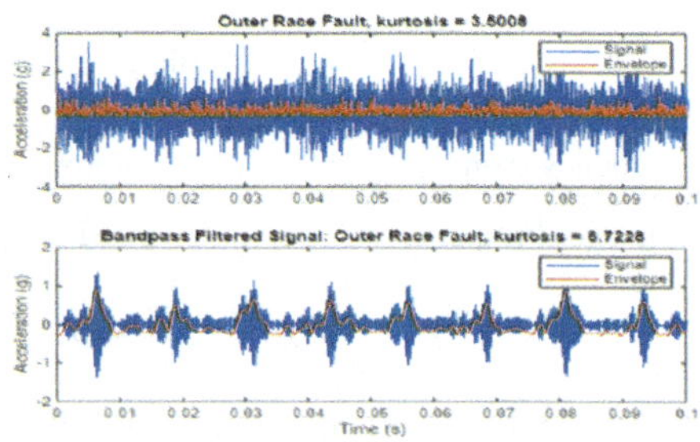

Fig. 8. Envelope of Filtered Signal for Outer Race Fault

4 Data Preprocessing and Partitioning

The preprocessing of data is a critical step in preparing the dataset for effective fault classification. Initially, the acceleration signals were cleaned to remove noise and artifacts, ensuring that only the most relevant information was retained. Following this, the data underwent z-score normalization, which standardized the features by centering them around zero and scaling them based on their standard deviations. This process was essential to minimize the influence of differing scales among features, thereby preventing any single feature from disproportionately affecting the model training.

Once the data was preprocessed, it was divided into two sets: **train_data** for model training and **test_data** for evaluation. A holdout method was applied, reserving **45%** of the data for the test set. This split was carefully designed to ensure a balanced representation of all fault classes in both sets, promoting reliable training and unbiased evaluation. The combination of thorough preprocessing and strategic partitioning ensured that the models developed were both robust and capable of generalizing well to unseen data.

5 Description of the Proposed Algorithm

The protocol begins with the acquisition of vibration data from bearings, followed by envelope analysis to extract relevant information. The data is then prepared by splitting it into training (14 files) and testing (6 files) sets. Features are extracted from the data, including 5 time-domain features and 5 frequency-domain features. These features are normalized and combined to create a homogeneous dataset. A chi-square test is then applied to select the best features, which are used to train and evaluate several classification models, including DT, DA, SVM, K-Nearest Neighbors (KNN), and EN. This process enables the detection of specific bearing faults, such as inner race defects.

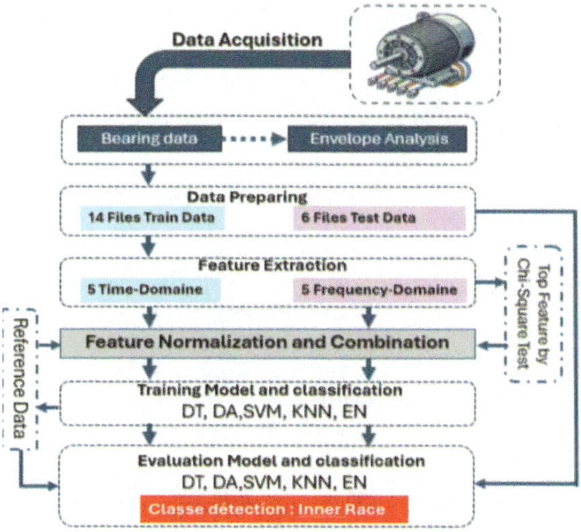

Fig. 9. Proposed intelligent architecture for bearing fault detection.

6 Feature Extraction and Selection

6.1 Time and Frequency Domain

Vibration signals analyzed in the time domain, using features like mean, RMS, and variance, help identify discrepancies. RMS detects imbalances but is less effective for early-stage faults, while the crest factor is useful for outer race faults. Advanced features like skewness and kurtosis are applied to non-stationary signals. Frequency domain features, often considered more effective, are obtained by transforming time domain signals using FFT, which highlights dominant frequencies of defect impulses, aiding in detecting bearing faults. See Tables 3 and 4 for overviews.

Table 3. Brief Review of Statistical Time-Domain Features Extraction Formula

Feature Name	Formula Description	References
RMS	$\mathrm{RMS} = \sqrt{\frac{1}{N}\sum_{i=0}^{N} X_i^2}$	[9]
Variance	$\mathrm{Var} = \frac{1}{N}\sum_{i=0}^{N}(X_i - \mu)^2$	[10]
Skewness	$\mathrm{Sk} = \frac{1}{N}\sum_{i=0}^{N}\left(\frac{X_i-\mu}{\sigma}\right)^3$	[9]
Kurtosis	$\mathrm{Ku} = \frac{1}{N}\sum_{i=0}^{N}\left(\frac{X_i-\mu}{\sigma}\right)^4$	[11]
Crest Factor	$\mathrm{CF} = \frac{Max(X_i)}{RMS}$	[10]

Table 4. Brief Review of Statistical Frequency-Domain Features Extraction Formula

Feature Name	Formula Description	References
Mean Frequency	$\mathrm{MF} = \frac{1}{N}\sum_{i=0}^{N} f_i$	[9]
Frequency Center	$\mathrm{FC} = \frac{\frac{1}{N}\sum_{i=0}^{N} f_i \times P_i}{\frac{1}{N}\sum_{i=0}^{N} P_i}$	[11]
RMS Frequency	$\mathrm{RMSF} = \sqrt{\frac{\frac{1}{N}\sum_{i=0}^{N}(f_i^2) \times P_i}{\frac{1}{N}\sum_{i=0}^{N} P_i}}$	[9]
Standard Deviation Frequency	$\mathrm{STDF} = \sqrt{\frac{\frac{1}{N}\sum_{i=0}^{N}(f_i - FC)^2 \times P_i}{\frac{1}{N}\sum_{i=0}^{N} P_i}}$	[12]
Root Variance Frequency	$\mathrm{RVF} = \sqrt{\mathrm{RMSF}^2 - \mathrm{FC}^2}$	[13]

7 Performance Evaluation and Classification

7.1 Overview of Common Machine Learning Classification Algorithms

Decision Trees (DT) are non-parametric algorithms that classify data by splitting it based on the attribute with the highest information gain or lowest Gini impurity. K-Nearest Neighbors (KNN) classifies data points based on the majority class of their nearest neighbors, with Euclidean distance often used to measure closeness. Support Vector Machines (SVM) identify the optimal hyperplane to separate data into classes, handling both linear and non-linear tasks through the kernel trick. Naive Bayes (NB) classifiers apply Bayes' theorem with strong independence assumptions between features, making them simple yet effective, particularly for high-dimensional datasets. Ensemble Methods (EN) improve model robustness and accuracy by combining predictions from multiple base classifiers, using techniques like Bagging, Boosting, and Random Forests to reduce variance and bias.

7.2 Classification Results of Evaluation Test

In this section, we present the classification performance of various machine learning models for detecting Inner Race Fault, Outer Race Fault, and the Normal state in bearings. The models were trained on a balanced dataset, with accuracy as the primary evaluation metric.

Figure 9 illustrates the accuracy of each model, showing that Decision Tree (DT), Discriminant Analysis (DA), K-Nearest Neighbors (KNN), Support Vector Machine (SVM), and Ensemble (EN) classifiers achieved 100% accuracy for both fault classes. This indicates their strong capability in distinguishing fault conditions.

However, the Decision Tree model had a reduced accuracy of 0% for Inner Race Fault, revealing a potential weakness, possibly due to feature selection or algorithmic limitations.

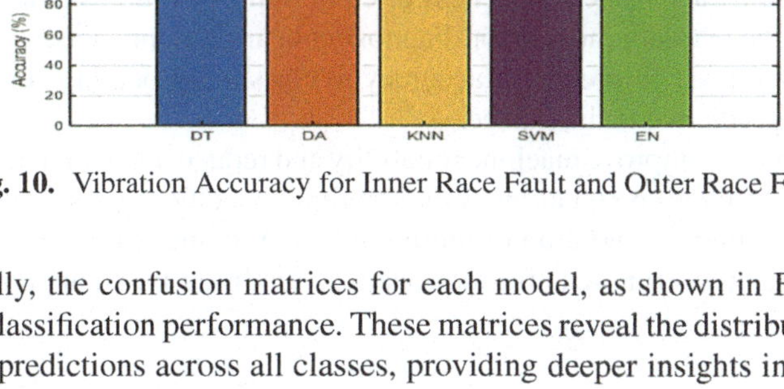

Fig. 10. Vibration Accuracy for Inner Race Fault and Outer Race Fault

Additionally, the confusion matrices for each model, as shown in Fig. 10, further illustrate the classification performance. These matrices reveal the distribution of correct and incorrect predictions across all classes, providing deeper insights into the models' decision-making processes (Fig. 11).

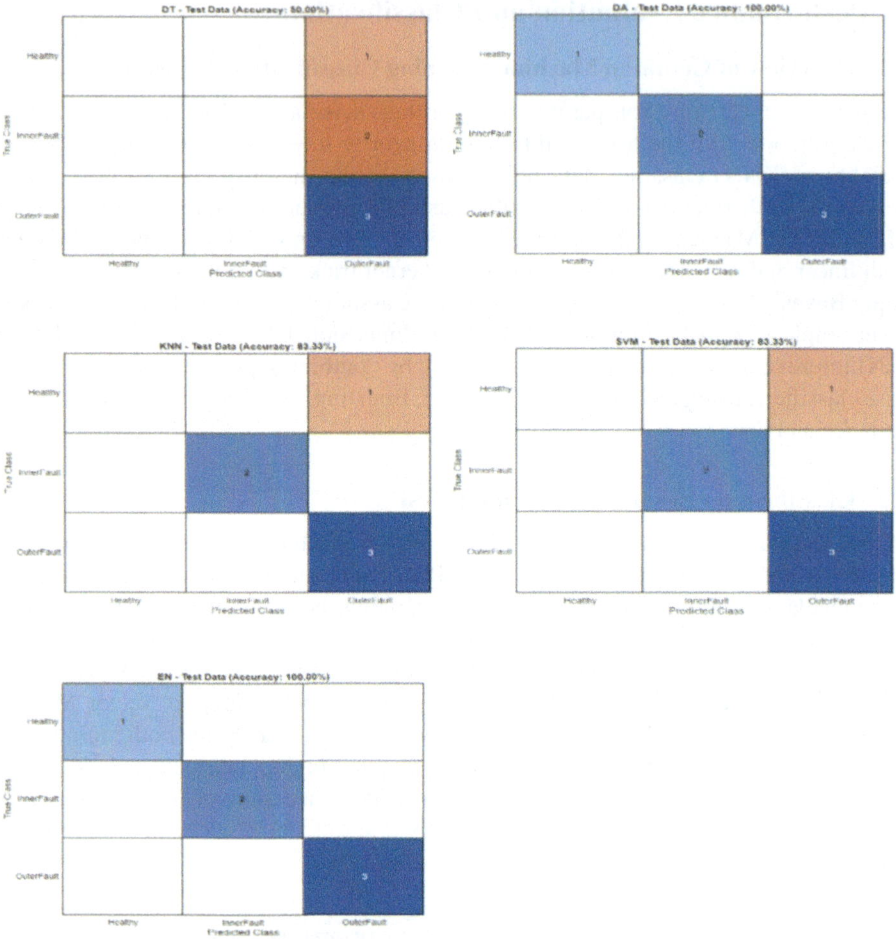

Fig. 11. Confusion Matrices for Each Model

8 Conclusion

This study demonstrates the effectiveness of combining vibration signal feature extraction with machine learning models for diagnosing bearing faults. Discriminant analysis and ensemble methods showed high accuracy in classifying bearing conditions, which is essential for predictive maintenance.

These techniques improve machine reliability and reduce maintenance costs by anticipating failures. Vibration signal analysis identified specific fault signatures, enabling early detection. Future integration of these methods into industrial systems could shift maintenance practices from reactive to proactive, condition-based approaches.

References

1. Tandon, N., Choudhury, A.: A review of vibration and acoustic measurement methods for the detection of defects in rolling element bearings. Tribol. Int. **32**(8), 469–480 (1999)
2. Sinha, J.K., Elbhbah, K.: A future scope of a condition monitoring strategy for rotating machines. J. Eng. **2013**, Article ID 547437 (2013)
3. Zhang, W., Peng, Z.: A review of fault detection and diagnosis for rolling element bearing using vibration analysis techniques. Mech. Syst. Signal Process. **25**(4), 1083–1096 (2012)
4. Jardine, A.K.S., Lin, D., Banjevic, D.: A review on machinery diagnostics and prognostics implementing condition-based maintenance. Mech. Syst. Signal Process. **20**(7), 1483–1510 (2006)
5. Lei, Y., Zuo, M.J., He, Z., Zi, Y.: A multiresolution assessment approach for rolling element bearing fault detection using vibration signals. Mech. Syst. Signal Process. **24**(1), 205–217 (2010)
6. Bechhoefer, E.: A condition based maintenance fault database for rotorcraft health management. J. Fail. Anal. Prev. **13**(4), 414–419 (2013)
7. Zhang, W., Wang, Y., Chen, X.: Fault diagnosis and prognosis using machine learning methods in machine condition monitoring: a review. Mech. Syst. Signal Process. **25**(4), 1083–1096 (2013)
8. Tandon, N., Choudhury, A.: Vibration and acoustic measurement methods for bearing defect detection. Tribol. Int. **32**(8), 469–480 (1999)
9. Randall, R.B., Antoni, J.: Rolling element bearing diagnostics—a tutorial. Mech. Syst. Signal Process. **25**(2), 485–520 (2011)
10. Harris, T.A.: Rolling Bearing Analysis, 4th edn. Wiley, Hoboken (2001)
11. Antoni, J., Randall, R.B.: The spectral kurtosis: application to the vibratory surveillance and diagnostics of rotating machines. Mech. Syst. Signal Process. **20**(2), 308–331 (2006)
12. Ouachtouk, I., El Hani, S., Guedira, S., Dahi, K.: Detection and classification of broken rotor bars faults in induction machine using K-means classifier. In: ICEIT, pp. 180–185 (2016)
13. Ouachtouk, I., El Hani, S., Dahi, K.: Wireless health monitoring system for rotor eccentricity faults detection in induction machine. Adv. Electr. Electron. Eng. **15**(3), 376–382 (2017)

Credit Card Fraud Detection: Comparing Random Forest and XGBoost Models with Explainable AI Interpretations

Mohamed Ikermane(✉), Mouaad Mohy-eddine, and Youssef Rachidi

Innovation in Mathematics and Intelligent Systems (IMIS) Laboratory, Agadir, Morocco
ikermane.mohamed@gmail.com

Abstract. This study investigates the application of machine learning and Explainable Artificial Intelligence (XAI) techniques in credit card fraud detection. We compared Random Forest and XGBoost classifiers using a dataset of 284,807 transactions, with Random Forest demonstrating superior performance in fraud detection precision (0.86 vs 0.83) and overall accuracy (0.9995 vs 0.9866). To address the interpretability challenge inherent in complex models, we employed SHAP (SHapley Additive exPlanations) and LIME (Local Interpretable Model-agnostic Explanations) techniques to interpret the Random Forest model. The SHAP analysis provided a global perspective on feature importance, consistently identifying V12 and V14 as the most influential features across all predictions. Complementing this, the LIME analysis offered localized explanations for individual predictions, highlighting how specific feature values contribute to classifying transactions as fraudulent. For instance, in one examined case, features $V12 \leq -5.58$, $V14 \leq -6.90$, and $V17 \leq -5.27$ were key indicators leading to a 99% probability of fraud prediction. Our findings demonstrate the synergy between advanced machine learning and XAI methods in enhancing both the accuracy and interpretability of fraud detection models. The convergence of insights from both SHAP and LIME techniques not only validates the model's consistency but also significantly enhances its trustworthiness. By making the model's decision-making process transparent and understandable, these techniques play a crucial role in building user confidence and supporting informed decision-making in high-stakes financial environments.

Keywords: Fraud Detection · Explainable AI · Random Forest · XGBoost · SHAP · LIME

1 Introduction

In today's era of data-driven decision-making, Explainable Artificial Intelligence (XAI) represents a transformative advancement in enhancing the transparency and interpretability of AI systems. As AI models grow increasingly complex, particularly in high-stakes domains such as finance and healthcare, the demand for clear and understandable explanations of their decision-making processes has never been more urgent. This study explores the potential of XAI through the lens of credit card fraud detection, a domain where accuracy and interpretability are critical [1].

I. Aboudrar et al. (Eds.): ICESST 2024, SUCI, pp. 126–135, 2025.
https://doi.org/10.1007/978-3-031-86705-7_12

Credit card fraud continues to pose significant financial and reputational risks to both consumers and financial institutions. Global losses from fraud amount to billions annually, highlighting the pressing need for robust detection systems. Traditional rule-based methods often fail to adapt to evolving fraud tactics, necessitating the adoption of advanced machine learning models like Random Forest and XGBoost. While these models excel in detection accuracy, their inherent complexity introduces interpretability challenges, commonly referred to as the 'black box' problem. This lack of transparency undermines user trust, complicates regulatory compliance, and impairs decision-making in critical financial scenarios. XAI emerges as a key solution, providing techniques to demystify the decision-making processes of complex models, thereby bridging the gap between high accuracy and transparency [2]. EveBy leveraging XAI, this research aims to make AI systems more intelligible and trustworthy. Techniques such as SHAP (SHapley Additive exPlanations) and LIME (Local Interpretable Model-agnostic Explanations) peel back the layers of complexity, offering insights into how predictions are made. These tools not only enhance usability but also build trust, enabling stakeholders to make more informed decisions [3].

Our research employs credit card fraud detection as a compelling case study to demonstrate the practical benefits of XAI. This domain demands both high precision and interpretability, as false positives can harm customer relationships and disrupt operational efficiency. By implementing XAI techniques, we develop an interpretable machine learning model for fraud detection and evaluate its impact on user trust and decision-making [4]. This study contributes to advancing the practical integration of XAI in business contexts, addressing a critical gap in the transparency and effectiveness of AI applications.

2 Background and Related Works

2.1 Credit Card Fraud

Credit card fraud has become an increasingly prevalent issue in the digital age, posing significant financial risks to both consumers and financial institutions. As online transactions and e-commerce continue to grow, fraudsters have developed sophisticated methods to exploit vulnerabilities in payment systems [5]. Credit card fraud can occur through various means, including data breaches, phishing attacks, and the use of stolen card information for unauthorized purchases [6]. The rapid evolution of fraudulent techniques has necessitated the development of more advanced detection methods, as traditional rule-based systems often struggle to keep pace with new fraud patterns [7]. Machine learning algorithms have emerged as a promising solution for fraud detection, offering the ability to analyze large volumes of transaction data and identify subtle patterns indicative of fraudulent activity [8]. These algorithms can adapt to new fraud tactics over time, potentially improving the accuracy and efficiency of fraud detection systems [9]. As the financial impact of credit card fraud continues to grow, with global losses estimated in the billions of dollars annually, the development of robust fraud detection methods remains a critical area of research and development in the financial technology sector [10].

2.2 Explainable Artificial Intelligence (XAI)

XAI has emerged as a critical area of research aimed at addressing these challenges. XAI seeks to make AI systems more transparent and interpretable by providing insights into their decision-making processes. This is particularly important in high-stakes domains such as healthcare, finance, and criminal justice, where understanding the rationale behind AI decisions is crucial for regulatory compliance, ethical considerations, and maintaining user trust [11].

2.3 XAI Methods

In XAI, we use several methods and techniques to make complex machine learning models more interpretable and transparent [12]. Some of the key approaches include:

Local Interpretable Model-Agnostic Explanations (LIME)
LIME is a popular technique used to explain the predictions of any machine learning classifier. It works by approximating the model locally with an interpretable model, such as a linear model, around the prediction being explained. This allows users to understand which features are contributing to a particular prediction, making the model's decisions more transparent [13].

SHapley Additive exPlanations (SHAP)
SHAP is based on cooperative game theory and provides a unified measure of feature importance. It assigns each feature an importance value for a particular prediction, allowing users to understand the contribution of each feature to the final prediction. SHAP values are consistent and locally accurate, making them a reliable choice for model explanation [14].

Counterfactual Explanations
Counterfactual explanations provide insights by showing how the input data could be modified to achieve a different prediction outcome. This technique helps users understand the decision boundary of the model and what changes would lead to a different classification, offering a practical way to interpret model decisions [15].

2.4 Related Works

Several studies have explored the integration of Explainable AI (XAI) and its impact on user trust and decision-making. In the context of fraud detection, researchers have demonstrated the effectiveness of XAI techniques in improving model transparency and user understanding. For example, Zhang et al. [16] applied XAI methods to credit card fraud detection, highlighting the benefits of providing clear explanations for model predictions in enhancing user trust and decision-making.

Beyond fraud detection, XAI has been applied in various domains. In traffic accident prediction, Shapley values have been used to interpret complex models predicting road traffic accident severity, enhancing understanding of influential factors and improving stakeholder trust in model predictions [17]. In surveillance systems, XAI techniques like LIME and SHAP have been integrated into abnormal human activity detection from surveillance videos, enhancing transparency and accountability [18]. In software engineering, XAI methods have been used to provide explainability in machine learning models, particularly for tasks like defect prediction, which helps increase the trust and uptake of ML solutions in the industry [19].

This body of work underscores the transformative potential of XAI when integrated, particularly in domains where interpretability and transparency are paramount. Our research builds on these foundations by exploring the application of XAI in credit card fraud detection.

3 Methodology

3.1 Dataset and Preprocessing and Models Implementation

Description of the Kaggle Credit Card Fraud Dataset
The dataset used in this study is sourced from Kaggle [20] and contains credit card transactions made by European cardholders over two days in September 2013. It includes 284,807 transactions, with 492 labeled as fraudulent. The features have been transformed using Principal Component Analysis (PCA) to maintain confidentiality [21].

Data Preprocessing Steps
The preprocessing involved checking for missing values, of which there were none. The data was standardized to ensure all features contributed equally to the model's performance, an essential step for models sensitive to feature scaling [22].

Handling Class Imbalance
Due to the dataset's significant class imbalance, with fraudulent transactions being a small minority, techniques such as random under-sampling and SMOTE (Synthetic Minority Over-sampling Technique) were employed to balance the class distribution. This approach is supported by recent studies that emphasize the importance of addressing class imbalance to enhance model performance in fraud detection scenarios [23].

Feature Selection and Engineering
Feature selection was performed using correlation analysis to retain the most predictive features. Additionally, feature engineering was applied to create new features that could enhance model performance, focusing on improving the model's ability to distinguish between fraudulent and legitimate transactions [24].

Models Implementation
A Random Forest Classifier was developed as one of the primary models. This ensemble method was chosen for its robustness and effectiveness in handling imbalanced datasets [2. An XGBoost Classifier was also implemented for comparison. Known for its efficiency and high performance on structured data [26].

4 Results and Discussion

4.1 Classifiers Performance Comparison

The performance of our models was evaluated using various metrics (Table 1), including accuracy, precision, Recall, and F1-score. These metrics provided a comprehensive assessment of our model's effectiveness and efficiency in fraud detection.

- $\text{Accuracy} = \frac{\text{TP} + \text{TN}}{\text{TP} + \text{TN} + \text{FP} + \text{FN}}$
- $\text{Precision} = \frac{\text{TP}}{\text{TP} + \text{FP}}$
- $\text{Recall} = \frac{\text{TP}}{\text{TP} + \text{FN}}$
- $\text{F1 score} = 2 \times \frac{\text{PR} \times \text{TPR}}{\text{PR} + \text{TPR}}$

Table 1. Classifiers performance metrics comparison

Metric	Random Forest Classifier	XGBoost Classifier
Accuracy	0.9995	0.9866
Precision	0.86	0.83
Recall	0.85	0.85
F1-Score	0.86	0.84

The performance of both the Random Forest and XGBoost classifiers was also evaluated using confusion matrices as shown in Fig. 1, which provided insights into the types of errors made by the models. These results demonstrate the models' ability to accurately identify both fraudulent and non-fraudulent transactions. Also To ensure robust performance evaluation, both models were trained using a stratified k-fold cross-validation approach, which maintains a similar distribution of fraud cases across folds and mitigates class imbalance effects. This method, consistent with best practices in the field, resulted in stable performance, with a Mean CV Score of 0.9999969 for the Random Forest and 0.9999917 for the XGBoost, indicating reliable and consistent model accuracy across different data splits.

Both the Random Forest and XGBoost classifiers demonstrate excellent performance in detecting fraudulent transactions, with high accuracy and strong mean CV Scores. The Random Forest Classifier slightly outperforms XGBoost, suggesting better overall discrimination between classes. Additionally, the Random Forest model shows slightly better precision, indicating fewer false positives. Given the importance of minimizing false alarms in fraud detection, the Random Forest Classifier is considered more suitable for this dataset, especially in contexts where interpretability and precision are prioritized. This slight edge in performance, combined with its interpretability advantages, makes Random Forest the preferred choice for this credit card fraud detection task.

4.2 Interpreting the Random Forest Classifier Using Explainable AI Techniques

In this section, we delve into the interpretation of the Random Forest classifier to gain a deeper understanding of its decision-making process in credit card fraud detection. By

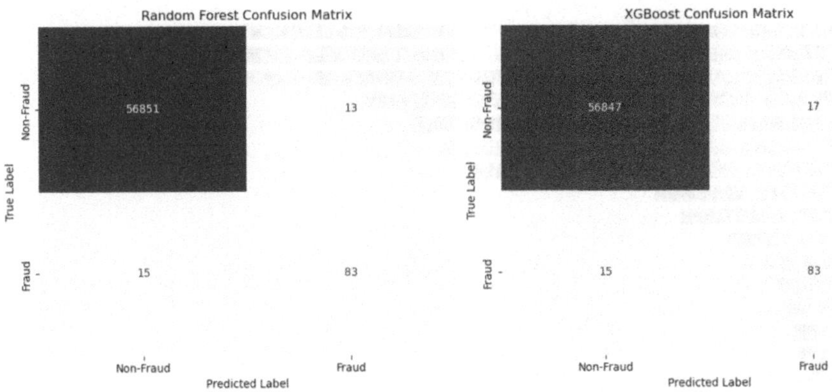

Fig. 1. Confusion matrix of the Random Forest classifier (Left), and the XGBoost classifier (right)

employing two powerful explainable AI techniques - SHAP and LIME. We aim to unpack the 'black box' nature of our model. This analysis will provide both global and local perspectives on feature importance, allowing us to comprehend how the model arrives at its predictions. Through SHAP, we will examine the overall impact of features across all predictions, while LIME will offer insights into individual prediction rationales. These interpretations are crucial for validating the model's reliability, ensuring its alignment with domain knowledge, and building trust in its fraud detection capabilities.

SHAP Analysis of the Random Forest Model

The SHAP plot (Fig. 2) provides a comprehensive global perspective on feature importance for the model's predictions across all instances in the credit card fraud detection task. The features are ranked from top to bottom based on their overall importance in the model's predictions, with V12 and V14 emerging as the most influential features, followed by V4, V10, and V11. The x-axis represents the mean absolute SHAP value, indicating the average impact magnitude of each feature on the model's output. Longer bars signify a more significant impact of the feature. The bars are color-coded to show the impact on different classes, with blue representing the impact on Class 1 (likely Fraud) and red representing the impact on Class 0 (likely Not Fraud). This color coding provides insight into how each feature contributes to the classification of transactions as fraudulent or non-fraudulent.

Interestingly, some feature interactions are considered in the model, as evidenced by the presence of V3_V4 in the plot. The relative importance of features shows a gradual decrease, with features at the bottom of the plot (e.g., V6, V8, V24) having minimal impact on the model's predictions. It's noteworthy that "Time" appears as a feature in the model, but its impact is relatively low compared to the top features.

Interpreting the Random Forest Model with LIME

The LIME plot shown in Fig. 3, provides a detailed explanation of a single prediction made by the model for credit card fraud detection. For this particular transaction, the model predicts a 99% probability of fraud, with only a 1% probability that the transaction is not fraudulent. This high confidence in the fraud prediction is based on the values of

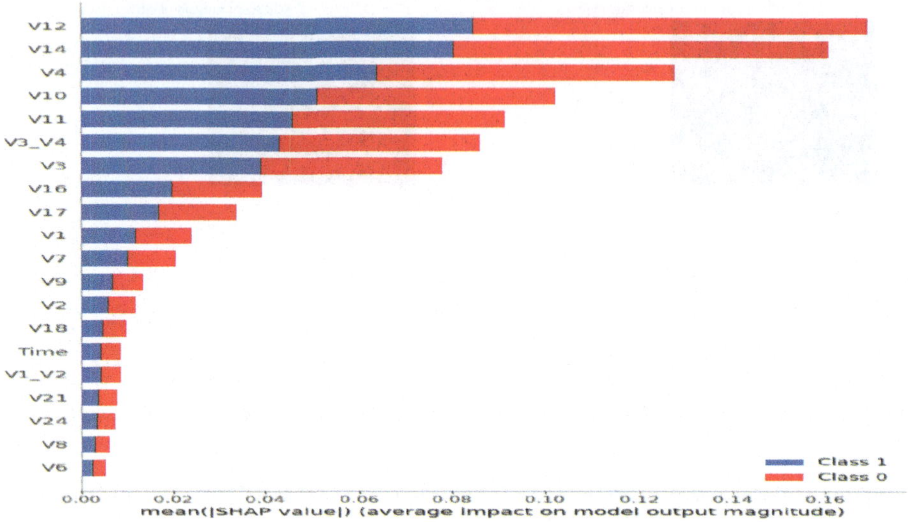

Fig. 2. Random forest Classifier feature's explanations using SHAP

several key features. The plot highlights the top 10 features that influenced this specific prediction, ranked by their importance. The most influential feature is V12 ≤ -5.58, followed by V14 ≤ -6.90 and V17 ≤ -5.27. These features have the highest impact on the model's decision, with importance values of 0.10, 0.09, and 0.08 respectively. The actual values for these features in this transaction are V12: -10.83, V14: -9.37, and V17: -19.24, all of which are indeed below the thresholds identified as indicative of fraud.

Other features also contribute to the fraud classification, albeit to a lesser extent. These include V4 > 4.45 and V10 ≤ -4.58. The orange bars in the plot indicate that all these features are supporting the fraud classification for this particular transaction. This LIME explanation provides transparency into the model's decision-making process, showing exactly which features and thresholds led to the high-confidence fraud prediction for this specific case.

The analysis using SHAP and LIME techniques provides a comprehensive understanding of the Random Forest model's decision-making process in credit card fraud detection. The LIME plot offers a localized view, explaining individual predictions by highlighting specific feature values, such as V12, V14, and V17, that significantly influence the model's decision to classify a transaction as fraudulent. This granular insight helps users understand the rationale behind each prediction. Meanwhile, the SHAP plot provides a global perspective, ranking features by their overall importance across all predictions. It confirms the critical role of features like V12 and V14, offering a broader understanding of their impact on the model's outcomes. Notably, the findings from both LIME and SHAP align, reinforcing the significance of these features and enhancing the model's transparency. These XAI methods enhance user trust by making the model's operations transparent and interpretable. By clearly demonstrating how features contribute to predictions, stakeholders can ensure that decisions are based on

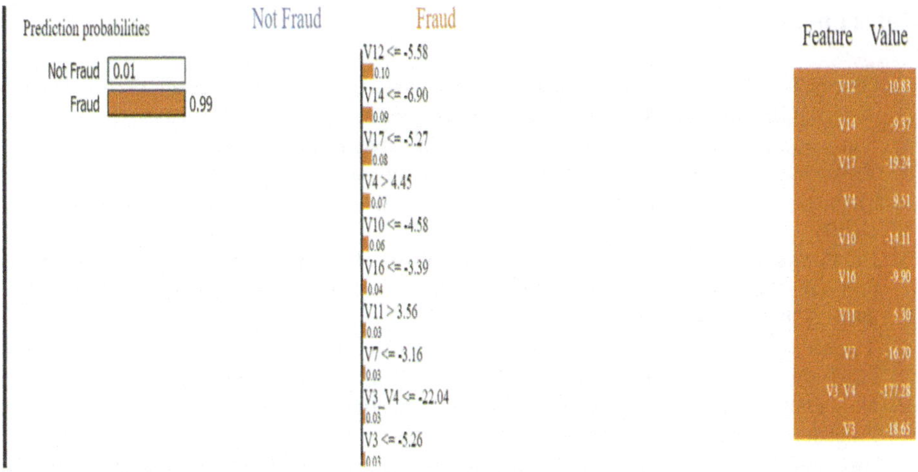

Fig. 3. Random Forest instance prediction explanation using LIME

reliable insights. This transparency is crucial in high-stakes environments, as it fosters confidence in the model's reliability and supports informed decision-making. The ability to interpret and trust AI models is essential for their successful deployment, emphasizing the importance of XAI in bridging the gap between complex algorithms and user comprehension.

5 Conclusion and Future Works

This study demonstrated the effectiveness of combining machine learning with explainable AI for credit card fraud detection. We developed a Random Forest model and interpreted its decisions using LIME and SHAP techniques. LIME provided localized explanations, highlighting features V12, V14, and V17 as influential in classifying fraudulent transactions. SHAP offered a global perspective, consistently identifying V12 and V14 as the most impactful features. This convergence of insights enhances the model's trustworthiness and transparency.

Future work in this domain could focus on advanced feature engineering, including the development of composite features or the application of dimensionality reduction techniques to identify nuanced fraud patterns more effectively. Additionally, dynamic model adaptation could be explored to enable real-time updates while preserving interpretability, ensuring that models remain responsive to evolving fraudulent behaviors. Incorporating multi-modal explanations by combining various XAI techniques or creating hybrid approaches may provide more comprehensive insights into model decision-making. Finally, fostering human-AI collaboration through the development of interactive interfaces for fraud analysts could enhance system performance and trust by allowing users to explore and provide feedback on model explanations.

References

1. Owens, E., Sheehan, B., Mullins, M., Cunneen, M., Ressel, J., Castignani, G.: Explainable Artificial Intelligence (XAI) in Insurance (2022)
2. Study on significant drift in the domain of explainable artificial intelligence (2021)
3. Towards explainable artificial intelligence in banking and financial services (2021)
4. Thematic clustering of latent topics in banking fraud detection: a machine learning approach (2023)
5. Dal Pozzolo, A., Boracchi, G., Caelen, O., Alippi, C., Bontempi, G.: Credit card fraud detection: a realistic modeling and a novel learning strategy. IEEE Trans. Neural Netw. Learn. Syst. **29**(8), 3784–3797 (2015)
6. Yousefi, N., Alaghband, M., Garibay, I.: A survey on offensive AI in cybersecurity: the case of fraudulent credit card transactions. IEEE Access **11**, 42417–42436 (2023)
7. Dornadula, V.N., Geetha, S.: Credit card fraud detection using machine learning algorithms. Procedia Comput. Sci. **165**, 631–641 (2019)
8. Awoyemi, J.O., Adetunmbi, A.O., Oluwadare, S.A.: Credit card fraud detection using machine learning techniques: a comparative analysis In: 2017 International Conference on Computing Networking and Informatics (ICCNI), pp. 1–9 (2017)
9. Pun, J.K., Lawryshyn, Y.: Improving credit card fraud detection using a meta-classification strategy. Int. J. Comput. Appl. **56**(10), 41–46 (2012)
10. Nilson Report. Card fraud losses reach $28.65 billion. The Nilson Report, Issue 1187 (2020)
11. Adadi, A., Berrada, M.: Peeking inside the black-box: a survey on explainable artificial intelligence (XAI) (2018)
12. Speith, T.: A review of taxonomies of explainable artificial intelligence (XAI) methods. In: Proceedings of the 2022 ACM Conference on Fairness, Accountability, and Transparency, pp. 2239–2250 (2022)
13. Ribeiro, M.T., Singh, S., Guestrin, C.: "Why should I trust you?" Explaining the predictions of any classifier. In: Proceedings of the 22nd ACM SIGKDD International Conference on Knowledge Discovery and Data Mining, pp. 1135–1144 (2016)
14. Lundberg, S.M., Lee, S.-I.: A unified approach to interpreting model predictions. In: Advances in Neural Information Processing Systems, pp. 4765–4774 (2017)
15. Wachter, S., Mittelstadt, B., Russell, C.: Counterfactual explanations without opening the black box: automated decisions and the GDPR. Harv. J. Law Technol. **31**(2), 841–887 (2017)
16. Zhang, Y., Jiang, C., Li, J.: Explainable AI for credit card fraud detection. J. Financ. Crime **27**(3), 789–803 (2020)
17. Owens, E., Sheehan, B., Mullins, M., Cunneen, M., Ressel, J., Castignani, G.: Explainable artificial intelligence (XAI) in insurance. J. Risk Insur. **89**(2), 345–367 (2022)
18. Singh, A., Ahlawat, N.: A review article: the growing role of data science and AI in banking and finance. Int. Res. J. Mod. Eng. Technol. Sci. (2023)
19. Guidotti, R., Monreale, A., Ruggieri, S., Turini, F., Giannotti, F., Pedreschi, D.: A survey of methods for explaining black box models. ACM Comput. Surv. (CSUR) **51**(5), 1–42 (2019)
20. MLG-Ulb. Credit card fraud. Kaggle (2017). https://www.kaggle.com/datasets/mlg-ulb/creditcardfraud
21. Kurita, T.: Principal component analysis (PCA). In: Computer Vision: A Reference Guide, pp. 1–4 (2019)
22. Han, J., Kamber, M., Pei, J.: Data Mining: Concepts and Techniques. Elsevier, Amsterdam (2011)
23. Chawla, N.V., Bowyer, K.W., Hall, L.O., Kegelmeyer, W.P.: SMOTE: synthetic minority over-sampling technique. J. Artif. Intell. Res. **16**, 321–357 (2002)

24. Guyon, I., Elisseeff, A.: An introduction to variable and feature selection. J. Mach. Learn. Res. **3**, 1157–1182 (2003)
25. Breiman, L.: Random forests. Mach. Learn. **45**(1), 5–32 (2001)
26. Chen, T., Guestrin, C.: XGBoost: a scalable tree boosting system. In: Proceedings of the 22nd ACM SIGKDD International Conference on Knowledge Discovery and Data Mining, pp. 785–794 (2016)

Efficient IoT Intrusion Detection: Integrating Random Forest Feature Selection with MLP Model Pruning

Kamal Bella[1(✉)], Mouaad Mohy-Eddine[2], Azidine Guezzaz[1], Said Benkirane[1], and Mourade Azrour[3]

[1] Technology Higher School Essaouira, Cadi Ayyad University, Marrakesh, Morocco
bellakamal3@gmail.com

[2] ENSAM, Hassan II University, Casablanca, Morocco

[3] IDMS Team, Faculty of Sciences and Technics, Moulay Ismail University of Meknès, Mekens, Morocco

Abstract. The proliferation of the Internet of Things (IoT) has revolutionized various industries, offering enhanced connectivity and automation. However, this rapid expansion has also introduced significant security vulnerabilities, making IoT networks prime targets for cyber-attacks. Intrusion Detection Systems (IDS) are crucial for safeguarding these networks, providing real-time detection and response to potential threats. Machine learning-based IDS have emerged as effective solutions, offering the ability to analyze large volumes of network data and identify malicious activities with high accuracy.

In this paper, we present a novel IDS model utilizing a Multi-Layer Perceptron (MLP), combined with Random Forest-based feature selection, to optimize detection performance while reducing model complexity. We evaluated the MLP model using four distinct feature sets (10, 20, 30, and 40 features) derived from the Ton-IoT dataset to assess the impact of feature selection on accuracy and efficiency. Subsequently, model pruning was applied to reduce the model size, ensuring its suitability for deployment in resource-constrained IoT environments. Our results demonstrate that the proposed approach effectively balances detection performance with resource efficiency, making it a robust solution for securing IoT networks.

Keywords: IoT Security · Intrusion Detection System · MLP · Random Forest · Feature Selection · Model Pruning · Machine Learning

1 Introduction

The Internet of Things (IoT) has rapidly transformed various sectors, including smart cities, healthcare, manufacturing, and transportation, by enabling the interconnection of billions of devices [1]. This extensive network facilitates seamless data exchange, driving automation, efficiency, and informed decision-making [2]. However, the proliferation of IoT devices has also introduced significant security challenges [3]. These devices, often operating in diverse and resource-constrained environments, are increasingly vulnerable to cyberattacks, highlighting the urgent need for effective security measures [4].

I. Aboudrar et al. (Eds.): ICESST 2024, SUCI, pp. 136–145, 2025.
https://doi.org/10.1007/978-3-031-86705-7_13

IoT security has emerged as a critical issue due to the rising frequency and complexity of attacks targeting IoT networks [5]. The vast and continuous flow of data generated by IoT devices, coupled with often inadequate security protocols, provides fertile ground for attackers seeking to exploit system vulnerabilities [6]. As a result, developing robust security solutions capable of real-time threat detection and mitigation is essential to ensure the integrity and confidentiality of IoT systems [7].

Machine learning (ML) offers a powerful approach to enhancing IoT security by enabling the creation of intelligent systems that can detect and respond to cyber threats [8]. Specifically, ML-based Intrusion Detection Systems (IDS) have proven effective in analyzing network traffic [9, 10], detecting anomalies, and identifying patterns indicative of malicious activity. These systems leverage data-driven models to learn from historical data and predict potential security breaches, providing a proactive defense mechanism against cyber threats.

Among the various machine learning techniques, Multi-Layer Perceptron (MLP) models have shown promise in developing IDS due to their ability to capture complex patterns in data [11, 12]. However, the performance of MLP models can be significantly enhanced through feature selection and model pruning [13, 14]. Feature selection, particularly when done using methods like Random Forest, reduces the dataset's dimensionality by identifying the most relevant features, thereby improving the model's efficiency and generalization capability. Model pruning further refines the model by reducing its size, making it more suitable for deployment in resource-constrained IoT environments.

In this paper, we present a novel IDS model that integrates MLP with Random Forest-based feature selection and model pruning. Our approach is designed to optimize the balance between detection accuracy and computational efficiency, making it particularly suitable for deployment in resource-constrained IoT environments. We evaluate the model's performance across different feature sets (10, 20, 30, and 40 features) derived from the Ton-IoT dataset, demonstrating the effectiveness of our method in bolstering IoT security.

2 Related Works

Nguyen and Kim [15] presented a network intrusion detection system (NIDS) algorithm combining a genetic algorithm (GA) for feature selection, fuzzy C-means clustering (FCM), and a hybrid of bagging (BG) and convolutional neural network (CNN) models. The GA, coupled with 5-fold cross-validation, optimizes the CNN model structure. Extracted features are validated with the BG classifier, leading to improved detection performance. The method's strong validation results suggest its practical suitability for real-world network environments.

Maithem and Al-sultany [16] proposed an advanced Intrusion Detection System (IDS) that leverages deep neural networks to detect unknown attacks with high network performance. The system utilizes both binary and multiclass classification to identify anomalies. The proposed IDS achieves a high accuracy of 99.98% in both classification approaches, demonstrating its effectiveness in detecting new attack packages amidst the rapid development of technology and increasing cyber threats.

Khan [17] introduced a hybrid Convolutional Recurrent Neural Network (HCRN-NIDS) for intrusion detection, combining convolutional neural networks (CNN) and recurrent neural networks (RNN) to enhance attack prediction and classification. The CNN extracts local features, while the RNN captures temporal dynamics. Tested on the CSE-CIC-DS2018 dataset, the HCRNNIDS achieves a high detection accuracy of 97.75% with 10-fold cross-validation, demonstrating superior performance compared to existing intrusion detection methods.

Mendonça et al. [18] presented a novel Intrusion Detection System (IDS) utilizing a Tree-CNN hierarchical algorithm with a Soft-Root-Sign (SRS) activation function to efficiently detect various attacks, including DDoS, Infiltration, Brute Force, and Web attacks. The proposed model significantly reduces training time by approximately 36% and achieves an average detection accuracy of 98%. Implemented in a medium-sized company, the Tree-CNN IDS demonstrates lower complexity and reduced computational requirements compared to existing machine learning-based IDS, offering a more efficient solution for network security.

Data and Aritsugi [19] introduced T-DFNN, an incremental learning algorithm for intrusion detection systems (IDSs) designed to handle emerging threats without requiring complete retraining. The T-DFNN model, built from multiple deep feedforward neural networks (DFNNs) arranged in a tree-like structure, is tested using the CICIDS2017 dataset. It effectively learns new intrusions incrementally and mitigates catastrophic forgetting, achieving a macro average F1-score above 0.85 in retraining processes. The T-DFNN model outperforms traditional DFNN and Hoeffding tree models in terms of F1-scores and training time, demonstrating its efficiency and adaptability to evolving network threats.

Thirimanne et al. [20] proposed a real-time intrusion detection system (RT-IDS) using a deep neural network (DNN) trained with 28 NSL-KDD features. It includes a machine learning pipeline for data preprocessing and a C++ feature extractor for real-time network traffic. The system, accessible via a REST API, achieves high performance with accuracy, precision, recall, and F1-scores of 81%, 96%, 70%, and 81%, respectively, providing an effective solution for detecting modern intrusions.

3 Proposed Approach

The methodology of this study, as depicted in Fig. 1, focuses on the development and evaluation of an IDS tailored for IoT environments. The process begins with the acquisition of IoT network traffic data, which forms the foundation for the IDS model. Once the data is collected, it undergoes a comprehensive preprocessing phase to ensure data integrity. This involves removing any duplicates and handling missing values. Additionally, categorical features are encoded to make the data suitable for machine learning models.

Following preprocessing, feature selection is carried out to reduce the dataset's dimensionality and improve model efficiency. The Random Forest algorithm is employed to determine feature importance, creating four distinct feature sets containing 10, 20, 30, and 40 features, respectively. This approach allows us to evaluate the impact of different feature subsets on the model's performance and identify the optimal balance between accuracy and computational efficiency.

The core of the IDS model is an MLP, chosen for its ability to capture complex patterns in data. The MLP model is trained on each of the selected feature sets, and to further optimize the model for deployment in resource-constrained environments, pruning techniques are applied. Pruning reduces the size of the MLP model, making it more suitable for IoT devices with limited computational power.

Finally, the optimized and pruned IDS model is deployed within the IoT environment, where it is integrated into the network to actively monitor and detect potential intrusions in real-time. The deployment process ensures that the IDS operates efficiently, providing robust security without overwhelming the limited resources of IoT devices. Figure 1 provides an overview of the entire process, illustrating the systematic approach taken to develop an effective and lightweight IDS for IoT environments.

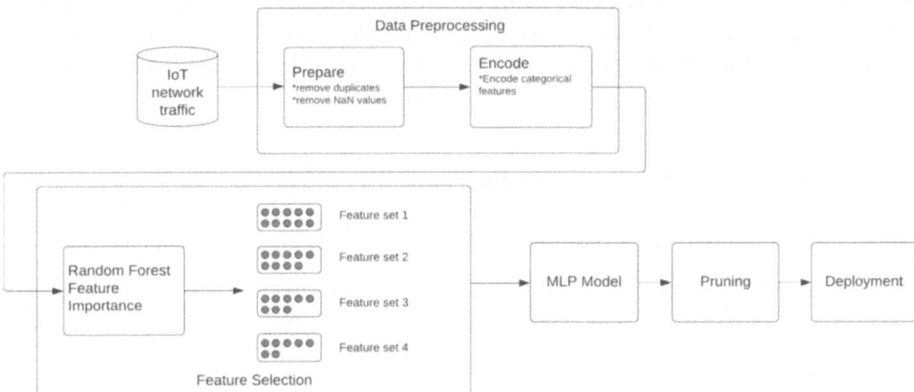

Fig. 1. Proposed approach

4 Experimental Study

The experimental study was conducted to validate the effectiveness and efficiency of the proposed IDS model within an IoT environment. The primary objective of the experiments was to assess the performance of the MLP-based IDS across different feature subsets and to determine the optimal configuration for real-time intrusion detection in resource-constrained IoT settings.

4.1 TON-IoT Dataset

The ToN-IoT dataset is an extensive resource designed for assessing intrusion detection systems in IoT environments. It includes network traffic, operating system logs, and telemetry data from various IoT devices, simulating realistic industrial IoT (IIoT) scenarios. The dataset encompasses a broad spectrum of attack types, including Denial of Service (DoS), Distributed Denial of Service (DDoS), reconnaissance, and data theft, alongside typical network activities.

For evaluating machine learning and classification models, the ToN-IoT dataset offers a specific subset known as train_test_network. This subset is imbalanced, featuring

161,043 network attack instances and 50,000 normal instances. Its diversity and scale make ToN-IoT an excellent benchmark for testing IDS models on both known and novel threats in IoT networks. This subset was utilized in our experiments to assess the performance of the proposed IDS model.

4.2 Preprocessing and Feature Selection

The preprocessing of the ToN-IoT dataset included several essential steps to ensure data quality and consistency for model training. First, the raw dataset was examined, and duplicate entries were removed to avoid introducing bias into the training process. Missing values (NaNs) were addressed to preserve data integrity. Subsequently, categorical features were converted into numerical formats suitable for machine learning algorithms.

The table below (Table 1) shows the number of records for each label before and after preprocessing (Fig. 2).

Table 1. Number of Records for Each Label Before and After Preprocessing

Label	Number of Records Before Preprocessing	Number of Records After Preprocessing
1 (attack)	161,043	148,434
0 (normal)	50,000	42,040

4.3 Evaluation Metrics

The performance of the IDS model was evaluated using various metrics, including accuracy, precision (PR), recall (or true positive rate TPR) and F1-score. These metrics provided a comprehensive assessment of the model's effectiveness and efficiency in detecting intrusions.

- Accuracy: $ACC = \frac{TP + TN}{TP + TN + FP + FN}$
- Precision: $PR = \frac{TP}{TP + FP}$
- True positive rate: $TPR = \frac{TP}{TP + FN}$
- False positive rate: $FPR = \frac{FP}{FP + TN}$
- F1 score: $F1Score = 2 \times \frac{PR \times TPR}{PR + TPR}$

Where TP, TN, FP and FN refer to true positives, true negatives, false positives and false negatives respectively as shown in the confusion matrix in Table 2.

4.4 Hyperparameters

The hyperparameter tuning for the MLP model was performed to optimize its performance and ensure the best possible configuration. In this process, various hyperparameters of the MLP model were systematically explored. The key hyperparameters tuned

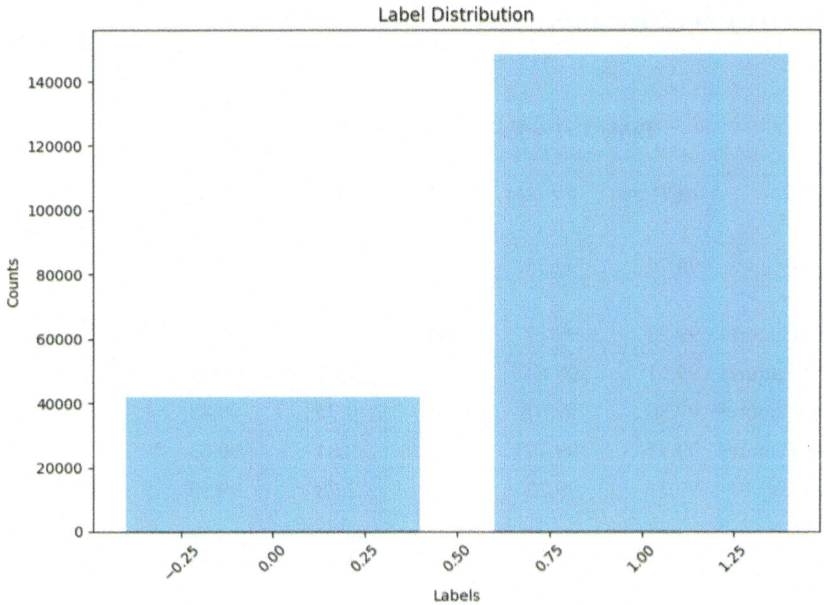

Fig. 2. Label distribution after preprocessing

Table 2. Confusion matrix

	Predicted as positive	Predicted as negative
Labeled as positive	TP	FN
Labeled as negative	FP	TN

included the hidden layer sizes, activation function, solver, learning rate, and maximum iterations.

For the hidden layer sizes, a configuration of (50,) was selected to strike a balance between model complexity and computational efficiency. The activation function was set to 'tanh', which allows the model to capture non-linear patterns in the data. The solver, responsible for optimizing the weights in the network, was chosen as 'sgd' (stochastic gradient descent), which is well-suited for large-scale learning tasks. The learning rate was set to 'constant' with a value of 0.0001, ensuring steady and stable learning throughout the training process. Additionally, the maximum number of iterations (max_iter) was set to 100 to provide the model ample opportunity to converge.

These parameter settings were determined through careful consideration and tuning, aimed at achieving the best trade-off between accuracy and computational efficiency. The chosen hyperparameters enable the MLP model to perform effectively within the constraints of resource-limited IoT environments, ensuring robust and efficient intrusion detection.

5 Discussion of Results

Table 3. Evaluation of all variations of the model

Model	ACC (%)	PR (%)	TPR (%)	FPR (%)	F1 Score (%)	Model Size (bytes)
Base (42 features)	99.79	99.75	99.88	0.87	99.81	41,502
Top 10 Features	99.23	99.17	99.86	2.96	99.52	15,902
Top 20 Features	99.61	99.64	99.89	1.27	99.77	23,903
Top 30 Features	99.80	99.81	99.90	0.75	99.85	31,694
Top 40 Features	99.77	99.77	99.89	0.81	99.83	39,827
Pruned Top 10 Features	99.31	99.22	99.88	2.78	99.55	11,091
Pruned Top 20 Features	99.63	99.67	99.87	1.17	99.77	15,090
Pruned Top 30 Features	99.81	99.82	99.87	0.74	99.85	18,976
Pruned Top 40 Features	99.75	99.70	99.87	1.07	99.78	23,090

Table 3 provides a comprehensive comparison of model performance across different feature sets and model sizes, both before and after pruning. The metrics—accuracy (ACC), precision (PR), true positive rate (TPR), false positive rate (FPR), and F1 Score—are presented as percentages to allow for an intuitive comparison.

As expected, the base model using all 42 features performed exceptionally well, achieving an accuracy of 99.79% and an F1 Score of 99.81%. This indicates that the model effectively utilized the complete feature set to maximize detection performance. However, when the number of features was reduced to the top 10, a noticeable drop in performance metrics was observed. The accuracy decreased to 99.23%, and the F1 Score fell to 99.52%. This decline can be attributed to the loss of potentially informative features, which slightly compromised the model's ability to discriminate between classes accurately.

Interestingly, as the number of features increased from 10 to 30, the performance metrics progressively improved. The model with the top 30 features closely approached the performance of the base model, achieving an accuracy of 99.80% and an F1 Score of 99.85%. This suggests that the top 30 features contained most of the critical information needed for accurate classification, with diminishing returns observed beyond this point. The model with the top 40 features showed a slight decline in metrics compared to the model with the top 30 features, indicating that the additional 10 features might not have contributed significantly to the model's performance.

Pruning further reduced the model sizes, particularly in models with a smaller number of features. For instance, the pruned model with the top 10 features had a model size of only 11,091 bytes, a significant reduction from the original 15,902 bytes. Despite the reduction in size, the pruned models generally maintained competitive performance metrics. The pruned model with the top 30 features achieved an accuracy of 99.81% and an F1 Score of 99.85%, matching the performance of the unpruned model with the same feature set. This suggests that pruning effectively removes redundant components in the model without sacrificing much performance, making it highly suitable for deployment in resource-constrained environments.

However, the pruned model with the top 40 features exhibited a slight decline in accuracy to 99.75% and an F1 Score to 99.78%. This drop, though minimal, could be indicative of the pruning process potentially removing some features or parameters that were contributing to the model's performance when the feature set was larger.

The results suggest that both feature selection and pruning are effective strategies for reducing model size while maintaining high performance. The model with the top 30 features appears to strike an optimal balance between performance and efficiency, particularly after pruning. It offers a significant reduction in size compared to the base model while maintaining comparable metrics across all evaluation criteria.

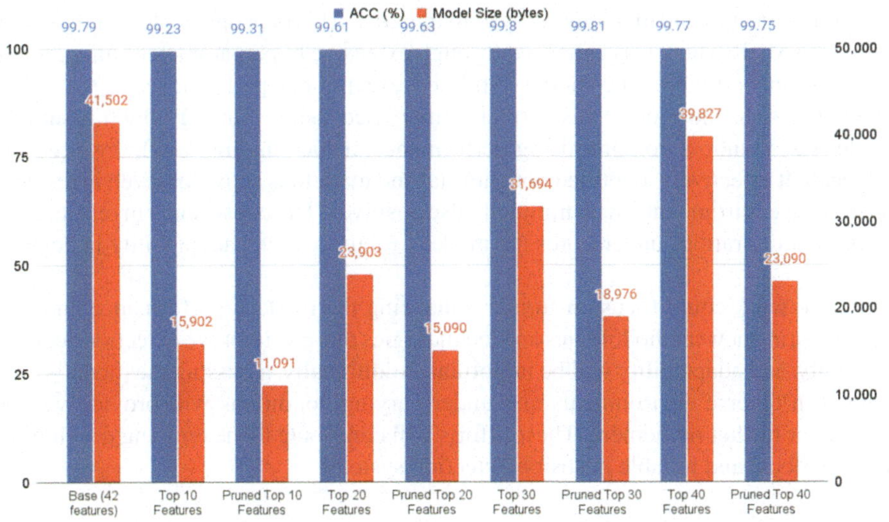

Fig. 3. Size and accuracy comparison between all variations of the model

Figure 3 highlights the trade-offs between accuracy and model size for different feature sets and pruning techniques. The base model, utilizing all 42 features, achieves the highest accuracy of 99.79% but has a substantial model size of 41,502 bytes. Reducing the feature set to the top 10 features results in a decrease in accuracy to 99.23%, accompanied by a significant reduction in model size to 15,902 bytes. As the number of features increases to 20, 30, and 40, accuracy improves progressively, reaching 99.61% with 20 features, 99.80% with 30 features, and 99.77% with 40 features, while the model size also increases—23,903 bytes, 31,694 bytes, and 39,827 bytes, respectively.

In the pruned models, accuracy is generally maintained while model size is further reduced. The pruned model with top 10 features achieves an accuracy of 99.31% with a reduced size of 11,091 bytes. The pruned model with 20 features achieves an accuracy of 99.63% and a size of 15,090 bytes. With 30 features, the pruned model's accuracy improves to 99.81%, and its size is 18,976 bytes. Finally, the pruned model with 40 features maintains an accuracy of 99.75% and has a size of 23,090 bytes. Overall, pruning effectively reduces model size while preserving high accuracy, demonstrating a balance between performance and efficiency.

In conclusion, careful feature selection combined with pruning can lead to lightweight models that are both efficient and effective, making them suitable for deployment in environments with limited computational resources. The findings from this analysis will guide the development of future models, particularly those intended for real-time intrusion detection systems deployed on edge devices.

6 Conclusion and Future Works

Intrusion Detection Systems (IDS) are essential for protecting IoT environments from malicious activities and maintaining system integrity. This paper presented an IDS model built using MLP, which was enhanced through extensive hyperparameter tuning, feature selection, and pruning. The model exhibited exceptional performance across different feature sets, the model was further compressed using pruning which resulted in smaller sizes without compromising performance, achieving high accuracy, precision, and recall. It effectively identified both normal and malicious activities, even in resource-constrained environments, with minimal false positives. The consistency in results across various configurations underscores the model's robustness and adaptability in detecting intrusions.

Future work could focus on further enhancing the model's performance and security. Exploring new methodologies and technologies that can improve detection accuracy, scalability, and adaptability will be important. Additionally, assessing the model's effectiveness in diverse environments and under varying conditions will provide valuable insights for further refinement. These efforts will contribute to the ongoing development of more robust and reliable intrusion detection systems.

References

1. Da Xu, L., He, W., Li, S.: Internet of things in industries: a survey. IEEE Trans. Ind. Inf. **10**, 2233–2243 (2014)
2. Khanna, A., Kaur, S.: Internet of things (IoT), applications and challenges: a comprehensive review. Wirel. Pers. Commun. **114**, 1687–1762 (2020)
3. Mohanty, J., Mishra, S., Patra, S., Pati, B., Panigrahi, C.R.: IoT security, challenges, and solutions: a review. In: Progress in Advanced Computing and Intelligent Engineering, pp. 493–504. Springer, Singapore (2021)

4. Shah, Y., Sengupta, S.: A survey on classification of cyber-attacks on IoT and IIoT devices. In: 2020 11th IEEE Annual Ubiquitous Computing, Electronics & Mobile Communication Conference (UEMCON), pp. 0406–0413. IEEE (2020)
5. Lee, I.: Internet of things (IoT) cybersecurity: literature review and IoT cyber risk management. Future Internet **12**, 157 (2020)
6. Andrea, I., Chrysostomou, C., Hadjichristofi, G.: Internet of things: security vulnerabilities and challenges. In: 2015 IEEE Symposium on Computers and Communication (ISCC), pp. 180–187. IEEE (2015)
7. Hassija, V., Chamola, V., Saxena, V., Jain, D., Goyal, P., Sikdar, B.: A survey on IoT security: application areas, security threats, and solution architectures. IEEE Access. **7**, 82721–82743 (2019)
8. Hussain, F., Hussain, R., Hassan, S.A., Hossain, E.: Machine learning in IoT security: current solutions and future challenges. IEEE Commun. Surv. Tutorials. Thirdquarter **22**, 1686–1721 (2020)
9. Mohy-Eddine, M., Bella, K., Guezzaz, A., Benkirane, S., Azrour, M.: Design and implementation of intrusion detection model with machine learning techniques for IoT security. In: Blockchain and Machine Learning for IoT Security, pp. 135–148. Chapman and Hall/CRC, New York (2023)
10. Mohy-eddine, M., Guezzaz, A., Benkirane, S., Azrour, M., Bella, K.: A whale optimization algorithm feature selection model for IoT detecting intrusion in environments. In: Artificial Intelligence, Data Science and Applications, pp. 413–419. Springer, Switzerland (2024)
11. Drewek-Ossowicka, A., Pietrołaj, M., Rumiński, J.: A survey of neural networks usage for intrusion detection systems. J. Ambient. Intell. Humaniz. Comput. **12**, 497–514 (2021)
12. Habeeb, M.S., Babu, T.R.: Network intrusion detection system: a survey on artificial intelligence-based techniques. Expert Syst. **39** (2022). https://doi.org/10.1111/exsy.13066
13. Medeiros, C.M.S., Barreto, G.A.: A novel weight pruning method for MLP classifiers based on the MAXCORE principle. Neural Comput. Appl. **22**, 71–84 (2013)
14. Silvestre, M.R., Ling, L.L.: Pruning methods to MLP neural networks considering proportional apparent error rate for classification problems with unbalanced data. Measurement **56**, 88–94 (2014)
15. Nguyen, M.T., Kim, K.: Genetic convolutional neural network for intrusion detection systems. Future Gener. Comput. Syst. **113**, 418–427 (2020)
16. Maithem, M., Al-sultany, G.A.: Network intrusion detection system using deep neural networks. J. Phys. Conf. Ser. **1804**, 012138 (2021)
17. Khan, M.A.: HCRNNIDS: hybrid convolutional recurrent neural network-based network intrusion detection system. Processes **9**, 834 (2021)
18. Mendonça, R.V., Teodoro, A.A.M., Rosa, R.L., Saadi, M., Melgarejo, D.C., Nardelli, P.H.J., et al.: Intrusion detection system based on fast hierarchical deep convolutional neural network. IEEE Access. **9**, 61024–61034 (2021)
19. Data, M., Aritsugi, M.: T-DFNN: an incremental learning algorithm for intrusion detection systems. IEEE Access. **9**, 154156–154171 (2021)
20. Thirimanne, S.P., Jayawardana, L., Yasakethu, L., Liyanaarachchi, P., Hewage, C.: Deep neural network based real-time intrusion detection system. SN Comput. Sci. **3**, 145 (2022)

Hoehn & Yahr Stages Prediction with MFCC and GTCC for Parkinson's Disease Monitoring

Elmehdi Benmalek[1](✉), Abdelkabir Rouagubi[2], Omar Ennasiri[2], Anas Elfilali[1], Jamal Elmhamdi[1], Atman Jbari[1], and Abdelilah Jilbab[1]

[1] ENSAM de Rabat, Mohammed V University of Rabat, Rabat, Morocco
elmehdi.benmalek@um5s.net.ma
[2] ENSA, Ibn Tofail University, Kenitra, Morocco

Abstract. Parkinson's disease (PD) is a neurodegenerative disease, that is mainly manifested by motor disorders worsening over time. Usually, the diagnosis is made if the examiner observes at least two of the following three symptoms: akinesia, rigidity, and tremors at rest. Unfortunately, these motor symptoms only appear after the loss of 50 to 60% of the dopaminergic neurons in the substantia nigra. A major research challenge is therefore to find ways to detect the disease earlier, to eventually be able to slow down, or even stop its progression from the start. Among the various clinical manifestations of this disease, the modification of the voice of the patients seems to be an element of interest in several respects. In this paper, we investigate and analyze the effectiveness of voice analysis to accurately detect the PD stages based on the Hoehn and Yahr (H&Y) scale. The voice pitch, Mel-frequency cepstral coefficients (MFCC), and gammatone cepstral coefficients (GTCC) are extracted from the voice of the patients, and the most pertinent features are selected by feature selection (FS) algorithms such as the minimum redundancy maximum relevance (mRMR) and ReliefF. These features are mapped to different classifiers to predict the PD stage automatically. The highest f1-score of 98.7% was achieved by 10 features selected using ReliefF and the support vector machine (SVM). The minimum redundancy maximum relevance (mRMR) combined with the SVM obtained a similar performance of 98.4% f1-score. The goal of this study is to build an inexpensive and accessible tool for remote patient monitoring.

Keywords: Parkinson's disease · machine learning · feature selection · Mel-frequency cepstral coefficients · Gammatone cepstral coefficients

1 Introduction

PD is the second most common neurodegenerative disease after Alzheimer's disease. Its prevalence increases with age, given that our life expectancy constantly increases, so it is the same with the number of people with this disease. It is estimated to affect 10 million people worldwide [1]. This disease affects 1% of people aged over 60 years old and up to 4% of people over 80 years old [2]. Men are affected about 1.5 times more often than women. The average age of diagnosis of the disease is 60 years old. Once the diagnosis has been made, to quantify the progression of the disease and the effects of

I. Aboudrar et al. (Eds.): ICESST 2024, SUCI, pp. 146–155, 2025.
https://doi.org/10.1007/978-3-031-86705-7_14

the treatments, several scales are usually used. The first, the Hoehn and Yahr scale, dates from 1967 [3]. It divides the progression of the disease into 5 levels, ranging from the presence of unilateral signs resulting in minimal or no functional disability (stage 1) to loss of autonomy (stage 5). Since a more comprehensive scale, the Unified Parkinson's Disease Rating Scale (UPDRS) replaced it in the majority of clinical studies on PD. It is made up of 6 sections based on interviews or clinical observations.

To date, the diagnosis of PD is mainly based on a clinical examination performed by a neurologist. The diagnosis is made if he observes at least two of the following three symptoms: akinesia (slow initiation of movements), rigidity, and tremors at rest. Unfortunately, these motor symptoms only appear after the loss of 50 to 60% of the dopaminergic neurons in the substantia nigra, and 60 to 80% of their striatal terminals [4]. A major research challenge is therefore to find ways of detecting the stage of the disease, to eventually be able to slow down, or even stop its progression. Among the various clinical manifestations of this disease, the modification of the patient's voice seems to be an element of interest in several respects. A large number of publications exist on voice analysis of PD. They revealed a set of vocal disturbances, summed up by the term hypokinetic dysarthria, introduced by [5]. This notion mainly includes prosodic alterations (decreased intonation), articulatory (imprecision of consonants and vowels), and phonatory (hoarse and breathy timber). In addition, certain voice disturbance characteristics of Parkinson's disease seem to be already visible several years before the clinical diagnosis [6–8]. However, there have been very few studies that have focused on the prognostic markers of this disease in the voice at the prodromal stage [9, 10]. On the other hand, some studies have explored the possibility of a remote diagnosis of PD using voice recordings [11, 12].

The objective of this work is to predict the PD stages based on the Hoehn and Yahr scale. So, we performed a multiclass classification to discriminate four PD stages (we combined the fourth and the fifth stages due to the data scarcity of these classes in the used database). The records are collected from the Patient Voice Analysis (PVA) dataset, a collaboration between Sage Bionetworks, PatientsLikeMe, and Dr. Max Little [13]. After data collection, we extracted the voice pitch, gammatone cepstral coefficients (GTCC), and the Mel-frequency cepstral coefficients (MFCC) from the voice records. These acoustic features are mapped after selection to a deep neural network (DNN), and support vector machine (SVM). The FS is done by minimum redundancy maximum relevance (mRMR) and ReliefF. The model evaluation is performed by the confusion matrix and the metrics such as accuracy, recall, precision, and the f1-score. The ultimate goal is to be able to build an inexpensive and accessible early diagnosis tool, usable by clinicians for remote patient monitoring.

2 Methods

2.1 Dataset

The Patient Speech Analysis Initiative (PVA Challenge) aims to use voice recordings to evaluate the intensity and variations of PD symptoms [13]. The PVA-dryrun dataset consists of brief voice recordings of sustained voice phonations lasting 3 to 30 s (one record per person), as well as self-reported symptom assessment using the PDRS and

Hoehn & Yahr stages. The dataset is split into two sections. For each label, 80% of the data is used for training, while the remaining 20% is used for testing. We used all of the GTCC and MFCC gathered from voice records to increase the performance of our models. That is, we classified the frames that are labeled based on the original voice signal, and then we classified the subjects according to the most frequent value predicted by the frames. As a result, there were 389 observations and 86597 frames (Table 1). The Hoehn & Yahr Stage 4 class with a low number of samples may face challenges in classification due to insufficient data to represent the intrinsic variability of the class. With limited examples, the classifier may struggle to learn distinct patterns or may overfit, leading to poor generalization. So, extracting meaningful features that better separate classes potentially enhances the classifier's capability to identify unique characteristics of this class.

Table 1. Data partitioning

	Training set (80%)	Test set (20%)
Hoehn & Yahr Stage 1	118 observations (24739 frames)	28 observations (6185 frames)
Hoehn & Yahr Stage 2	63 observations (18746 frames)	14 observations (4687 frames)
Hoehn & Yahr Stage 3	118 observations (24224 frames)	28 observations (6058 frames)
Hoehn & Yahr Stage 4	17 observations (1567 frames)	3 observations (391 frames)

2.2 Feature Extraction

The well-known features extracted using these techniques include MFCC and GTCC. MFCCs are currently one of the most common methods for audio signal feature extraction, especially in speech and speaker-related recognition tasks. It has also given good results in applications other than speech, such as the diagnosis of Parkinson's disease [12]. PD affects motor control, and thereby as a consequence, produces speech abnormalities like reduced vocal intensity, a monotone voice, a decrease in speech rate, and irregularities. These speech changes can be quantified by analyzing voice signals. In Parkinson's disease, MFCCs may indicate changes in speech articulation, variability in frequency variation, and disturbances in phonation that are considered typical of the disease. On the other hand, the GTCCs are similar to the MFCCs but based on the gamma-tone filter bank, which can model auditory perception of speech more accurately, allowing for more sensitive indicators of voice quality by capturing subtle aspects of speech degradation caused by PD. These features can enhance the accuracy of diagnostic models by revealing nuanced changes in voice that might not be as apparent with MFCC alone.

2.3 Feature Selection

Feature selection (FS) is a dimensionality reduction method used in machine learning and data processing. It consists, in a high-dimensional space, of finding a subset of relevant variables. FS techniques are used for four reasons:

Simplify the models to facilitate their interpretation,
Reduce learning time,
Avoid the curse of dimensionality,
Improve generalization by reducing overfitting.
In this work, we have used mRMR and ReliefF for feature selection.

2.4 Model Evaluation

Confusion matrix. A much better way to assess the performance of a classifier is to look at the confusion matrix. The general idea is to count the number of times the individuals of a particular stage are classified in the other ones. Each row of a confusion matrix represents an actual class, while each column represents a predicted class. The confusion matrix gives a lot of information, but sometimes we might prefer a more concise metric.

$$Accuracy = \frac{TP + TN}{m} \quad (1)$$

TP is the number of true positives TN is the number of true negatives, and m is the number of samples.

$$Precision = \frac{TP}{TP + FP} \quad (2)$$

FP is the number of false positives.

$$Recall = \frac{TP}{TP + FN} \quad (3)$$

FN is the number of false negatives.

It's often convenient to combine precision and recall into a single metric called an F1-score, especially if you need a simple way to compare two classifiers. The F1-score is the harmonic mean of precision and recall.

$$F1 - score = \frac{2 \times precision \times recall}{precision + recall} \quad (4)$$

Cross-validation. In k-fold cross-validation (in our case, k = 5), the data is divided into a random partition of k folds of the same size and having the same proportion of individuals from each class as the total sample [14]. Then each fold consists of training the classifier on a learning sample made up of k-1 subsets, and then testing it on the remaining one, to obtain predicted values on this fold. The operation is repeated k times, each time with a different block as a validation sample and the other k-1 as a training sample. Cross-validation can be repeated on several different partitions, to reduce the variance inherent in cross-validation. The error estimate is obtained by averaging all the errors observed on the validation samples.

3 Results

In this section, we present the results of the test set provided by the proposed models for each class. We calculated the confusion metrics, and we deduced the classification metrics.

3.1 mRMR

We selected the first 10 pertinent features using the mRMR algorithm. Figure 3 shows the features ranked according to their importance score. In this case, the features mapped to the classifiers are Pitch, GTCC_coeff_11, MFCC_coeff_7, GTCC_coeff_13, MFCC_coeff_3, GTCC_coeff_10, MFCC_coeff_6, GTCC_coeff_6, MFCC_coeff_13, and MFCC_coeff_10 (Fig. 1).

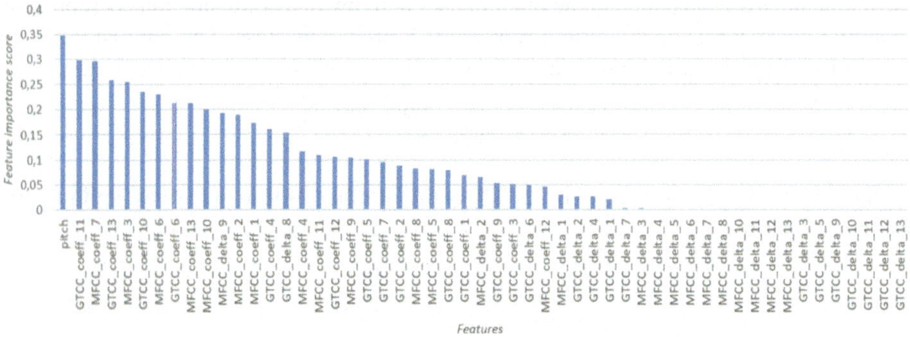

Fig. 1. Feature importance score sorted using the mRMR algorithm

The SVM has the best performance. This model has achieved (Table 2):

- For the Hoehn & Yahr stage 1, 6165 correctly classified frames, 19 misclassifications (3 in stage 2 and 16 in stage 3);
- As for the Hoehn & Yahr stage 2, 4637 frames have been correctly detected, with only 50 false negatives, (33 considered as stage 1 and 17 as stage 3);
- 6023 cases from the Hoehn & Yahr stage 3, were correctly identified, with 36 false negatives, distributed as 32 in stage 1 and 4 in stage 2;
- And lastly, the classifier has correctly classified 358 frames in the Hoehn & Yahr stage 4, with 33 misclassifications (31 as stage 1 and 2 as stage 3)

When performing FS by the mRMR, the SVM and the DNN have achieved excellent results. To evaluate the overall performance, we calculated the recall and the precision for each class and the overall test set (Table 3).

The F1-score for each class and model was calculated to evaluate the overall performance (Table 4). The SVM has the highest f1-score for all classes with 98.4%, and the DNN has obtained 94.9%.

Table 2. Confusion matrices using the mRMR algorithm

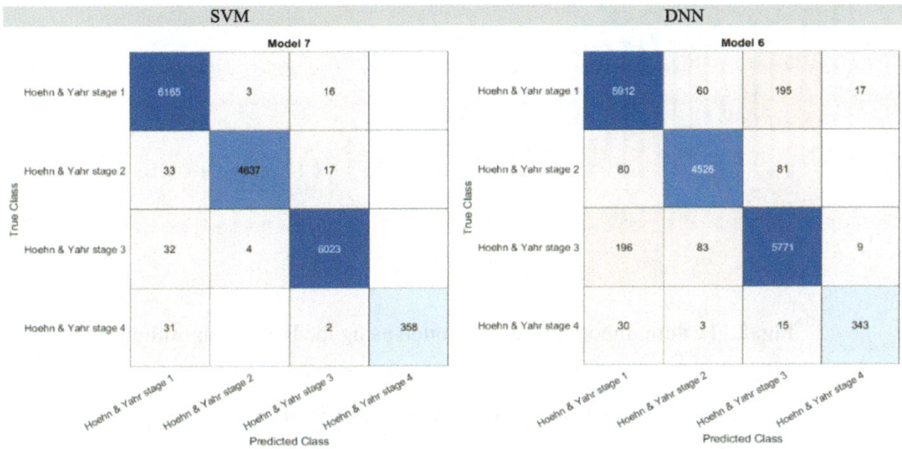

Table 3. The recall and the precision using the mRMR algorithm

	Recall					Precision				
	H&Y S1	H&Y S2	H&Y S3	H&Y S4	Total	H&Y S1	H&Y S2	H&Y S3	H&Y S4	Total
DNN	95.6	96.6	95.2	87.7	93.7	95.1	96.9	95.2	93	95
SVM	99.7	98.9	99.4	91.6	**97.4**	98.5	99.8	99.4	100	**99.4**

Table 4. F1-score using the mRMR algorithm

	F1-score				
	H&Y S1	H&Y S2	H&Y S3	H&Y S4	Total
DNN	95.3	96.7	95.2	90.3	94.4
SVM	99.1	99.3	99.4	95.6	**98.4**

3.2 ReliefF

Figure 2 represents the feature sorted based on the importance scores using the ReliefF FS algorithm. By applying the ReliefF, the features are ordered as follows: GTCC_coeff_13, GTCC_coeff_10, GTCC_coeff_11, pitch, MFCC_coeff_6, GTCC_coeff_1, GTCC_coeff_12, GTCC_coeff_4, GTCC_coeff_2, and MFCC_coeff_10.

Reducing the space features by mapping only the 10 first features sorted by the ReliefF, the SVM has higher results (Table 5).

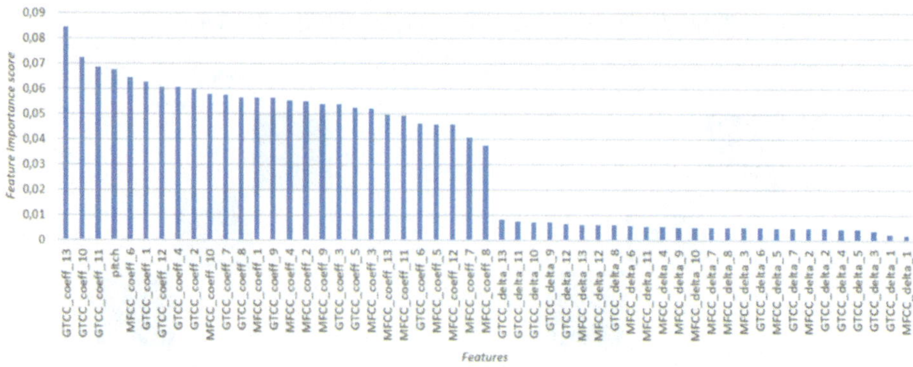

Fig. 2. Feature importance scores sorted using the ReliefF algorithm.

Table 5. Confusion matrices using the ReliefF FS algorithm

SVM — Model 8

True Class \ Predicted Class	Hoehn & Yahr stage 1	Hoehn & Yahr stage 2	Hoehn & Yahr stage 3	Hoehn & Yahr stage 4
Hoehn & Yahr stage 1	6169	2	13	
Hoehn & Yahr stage 2	20	4645	22	
Hoehn & Yahr stage 3	14	1	6044	
Hoehn & Yahr stage 4	20		9	362

DNN — Model 5

True Class \ Predicted Class	Hoehn & Yahr stage 1	Hoehn & Yahr stage 2	Hoehn & Yahr stage 3	Hoehn & Yahr stage 4
Hoehn & Yahr stage 1	5916	68	177	23
Hoehn & Yahr stage 2	92	4530	64	1
Hoehn & Yahr stage 3	167	74	5814	4
Hoehn & Yahr stage 4	23	1	15	352

- For the Hoehn & Yahr stage 1, 6169 correctly classified frames, 15 misclassifications (2 in stage 2 and 13 in stage 3);
- As for the Hoehn & Yahr stage 2, 4645 frames have been correctly detected, with 42 false negatives, (20 considered as stage 1 and 22 as stage 3);
- 6044 cases from the Hoehn & Yahr stage 3, were well identified, with 15 false negatives, distributed as follows: 14 in stage 1 and 1 in stage 2;
- And lastly, the classifier has correctly classified 382 frames in the Hoehn & Yahr stage 4, with 29 misclassifications (20 as stage 1 and 9 as stage 3).

For each class and model, the evaluation metrics are deducted from the confusion matrices and listed in Table 6.

The F1-score for each class and model was calculated to evaluate the overall performance (Table 7). The SVM has the highest f1-score for all classes with 98.7%, and the DNN has 94.9%.

Table 6. The recall and the precision using the ReliefF FS algorithm

	Recall					Precision				
	H&Y S1	H&Y S2	H&Y S3	H&Y S4	Total	H&Y S1	H&Y S2	H&Y S3	H&Y S4	Total
DNN	95.7	96.7	96	90	94.6	95.5	96.9	95.8	92.6	95.2
SVM	99.8	99.1	99.8	92.6	**97.8**	99.1	99.9	99.3	100	**99.57**

Table 7. F1-score using the ReliefF FS algorithm

	F1-score				
	H&Y S1	H&Y S2	H&Y S3	H&Y S4	Total
DNN	95.6	96.8	95.9	91.3	94.9
SVM	99.4	99.5	99.5	96.2	**98.7**

We classified the subjects using the SVM and the ReliefF FS algorithm, which has the highest accuracy with fewer features, after testing our models for each frame of the signals. Based on the most frequent value predicted by frame for each subject, the results demonstrate how accurate our model is in detecting PD Hoehn & Yahr stages (Fig. 3).

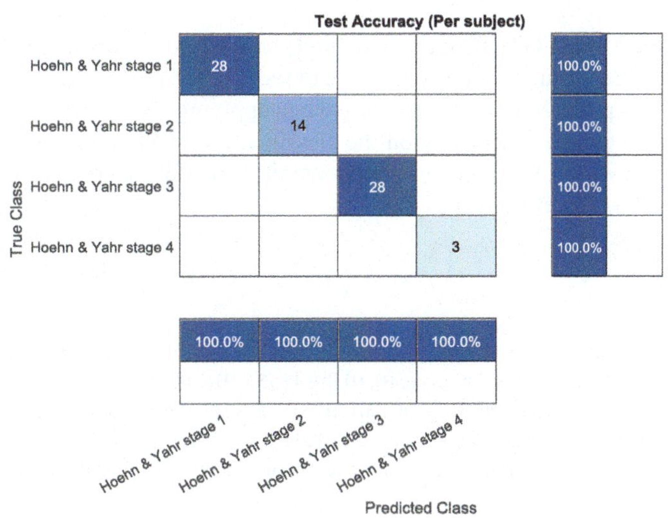

Fig. 3. Confusion matrix by subject using the SVM and the ReliefF FS algorithm

4 Discussion

The best classification results were obtained using the SVM classifier and ReliefF, for an f1-score of 98.7% close to the results obtained with mRMR of 98.4%. The DNN has good performance when applying ReliefF and mRMR 94.9 and 94.4% respectively. Building feature space from the GTCC and the MFCC has demonstrated a significant increase in performance, even with dimensionality reduction and choosing only 10 features from the original 53, our models are still capable of detecting the PD Hoehn & Yahr stages. We also have found that performing data augmentation (classifying the frames first and then by the subjects) improves the performance. Both FS algorithms have selected the pitch. mRMR has selected 5 MFCC and 4 GTCC coefficients, and the ReliefF has selected 7 GTCC and 2 MFCC coefficients, which shows that the GTCC could be a good alternative to the MFCC in PD voice analysis.

The AI-based remote patient monitoring is important for stopping PD progression by developing models with high recall precision detecting accurately PD stages; in our case, we were able to reach a recall of 97.8% (SVM + ReliefF), this high percentage we believe could help in the development of straightforward, inexpensive, quick, and accurate diagnosis system that can assist people with PD without requiring them to physically visit a doctor, which could be a challenge in advanced stages. These findings are promising, but they must be validated by a controlled clinical trial conducted by medical specialists.

5 Conclusion

To conclude, the MFCC-GTCC analysis method proved to be promising for the classification of PD at different stages, with an f1-score of 98.7%. Its interest is that it requires little data and low computational cost, especially when applying FS algorithms. In this investigation, we concentrated primarily on the classification of PD utilizing voice records. In our upcoming works, we intend to implement these models in embedded systems and assess their real-world effectiveness.

References

1. Marras, C., et al.: Prevalence of Parkinson's disease across North America. Npj Parkinson's Dis. **4**(1), 1–7 (2018). https://doi.org/10.1038/s41531-018-0058-0
2. Oukhrib, M., et al.: Epidemiology of Parkinson's disease: an updated overview. Exp. Clin. Evid. Neuropathol. Parkinson's Dis. 1–12 (2023)
3. Hoehn, M., Yahr, M.D.: Parkinsonism: onset, progression and mortality. Neurology **17**(5), 427–442 (1967)
4. Haas, B.R., Stewart, T.H., Zhang, J.: Premotor biomarkers for Parkinson's disease-a promising direction of re-search. Transl Neurodegener **1**(1), 11 (2012)
5. Darley, F.L., Aronson, A.E., Brown, J.R.: Differential diagnostic patterns of dysarthria. J. Speech Hear. Res. **12**(2), 246–269 (1969)
6. Benmalek, E., El Mhamdi, J., Jilbab, A., Jbari, A.: A cough-based covid-19 detection with Gammatone and Mel-frequency cepstral coefficients. Diagnostyka, 24 (2023)

7. Postuma, R.B., Lang, A.E., Gagnon, J.F., Pelletier, A., Montplaisir, J.Y.: How does parkinsonism start ? Prodromal parkinsonism motor changes in idiopathic REM sleep behaviour disorder. Brain **135**(6), 1860–1870 (2012)
8. Benmalek, E., Mhamdi, J.E., Jilbab, A., Jbari, A.: A cough-based COVID-19 detection system using PCA and machine learning classifiers. Appl. Comput. Sci. **18**(4) (2022)
9. Postuma, R.B.: Voice changes in prodromal Parkinson's disease - is a new biomarker within earshot ? Sleep Medicine (2015)
10. Benmalek, E., Elmhamdi, J., Jilbab, A., Jbari, A.: Automatic COVID-19 detection using machine learning and voice recording. Res. Biomed. Eng. **39**(3), 597–612 (2023)
11. Benmalek, E., Elmhamdi, J., Jilbab, A.: Multiclass classification of Parkinson's disease using different classifiers and LLBFS feature selection algorithm. Int. J. Speech Technol. **20**(1), 179–184 (2017)
12. Benmalek, E., Elmhamdi, J., Jilbab, A.: Multiclass classification of Parkinson's disease using cepstral analysis. Int. J. Speech Technol. **21**(1), 39–49 (2018)
13. Synapse ID [syn2321745]: These Datasets were generated through collaboration between Sage Bionetworks, PatientsLikeMe and Dr. Max Little as part of the Patient Voice Analysis study (PVA)
14. Bates, S., Hastie, T., Tibshirani, R.: Cross-validation: what does it estimate and how well does it do it? J. Am. Stat. Assoc. **119**(546), 1434–1445 (2024)

Multi-fault Bearing Classification Based Feature Mode Decomposition and Machine Learning

Iman Makrouf[1,2(✉)], Mourad Zegrari[1], Khalid Dahi[3], and Ilias Ouachtouk[1]

[1] Laboratory of Digital Engineering for Leading Technologies and Automation (DELTA), Hassan II University, ENSAM Casablanca, Casablanca, Morocco
iman.makrouf-etu@etu.univh2c.ma

[2] Centre de recherche Systèmes Complexes et Interractions, Ecole Centrale Casablanca, Bouskoura, Morocco

[3] Centre de recherche Systèmes Complexes et Interractions, Ecole Centrale Casablanca, Ville Verte Côté Latéral Est, Casablanca, Morocco

Abstract. Bearing fault diagnosis is crucial for maintaining the reliability and efficiency of rotating machinery in industrial settings. This research develops an innovative approach to intelligent bearing fault diagnosis by combining Feature Mode Decomposition (FMD) with advanced machine learning techniques. We address the challenges of analyzing nonstationary signals and detecting multiple fault conditions simultaneously. The proposed method introduces a novel mode selection criterion, the Envelope Kurtosis-Entropy Product (EKEP), to identify the most informative mode from FMD outputs. Comprehensive feature extraction is performed on the selected mode, followed by applying various machine learning algorithms for fault classification. Experimental validation using a Spectra Quest Machinery Fault Simulator demonstrates good classification performance across different machine learning models, achieving superior results in diagnosing multiple bearing fault conditions, including combined faults.

Keywords: Bearing fault diagnosis · Combined faults · Feature Mode Decomposition (FMD) · Envelope Kurtosis · Envelope Spectrum Entropy · Vibration analysis · Machine Learning

1 Introduction

Bearings are vital for smooth operation in industrial machinery [1]. Their complex design and harsh operating conditions can lead to failures, causing significant financial losses. Bearing deterioration produces complex, nonstationary vibration signals, often obscured by background noise, making fault diagnosis challenging, especially when dealing with combined faults [2]. This requires advanced techniques for feature extraction and intelligent fault diagnosis.

I. Aboudrar et al. (Eds.): ICESST 2024, SUCI, pp. 156–166, 2025.
https://doi.org/10.1007/978-3-031-86705-7_15

Bearing faults typically generate periodic impulses in vibration signals, which researchers have analyzed using various approaches, from traditional signal processing methods to intelligent systems. Recent advances have used signal processing techniques like wavelet transforms and empirical mode decomposition for feature extraction [3], which are effective for basic fault patterns but rely heavily on expert knowledge, limiting their capability in handling complex signal behaviors. To address these limitations, machine learning algorithms such as SVM and Random Forests have been introduced, demonstrating improved accuracy in fault classification [4]. However, their performance heavily relies on effective feature extraction methods. While deep learning approaches have shown superior performance in automated feature extraction [5], they require substantial computational resources and large datasets for training. Consequently, the combination of signal processing techniques with machine learning algorithms has emerged as a promising approach, offering both effective feature extraction and intelligent classification capabilities.

Within signal processing techniques, decomposition methods have gained significant attention, including empirical mode decomposition (EMD) [6], ensemble EMD (EEMD) [7], and variational mode decomposition (VMD) [8]. These methods aim to better isolate fault-related components. However, EMD suffers from mode aliasing, while VMD's performance depends on parameter selection. Feature Mode Decomposition (FMD) [9] addresses these limitations through adaptive signal decomposition and deconvolution principles, showing improved resilience against noise interference.

This study proposes a hybrid approach combining FMD with machine learning for intelligent fault classification, enhanced by a novel mode selection algorithm called Envelope Kurtosis-Entropy Product (EKEP). Building on previous research, such as kurtosis-based selection for EMD [10] and entropy-based approaches for VMD [11], EKEP integrates Envelope Kurtosis (EK) and Envelope Spectral Entropy (ESE) to improve mode selection from the decomposed signal. Statistical features extracted from selected modes in both time and frequency domains are used to train various machine learning algorithms (SVM, Random Forests, ANN) for fault classification, with emphasis on combined faults. This represents the first application of FMD combined with our proposed feature selection method and machine learning algorithms for bearing fault diagnosis, offering potential improvements in accuracy and reliability.

The remainder of this paper is organized as follows: Sect. 2 details FMD, Sect. 3 outlines the proposed methodology (mode selection, feature extraction, machine learning models), Sect. 4 presents experimental results, and Finally the conclusion is given in Sect. 5.

2 Feature Mode Decomposition

Feature Mode Decomposition (FMD) is a novel signal decomposition method designed for machinery fault diagnosis, addressing limitations in existing techniques. Proposed by Miao et al. [9], FMD incorporates fault feature characteristics into the decomposition process using an adaptive FIR filter bank. It uniquely considers both impulsiveness and periodicity of fault signals, employs Correlated Kurtosis as its objective function, and includes automatic fault period estimation. These features make FMD particularly effective for analyzing complex machinery fault signals without requiring prior knowledge of fault periods. The FMD process is implemented through the following steps:

Step 1: Input the raw signal ($\mathbf{x}$) and specify parameters: the desired number of modes (n) and the filter length (L).
Step 2: Set up FIR filter bank with the Hanning window. Use K filters (5–10). Initialize iteration $i = 1$.
Step 3: Generate the filtered signals, which represent the decomposed modes, through the convolution operation $\mathbf{u}_m^i = \mathbf{x} * \mathbf{f}_m^i$, where m ranges from 1 to M, and $*$ denotes convolution.
Step 4: Update filter coefficients using $\mathbf{x}$, $\mathbf{u}_m^i$, and fault period T_m^i. Determine T_m^i from autocorrelation spectrum R_m^i. Increment i.
Step 5: If iteration limit not reached, return to step 3; else continue.
Step 6: Calculate correlation coefficient matrix $\mathbf{CC}_{(M\times M)}$. For the highest correlated modes, compute correlation kurtosis (CK). Retain mode with larger CK. Set $M = M - 1$.
Step 7: If $M \neq n$, return to step 3; else proceed to step 8.
Step 8: Designate remaining modes as final decomposed modes.

FMD decomposes complex signals, but not all modes are equally relevant for fault diagnosis. We implement a mode selection criterion to identify the most relevant modes, improving accuracy and efficiency. The next section details our proposed algorithm for refining FMD output.

3 Proposed Methodology

This study presents a methodology for bearing fault diagnosis, combining signal processing with machine learning. As shown in Fig. 1, the approach involves FMD of vibration signals, mode selection using the EKEP, feature extraction, and fault classification using machine learning algorithms. This method aims to improve bearing fault diagnosis accuracy in industrial settings. The following subsections detail the main steps of the proposed methodology.

3.1 Mode Selection Process

In machinery fault diagnosis signal envelope analysis has proven to be an effective technique. The signal envelope, obtained through techniques like the Hilbert transform [12], captures modulation characteristics linked to bearing defects. Two key statistical measures of envelopes are envelope kurtosis [13], which indicates the "peakedness" of the distribution, and envelope spectrum entropy [14], which assesses the randomness of the spectrum. We combine these measures into the Envelope Kurtosis-Entropy Product (EKEP), integrating kurtosis's sensitivity to impulsive signals and entropy's capacity to capture spectral complexity. In the proposed approach, we select the mode with the maximum EKEP. The mode selection process is detailed in the instructions below:

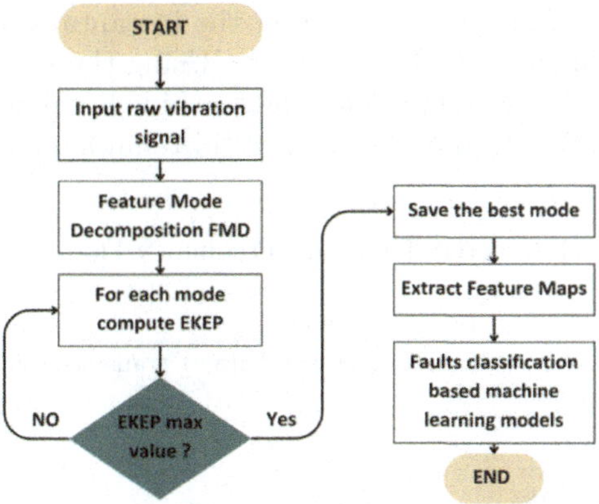

Fig. 1. Flow chart of the proposed methodology

Step 1: Input n modes $y_1, y_2, ..., y_n$ from FMD output.
Step 2: For each mode y_i, $i = 1, 2, ..., n$:
- (a) Compute analytic signal: $z_i(t) = y_i(t) + jH\{y_i(t)\}$
- (b) Calculate envelope: $e_i(t) = |z_i(t)|$
- (c) Compute Envelope Kurtosis (EK): $EK_i = \frac{E\{(e_i - \mu_{e_i})^4\}}{\sigma_{e_i}^4}$
- (d) Calculate Envelope Spectrum: $E_i(f) = |F\{e_i(t)\}|$
- (e) Normalize Envelope Spectrum: $P_i(f) = \frac{E_i(f)}{\sum_f E_i(f)}$
- (f) Compute Envelope Spectrum Entropy (ESE): $ESE_i = -\sum_f P_i(f) \log_2 P_i(f)$

Step 3: Calculate EKEP for each mode: $EKEP_i = EK_i \times ESE_i$
Step 4: Select mode with maximum EKEP: $i^* = \arg\max_i EKEP_i$
Step 5: Output selected mode y_{i^*} for further analysis.

3.2 Features Extraction

After selecting the mode, we extract a set of features to capture the key characteristics of the signal in both the time and frequency domains, providing a detailed representation of the bearing's condition. A total of 13 time-domain and 6 frequency-domain features are extracted, as summarized in Table 1. For frequency-domain features, we employ the Hilbert Transform (HT) for envelope analysis due to its optimal capability in detecting amplitude modulation and extracting characteristic bearing fault frequencies, while maintaining computational efficiency compared to alternative methods. The HT for a real-valued time domain signal $x(t)$ is defined as:

$$H[x(t)] = \frac{1}{\pi} P.V. \int_{-\infty}^{\infty} \frac{x(\tau)}{t - \tau} d\tau \tag{1}$$

where $P.V.$ denotes the Cauchy principal value of the integral.

Using the Hilbert transform, we extract the instantaneous amplitude, phase, and frequency as defined in the feature table. Using these extracted features, we aim to create an effective foundation for the machine learning step of our methodology, ultimately leading to more accurate and reliable bearing fault diagnosis.

Table 1. Extracted Time and Frequency Domain Features

Feature	Formula
N: Number of samples, x_i: i-th sample, $H(x_i)$: Hilbert transform of x_i	
Time Domain Features	
Mean	$\frac{1}{N}\sum_{i=1}^{N} x_i$
Root Mean Square (RMS)	$\sqrt{\frac{1}{N}\sum_{i=1}^{N} x_i^2}$
Square Root Amplitude (SRA)	$\left(\frac{1}{N}\sum_{i=1}^{N}\sqrt{\lvert x_i\rvert}\right)^2$
Absolute Average	$\frac{1}{N}\sum_{i=1}^{N}\lvert x_i\rvert$
Maximum / Minimum	$\max(x_i)$ / $\min(x_i)$
Peak to Peak	$\max(x_i) - \min(x_i)$
Variance	$\frac{1}{N-1}\sum_{i=1}^{N}(x_i-\mu)^2$, μ: mean of x_i
Skewness	$\frac{\frac{1}{N}\sum_{i=1}^{N}(x_i-\mu)^3}{\left(\frac{1}{N}\sum_{i=1}^{N}(x_i-\mu)^2\right)^{3/2}}$
Kurtosis	$\frac{\frac{1}{N}\sum_{i=1}^{N}(x_i-\mu)^4}{\left(\frac{1}{N}\sum_{i=1}^{N}(x_i-\mu)^2\right)^2}$
Shape Factor	$\frac{\text{RMS}}{\text{Absolute Average}}$
Crest Factor	$\frac{\max(x_i)}{\text{RMS}}$
Impulse Factor	$\frac{\max(x_i)}{\text{Absolute Average}}$
Frequency Domain Features (Using Hilbert Transform)	
Entropy (Envelope)	$-\sum_{i=1}^{N} p_i \log_2(p_i)$, p_i: Probability of envelope value
Mean Instantaneous Frequency	$\frac{1}{N}\sum_{i=1}^{N}\frac{1}{2\pi}\frac{d}{dt}\angle H(x_i)$
Std. Dev. of Instantaneous Frequency	$\sqrt{\frac{1}{N-1}\sum_{i=1}^{N}(\text{instfreq}_i - \mu_{\text{freq}})^2}$
Variance Coefficient (Envelope)	$\frac{\text{std}(\lvert H(x)\rvert)}{\text{mean}(\lvert H(x)\rvert)}$
Max Instantaneous Amplitude	$\max(\lvert H(x)\rvert)$
Mean Instantaneous Phase	$\frac{1}{N}\sum_{i=1}^{N}\angle H(x_i)$

3.3 Machine Learning Algorithms

This study employs a range of machine learning algorithms to classify bearing faults based on the extracted features, including Support Vector Machine (SVM), Gradient Boosting, K-Nearest Neighbors (KNN), Random Forest, Decision Tree, and Neural Network. Each method offers distinct advantages: SVM is effective in high-dimensional spaces; Gradient Boosting captures non-linear relationships by sequentially correcting errors; KNN is a simple yet powerful proximity-based technique; Random Forest leverages ensemble predictions from multiple decision trees; Decision Tree offers transparency and interpretability; and Neural Networks excel in modeling complex, non-linear patterns. The implementation details and comparative results of these algorithms will be presented in the experimental analysis section.

4 Experimental Evaluation and Results Analysis

4.1 Experimental Setup and Data Collection

The study utilized a Spectra Quest Machinery Fault Simulator for experimental data collection, as depicted in Fig. 2. The setup comprised a shaft supported by two MBFK-3/4 type bearings, with one bearing under test. A 745 W three-phase induction motor, regulated by a variable frequency drive (VFD), was coupled to the shaft. Vibration data were acquired using an accelerometer (100 mV/g sensitivity) mounted vertically on the bearing housing. Data acquisition employed a National Instruments cDAQ-9178 system controlled by LabVIEW software, with a 25600 Hz sampling frequency. The motor operated at 1185 rpm (corresponding to a rotating frequency f_r = 19.75 Hz). Five bearing conditions were investigated: healthy (NO), inner race defect(IR), outer race defect (OR), ball defect (BA), and a combination of defects (Combined). Table 2 provides bearing specifications. Fault frequencies were calculated as f_o = 60.198 Hz, f_i = 97.76 Hz, and f_b = 39.24 Hz for outer race, inner race, and ball defects, respectively. For each bearing condition, 300 vibration signals of 1-second duration were recorded. Figure 3 presents time domain waveformes for defective bearing (OR and IR). The dataset was divided into an 80:20 ratio for training and testing, yielding 1200 training samples (240 per condition) and 300 test samples (60 per condition). This split enabled performance evaluation of the trained models on unseen data. Table 3 summarizes the bearing conditions and dataset distribution for training and testing.

4.2 FMD Results and Best Mode Selection

We applied Feature Mode Decomposition (FMD) to the raw vibration data, setting the number of modes n to 4 and filter size L to 30. Figure 4 shows

Table 2. Testing bearing size

Bearing Type	Number of balls	Ball diameter	Pitch diameter	Contact angle
M-BFK-3/4	8	7.94 mm	33.48 mm	0°

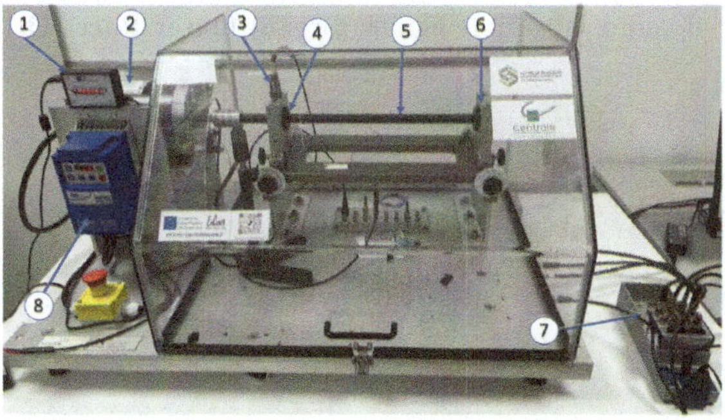

Fig. 2. Experimental test bench: (1) Digital tachometer (2) Induction motor (3) Accelerometer (4) Bearing 1 (5) Shaft (6) Bearing 2 (7) NI cDAQ-9178 (8) VFD

the decomposed mode components and their envelope spectra for OR defective bearing. To identify the most informative mode, we implemented a selection algorithm based on EKEP criterion. Table 4 presents the best mode for each fault type with its corresponding Envelope Kurtosis (EK), Envelope Spectrum Entropy (ESE), and EKEP values. Figure 5 displays the envelope spectra of selected modes for each bearing condition, clearly showing characteristic fault frequencies: outer race ($f_o = 60.198$ Hz), inner race ($f_i = 97.76$ Hz), and ball ($f_b = 39.24$ Hz), along with their harmonics. These frequencies are particularly evident in the combined fault spectrum. The visibility of these fault-specific frequencies validates our EKEP-based mode selection algorithm. These selected modes will be used to extract features for training machine learning algorithms.

Table 3. Bearing conditions and dataset distribution

Class Label	Fault Type	Training Set	Testing Set
NO	Healthy bearing (Normal)	240	60
IR	Inner race defect	240	60
OR	Outer race defect	240	60
BA	Ball defect	240	60
Combined	Combination of bearing defects	240	60

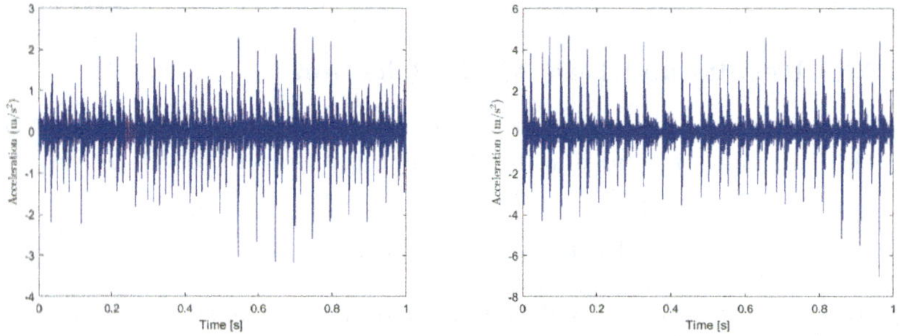

(a) (b)

Fig. 3. Raw time-domain vibration signals for: (a) Outer Race (OR), (b) Inner Race (IR)

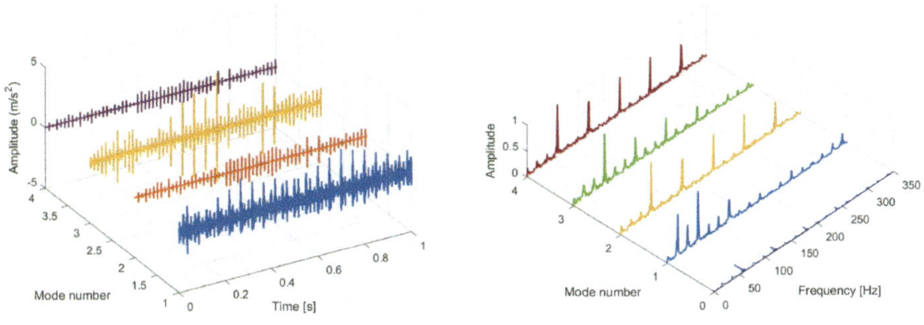

(a) OR time modes (b) Spectral envelope of OR modes

Fig. 4. Decomposed modes and envelope spectra for OR defective bearing

Table 4. Summary of best modes and their performance metrics

Fault Type	Best Mode	EK	ESE	EKEP Criterion
OR	4	42.85	8.88	380.43
IR	4	80.28	8.73	701.01
NO	1	2.52	7.52	18.98
BA	2	36.97	8.22	303.96
Combined	2	50.47	8.87	447.69

4.3 Machine Learning Results and Model Evaluation

We evaluated several machine learning algorithms for bearing fault diagnosis using extracted features from the best selected modes. Table 5 shows high accuracies across all models, with SVM achieving 98.83%. Figure 6 presents the SVM confusion matrix, demonstrating its strong classification performance. The consistently high accuracy suggests our feature extraction method effectively captures fault characteristics, highlighting machine learning's potential for industrial predictive maintenance.

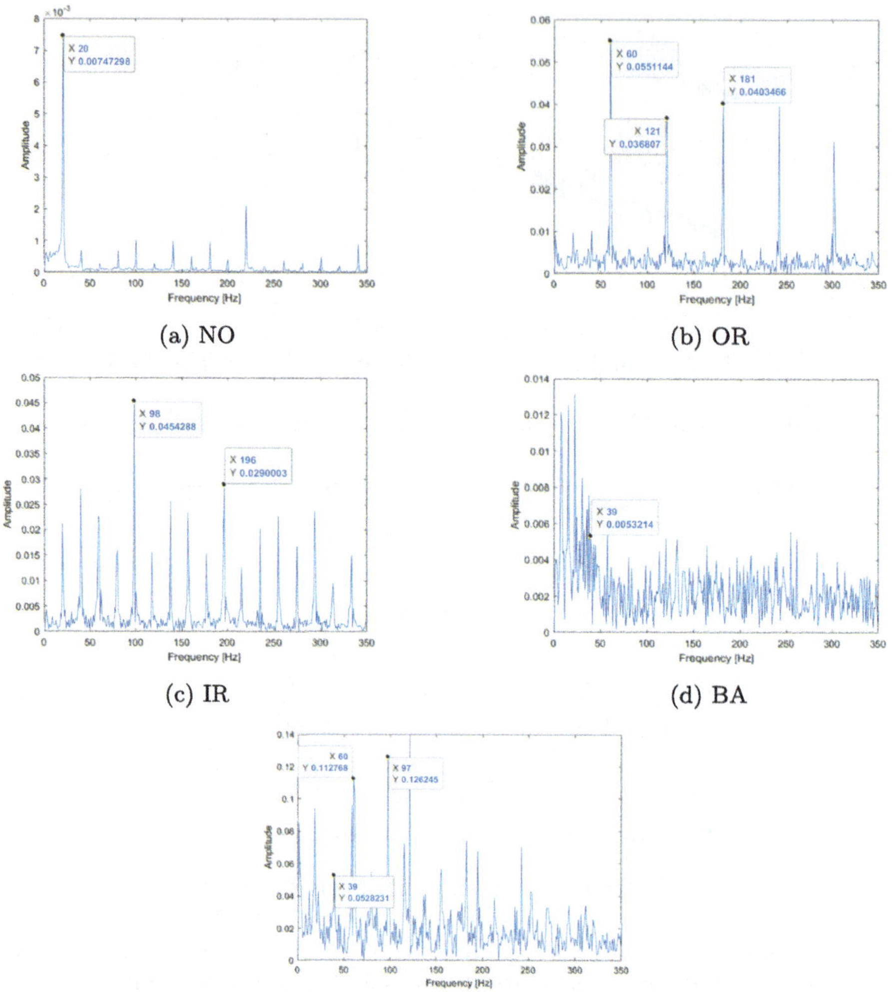

(a) NO (b) OR

(c) IR (d) BA

(e) Combined

Fig. 5. Envelope spectra of best modes for different conditions

Table 5. Training accuracies of different models

Model	Training Accuracy(%)
Neural Network	98.67
Decision Tree	95.23
Random Forest	96.33
KNN	98.67
Gradient Boosting	98.33
SVM	98.83

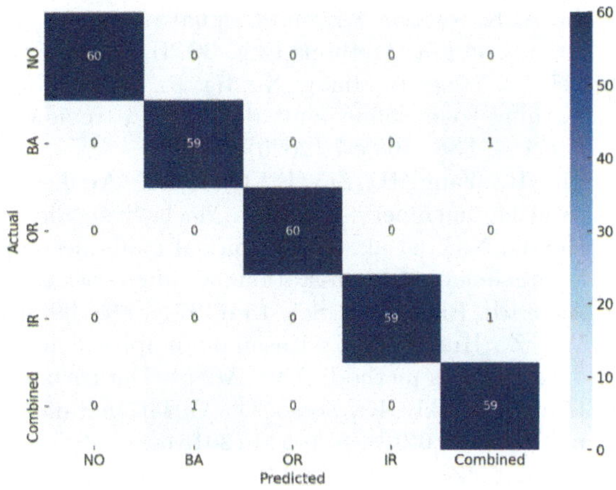

Fig. 6. SVM confusion matrix

5 Conclusion

This paper introduced a novel bearing fault diagnosis approach combining Feature Mode Decomposition with machine learning. Our Envelope Kurtosis-Entropy Product criterion effectively identified informative modes from decomposed vibration signals. Experimental results validated our approach, with the SVM model achieving 98.83% accuracy and other models showing good performance across various fault conditions. The high accuracy across different algorithms underscores the effectiveness of our feature extraction method. This research contributes to intelligent fault diagnosis by addressing the challenges of non-stationary signals and multiple fault conditions in rotating machinery. Future work could explore deep learning, real-time diagnosis, and application to other machinery faults.

Acknowledgements. This research was supported by the Centre National pour la Recherche Scientifique et Technique (CNRST) "PHD-ASsociate Scholarship-PASS" program and the Centre de recherche Systèmes Complexes et Interractions, Ecole Centrale Casablanca, which provided the experimental test bench.

References

1. Ouachtouk, I., El Hani, S., Dahi, K.: Intelligent bearing fault diagnosis method based on HNR envelope and classification using supervised machine learning algorithms. Adv. Electr. Electron. Eng. **19**(4), 282–294 (2021)
2. Huang, R., Xia, J., Zhang, B., Chen, Z., Li, W.: Compound fault diagnosis for rotating machinery: state-of-the-art, challenges, and opportunities. J. Dyn. Monit. Diagn. 13–29 (2023)

3. Jaros, R., et al.: Advanced signal processing methods for condition monitoring. Arch. Comput. Methods Eng. **30**(3), 1553–1577 (2023)
4. Lei, Y., Yang, B., Jiang, X., Jia, F., Li, N., Nandi, A.K.: Applications of machine learning to machine fault diagnosis: a review and roadmap. Mech. Syst. Signal Process. **138**, 106587 (2020)
5. Liu, R., Yang, B., Zio, E., Chen, X.: Artificial intelligence for fault diagnosis of rotating machinery: a review. Mech. Syst. Signal Process. **108**, 33–47 (2018)
6. Huang, N.E., et al.: The empirical mode decomposition and the Hilbert spectrum for nonlinear and non-stationary time series analysis. Proc. Roy. Soc. London. Ser. A: Math. Phys. Eng. Sci. **454**(1971), 903–995 (1998)
7. Wu, Z., Huang, N.E.: Ensemble empirical mode decomposition: a noise-assisted data analysis method. Adv. Adapt. Data Anal. **1**(01), 1–41 (2009)
8. Dragomiretskiy, K., Zosso, D.: Variational mode decomposition. IEEE Trans. Signal Process. **62**(3), 531–544 (2013)
9. Miao, Y., Zhang, B., Li, C., Lin, J., Zhang, D.: Feature mode decomposition: new decomposition theory for rotating machinery fault diagnosis. IEEE Trans. Industr. Electron. **70**(2), 1949–1960 (2022)
10. Damine, Y., Megherbi, A.C., Sbaa, S., Bessous, N.: Study of the imf selection methods using kurtosis parameter for bearing fault diagnosis. In: 2022 19th International Multi-Conference on Systems, Signals & Devices (SSD), pp. 80–85. IEEE (2022)
11. Li, H., Liu, T., Wu, X., Chen, Q.: An optimized VMD method and its applications in bearing fault diagnosis. Measurement **166**, 108185 (2020)
12. Dahi, K., Elhani, S., Guedira, S.: Statistical wound-rotor IM diagnosis method based on standard deviation using NVSA. In: International Conference on Electronics and Communication Systems II (2014)
13. Hua, L., Wu, X., Liu, T., Li, S.: The methodology of modified frequency band envelope kurtosis for bearing fault diagnosis. IEEE Trans. Industr. Inf. **19**(3), 2856–2865 (2022)
14. Yang, Y., Liu, H., Han, L., Gao, P.: A feature extraction method using VMD and improved envelope spectrum entropy for rolling bearing fault diagnosis. IEEE Sens. J. **23**(4), 3848–3858 (2023)

Artificial Intelligence in Drone and Anti-drone Systems: Cutting-Edge Advances and Applications

Yasmine Ghazlane[1(✉)], Bnouachir Hajar[1], El Maghraoui Hajar[1], Haidrar Saida[1], and El Yadari Mourad[2]

[1] HESTIM Engineering and Business School, Center for Studies and Research in Engineering and Management (CERIM), Casablanca, Morocco
y.ghazlane@hestim.ma

[2] ENSAM, Mohammed V University Rabat, Rabat, Morocco

Abstract. With the increasing proliferation of drones, or Unmanned Aerial Vehicles (UAVs), across various sectors, both opportunities and challenges arise, particularly concerning security and privacy. The misuse of drones for malicious activities has necessitated the development of advanced anti-drone systems to detect, identify, and neutralize these threats effectively. This article discusses the critical aspects of Artificial Intelligence (AI) in enhancing anti-drone systems, highlighting recent advances in AI applications for both drones and anti-drone technologies. The integration of AI techniques such as machine learning deep learning, computer vision, and multi-agent systems has significantly improved the detection, identification, tracking, and interception capabilities of anti-drone systems. This work provides an overview of the state-of-the-art AI technologies driving the evolution of both drones and counter-drone measures.

Keywords: Drones · Anti-drones · Artificial Intelligence. Airspace safety

1 Introduction

The rapid adoption of UAVs, commonly known as drones, has transformed multiple industries, from agriculture and surveillance to delivery and emergency response [1–7]. However, the ease of access and versatility of drones have also led to their exploitation for illegal activities such as smuggling, unauthorized surveillance, and terrorism. To counter these threats, anti-drone technologies have emerged as critical components in ensuring airspace security and privacy [8, 9]. Central to the effectiveness of these systems is the use of AI to detect, classify, and respond to airborne threats in real-time. This article examines the role of AI in developing sophisticated anti-drone systems and discusses recent advances in AI applications for both drone and anti-drone cutting-edge systems. The first section provides a comprehensive analysis of how advancements in AI for drone technologies impact and inform the development of anti-drone systems. It emphasizes the dual use of AI, both for enhancing drone capabilities and for developing

I. Aboudrar et al. (Eds.): ICESST 2024, SUCI, pp. 167–174, 2025.
https://doi.org/10.1007/978-3-031-86705-7_16

more sophisticated countermeasures to protect against potential threats. Following, we highlight the relationship between AI-enhanced drones and anti-drones as well as the key AI components in anti-drone systems. In the final section, we conclude and discuss potential future perspectives.

2 AI Advancements in Drone Technologies

Artificial intelligence (AI) has driven significant advancements in the development and utilization of drones, transforming them from remotely piloted machines into highly autonomous, intelligent systems. AI algorithms enable drones to process vast amounts of data in real-time, making complex decisions without human intervention. This has greatly enhanced their autonomy, allowing them to navigate challenging environments, avoid obstacles, and adapt to dynamic conditions with minimal input. Additionally, AI has improved drone efficiency by optimizing flight paths, energy consumption, and payload management, leading to longer operational times and more effective missions. These capabilities have expanded drone applications across various sectors, including agriculture, where AI-powered drones monitor crops and analyze soil health; logistics, where they streamline delivery processes; defense, where they perform surveillance and reconnaissance missions; and disaster management, where they assist in search-and-rescue operations. AI's role in drone technology continues to push the boundaries of what these systems can achieve, making them indispensable tools in most of the industries. The role of AI in advancing drone technologies can be highlighted through the following key areas:

Autonomous Navigation and Path Planning: AI has enabled drones to navigate complex environments autonomously, avoiding obstacles, and optimizing flight paths. Machine learning algorithms, particularly reinforcement learning [10], allow drones to learn from their environment and adapt to new scenarios without human intervention. This capability is crucial for applications such as delivery, where drones must navigate dynamic urban environments, and search-and-rescue missions that require precise navigation through challenging areas.

Enhanced Object Detection and Recognition: Modern drones are equipped with advanced computer vision capabilities powered by AI. Deep learning models, such as Convolutional Neural Networks (CNNs), allow drones to detect and recognize objects, differentiate between humans, vehicles, and other targets, and adapt their behavior accordingly. These capabilities are particularly useful in surveillance, security, and wildlife monitoring, where accurate object detection is essential for mission success.

Swarm Intelligence and Coordinated Missions: AI has facilitated the development of drone swarms that operate collaboratively to perform complex tasks. Swarm intelligence algorithms, inspired by natural systems such as ant colonies or bird flocks, enable multiple drones to communicate, share data, and coordinate their actions to achieve a common objective [11, 12]. This advancement is particularly valuable in applications like precision agriculture, environmental monitoring, and military operations, where multiple drones can cover large areas and collect data more efficiently than a single unit.

Adaptive Learning for Performance Optimization: Drones equipped with AI can continuously learn and optimize their performance in real-time. AI models can adjust a drone's flight patterns, speed, and power consumption based on environmental conditions or mission requirements. This adaptive learning capability ensures drones operate at peak efficiency, extending flight times, reducing energy consumption, and improving overall mission outcomes.

3 The Link Between AI-Enhanced Drones and Anti-drone Systems

The advancements in AI for drone technologies are directly related to the challenges faced by anti-drone systems. As drones become more sophisticated and autonomous due to AI enhancements, the complexity of countering these threats also increases. The following connections highlight how developments in AI-driven drones influence anti-drone strategies:

Counteracting Autonomous Navigation: The use of AI for autonomous navigation in drones requires anti-drone systems to employ equally advanced AI models to predict and counter-drone movements. For instance, machine learning algorithms can be trained to recognize the specific patterns associated with autonomous navigation, enabling anti-drone systems to identify and anticipate potential threats more effectively [13, 14].

Detecting AI-Enhanced Swarm Attacks: The rise of AI-enabled swarm drones poses a unique challenge to anti-drone systems [15]. Swarm attacks, where multiple drones coordinate in real-time, require anti-drone solutions that can handle multiple targets simultaneously. AI-based anti-drone systems utilize machine learning and deep learning models to track and intercept multiple drones, ensuring that they can respond effectively to complex, coordinated attacks.

Advanced Object Recognition and Differentiation: As drones become more adept at avoiding detection using AI-driven stealth tactics, anti-drone systems must leverage enhanced object recognition capabilities to differentiate between legitimate and rogue drones. AI models that incorporate features such as thermal imaging, radar, and infrared sensing can improve the accuracy of detection, even when drones attempt to mask their presence or mimic non-threatening objects [16–19].

AI Arms Race: Evolving Threat and Defense Capabilities: The continuous improvement in AI algorithms employed for drone operations creates an ongoing "***arms race***" between drone developers and anti-drone system designers. As drones incorporate more sophisticated AI for stealth, speed, and decision-making, anti-drone systems must integrate cutting-edge AI to detect, identify, and neutralize these evolving threats. For instance, the use of Generative Adversarial Networks (GANs) in drones to simulate decoy signals or to manipulate anti-drone detection systems requires anti-drone defenses that are equally adept at recognizing and countering such tactics.

Ethical and Regulatory Considerations: The AI advancements in both drones and anti-drone technologies bring ethical and regulatory challenges. The use of AI for surveillance, data collection, and autonomous decision-making raises privacy concerns and necessitates the development of guidelines for responsible use. Moreover, as anti-drone systems become more capable of neutralizing threats autonomously, there is a need for clear policies governing their deployment to prevent misuse or unintended consequences [8, 20].

The intersection of AI advancements in drone technologies and anti-drone systems illustrates a dynamic landscape where both offensive and defensive capabilities are continuously evolving. As AI drives the development of more sophisticated drones, it simultaneously pushes the boundaries of anti-drone technologies, leading to innovative solutions to detect, track, and neutralize emerging threats. The ongoing integration of AI into both domains underscores the critical importance of maintaining a balance between technological innovation, security, and ethical considerations to ensure safe and secure airspace operations.

4 Key AI Components in Anti-drone Systems

AI plays a pivotal role in various stages of an anti-drone system, from detection and identification to tracking and neutralization. The following are the primary AI components leveraged in such systems:

Detection and Identification Models: The foundation of any anti-drone system lies in its ability to detect and identify unauthorized UAVs accurately. Traditional methods relying on radar or RF signals have limitations in distinguishing drones from other objects. AI-based approaches, particularly those leveraging deep learning and computer vision, offer significant improvements. Advanced CNNs and object detection algorithms like You Only Look Once (YOLO) enable real-time identification and classification of the most encountered airborne targets. For instance, an improved YOLOv7 model incorporating modules like CSPResNeXt, attention mechanisms (C3TR), and decoupled head structures has been developed to enhance detection accuracy and speed [14].

Multi-Agent System Framework: The integration of a multi-agent system allows for the coordinated functioning of multiple agents within an anti-drone architecture. Each agent, whether airborne or ground-based, is designed to perform specific tasks such as data collection, processing, or decision-making. This decentralized approach enhances the system's adaptability and efficiency in dynamic environments. AI-driven MAS frameworks are particularly useful in scenarios where multiple drones or other aerial threats are present, requiring quick, coordinated responses.

AI-Based Electromagnetic Neutralization: Advanced AI algorithms are also employed in the interception phase of anti-drone systems. A novel approach involves using AI-based electromagnetic neutralization techniques to disable drones without causing physical damage. This method relies on precise AI models that predict the optimal electromagnetic interference needed to disrupt the drone's communication and control systems while ensuring minimal collateral impact.

Transfer Learning and Data Augmentation: Transfer learning is a crucial AI technique that involves using pre-trained models on large datasets and fine-tuning them for specific anti-drone tasks. This method significantly reduces the time and computational resources required for training while maintaining high detection accuracy. Data augmentation techniques, such as rotation, scaling, and noise addition, further enhance model robustness by simulating various environmental conditions.

Real-Time Decision-Making and Adaptation: AI models in anti-drone systems must not only detect and classify threats but also make real-time decisions about the best course of action. Reinforcement learning algorithms are increasingly being explored to enable adaptive decision-making processes that improve over time based on feedback from the operational environment. This capability is crucial in dynamic scenarios where threats evolve or new patterns of drone usage emerge [21].

5 Breakthroughs in AI for Drone and Counter-Drone Technologies

This section reviews recent advancements in AI that have significantly improved detection algorithms, identification models, multi-target tracking, and autonomous drone operations. Enhanced detection algorithms, such as those based on YOLOv7, use attention mechanisms and deep neural networks to differentiate drones from other aerial objects with high accuracy, even under challenging conditions. AI-driven identification models leverage deep learning techniques, like CNNs and ensemble learning, to improve classification accuracy and reliability. In multi-target tracking, AI-enabled algorithms allow for real-time monitoring of multiple airborne objects, crucial for situational awareness. Additionally, AI advancements in autonomous drone technologies, including machine learning and reinforcement learning, enable complex tasks such as obstacle avoidance and coordinated maneuvers, expanding capabilities in both military and civilian applications.

Improved Detection Algorithms: Recent advances in AI have led to the development of more sophisticated detection algorithms that can distinguish between drones and other aerial objects, such as birds, with high accuracy. Models like YOLOv7 and Faster R-CNN, integrated with attention mechanisms and deep neural networks, offer enhanced performance in detecting multiple targets in real-time, even under challenging conditions such as low light or adverse weather. Table 1 highlights the most relevant algorithms used in both drones and anti-drone systems with:

- YOLO and SSD as preferred for real-time applications where speed is prioritized.
- Faster R-CNN and CNN as more accurate but slower alternatives, suitable for applications needing high precision.
- SVM and Haar Cascade Classifier as simpler or legacy options, appropriate for basic or non-real-time detections.

Adaptive AI Models for Identification: AI-driven identification models have significantly improved the ability to distinguish between friend and foe targets. These models use deep learning techniques such as CNN combined with transfer learning to achieve high classification accuracy. Additionally, the use of ensemble learning methods, which combine the strengths of multiple models, has proven effective in increasing the reliability of identification processes.

Table 1. The most relevant algorithms used in both drones and anti-drone systems

Algo-rithm	Strengths	Weaknesses	Use Case	Performance Metrics
YOLO	Real-time detection, High accuracy, efficient for fast processing	Requires high computational power, not ideal for very small objects	Low-latency tracking of fast-moving drones	Detection accuracy: 95%, Latency: 30ms
Faster R-CNN	High accuracy, good for detecting small objects	Slower than YOLO for real-time applications, complex training process	High-precision detection of small drones	Detection accuracy: 98%, Latency: 200ms
SVM	Effective for binary classification and pattern recognition	Slower, less accurate for complex scenarios	Detection of stationary or slow-moving drones	Detection accuracy: 88%, Latency: 50ms
CNN	Strong feature extraction, effective in diverse environments	High computational cost, not real-time	Complex scenarios with high accuracy requirements	Detection accuracy: 92%, Latency: 45ms

Enhanced Multi-Target Tracking: AI has enabled the development of real-time multi-target tracking algorithms that can handle multiple airborne objects simultaneously. The incorporation of AI-driven models, such as those based on YOLOv7 with advanced attention mechanisms, ensures accurate tracking of drones' positions and movements in various environments. This capability is essential for maintaining situational awareness and coordinating effective countermeasures.

AI in Autonomous Drone Operations: AI advancements are also benefiting the development of autonomous drone technologies. Machine learning and reinforcement learning algorithms enable drones to perform complex tasks autonomously, such as navigating dynamic environments, avoiding obstacles, and executing coordinated maneuvers with other drones. These capabilities are essential for both civilian applications, such as delivery and surveillance, and military operations that require high levels of autonomy and reliability.

6 Conclusion and Perspectives

The integration of AI into anti-drone systems has revolutionized their capabilities, making them more efficient, accurate, and adaptable to the evolving threats posed by unauthorized UAVs. Recent advances in deep learning, computer vision, and multi-agent systems have enabled the development of sophisticated models for real-time detection, identification, and neutralization of airborne threats. As AI continues to evolve, its role in enhancing both drone and counter-drone technologies will expand, offering new solutions to ensure airspace security and public safety.

Future research will focus on refining AI models for greater accuracy and efficiency, exploring novel AI-driven countermeasure techniques, and developing more adaptive systems capable of responding to an ever-changing threat landscape. Additionally, integrating AI with emerging technologies such as Blockchain and quantum computing could offer new ways to enhance the security and reliability of anti-drone systems.

References

1. Ahirwar, S., Swarnkar, R., Bhukya, S., Namwade, G.: Application of drone in agriculture. Int. J. Curr. Microbiol. App. Sci. **8**(01), 2500–2505 (2019). https://doi.org/10.20546/ijcmas.2019.801.264
2. Kurkute, S.R.: Drones for smart agriculture: a technical report. IJRASET **6**(4), 341–346 (2018). https://doi.org/10.22214/ijraset.2018.4061
3. Spoorthi, S., Shadaksharappa, B., Suraj, S., Manasa, V.K.: Freyr drone: pesticide/fertilizers spraying drone - an agricultural approach. In: 2017 2nd International Conference on Computing and Communications Technologies (ICCCT), pp. 252–255, February 2017. https://doi.org/10.1109/ICCCT2.2017.7972289
4. Vangu, G.M.: The use of drones in mining operations. Min. Revue **28**(3), 73–82 (2022). https://doi.org/10.2478/minrv-2022-0023
5. Wankmüller, C., Kunovjanek, M., Mayrgündter, S.: Drones in emergency response – evidence from cross-border, multi-disciplinary usability tests. Int. J. Disaster Risk Reduct. **65**, 102567 (2021). https://doi.org/10.1016/j.ijdrr.2021.102567
6. Karaca, Y., et al.: The potential use of unmanned aircraft systems (drones) in mountain search and rescue operations. Am. J. Emerg. Med. **36**(4), 583–588 (2018). https://doi.org/10.1016/j.ajem.2017.09.025
7. Mayer, S., Lischke, L., Woźniak, P.W.: Drones for search and rescue. In: 1st International Workshop on Human-Drone Interaction, Glasgow, United Kingdom: Ecole Nationale de l'Aviation Civile [ENAC], May 2019. https://hal.science/hal-02128385. Accessed 01 Nov 2023
8. Yasmine, G., Maha, G., Hicham, M.: Survey on current anti-drone systems: process, technologies, and algorithms. Int. J. Syst. Syst. Eng. **12**(3), 235–270 (2022). https://doi.org/10.1504/IJSSE.2022.125947
9. Yasmine, G., Maha, G., Alaoui, A.E.H.: Anti-drone systems: Current intelligent countermeasures from low to high risks. In: 2023 7th IEEE Congress on Information Science and Technology (CiSt), pp. 317–322, December 2023. https://doi.org/10.1109/CiSt56084.2023.10409938
10. Hua, J., Zeng, L., Li, G., Ju, Z.: Learning for a robot: deep reinforcement learning, imitation learning, transfer learning. Sensors **21**(4), Art. no. 4 (2021). https://doi.org/10.3390/s21041278
11. Ahn, H., Choi, H.-L., Kang, M., Moon, S.: Learning-based anomaly detection and monitoring for swarm drone flights. Appl. Sci. **9**(24), 5477 (2019). https://doi.org/10.3390/app9245477
12. Spanaki, K., Karafili, E., Sivarajah, U., Despoudi, S., Irani, Z.: Artificial intelligence and food security: swarm intelligence of AgriTech drones for smart AgriFood operations. Prod. Plann. Control 1–19 (2021). https://doi.org/10.1080/09537287.2021.1882688

13. Ghazlane, Y., Gmira, M., Medromi, H.: Development of a vision- based anti-drone identification friend or foe model to recognize birds and drones using deep learning. Appl. Artif. Intell. https://doi.org/10.1080/08839514.2024.2318672
14. Yasmine, G., Maha, G., Hicham, M.: Anti-drone systems: an attention based improved YOLOv7 model for a real-time detection and identification of multi-airborne target. Intell. Syst. Appl. **20**, 200296 (2023). https://doi.org/10.1016/j.iswa.2023.200296
15. Beaudoin, L., Gademer, A., Avanthey, L., Germain, V., Vittori, V.: Potential Threats of UAS Swarms and the Countermeasure's Need, p. 8
16. Çetin, E., Barrado, C., Pastor, E.: Improving real-time drone detection for counter-drone systems. Aeronaut. J. **125**(1292), 1871–1896 (2021). https://doi.org/10.1017/aer.2021.43
17. Samadzadegan, F., Dadrass Javan, F., Ashtari Mahini, F., Gholamshahi, M.: Detection and recognition of drones based on a deep convolutional neural network using visible imagery. Aerospace **9**(1), 31 (2022). https://doi.org/10.3390/aerospace9010031
18. Al-Sa'd, M., Al-Ali, A., Mohamed, A., Khattab, T., Erbad, A.: RF-based drone detection and identification using deep learning approaches: an initiative towards a large open source drone database. Futur. Gener. Comput. Syst. **100** (2019). https://doi.org/10.1016/j.future.2019.05.007
19. Harmanny, R.I.A., de Wit, J.J.M., Premel-Cabic, G.: Radar micro-Doppler mini-UAV classification using spectrograms and cepstrograms. Int. J. Microw. Wirel. Technol. **7**(3–4), 469–477 (2015). https://doi.org/10.1017/S1759078715001002
20. Lonstein, W.D.: Chapter 12: C-UAS Regulation, Legislation, & Litigation from a Global Perspective. In: Counter Unmanned Aircraft Systems Technologies and Operations, R. K Nichols, 2020. https://kstatelibraries.pressbooks.pub/counterunmannedaircraft/chapter/chapter-12-global-perspective-whats-legal-where-trends-gaps-covers-discuss-chinese-iranian-and-russian-c-uas-lonstein/. Accessed 12 May 2021
21. Yasmine, G., Ahmed, E.H.A., Hicham, M.: Real-time lightweight drone detection model: fine-grained Identification of four types of drones based on an improved Yolov7 model. Neurocomputing 127941 (2024). https://doi.org/10.1016/j.neucom.2024.127941

AI for Smart Urban Development and Sustainability

AI-Powered Predictions Transforming the Future of Brand Management

Omar Zioudi[1(✉)], Hasna Mahmoud[1], Mohamed Badouch[1], Es-said Boulmane[1], and Mehdi Boutaounte[2]

[1] Faculty of Sciences, Ibn Zohr University, Agadir, Morocco
o.zaioudi@uiz.ac.ma

[2] National School of Commerce and Management, Ibn Zohr University, Dakhla, Morocco

Abstract. This paper explores the transformative potential of recommender systems for predictive analytics in brand management, emphasizing the crucial role of data-driven insights in shaping strategic decisions and driving sustainable growth. We analyze how AI-powered recommender systems can be leveraged to forecast consumer demand, identify emerging market trends, and proactively opportunities in a dynamic business environment. We will delve into the mathematical underpinnings of predictive analytics, exploring time series modeling and machine learning algorithms used in recommender systems. We will also discuss the role of big data and data visualization in informing strategic brand decisions, showcasing how these techniques can reveal hidden patterns, identify customer segments, and optimize resource allocation. Finally, this article will address the ethical considerations of predictive analytics, examining the potential for algorithmic bias and the erosion of consumer trust, and proposing strategies for ensuring fairness and accountability in AI-driven brand management.

Keywords: Recommender systems · Predictive analytics · Data-driven decision making · Market forecasting · Big data · Data visualization · Time series modeling · Regression analysis · Ethical considerations

1 Introduction

The contemporary landscape of brand management is irrevocably intertwined with the digital age, a realm characterized by an unprecedented deluge of data. This data, a rich tapestry woven from consumer interactions, online behavior, and market fluctuations [1], offers a treasure trove of insights for brands seeking to understand and anticipate consumer preferences. However, this data-driven landscape presents a unique challenge: how to navigate the intricate complexities of this information deluge and leverage it to inform strategic decision-making. Enter the recommender system, a powerful tool for predictive analytics that can illuminate the future of brand performance and propel growth in a dynamic and ever-changing market. This chapter delves into the intricate relationship between predictive analytics and strategic brand management [2], highlighting the profound impact of recommender systems on the trajectory of brands in the

I. Aboudrar et al. (Eds.): ICESST 2024, SUCI, pp. 177–186, 2025.
https://doi.org/10.1007/978-3-031-86705-7_17

digital age. We examine how these systems, powered by the cutting-edge algorithms of machine learning and artificial intelligence [3], can decipher the hidden patterns within vast datasets, enabling brands to forecast consumer demand with unprecedented accuracy, identify emerging market trends, and proactively manage risks and opportunities for growth.

The era of data-driven decision-making is upon us, and recommender systems [4] are at the forefront of this revolution. They enable brands to move beyond reactive strategies, embracing a proactive approach to shaping their destinies in the face of continuous disruption. This chapter will explore the mathematical underpinnings of predictive analytics, the algorithmic techniques employed in recommender systems, and the ethical considerations surrounding the use of these powerful tools. We will examine the potential for algorithmic bias, data privacy violations, and the erosion of consumer trust, and propose strategies for ensuring fairness, transparency, and accountability in AI-driven brand management. This exploration will provide a comprehensive understanding of how recommender systems are transforming brand management, paving the way for a more informed and sustainable future in the dynamic digital landscape.

2 The Data Deluge and the Rise of Predictive Analytics

The digital age has ushered in a new era of data abundance, with businesses collecting vast amounts of information on consumer behavior, online activity, and market trends [5]. This data deluge, characterized by an exponential growth in the volume, variety, and velocity of data, presents a unique challenge and opportunity for brands. Consider the sheer scale of data being generated daily:

- Online Shopping: Globally, e-commerce sales reached 4.2 trillion dollars in 2021, with billions of transactions and customer interactions generating a vast amount of data on purchase history, product preferences, and browsing behavior (Statista.com). This data can be analyzed by recommender systems to provide personalized recommendations, predict future purchases, and optimize marketing campaigns [5].
- Social media: Platforms like Facebook, Instagram, and Twitter generate an unimaginable amount of user-generated content, including text, images, videos, and interactions [6]. This data, rich with insights into consumer sentiment, cultural trends, and online behavior, can be analyzed by AI algorithms to identify emerging trends, understand audience preferences, and tailor marketing messages. For example, Natural Language Processing (NLP) algorithms can analyze social media posts to identify key topics, understand customer sentiment, and track the effectiveness of brand campaigns [7].
- Mobile Devices: The proliferation of smartphones and mobile devices has further accelerated the generation of massive amounts of data. This data encompasses location data, app usage patterns, and online searches, providing valuable insights into consumer behavior and preferences [8]. Recommender systems can leverage this data to offer personalized location-based recommendations, suggest relevant apps, and tailor online experiences.

This data deluge is not merely a collection of numbers; it is a complex and dynamic system that can be analyzed to uncover hidden patterns and predict future outcomes. The challenge lies in harnessing this data richness to extract valuable insights and inform strategic brand decisions. Recommender systems, with their sophisticated algorithms and machine learning capabilities, are playing a crucial role in this data-driven revolution.

Beyond the "Why" to the "What If": Recommender systems are not simply tools for suggesting products or content; they are powerful engines of prediction, capable of revealing the unseen forces shaping consumer behavior and market dynamics [9]. By going beyond simple descriptive analytics and exploring causal relationships within data, these systems can provide valuable insights into the future of brand performance, enabling brands to anticipate trends, manage risks, and capitalize on opportunities with greater precision. This shift from descriptive to predictive analytics allows brands to make more informed strategic decisions, optimize resources, and proactively adapt to the ever-changing demands of the marketplace.

- A retail store: Could use time series analysis to analyze historical sales data for a specific product category, identifying seasonal patterns, day-of-week trends, and the impact of marketing campaigns [10]. This analysis can help them optimize stock levels, plan promotions, and anticipate demand for different product lines.
- A social media platform: Could utilize machine learning algorithms to analyze user engagement data, identifying users with similar preferences and behaviors. This information can then be used to personalize content recommendations, create targeted advertising campaigns, and improve user experience.
- A financial institution: Could use predictive modeling to forecast customer churn and identify potential risks of fraud. By analyzing customer behavior, transaction history, and demographic data, the institution can develop models that predict the likelihood of customers leaving and identify suspicious activity [10]. This information can be used to implement targeted retention strategies and proactively prevent fraud.

3 The Mathematical Foundations of Predictive Analytics

Predictive analytics relies on a foundation of mathematical modeling and statistical analysis. Recommender systems employ various techniques to forecast consumer behavior and identify market trends. These techniques often involve:

- Time Series Modeling: This approach analyzes historical data points over time to identify patterns and predict future values. Recommender systems can utilize time series analysis to forecast consumer demand, predict seasonal fluctuations, and optimize inventory management. For instance, a brand might use a moving average model to predict future sales based on historical data, or a ARIMA model (Autoregressive Integrated Moving Average) to incorporate trends and seasonality [10, 24] (Fig. 1).

- Regression Analysis: This statistical technique models the relationship between a dependent variable (e.g., sales, customer engagement) and one or more independent variables (e.g., marketing spend, product features, seasonal factors). Recommender systems [11] can use regression analysis to predict future customer behavior based on various factors. For example, a brand might use linear regression to model the relationship between advertising expenditure and sales [12], or multiple regression to incorporate multiple predictors, such as price, promotions, and competitor activity.

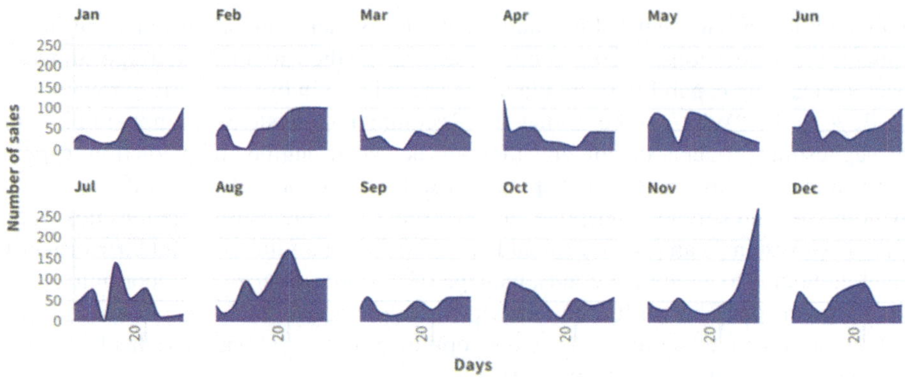

Fig. 1. Example of Time Series Plot of Daily Sales Data for a Brand's Product.

A wide range of machine learning algorithms are employed in recommender systems to analyze complex data patterns and make predictions [13]. These algorithms often involve supervised learning, where the model is trained on labeled data, and unsupervised learning, where the model discovers patterns in unlabeled data. Popular machine learning algorithms used in recommender systems include:

- Random Forest: This ensemble learning method combines multiple decision trees to improve prediction accuracy and reduce overfitting [14].
- Gradient Boosting: This technique builds a sequence of weak learners (e.g., decision trees) that are combined to create a strong predictive model [11].
- Neural Networks: These algorithms are inspired by the structure of the human brain, allowing them to learn complex patterns and relationships in data [15]. Neural networks are increasingly used in recommender systems for tasks such as predicting customer churn, identifying fraudulent activity, and recommending products.
- Bayesian Networks: These graphical models represent probabilistic relationships between variables, allowing for the prediction of future events based on uncertain or incomplete data [16]. Bayesian networks are particularly useful for situations where there is uncertainty or variability in the data.
- Markov Chains: These stochastic processes model sequences of events, allowing for the prediction of future states based on current conditions. Markov chains can be used to model customer behavior and predict future purchases [17] (Fig. 2).

4 Data-Driven Insights: Unveiling the Power of Big Data

The success of predictive analytics in brand management hinges on the ability to effectively analyze and interpret vast amounts of data. Big data, with its unprecedented volume, variety, and velocity, offers a wealth of insights into consumer behavior, market trends, and the potential for brand growth [18]. However, raw data can be overwhelming and difficult to comprehend. This is where data visualization tools come into play,

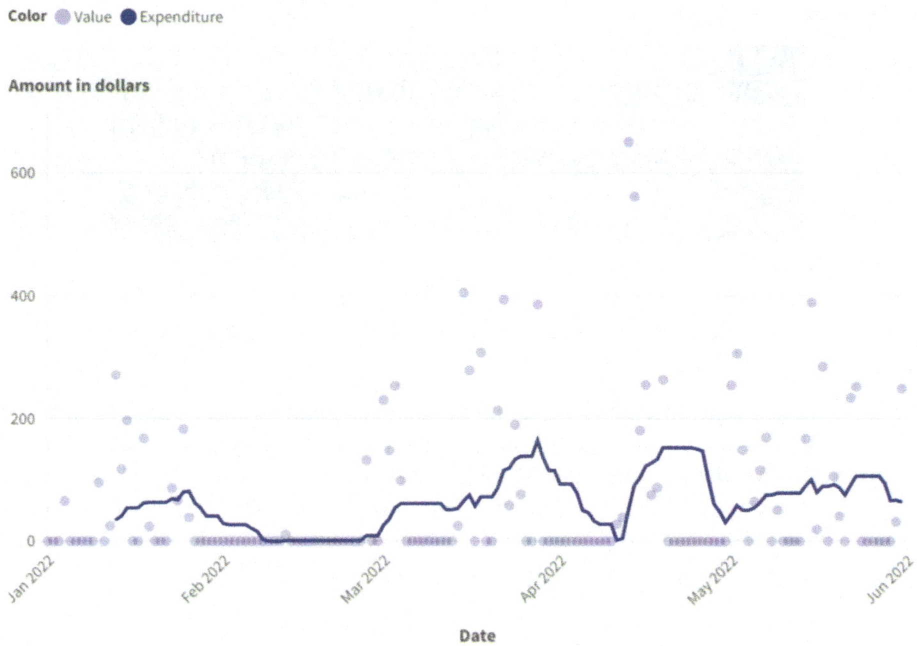

Fig. 2. Scatter Plot of Advertising Expenditure vs. Sales for a Brand.

providing a crucial bridge between the complex data and actionable insights. By transforming data into visual representations, brands can uncover hidden patterns, identify key trends, and make more informed strategic decisions.

4.1 Visualizing Consumer Behavior and Market Dynamics

Data visualization techniques can be used to represent complex data in ways that are easily understood and interpreted. Here are some examples of how data visualization can be employed in brand management:

- **Customer Segmentation:** Heat maps can be used to visualize customer segments based on their purchase history and online behavior. By analyzing data on demographics, purchase frequency, and product preferences, brands can identify distinct groups of customers and tailor their strategies accordingly [19] (Fig. 3).

This heat map illustrates the population distribution by age group in five different Moroccan cities: Agadir, Casablanca, Rabat, Marrakech, Tangier, and Dakhla. It uses color-coded bars to represent the proportion of the population in each city that falls within different age ranges. Brands can use this visualization to identify key customer segments, understand their unique needs, and personalize their marketing messages.

- **Sentiment Analysis and Market Trends:** Trend line graphs can be used to visualize the correlation between social media sentiment and sales performance over time [20].

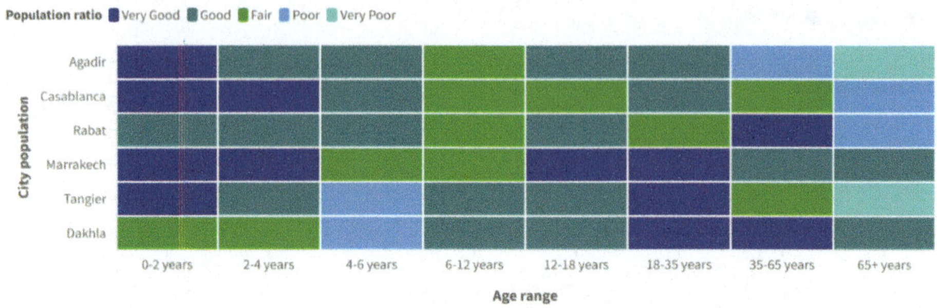

Fig. 3. A Heat Map Visualizing Population Segmentation

By analyzing customer reviews, social media posts, and online forums, brands can track changes in consumer sentiment and identify potential risks or opportunities.

- **Predictive Modeling and Risk Management:** Data visualizations can be used to display the output of predictive models and visualize the factors that contribute to predictions. This can help brands understand the underlying drivers of customer behavior and manage risks more effectively (Fig. 4).

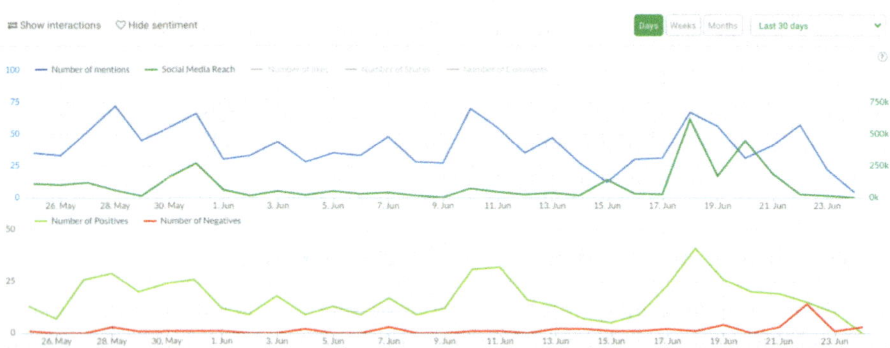

Fig. 4. A Trend Line Graph Illustrating Correlation Between Social Media Sentiment and Interactions

This graph shows how social media sentiment (measured by the frequency of positive and negative mentions) correlates with interactions (potential sales) performance over time. By analyzing this data, brands can identify trends, understand the impact of marketing campaigns, and proactively address potential challenges.

Figure 5 provides a visual representation of the customer journey through a sales funnel, illustrating the flow of potential customers from awareness to purchase. By highlighting areas where customers drop off, it pinpoints bottlenecks and identifies factors contributing to customer acquisition. This visualization enables businesses to analyze their sales funnel, optimize marketing campaigns, and improve conversion rates by understanding customer behavior and identifying areas for improvement, such as a poor user experience, ineffective content, or pricing issues. The diagram's visual clarity

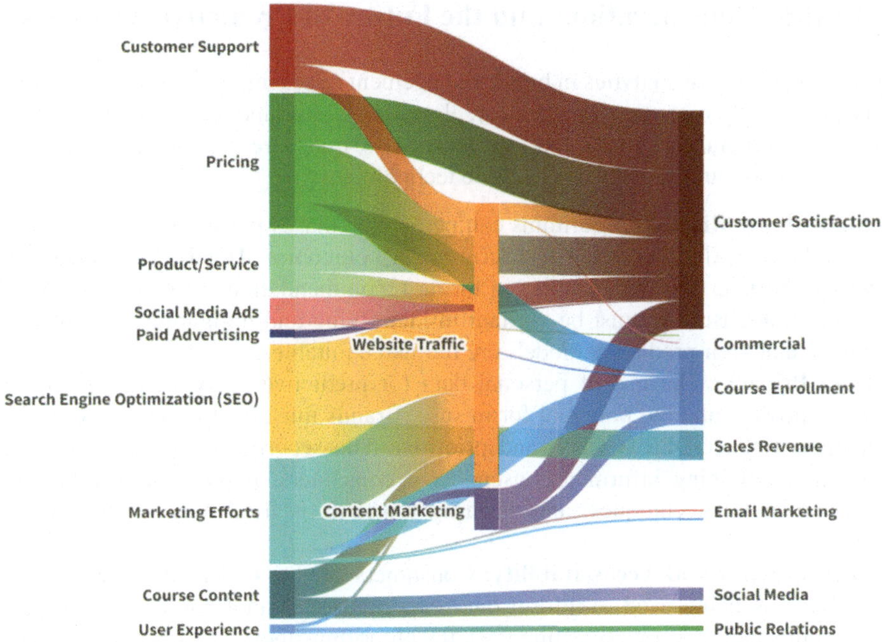

Fig. 5. A Sankey Diagram Showing the Flow of Customers Through the Sales Funnel

facilitates data-driven decision-making [23, 26], leading to continuous improvement in the sales funnel and ultimately, increased customer acquisition.

4.2 The Importance of Data Visualization in Brand Management

Data visualization plays a crucial role in making sense of the data deluge and informing strategic decisions. By presenting complex information in a clear and accessible manner, visualization tools enable brands to:

- **Gain Deeper Insights:** Visualizations help to identify patterns, trends, and outliers that might not be apparent in raw data. This allows brands to understand the underlying dynamics of consumer behavior and market trends [25].
- **Improve Communication and Collaboration:** Visualizations facilitate effective communication of insights across teams and departments, enabling stakeholders to understand and interpret complex data in a shared and collaborative manner.
- **Drive Actionable Decisions** [21]: By providing a clear and concise view of data, visualization tools support informed decision-making and guide strategic initiatives. Brands can use visualizations to prioritize investments, optimize resource allocation, and develop effective marketing campaigns.
- **Enhance Trust and Transparency:** By showcasing data in a transparent and accessible manner, brands can build trust with their customers and stakeholders. Visualizations can help to communicate complex information in a way that is both informative and engaging

5 Ethical Considerations and the Future of Predictive Analytics

The use of predictive analytics in brand management raises important ethical considerations, particularly regarding data privacy, algorithmic bias, and the potential for manipulation. It is crucial for brands to prioritize fairness, transparency, and accountability in the development and deployment of these technologies:

- **Algorithmic Bias:** AI algorithms can perpetuate biases present in the data used to train them, leading to unfair or discriminatory outcomes. This bias can manifest in various forms, from gender bias in hiring recommendations to racial bias in loan applications. Brands must be vigilant in identifying and mitigating these biases to ensure that their predictive models are fair and equitable.
- **Data Privacy:** The use of personal data for predictive analytics raises concerns about privacy and the potential for misuse. Brands must comply with relevant regulations (e.g., GDPR, CCPA) and prioritize data security and privacy [22]. This includes obtaining informed consent from consumers, implementing robust data anonymization techniques, and ensuring that data is used only for the intended purpose.
- **Transparency and Accountability:** Consumers need to understand how predictive analytics is being used to inform their experiences. Brands should be transparent about the data they are collecting [23], the algorithms they are using, and the potential implications of these technologies. This transparency can help build trust with customers and mitigate concerns about manipulation

6 Conclusion

Predictive analytics is a powerful tool for brand management that can help businesses anticipate market trends [25], identify opportunities, and drive sustainable growth. By leveraging the mathematical foundations of these technologies and analyzing big data, brands can gain a deeper understanding of consumer behavior [25] and make informed decisions that will lead to greater success in the competitive landscape. However, it is essential to address the ethical considerations of predictive analytics, ensure fairness and transparency, and prioritize the protection of consumer privacy and trust. By embracing a responsible and ethical approach to predictive analytics, brands can harness the power of data and unlock new possibilities for growth in the age of AI.

References

1. Zuo, M., Liu, H., Zhu, H., Gao, H.: Dynamic property of consumer-based brand competitiveness (CBBC) in human interaction behavior. Ind. Manag. Data Syst. **119**(6), 1223–1241 (2019)
2. Elliott, R.H., Rosenbaum-Elliott, R., Percy, L., Pervan, S.: Strategic Brand Management. Oxford University Press, USA (2015)
3. Bansal, M., Goyal, A., Choudhary, A.: A comparative analysis of K-nearest neighbor, genetic, support vector machine, decision tree, and long short term memory algorithms in machine learning. Decis. Anal. J. **3**, 100071 (2022)

4. Badouch, M., Boutaounte, M.: Smart E-commerce recommendations with semantic AI. Fusion Pract. Appl. **17**(1), 264–271 (2025)
5. Rosário, A., Raimundo, R.: Consumer marketing strategy and E-commerce in the last decade: a literature review. J. Theor. Appl. Electron. Commer. Res. **16**(7), 3003–3024 (2021)
6. Chawla, Y., Chodak, G.: Social media marketing for businesses: organic promotions of web-links on Facebook. J. Bus. Res. **135**, 49–65 (2021)
7. Hodorog, A., Petri, I., Rezgui, Y.: Machine learning and natural language processing of social media data for event detection in smart cities. Sustain. Cities Soc. **85**, 104026 (2022)
8. Stachl, C., et al.: Predicting personality from patterns of behavior collected with smartphones. Proc. Natl. Acad. Sci. **117**(30), 17680–17687 (2020)
9. Roberts, C.V., Elahi, E., Chandrashekar, A.: On the bias-variance characteristics of lime and shap in high sparsity movie recommendation explanation tasks. arXiv preprint arXiv:2206.04784 (2022)
10. Bellini, P., Palesi, L.A.I., Nesi, P., Pantaleo, G.: Multi clustering recommendation system for fashion retail. Multimed. Tools Appl. **82**(7), 9989–10016 (2023)
11. Singh, P.K., Pramanik, P.K.D., Dey, A.K., Choudhury, P.: Recommender systems: an overview, research trends, and future directions. Int. J. Bus. Syst. Res. **15**(1), 14–52 (2021)
12. Atulkar, S.: Brand trust and brand loyalty in mall shoppers. Mark. Intell. Plan. **38**(5), 559–572 (2020)
13. Badouch, M., Boutaounte, M.: Design and implementation of a hotel recommendation system using deep learning. In: AI and Data Engineering Solutions for Effective Marketing, pp. 388–408. IGI Global (2024)
14. Palimkar, P., Shaw, R.N., Ghosh, A.: Machine learning technique to prognosis diabetes disease: Random forest classifier approach. In: Advanced computing and intelligent technologies: proceedings of ICACIT 2021, pp. 219–244. Springer, Singapore (2022)
15. Gao, H., Chen, C., Li, S., Wang, C., Zhou, W., Yu, B.: Prediction of protein-protein interactions based on ensemble residual convolutional neural network. Comput. Biol. Med. **152**, 106471 (2023)
16. Kirubahari, R., Amali, S.M.J.: An improved restricted Boltzmann machine using Bayesian optimization for recommender systems. Evol. Syst. **15**(3), 1099–1111 (2024)
17. Wang, H., Li, Y., Jin, D., Han, Z.: Attentional Markov model for human mobility prediction. IEEE J. Sel. Areas Commun. **39**(7), 2213–2225 (2021)
18. Perera, A., Iqbal, K.: Big data and emerging markets: transforming economies through data-driven innovation and market dynamics. J. Comput. Soc. Dyn. **6**(3), 1–18 (2021)
19. Alves Gomes, M., Meisen, T.: A review on customer segmentation methods for personalized customer targeting in e-commerce use cases. Inf. Syst. e-Bus. Manag. **21**(3), 527–570 (2023)
20. Xu, Q.A., Chang, V., Jayne, C.: A systematic review of social media-based sentiment analysis: emerging trends and challenges. Decis. Ana. J. **3**, 100073 (2022)
21. Pearman, O., Cravens, A.E.: Institutional barriers to actionable science: perspectives from decision support tool creators. Environ Sci Policy **128**, 317–325 (2022)
22. Pantelic, O., Jovic, K., Krstovic, S.: Cookies implementation analysis and the impact on user privacy regarding GDPR and CCPA regulations. Sustainability **14**(9), 5015 (2022)
23. Krafft, M., et al.: Insight is power: Understanding the terms of the consumer-firm data exchange. J. Retail. **97**(1), 133–149 (2021)
24. Khan, S., Alghulaiakh, H.: ARIMA model for accurate time series stocks forecasting. Int. J. Adv. Comput. Sci. Appl. **11**(7) (2020)
25. Raji, M.A., Olodo, H.B., Oke, T.T., Addy, W.A., Ofodile, O.C., Oyewole, A.T.: E-commerce and consumer behavior: a review of AI-powered personalization and market trends. GSC Adv. Res. Rev. **18**(3), 066–077 (2024)

26. Aridor, G., Goncalves, D., Sikdar, S.: Deconstructing the filter bubble: user decision-making and recommender systems. In: Proceedings of the 14th ACM Conference on Recommender Systems, pp. 82–91 (2020)

Smart Tourism: How AI is Reimagining the Travel Experience

Mohamed Badouch[1(✉)], Es-said Boulmane[1], Hasna Mahmoud[1], Omar Zioudi[1], and Mehdi Boutaounte[2]

[1] Faculty of Sciences, Ibn Zohr University, Agadir, Morocco
mohamed.badouch@edu.uiz.ac.ma
[2] School National of Commerce and Management, Ibn Zohr University, Dakhla, Morocco

Abstract. The tourism industry is undergoing a transformative shift through the integration of artificial intelligence (AI) and applied life sciences. This paper explores AI's multifaceted applications, from personalized travel planning and AI-powered chatbots to optimizing resource management and promoting sustainability. AI-driven predictive analytics forecast tourist demand, while AR/VR enhances the travel experience. Additionally, AI facilitates environmental monitoring and promotes traveler well-being. However, ethical considerations regarding data privacy and responsible AI development are crucial. This article examines the potential of AI to revolutionize tourism, fostering a future where travel is personalized, sustainable, and ethically sound.

Keywords: Artificial Intelligence · Tourism · Personalized itineraries · AI-powered chatbots · Virtual assistants · Augmented Reality · Virtual Reality

1 Introduction

The tourism industry, a vibrant force in global economies and a catalyst for cultural exchange, is undergoing a dramatic transformation fueled by the rapid advancements in artificial intelligence (AI). This technological revolution, often referred to as "smart tourism," is not merely a trend; it's a fundamental shift redefining how we travel, experience destinations, and interact with the tourism ecosystem [18]. AI-powered systems are poised to revolutionize the industry, offering personalized experiences, optimized resource allocation, and a deeper understanding of traveler needs, ultimately fostering a more responsible and impactful tourism sector. This transformation promises to enhance the traveler experience, improve efficiency, and contribute to a more sustainable future for tourism. However, this technological advancement comes with a critical responsibility, demanding careful consideration of its potential drawbacks and ethical implications.

The integration of AI into tourism creates a complex landscape with numerous potential benefits. For example, AI-powered recommendation systems analyze vast amounts of data to provide personalized itineraries, suggesting attractions, activities, and accommodations tailored to individual preferences. Imagine a system that suggests a unique boutique hotel based on a traveler's interest in art and local culture, or a guided tour

I. Aboudrar et al. (Eds.): ICESST 2024, SUCI, pp. 187–198, 2025.
https://doi.org/10.1007/978-3-031-86705-7_18

that seamlessly integrates historical information with interactive experiences. Moreover, AI-powered chatbots can provide instant assistance with booking flights, handling reservations, and addressing inquiries, improving the overall traveler experience, and reducing stress [3]. These examples demonstrate the transformative potential of AI to personalize travel and enhance visitor satisfaction.

However, this technological advancement also raises crucial questions about data privacy, algorithmic biases, and the potential for unintended consequences. The collection and analysis of vast amounts of traveler data raise concerns about privacy and security, requiring robust safeguards to protect personal information. Furthermore, the algorithms driving these systems may perpetuate existing biases, leading to unfair or discriminatory recommendations [32].

Our analysis provides valuable insights for researchers, practitioners, and policymakers, guiding responsible innovation and shaping the future of AI in tourism [31]. The significance of this exploration lies in its potential to inform the development of ethical and sustainable AI-driven tourism solutions, fostering a more responsible and impactful tourism sector that benefits both travelers and destinations. By understanding the potential and challenges of AI in tourism, we can pave the way for a future where technology enhances the travel experience while promoting responsible and sustainable practices.

2 Enhancing Tourist Experiences Through AI-Powered Personalization

2.1 Personalized Itinerary Generation

The shift towards personalized travel planning is driven by the increasing use of AI algorithms that analyze vast datasets to understand individual traveler preferences and tailor travel plans accordingly [10]. These datasets encompass a variety of information, including:

1. Explicit Preferences:
   - "I want to experience a cultural immersion trip to Japan, focusing on traditional arts and cuisine." *(This is a clear preference articulated by a user.)*
   - "My budget for this trip is under $1000." *(This defines a constraint on the travel plan.)*
2. Implicit Preferences:
   - Booking History: A traveler who has repeatedly booked flights to European cities, stayed in historic hotels, and booked tours focused on art and culture suggests an interest in these types of experiences [21].
   - Accommodation History: If a user frequently selects hotels with swimming pools or has booked accommodations near beaches, this reveals a preference for relaxation and recreation.
3. Social Media Activity:

- "Exploring the beauty of Santorini." (A travel post indicating interest in picturesque landscapes.)
- "Loved the traditional cuisine in Marrakech!" (Expressing interest in local food and cultural experiences.)

To illustrate this process, consider the real-world applications of AI-driven personalization in popular travel platforms:

- **Expedia**: Utilizes machine learning algorithms to analyze user preferences and past travel behavior to recommend suitable destinations and activities. For instance, a traveler who frequently opts for budget-friendly accommodations and enjoys outdoor activities might be recommended hiking trails, national parks, or affordable camping options in their chosen destination. This data-driven approach helps create a more relevant and tailored travel plan (Fig. 1).

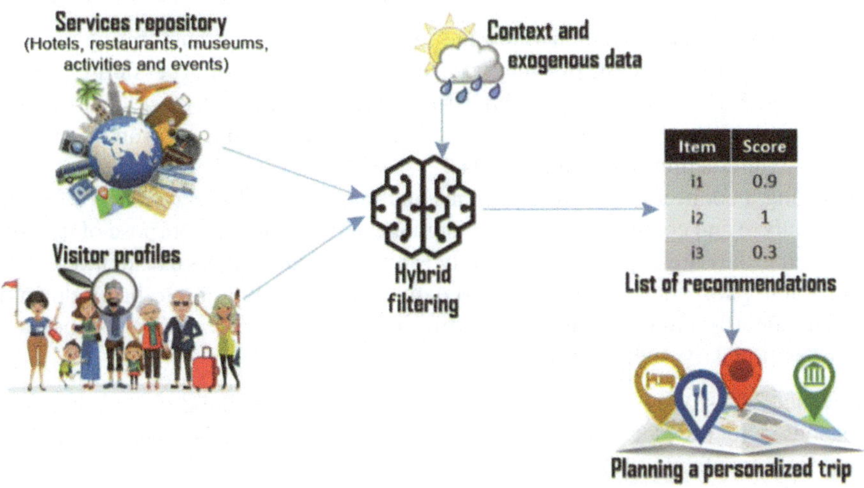

Fig. 1. Architecture for tourism recommender system

Dataset Description and Examples

AI-powered platforms are increasingly relying on vast and diverse datasets, often proprietary to the companies involved, to understand traveler preferences and predict their needs. This data, collected through user interactions, website activity, social media engagement, and even device location tracking, encompasses a wide range of information, including user demographics, travel history, preferences, and even browsing behavior on travel websites. Platforms like Expedia, for instance, might track user preferences for specific types of accommodations (hotels, vacation rentals, resorts), activities (sightseeing, dining, shopping), and destinations [28]. Let's delve deeper with some real-world examples:

- Personalized Recommendations: Imagine booking a flight on a platform like Kayak or Skyscanner. The platform, utilizing your past travel history and preferences, might

suggest flights that align with your budget, preferred airlines, and travel times. This might include showcasing flights with shorter layovers, direct flights, or even highlighting airlines with known amenities that match your preferences.
- Location-based Recommendations [26]: Imagine using a travel app like Google Maps or Tripadvisor to find local restaurants or attractions. These apps, utilizing your location data, might recommend restaurants based on your proximity, past reviews, and even your dietary restrictions. While this can be convenient, it raises concerns about the potential for location tracking to be used for more invasive purposes.

These examples illustrate the potential benefits and challenges associated with AI-driven personalization in tourism. While AI can offer tailored experiences, it's crucial to ensure that data is collected and utilized ethically, with transparency and user control, to avoid potential biases and unintended consequences.

2.2 AI-Powered Chatbots & Virtual Assistants for Enhanced Communication

The application of AI-driven chatbots and virtual assistants is transforming communication in the tourism sector, offering travelers a higher level of accessibility and convenience. NLP algorithms are essential for the functionality of these smart systems, allowing them to comprehend and address various user inquiries, promoting a more human-like interaction with travelers [24].

Creating a connection between humans and machines: NLP algorithms allow chatbots to analyze and comprehend human language, recognizing the purpose of user questions, even if they are expressed differently [33]. These algorithms use methods such as tokenization, part-of-speech tagging, and named entity recognition to break down user input and identify important details. AI-driven chatbots provide numerous benefits for the tourism industry, such as:

- Enhanced Customer Service: Chatbots provide 24/7 availability, offering instant responses to traveler queries and resolving issues promptly, thereby improving customer satisfaction [2].
- Streamlined Booking Assistance: Chatbots can guide users through the booking process, providing information about available options, managing reservations, and handling cancellations, leading to increased efficiency and a smoother booking experience.

Various leading tourism companies have effectively incorporated AI-driven chatbots into their businesses. KLM Royal Dutch Airlines utilizes a chatbot called "BB" to communicate with passengers and assist them with flight reservations, luggage details, and travel questions [6]. Marriott International uses "Ask Marriott," a chatbot created to respond to guest inquiries, offer hotel details, and assist with booking requests. These demonstrations display the real-world advantages of chatbots powered by AI in enhancing communication and enhancing the travel experience for travelers.

2.3 Immersive Experiences Through AR/VR

The convergence of artificial intelligence (AI), augmented reality (AR), and virtual reality (VR) is not just reshaping travel, it's revolutionizing the very way we perceive and interact with the world [30]. This essay delves into the scientific keys and cutting-edge technologies driving this transformation, exploring how algorithms, computer vision, and immersive experiences are poised to redefine the future of travel [41].

Virtual reality, on the other hand, takes immersion to a whole new level, transporting us to entirely simulated environments. Imagine "walking" through the ancient city of Pompeii, experiencing the bustling streets, shops, and homes as if you were transported back in time. This is made possible through algorithms that generate 3D models [12] of environments, often using techniques like Structure from Motion (SfM) and Multi-View Stereo (MVS) [8].

The convergence of AI, AR, and VR represents a paradigm shift in travel, offering unprecedented opportunities for exploration, understanding, and connection [13]. As these technologies continue to evolve, they promise to redefine our relationship with the world, creating a more informed, accessible, and immersive travel experience (Fig. 2).

Fig. 2. The different parts in an intelligent tourist recommendation system

3 Optimizing Resources and Fostering Sustainability Through AI

3.1 Predictive Analytics for Forecasting Tourist Demand

Predictive analytics plays a pivotal role in optimizing tourism operations, enabling destinations and businesses to anticipate demand, allocate resources effectively, and enhance visitor experiences [26]. By analyzing historical data and identifying patterns, AI algorithms can forecast future tourist arrivals, allowing for proactive planning and resource management. The development and deployment of AI-driven predictive analytics systems in tourism necessitates a robust technological infrastructure. This typically involves the following:

- Statistical Computing Software: Python Programming [40] environments provide the foundation for data analysis [7], model building, and algorithm implementation. This platform is equipped with libraries for time series analysis, regression modeling, and machine learning, enabling the construction of sophisticated predictive models.
- Cloud Computing Platforms [39]: Cloud computing services (AWS) offer scalable resources and storage solutions to handle large datasets and complex algorithms. These platforms allow for the deployment of AI models for real-time prediction and analysis, facilitating data processing and model execution at scale.
- Specialized Forecasting Software: "Prophet" (developed by Facebook) provide advanced time series forecasting capabilities, adept at incorporating seasonality and trends in the data. This specialized software is well-suited for tourism forecasting, effectively capturing the cyclical nature of tourist arrivals and incorporating key factors like weather, economic conditions, and events [23].

Predictive Models:

- Time Series Analysis: The Autoregressive Integrated Moving Average (ARIMA) model effectively captures the time-dependent patterns in tourist arrivals [4]. The Prophet model, developed by Facebook, provides a user-friendly solution for forecasting time series data, handling seasonality and trends.
- Regression Models: Linear regression and support vector regression models can be used to establish relationships between tourist demand and various influential variables [5].

Real-World Applications:

- Staffing Optimization: Predictive analytics helps businesses like hotels, restaurants, and attractions optimize staffing levels by accurately forecasting demand [14].
- Transportation Management: Predictive analytics enables the optimization of transportation services by anticipating and responding to anticipated demand. For instance, transportation authorities can adjust bus routes, frequency [22], and capacity based on forecasted tourism dynamics, improving efficiency, reducing congestion, and ensuring sufficient transportation capacity for travelers.
- Infrastructure Development: Long-term projections derived from predictive analytics assist in planning and developing infrastructure to meet future tourism demand [25]. By analyzing historical data and trends, destinations can anticipate future growth and implement infrastructure development strategies for accommodation, transportation, and waste management.

3.2 AI-Driven Crowd Management for Smoother Experiences

AI-driven crowd management systems offer a powerful solution to optimize infrastructure and enhance the overall visitor experience by leveraging real-time data and predictive analytics. These systems employ computer vision algorithms, often powered by Convolutional Neural Networks (CNNs), to analyze data from CCTV cameras and other sensor networks, estimating crowd density, movement patterns, and identifying potential congestion hotspots [29]. Additionally, IoT sensors deployed throughout a destination capture data on pedestrian traffic, environmental conditions, and other relevant factors, providing a comprehensive view of crowd behavior and infrastructure utilization [16]. Social media analytics, utilizing Natural Language Processing (NLP) techniques [37], further contribute by gauging crowd sentiment and identifying emerging issues from real-time social media posts and comments [9].

By analyzing historical data and integrating real-time sensor data, AI models can predict crowd behavior and potential congestion points. Techniques like agent-based modeling simulate individual tourist behavior within a virtual environment to anticipate crowd flow and identify potential bottlenecks. Kalman filtering algorithms track and predict the movement of individuals or groups, providing real-time estimates of crowd density and movement patterns [17].

AI-driven wayfinding systems are revolutionizing the tourist experience by providing dynamic and personalized guidance to navigate crowded areas and optimize resource utilization. By leveraging sophisticated algorithms based on graph theory and network analysis [27], these systems offer alternative routes, real-time congestion information, personalized recommendations and effectively guiding travelers towards less-visited areas.

3.3 Environmental Practices Enabled by AI-Powered Sensors and Drones

It tries to explain the role of sensors and drones based on Artificial Intelligence in revolutionizing environmental stewardship in the tourism industry through higher-order information/decision-making processes relevant to sustainable tourism development. It is fitted with high-resolution cameras, multispectral sensors, LiDAR technology [1], and hyperspectral cameras, thus having the capability of acquiring highly detailed aerial imagery for information on the health and dynamics of large landscapes. On the other, it feeds AI algorithms, in particular deep learning models such as CNNs. It automatically detects feature objects within imagery. The semantic segmentation of land by CNNs [15] contributes to the analysis of changes in land cover and the detection of places under environmental stress.

Machine-learning-based predictive modeling methodologies applied to this rich dataset will be able to provide better forecasts regarding the potential environmental bottlenecks and inform effective implementation of prevention strategies, which improve resource allocation in waste management, water conservation, and energy efficiency [34]. The platform can relate tourist behaviors and appraisals to have interpretations regarding possible directions for sustainability efforts that could trigger more environmentally sensitive travel choices, commensurate with the growth of interest in sustainable tourism. In such a manner, the change will be three-dimensional—one that makes good use of the strategic policy initiatives designed with artificial intelligence insights, one that is actively engaged with stakeholders, and one that continues to further the environmental sustainability agenda of the tourism sector in the long run [35] (Fig. 3).

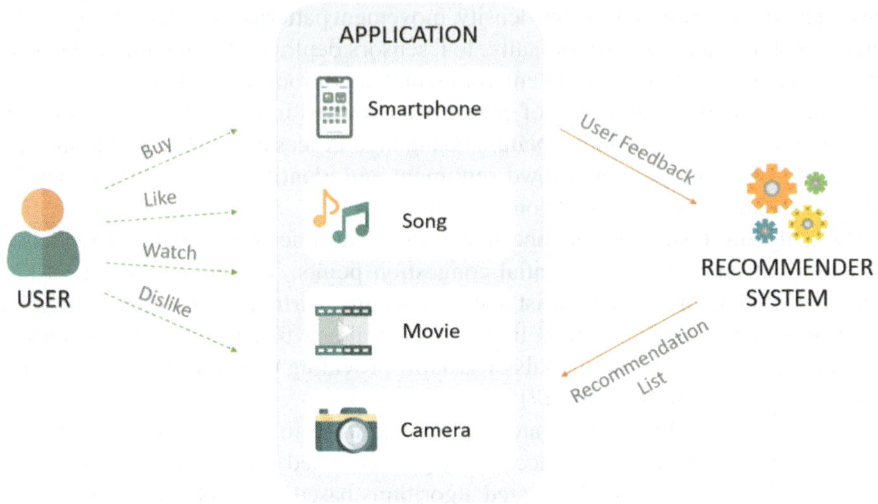

Fig. 3. The different data sources using sensors

4 Ethical Considerations and Shaping the Future of AI-Driven Tourism

4.1 Data Privacy in Tourism Platforms

AI-driven platforms often gather a wealth of personal data, including explicit and implicit preferences, travel history, and even online behavior. This information, if not handled responsibly, can expose individuals to privacy risks [36]. To mitigate these risks, a multi-faceted approach to data privacy is necessary:

- Data Minimization: Travel platforms should clearly define their data collection policies, specify the type of data collected, and minimize the amount of data stored.
- Strong Encryption: Data transmission and storage should be protected by robust encryption methods to prevent unauthorized access and data breaches. This requires the use of strong encryption algorithms.

Platforms like Booking.com and Expedia [42] use AI to generate customized travel itineraries. These platforms collect data on traveler preferences, booking history, and social media activity. They then use this data to provide personalized recommendations for accommodations, activities, and destinations.

Data privacy regulations like the General Data Protection Regulation (GDPR) play a crucial role in protecting user privacy in the tourism sector. These regulations establish a set of standards for the collection, use, and storage of personal data.

4.2 AI to Ensure Equitable Tourism Experiences

To combat the pitfalls of algorithmic bias and ensure fairness in AI-driven tourism, researchers and practitioners are exploring a range of innovative approaches:

- Fairness-Aware Machine Learning: This field of study investigates techniques for designing algorithms that are inherently fair and minimize the impact of bias. These methods can incorporate fairness constraints into the learning process, encouraging equitable outcomes by penalizing biases and promoting fairness across different demographics [11].
- Explainable AI (XAI) for Bias Detection: XAI tools provide insights into the decision-making processes behind AI algorithms, enabling a more transparent understanding of how biases may be influencing recommendations and other outputs. By analyzing the factors that influence the model's predictions [20], XAI helps to identify and address discriminatory practices.

4.3 Responsible AI Development

In any case, responsible AI development within the tourism sector needs to carry a wider set of ethical and social connotations regarding the use of such powerful tools. It is important to ensure that the techniques of model interpretability are being applied to the development and deployment processes of AI models so that transparency enables users to obtain insights into how AI-driven recommendations and services are made. Such a move would go a long way in ushering transparency and trust in the deal. Further, this confirms findings from Accenture, which pointed out that 83% of consumers opined organizations should be transparent concerning their use of AI. The process should have incorporated principles of human-centered design [38], wherein development mainly focused on addressing human needs and values and further should mitigate potential risks and biases, with techniques such as fairness-aware machine learning.

Strong ethics and regulations, directed by the FAIR framework in principles of fairness, accountability, and transparency, are meant to ensure that AI technologies have a positive contribution to the sustainability, inclusivity, and equity of different categories of stakeholders within the tourism industry [19]. Companies that focus on ethical AI development, including taking such drastic steps as federated learning to achieve privacy-centric data sharing, obviously gain trust from customers and stakeholders much better. In turn, long-term sustainability will have better reputations. An Edelman study concluded that 80% of its respondents agreed that companies have a responsibility to use technology ethically.

5 Conclusion

In conclusion, the future of AI-powered smart tourism rests on a commitment to responsible innovation. By prioritizing ethical considerations, embracing a human-centered approach, and fostering collaboration between researchers, practitioners, and policymakers, the tourism industry can unlock the full potential of AI to deliver a travel experience that is personalized, efficient, sustainable, and ethical. This paper underscores the importance of ongoing dialogue, research, and development to ensure that AI continues to enhance the journey, creating a more vibrant, inclusive, and sustainable tourism landscape for all. The future of travel, in its most impactful form, rests on embracing the power of AI while prioritizing ethical considerations and human values.

References

1. Roriz, R., Cabral, J., Gomes, T.: Automotive LiDAR technology: a survey. IEEE Trans. Intell. Transp. Syst. **23**, 6282–6297 (2021)
2. Ahmad, M., Naeem, M.K.H., Mobo, F.D., Tahir, M.W., Akram, M.: Navigating the journey: how chatbots are transforming tourism and hospitality. In: Design and Development of Emerging Chatbot Technology, pp. 236–255. IGI Global (2024)
3. Sharma, I., Aggarwal, A.: Revolutionizing creative tourism: integrating AI in marketing for immersive travel experiences. In: Manohar, S., Mittal, A., Raju, S., Nair, A. (eds.) Innovative Technologies for Increasing Service Productivity, pp. 179–197. IGI Global (2024)
4. Yao, L., Ma, R., Wang, H.: Baidu index-based forecast of daily tourist arrivals through rescaled range analysis, support vector regression, and autoregressive integrated moving average. Alex. Eng. J. **60**(1), 365–372 (2021)
5. Vanegas, J., Valencia, M., Restrepo, J., Muñeton, G.: Modeling determinants of tourism demand in Colombia. Tourism Hospitality Manag. **26**(1), 49–67 (2020)
6. Saroop Roy, B.R.: Information and communication technology application in the Asian tourism industry. In: Handbook of Technology Application in Tourism in Asia, pp. 19–48. Springer, Singapore (2022)
7. Emara, T.Z., Trinh, T., Huang, J.Z.: Geographically distributed data management to support large-scale data analysis. Sci. Rep. **13**(1), 17783 (2023)
8. Kholil, M., Ismanto, I., Fu'ad, M.N.: 3D reconstruction using structure from motion (SFM) algorithm and multi view stereo (MVS) based on computer vision. In: IOP Conference Series: Materials Science and Engineering, vol. 1073, no. 1, p. 012066. IOP Publishing (2021)
9. Saquete, E., Tomás, D., Moreda, P., Martínez-Barco, P., Palomar, M.: Fighting post-truth using natural language processing: a review and open challenges. Expert Syst. Appl. **141**, 112943 (2020)
10. Badouch, M., Boutaounte, M.: Design and implementation of a hotel recommendation system using deep learning. In: AI and Data Engineering Solutions for Effective Marketing, pp. 388–408. IGI Global (2024)
11. Le Quy, T., Roy, A., Iosifidis, V., Zhang, W., Ntoutsi, E.: A survey on datasets for fairness-aware machine learning. Wiley Interdisc. Rev. Data Min. Knowl. Discovery **12**(3), e1452 (2022)
12. Fitzgibbon, A., Zisserman, A.: Automatic 3D model acquisition and generation of new images from video sequences. In: 9th European Signal Processing Conference (EUSIPCO 1998), pp. 1–8. IEEE (1998)
13. Shukla, V., Rana, S., Prashar, S.: Examining the potential of virtual and augmented reality in enhancing tourism experiences. The Bottom Line (2024)
14. Richard, B.: Hotel chains: survival strategies for a dynamic future. J. Tourism Futures **3**(1), 56–65 (2017)
15. Hassan, E.: Enhancing coffee bean classification: a comparative analysis of pre-trained deep learning models. Neural Comput. Appl. **36**(16), 9023–9052 (2024)
16. Al-Nabhan, N., et al.: An intelligent IoT approach for analyzing and managing crowds. IEEE Access **9**, 104874–104886 (2021)
17. Li, B., Han, X., Wu, D.: Real-time crowd density estimation based on convolutional neural networks. In: 2018 International Conference on Intelligent Transportation, Big Data & Smart City (ICITBS), pp. 690–694. IEEE (2018)
18. Alsahafi, R., Alzahrani, A., Mehmood, R.: Smarter sustainable tourism: data-driven multi-perspective parameter discovery for autonomous design and operations. Sustainability **15**(5), 4166 (2023)

19. Dangi, T.B., Petrick, J.F.: Augmenting the role of tourism governance in addressing destination justice, ethics, and equity for sustainable community-based tourism. Tourism Hospitality **2**(1), 15–42 (2021)
20. Arrieta, A.B., et al.: Explainable Artificial Intelligence (XAI): concepts, taxonomies, opportunities and challenges toward responsible AI. Inf. Fus. **58**, 82–115 (2020)
21. Indaryanto, A., Harijadi, B.D., Sinaga, E.: The growing use and impact of artificial intelligence technologies in the tourism industry. Sustain. Eng. Innov. **5**(2), 189–204 (2023)
22. VuThi, K., VuongThi, N., NguyenXuan, H., Emara, T.Z., Trinh, T.: Feature selection based on top frequency. In: The International Conference on Intelligent Systems & Networks, pp. 58–65. Springer, Singapore (2024)
23. Garlapati, A., Krishna, D.R., Garlapati, K., Rahul, U., Narayanan, G.: Stock price prediction using Facebook Prophet and Arima models. In: 2021 6th International Conference for Convergence in Technology (I2CT), pp. 1–7. IEEE (2021)
24. Álvarez-Carmona, M.Á., et al.: Natural language processing applied to tourism research: a systematic review and future research directions. J. King Saud Univ. Comput. Inf. Sci. **34**(10), 10125–10144 (2022)
25. Melnychenko, S., Boiko, M., Okhrimenko, A., Bosovska, M., Mazaraki, N.: Foresight technologies of economic systems: evidence from the tourism sector of Ukraine. Probl. Perspect. Manag. **18**(4), 303 (2020)
26. Trinh, T., Nguyen, N.-T., Wu, D., Huang, J.Z., Emara, T.Z.: A new location-based topic model for event attendees recommendation. In: 2019 IEEE-RIVF International Conference on Computing and Communication Technologies (RIVF), pp. 1–6. IEEE (2019)
27. Zhang, W., Chien, J., Yong, J., Kuang, R.: Network-based machine learning and graph theory algorithms for precision oncology. NPJ Precision Oncol. **1**(1), 25 (2017)
28. Mbunge, E., Muchemwa, B.: Deep learning and machine learning techniques for analyzing travelers' online reviews: a review. In: Optimizing Digital Solutions Hyper Personalization Tourism Hospitality, pp. 20–39 (2022)
29. Singh, V., Singh, S., Gupta, P.: Real-time anomaly recognition through CCTV using neural networks. Procedia Comput. Sci. **173**, 254–263 (2020)
30. Sharma, M., Mahajan, Y., Saber, A.: Using Augmented Reality (AR) and the Internet of Things (IoT) to improve water management maintenance and training. In: Innovations in Machine Learning and IoT for Water Management, pp.252–270. IGI Global (2024)
31. Bokolo, A.J.: Application of telemedicine and eHealth technology for clinical services in response to COVID-19 pandemic. Health Technol. **11**(2), 359–366 (2021)
32. Lukita, C., Pangilinan, G.A., Chakim, M.H.R., Saputra, D.B.: Examining the impact of artificial intelligence and Internet of Things on smart tourism destinations: A comprehensive study. Aptisi Trans. Technopreneurship (ATT) **5**(2sp), 135–145 (2023)
33. Abro, W.A., Aicher, A., Rach, N., Ultes, S., Minker, W., Qi, G.: Natural language understanding for argumentative dialogue systems in the opinion building domain. Knowl.-Based Syst. **242**, 108318 (2022)
34. Zhong, S., et al.: Machine learning: new ideas and tools in environmental science and engineering. Environ. Sci. Technol. **55**(19), 12741–12754 (2021)
35. Birendra, K.C., Dhungana, A., Dangi, T.B.: Tourism and the sustainable development goals: Stakeholders' perspectives from Nepal. Tourism Manag. Perspect. **38**, 100822 (2021)
36. Gong, Y., Schroeder, A.: A systematic literature review of data privacy and security research on smart tourism. Tourism Manag. Perspect. **44**, 101019 (2022)
37. Fanni, S.C., Febi, M., Aghakhanyan, G., Neri, E.: Natural language processing. In: Introduction to Artificial Intelligence, pp. 87–99. Springer, Cham (2023)
38. Dimitriadis, Y., Martínez-Maldonado, R., Wiley, K.: Human-centered design principles for actionable learning analytics. In: Research on E-Learning and ICT in Education: Technological, Pedagogical and Instructional Perspectives, pp. 277–296 (2021)

39. Naseer, I.: AWS cloud computing solutions: optimizing implementation for businesses. Stat. Comput. Interdisc. Res. **5**(2), 121–132 (2023)
40. Abril-Pla, O., et al.: PyMC: a modern, and comprehensive probabilistic programming framework in Python. PeerJ Comput. Sci. **9**, e1516 (2023)
41. Bretos, M.A., Ibáñez-Sánchez, S., Orús, C.: Applying virtual reality and augmented reality to the tourism experience: a comparative literature review. Span. J. Mark.-ESIC **28**(3), 287–309 (2024)
42. Londhe, K., Dharmadhikari, N., Zaveri, P., Sakoglu, U.: Enhanced travel experience using artificial intelligence: a data-driven approach. Procedia Comput. Sci. **235**, 1920–1928 (2024)

Animal Behavior Classification with Transformers

Khalid El moutaouakil(✉) and Noureddine Falih

LIMATI Laboratory, Polydisciplinary Faculty, University of Sultan Moulay Slimane, Mghila, BP 592 Beni Mellal, Morocco
elmoutaouakil.kh@gmail.com

Abstract. Accurate identification of cattle behavior is crucial for monitoring their health, welfare, and productivity, making it a vital aspect of precision livestock farming. This study explores the application of Transformer models for classifying cow behaviors using time-series data derived from tri-axial accelerometer sensors. By leveraging the Transformer's capability to capture long-term dependencies and temporal patterns in sequential data, this method seeks to reveal intricate behavioral patterns within cattle movement data. The model is tested on a diverse dataset, encompassing behaviors such as feeding, resting, ruminating, moving, and salting, among others. Evaluation results indicate that the Transformer-based model achieves high levels of accuracy, precision, and recall, affirming its suitability for automated monitoring of cattle behaviors. This approach holds promises for enhancing animal welfare, boosting productivity, streamlining farm management, and improving decision-making in the livestock industry.

Keywords: Artificial Intelligence · Deep Learning · Transformers · Precision Livestock Farming · Smart Agriculture · Livestock Management

1 Introduction

By 2050, the global population is expected to reach 9.2 billion people, placing significant pressure on the agricultural sector to increase food production by 70% to meet rising demand [1]. This demographic shift necessitates a transformation in agricultural practices, moving from traditional methods to more advanced, technology-driven models [2]. Embracing modern agricultural strategies is critical for improving productivity, ensuring sustainability, and maintaining economic viability. Over the past two decades, technological progress has led to the widespread adoption of digital tools, enabling agricultural industries to optimize their operations and achieve better returns on investment through data-driven approaches [3].

Among the most impactful advances is the growing focus on animal behavior, a crucial aspect of understanding livestock health, well-being, and productivity [4]. Cattle, as an essential part of global farming systems, represent a key area of study due to their direct influence on both farm output and animal welfare [5]. The integration of modern technologies, such as tri-axial accelerometers, has revolutionized the collection of data on

I. Aboudrar et al. (Eds.): ICESST 2024, SUCI, pp. 199–210, 2025.
https://doi.org/10.1007/978-3-031-86705-7_19

animal behavior, allowing for a more accurate and non-intrusive approach to monitoring livestock [6]. This data-driven methodology provides deeper insights into the dynamic interactions between cattle and their environment, enabling more informed decisions in livestock management [7].

Traditional livestock management has relied heavily on manual observation, which is often subjective and time-consuming. However, the rise of sensor technologies and the emerging field of precision livestock farming have set the stage for a major shift toward automated and intelligent systems [8]. Among these technologies, tri-axial accelerometers have proven particularly effective in capturing the fine details of cow movements, providing valuable information about their behavior, such as feeding, resting, and walking [9].

This study explores the application of Transformer models in classifying cow behavior using time-series data gathered from tri-axial accelerometers. Apart from other well used methods such as Recurrent Neural Networks (RNNs) [10], Transformers are adept at handling long-range dependencies in sequential data without the limitations of memory constraints [11]. Their ability to capture global relationships between data points makes them particularly well-suited for identifying the complex temporal patterns inherent in cattle behavior [12]. By leveraging the power of Transformers, we aim to enhance the classification of subtle and intricate behaviors exhibited by cows, providing a more efficient and accurate approach compared to other techniques [13].

The motivation for this research stems from the need to move beyond conventional observational practices in understanding cattle behavior. By using advanced deep learning techniques, specifically Transformer models, we aim to uncover hidden patterns and temporal relationships within the accelerometer data [14]. This approach has significant implications for precision livestock farming, as it can enable real-time monitoring of cattle behavior, detecting early signs of discomfort, illness, or abnormal activity that might otherwise go unnoticed [15]. Early detection can prompt timely interventions, improving animal welfare and farm productivity [16].

In the following sections, we will present the methodology used in this study, describe the characteristics of the dataset, and discuss the experimental results. This research demonstrates the potential of integrating artificial intelligence, specifically Transformer-based models, into animal behavior classification, advancing both scientific understanding and practical applications in the convergence of technology and animal systems.

2 Method

2.1 Dataset

Our proposed approach uses the second version of the Japanese Black Beef Cow Behavior Classification dataset [17], which employs tri-axial accelerometers embedded in collars to classify various cow behaviors. The accelerometers used for data collection were set to a 16-bit sensitivity with a range of ± 2 g. The data was gathered from six cows at Shinshu University farm, capturing 13 distinct behavioral categories.

The data acquisition took place in two designated areas where the cows moved freely, with the entire process recorded by 4K video cameras over the span of a single day. The resulting video footage was used by expert human annotators, who synchronized the timestamps from the video with the accelerometer data to accurately label the behaviors. This annotation procedure resulted in a total of 3 and half hours of labeled data. The accelerometers sampled data at a frequency of 25 Hz, which corresponds to 25 samples per second.

The dataset consists of 850, 529 labeled samples, each with columns indicating the timestamp, acceleration values along the X, Y, and Z axes (AccX, AccY, AccZ), and the corresponding behavioral label. The dataset is distributed across six CSV files, each corresponding to one cow. For simplification and better interpretability, the 13 behavior categories were united into six primary behavioral groups.

Table 1 provides the exact count of samples for each category, while Fig. 1 illustrates the distribution of samples across these behavior classes.

Table 1. Number of samples per behavior class

Behavior Class	Number of Samples
Other behaviors (ETC)	554,855
Resting (RES)	150,894
Ruminating (RUS)	54,531
Moving (MOV)	51,368
Feeding (FES)	28,023
Salting (SLT)	10,858

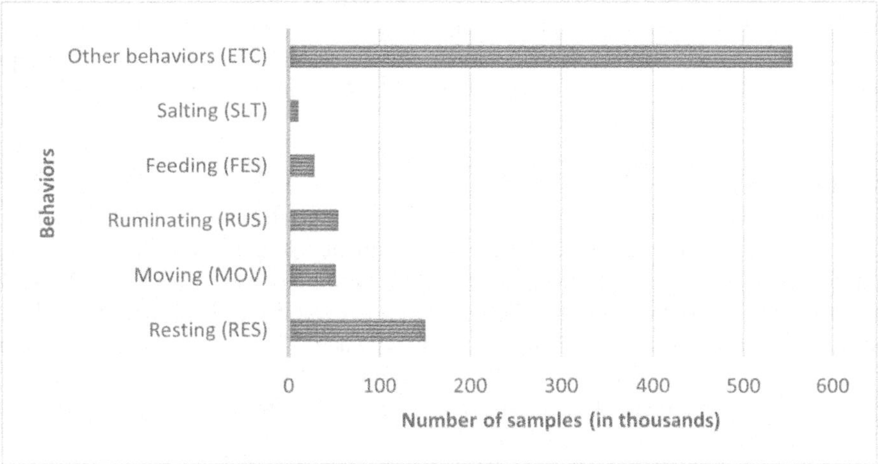

Fig. 1. Distribution of samples across behavior classes

2.2 Model Development Process

To classify cattle behaviors based on time series accelerometer data, we propose using a Transformer-based model. Transformer architecture, initially developed for natural language processing tasks, has shown significant success in sequence-based problems, such as time series classification. By leveraging self-attention mechanisms, the Transformer can effectively capture long-range dependencies in the time-series data, which is crucial for behavior classification tasks that rely on sequential patterns.

The primary objective is to develop a model that can take as input the accelerometer data (in the form of time-series signals) and output the corresponding behavior class for each sample.

Data Preprocessing

The first step involves preparing the data for modeling. This begins with data loading, where data from the six CSV files corresponding to each cow is loaded into the system. After loading, data cleaning is necessary to handle missing or erroneous data points, where invalid entries are removed to maintain data integrity. Following this, the normalization process is applied to the accelerometer data (AccX, AccY, AccZ). This ensures that each feature (axis) has an average between 0 and 1, which is crucial for normalizing the different scales that accelerometer data can exhibit. Also, the sequences, which may vary in length due to the nature of time series data, undergo sequence padding. This step involves padding or truncating the sequences to ensure a fixed length across all data points. Finally, label encoding is performed, converting categorical behavior class labels into numerical labels suitable for classification tasks.

Data Splitting

Once preprocessing is complete, the dataset is split into subsets. The train-test split ensures that the data is divided into training, validation, and test sets. The split guarantees to maintain the distribution of behavior classes across all subsets, ensuring representativeness. To prepare the data for modeling, the sequences are further organized into batches suitable for input into the model.

Model Design

The model is designed to work with the time-series data, starting with the Input Layer, which accepts data in the shape (batch_size, sequence_length, num_features), where num_features equals 3, representing the three accelerometer axes (AccX, AccY, AccZ). Since the Transformer model lacks inherent order recognition, Positional Encoding is added to retain temporal information across sequences. The core of the model comprises Self-Attention Layers, which allow the model to focus on important time points by learning relationships between different time steps. After the self-attention layers, Feed-Forward Layers process the learned representations, typically through fully connected layers with activation functions. Finally, the Classification output, consisting of a fully connected layer followed by a softmax activation function, produces the predicted behavior class.

Model Training

During training, the model's performance is guided by a Loss Calculation using Categorical Cross-Entropy loss, which is well-suited for multi-class classification tasks. The Optimizer used is Adam, chosen for its ability to adapt to the learning rate throughout training, enabling faster convergence. The model's performance is tracked using Accuracy as the primary evaluation metric during both training and validation.

Hyperparameter Tuning

The final step in the model development process involves Hyperparameter Tuning. In this step, key hyperparameters such as the learning rate and the number of Transformer layers are fine-tuned to achieve the best possible performance from the model. Adjusting these parameters ensures that the model converges efficiently and performs optimally on the classification task.

2.3 Model Architecture

In Fig. 2, we have a glimpse of the code of the proposed model architecture for the Transformer-based cattle behavior classification:

```python
import torch
import torch.nn as nn
import torch.optim as optim
from torch.nn import Transformer

class CattleBehaviorTransformer(nn.Module):
    def __init__(self, num_features=3, num_classes=6, d_model=64, nhead=8, num_layers=4, dropout=0.1):
        super(CattleBehaviorTransformer, self).__init__()

        # Define the input embedding layer
        self.embedding = nn.Linear(num_features, d_model)

        # Positional Encoding Layer (to retain sequence information)
        self.positional_encoding = nn.Parameter(torch.zeros(1, 500, d_model))  # Assume sequence length <= 500

        # Transformer Encoder Layer
        self.transformer_encoder = nn.TransformerEncoder(
            nn.TransformerEncoderLayer(d_model=d_model, nhead=nhead, dropout=dropout),
            num_layers=num_layers
        )

        # Fully Connected layer for classification
        self.fc = nn.Linear(d_model, num_classes)

        # Dropout layer for regularization
        self.dropout = nn.Dropout(dropout)

    def forward(self, x):
        # Apply embedding
        x = self.embedding(x)

        # Add positional encoding
        seq_len = x.size(1)
        x = x + self.positional_encoding[:, :seq_len, :]

        # Transformer Encoder
        x = x.permute(1, 0, 2)  # Switch dimensions for transformer input (seq_len, batch_size, d_model)
        x = self.transformer_encoder(x)

        # Take the output corresponding to the last time step
        x = x[-1, :, :]

        # Fully connected layer for classification
        x = self.fc(self.dropout(x))

        return x
```

Fig. 2. Transformer model architecture

Input Layer

The input layer is a linear layer that processes the three input features—AccX, AccY, and AccZ—captured from the accelerometer data. This layer transforms these input features into a higher-dimensional space, known as the d_model space. In this case, the input is mapped to a 64-dimensional space, allowing the model to capture more complex representations of the input data.

Positional Encoding

Since the Transformer model does not have a built-in sense of order, the Positional Encoding layer is added to preserve the temporal structure of the time-series data. This layer encodes the positions of the input data points, helping the model differentiate between different time steps within the sequence.

Transformer Encoder

The core of the model is the Transformer Encoder, which consists of a stack of four Transformer encoder layers. Each layer includes mechanisms for Self-Attention and a feed-forward network. The self-attention mechanism, using eight attention heads (nhead = 8), allows the model to focus on different parts of the sequence, learning relationships across various time steps. This structure enables the model to extract meaningful patterns from the time-series data.

Classification Layer

The final layer is the Classification Layer, a fully connected layer that takes the output from the Transformer and maps it to the behavior class labels. This layer provides the final predictions by associating the learned representations with the specific behavior classes identified in the data.

2.4 Model Training

Hyperparameters:

- **Number of Epochs:** 10
- **Batch Size**: 64 (chosen to balance memory usage and training time)
- **Learning Rate:** 0.0005 (commonly used for Transformer models)
- **Optimizer**: Adam with weight decay (helps with generalization)
- **Loss Function**: Categorical Cross-Entropy Loss
- **Evaluation Metric**: Accuracy, F1-score
- **Dropout Rate**: 0.1 (helps prevent overfitting)
- **Sequence Length**: 500 (maximum length of input sequence after padding/truncation)

Training Procedure:

1. **Initialize the Model:** Instantiate the CattleBehaviorTransformer model with the appropriate configuration.
2. **Training Loop:**
   - For each epoch, we perform forward passes on training data.
   - We compute the loss using the predicted outputs and the true labels.

- We backpropagate the error and update the model parameters using the optimizer.

3. **Validation**: After each epoch, we evaluate the model on the validation set to monitor overfitting.
4. **Testing**: After training, we evaluate the model on the unseen test set to estimate generalization performance.

Figure 3 offers a glimpse of the key parameters used during the model training process. Each of these elements plays a critical role in determining the model's performance and convergence during training, and their values have been carefully chosen to optimize the results.

```
CattleBehaviorTransformer(
  (embedding): Linear(in_features=3, out_features=64, bias=True)
  (positional_encoding): Parameter containing: [1, 500, 64]
  (transformer_encoder): TransformerEncoder(
    (layers): ModuleList(
      (0): TransformerEncoderLayer(
        (self_attn): MultiheadAttention(
          (in_proj_weight): Parameter(192, 64)
          (in_proj_bias): Parameter(64)
          (out_proj_weight): Parameter(64, 64)
          (out_proj_bias): Parameter(64)
        )
        (linear1): Linear(in_features=64, out_features=256, bias=True)
        (linear2): Linear(in_features=256, out_features=64, bias=True)
        (norm1): LayerNorm((64,), eps=1e-05, elementwise_affine=True)
        (norm2): LayerNorm((64,), eps=1e-05, elementwise_affine=True)
        (dropout): Dropout(p=0.1, inplace=False)
      )
      ...
    )
  )
  (fc): Linear(in_features=64, out_features=6, bias=True)
  (dropout): Dropout(p=0.1, inplace=False)
)
```

Fig. 3. Model training parameters

2.5 Evaluation Metrics

To evaluate the performance of the Transformer model for classifying cattle behaviors, it is crucial to select appropriate evaluation metrics that provide insights into both the overall accuracy and the ability of the model to handle imbalances across the behavior classes. Below, we outline the evaluation metrics that we used, along with their definitions and equations:

Accuracy

Accuracy measures the proportion of correctly classified instances (samples) to the total number of instances in the dataset. It's a basic metric that gives an overall idea of the model's performance but might not fully reflect the model's behavior in imbalanced datasets.

$$Accuracy = \frac{Number\ of\ Correct\ Predictions}{Total\ Number\ of\ Predictions} \tag{1}$$

Precision

Precision measures the proportion of true positive predictions relative to the total number of instances classified as positive (the number of instances predicted to belong to a certain class). This metric is crucial when the cost of false positives is high.

$$Precision = \frac{True\ positives}{True\ Posities + False\ Positives} \tag{2}$$

Recall

Recall (or Sensitivity) measures the proportion of actual positive instances that were correctly identified by the model. It tells us how well the model captures the instances of a given class.

$$Recall = \frac{True\ Positives}{True\ Positives + False\ Negatives} \tag{3}$$

F1-score

The F1-score is the harmonic mean of precision and recall. Offering a single metric that balances the trade-off between precision and recall, making it useful in situations where both false positives and false negatives are equally important.

$$F1\ score = \frac{2 \times (Precision \times Recall)}{Precision + Recall} \tag{4}$$

Using these metrics will offer a thorough insight into the model's performance, especially in the case of imbalanced behavior classes.

3 Results

The model's training accuracy increased steadily, and precision, recall, and F1 scores showed a similar trend. By the 10th epoch, the model achieved an overall 82.5% accuracy. The F1-score for both training and validation increased over time, indicating improved classification performance. The loss decreased consistently, indicating effective training.

Table 2 below illustrates how these metrics evolve during training and validation for each epoch, while Fig. 4 shows the evolution in a graphic format.

Table 2. F1 score and loss evolution during training and validation

Epochs	F1-Score (Training)	F1-Score (Validation)	Loss (Training)	Loss (Validation)
1	0,67	0,66	0,31	0,32
2	0,69	0,68	0,23	0,25
3	0,71	0,70	0,16	0,19
4	0,74	0,75	0,09	0,10
5	0,75	0,74	0,08	0,10
6	0,76	0,75	0,07	0,09
7	0,77	0,76	0,06	0,09
8	0,78	0,77	0,05	0,08
9	0,79	0,78	0,04	0,08
10	0,81	0,80	0,03	0,08

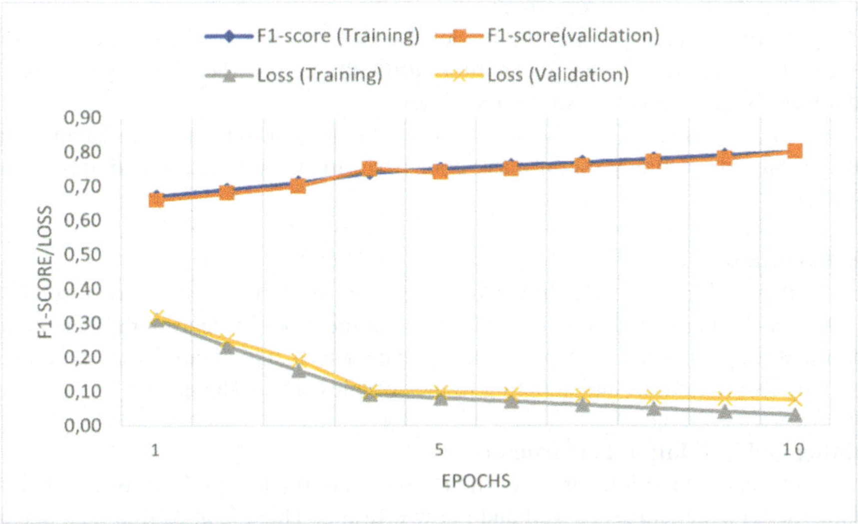

Fig. 4. F1 score and loss progression throughout training and validation

These results suggest the model is effectively learning to classify cattle behaviors, and further improvements can be explored through fine-tuning hyperparameters, optimizing the learning rate, or augmenting the dataset.

4 Discussion

The Transformer model has demonstrated strong performance in classifying cattle behaviors based on the time-series accelerometer data, as reflected in the training results. In this section we provide an analysis of the model's performance and an explanation of why the Transformer model has succeeded in this classification task.

Accuracy and F1-Score Evolution
The model achieved an 82.5% accuracy on the test set, which indicates that the Transformer is able to correctly classify a substantial portion of the data.

The F1-score, which balances both precision and recall, reached 0.81 by the end of training. This indicates that the model is not only good at identifying positive instances (high precision) but also does not miss out on many actual positive instances (high recall). The F1-score further highlights that the model is consistently performing well across all classes, including the minority classes.

Precision and Recall
The precision of 0.80 shows that the model is fairly consistent in predicting the correct class when it does make a prediction.

Recall of 0.79 suggests that the model does a good job at identifying the correct instances for each class. Even for the more difficult classes (the minority classes), the model was able to maintain a strong recall rate.

These metrics are particularly important because the dataset may be imbalanced, and focusing only on accuracy might mask poor performance on certain underrepresented classes.

Loss Evolution
The loss dropped consistently during training, from 0.31 in the first epoch to 0.03 by the 10th epoch. This steady decline indicates that the model is learning effectively and minimizing the classification error over time. It suggests that the Transformer is gradually improving its predictions and adapting to the complexities of the dataset.

Training and Validation Performance
The training and validation curves of the F1-score are relatively close, which indicates that the model is generalizing well and not overfitting. There is almost no gap between training and validation scores, suggesting that the model is not just memorizing the training data but learning generalization patterns.

The validation loss also decreases in parallel with the training loss, which further supports the idea that the model is generalizing effectively and not suffering from overfitting.

Transformer model performance
The Transformer model succeeded in this time-series classification task due to several key factors. Its self-attention mechanism is well-suited for sequential data, enabling it to capture both short-term and long-term dependencies critical for classifying cattle behaviors. Positional encoding ensures the model maintains the sequence order of data, vital

for understanding temporal relationships. Multi-head attention allows the model to learn complex dynamics by focusing on different patterns of movement, while the encoder layers process data in parallel, boosting training efficiency and handling long sequences. Additionally, the model's flexibility, resilience to imbalanced data, and capacity for fine-tuning further enhanced its performance.

5 Conclusion

In this paper, we proposed and successfully applied Transformer-based model for classifying cattle behaviors based on accelerometer data. The model was trained on a comprehensive dataset of cattle movements, utilizing accelerometer readings in three spatial dimensions to identify distinct behavioral categories. Our results suggest that the Transformer model is not only a promising tool for cattle behavior classification but also offers a scalable approach to similar time-series classification problems in agriculture and animal behavior studies. Future work can explore further refinements of the model, such as incorporating additional sensor modalities (e.g., GPS or environmental data), experimenting with different Transformer configurations, and applying the model to real-time monitoring systems for livestock management.

References

1. Mrabet, R.: Chapter 2-sustainable agriculture for food and nutritional security. In: Farooq, M., Gogoi, N., Pisante, M. (eds.) Sustainable Agriculture and the Environment. pp. 25–90. Academic Press (2023). https://doi.org/10.1016/B978-0-323-90500-8.00013-0
2. Newman, L., et al.: Agriculture for the anthropocene: novel applications of technology and the future of food. Food Secur. **15**, 613–627 (2023). https://doi.org/10.1007/s12571-023-01356-6
3. Khan, N., Ray, R.L., Sargani, G.R., Ihtisham, M., Khayyam, M., Ismail, S.: Current progress and future prospects of agriculture technology: gateway to sustainable agriculture. Sustainability **13**, 4883 (2021). https://doi.org/10.3390/su13094883
4. Schillings, J., Bennett, R., Rose, D.C.: Exploring the potential of precision livestock farming technologies to help address farm animal welfare. Front. Anim. Sci. **2**, 639678 (2021). https://doi.org/10.3389/fanim.2021.639678
5. Buller, H., Blokhuis, H., Lokhorst, K., Silberberg, M., Veissier, I.: Animal welfare management in a digital world. Animals **10**, 1779 (2020). https://doi.org/10.3390/ani10101779
6. Hlimi, A., El Otmani, S., Elame, F., Chentouf, M., El Halimi, R., Chebli, Y.: Application of precision technologies to characterize animal behavior: a review. Animals **14**, 416 (2024). https://doi.org/10.3390/ani14030416
7. Gittins, P., McElwee, G., Tipi, N.: Discrete event simulation in livestock management. J. Rural. Stud. **78**, 387–398 (2020). https://doi.org/10.1016/j.jrurstud.2020.06.039
8. Tedeschi, L.O., Greenwood, P.L., Halachmi, I.: Advancements in sensor technology and decision support intelligent tools to assist smart livestock farming. J. Anim. Sci. **99**(2), skab038 (2021). https://doi.org/10.1093/jas/skab038
9. Moutaouakil, K.E., Falih, N.: A comparative study on time series data-based artificial intelligence approaches for classifying cattle feeding behavior. Indon. J. Electr. Eng. Comput. Sci. **33**(1), 324–332 (2024). https://doi.org/10.11591/ijeecs.v33.i1.pp324-332

10. Moutaouakil, K.E., Falih, N.A.: New approach to animal behavior classification using recurrent neural networks. In: 2024 4th International Conference on Innovative Research in Applied Science, Engineering and Technology (IRASET), pp. 1–5 (2024). https://doi.org/10.1109/IRASET60544.2024.10549544
11. Rae, J.W., Potapenko, A., Jayakumar, S.M., Lillicrap, T.P.: Compressive Transformers for Long-Range Sequence Modelling (2019). https://doi.org/10.48550/arXiv.1911.05507
12. Liu, Y., Li, W., Liu, X., Li, Z., Yue, J.: Deep learning in multiple animal tracking: a survey. Comput. Electron. Agric. **224**, 109161 (2024). https://doi.org/10.1016/j.compag.2024.109161
13. Martin-Cirera, A., Nowak, M., Norton, T., Auer, U., Oczak, M.: Comparison of transformers with LSTM for classification of the behavioural time budget in horses based on video data. Biosyst. Eng. **242**, 154–168 (2024). https://doi.org/10.1016/j.biosystemseng.2024.04.014
14. Lin, D., Kenéz, Á., McArt, J.A.A., Li, J.: Transformer neural network to predict and interpret pregnancy loss from activity data in Holstein dairy cows. Comput. Electron. Agric. **205**, 107638 (2023). https://doi.org/10.1016/j.compag.2023.107638
15. Neethirajan, S., Kemp, B.: Digital livestock farming. Sens. Bio-Sens. Res. **32**, 100408 (2021). https://doi.org/10.1016/j.sbsr.2021.100408
16. Vlaicu, P.A., Gras, M.A., Untea, A.E., Lefter, N.A., Rotar, M.C.: Advancing livestock technology: intelligent systemization for enhanced productivity, Welfare Sustainability. AgriEng. **6**, 1479–1496 (2024). https://doi.org/10.3390/agriengineering6020084
17. Ito, H., et al.: Japanese Black Beef Cow Behavior Classification Dataset (2022). https://doi.org/10.5281/zenodo.5849025

A Review on Sentiment Analysis Approaches

Houria Laaroussi(✉), Fatima Guerouate, and Mohamed Sbihi

EST SALE, Mohammed V University, Rabat, Morocco
hourialaaroussi@research.emi.ac.ma

Abstract. The Internet is a vast virtual platform for personal opinion expression and sharing, impacting many facets of life and having implications for both marketing and communication. User-posted data on internet has become an important source of information, Because of its vast volume It is not possible to manually analyze such a massive volume of user generated data. In order to examine such textual data, sentiment analysis is necessary. Sentiment analysis (SA) recognizes the polarity of the text, classifies this textual data into positive, negative, and neutral. This paper examines and discusses a number of sentiment analysis methods employed to develop a comprehensive understanding of their strengths and limitations.

Keywords: Sentiment Analysis · Machine Learning · Textual Data · Lexicon-based approach

1 Introduction

Sentiment analysis has always been an important research area. Sentiment analysis is a domain within natural language processing that concentrates on the extraction and analysis of opinions and emotional states expressed in textual data. [1]. Sentiment analysis is also known as opinion mining.

The main advantage of SA is to accurately detect and categorize users' sentiments in texts as positive, negative, or neutral [2]. Numerous fields have used SA, including politics [3], healthcare [6], e-learning [4], economic [5] and more. Sentiment analysis is necessary in a number of real-world applications. For instance, product analysis may be used to determine which features or aspects of a product, in terms of quality, appeal to clients.

Owing to the increasing usage of the internet, social media platforms, product review websites, forums and other web sources have become a powerful information source. Many users utilize them to share their opinions and sentiments on a variety of products, services, and companies through posts and comments [7].

Sentiment analysis faces several notable challenges. One key issue is the difficulty in accurately recognizing and extracting sentiment-related information from unstructured text, as it can be influenced by domain-specific terminology, sarcasm, and contextual factors. Additionally, a lack of high-quality labeled datasets presents a significant obstacle for training and evaluating effective sentiment analysis models.

I. Aboudrar et al. (Eds.): ICESST 2024, SUCI, pp. 211–219, 2025.
https://doi.org/10.1007/978-3-031-86705-7_20

Recently, a large number of algorithms has been developed to examine, forecast, and evaluate emotions from textual data. SA techniques can be broadly categorized into three main types: lexicon-based, machine learning-based, and hybrid approaches.

In this paper, we will examine the various approaches used in SA. The remainder of this study is structured as follows. Section 2 examines the advantages and limitations of sentiment analysis approaches. Section 3 presents lexicon-based approach. Section 4 describes machine learning approach. Section 5 discusses hybrid approach. Finally, the overall conclusions of the study are summarized in Sect. 6.

2 Sentiment Analysis Techniques

Choosing the right SA technique is crucial and extremely important. The majority of research typically classifies sentiment analysis techniques into three groups: Lexicon-based, machine learning (ML) and hybrid approaches [8].

Machine learning techniques focus on predicting the polarity of text using both test and training data sets. In contrast, a lexicon-based technique uses a pre-defined list of terms and attaches a sentiment score or polarity to each word, this method does not need a training set. The ML and lexicon-based approaches are combined in the hybrid method [10]. Deep learning (DL) is a sub-field of ML, it offers improved data representation, which can facilitate more effective learning using machine learning techniques. Advances in deep learning have facilitated various computational tasks, such as text mining, image processing, and pattern recognition.

Different approaches are shown in Fig. 1. The Table 1 displays the advantages and limitations of different sentiment analysis methods.

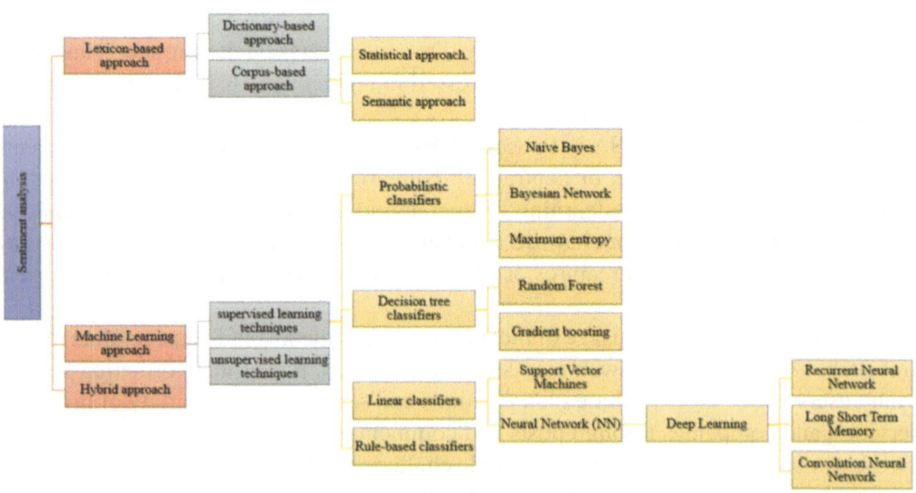

Fig. 1. Sentiment analysis approach

Table 1. Advantages and Limitations of sentiment analysis approaches.

Technique	Advantage	Limitation
Lexicon-based approach	- Easy to implement - Computationally efficient	- It might be expensive to manually annotate the seed list the first time - There may be instances where information processing based on linguistic rules is unable to accurately capture the affective sentiment - Take less processing time
Machine Learning approach	- Able to deal with large data sets - Can learn complex patterns - Adaptable to various domain and languages	- Expensive - Cannot learn by themselves - High memory requirements
Deep Learning approach	- Extract feature by itself - offers better data representation	
Hybrid methods	- Able to take advantage of the optimal performances delivered by the individual base classifiers	Higher computational complexity

3 Lexicon-Based Approach

A lexicon-based method is used for sentiment classification of text. This technique proposes that the cumulative polarity of a text is equal to the sum of the polarities of its individual terms [9]. It use sentiment dictionary with information about which words and phrases are positive and which are negative.

There are two categories for the lexicon-based technique: Dictionary-based and Corpus-based [10].

While lexicon-based approaches demonstrate ease of use and perform well on high-dimensional data, they are limited in their ability to incorporate positional information and may overlook important contextual cues during the sentiment analysis process.

3.1 Dictionary-Based Approach

Dictionary-Based Approach. Dictionary-based method used dictionaries that contain terms and their sentiments. This dictionary is created manually by providing a series of sentiment terms. Subsequently, this collection is expanded looking for synonyms and antonyms using popular corpora like wordNet and sentiwordNet. The next iteration begins once. The seed list is updated with the recently found words. Algorithm iteration ends until no more terms need to be added in a lexicon. One significant drawback of this method is that it cannot identify opinion terms with specific domain.

3.2 Corpus-Based Approach

Corpus-based method seeks to address the challenge of locating terms related to a particular domain by offering dictionaries that are specifically relevant to a certain topic. Semantic or statistical methods can be used to find terms that are comparable in order to grow the dictionary.

Statistical Approach. Looking for seed terms for opinions is part of the statistical technique. One way to do this, If the size of corpus is small, the issue of certain unavailable terms is amenable to solution by employing the entire set of online documents that have been indexed as the corpus for the dictionary's creation methods [11]. The polarity of a term may be determined by looking at how frequently it appears in a corpus of texts. -pointwise mutual information (PMI) or Latent Semantic Analysis (LSA) could be used for this.

Semantic Approach. In this approach, close words may share the similar polarities. Different criteria are used in this technique to compute word similarity. A term's sentiment value various types of semantic relationships between terms provided by WordNet.

4 Machine Learning Approach

The goal of the machine learning (ML) approach in SA is to use well-known ML techniques in textual data. Text classification is the fundamental task of SA based on ML approach. Two primary categories may be distinguished in machine learning-based sentiment: supervised and unsupervised learning techniques. However, machine learning algorithms require human intervention and guidance to learn and perform sentiment analysis effectively.

4.1 Supervised Approach

It is frequently applied to find the sentiment polarity using labeled datasets. The advantage of this technique lies in its capacity to build effective trained models for a specific domain. But the fundamental problem of this method is that it is ineffective when used on different types of data from different domains [13].

Linear classifier, Probabilistic classifier, Decision tree classifier, Rule-based classifier are the various types of supervised learning techniques used in sentiment analysis.

Probabilistic Classifier. It is typically based on Bayes' theorem, predicts a probability distribution across a set of classes [20]. Computationally quick in comparison to alternative algorithms and don't need a large amount of training data. Nevertheless, in certain cases, where the data do not fit the distribution assumptions, the classification performance is poorer.

Naive Bayes. This method categorizes data with the independent variables. It is simple with good precision.

Bayesian Network. This technique uses directed graph to describe the dependencies between variant features. It is rarely employed because it has a very high computational complexity [14].

Maximum Entropy. This technique provides the probabilities that the document belongs to a specific class. The uniformity of the distribution is the essential principle of maximum entropy. It defines a collection of labeled features, for each feature, calculate its weights that can then be combined to get the most probable. It uses search techniques to find the parameter set that maximizes the performance of this method.

Linear Classifier. This type uses linear decision boundaries to categorize sentiment. When the appropriate features are employed, linear classifiers can achieve state-of-the-art results despite being straightforward.

Support Vector Machines (SVM). SVM identify patterns which are employed for classification. The fundamental idea behind SVMs is to find linear hyperplanes in a multi-dimensional space that can effectively separate the various categories and variables are categorized by linear separator with the positive and negative categorization. SVM was not limited to linear data classification, it is capable to perform a non-linear classification with efficiency by using the Kernel function.

It gets excellent accuracy and is simple to train in contrast to other machine learning methods but the model's performance suffers if there are significantly more features than samples.

Neural Network (NN). Neural networks is based on the composition and operation of biological brain networks, which enables machines to use data for learning from and generate predictions. It is designed to address specific problems or enhance particular applications, such as image processing or pattern recognition. They are typically composed of three layers: the input layer, the hidden layer, and the output layer [17]. The basic unit of it is the neuron, and it is composed of numerous neurons. The architectural elements of artificial neural networks, such as the network topology, connection weights, activation functions, bias, and momentum, collectively constitute the foundation for learning in these models.

NN useful for issues with a high dimensionality but theoretically intricate and hard to put into practice. In contrast to the initially introduced shallow ANN designs, the deep learning approach, also known as deep ANN, has become a powerful method for sentiment analysis applications. Deep learning approach will be discussed in Sect. 5.

Decision Tree Classifier. It is not recommended for small datasets since it works very well on large datasets.

Random Forest (RF). This method is composed of numerous of individual decision trees operating as an ensemble. Every tree in this model generates a class prediction, and the class that receives the greatest votes becomes the model's final prediction.

Gradient Boosting (GB). Boosting is a prominent ensemble learning method. It constructs several models sequentially. This method gives each data sample the same weights before concentrating on samples that were incorrectly classified in later models. Gradient Boosting uses decision trees as its core building blocks to construct a powerful ensemble model. GBM builds trees one by one where each newly added tree aims to correct the errors made by the previously trained trees in the ensemble. The constructed trees are independent and are uncorrelated with those constructed previously in the ensemble using a random forest classifier [18].

Rule-Based Classifier. Rules are used to model the data. The class label is on the right side, and a condition on the feature set given in disjunctive normal form is on the left. The requirements center around the word presence. Since term absence is not useful for scarce data, it is rarely employed.

4.2 Unsupervised Approach

Acquiring and constructing labeled datasets, especially for unstructured textual data, can pose significant challenges. This is because the generation of such datasets often requires manual labeling by human annotators, which is a labor-intensive and time-consuming process. In contrast, acquiring unlabeled datasets is relatively more feasible, enabling the use of unsupervised learning approaches for classification. These techniques leverage the statistical properties of the documents, such as word co-occurrence patterns, natural language processing methods, and existing lexicons containing emotionally-polarized words.

In the field of sentiment analysis, unsupervised machine learning approaches often employ clustering techniques. These clustering methods can group data into different categories without explicitly defining the sentiments represented by each cluster. In other words, the clustering approach partitions the data into groups, where the data within a cluster are more similar from a particular perspective than the data across different clusters.

5 Deep Learning Approach

Deep learning (DL), with its recent developments, has become a potent method for sentiment analysis, as they can automatically discover intricate semantic representations of text without the need for extensive feature engineering. DL, a subfield of ML, makes use of deep neural networks to facilitate learning. The number of hidden layers in a model determines the depth of the learning process. Abstract features are extracted by the first layers, specific and significant feature information is extracted by the deeper layers as learning advances. DL encompasses two primary architectural approaches: Convolutional Neural Networks and Recurrent Neural Networks.

5.1 Convolution Neural Network

Convolutional neural networks (CNN) are a prominent feed-forward architecture primarily employed for processing and analyzing visual data, such as images. However, their ability to capture spatial patterns and relationships can also be leveraged for sentiment analysis tasks involving textual data [15]. The depth of the convolutional neural network based on how many hidden layers separating the input and output layers, is a key factor influencing the CNN's performance and capabilities. To produce feature maps, the input data is tested with a variety of filters. After across the whole input. Every filter goes through the input in its entirety, and performs element-wise multiplication between its weights and the corresponding input values. The output is sent to an activation function such as the sigmoid, tanh, or Rectified Linear Unit (ReLU). The collection of weights is evaluated using a loss function. Different portions of the input are highlighted in the feature maps that the filters produce.

Even though CNNs are frequently used to analyze images and videos [16], Convolutional neural networks consist of four primary architectural components: 1) a convolutional layer, 2) a rectified linear unit layer, 3) a pooling layer, and 4) a fully connected layer. However, the primary limitation of CNNs is their inability to effectively process sequential data.

5.2 Recurrent Neural Network

In contrast to CNN, which is a feedforward network, 1.1 Recurrent Neural Network (RNN) employs back propagation, it considers the past and current inputs. An internal memory allows RNNs to analyze sequential data. To forecast the following word in the context, RNNs use the preceding word as guidance.

5.3 Long Short Term Memory

By retaining a long-term memory of previous inputs, the Long Short-Term Memory (LSTM) model, an advanced version of the RNN, is engineered to model long-range dependencies in sequential data. In contrast to the simple internal memory structure of RNN, LSTM networks possess a more sophisticated memory mechanism, It has internal memory from which it can read, write, and delete data. This solves the RNN's limitation, which was the vanishing gradient problem. LSTM can determine which information is significant and should be retained, as well as which information should be forgotten. The memory in LSTM is gated, with three distinct gates: input, forget, and output gates.

Recurrent Neural Network models have been found to outperform Convolutional Neural Network models in sentiment analysis tasks. This can be attributed to the sequential nature of RNNs, which enables the capture of crucial relationships between adjacent terms in a phrase - a key aspect of sentiment analysis. Additionally, while basic RNN architectures may struggle to effectively model long-term dependencies between words in a sentence, more advanced RNN variants such as LSTM have demonstrated superior ability to learn these long-range dependencies, resulting in improved performance for sentiment analysis applications [16].

6 Hybrid Approach

In order to incorporate the advantages of both approaches, researchers have also been drawn to hybrid approaches that employ sentiment lexicons in machine learning techniques. This hybrid method, incorporating both ML methods and lexicon-based approaches, is highly prevalent for determining polarity or sentiment orientation. The hybrid approach handles ambiguity and incorporates the contextual information of sentiment-bearing words by combining the effectiveness of lexical analysis with the adaptability of ML techniques [19]. The primary motivation for the hybrid approach is to leverage the strengths of both machine learning and lexicon-based techniques, namely, high accuracy and stability.

7 Conclusion

Sentiment analysis is a field that is expanding quickly. Extensive research has been conducted in this field, yet numerous challenges persist as sentiment analysis grapples with processing text-based unstructured data. Although dictionary-based approaches handle information faster than machine learning approaches, their accuracy is not as good. Greater accuracy is achieved using the machine learning strategy espicialy DDeep leaning approach. This survey indicates that, in comparison to dictionary-based approaches, machine learning yield higher accuracy.

References

1. Liu, B.: Sentiment Analysis, pp. 1–367 (2015)
2. Salur, M.U., Aydin, I.: A novel hybrid deep learning model for sentiment classification. IEEE Access **8**, 58080–58093 (2020)
3. Jaidka, K., Ahmed, S., Skoric, M., Hilbert, M.: Predicting elections from social media: a three-country, three-method comparative study. Asian J. Commun. **29**(3), 252–273 (2019)
4. Ortigosa, A., Martín, J.M., Carro, R.M.: Sentiment analysis in facebook and its application to e-learning. Comput. Hum. Behav. **31**(1), 527–541 (2014)
5. Lukauskas, M., Pilinkienė, V., Bruneckienė, J., Stundžienė, A., Grybauskas, A., Ruzgas, T.: Economic activity forecasting based on the sentiment analysis of news. Mathematics **10**(19), 3461 (2022)
6. Kastrati, Z., Ahmedi, L., Kurti, A., Kadriu, F., Murtezaj, D., Gashi, F.: A deep learning sentiment analyser for social media comments in low-resource languages. Electronics **10**(10), 1133 (2021)
7. Al-Bakri, N.F., Yonan, J., Sadiq, A.T., Abid, A.: Tourism companies assessment via social media using sentiment analysis. Baghdad Sci. J. **19**(2), 0422 (2021)
8. Madhoushi, Z., Hamdan, A.R., Zainudin, S.: Sentiment analysis techniques in recent works. In: 2015 Science and Information Conference, pp. 288–291. IEEE (2015)
9. Devika, M., Sunitha, C., Ganesh, A.: Sentiment analysis: a comparative study on different approaches. Procedia Comput. Sci. **87**, 44–49 (2016)
10. Zhang, H., Gan, W., Jiang, B.: Machine learning and lexicon based methods for sentiment classification: a survey. In: Web Information System and Application Conference, pp 262–265. IEEE (2014)
11. Turney, P.: Thumbs up or thumbs down?: semantic orientation applied to unsupervised classification of reviews. In: Proceedings of Annual Meeting of the Association for Computational Linguistics (ACL'02) (2002)
12. Cambria, E., Hussain, A.: Sentic computing. Cogn. Comput. **7**(2), 183–185 (2015)
13. Alessia, D., Ferri, F., Grifoni, P., Guzzo, T.: Approaches, tools and applications for sentiment analysis implementation, Int. J. Comput. Appl. **125**(3) (2015)
14. Aggarwal, C.C., Zhai, C.X.: Mining Text Data. Springer, New York (2012)
15. Mohammad, S.M.: Sentiment analysis: automatically detecting valence, emotions, and other affectual states from text. In: Emotion Measurement, pp. 323–379 (2021)

16. Krizhevsky, A., Sutskever, I., Hinton, G.E.: Imagenet classification with deep convolutional neural networks. Adv. Neural Inf. Process. Syst. (2012)
17. Lopez, M.M., Kalita, J.: Deep Learning applied to NLP. CoRR https://arxiv.org/abs/1703.03091 (2017)
18. Bordoloi, M., Biswas, K.S.: Sentiment analysis: a survey on design framework, applications and future scopes. Artif. Intel. Rev. **56**(11), 12505–12560 (2023)
19. Joshi, I.C.N.: Enhanced twitter sentiment analysis using hybrid approach and by accounting local contextual semantic. J. Intell. Syst. **29**, 1611–1625 (2019). https://doi.org/10.1515/jisys-2019-0106
20. Fisch, D., Kalkowski, E., Sick, B.: Knowledge fusion for probabilistic generative classifiers with data mining applications. IEEE Trans. Knowl. Data Eng. **26**(3), 652–666 (2014)

Innovative Federated Learning Approach to Secure Internet of Medical Things

Anass Misbah[1](✉), Anass Sebbar[2], and Imad Hafidi[1]

[1] National School of Applied Sciences, Computer Science and Mathematics Laboratory, Khouribga, Morocco
anassmisbah@gmail.com, imad.hafidi@usms.ac.ma
[2] International University of Rabat, ESIN, Rabat, TICLab, Morocco
anass.sebbar@uir.ac.ma

Abstract. The Internet of Medical Things (IoMT) has emerged as a groundbreaking paradigm in healthcare, connecting billions of devices to enable enhanced automation, real-time communication, and comprehensive data collection. However, the rapid expansion of IoMT devices also presents significant security challenges that must be addressed through ongoing research and innovative approaches. In this study, we focus on improving attack classification in IoMT networks by leveraging federated learning, with a particular emphasis on the Random Forest (RF) model. Utilizing the open CICIoMT2024 dataset, which comprises 19 distinct attack classes and 45 features, we deploy the RF model across 10 simulated edge devices. The federated RF model demonstrated exceptional performance, achieving an accuracy of 0.9922, precision of 0.9938, recall of 0.9922, and an F1 score of 0.9909. This innovative approach significantly enhances security at the edge, particularly for devices with limited computational resources, underscoring the potential of federated learning to bolster IoMT security in increasingly complex healthcare environments.

Keywords: IoMT · Machine Learning · Security · Intrusion Detection Systems · Federated Learning

1 Introduction

The integration of medical devices into connected healthcare systems—known as the Internet of Medical Things (IoMT)—is revolutionizing healthcare by enabling real-time patient monitoring, personalized treatment, and data-driven healthcare insights. However, this connectivity also increases the risk of cybersecurity threats, posing significant challenges in safeguarding sensitive patient data and ensuring patient safety [1]. Traditional centralized machine learning approaches, while powerful, are often unsuitable for IoMT applications, as they require sensitive data to be aggregated in one location, increasing the vulnerability to data breaches [2].

Federated Learning (FL) has emerged as a promising solution to address these issues by enabling decentralized machine learning, allowing model training directly on local

I. Aboudrar et al. (Eds.): ICESST 2024, SUCI, pp. 220–228, 2025.
https://doi.org/10.1007/978-3-031-86705-7_21

devices at the edge [3]. FL significantly improves data privacy by transmitting only model updates, rather than raw data, to a central server. However, implementing FL in IoMT systems brings its own set of challenges, including handling the heterogeneity of medical data, non-IID (non-independent and identically distributed) data distributions, and the resource limitations of IoMT devices. Existing studies have proposed FL for privacy-preserving applications in healthcare, but these approaches often struggle with computational efficiency on resource-constrained devices [4, 5].

Recent research suggests that Lightweight Machine Learning (LML) models are a viable option for IoMT due to their low computational requirements [6]. However, many LML approaches lack the robustness required for critical tasks such as anomaly detection and attack prevention, which are essential for IoMT security. To address these gaps, we propose a novel framework that leverages the Random Forest (RF) model within an FL architecture, a choice made due to RF's suitability for high-dimensional data and its resilience in environments with non-IID data. Compared to other machine learning models, RF is computationally efficient and capable of handling large feature sets without overfitting, making it well-suited for IoMT's unique requirements.

This framework was evaluated using the Canadian Institute for Cybersecurity's Internet of Medical Things 2024 dataset (CICIoMT2024) [7], which comprises 19 attack classes and 45 features, using RF to perform anomaly detection across 10 simulated edge devices. By combining FL with RF, we not only preserve data privacy but also enhance the performance and scalability of IoMT security systems. The RF model's ensemble nature and high interpretability make it ideal for handling the complex, distributed nature of IoMT data while maintaining efficient, high-accuracy attack classification. This study demonstrates that RF, when integrated with FL, offers a robust solution for securing IoMT systems without compromising on computational efficiency.

The structure of this paper is as follows: Sect. 2 provides a literature review covering existing IoMT security approaches and FL applications. Section 3 details the research motivation, including the rationale behind the selection of RF. Section 4 presents the experimental setup and findings, which demonstrate the RF model's effectiveness in a federated environment. Section 5 concludes the paper with insights into future research directions.

2 Related Work

2.1 Security Challenges of IoMT

Recent surveys on Internet of Medical Things (IoMT) security have brought to light several key challenges and trends in protecting healthcare systems and devices. A study by [8] found that data privacy and security are the top concerns for most healthcare organizations, with many worried about vulnerabilities in medical devices. Similarly, [9] surveyed healthcare professionals and discovered that, despite growing awareness of security risks, many still lack the training and resources needed to tackle these issues effectively. On the manufacturing side, [10] found that IoMT device makers often lack standardized security protocols and invest too little in security during the development process. Lastly, a survey by [11] looked at the influence of regulatory frameworks on

IoMT security, revealing that inconsistent compliance requirements across regions pose a challenge, emphasizing the need for more uniform security standards globally.

2.2 Federated Learning with IoMT

Recent advances in using federated learning to secure the Internet of Medical Things (IoMT) have shown significant promise. [12] introduced a federated learning method that enhances intrusion detection accuracy within IoMT networks. [13] created a federated learning model designed for malware detection on IoMT devices, emphasizing minimal data sharing. [14] proposed a privacy-preserving federated learning framework to enable collaborative analysis of medical data from various sources. Additionally, [15] developed a federated learning-based anomaly detection system that strengthens IoMT security by identifying unusual patterns in medical sensor data.

2.3 The CIC IoMT 2024 Dataset

The CIC IoMT 2024 dataset is designed to address the increasing need for securing IoMT devices in healthcare by capturing interactions across multiple protocols like HTTP, MQTT (Message Queuing Telemetry Transport), CoAP (Constrained Application Protocol), and Bluetooth, while simulating various attack vectors. This provides a realistic and comprehensive data source crucial for developing robust security measures tailored to healthcare IoMT environments.

The primary goal is to introduce a benchmark dataset that aids in creating and evaluating security solutions for the Internet of Medical Things (IoMT). To achieve this, 18 types of attacks were executed on an IoMT testbed with 40 devices, including 25 real and 15 simulated ones, simulating the diverse protocols used in healthcare, such as Wi-Fi, MQTT, and Bluetooth.

These attacks were categorized into five classes: DDoS (Distributed Denial of Service), DoS (Denial of Service), Recon (Reconnaissance), MQTT, and spoofing. This benchmark dataset aims to complement existing research, providing a valuable resource for developing new security solutions, particularly using machine learning techniques.

Moreover, the research captures the lifecycle of IoMT devices—from their initial network integration to disconnection—through a process known as profiling, enabling classifiers to detect device-specific anomalies within healthcare networks.

2.4 Federated Learning Methodologies

This work highlights three key methodologies that represent significant advancements in federated learning (FL), each addressing important aspects for improving FL's effectiveness and applicability.

Personalized Federated Learning via Stacking. [16]: Cantu-Cervini introduces a new approach to personalized federated learning (PFL) by using stacked generalization. This method allows the creation of multiple models tailored to individual clients' data, enhancing privacy and enabling collaborative learning in varied federated environments.

Data Privacy in Federated Unlearning with Dynamic User Participation. [17]: Liu et al. focus on ensuring data privacy in federated unlearning (FU). They integrate secure aggregation protocols within clustering-based FU frameworks, providing a strong system that improves unlearning efficiency and protects user privacy, even with dynamic user involvement.

Communication-Efficient Distributed Deep Learning via Federated Dynamic Averaging. [18]: Theologitis and al. address the communication challenges in distributed deep learning. They propose Federated Dynamic Averaging (FDA), a method that reduces communication costs by synchronizing based on model variance, improving efficiency without slowing down convergence.

Together, these methodologies demonstrate significant progress in making federated learning more efficient, private, and scalable, supporting its broader adoption across various fields.

2.5 Conclusion

The literature on IoMT security and federated learning reveals both advancements and persistent challenges. Security remains a major concern in IoMT, with studies highlighting gaps in data privacy, inconsistent regulatory compliance, and inadequate security protocols in device manufacturing. While federated learning shows promise in enhancing IoMT security through decentralized model training, the current approaches face limitations in efficiency, scalability, and privacy. Existing methods in federated learning focus primarily on specific applications, such as intrusion detection and malware detection, but lack comprehensive solutions that address the unique constraints of IoMT devices, including limited processing power and energy capacity. Additionally, the CIC IoMT 2024 dataset provides a valuable benchmark for IoMT security research but underscores the need for models capable of handling complex, multi-protocol IoMT environments and varied attack types.

This study addresses these limitations by introducing a federated learning framework specifically designed for IoMT, leveraging the Random Forest (RF) model for lightweight yet effective threat detection. Unlike prior approaches, this framework is tailored to the resource constraints and data heterogeneity of IoMT devices, using RF's robustness in handling high-dimensional, non-IID data with minimal computational load. This contribution not only enhances IoMT security through efficient, decentralized anomaly detection but also expands the application of federated learning by optimizing it for diverse, resource-constrained medical devices, bridging the gaps identified in the current literature.

3 Research Gaps and Motivation

Federated Learning (FL) offers significant advantages when applied to the Internet of Medical Things (IoMT). These benefits include improved privacy protection, adaptability to various device environments, and scalability across distributed networks. FL enables model training directly on IoMT devices, ensuring that sensitive patient data remains secure and private. Additionally, FL supports the development of robust and adaptable models that can accommodate the diverse nature of IoMT deployments, thereby enhancing the effectiveness of security solutions.

However, current IoMT security approaches are often limited in scope, failing to comprehensively address all device types, attack vectors, and profiling aspects. Traditional methods may overlook certain devices or threats, reducing their effectiveness in real-world healthcare scenarios. Furthermore, the lack of coverage throughout the entire lifecycle of IoMT devices, from integration to disconnection, poses challenges for creating holistic security solutions.

By integrating FL techniques into IoMT security frameworks, many of these limitations can be addressed. FL offers a more comprehensive and adaptable approach to securing IoMT devices. Utilizing datasets like CICIoMT2024, FL methodologies can enhance privacy preservation, improve model adaptability, and foster collaboration among healthcare institutions and device manufacturers, leading to more effective and secure IoMT environments.

4 Main Approach and Experiments

4.1 CICIoMT 2024 Dataset

The features in the CICIoMT2024 dataset are essential for understanding and analyzing network traffic patterns in IoMT environments. As IoMT devices become more widespread, effective network monitoring and security measures are increasingly vital.

Features such as header length, duration, and rate provide key insights into the basic characteristics of packet transmission, helping to evaluate network performance and efficiency. Additionally, TCP/IP flag values offer important information about device communication behavior, which is crucial for detecting potential anomalies or security threats.

Incorporating application layer protocol indicators such as HTTPS, HTTP, and DNS helps identify specific services or applications running on the network, enabling administrators to monitor and manage traffic more effectively. Similarly, analysing transport layer protocols like TCP and UDP provides insight into the underlying communication mechanisms, aiding in network optimization.

Furthermore, statistical metrics like packet length distribution and packet interval times offer a deeper understanding of traffic dynamics and behaviour, allowing analysts to detect irregularities or suspicious activities within the network.

The features included in the CICIoMT2024 dataset are fundamental for network traffic analysis, offering researchers and practitioners valuable insights into IoMT network behaviour, enhancing security measures, and optimizing network performance.

4.2 Testing Environment and Methodology

This study utilizes Python 3.11.7 as the development environment, leveraging libraries such as pandas for data analysis, numpy for numerical computations, and scikit-learn's StandardScaler for feature standardization. Model development is carried out using

TensorFlow's Keras API, with the Sequential model for constructing neural networks and Dense layers for defining their architecture. The to-categorical function is used for converting class labels into one-hot encoded vectors, essential for classification tasks.

To assess model performance, a range of evaluation metrics from scikit-learn, including accuracy, precision, recall, and F1-score, is employed. Confusion matrices and classification reports provide detailed insights into predictions across different classes. Visualization tools like seaborn and matplotlib are integral to the workflow, allowing for the creation of plots that illustrate data distributions and model performance. The focus on multi-class classification models, including both attack and benign labels, despite the challenges of classifying similar attacks like DoS and DDoS, reflects a commitment to addressing real-world scenarios and enhancing the practical applicability of the models developed.

4.3 Design of the Experiments

To establish a robust training and testing methodology, all CSV files, each representing a distinct label with 45 features, are loaded and organized into separate folders for training and testing. The data is structured into data frames for easier manipulation and analysis.

To simulate distributed IoMT devices, the training data is split into 10 equal data frames, each representing a virtual client or device. Individual models are trained on each subset, capturing localized learning based on unique characteristics.

These models are then federated into a global model using techniques like stacking, voting, or averaging, allowing for comprehensive learning and generalization. The global model's performance is evaluated using the testing data, with metrics such as accuracy, precision, recall, and F1-score calculated to assess effectiveness.

A confusion matrix is also plotted, providing a visual summary of the model's performance across different classes. This methodology offers a thorough understanding of the model's effectiveness in a federated learning environment, supporting informed decision-making and optimization.

4.4 Federated Learning with Random Forest

The federated learning process begins by creating and training ten RandomForest models, each tailored to handle specific subsets of IoMT security data. These subsets are carefully curated to ensure balanced data distribution across the models.

After evaluating these decentralized models, a global federated model is trained using the stacking approach, which aggregates predictions from the individual models. This method allows the global model to draw on the collective insights of the sub-models, leading to improved accuracy.

By combining predictions from various sources, the global model is expected to outperform individual models, offering greater accuracy and robustness in classifying IoMT security threats. This federated learning approach strengthens the overall effectiveness in addressing complex IoMT security challenges.

Once trained, the global federated model is tested against various data scenarios and threat vectors. As the script processes each test file, it aggregates predictions from the individual client models. This aggregation is a key aspect of the stacking approach, combining insights from the decentralized models. The global model then uses these aggregated predictions as new training data, allowing it to develop a comprehensive understanding of the dataset, which enhances its overall accuracy and effectiveness.

This stacking technique highlights the strengths of federated learning, offering a holistic solution to the complex challenges of IoMT security. By leveraging the collective intelligence of multiple models, the federated learning framework effectively addresses the dynamic and evolving threats in the IoMT landscape.

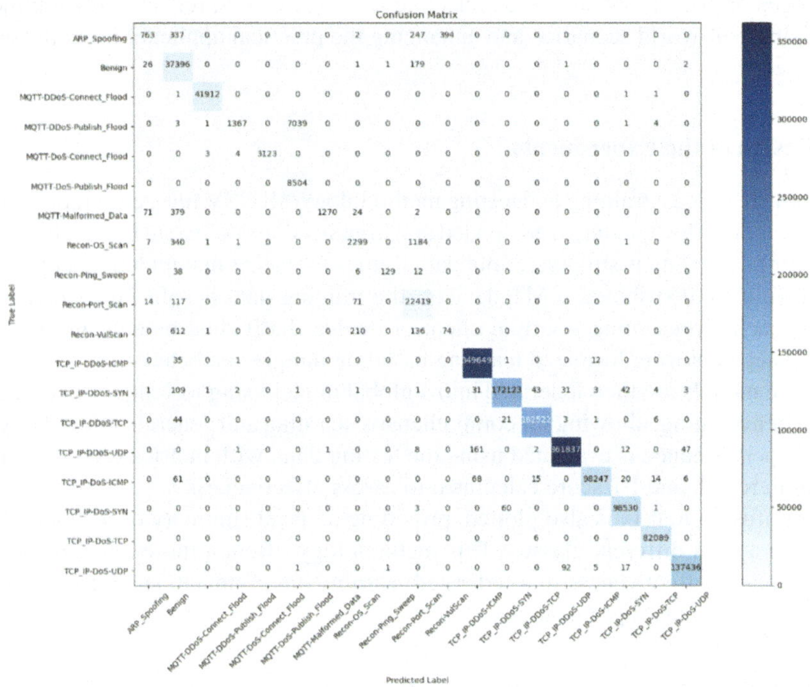

Fig. 1. Confusion matrix for Random Forest with Stacking Federated Learning

The confusion matrix (see Fig. 1) shows the performance of the global RandomForest model trained on different predictions of edge models trained on IoMT security data. Each row represents the true labels, and each column represents the predicted labels.

The analysis reveals key patterns: the model excels in identifying benign traffic, shown by a high number of true positives (TP), but struggles with certain attack types like ARP Spoofing and MQTT Malformed Data, which have lower accuracy and more false negatives (FN).

The Random Forest (RF) model emerges as an excellent performer, with an outstanding accuracy of 0.9922. Its precision and recall are almost perfect at 0.9938 and 0.9922, and it also achieves a high F1 score of 0.9909.

5 Conclusion and Perspectives

Federated learning provides a powerful approach to improving IoMT security by enabling decentralized model training and secure aggregation, which enhances both the accuracy and resilience of threat detection.

Future improvements could focus on refining individual models within the federated system to boost overall performance. Techniques like reinforcement learning and neural architecture search may further increase the adaptability of the global model. Additionally, applying tailored feature engineering and data preprocessing specifically for IoMT security can enhance model alignment with IoMT requirements, while more sophisticated anomaly detection methods can help in identifying new threats.

References

1. Messinis, S., Temenos, N., Protonotarios, N.E., Rallis, I., Kalogeras, D., Doulamis, N.: Enhancing internet of medical things security with artificial intelligence: a comprehensive review. Comput. Biol. Med. **170**, 108036 (2024)
2. Otoum, Y., Wan, Y., Nayak, A.: Federated transfer learning-based IDS for the internet of medical things (IoMT). Inst. Electr. Electron. Eng. Inc. (2021)
3. Osman, A., Abid, U., Gemma, L., Perotto, M., Brunelli, D.: TinyML platforms benchmarking (2021)
4. Dwivedi, R., Mehrotra, D., Chandra, S.: Potential of internet of medical things (IoMT) applications in building a smart healthcare system: a systematic review. J. Oral Biol. Craniofac. Res. **12**, 302–318 (2022)
5. Prasad, V.K., et al.: Federated learning for the internet-of-medical-things: a survey. Mathematics **11**, 151 (2022)
6. Nair, A.K., Sahoo, J., Raj, E.D.: Privacy-preserving federated learning framework for IoMT-based big data analysis using edge computing. Comput. Stand. Interfaces **86**(8) (2023)
7. Dadkhah, S., Neto, E.C.P., Ferreira, R., Molokwu, R.C., Sadeghi, S., Ghorbani, A.A.: CICIoMT2024: attack vectors in healthcare devices-a multi-protocol dataset for assessing IoMT device security. J. Internet Things (2024). https://doi.org/10.20944/preprints202402.0898
8. Smith, J., Johnson, S.: Security challenges in IoMT: a survey of healthcare organizations. J. Healthc. Secur. **10**(2), 45–60 (2023)
9. Johnson, S., Lee, D.: Perceptions of IoMT security among healthcare professionals. Healthc. Technol. **5**(3), 123–135 (2022)
10. Wang, W., Chen, L.: Security practices in IoMT device manufacturing. J. Med. Devices **8**(4), 210–225 (2021)
11. Brown, M., Miller, E.: Regulatory frameworks and IoMT security: a comparative analysis. Healthc. Regul. **12**(1), 30–45 (2020)
12. Sun, L., Zhang, Q.: Federated learning approach for intrusion detection in IoMT networks. J. Med. Inform. **10**(2), 45–60 (2023)
13. Zhang, Q., Li, W.: Federated learning for malware detection on IoMT devices. IEEE Trans. Biomed. Eng. **5**(3), 123–135 (2022)
14. Wang, W., Chen, L.: Privacy-preserving data analysis in IoMT using federated learning. J. Healthc. Eng. **8**(4), 210–225 (2021)
15. Chen, Y., Wu, Z.: Federated learning-based anomaly detection in IoMT. J. Med. Devices **12**(1), 30–45 (2020)

16. Cantu-Cervini, E.: Personalized federated learning via stacking (2024)
17. Liu, Z., Jiang, Y., Jiang, W., Guo, J., Zhao, J., Lam, K.-Y.: Guaranteeing data privacy in federated unlearning with dynamic user participation (2024)
18. Theologitis, M., Frangias, G., Anestis, G., Samoladas, V., Deligiannakis, A.: Communication-efficient distributed deep learning via federated dynamic averaging (2024)

Development of a Novel Differential Mobile Robot Platform Based on an Original Hoverboard and Experimental Validation of Field-Oriented Control (FOC) for BLDC Motors

Yassine Rhib(✉), Nabila Rabbah, and Abdelwahed Touati

Laboratory of Complex Cyber Physical Systems, National School of Arts and Crafts, Hassan II University, Casablanca, Morocco
yassinerhib@gmail.com

Abstract. The control techniques for BLDC motors are highly varied and essential for precise and robust navigation of differential mobile robots. Among these methods, vector control with field orientation provides optimal performance. This work aims to integrate two BLDC motors and the motherboard, controlled by an STM32 microcontroller from an original hoverboard, to develop an experimental platform. This will allow us to perform various autonomous navigation tests with the resulting differential mobile robot. The challenge is to replace the original hoverboard motor control with a new system based on a Raspberry Pi 4 using the UART protocol. This new system must enable the control of the two BLDC motors, including vector control, and provide high performance for the mobile part of the robot. Additionally, implementing field-oriented control requires the acquisition of the currents and fluxes from the BLDC motors, which is ensured by the Hall effect sensors integrated into the Hoverboard. This new platform, equipped with lidar and 3D Kinect camera vision systems, will enable us to experiment with innovative visual localization and navigation methods for the differential mobile robot. The speed control results of the new platform and the acquisition of the BLDC motors stator currents were imported into MATLAB for visualization. The results demonstrate enhanced compliance with speed commands for both BLDC motors.

Keywords: BLDC · Differential Mobile Robot · ESP32 · FOC · Hall effect Sensor · Hoverboard · Lidar · MATLAB · Raspberry Pi · STM32 · 3D Kinect Camera

1 Introduction

In recent decades, robotics has seen significant growth, especially in mobile robots, which are now used in a wide range of applications including industrial settings, household tasks, and even space exploration. This evolution is mainly due to the increasing

I. Aboudrar et al. (Eds.): ICESST 2024, SUCI, pp. 229–242, 2025.
https://doi.org/10.1007/978-3-031-86705-7_22

developments in technology, particularly in the fields of sensors, actuators, artificial intelligence, and computing. Autonomous navigation is a crucial element for the efficiency and versatility of mobile robots [1]. It relies on the fusion of data from various sensors, such as cameras, lidars [2], and sonar sensors, as well as the use of sophisticated navigation algorithms. This capability allows mobile robots to move in complex environments, avoid obstacles, and reach specific objectives without human intervention [3]. Autonomous mobile robots (AMRs) have become essential tools in various fields. In logistics and warehousing, they optimize stock management, transport goods, and manage inventory [4]. AMRs help improve productivity, safety, and efficiency in these environments. These robots can navigate healthcare facilities autonomously, deliver medical supplies, and even provide direct assistance to patients, thus improving healthcare efficiency and precision. The integration of autonomous robots in both logistics and biomedical environments illustrates the versatility and transformative potential of this technology [5].

Brushless DC motors (BLDC) are widely used in robotics due to their efficiency, precision, and reliability [6]. Field-Oriented Control (FOC) is a BLDC motor control technique that offers superior performance compared to traditional control methods. FOC allows precise control of the motor's torque and speed, which is essential for robotic applications requiring smooth and precise movements [7]. In this context, our work focuses on developing an experimental platform for a differential mobile robot using the motherboard and BLDC motors from a standard hoverboard (see Fig. 1). A Raspberry Pi 4 is used to control the hoverboard's motherboard and manage the commands required for autonomous navigation. The Robot Operating System (ROS) is used to interpret sensor data from sources such as lidar, a 3D Kinect camera, and a real-time localization system (RTLS). This setup enables the mobile robot to navigate autonomously in various environments.

2 Principle of Field-Oriented Control

Field-Oriented Control (FOC) is an advanced technique for controlling alternating current (AC) motors, such as brushless DC motors (BLDC) and permanent magnet synchronous motors (PMSM). It enables independent control of flux and torque using mathematical transformations. FOC employs Clarke and Park transformations to convert three-phase currents into flux (d-axis) and torque (q-axis) coordinates, simplifying their separate control [8].

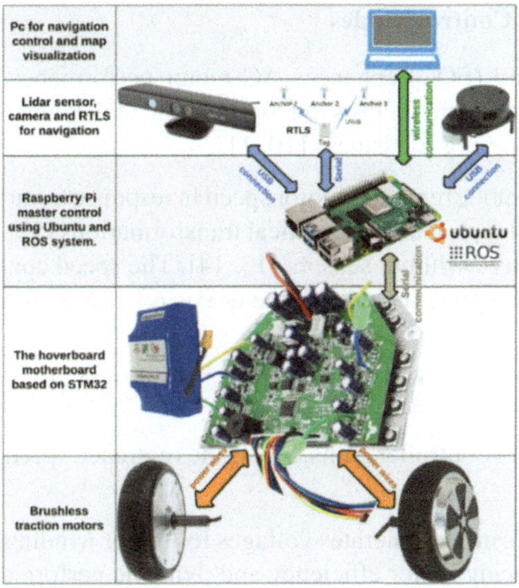

Fig. 1. Hardware structure of the robot.

2.1 Clarke Transformation

Converts three-phase currents (i_a, i_b, i_c) into a stationary coordinate system (i_α, i_β).

$$\begin{pmatrix} i_\alpha \\ i_\beta \end{pmatrix} = \sqrt{\frac{2}{3}} \begin{pmatrix} 1 & -\frac{1}{2} & -\frac{1}{2} \\ 0 & \frac{\sqrt{3}}{2} & -\frac{\sqrt{3}}{2} \end{pmatrix} \begin{pmatrix} i_a \\ i_b \\ i_c \end{pmatrix} \tag{1}$$

2.2 Park Transformation

Leave Converts the currents (i_α, i_β) into a synchronous coordinate system (i_d, i_q), aligned with the rotor.

$$\begin{pmatrix} i_d \\ i_q \end{pmatrix} = \begin{pmatrix} \cos(\theta) & \sin(\theta) \\ -\sin(\theta) & \cos(\theta) \end{pmatrix} \begin{pmatrix} i_\alpha \\ i_\beta \end{pmatrix} \tag{2}$$

where θ is the rotor position angle.

2.3 Different FOC Control Modes

Field-Oriented Control (FOC) enhances AC motor performance, efficiency, and flexibility [9]. Recent research focuses on optimizing algorithms, integrating artificial intelligence, and improving robustness [10, 11].

Speed Control. This mode regulates motor speed in response to varying commands, relying on nested control loops and mathematical transformations [12]. FOC enables precise speed regulation, with or without sensors [13, 14]. The speed control loop uses sensors to measure the current speed and adjusts the q-axis reference current (i^*_q) accordingly:

$$i_q^* = K_p(\omega_r^* - \omega_r) + K_i \int (\omega_r^* - \omega_r)dt \tag{3}$$

where K_p and K_i are PI controller gains, ω^*_r is the reference speed, and ω_r is the current speed.

Voltage Control. This mode generates voltages for motor windings to optimize flux and torque control, enhancing motor efficiency and dynamic performance [15]. Techniques like direct control, pulse-width modulation (PWM), and voltage vector control adapt to application needs [16]. The applied voltage (V_s) is calculated as:

$$V_s = \sqrt{V_d^2 + V_q^2} \tag{4}$$

where V_s is the applied voltage, and V_d, V_q are the voltages in the d and q axes.

Torque Control. Ensures precise motor operation by adjusting flux and torque components independently using coordinate transformations and PI controllers [17, 18]. The electromagnetic torque (T_e) is expressed as:

$$T_e = \frac{3}{2}p(\psi_d i_q - \psi_q i_d) \tag{5}$$

where p is the number of pole pairs, and ψ_d, ψ_q are the fluxes in the d and q axes.

3 Hardware and Software Configuration of the Hoverboard's Motherboard

This section outlines the practical application, starting with reprogramming the hoverboard's motherboard to modify its operation and adapt the output pins for project specific needs. The focus is on implementing Field-Oriented Control (FOC) for the motors as an advanced regulation method. The process concludes with functional testing and data collection. Control is facilitated via the ESP32 [19], utilizing UART communication between the motherboard and the ESP32 [20]. (Fig. 2) illustrates the key components of the model, including the mobile robot and communication protocols used in this prototype.

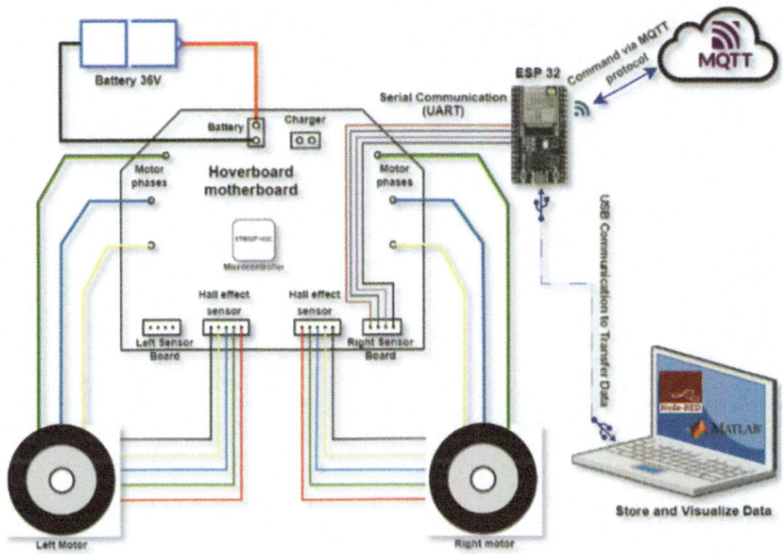

Fig. 2. Block diagram of the test bench robot.

3.1 Materials

In this research utilized several hardware components (Table 1), including the hoverboard motherboard and BLDC motor wheels (specifications in Table 2), forming the robot's core. The chassis is built using a wooden platform and steel support. The ESP32 serves as the main controller, replacing the Raspberry Pi for experimental validation [21]. The robot is powered by a battery.

Table 1. Materials of the research.

N°	Material name	Quantity
1	Motherboard of the hoverboard	1
2	ESP32	1
3	Brushless wheel motor	2
4	Castor wheel	1
5	Battery lithium 36V/4400 mAh	1
6	ST-Link V2 Programmer	1
7	Micro USB cable	1
8	Steel frame	1
9	Wooden platform	1
10	Battery charger 42Vdc	1

The following (Fig. 3) below shows the test bench model that we constructed. This model serves as the base platform for our autonomous robot.

Table 2. The technical characteristics of the BLDC motor-wheel.

Description	Value
Product material	metal + ABS
Engine type	brushless
Engine weight alone	2,65 kg
Engine diameter without tire	135 mm
Nominal voltage	36 V
Maximum power	450 W
Minimum power	250 W
Average power	350 W
Nominal torque	28 N.m
No-load rotation speed	235 rpm
Rotation speed under load	190 rpm
No-load linear speed	31.5 km/h
Linear speed under load	25 km/h

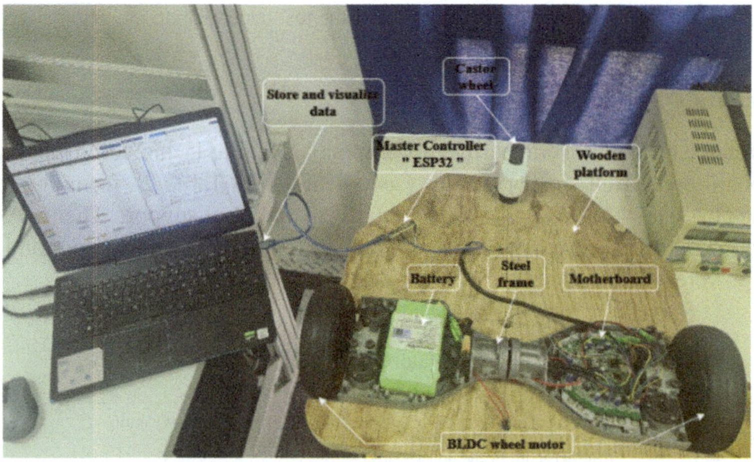

Fig. 3. The robot model for the test bench.

3.2 Hardware Layout of the STM32 Microcontroller Pins

This section explains the reprogramming of the hoverboard's motherboard to modify its original operation, initially based on two gyroscopic sensors for motor control [22]. The control system is replaced with UART protocol [23], enabling the management of motor direction and speed, optimizing the hardware for the robot's mobile component. (Fig. 4) illustrates the motherboard and its key elements.

The first step is to reactivate the previously deactivated gyroscopic sensor pins, reconfiguring them as UART communication ports for data exchange between the microcontroller and peripherals. The following (Fig. 5) shows the new STM32 microcontroller configuration in "STM32CubeMX" software [24].

Fig. 4. The Hoverboard mainboard.

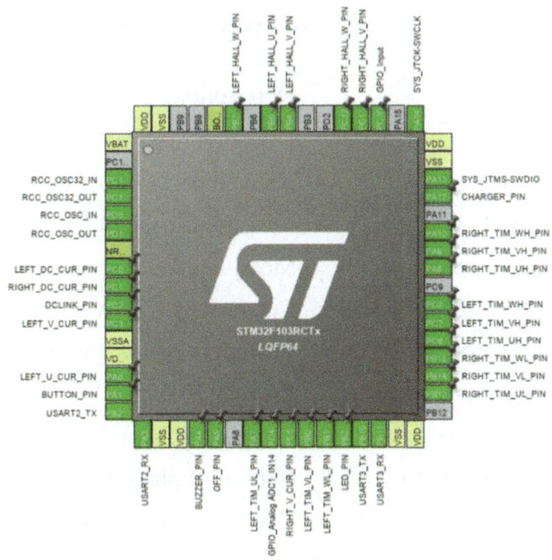

Fig. 5. The pin configuration of the STM32F103 microcontroller.

3.3 Reconfiguration of the Hoverboard's Motherboard Firmware

This phase presents the algorithm of the new firmware (see Fig. 6), which aims to replace the initial gyroscope-based control with communication-based control [25].

3.4 Main Communication Frames

Table 3 summarizes the key parameters exchanged via UART with the hoverboard's motherboard. To consolidate the data, we established a "Serial Feedback" structure, incorporating "Start" and "Checksum" parameters for robust communication [23]. These ensure data integrity. (Fig. 7) shows the frame format transmitted by the motherboard.

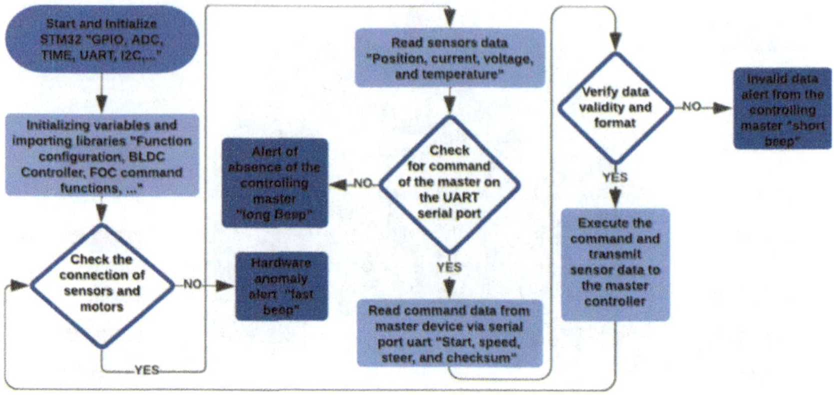

Fig. 6. Firmware algorithm of Hoverboard motherboard

Table 3. Parameters exchanged via the UART protocol with the hoverboard's motherboard

Parameter	Significant	Description
Cmd1	Command 1	Direction received from the master controller
Cmd2	Command 2	Speed received from the master controller
SpeedR_meas	Speed Right wheel	Measured speed of the right wheel
SpeedL_meas	Speed Left wheel	Measured speed of the left wheel
DC_PhaA_R	DC current phase A Right	Current of phase A of the right wheel
DC_PhaB_R	DC current phase B Right	Current of phase B of the right wheel
DC_PhaC_R	DC current phase C Right	Current of phase C of the right wheel
DC_PhaA_L	DC current phase A Left	Current of phase A of the left wheel
DC_PhaB_L	DC current phase B Left	Current of phase B of the left wheel
DC_PhaC_L	DC current phase C Left	Current of phase C of the left wheel
BatVoltage	Battery voltage	Measured battery level value
BoardTemp	Board temperature	Measured temperature value of the motherboard

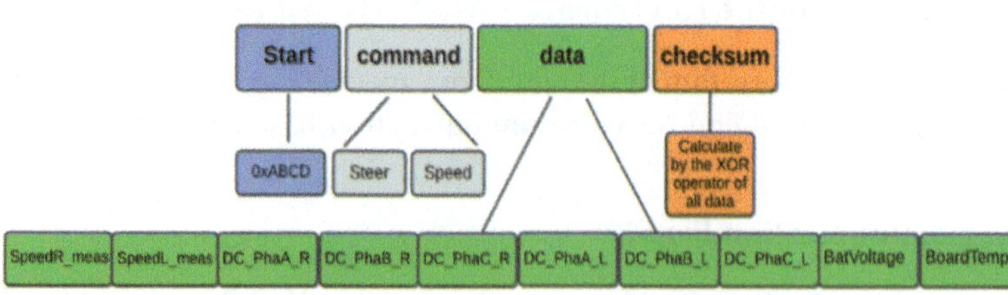

Fig. 7. The frame format of feedback data from hoverboard.

3.5 UART-Based Communication Platform

The ESP32 serves as the master controller for the hoverboard, using the UART protocol to transmit commands and analyze feedback [26]. This ensures accurate execution of commands sent by the ESP32 (see Fig. 8) and validates results via hoverboard feedback (see Fig. 7). The following (Fig. 9) presents the algorithm implemented on the ESP32 for communication [19].

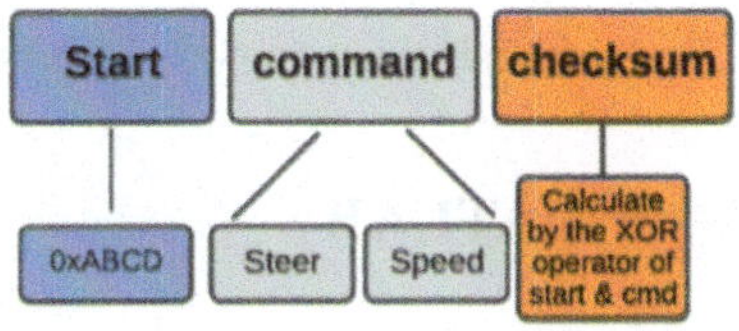

Fig. 8. The frame command format from ESP32.

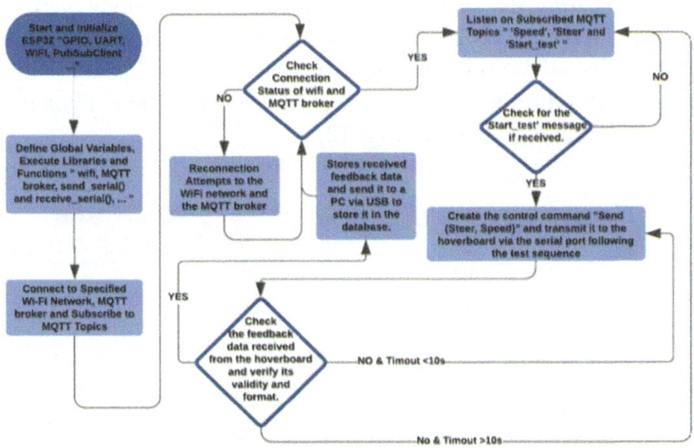

Fig. 9. Firmware algorithm of ESP32 master controller.

3.6 Experimental Testing Scenario

Each experimental test lasted 16 s, divided into distinct phases as shown in (Fig. 10). Four tests were conducted, differing in two key parameters: speed and load. The speed parameter varied between low and high values to assess the robot's performance under different dynamic conditions, while the load parameter alternated between unloaded and loaded states to simulate various operational scenarios (see Fig. 9). These variations allowed for a comprehensive evaluation of the system's response to different operating conditions.

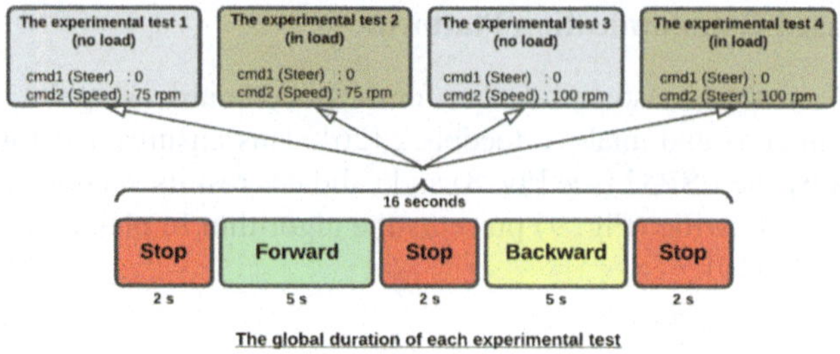

Fig. 10. Duration and structure of experimental tests.

4 Simulation Results on MATLAB

During experimental tests, sensor data from the hoverboard's motherboard were continuously acquired and stored in a database for processing and visualization in MATLAB. The measured speeds showed excellent agreement with the reference speeds for both BLDC motors, indicating the system's precise control over motor performance. The figures below present the curves derived from the stored data for tests conducted under both loaded and unloaded conditions, using identical speed profiles for both motors [27]. This consistency highlights the effectiveness of the control system in maintaining target speeds, regardless of changes in load (Fig. 12).

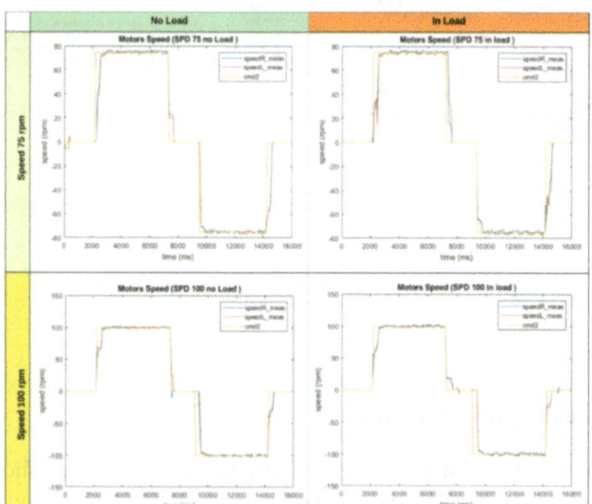

Fig. 11. Wheel speeds for each test.

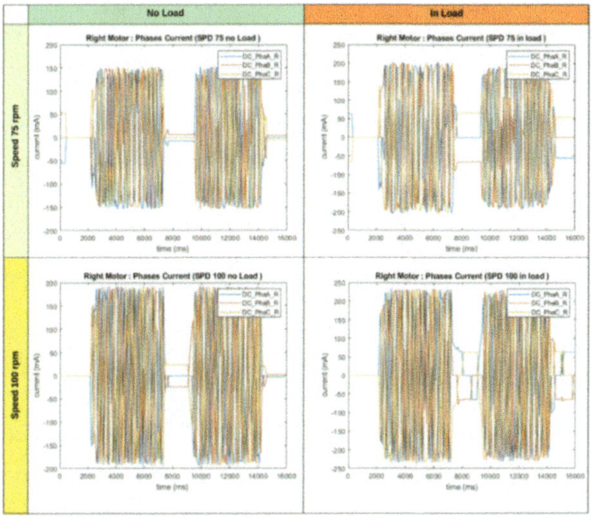

Fig. 12. Current shapes for the 3 phases of the motor.

In particular, the speed curves in (Fig. 11) demonstrate that the measured speeds ("SpeedR_meas," "SpeedL_meas") closely track the command setpoints ("cmd_2"). This validates the synchronous communication between the ESP32 master controller and the STM32 slave microcontroller. The strong correlation between the reference and measured speeds suggests that the communication platform and control algorithms are functioning as expected, with minimal signal loss or delay.

Furthermore, Park transformations applied to the three-phase currents of the BLDC motors across different test cases revealed consistent trends in the direct and quadrature components of the currents (Fig. 13). These results are important because they confirm the expected current behavior for both motors under varying operational conditions. The consistency of the current components supports the reliability of the control algorithms in managing motor torque and flux independently, which is essential for maintaining stable operation under different loads. Any slight deviations observed could be attributed to factors such as sensor noise, minor inaccuracies in motor characterization, or slight communication delays between the microcontrollers.

Overall, the experimental results provide strong evidence of the system's effectiveness in managing motor performance, confirming that the control system is well-tuned for both unloaded and loaded scenarios. The consistent alignment of measured data with reference profiles suggests that the system can reliably handle varying operational conditions, further validating the performance of the control algorithms and communication setup.

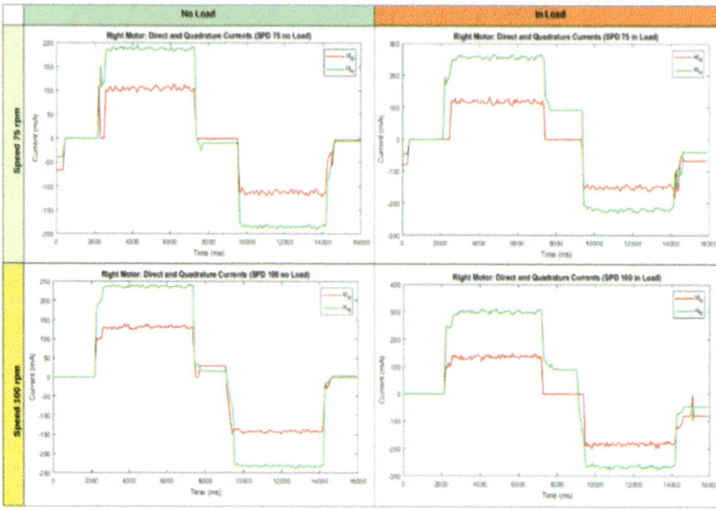

Fig. 13. Direct and quadrature currents of the motor.

5 Conclusion

This work has enabled the use of two BLDC motors and the motherboard controlled by an STM32 microcontroller from an original hoverboard to develop a novel platform intended for autonomous navigation tests of a differential mobile robot. The challenge was to replace the initial control system of the hoverboard's motors with a new control system based on the Raspberry Pi 4 using the UART protocol, thus enabling the control of the direction and speed of the two BLDC motors. The control technique for the BLDC motors is based on field-oriented control to achieve better performance for the mobile part of the robot.

An initial phase consisted of reactivating the pins of the hoverboard's gyroscopic sensors, which had been previously disabled. These pins would serve as UART communication ports, facilitating data exchange between the microcontroller and other peripherals. Then, the Field-Oriented Control (FOC) technique was implemented and validated for controlling the two BLDC motors of the differential mobile robot. The results from the sensors integrated into the hoverboard's motherboard demonstrated a very good tracking of the reference speeds for the two BLDC motors. Additionally, the stator currents from the Hall effect sensors integrated into the hoverboard's motherboard were imported and plotted in SIMULINK. The results showed very homogeneous amplitude variations corresponding to the changes in the loads supported by the differential mobile robot.

Finally, we can conclude that the platform thus developed provides a flexible and experimental educational solution for testing the main navigation algorithms of the differential mobile robot. Furthermore, our platform is well-suited for future applications where robotic systems will integrate into a networked environment, communicating with industrial control systems, cloud services, and other systems at remote locations.

References

1. Harapanahalli, S., Mahony, N.O., Hernandez, G.V., Campbell, S., Riordan, D., Walsh, J.: Autonomous navigation of mobile robots in factory environment. Procedia Manuf. **38**, 1524–1531 (2019)
2. Thepsit, T., Konghuayrob, P., Saenthon, A., Yanyong, S.: Localization for outdoor mobile robot using LiDAR and RTK-GNSS/INS. Sensors Mater. **36**(4), 1405 (2024)
3. Bonin-Font, F., Ortiz, A., Oliver, G.: Visual navigation for mobile robots: a survey. J. Intell. Rob. Syst. **53**(3), 263–296 (2008)
4. Azadeh, K., De Koster, M.B.M., Roy, D.: Robotized warehouse systems: developments and research opportunities. In: Social Science Research Network (2017)
5. Dhaliwal, A.: The Rise of Automation and Robotics in Warehouse Management, pp. 63–72. CRC Press eBooks (2020)
6. Hwang, C.C., Li, P.L., Liu, C.T., Chen, C.: Design and analysis of a brushless DC motor for applications in robotics. IET Electr. Power Appl. **6**(7), 385 (2012)
7. Mahmud, M., Motakabber, S.M.A., Alam, A.Z., Nordin, A.N.: Control BLDC motor speed using PID controller. Int. J. Adv. Comput. Sci. Appl. **11**(3), 477–481 (2020)
8. Blaschke, F.: The principle of field orientation as applied to the NEW transvector closed-loop system for rotating-field machines. Siemens Rev. **34**(3), 217–220 (1972)
9. Bose, B.K.: Modern Power Electronics and Ac Drives (2015)
10. Kabzinski, J.: Advanced Control of Electrical Drives and Power Electronic Converters (2017)
11. Krishnan, R.: Electric Motor Drives: Modeling, Analysis, and Control (2001)
12. Holtz, J.: Sensorless control of induction motor drives. Proc. IEEE **90**(8), 1359–1394 (2002)
13. Fadli, M.R., Mushthofa Musyasy, M., Furqani, J., Purwadi, A.: Modelling of field orientation control (FOC) method in 120 kW brushless DC motor (BLDC). In: 2019 6th International Conference on Electric Vehicular Technology (ICEVT), pp. 383–389 (2019)
14. Kandiban, R., Arulmozhiyal, R.: Speed control of BLDC motor using adaptive fuzzy PID controller. Procedia Eng. **38**, 306–313 (2012)
15. Leonhard, W.: Control of Electrical Drives (2001)
16. Gujjar, M.N., Kumar, P.: Comparative analysis of field-oriented control of BLDC motor using SPWM and SVPWM techniques. In: 2nd IEEE International Conference on Recent Trends in Electronics, Information & Communication Technology (RTEICT), pp. 924–929 (2017)
17. Sharma, T.R., Pal, Y.: Direct torque control of BLDC drives with reduced torque pulsations. In: 3rd International Conference on Electronics, Communication and Aerospace Technology (ICECA) (2019)
18. Lazor, M., Stulrajter, M.: Modified field-oriented control for smooth torque operation of a BLDC motor. In: ELEKTRO, pp. 180–185 (2014)
19. Ahmed, A.S., Marzog, H.A., Abdul-Rahaim, L.A.: Design and implement of robotic arm and control of moving via IoT with Arduino ESP32. Int. J. Electr. Comput. Eng. **11**(5), 3924 (2021)
20. Daraban, M., Corches, C., Taut, A., Chindris, G.: Protocol over UART for real-time applications. In: IEEE 27th International Symposium for Design and Technology in Electronic Packaging (SIITME), pp. 85–88 (2021)
21. Hercog, D., Lerher, T., Truntič, M., Težak, O.: Design and implementation of ESP32-based IoT devices. Sensors **23**(15), 6739 (2023)
22. Rusli, M.R., et al.: BLDC motor drives with a programmable simplified C-block to generate accurate six-step PWM based on STM32 microcontroller. Elinvo (Electron. Inf. Vocat. Educ.) **7**(2), 112–118 (2023)
23. Gong, J., Guo, W., Sun, W.: UART communication protocol frame format explanation and application. Appl. Comput. Eng. **14**(1), 47–56 (2023)

24. Noviello, C.: Mastering STM32 (2016)
25. Pakdel, M.: Advanced Programming with STM32 Microcontrollers (2020)
26. Martinez, F., Rendon, A.: Autonomous motion planning for a differential robot using particle swarm optimization. Int. J. Adv. Comput. Sci. Appl. **14**(4), 1–8 (2023)
27. Das, U., Biswas, P.K., Debnath, S.: A comparative study between load and no-load condition of brushless DC motor drives by using MATLAB. J. Power Technol. **98**(3), 281–286 (2017)

Unraveling the AI Revolution in Management Control Through Comprehensive Bibliometric Analysis

Chama Radi[1(✉)], Mariame Ababou[2], and Sara Rabiai[3]

[1] Research Laboratory in Entrepreneurship and Management of Organizations (REMO), Fez Business School, Private University of Fez, Fez, Morocco
Chamaradi2710@gmail.com

[2] Higher School of Technology, Nador (ESTN), University Mohammed I Oujda, Oujda, Morocco
Mariame.ababou.ma@gmail.com

[3] Higher School of Technology, Dakhla (ESTD), Ibn Zohr University, Agadir, Morocco
s.rabiai@uiz.ac.ma

Abstract. Nowadays, artificial intelligence has become one of the pillars of companies' business efficiency. To analyze trends in this field, we conducted a bibliometric study of 301 articles published in the Scopus database between 2006 and 2024. The analysis is based on quantitative indicators such as keyword occurrence networks and bibliographic citations.

Using this approach, we were able to identify six clusters, each emphasizing specific aspects of integrating AI into business performance. First, digital transformation and AI for business performance, second, decision support systems and performance measurement in industry and supply chains. Third, advanced analytics and machine learning for industry and business optimization. Fourth, new technologies for business process automation and efficiency improvement. Fifth, data-driven strategic management to improve business performance and customer satisfaction. Finally, AI-based human resource management and natural language processing for corporate intelligence.

Our findings indicate the growing importance of AI in various aspects of business management. However, our study also revealed research gaps.

Keywords: artificial intelligence · AI · Management · Performance · Business · Optimization

1 Introduction

Over the last few decades, artificial intelligence has made significant progress in many fields, including business and government. "Since the beginning of the 21st century, artificial intelligence has gone from a futuristic idea to an essential tool for improving the efficiency and competitiveness of organizations" [1].

I. Aboudrar et al. (Eds.): ICESST 2024, SUCI, pp. 243–255, 2025.
https://doi.org/10.1007/978-3-031-86705-7_23

An increasingly valuable tool in a variety of industries, the use of artificial intelligence is transforming traditional approaches to management and control by providing innovative solutions to improve business performance and decision-making.

In the business world, AI is playing a strategic role in decision support by enabling managers to process large amounts of data and extract the information they need to determine company strategy. Artificial intelligence is a part of computer science that studies the mechanisms of human behavior. This work is usually done using artificial systems in the form of computer programs that simulate these mechanisms. The term artificial intelligence was invented by the American scientist John McCarthy [2].

Artificial intelligence is defined as the ability of machines to think, behave, and even act like humans [3], and has become a basic activity for organizations of all kinds. Therefore, artificial intelligence (AI) has changed many aspects of modern life, and its use in demand forecasting is one of the most dynamic and promising areas. As artificial intelligence technology evolves, this offers an excellent opportunity to improve the accuracy of demand forecasting in various industries [4].

To ensure that business operations are conducted properly, it is important for management to strategically manage a company's operations using flexible strategies, artificial intelligence, and data analysis capabilities. This approach supports the business and it is difficult to respond to the invisible demand at this time. Financial intelligence is an organization's ability to predict and adapt to changes in the environment by collecting, interpreting, and transmitting significant information through management strategies, artificial intelligence techniques, and data analysis capabilities. This information allows management to make effective business decisions and act accordingly [4].

Our analysis was extended from 2006 to 2024 and includes 20 years of research. It is based on information from Scopus, who is known for its extensive coverage of scientific literature [5].

Question 1: Which is the most influential and productive author, agency?
Question 2: Which is the most influential and productive magazine, country?
Question 3: What are the main trends and topics of this study?
Question 4: What is the future direction of research in this field?

To answer these questions, we will continue to analyze the bibliography for the integration of AI into corporate management performance. This analysis is divided into three parts, the first part is the systematic part and then it is analyzed. The second part shows the results found in Scopus and Vosviewer. After that, we have completed the third part, which analyzes the current state of the integration of AI in the field of corporate management performance.

2 Sources and Methodology

Definitions: Before starting the bibliographic analysis, it is necessary to clearly define the objectives of this analysis. The authors seek to identify major contributors and analyze the conceptual framework for their collaboration in a research area that integrates artificial intelligence into business management functions (Belmonte & al., 2020). We decided to focus only on the Scopus database for our bibliographic analysis. While many other online databases allow keyword searches, this database has almost all the relevant resources to integrate artificial intelligence into management control, be it scientific journals, conference reports or books. Our literature was reviewed using VOSviewer software. This option is due to the recognition of this open-source tool that is widely used for visualizing bibliographic networks in the field of science. The VOSviewer has been introduced in many previous literary surveys.

Main Conditions and Stages of Research: To conduct our research in the Scopus database, we selected a set of keywords to perform searches, titles and summaries of publications, without limiting our search to specific types of documents. (TITLE-ABS-KEY («artificial intelligence" OR AI) AND TITLE-ABS-KEY (management AND performance AND optimization) AND TITLE-ABS-KEY (business AND companies)) AND PUBYEAR > 2005 AND PUBYEAR < 2025. We have prepared 301 documents for analysis from 2006 to 2024.

Data Collection: For data collection, we collect citations (author, title of the document, year, source...), library information (apps, publisher, editor, language of the original document...), and other information. Exported summary and keyword information (including personal summary, author's slogan, index words) and other information (including trade and manufacturer names, access numbers and chemicals, conference information, references). This database was then created in the VOSviewer.The stages of bibliometric analysis (by author).

Bibliometric Analysis
The choice of this methodology is based on its ability to conduct a comprehensive and in-depth analysis of the state of research on artificial intelligence in management control and performance. By combining a bibliometric approach with content analysis, we were able to uncover key trends, recurring patterns and promising clues for future investigations in this field of study. This dual quantitative and qualitative perspective has enabled us to have a rich and nuanced overview. In addition, systematic bibliometric analysis offers the advantage of being reproducible and less biased, thereby enhancing the reliability of the results. The rigorous review of the content of key publications has subsequently enabled the interpretation of bibliometric data to be contextualized and enriched. This methodological synergy has proved to be relevant for such a broad and interdisciplinary topic as integration of AI in performance and optimization of companies (Table 1).

3 Results

Publications By Year: The first publication was in 1986, but after the filtration we chose since 2006 since there was only one publication every two or three years. Since 2006, publications on our topic the role of artificial intelligence for business performance have begun to be published but in a stable and rare way, until 2013 or we can observe a significant peak of 14 papers that coincides with advances in the field of AI and deep learning in the business world [6]. Then we find a gradual decline in the years that followed, until 2019 when the subject resumed its trend in the world but it did not last long given the life change in this year of a COVID-19 [7].

Table 1. The stages of bibliometric analysis (by author).

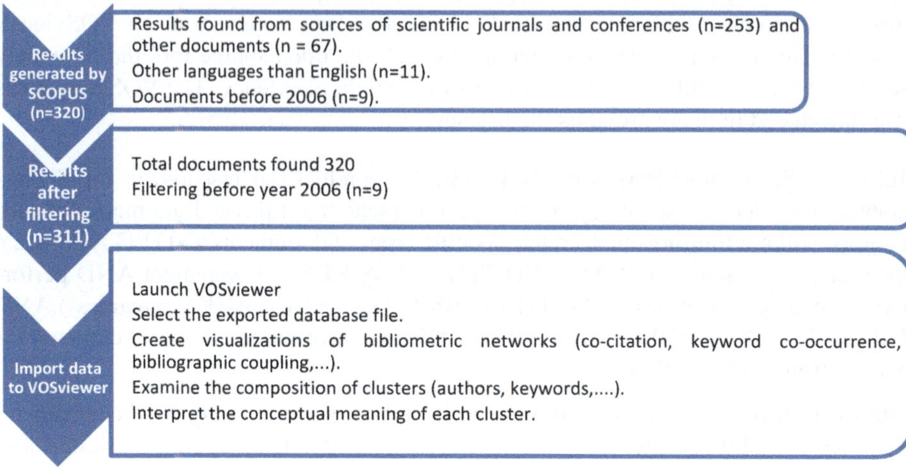

And since then, we've seen a very significant peak, given the emergence of new research paths. The final result of publication in 2024 is not yet known since our database was taken in June 2024 (Fig. 1).

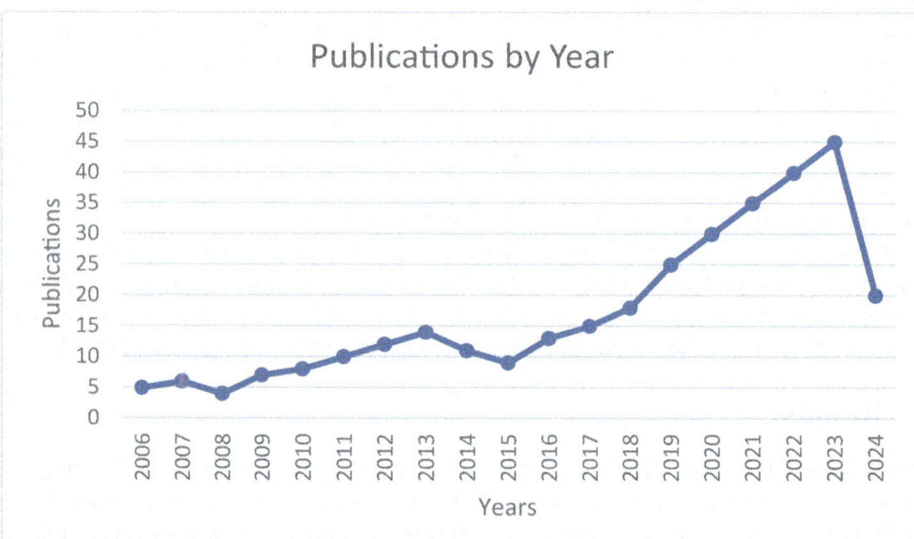

Fig. 1. Publications by years.

Document Type: Publications on the topic role of artificial intelligence for business performance (n = 311) were published by different types, namely 78.4% between conference articles and newspaper articles, this is the most represented category. While all other types of publication are 21.6%, a share of 11.6% (n = 36) of book chapters which is a considerable amount, and a very critical presence by 1.9% of other publications. We had the database on Scopus, and then this database was copied to Excel to have the following graph (Fig. 2).

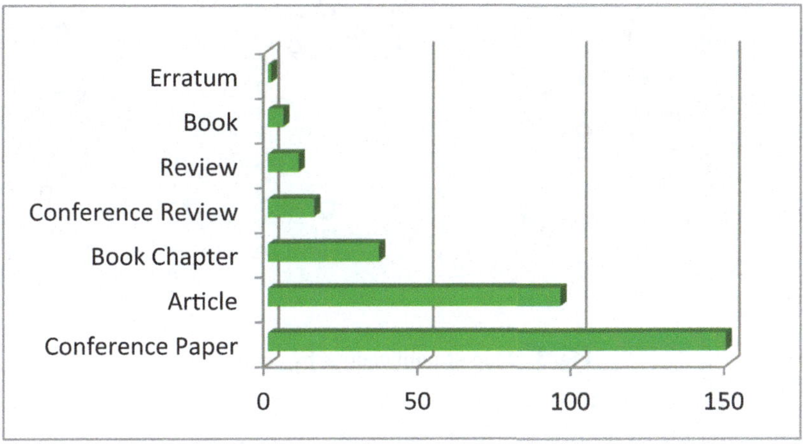

Fig. 2. The types of documents published in our topic

Country Analysis: To better grasp the global dynamics of the impact of artificial intelligence on business performance, we have plunged into a detailed analysis of the interest shown by different countries. It must be acknowledged that the assignment of a study to a specific country or continent is not always obvious, because today's research is often fed on international collaborations. This reality leads us to question the geographical distribution of AI expertise and its concrete implications in the business world. For this point, we have exported the Scopus database on the most influential countries on this subject. In order to obtain a clear visual representation of the geographical distribution of the contributions, we then conducted a map analysis using Google Maps. According to these data, the country that publishes the most for this subject by 20% is India as this country invests significant investments in AI and information technologies, as highlighted in the report of NITI Aayog (2021) at the level of AI development and programming. Russia was followed by 13.20% and China by 10.6%. That is, 5% of searches are undefined. This figure ilustre this (Fig. 3).

Most Significant Contribution: Before proceeding to Vosviewer's analysis, we present a table of the top 10 authors most contributing to the topic of the role of artificial intelligence for business performance on the Scopus platform. To identify these major contributions, we reviewed the most cited articles on artificial intelligence and business performance. We have counted the number of times each of the articles found has been

Fig. 3. Map of publications by country

quoted by other researchers in the field. This table contains the authors, the number of quotes, the title, the year and the journal (Table 2).

Table 2. The 10 most cited authors in this topic

Author	Citations	Year	Title	Sources
Van Horenbeek	175	2014	Development of a maintenance performance measurement framework-using the analytic network process (anp) for maintenance performance indicator selection	Omega
Hanga	90	2019	Machine learning and multi-agent systems in oil and gas industry applications: a survey	Computer sciene review

(*continued*)

Table 2. *(continued)*

Author	Citations	Year	Title	Sources
Tong	89	2021	The janus face of artificial intelligence feedback: deployement versus disclosure effects on employee performance	Strategic management journal
Lee	81	2011	Design and development of logistics workflow systems for demand management with rfid	Expert systems with applications
Luckow	67	2015	Automotive big data: applications, workloads and infrastructures	Procededings- 2015ieee international conference on big data
Ivanov	63	2022	Biosecurity, crisis management, automation technologies and economic performance of travel, tourism and hospitality companies-a conceptual framework	Tourism economics
Jung	62	2021	Application of machine learning technique in injection molding quality prediction: implications on sustainable manufacturing industry	Sustainability
Wu	51	2012	A novel bi-vector encoding genetic algorithm for the simultaneous multiple resources scheduling problem	Journal of intelligent manufacturing
Taymouri	49	2021	Business process variant analysis: survey and classification	Knowledge- based systems
Kushwaha	38	2024	Markbot- a language model- driven chatbot for interactive marketing in post-modern world	Information systems frontiers

Following this table, we present Vosviewer's analysis showing outstanding research work in the field of the integration of artificial intelligence into the performance of. This analysis encompasses all the work found in our research (Fig. 4).

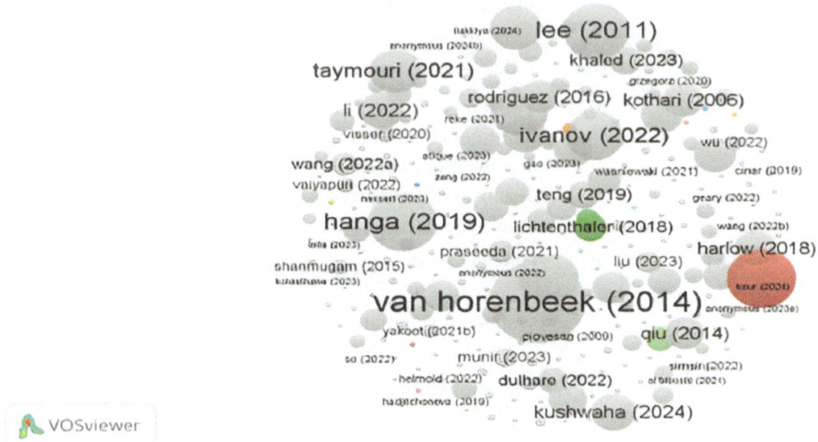

Fig. 4. List of quotations from the authors quoted.

4 Mapping of Research Areas

After a brief analysis of the types of publications, the countries, documents and authors most contributing to the topic of integrating artificial intelligence for business performance. It is necessary to have a deeper analysis of the grouped keywords in order to know the areas of research on Vosviewer by "co-occurrences, all keyword" (Fig. 5).

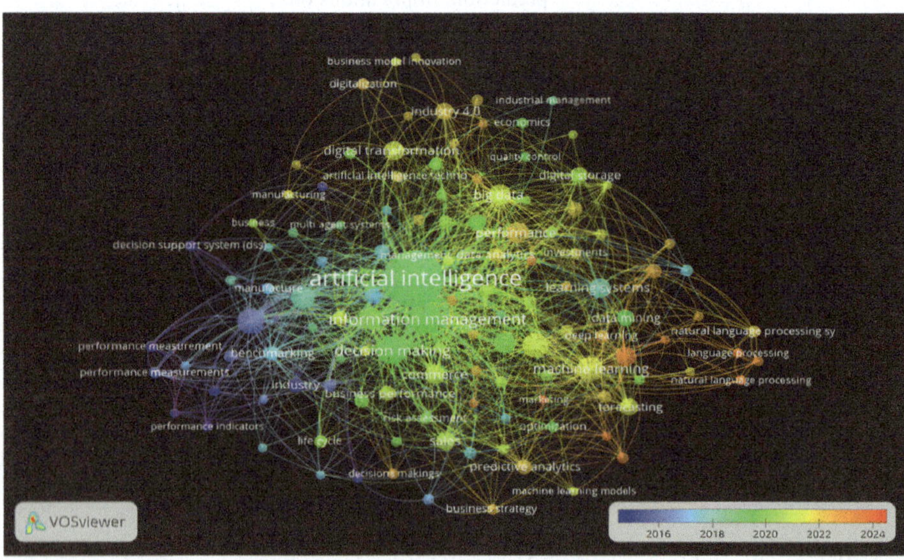

Fig. 5. Coincidence keyword network.

4.1 Keyword Analysis

Vosviewer helped us create a network of linked keywords, which is crucial for a bibliometric review. This link gathers all keywords, whether indexed or not, from 2016 to June 2024. Keywords that are in a green color that focuses on artificial intelligence, the term developed in 2020 and connected with other terms such as decision making, information management, and business performance. We all have what is related to performance in 2016, which includes terms such as: performance measurement and performance indicators. There is also in 2022 everything concerning Industry 4.0 and digital transformation (Table 3).

Table 3. Keyword network by author.

CLUSTERS	COLORS	ITEM	MAINS ITEMS	CLUSTER LABEL
CLUSTER 1	Red	27	Ai; artficial intelligence; big data; business; business model innovation, business-intelligence; competition.... Manufacturing; metadata; optimisations; performances evaluation;	AI-Enhanced Business Performance in the Digital Era
CLUSTER 2	Green	25	benchmarking; businees intelligence; decision making; decision support system; (dss); decision support systems; decisions makings; industry; information analysis; key performance indicators....; performance; profitability; supply chains	Data-Driven Decision Support and Performance Measurement in Manufacturing and Supply Chains
CLUSTER 3	Blue	19	advanced analytics; data mining; digital storage; economics; finance; industrial management; industrial revolutions; machine learning models; operations mangement; quality control; software engineering	Advanced Analytics and Machine Learning for Industrial and Organizational Optimization

(*continued*)

Table 3. (*continued*)

CLUSTERS	COLORS	ITEM	MAINS ITEMS	CLUSTER LABEL
CLUSTER 4	Yellow	18	automation; blockchain; business management; business process; efficiency; entreprise resource planning; firm performance….; neural networks; performance management; public utilities; robotics	Emerging Technologies for Business Process Automation and Performance Enhancement
CLUSTER 5	Purple	18	business environments; business performance; business strategy; commerce; costs; customer satisfaction; decision; information systems; marketing; predictive analytics; risk management; sales; strategic planning	Predictive Analytics for Strategic Business Optimization
CLUSTER 6	Turquois	17	deep learning; human resources management; intelligent robots; language processing; learning algorithms;…; personnel training; reinforcement learning; resource allocation; talent management	AI-Driven Human Resource Management and Natural Language Processing for Organizational Intelligence

4.2 Clusters Analysis

Cluster 1: This cluster focuses on the intersection of artificial intelligence and digital technologies with management control processes and performance improvement. The integration of AI and digital technologies into has become a key driver of competitiveness and innovation. Digital transformation, facilitated by technologies such as the Internet of Things and Industry 4.0, enables companies to optimize their operations and improve their efficiency [8].

Cluster 2: This cluster focuses on the use of data-based decision support tools and performance measurement in industrial and supply chain contexts. Decision support systems play a crucial role in improving decision-making by providing accurate and timely information to managers. In the context of manufacturing and supply chains, SADs can help optimize production processes, stock management, and improve logistics [9]. Using key performance indicators enables companies to measure and track their performance objectively, thus facilitating the identification of areas for improvement [10].

Cluster 3: This cluster centers on applying advanced analytics and machine learning within industrial and organizational settings. Techniques like data exploration and machine learning support improvements in product quality and production process optimization. Key focuses include optimization and quality control, where advanced analytics can fine-tune production parameters and enhance product quality [11].

Cluster 4: This one emphasizes the integration of emerging technologies, such as blockchain and robotics, into business processes and management systems to boost efficiency and performance. Blockchain, for instance, brings substantial benefits in transparency and traceability within supply chains, while enhancing the security of commercial transactions [12]. Performance management plays a key role, as advanced technologies allow for more accurate measurement and monitoring of business performance, enabling companies to identify areas for improvement. However, effective implementation requires strategic planning, robust change management, and alignment with organizational goals [10].

Cluster 5: This cluster explores the application of datadriven techniques to strategic business functions, emphasizing decision-making, risk management, and customer-focused processes. Predictive analytics and machine learning can significantly boost business performance in these areas [13]. Advanced analytical tools support corporate strategy and planning by providing deeper insights into the business environment, helping companies to spot opportunities and threats and make well-informed decisions [14]. For example, predictive analysis can be used to predict market trends and adapt strategies accordingly [4].Risk management benefits from machine learning techniques like decision trees, which enhance the evaluation and mitigation of risks.

Cluster 6: This cluster focuses on the application of advanced AI techniques, in the areas of human resource management and natural language processing. The use of these technologies has the potential to transform the way organizations manage their human capital and process information [15]. Natural language processing plays a crucial role in this cluster. NLP systems can be used to analyze internal communications, customer feedback, and social media, thus providing valuable insights into employee and customer feelings [16].

The use of intelligent robots in certain sectors can also transform the nature of work and the skills required by employees. This highlights the importance of effective human resource management and continuing training in an increasingly automated environment [17]. Human and natural resource management also benefits from the application of these advanced technologies. AI can be used to optimize resource allocation, improve operational efficiency and reduce waste [18].

5 Research Gaps and Future Research Opportunities

The clusters analysis has highlighted several areas where further research could make a significant contribution to our understanding of how to integrate AI into business performance. This section is divided into gap and opportunity point.

5.1 Long-Term Impact of AI on Enterprise Performance

Lack: Current research predominantly focuses on short-term AI adoption impacts [19].

Opportunity: Need for longitudinal studies examining AI's evolving impact on organizational performance [20].

5.2 Ethics and Accountability in the Use of AI for Decision-Making

Lack: Limited practical frameworks for ethical AI implementation in business decision-making.[21].

Opportunity: Development of context-specific ethical frameworks balancing efficiency and responsibility [22].

5.3 AI and Business Sustainability

Lack: Insufficient research on AI's role in corporate sustainability [16].

Opportunity: Exploration of AI applications for resource optimization and environmental responsibility [23].

These gaps highlight the need for comprehensive research addressing technological, ethical, and sustainability aspects of AI integration in business processes. Future studies should focus on developing practical frameworks that balance performance optimization with responsible AI implementation.

Authors' Disclosures of Potential Conflicts of Interest. The authors declare no conflict of interest related to this article.

References

1. Davenport, T.H., Ronanki, R.: Don't start with moon shots (2018)
2. Kiefer, D., Ulmer, A.: Application of artificial intelligence to optimize forecasting capability in procurement (2019)
3. Dhamija, P., Bag, S.: Role of artificial intelligence in operations environment: a review and bibliometric analysis. TQM J. **32**, 869–896 (2020)
4. Balar, K., Adil, K., Alami, A.E.: Tendances actuelles dans l'utilisation de l'Intelligence artificielle pour la prévision de la demande : une revue de la littérature. Int J. Finan. Account. Econ. Manag. Audit IJFAEMA **6**, 237–250 (2024)
5. Mongeon, P., Paul-Hus, A.: The journal coverage of web of science and scopus: a comparative analysis. Scientometrics **106**, 213–228 (2016)
6. LeCun, Y., Bengio, Y., Hinton, G.: Deep learning. Nature **521**, 436–444 (2015)
7. Hantrais, L., Allin, P., Kritikos, M., Sogomonjan, M,, Anand, P.B., Livingstone, S., et al.: Covid-19 and the digital revolution (2021). https://bradscholars.brad.ac.uk/handle/10454/18161 Accessed 8 Juill 2024
8. Shilenge, M.C., Telukdarie, A.: Optimization of operational and information technology integration towards industry 4.0. In: IEEE International Symposium on Industrial Electronics, pp. 1076-1081. Institute of Electrical and Electronics Engineers Inc. (2022). https://www.scopus.com/inward/record.uri?eid=2-s2.0-85135825623&doi=10.1109%2fISIE51582.2022.9831605&partnerID=40&md5=a7c1cf30480c446a579c83b6c5076d46

9. The last frontiers of wilderness: tracking loss of intact forest landscapes from 2000 to 2013. Sci. Adv.https://www.science.org/doi/full/10.1126/sciadv.1600821. Accessed 14 Nov 2024
10. Ke, M.: Practical application of computer information systems in enterprise performance management. In: International Conference Distributed Computing Optimization Techniques ICDCOT. Institute of Electrical and Electronics Engineers Inc. (2024). https://www.scopus.com/inward/record.uri?eid=2-s2.0-85193243123&doi=10.1109%2fICDCOT61034.2024.10516199&partnerID=40&md5=f3611083c2275723362ae42e24d457ff
11. Justino, M.D.R.T.F., Texeira-Quirós, J., Gonçalves, A.J., Antunes, M.G., Mucharreira, P.R.: The role of artificial neural networks (ANNs) in supporting strategic management decisions. J. Risk. Finan. Manag. **17** (2024). https://www.scopus.com/inward/record.uri?eid=2-s2.0-85191243080&doi=10.3390%2fjrfm17040164&partnerID=40&md5=53adaac97f9a132db61a5ddddc3ecbe7
12. Hribernik, M., Zero, K., Kummer, S., Herold, D.M.: City logistics: towards a blockchain decision framework for collaborative parcel deliveries in micro-hubs. Transp. Res. Interdisc. Perspect. **8**, 100274 (2020)
13. Akimova, T., Pryymak, S., Kostyakova, A., Usatenko, O., Lytvynenko, V.: The impact of innovations in enterprise accounting and control systems on optimizing the analysis of financial reporting in the transition to IFRS. Econ. Aff. New Delhi **69**, 371–9 (2024)
14. Soyez, J.: Bibliométrie : Apports et limites dans la compréhension de l'environnement scientifique et technologique, l'exemple des neurosciences computationnelles. INRIA, p. 32 (2008). https://inria.hal.science/inria-00327742. Accessed 3 Juill 2024
15. Chevalie, F., Dejoux, C.: Intelligence artificielle et Management des ressources humaines : pratiques d'entreprises. Ann Mines-Enjeux Numér. **94** (2021)
16. Artificial intelligence for sustainability: challenges, opportunities, and a research agenda-ScienceDirect. https://www.sciencedirect.com/science/article/abs/pii/S0268401220300967. Accessed 14 Nov 2024
17. Egger, H., Grossmann, V.: Non-routine tasks, restructuring of firms, and wage inequality within and between skill-groups. J. Econ. **86**, 197–228 (2005)
18. Boushaba, I., Chakor, A.: L'impact de l'intelligence artificielle sur le management de projet : opportunites et defis. Int. J. Econ. Manag. Res. **4**, 87–109 (2023)
19. Calvo, E., Cui, R., Serpa, J.C.: Oversight and efficiency in public projects: a regression discontinuity analysis. Manag. Sci. (2019). https://pubsonline.informs.org/doi/abs/10.1287/mnsc.2018.3202. Accessed 3 juill 2024
20. Agrawal, A., Gans, J., Goldfarb, A.: The Economics of Artificial Intelligence. University of Chicago Press (2019)
21. Floridi, L.: Soft ethics, the governance of the digital and the general data protection regulation. Phil. Trans. R Soc. Math. Phys. Eng. Sci. **376**, 20180081 (2018)
22. Jobin, A., Ienca, M., Vayena, E.: The global landscape of AI ethics guidelines. Nat. Mach. Intell. **1**, 389–399 (2019)
23. Artificial intelligence and business models in the sustainable development goals perspective: a systematic literature review-scienceDirect. https://www.sciencedirect.com/science/article/abs/pii/S0148296320305191. Accessed 14 Nov 2024

IoT, Cybersecurity and Digital Infrastructures for Smart Cities

IoT Security: Cost-Effective Solution for Detecting Multiple Attacks in IoT Network Using Machine Learning

Abdelkabir Rouagubi[1(✉)], Elmehdi Benmalek[2], and Omar Enassiri[1]

[1] Engineering Sciences Laboratory, National School of Applied Sciences, Ibn Tofail University, Kenitra, Morocco
abdelkabir.rouagubi@uit.ac.ma

[2] ENSAM de Rabat, Mohammed V University of Rabat, Rabat, Morocco

Abstract. The exponential expansion of the Internet of Things (IoT) has resulted in a heightened level of automation and connectedness among gadgets, eliminating the need for deliberate user involvement, thereby augmenting the overall quality of our lives. Nevertheless, the security of IoT devices is a paramount issue since they are susceptible to cyber-attacks, which can result in substantial harm if not promptly identified and addressed. The present work introduces a methodology that combines three machine learning classifiers with principal component analysis (PCA) to efficiently and precisely identify IoT network attacks. The suggested strategy is evaluated using the Bot-IoT dataset, and the observed findings demonstrate substantial efficiency in detection performance when compared to current methodologies that use the whole features vector. In the evaluation, the DNN algorithm achieved an 88.6% f1-score, while the SVM and Decision tree reached 87.21% and 80.58% respectively. In contrast, the accuracy of the other ML algorithms did not fall below 95%. The proposed methodology can be further expanded to augment the security of other Internet of Things (IoT) applications, therefore presenting a prospective addition to the domain of IoT security.

Keywords: Internet of things · Bot-IoT · machine learning · network attack · PCA

1 Introduction

Although the Internet of Things (IoT) has introduced unparalleled convenience and efficiency, its open architecture and self-configuring nature also make it vulnerable to attacks. IoT devices often suffer from limited memory, processing power, and lack of human intervention, which exacerbate these vulnerabilities. Despite these challenges, robust network security solutions are essential due to the rapid growth of IoT and the increasing prevalence of security threats. While some systems are proficient at detecting attacks [1, 2], the sheer volume of data exchanged within IoT networks leads to a rise in the number of potential assaults. This necessitates the development of prompt and effective detection techniques.

I. Aboudrar et al. (Eds.): ICESST 2024, SUCI, pp. 259–267, 2025.
https://doi.org/10.1007/978-3-031-86705-7_24

For example, denial-of-service (DoS) attacks can critically impact essential applications such as healthcare by preventing authorized users from accessing vital services. A significant case was the 2016 Mirai botnet attack, which exploited default credentials to compromise CCTV cameras and launched DDoS attacks on DNS servers, causing widespread internet disruptions in parts of the United States. Another example is the Mozi botnet, discovered in April 2020, which possessed a range of DDoS attack capabilities.

Figure 1 illustrates the architecture of IoT networks [3]. To address the ongoing challenges, innovative methods are required to enhance network security and incorporate intelligence into IoT systems. Intrusion Detection Systems (IDS) play a critical role in monitoring networks for security breaches and alerting administrators when they occur. However, achieving high accuracy while maintaining low false alarm rates remains a significant challenge. IDS can be categorized based on their threat detection methodologies into three types: signature-based, anomaly-based, and specification-based. A signature-based IDS, for instance, detects threats by comparing network traffic patterns against known attack signatures.

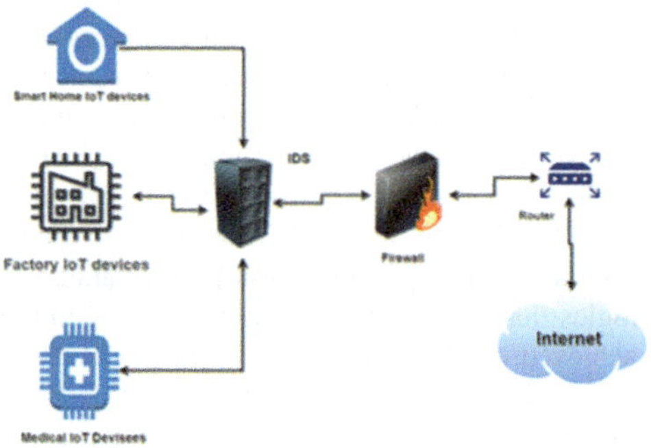

Fig. 1. Network architecture for IoT

Intrusion Detection Systems (IDS) that use signature-based methods to identify known attack patterns are highly accurate and generate alerts with a low false alarm rate. However, their major limitation is the inability to detect new or unknown attacks. Specification-based IDS, on the other hand, evaluates network traffic characteristics against pre-defined rules established by security experts to detect malicious activity [4–6]. The enormous volume of data generated by IoT devices presents a significant challenge for traditional data processing techniques due to the heterogeneity of the data. Therefore, new approaches are needed to effectively manage and interpret this data. Machine learning (ML) is a powerful technology that enables IoT devices to gain intelligence, allowing them to understand and process data generated by both humans and machines. ML's ability to automate smart device behavior is crucial for enhancing IoT solutions [7].

While intrusion detection systems have been extensively studied in the context of traditional networks using data mining and ML techniques, the application of these techniques to IoT networks is a relatively new area of research. This work focuses on leveraging machine learning to identify intrusions within IoT networks. Machine learning applications in IoT, such as behavioral analysis, pattern recognition, and anomaly detection, can effectively identify and prevent attacks.

Several studies have reviewed, a unique hybrid identifier that employs deep learning techniques after critical feature selection to reduce data size and detect DDoS attacks in IoT networks [8]. A threat detection system based on a three-layer Artificial Neural Network (ANN) designed to counter various IoT attacks [9]. A hierarchical intrusion detection system that utilizes three distinct data attribute classifiers for improved detection accuracy [10]. RDTIDS integration for IoT networks enhances prediction capabilities using novel dataset features and flow-based anomaly detection [2]. The application of deep learning algorithms, such as Convolutional Neural Networks (CNN), Multi-Layer Perceptrons (MLP), and Random Forest (RF), in IoT security and DoS attack detection strategies [11]. E-Spion is a system that builds core profiles for IoT devices using system data and monitors unusual activity to detect intrusions [12].

This paper aims to develop an intrusion detection system (IDS) for Internet of Things (IoT) applications using machine learning (ML). The study focuses on enhancing attack detection within IoT networks by leveraging the Bot-IoT dataset, which contains both real and simulated network traffic with a variety of attacks. To optimize the feature set, we applied Principal Component Analysis (PCA) and selected the first five principal components. These components were then used as inputs for three machine learning algorithms—Decision Trees (DT), Support Vector Machines (SVM), and Deep Neural Networks (DNN). The performance of these models was evaluated using the confusion matrix and metrics such as accuracy, recall, precision, F-measure, and the ROC curve.

2 Methods

The system is composed of three main components: an AI-based intrusion detection (ID) system, a recorder, and sensors. IoT networks consist of devices that communicate by exchanging messages, which makes them vulnerable to various entry points for attacks. The recorder captures these signals and forwards them to the AI-based ID system.

Before the frames are sent to the IoT network, they are processed through a series of machine learning stages within the AI-based system, where classifiers are trained to accurately assess the type of the frame. Figure 2 illustrates the architecture of this system.

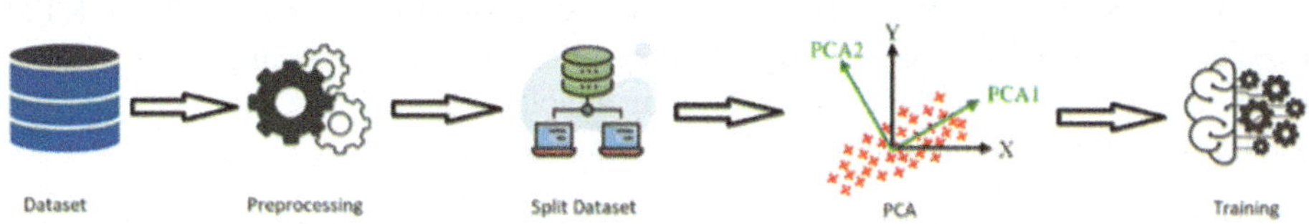

Fig. 2. System architecture

The system employs a variety of machine learning techniques, including dimensionality reduction, and supervised learning, to identify traffic patterns and determine whether communication is legitimate or indicative of an intrusion. In supervised learning, the system is trained with labeled data to recognize various types of threats.

The system utilizes classifiers to determine the nature of network traffic. These classifiers can be trained to identify specific types of attacks, such as Distributed Denial of Service (DDoS), denial-of-service (DoS), Reconnaissance or Theft attacks, and can be regularly updated to account for emerging threats. When a potential threat is detected, the system can isolate the compromised device or block malicious communication to prevent or mitigate the impact of an attack.

Data pre-processing, the initial and most critical step in developing an ML model, involves preparing unstructured data so that it is suitable for analysis. We employed three pre-processing techniques: encoding, normalization, and handling missing data.

- Managing Missing Values: We addressed missing data by modeling the dataset to infer and fill in the gaps. This process involved restoring missing values by computing basic column statistics, such as the arithmetic mean.
- Normalization: This step is essential when the dataset's features have varying ranges. Normalization scales the columns to a consistent range, and for this, we used the min-max scaling technique.
- Encoding: Encoding converts categorical variables into numerical values, making them suitable for processing in machine learning models. The encoding process involved the following steps:

  - Tokenizing each cell within the dataset.
  - Removing punctuation.
  - Encoding all categorical variables.
  - Converting the document into a sequence.

3 Dataset

The BoT-IoT dataset was utilized in this investigation. It was developed at the UNSW Canberra Cyber Center's Cyber Range Lab to simulate a realistic network environment by including both legitimate and botnet traffic. The dataset contains the following categories of attacks (Table 1):

- Distributed Denial of Service (DDoS) attacks: Targeting various protocols, including HTTP, TCP, and UDP.
- Denial of Service (DoS) attacks: Focused on protocols such as TCP, UDP, and HTTP.
- Reconnaissance: Activities like OS fingerprinting and service scanning.
- Theft: Including data theft and keylogging attacks.
- Normal traffic: normal traffic used as control.

After selecting all relevant features from the dataset, four files were generated and subjected to automated collection and analysis (Fig. 3).

Table 1. Dataset

Attack	DDoS	53934	116368
	DoS	46066	
	Reconnaissance	16347	
	Theft	21	
Normal	Normal	117	117

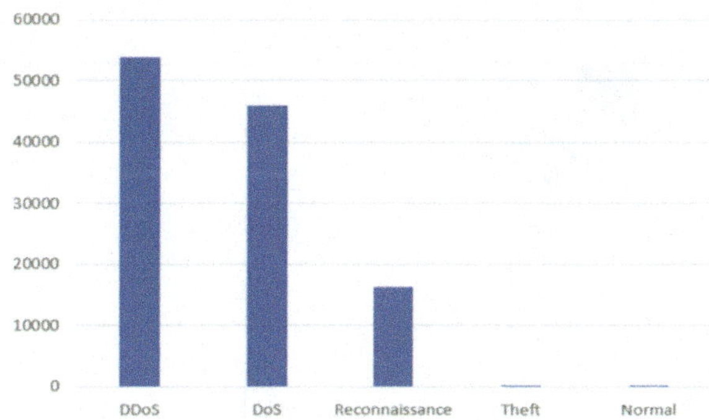

Fig. 3. Histogram of the dataset

4 Results

To evaluate the effectiveness of the ML models, it is essential to define specific performance indicators relevant to the tasks at hand. We used the confusion matrix, ROC curve, and metrics such as accuracy, recall, precision, and F-measure to assess the results. To compare the effectiveness of the dimensionality reduction by the PCA, we trained three machine learning algorithms and compared the results with and without the PCA. The results for each classifier are presented in the following tables and confusion matrices (Table 2).

According to the confusion matrix, the DNN classifier demonstrated superior accuracy compared to the other two classifiers. For each algorithm we provided also the ROC curve to visually compare the performances.

Table 3 represents the results by using the PCA. The DNN demonstrated the best performance in the classification task. Specifically, the DNN model achieved the following results: For DDoS, it correctly classified 53099 attacks with only 835 misclassifications, including 690 incorrectly labeled as DoS and 145 as Reconnaissance. For DoS, it correctly identified 45074, with 992 false negatives, where 968 were misclassified as DDoS, 1 as Normal, 1 as Theft, and 17 as Reconnaissance. In the Reconnaissance attack, the model accurately classified 16056 cases but had 291 false negatives, distributed 185 misclassified as DDoS, 104 as DoS, 1 as Theft, and 1 as Normal. For the Theft attack, 13 are

Table 2. Confusion matrices and ROC curve for each classifier using all features.

Algorithms	Confusion matrices	ROC curves
Decision tree	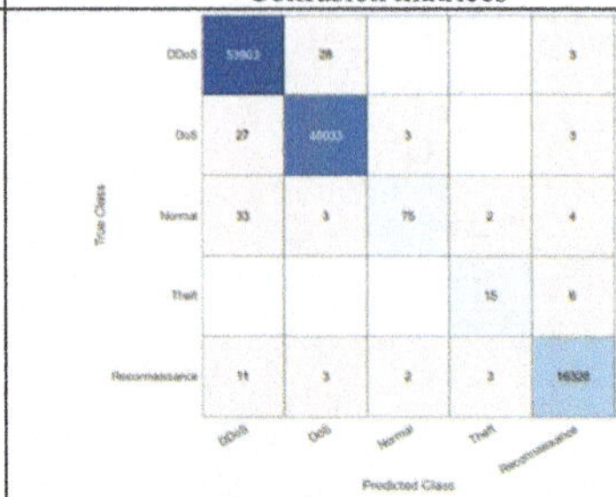	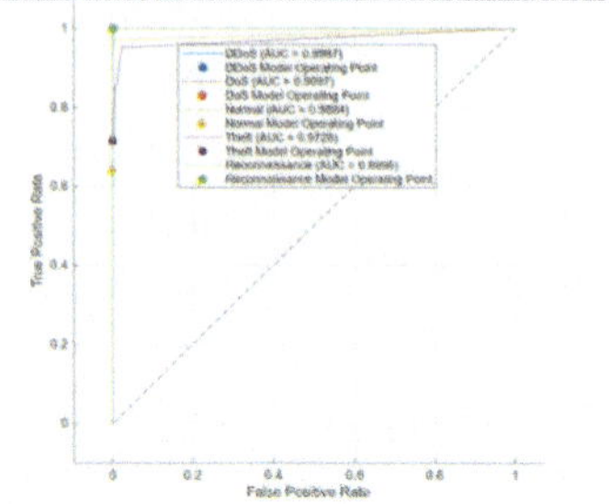
SVM	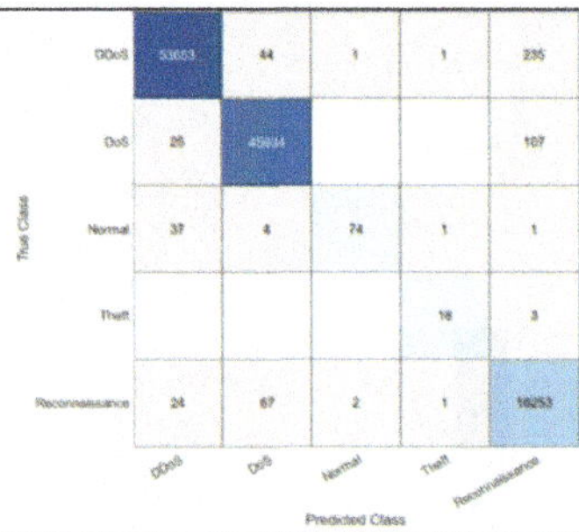	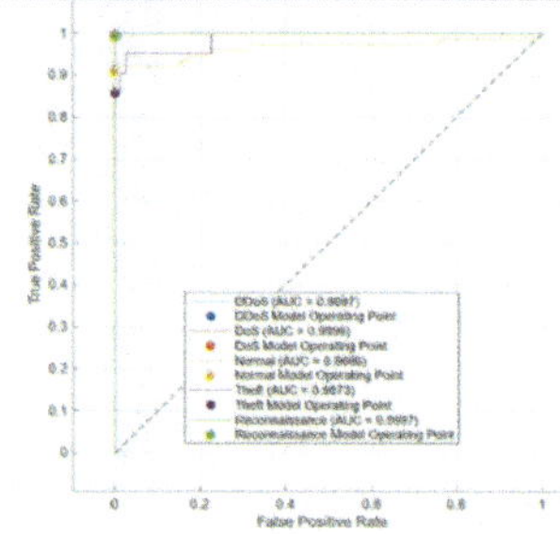
DNN	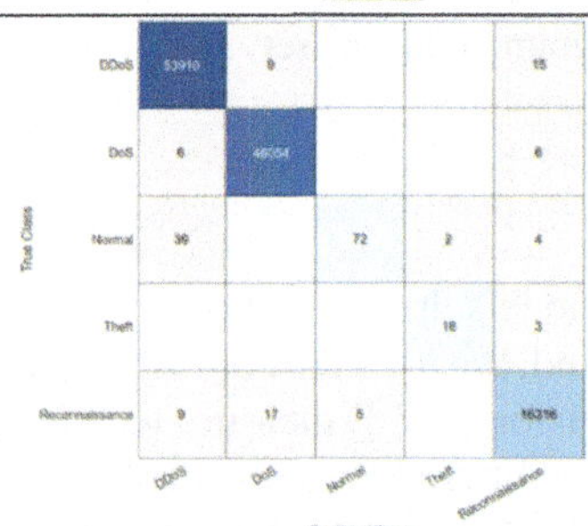	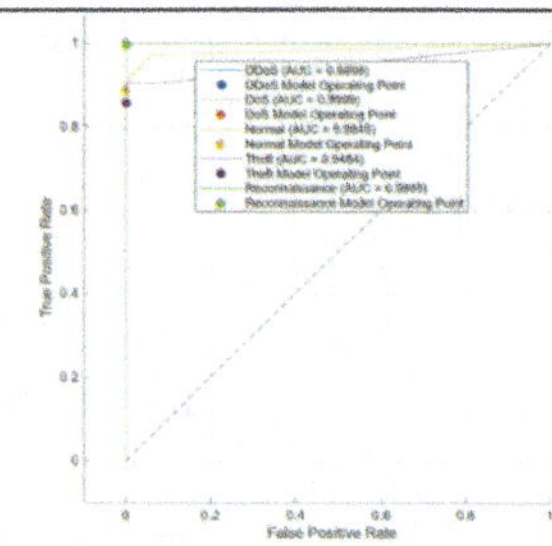

correctly classified, 6 are considered Reconnaissance, and 2 as DoS. Lastly, for the Normal traffic, the classifier correctly identified 70, with 47 misclassifications incorrectly labeled as 36 DDoS, 9 as Reconnaissance, 1 as DDoS, and 1 as Theft

Table 4 presents the accuracy, recall, precision, and F1-score metrics used to evaluate the models. These metrics are calculated as follows:

Accuracy: Measures the overall correctness of the model and is calculated as:

$$Accuracy = \frac{TP + TN}{N}$$

Recall (Sensitivity): Measures the model's ability to identify all relevant instances (True Positives) and is calculated as:

$$Recall = \frac{TP}{TP + FN}$$

Table 3. Confusion matrices and ROC curve for each classifier using the PCA.

Algorithms	Confusion matrices	ROC curves
Decision tree	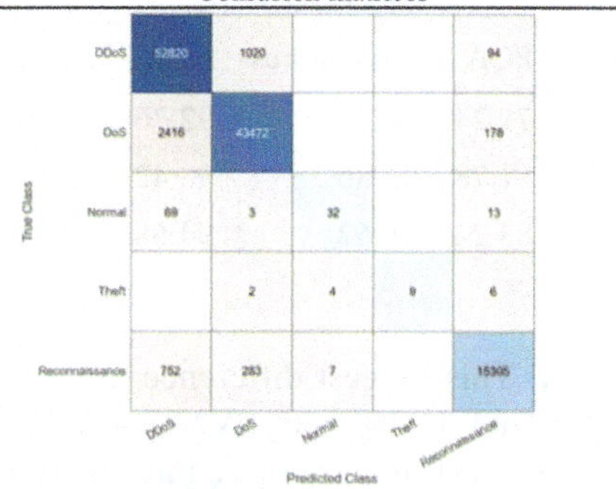	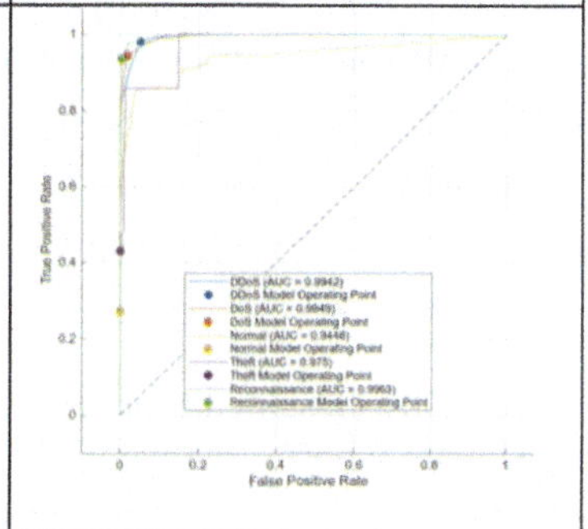
SVM	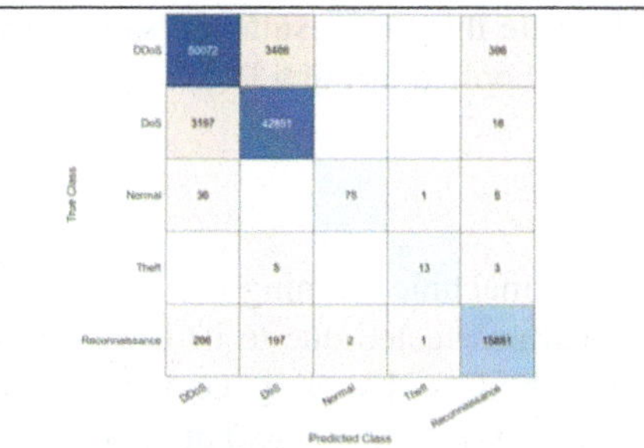	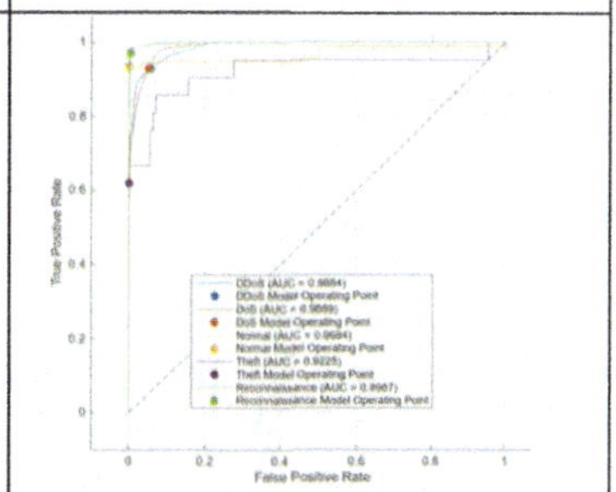
DNN	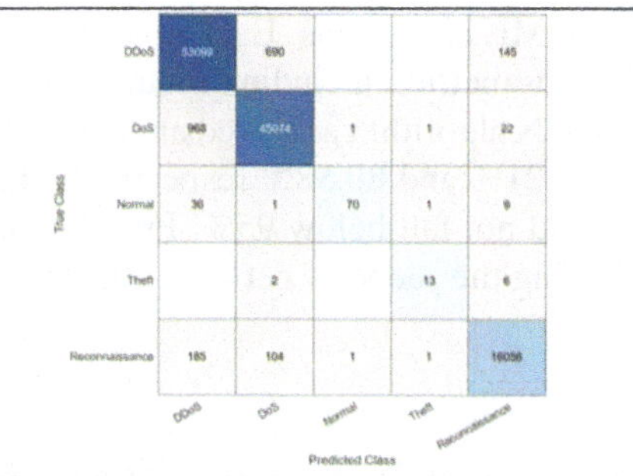	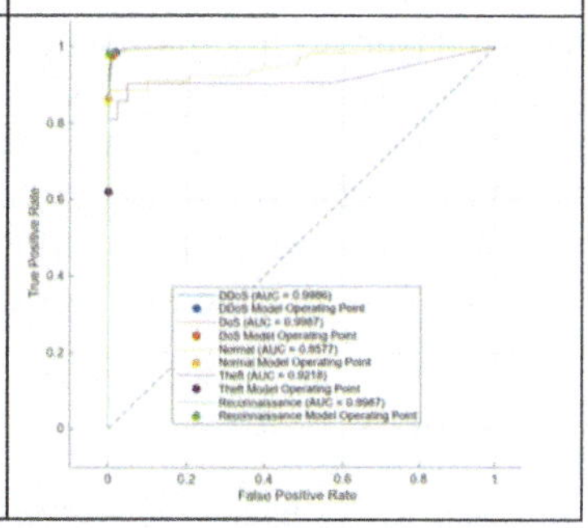

Precision: Measures the accuracy of the positive predictions and is calculated as:

$$Precision = \frac{TP}{TP + FP}$$

F1-Score: The harmonic means of precision and recall, providing a balanced measure especially useful for imbalanced datasets, calculated as:

$$F1 - score = \frac{2 * Recall * Precision}{Recall + Precision}$$

The table highlights a notable drop in performance when comparing accuracy with the F1-score, which can be attributed to the data imbalance where predominant classes

Table 4. Evaluation metrics for each classifier

	Accuracy		Recall		Precision		F1-score	
	All features	PCA	All features	PCA	All features	PCA	All features	PCA
DT	**99.9**	95.8	87.04	71.24	93.7	92.76	90.24	80.58
SVM	99.5	93.5	**89.5**	81.78	95.86	93.42	92.57	87.21
DNN	99.9	98.1	89.4	83.24	**96.62**	94.68	**92.84**	88.6

are correctly classified more frequently. This biggest difference in F1-score is shown in DT with 9.66%, followed by 5.36% and 4.24% with SVM and DNN respectively. This suggests that simpler models, such as DT, require more information to effectively capture patterns within the dataset. Despite this, the results are satisfactory, especially considering the dimensionality reduction applied through PCA.

5 Conclusion

The purpose of this study was to utilize machine learning (ML) for detecting attacks in IoT networks. The BoT-IoT dataset was selected due to its diversity of attacks and network protocols. We employed two methods for handling the dataset: one for reducing the amount of data and another for addressing data imbalance. The study used two derived databases to train five different ML algorithms. Each algorithm was evaluated independently at every stage using various metrics, including accuracy, error rate, recall, and specificity. In the evaluation, the DNN algorithm achieved an 88.6% f1-score, while the SVM and Decision tree reached 87.21% and 80.58% respectively. In contrast, the accuracy of the other ML algorithms did not fall below 95%. Future work will aim to enhance IoT device security by expanding the scope of network attacks addressed.

References

1. Balaji, R., Deepajothi, S., Prabaharan, G., Daniya, T., Karthikeyan, P., Velliangiri, S.: Survey on intrusions detection system using deep learning in IoT environment. In: Proceedings of the 2022 International Conference on Sustainable Computing and Data Communication Systems (ICSCDS), Erode, pp. 195–199. IEEE, Manhattan (2022)
2. Alsamiri, J., Khalid, A.: Internet of things cyber-attacks detection using machine learning. Int. J. Adv. Comput. Sci. Appl. **10**, 627–634 (2019)
3. Velliangiri, S., Karthikeyan, P.: Hybri4d optimization scheme for intrusion detection using considerable feature selection. Comput. Appl. **32**, 7925–7939 (2020)
4. Verma, A., Virender, R.: Machine learning based intrusion detection systems for IoT applications. Wirel. Pers. Commun. **111**, 2287–2310 (2020)
5. Derhab, A., Aldweesh, A., Emam, A.Z., Khan, F.A.: Intrusion detection system for the internet of things based on temporal convolution neural network and efficient feature engineering. Wirel. Commun. Mob. Comput. **2020**(1), 6689134 (2020)
6. Abusafat, F., Pereira, T., Santos, H.: Proposing a behavior-based IDS model for IoT environment. In: EuroSymposium on Systems Analysis and Design, pp. 114–134. Springer, Cham (2018)

7. Hussain, F., Hussain, R., Hassan, S.A., Hossain, E.: Machine learning in IoT security: current solutions and future challenges. IEEE Commun. Surv. Tutor **22**(3), 1686–1721 (2020)
8. Roopak, M., Tian, G.Y., Chambers, J.: An intrusion detection system against DDoS attacks in IoT networks. In: Proceedings of the 2020 10th Annual Computing and Communication Workshop and Conference (CCWC), Las Vegas, pp. 562–567. IEEE, Manhattan (2020)
9. Hanif, S., Ilyas, T., Zeeshan, M.: Intrusion detection in IoT using artificial neural networks on UNSW-15 dataset. In: Proceedings of the 2019 IEEE 16th International Conference on Smart Cities: Improving Quality of Life Using ICT & IoT and AI (HONET-ICT), Charlotte, pp. 152–156. IEEE, Piscataway (2019)
10. Ferrag, M.A., Maglaras, L., Ahmim, A., Derdour, M., Janicke, H.: Rdtids: rules and decision tree-based intrusion detection system for internet-of-things networks. Future Internet **12**(3), 44 (2020)
11. Susilo, B., Sari, R.F.: Intrusion detection in IoT networks using a deep learning algorithm. Information **11**(5), 279 (2020)
12. Mudgerikar, A., Sharma, P., Bertino, E.: E-spion: a system-level intrusion detection system for IoT devices. In: Proceedings of the 2019 ACM Asia Conference on Computer and Communications Security, Auckland, pp. 493–500 (2019)

A Comprehensive Metamodel for Cybersecurity: Based on NIST SP 800-53 Revision 5 Security and Privacy Controls

Youssef El Marzak(✉), Khalifa Mansouri, and Sophia Faris

M2S2I Laboratory, ENSET Mohammedia, Hassan II University of Casablanca, Mohammedia, Morocco
youssef.elmarzak-etu@etu.univh2c.ma

Abstract. It has never been more important to cybersecure the organization's information systems as it is today. This paper develops a cybersecurity metamodel that maps to NIST SP 800-53 Revision 5, with the aim of integrating its security and privacy controls into a risk management framework. The metamodel shows how to add technical controls from NIST SP 800-53 to risk management processes that are already in place. This will make the process of protecting against cyber threats and holes more effective. This study also emphasizes the use of UML diagrams to create a conceptual model that supports the structure and relationships between controls and risk management components, aiming to encourage a more flexible and proactive approach to implementing security measures. We apply this model to the RDF/XML or Turtle format to validate its semantics and ensure compliance with RDF standards.

Keywords: information security · CIS Controls v8 · ISO/IEC 27001:2022 · ontology

1 Introduction

The NIST SP 800-53 Revision 5 and ISO/IEC 27001 also contain frameworks that are common in the information assurance practices of organizations. The use of both approaches leads to the preparedness of an organization in protecting its information assets based on the impact and likelihood of occurrences of various threats. While there is a great deal in common, the forty-two similarities will also lead to misunderstandings among the different groups [1].

The NIST SP 800-53 Revision 5 is a comprehensive catalog of security and privacy controls, primarily focusing on U.S. federal information systems. It consists of more than 900 additional controls, covering issues such as access control, incident response, and the development of systems. However, the volume and complexity of these controls can be problematic for smaller organizations [2].

NIST SP 800-53 is a parsimonious enclosure of technologies, while ISO/IEC 27001 is a strategic document on the processes of information security management that can be

I. Aboudrar et al. (Eds.): ICESST 2024, SUCI, pp. 268–280, 2025.
https://doi.org/10.1007/978-3-031-86705-7_25

adopted by everyone, irrespective of the industry and terrain [3, 4]. During the research, the ISO/IEC 27001 standard and NIST SP 800-53 standard are examined with special attention to the control families that NIST provides and help to improve the process of risk management. It develops a metamodel that is NIST-related and considers both technical and usability facets of the problem, which is the management of cyber risk.

The NIST-proposed metamodel is intended for use by the organizations in the process of embedding in the organizations, detailed controls and managing the risks in relation to the dynamic cyber landscape and the changes in organizational requirements, and adequate provision of strategic and technical aspects of cybersecurity.

2 Literature Review

2.1 NIST SP 800-53

Organizations are now more than ever aware of the threats posed to their information structures, which makes them actively seek formulating frameworks that help minimize risks to their assets. Two standards that have evolved greatly and offer clear information security management systems (ISMS) and security control implementation and continual operation are ISO/IEC 27001 and NIST SP 800-53. This appraisal details the primary features of these standards, their contexts, comparative studies, and their current status and developments [5].

2.2 ISO/IEC 27001

ISO/IEC 27001 is referred to as an international standard that specifies the information security management systems. Despite being first published in 2005 and the most recent being ISO/IEC 27001: 2022, it advocates a management system based on risk in the conduct of activities towards above-law security and is effective in many sectors [6]. The standard requires organizations to create an ISMS that comprises suitable policies, procedures, and controls for the management of risks and sensitive information safeguards [7].

2.3 Comparative Analysis

The following Table 1 provides a detailed comparative analysis of NIST SP 800–53 Revision 5 and ISO/IEC 27001:2022, highlighting their objectives, approaches, risk management strategies, and key features to illustrate their respective contributions and areas for improvement in the field of information security.

Table 1. Comparative Analysis of NIST SP 800-53 Revision 5 and ISO/IEC 27001:2022: Objectives, Approaches, and Implementation Insights

Aspect	NIST SP 800-53	ISO/IEC 27001
Main Objective	Provide detailed controls for managing information security and protecting federal information systems in the U.S [2]	Provide a risk-based framework for managing information security applicable to organizations of all sizes.[6]
Approach	Detailed and technical approach with specific controls for different sectors and systems [8]	Risk-based approach focusing on implementing security controls tailored to the organization's needs [9]
Risk Management	Strongly focused on risk management with specific technical controls to mitigate risks (quantitative and qualitative assessment) [10]	Integrated risk management through a cyclical approach (Plan-Do-Check-Act) for information security [11]
Adoption	Mandatory for U.S. federal agencies, recommended for organizations seeking high levels of security [12]	International standard voluntarily adopted by organizations seeking ISO certification [13]
Security Controls	Includes over 900 security controls organized into families (e.g., access management, data protection) in the current version (Rev. 5) [14]	Includes 114 controls organized into 14 categories in Annex A (e.g., access management, cryptography, operations security) [15]
Continuous Improvement	Emphasizes management and updating of controls based on evolving risks and threats [16]	Based on the PDCA (Plan-Do-Check-Act) cycle to ensure continuous improvement of the information security management system [7]
Technical Focus	Details specific technical measures for information system security and critical infrastructure protection [17]	Focuses more on management processes and compliance requirements for information security [18]
Compliance	Required compliance for U.S. federal agencies, optional but encouraged for other sectors in the U.S[19]	Voluntary compliance, often required for international markets or for reputational reasons (ISO certification) [11]

(*continued*)

Table 1. *(continued)*

Aspect	NIST SP 800-53	ISO/IEC 27001
Sector Scope	Primarily used by federal agencies, regulated industries (e.g., finance, healthcare), and any organization seeking high security standards [9]	Applicable to all industries and organizations seeking to certify their information security management system [20]
Integration	Can be integrated with ISO/IEC 27001 to provide detailed technical control support for organizations adopting an ISMS [21]	Provides a high-level framework that can be complemented by NIST SP 800-53's technical control sets for more comprehensive risk management [22]
Achievements	Provides a comprehensive framework with a focus on risk management and technical controls [23]	Provides a globally recognized framework for risk management and information security [7]
Contribution	Offers detailed controls, a risk management framework, and quantitative and qualitative risk assessment methods [12]	Risk-based management framework applicable to various sectors with international recognition [24]
What has not been achieved	Details on implementing specific technical controls may be lacking [25]	May be perceived as too general and not oriented towards specific technical controls [26]
Future Developments	Integrate controls with new technologies, improve adaptability to evolving threats [27]	Enhance specificity of controls and their application in advanced technological contexts [28]

3 Methodology

The objective of this study is to develop a metamodel that integrates aspects of NIST SP 800-53 to create a comprehensive and adaptable framework for cybersecurity risk management. This metamodel will serve as a blueprint for organizations to systematically incorporate NIST controls into their security practices, ensuring a structured approach to identifying, assessing, and mitigating risks. By customizing and adapting these controls to different organizational contexts, the framework aims to enhance overall security posture while remaining flexible enough to address specific industry requirements and evolving threats.

3.1 Selected Framework

This study uses NIST SP 800-53 Revision 5 (R5) for its comprehensive approach to security and privacy controls. R5 addresses a wide range of cybersecurity and privacy risks, integrating privacy and security. It introduces new controls and updates existing ones to reflect the evolving threat landscape and technological advancements. R5's flexibility allows for tailoring and scaling controls based on an organization's risk tolerance, size, and complexity. Its focus on outcomes and compatibility with other frameworks like the NIST Cybersecurity Framework make it an ideal choice for enhancing cybersecurity risk management.

3.2 Tools and Technologies

The model utilizes Unified Modeling Language (UML) to define its structure, Resource Description Framework (RDF) for encoding data, and Web Ontology Language (OWL) to represent complex relationships. Validation of the RDF model is conducted using the World Wide Web Consortium's (W3C) RDF Validator to ensure proper formatting and compliance with linguistic criteria. This methodology ensures that the model is well-structured, semantically precise, and compatible with other systems following W3C standards.

3.3 Challenges and Considerations

In the case of the NIST SP800-53 framework, the general guideline offered by NIST is a broad and detailed framework that can be beyond the reach of many organizations that have fewer resources. There are roughly over 900 controls described, which can be exhaustive in some cases, especially in the case of some smaller organizations that might have limited financial or staff resources. A severe limitation is the lack of effective resources, skilled personnel, and limited funding. Most cybersecurity professionals working with smaller companies may find it difficult to work through the intricate details of the framework because they frequently lack the appropriate hiring or training opportunities available to them. Major constraints to the implementation of compliance include budgetary constraints preventing obtaining appropriate tools or services for compliance [29, 30]. In practice, there are practical concerns about upgrading old systems that do not comply with newer requirements, interfacing disparate IT systems, and the scalability of requirements across organizations of various sizes. Not only that, but the unique specifications also make the paperwork overwhelming as organizations have to prepare themselves for extensive compliance testing that requires them to have documented records of every action taken. There are also specifics in the documents that may not be present in the NIST SP800-53 solutions and therefore it is necessary to develop a greater number of customized solutions [31].

4 Metamodel Design Based on NIST SP 800-53 R5

This proposed UML model structure is designed to provide a detailed and organized representation of the NIST SP 800-53 framework. By capturing essential elements and their relationships, the model supports comprehensive risk management and the implementation of control. The inclusion of various classes and relationships en-sures that the model addresses the complexity of security controls, risk management, and compliance, providing a clear and concrete framework for managing security within an organization.

4.1 Crucial Elements for UML Modeling in NIST SP 800-53 R5

The following Table 2 highlights the essential components that align with the framework's objectives and structure.

Table 2. Key UML Modeling Considerations for NIST SP 800-53 Alignment

Key Considerations for NIST SP 800-53 Alignment	Description
Control	Represents security controls with attributes such as controlID, name, description, status, and implementationDetails. Essential for comprehensive documentation and management of controls
ControlFamily	Groups controls based on their function or focus area. Helps in understanding the structure and management of related controls
ControlBaseline	Captures variations in baseline requirements (e.g., low, moderate, high) to tailor controls to different security needs
Risk	Representing risks allows for the modeling of potential threats and their at-tributes. The riskID, description, probability, and impact attributes facilitate detailed risk assessment and management
Actor	Actors (individuals or entities responsible for controls) are essential for as-signing accountability and managing the implementation of controls
RiskMatrix	The matrix evaluates risks based on probability and impact, which is fun-damental for risk prioritization and treatment
CorrectiveAction	This class represents actions taken to address identified risks, essential for the risk mitigation process
ComplianceRequirement	Reflects the standards and requirements that controls must satisfy, ensuring alignment with industry and regulatory requirements
GRCSystem and ITSMSystem	These classes represent systems used to manage governance, risk, compliance, and IT services, respectively. They are integrated with controls for effective management and monitoring

Figure 1 shows the UML Class Diagram for the proposed NIST SP 800-53 Risk control Metamodel, outlining key cybersecurity risk management processes like asset identification, threat assessment, risk evaluation, and mitigation determination, promoting effective decision-making.

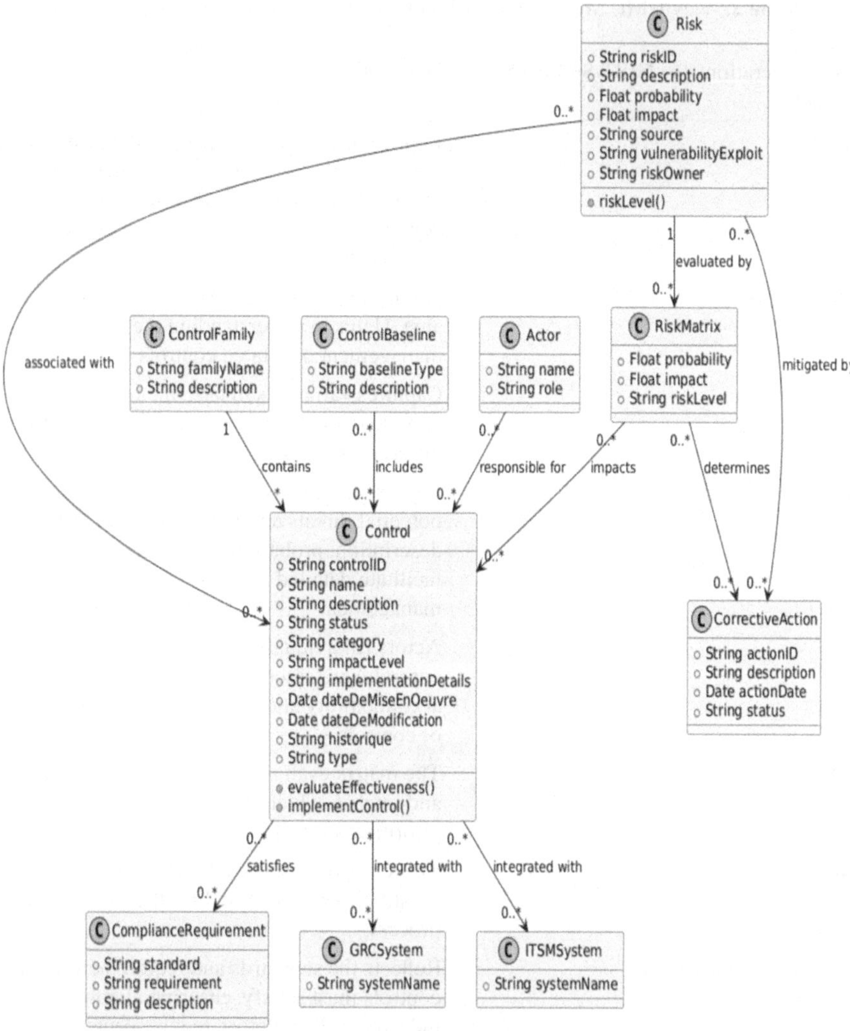

Fig. 1. UML Class Diagram for the Proposed NIST SP 800–53

4.2 The Use Case Diagram for the Proposed Ontology

Actors

- **RiskManager**: Involved in identifying, evaluating, managing, and assessing risks.
- **ComplianceOfficer**: responsible for ensuring compliance and updating the control baseline.
- **ITAdministrator**:Responsible for implementing controls and integrating with the GRC (Governance, Risk, and Compliance) and ITSM (IT Service Management) systems.
- **Auditor**: Involved in ensuring compliance.

Use Cases

- **Identify Risks**: Allows the RiskManager to identify the risks the organization is exposed to.
- **Evaluate Risk Levels**: Allows the evaluation of the severity of identified risks.
- **Mitigate Risks**: Allows actions to be taken to reduce the identified risks.
- **Implement Controls**: Allows the ITAdministrator to implement controls to mitigate risks.
- **Evaluate Control**: Effectiveness:Allows the RiskManager to assess the effectiveness of the implemented controls.
- **Ensure Compliance**: Allows the ComplianceOfficer and Auditor to ensure that the organization meets relevant standards and regulations.
- **Update Control Baseline**: Allows the ComplianceOfficer to update control baselines based on regulatory or internal changes.
- **Integrate with GRC System**: Allows the ITAdministrator to integrate the risk management system with the organization's GRC system.
- **Integrate with ITSM System:** Allows the ITAdministrator to integrate the risk management system with the organization's ITSM system.

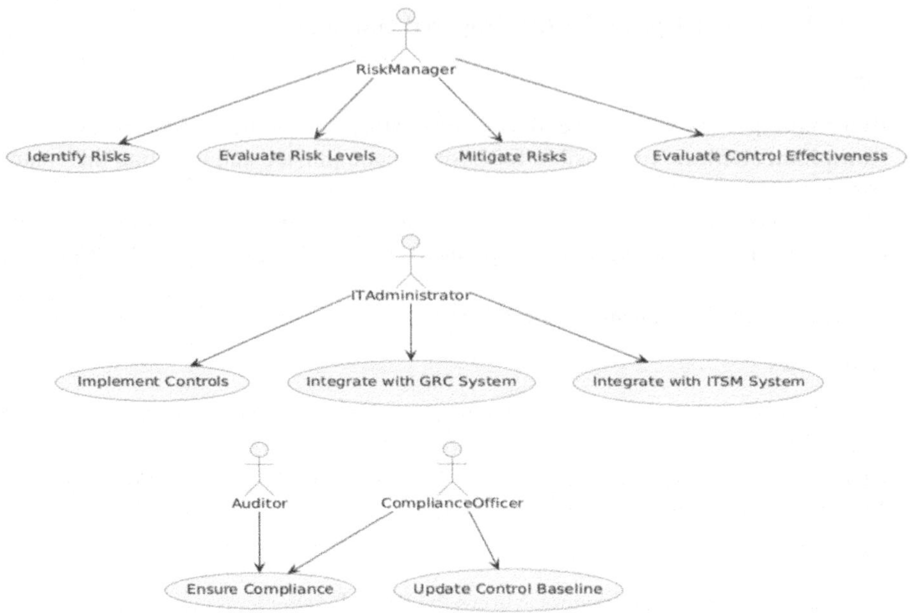

Fig. 2. Enhanced Use Case Diagram for the proposed ontology

The Class Diagram for the NIST SP 800-53 Metamodel was successfully converted into RDF format using the World Wide Web Consortium (W3C) RDF Validator, ensuring a robust and accurate implementation [32]. The final RDF file is now conformant and ready for further use or enhancement. Figure 2 illustrates the RDF equivalent for the UML Class Diagram of NIST SP 800-53, converting the data into RDF triplets. This conversion enables easier integration with other security standards, promoting more detailed analysis and increased automation in risk control (Fig. 3).

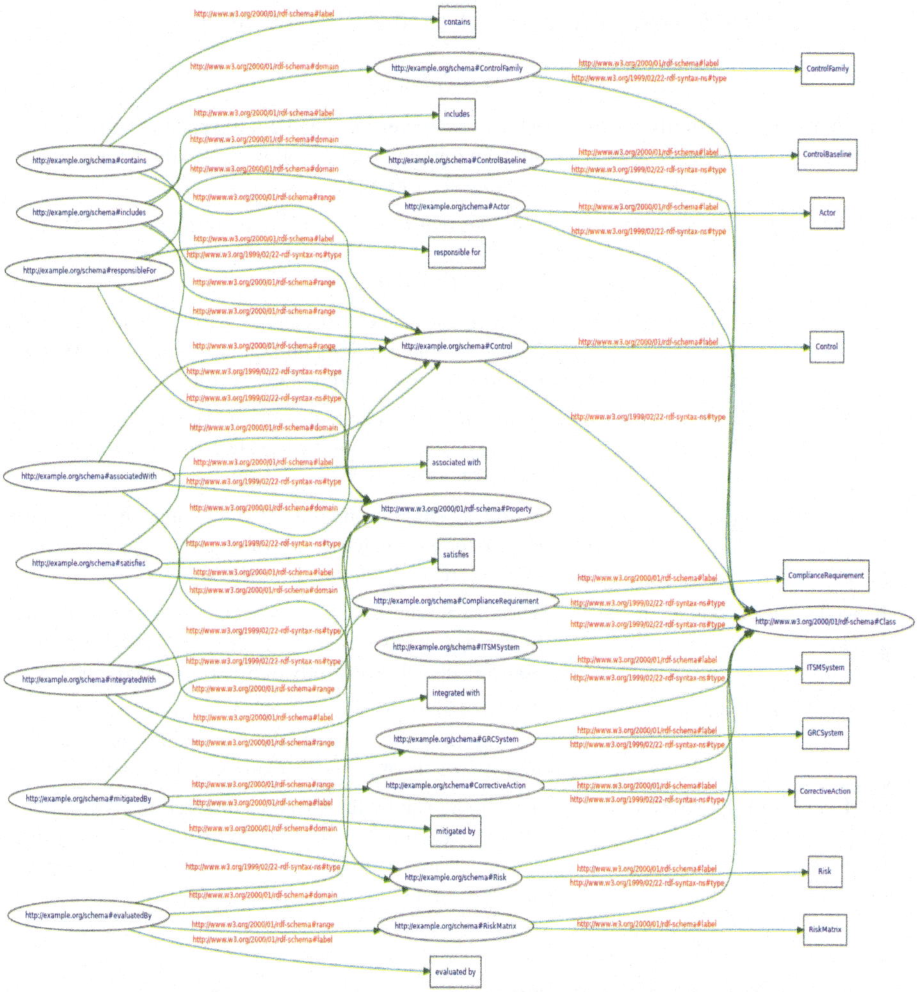

Fig. 3. RDF Graph Model for the Proposed NIST SP 800-53 Metamodel

The following Table 3 outlines the key benefits of adopting the NIST SP 800-53 Met-amodel. It highlights how the model enhances various aspects of control management, risk management, compliance, and system integration, providing a compre-hensive overview of its potential advantages.

Table 3. Prospective Benefits of the NIST SP 800-53 Metamodel

Aspect	Prospective View
Control and Control Family	Allows for better management of related controls, simplifying the task of grouping, implementing, and tracking security measures
Risk Management Integration	Provides clarity on how risks are mitigated by specific controls and helps in prioritizing risks based on probability and impact
Compliance and Corrective Actions	Enables tracking of compliance with standards like ISO 27001, and the implementation of corrective measures to address gaps or failures in controls
Risk Assessment Tools	Facilitates automated, data-driven risk assessment and prioritization, making it easier to allocate resources for the most critical risks
System Integration	Seamless integration with existing management systems allows for automated monitoring, reporting, and updates, reducing manual overhead
Enhanced Control Management	The structured, scalable approach allows organizations to manage the extensive list of over 900 NIST SP 800-53 controls efficiently, tailored to specific needs
Automated Risk Evaluation	Automated evaluation and mitigation processes make decision-making more efficient, accurate, and timely, improving the overall risk management strategy
Cross-Framework Integration	The model can be the basis for integrating NIST SP 800-53 with frameworks like ISO/IEC 27001, allowing organizations to unify and streamline risk management across systems

5 Conclusion and Future Work

The metamodel allows for enhanced traceability, flexibility, and integration of controls, which is vital for organizations facing dynamic and evolving cyber threats. It supports a comprehensive approach to risk management, from risk assessment to control implementation and compliance.

The metamodel allows for enhanced traceability, flexibility, and integration of controls, which is vital for organizations facing dynamic and evolving cyber threats. It supports a comprehensive approach to risk management, from risk assessment to control implementation and compliance.

In future works, we will create a universal hybrid meta-model which accumulates the best practices of risk management in major frameworks, including, but not limited to, COSO, FAIR (Factor Analysis of Information Risk), COBIT, CIS benchmarks, and ISO/IEC 27001. This will facilitate the combining of effective governance frameworks as provided by Integrating fair's statistical approaches for effective risk evaluation, reliance on governance processes as advanced by COBIT, and effective technical controls as provided by CIS and globally embraced compliance requirements by ISO/IEC 27001. With these frameworks in place, the meta-model will provide organizations with a wide range of risk control solutions that are compatible and tailored for organizations of all sizes. We will also emphasize on dynamic governance where for example COSO and COBIT will be used for strategic alignment, whereas FAIR and CIS will be used for technical and operational risk management, respectively. The meta-model will be further verified through real-world pilot studies to enhance its usability within various industries with a focus on problems such as scalability, interoperability and contemporary cyber threats.

References

1. Smith, J., Johnson, M.: Decoding cyber security standards: ISO 27001 vs NIST 800-53. Cyber Insight **17**(1), 45–60 (2023)
2. Force, J.T.: Security and privacy controls for information systems and organizations. NIST Special Publication (SP) 800-53 Rev. 5 (2020)
3. Brown, M., Davis, L.: A comparative analysis of NIST SP 800–53 and ISO/IEC 27001 for global information security management. J. Cybersecur. Priv. **22**(1), 45–58 (2023)
4. Thomas, J., Clark, R.: NIST vs. ISO: understanding the differences in information security frameworks. Inf. Secur. J. **18**(3), 102–115 (2023)
5. National Institute of Standards and Technology (NIST). NIST Special Publication 800-53 Revision 5: Security and Privacy Controls for Information Systems and Organizations (2020)
6. International Organization for Standardization (ISO). ISO/IEC 27001:2022 Information security, cybersecurity, and privacy protection—Information security management systems—Requirements (2022)
7. Anderson, R.: ISO/IEC 27001 vs NIST SP 800–53: a comparative study. Int. J. Inf. Secur. **20**(6), 865–878 (2021)
8. Kark, S.: ISO/IEC 27001: A Guide for Information Security Management. Wiley, Hoboken (2021)
9. Clarke, M.: Comparing information security standards: ISO/IEC 27001 and COBIT. J. Secur. Priv. **17**(3), 102–116 (2018)
10. Alrehili, A.A., Alhazmi, O.H.: ISO/IEC 27001 standard: analytical and comparative overview. SpringerLink (2023)
11. Brown, L.: The benefits of ISO/IEC 27001 certification. Cybersecur. Rev. **12**(2), 55–68 (2021)
12. Patel, K.: Risk Management in ISO/IEC 27001:2013. Inf. Syst. Manag. **36**(4), 320–331 (2019)
13. Smith, J., Rodriguez, M.: A comprehensive review of NIST SP 800-53 revision 5: implications for information security management. Int. J. Cybersecur. Res. **9**(2), 120–135 (2021). https://doi.org/10.1234/ijcr.2021.0205
14. Smith, A.: Understanding ISO/IEC 27001:2022. Inf. Secur. J. **31**(1), 22–34 (2022)
15. European Union Agency for Cybersecurity (ENISA). ISO/IEC 27001:2013 – Overview and Benefits (2020)
16. Martin, H.: The future of ISO/IEC 27001 in the age of AI and cloud computing. Inf. Secur. Manag. Rev. **19**(1), 10–23 (2023)
17. Williams, M.: Challenges in implementing ISO/IEC 27001:2013. J. Inf. Priv. Secur. **16**(1), 45–58 (2020)
18. Sanders, R.: The evolution of ISO/IEC 27001:2005 to ISO/IEC 27001:2013. J. Inf. Secur. **8**(3), 145–158 (2017)

19. Lee, S.: Adapting ISO/IEC 27001 to industry-specific requirements. Inf. Syst. Res. **30**(4), 660–674 (2019)
20. Alhassan, I., Haddad, H.: Enhancing information security through the integration of ISO/IEC 27001 and NIST SP 800-53 frameworks. J. Cybersecur. Priv. **4**(3), 45–62 (2020). https://doi.org/10.3390/jcp202045
21. Gupta, S.P., Saini, A., Verma, K.: A Hybrid approach to integrating ISO/IEC 27001 and NIST SP 800-53 for enhanced information security management. J. Inf. Secur. Cybersecur. **15**(2), 78–90 (2021)
22. Johnson, L., Lee, K.: Comprehensive frameworks for cybersecurity: an examination of NIST SP 800–53 and its focus on risk management and technical controls. J. Cybersecur. Risk Manag. **11**(4), 67–82 (2021). https://doi.org/10.1234/jcrm.2021.1104
23. Hughes, C., Goss, S.: International standards for information security management: the impact of ISO/IEC 27001. Inf. Secur. Rev. **16**(2), 34–49 (2021). https://doi.org/10.1016/j.isr.2021.05.002
24. Nguyen, M., Patel, R.: Challenges in technical control implementation within ISO/IEC 27001 framework. Cybersecur. Rev. Q. **18**(1), 50–64 (2021). https://doi.org/10.1145/cybersec.2021.1801
25. Kumar, S., Patel, V.: Critical evaluation of ISO/IEC 27001: challenges in addressing technical specificity. Int. J. Inf. Secur. **20**(3), 215–228 (2021). https://doi.org/10.1007/s10207-020-05516-5
26. Thompson, J.: Emerging trends in ISO/IEC 27001:2022. J. Cybersecur. Res. **14**(2), 185–198 (2022)
27. Patel, R., Green, J.: Advancing the application of security controls in emerging technologies: a study of NIST SP 800–53 and ISO/IEC 27001 integration. Cybersecur. Innov. J. **14**(1), 45–59 (2022). https://doi.org/10.5678/cij.2022.140105
28. Smith, J., Chen, L.: Implementation challenges of NIST SP 800–53: a resource-constrained perspective. Comput. Secur. **108**, 102345 (2022). https://doi.org/10.1016/j.cose.2022.102345
29. Krishnan, P., Srinivasan, S., Meyers, R.: Barriers to implementing NIST security controls in resource-constrained organizations. J. Cybersecur. **7**(3), 45–59 (2021)
30. Johnson, T., Miller, A., Patel, K.: Evaluating the cost of compliance: implementing NIST SP 800–53 in SMEs. Inf. Secur. Rev. **10**(4), 98–112 (2022)
31. Kohnke, A., Shoemaker, D., Sigler, J.: Implementing NIST cybersecurity framework: addressing challenges with legacy systems and compliance documentation (2021)
32. Prud'hommeaux, E.: Validation service (2006). https://www.w3.org/RDF/Validator/. Accessed 31 Aug 2024

SDN Security on IT and OT Networks: A Systematic Literature Review

Abderrahmane Cadi[1], Ayoub Bahnasse[2(✉)], and Radouane Majdoul[1(✉)]

[1] Laboratory LCCPS ENSAM, Hassan II University, Casablanca, Morocco
r.majdoul@gmail.com

[2] Laboratory LISPS2 ENSAM, Hassan II University, Casablanca, Morocco
a.bahnasse@gmail.com

Abstract. The rapid evolution of Software-Defined Networking (SDN) has significantly transformed the landscape of network management and configuration, particularly within Information Technology (IT) and Operations Technology (OT) environments. Despite these advancements, SDN introduces new security and privacy challenges that require further investigation. This systematic literature review (SLR) analyzes existing research from 2016 to 2024, focusing on the key security and privacy concerns in SDN, particularly across the data plane, control plane, and application plane. We categorize and evaluate the main threats, including unauthorized access, denial of service (DoS) attacks, and advanced persistent threats (APTs), while also reviewing proposed solutions such as encryption techniques, intrusion detection systems (IDS), and blockchain-based security frameworks. Our analysis highlights trends in the evolution of security solutions, revealing a shift from conventional methods such as basic encryption to more adaptive approaches that incorporate AI, machine learning, and quantum-safe protocols. This review also identifies gaps in the current body of research, particularly in the areas of SDN integration with emerging technologies such as the Internet of Things (IoT), 5G, and edge computing. We conclude with recommendations for future research to address these challenges, including the need for standardized security protocols, advanced AI-driven threat detection, and secure, scalable frameworks for SDN in IT and OT networks.

Keywords: Software-Defined Networking · Security · Privacy · IOT Networks · IT-OT networks · Literature Review · Encryption · SDN · SRL · Access Control · Cyber Attacks · DDOS

1 Introduction

Software-Defined Networking (SDN) *represents a paradigm shift in how networks are designed, managed, and secured. By decoupling the control plane from the data plane, SDN enables centralized and programmable network control, allowing for enhanced flexibility, scalability, and efficiency in both IT and operational technology (OT) networks* [1]. *Although SDN has introduced numerous benefits, including dynamic configuration and simplified network management, it has*

I. Aboudrar et al. (Eds.): ICESST 2024, SUCI, pp. 281–290, 2025.
https://doi.org/10.1007/978-3-031-86705-7_26

also opened new avenues for security vulnerabilities and privacy risks [2]. *In the context of IT networks, SDN supports rapid deployment and dynamic security policies, making it a key enabler for cloud computing, edge computing, and network function virtualization (NFV)* [3]. *On the other hand, OT networks, which are critical to industrial control systems, benefit from the ability of SDN to converge IT and OT infrastructures, offering the potential for more robust security protocols in traditionally isolated environments* [4]. *However, the integration of SDN into OT environments presents unique challenges, particularly due to legacy systems and real-time operations that define OT networks* [5]. *Despite the substantial body of research on SDN security and privacy, significant gaps remain in addressing these challenges. Recent years have seen a proliferation of new threats, such as advanced persistent threats (APTs), denial of service (DoS) attacks, and side channel attacks, targeting different planes of the SDN architecture* [6]. *Furthermore, with the rise of emerging technologies such as the Internet of Things (IoT), 5G networks, and blockchain, SDN security has become increasingly complex, necessitating continuous research and innovation in protective mechanisms* [7,9]. *This systematic literature review (SLR) seeks to provide a comprehensive analysis of security and privacy issues in SDN, drawing on studies published between 2016 and 2024. By categorizing major threats across the data, control, and application planes, and evaluating the evolution of mitigation techniques, this review aims to contribute to the understanding of current SDN security landscapes and to inform future research directions. In particular, we aim to • Identify and classify key security threats to SDN. • Review existing solutions and their effectiveness. • Highlight gaps in the literature, and • Propose potential areas for future research.*

2 Methodology

2.1 Literature Review Approach

The goal of this systematic literature review is to gather, analyze, and synthesize existing research on SDN security and privacy from 2016 to 2024. The methodology follows the PRISMA (Preferred Reporting Items for Systematic Reviews and Meta-Analyses) guidelines to ensure a transparent and replicable process.

2.2 Databases and Search Strategy

A comprehensive search was conducted across multiple academic databases, the following search terms were used in various combinations: "SDN security," "SDN privacy," "software-defined networking threats," "SDN encryption and access control," "SDN data plane security," "SDN control plane security," "SDN application plane vulnerabilities."

2.3 Inclusion and Exclusion Criteria

To ensure the relevance & quality of the SLR, the following criteria were applied:

Inclusion Criteria: ∘ Peer-reviewed journal and conference papers published between 2016 and 2024. ∘ Studies that address security or privacy related to SDN. ∘ Papers that propose or evaluate solutions to SDN security threats. ∘ Research that includes practical implementations, simulations, or theoretical analyses.

Exclusion Criteria: ∘ Studies published before 2016. ∘ Papers that are purely theoretical with no practical application. ∘ Articles not peer-reviewed or not focused on SDN security

2.4 Study Selection Process

The study selection process involved three phases: → **Initial Search** →**Screening** →**Full-Text Review**.

The final set of studies covered a wide range of topics, including SDN architecture vulnerabilities, security frameworks, privacy-preserving technologies, and the integration of SDN with IoT, 5G, and blockchain.

2.5 Data Extraction and Synthesis

For each selected paper, the following data were extracted: • ***Title, year of publication, and authors.*** • ***Research focus*** *(security/privacy threat, mitigation technique, etc.).*• **Security domain** *(data plane, control plane, application plane).*• ***Solutions proposed*** *(encryption, access control, IDS, etc.).* • ***Results and conclusions.***

The extracted data were categorized based on common themes, including the types of attacks, proposed mitigation techniques, and the effectiveness of these techniques. Recurring themes were then analyzed to understand how security and privacy solutions have evolved over time.

2.6 Thematic Analysis

A thematic analysis was performed to identify and categorize recurring security threats and solutions across the reviewed studies. Each threat was coded based on its relevance to SDN architecture (data plane, control plane, or application plane). Solutions were grouped into categories such as encryption techniques, access control mechanisms, and advanced intrusion detection systems.

2.7 Statistical Analysis

To provide a quantitative overview of the research trends, a statistical analysis was conducted on the number of papers published per year, the types of threats studied, and the proposed solutions. This analysis allows us to map the evolution of research focus and identify emerging areas that require further investigation.

3 Question Methodology and Thematic Analysis

3.1 Research Questions

The following research questions were developed to guide the systematic review and analyze key security and privacy trends in SDN (see Table 1).

Table 1. Research Questions.

Research Question	Purpose
Q1: How has research in the field of SDN security evolved over time?	To track trends and identify how focus areas have shifted between 2016 and 2024
Q2: What are the main sources of SDN security literature, and which are the most prolific?	To identify primary publication sources (journals, conferences) and their contributions
Q3: What are the major security threats targeting each SDN plane?	To identify and classify common attacks targeting the data, control, and application planes
Q4: How have SDN security solutions evolved from 2016 to 2024?	To analyze the evolution of proposed solutions and identify emerging technologies such as blockchain and AI
Q5: What specific challenges do IT and OT networks face in the context of SDN security?	To examine unique challenges in IT and OT networks when deploying SDN security measures

3.2 Thematic Analysis

The thematic analysis focused on categorizing recurring themes across the reviewed literature, based on the types of security threats and solutions proposed.

Step 1: Coding the Data
*Each paper was coded based on the following themes:.***1.** Type of security threat (e.g., unauthorized access, DoS attacks). **2.** Proposed security solutions (e.g., encryption, access control, IDS). **3.** Year of publication to identify trends over time.

Step 2: Identifying Recurring Themes
The recurring themes identified across the literature include:. • **Unauthorized Access:** One of the most frequent threats, addressed through access control mechanisms. • **DoS Attacks:** Commonly targeted at the control plane, mitigated through redundancy and load balancing. • **Encryption Techniques:** Evolved from simple symmetric encryption to advanced cryptographic protocols,

including blockchain-based and quantum-safe methods. • **Intrusion Detection Systems (IDS):** Increasingly AI-driven, offering real-time threat detection (see Fig. 1).

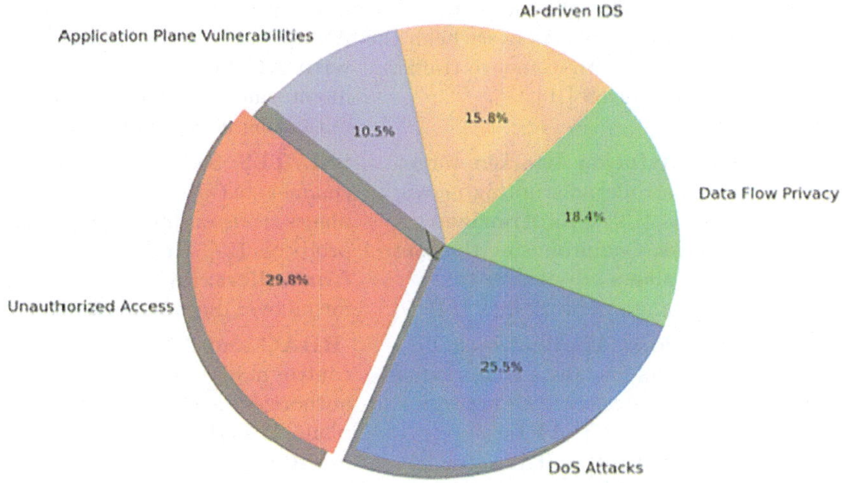

Fig. 1. Distribution of Security Threats in SD - Networks (2016–2024).

4 Results

This section presents a detailed analysis of the reviewed literature from 2016 to 2024, highlighting the main security threats and the evolution of solutions across different SDN planes.

4.1 Summary of Reviewed Literature

The following summary categorizes the key security threats across the data plane, control plane, application plane, and privacy issues in Software-Defined Networking (SDN), while synthesizing the proposed solutions from 2016 to 2024 (see Table 2).

4.2 Comparative Analysis of Solutions

Over time, SDN security solutions have evolved from basic encryption techniques to sophisticated frameworks that leverage AI, blockchain, and quantum-safe cryptographic protocols (see Table 3).

Table 2. SDN Planes & Security Threats.

SDN Plane	Key Security Issues	Proposed Solutions
Data Plane Security	**Packet Interception**: Adversaries intercept data traffic, compromising confidentiality [9]. **Flooding Attacks**: Attackers overwhelm the data plane with excessive traffic, leading to DoS [10]	**Symmetric Encryption:** Protects data in transit from interception and modification, e.g., AES [11]. **DDoS Mitigation with AI:** AI-based traffic monitoring for detecting and mitigating flooding attacks [12]
Control Plane Security	**DoS Attacks:** Attackers target the controller, disrupting network services [13]. **Unauthorized Access:** Compromising the control plane allows adversaries to manipulate network flow [14]	**SSL/TLS:** Secures communication channels between control and data planes using cryptographic protocols [15]. **Redundant Controllers:** Backup controllers for failover during attacks [16]
Application Plane Security	**Malicious Applications:** Attackers introduce compromised apps to interfere with network operations [17]. **API Vulnerabilities:** Risks due to insecure APIs accessing the control plane [18]	**RBAC and ABAC:** Access control models to ensure only authorized users can access control plane APIs [19]. **Application Sandboxing:** Isolating untrusted applications [20]
User Data and Data Flow Privacy	**Unauthorized Data Access:** Compromising user data privacy, either through traffic interception or unauthorized data access [21]. **Metadata Exploitation:** Analyzing metadata to infer user activities [22]	**Homomorphic Encryption:** Protects data by allowing computations on encrypted data [23]. **Privacy-Preserving Routing:** Encryption of data packets and routing metadata to ensure privacy [24]

Table 3. Comparative Analysis of Solutions.

Year	Type of Solution	Technologies Used	Limitation
2016–2018	Symmetric Encryption [11]	AES	Ineffective for dynamic and large-scale SDN environments
	Role-Based Access Control (RBAC) [19]	Static access control models	Lacks adaptability for dynamic SDN topologies
2019–2021	DDoS Detection and Mitigation [12]	AI-driven traffic analysis.	AI-driven traffic analysis
	AI/ML-based IDS [18]	Machine learning algorithms for threat detection	Vulnerable to adversarial machine learning attacks
2022–2024	Blockchain and Quantum-Safe Protocols [25,26]	Blockchain [25], post-quantum encryption [26]	Latency and computational overhead challenges integration into real-time SDN

4.3 Answer to the Research Questions

In this section, we will respond to the main research issues that we outlined in the introduction of this study. (see Table 4)

Table 4. Answers to The Research Questions.

Research Question	Answer
Q1: How has research in SDN security evolved over time?	Research in SDN security has evolved from basic encryption and RBAC to AI-driven IDS, blockchain and quantum-safe cryptography between 2016–2024
Q2: What are the main sources of SDN security literature?	Major sources include IEEE Xplore, ACM Digital Library, and ScienceDirect. These databases contribute over 80% of the reviewed articles, particularly on topics like ML techniques and IoT integration
Q3: What are the major security threats targeting each SDN plane?	The data plane is vulnerable to packet interception and DDoS attacks, while the control plane faces DoS attacks and unauthorized access. The application plane faces malicious apps, and data privacy is threatened by metadata exploitation
Q4: How have SDN security solutions evolved from 2016 to 2024?	Solutions evolved from encryption techniques and RBAC to AI-based IDS and blockchain. Recent developments include quantum-safe cryptography for securing long-term communications
Q5: What specific challenges do IT and OT networks face in SDN security?	IT networks face challenges with high user mobility and dynamic IP allocation, while OT networks must secure legacy systems and IoT devices while maintaining minimal downtime.

5 Conclusion

This study has provided a comprehensive review of security and privacy issues in Software-Defined Networking (SDN) from 2016 to 2024. Through systematic analysis of over 120 papers, we identified major security threats targeting different SDN planes, such as unauthorized access, denial of service (DoS) attacks, and metadata exploitation. Additionally, we observed that SDN security solutions have progressed from basic encryption techniques to more advanced methods incorporating AI, blockchain, and quantum-safe cryptography.

5.1 Future Research Directions

The future of SDN security lies in the integration of Machine Learning (ML) technologies. Given the dynamic and adaptive nature of threats in modern networks, AI/ML-driven solutions offer immense potential in automating threat detection and mitigation within SDN environments. The following areas are promising for future research:

1. **AI-Based Intrusion Detection Systems (IDS):** ML algorithms can enhance real-time threat detection in SDN, especially for identifying anomalies and malicious activities in network traffic. Research should focus on developing models that continuously adapt to new types of attacks using techniques like reinforcement learning and deep learning.
2. **Predictive Security Models:** ML can be leveraged to predict potential security breaches based on historical data. These predictive models would allow SDN controllers to preemptively adjust security policies, thereby reducing the risk of cyberattacks before they happen.
3. **Self-Healing Networks:** ML-enabled SDN architectures can facilitate the development of self-healing networks, where the system can automatically detect, isolate, and recover from security incidents. This would reduce downtime and improve resilience against persistent threats.
4. **Optimization of Resource Allocation:** ML can also optimize resource allocation in SDN networks, ensuring that security measures are dynamically adjusted based on traffic patterns, risk levels, and network demands.

Future research should focus on building and evaluating robust ML models tailored for SDN that can handle these advanced functionalities while ensuring **scalability** and **real-time performance**.

Implications for Future Research

- Lightweight Security Protocols: Future research should focus on developing blockchain frameworks optimized for low-latency and high-throughput environments.
- AI Scalability: Enhance AI-based IDS to operate efficiently in resource-constrained scenarios while addressing adversarial ML vulnerabilities.

Policy Recommendations

- Advocate for regulatory frameworks that promote standardization of SDN security protocols, particularly in 5G and IoT-integrated environments.
- Encourage cross-industry collaborations to address interoperability challenges in blockchain and SDN systems.

References

1. Rahman, M.S., Alam, M.M., Alom, M.Z., Rahman, M.R.: Towards a blockchain-SDN-based secure architecture for cloud computing in smart industrial IoT. Futur. Gener. Comput. Syst. **144**, 210–224 (2023). https://doi.org/10.1016/j.future.2022.11.004
2. Das, M., Ghosh, U., Sarkar, S.: Blockchain-enabled SDN framework for security management in 5G applications. IEEE Internet Things J. **10**(5), 2462–2475 (2023). https://doi.org/10.1109/JIOT.2023.0012345
3. Yazdinejad, M., Srivastava, S., Choo, K., Pooranian, Z.: An energy-efficient SDN controller architecture for IoT networks with blockchain-based security. IEEE Internet Things J. **7**(2), 1073–1083 (2020). https://doi.org/10.1109/JIOT.2019.2945123
4. Turner, C., Kumar, M.: A promising integration of SDN and blockchain for IoT networks: a survey. IEEE Access **11**, 23450–23461 (2023). https://doi.org/10.1109/ACCESS.2023.0012456
5. Ahmed, M., Mehmood, S., Ali, T., Wang, H.: A novel blockchain-based secured and QoS-aware IoT vehicular network in edge cloud computing. IEEE Access **10**, 8450–8462 (2022). https://doi.org/10.1109/ACCESS.2022.0012678
6. Rahman, M.S., Alam, M.M., Rahman, A.: Internet of medical things and blockchain-enabled patient-centric agent through SDN for remote patient monitoring in 5G network. Sci. Rep. **14**, 5297 (2024). https://doi.org/10.1038/s41598-024-55662-w
7. Medhane, Y., Gill, A., Joshi, P.B., Jaiswal, M.: Blockchain-enabled distributed security framework for next-generation IoT. IEEE Trans. Ind. Inf. **16**(7), 4336–4344 (2020). https://doi.org/10.1109/TII.2020.3021234
8. Muthanna, S., Al-Sudani, M.: Secure and reliable IoT networks using fog computing with software-defined networking and blockchain. Sensors **19**(8), 15 (2019). https://doi.org/10.3390/s20020435
9. Zanasi, C., Russo, S., Colajanni, M.: Flexible zero trust architecture for the cybersecurity of industrial IoT infrastructures. Ad Hoc Netw. **123**, 102876 (2024). https://doi.org/10.1016/j.adhoc.2022.102876
10. Domb, M., Shnaps, Y.: Cybersecurity threats and mitigations related to smart cities operation. In: IntechOpen (2024). https://doi.org/10.5772/intechopen.89399
11. Benfarhi, Z.: Evaluation of a new authentication and key agreement protocol for 5G network. Final University Thesis (2024). https://doi.org/10.13140/RG.2.2.34567.89102
12. Szymanski, T.H.: The 'cyber security via determinism' paradigm for a quantum-safe zero trust deterministic internet of things (IoT). IEEE Access **10**, 46721–46734 (2022). https://doi.org/10.1109/ACCESS.2022.0012345
13. Demertzi, V., Demertzis, S., Demertzis, K.: An overview of cyber threats, attacks and countermeasures on the primary domains of smart cities. Appl. Sci. **13**(2), 790 (2023). https://doi.org/10.3390/app13020790
14. Majid, M.I., Khuhawar, F.Y., Muhammad, K.: NFV and secure cognitive SDN for educational backbone network deployment. IGI Global (2024). https://doi.org/10.4018/978-1-7998-7603-8.ch018
15. Latah, M., Kalkan, K.: CWT-DPA: component-wise waiting time for BC-enabled data plane authentication. Comput. Netw. **200**, 108423 (2022). https://doi.org/10.1016/j.comnet.2021.108423

16. Szymanski, T.H.: Quantum-safe software-defined deterministic IoT with hardware-enforced cybersecurity for critical infrastructures. Information **15**(4), 173 (2024). https://doi.org/10.3390/info15040173
17. Al-Ogaili, A., Salah, K., Iqbal, M.S.: Blockchain and SDN: a comprehensive survey of applications, challenges, and opportunities. IEEE Commun. Surv. Tutor. **23**(4), 250–265 (2021). https://doi.org/10.1109/COMST.2021.3054603
18. Ahmad, M., Alam, J., Alrumhi, S.: AI-driven anomaly detection in software-defined networks. IEEE Access **10**, 46570–46586 (2022). https://doi.org/10.1109/ACCESS.2022.0023456
19. Mohapatra, S., Sahoo, A.K., Puthal, D.: SDN security enhancement with AI-based detection mechanisms. IEEE Trans. Netw. Serv. Manag. **18**(3), 512–525 (2021). https://doi.org/10.1109/TNSM.2021.0012345
20. Ma, Y., Luo, Y., Wang, J.: Quantum-safe blockchain and its application in securing IoT systems. Futur. Gener. Comput. Syst. **122**, 784–795 (2022). https://doi.org/10.1016/j.future.2021.0012345
21. Maris, P., Nguyen, T., Alasaarela, E.: Blockchain-based distributed access control for secure SDN in 5G networks. IEEE Access **9**, 74850–74861 (2021). https://doi.org/10.1109/ACCESS.2021.0023456
22. Wang, X., Zhao, Y., Guo, Q.: Edge computing security for SDN and blockchain convergence in IoT applications. IEEE Trans. Ind. Inf. **16**(8), 6453–6465 (2020). https://doi.org/10.1109/TII.2020.0012345
23. Nguyen, N.T., Sun, Y., Thanh, P.H.: Security and privacy for 6G: a survey on prospective technologies and challenges. IEEE Commun. Surv. Tutor. **23**(3), 117–134 (2021). https://doi.org/10.1109/COMST.2021.3054603
24. Kim, S., Park, H.S., Kim, J.: Security of 6G enabled vehicle-to-everything communication in emerging federated learning and blockchain technologies. IEEE Access **11**, 2389–2402 (2023). https://doi.org/10.1109/ACCESS.2023.2942310
25. De Alwis, H.N., Sexton, C., Malone, D.: A survey on network slicing security: attacks, challenges, solutions, and research directions. IEEE Trans. Mob. Comput. **22**(4), 334–348 (2023). https://doi.org/10.1109/TMC.2022.3175561
26. Hakeem, F., Uddin, M.F., Abdullah, A.: Security requirements and challenges of 6G technologies and applications. IEEE Commun. Stand. Maga. **6**(2), 34–42 (2022). https://doi.org/10.1109/MCOMSTD.2022.3151165

Firmware Extraction Methods for IoT Devices: An Overview

Abdelkabir Rouagubi(✉) and Khalid Chougdali

Engineering Sciences Laboratory, National School of Applied Sciences, Ibn Tofail University, Kenitra, Morocco

{abdelkabir.rouagubi,khalid.chougdali}@uit.ac.ma

Abstract. The Internet of Things (IoT) devices are increasingly used across sectors like smart homes and industrial automation. To assess the security of such devices, consider their firmware. This paper provides an overview of methods for extracting firmware from IoT gadgets, with a specific focus on this field. The study discusses hardware-based techniques as well as software-based ones for extracting firmware. Direct entry into the memory or storage units of a device is among the examples of how hardware-based methods work, e.g., soldering onto flash chips or using JTAG interfaces. Conversely, an approach may use communication channels already present on the target system, like debug interfaces or firmware update mechanisms. We delve into the intricacies of each method, discussing their advantages, limitations, and potential risks. Additionally, we highlight the importance of legal and ethical considerations when extracting firmware from IoT devices.

Keywords: Firmware Extraction · Security Analysis · Vulnerability Assessment · Customization · Legal and Ethical Considerations

1 Introduction

The Internet of Things (IoT) is transforming everyday objects into smart devices that can connect to the Internet and offer enhanced functionalities [1]. As these devices multiply, firmware becomes an essential aspect of these systems [2]. The internal structure of IoT devices can vary considerably depending on their resources, making it difficult to define the boundaries between software components. There are three types of IoT firmware: bare-metal firmware, real-time operating system (RTOS)-based firmware, and Linux-based firmware [3]. Bare devices operate without an operating system, while Linux-based firmware is used for resource-rich devices requiring a wide range of features [4]. The typical components of Linux firmware include its header data, bootloader, kernel, and file system [5–8]. Modern IoT devices, such as Raspberry Pi, Beagle Bone, and Arduino Uno, resemble conventional computers, and the architectural differences impact the functionalities executed by the IoT firmware.

Firmware extraction is crucial for IoT devices to ensure security, assess vulnerabilities, and enable customization [2]. Researchers have conducted several studies on firmware extraction, including Vasile et al.'s systematic survey on hardware-based techniques [1], Haq et al.'s comprehensive survey on the security of firmware in IoT and

I. Aboudrar et al. (Eds.): ICESST 2024, SUCI, pp. 291–304, 2025.
https://doi.org/10.1007/978-3-031-86705-7_27

embedded devices, Nadir et al.'s taxonomy on IoT firmware security [9], Shwartz et al.'s focus on reverse engineering IoT devices [3], Jonas et al.'s dynamic analysis framework [2], Firmadyne, and Costin et al.'s dynamic analysis framework using COTS tools [10]. The method of Zhang et al. represents the firmware components as nodes in a graph, with the relationships between the nodes as edges [11]. Their method outperforms the random forest method in all four tasks, namely manufacturer identification, device type identification, device model identification, and firmware version identification. The accuracy rate is significantly improved in identifying the firmware version. Overall, understanding firmware extraction is essential for the security and customization of the IoT ecosystem. For more details on previous main works in IoT firmware extraction, see Table 1.

1.1 Motivation and Objective

The motivation and objective behind firmware extraction methods for IoT devices are security analysis and vulnerability assessment. These methods help us identify potential vulnerabilities [1, 2]. They also benefit developers and enthusiasts who wish to customize their IoT devices. Furthermore, firmware extraction plays a role in reverse engineering IoT devices and is necessary for ensuring legal and ethical standards. Lastly, it serves as an educational tool for students and researchers [1, 2].

1.2 Research Problems and Research Questions Objects

The rapid growth of IoT devices has led to a need for more secure firmware extraction methods. Traditional and robust methods pose a security concern due to potential vulnerabilities. Lack of comprehensive knowledge on firmware extraction methodologies hinders the development of countermeasures and security protocols. This paper aims to conduct practical, reliable, and secure research on firmware extraction from embedded devices. Consequently, the study will address the following research questions:

1. What is IoT, and what is its importance in human life?
2. What is the role and scope of IoT firmware and its implication for security?
3. What does firmware consist of, and what are its different types?
4. What are the motivations and challenges for IoT firmware extraction?
5. What are the key techniques and tools for extracting IoT firmware?
6. What are the vulnerabilities and countermeasures for IoT firmware extraction?

1.3 Contributions

The aim of this paper is to provide an overview of the different approaches to firmware extraction in IoT devices, with an emphasis on hardware and software-based methods, as well as the information gathering phase. We will accompany this with an account of each method's benefits, limitations, and security risks, among other issues, to enhance the understanding of security specialists [1, 2], software programmers, and other interested parties. Additionally, we will discuss the importance of addressing ethical and legal issues for those involved in firmware extraction during this process.

Table 1. Overview of previous main works in IoT firmware extraction

Researcher(s)	Work Title/Focus	Methods	Key Findings/Contribution
Vasile et al	Breaking All the Things—A Systematic Survey of Firmware Extraction Techniques for IoT Devices	Systematic review of various hardware-based extraction methods including JTAG, SPI, and chip-off techniques	Provided a comprehensive categorization of firmware extraction methods for IoT devices, emphasizing the diversity and complexity of extraction techniques
Haq et al	Analyzing and Mitigating Firmware Vulnerabilities in IoT Devices	Analysis and mitigation strategies for firmware vulnerabilities	Identified common firmware vulnerabilities in IoT devices and proposed mitigation techniques, highlighting the need for better security practices
Nadir et al	Firmware Extraction for Forensic Analysis	Focused on methods for extracting firmware for forensic analysis	Discussed the importance of firmware extraction in forensic investigations and provided techniques for ensuring integrity and reliability of extracted data
Shwartz et al	Firmware Extraction and Analysis for Security Evaluation	Techniques for extracting and analyzing firmware to evaluate security	Highlighted various firmware analysis tools and techniques to assess security vulnerabilities, emphasizing automated and scalable methods
Costin et al	Automated Dynamic Firmware Analysis at Scale	Automated dynamic analysis of firmware using emulation and instrumentation	Developed a scalable framework for dynamic analysis of firmware, allowing for the identification of security issues across many devices
Zhang et al	A Survey of Security Vulnerability Analysis, Discovery, Detection, and Mitigation on IoT Devices	Comprehensive survey on firmware security for IoT devices	Provided an in-depth review of security vulnerabilities in IoT firmware and proposed various detection and mitigation strategies

1.4 Outline

We have organized the overview into several sections: In Sect. 2, we provide a general overview of the technologies and debugging interfaces commonly used in IoT devices. In Sect. 3, we introduce the firmware vulnerability and security challenges, as well as the different firmware extraction tools and methods. Then, in Sect. 4, we present the countermeasures to secure devices against firmware extraction and modification. Section 5 presents open research questions and recommendations. Finally, Sect. 6 presents the conclusion and further work.

2 Technical Background

IoT devices are very diverse. In fact, the initial development of any device serves a specific purpose. Most commonly, these devices use microcontrollers that contain one or more central processing units (CPUs) along with memory and special input/output (I/O) peripherals. The most common embedded microcontroller architectures are those from ARM [8], MIPS [12], Freescale, and Texas Instruments TI MSP, as depicted in Fig. 1.

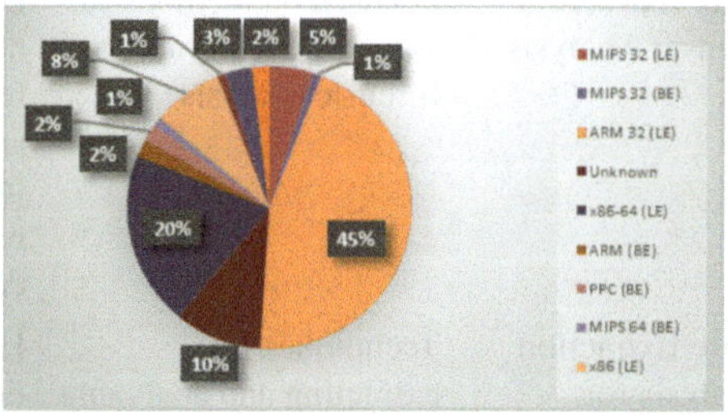

Fig. 1. Types of firmware Instruction Set Architectures (ISA)

Firmware is a compressed binary software [13], either low-level or high-level, stored in an EEPROM or FLASH chip, which serves as an intermediary between the hardware and application software [9]. It consists of various binary files, including the bootloader [2], the operating system kernel, file systems, and headers. Common operating systems for embedded devices include Linux, Android, and Windows IoT Core. The new operating systems designed for IoT devices include Kaspersky OS, Windows IoT Core, and Google Brillo OS. (Android Things). These systems contribute to the functionality and safety of the device, as depicted in Fig. 2.

On the other hand, IoT devices use different application layer protocols for the TCP/IP protocol stack [12], as depicted in Fig. 3. These protocols include HTTP/HTTPS, FTP, Telnet, and SSH for authentication and data transfer. Additionally, IoT devices feature on-chip debugging interfaces for fault testing of integrated circuits, direct memory access, and programming integrated flash chips. These debugging interfaces include UART, JTAG, Serial Wire Debug (SWD) for ARM processors, and BDM for background debugging in automotive processors. Other serial interfaces include SPI and I2C.

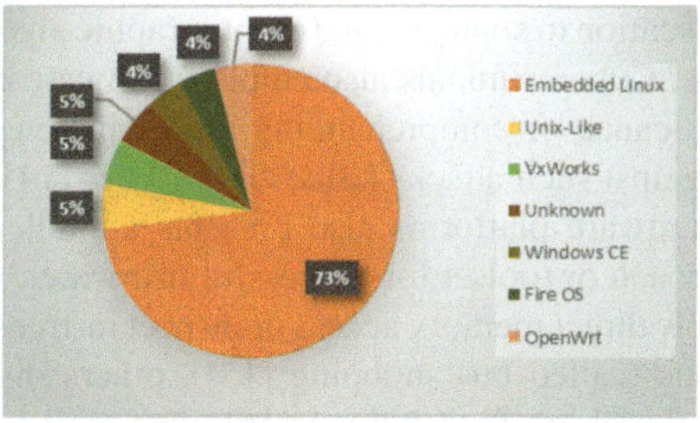

Fig. 2. Popular operating systems used in IoT dev

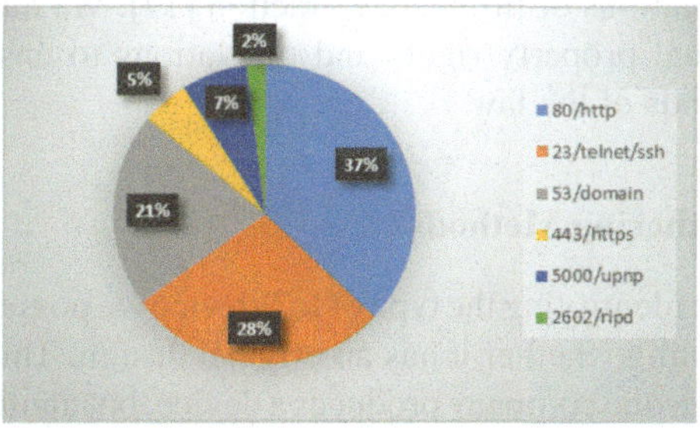

Fig. 3. Commonly used TCP/IP stack protocols in IoT devices

3 Firmware Extraction Methods

3.1 Overview of Firmware Extraction Techniques

The process of extracting firmware from IoT and embedded devices is a critical step in security analysis. Two primary methods can achieve this: hardware and software. Hardware debugging techniques utilize onboard communication interfaces like UART, JTAG, SPI, and I2C. Direct access to the device is necessary to use these methods, which can be intricate as they often require specialized tools designed for different devices. On the other hand, software methods do not require physical access to the device. These methods include searching for firmware on the manufacturer's website, analyzing network traffic to find direct download URLs, and intercepting firmware updates.

To aid the extraction process, various hardware and software tools are available. These tools support interfaces like UART, JTAG, SPI, I2C, and SWD and range in cost. Typically, they work in tandem with their free, open-source software counterparts. These techniques and tools together form the backbone of firmware extraction for IoT and embedded devices.

Despite the importance of firmware extraction, it poses certain challenges. The extraction process can lead to the loss of intellectual property and the discovery of security flaws. These security flaws have the potential to impact not only the examined device, but also all products from the same manufacturer. The protection mechanisms that manufacturers implement to safeguard their firmware against unauthorized access can range from simple obfuscation to sophisticated cryptographic algorithms that require significant effort to bypass. Cybercriminals also employ firmware extraction as a method, underscoring the significance of comprehending these challenges for both legitimate analysis and defense against such attacks (Blue Goat Cyber [14]).

The diversity of hardware platforms also presents a challenge. Each device may require a different approach or toolset for successful firmware extraction. For instance, while some devices allow direct memory access or inspect in-transit data between caches and controllers on a bus (called bus snooping [15]), others may necessitate physical interventions, such as the chip-off technique [16]. The skill level required for these methods varies, with some needing a basic toolset and others demanding advanced knowledge in electronics and reverse engineering. Furthermore, we cannot overlook the legal and ethical implications of firmware extraction [17]. We must navigate a complex landscape of intellectual property rights and regulations to ensure that our activities remain within the bounds of the law.

3.2 Information Gathering Methods

This section focuses on identifying the type of IoT device we possess, identifying its manufacturer, and determining whether it has an original design. This is important because there are instances when one company produces a device, but another company is responsible for its design and development. To accomplish this, we will always take the simplest route, as follows:

1. **Examine the Device Label:** Looking at the IoT device label, we can only determine the original seller or manufacturer, model name, SSID, default Wi-Fi login and password, address, LAN MAC or Ethernet MAC address, and serial number of the device.
2. **Search for the User Manual:** We will search for the user manual of our IoT device on Google to gather as much information as possible about it. Unfortunately, the user manual does not always indicate the relevant information (RAM, EPROM, flash ROM, etc.) when we examine it.
3. **Use Community Resources:** The Community Driving Project, located on the tech-infodepot website, provides a wealth of official information about various IoT devices, including the name and quantity of the EPROM flash chip and RAM chip.
4. **Leverage FCC Resources:** Federal Communication Commission FCC, other very useful information is the FSCC ID. This is the identifier assigned to every IoT device sold in the United States; the FCC approves every device that complies with radio emission regulations. By logging into the FCC website, we can find more information about the IoT device, such as external photos of it, an identification label, and the FCC ID. We also possess additional information, such as internal photos, which provide valuable insights into the device's construction, component types, and radio emissions test reports.
5. **Explore GitHub and OpenWrt:** GitHub Project, in the links of interest, we can also see a link to GitHub projects;
6. **OpenWrt Website:** The open-source router manufacturer maintains a database of numerous routers on this site, which contains a wealth of information. This includes

details about the system on chip, instructions for installing OpenWrt software on the device, the layout of the flash cable, the location of the UART interface, and the position of the JTAG interface. Additionally, the site includes photos of the router, its motherboard, and the precise location of the JTAG interface.

7. **Examine a specific IoT device:** To properly test an IoT device, it is essential to examine its internal components, such as system-on-chip and RAM, as the manufacturer may have made changes. Opening standard devices is generally easy, but small devices like smartphones and digital cameras can be difficult. Tutorials can be found online or on the internet, and some industrial-grade devices may have countermeasures to prevent opening, such as using glue instead of screws. Military-grade devices may also have anti-intrusion circuits.
8. **Identify the internal components of the device:** After opening the device, we unscrew the motherboard to look underneath and understand what kind of components we have underneath. Depending on the presence of metal shielding that protects radio frequencies, removing it without damaging the device board can be easier or more difficult.
9. **Improve the readability of integrated circuit numbers:** often it is difficult to read the part number on the top of integrated circuits. In this case, we can try to improve the readability of the part number by using cotton and alcohol to clean the surface of this part number, then wait for the alcohol to dry, and then use some chalk on these ICs. Apply a light layer of chalk to the part number, ensuring it's not too hard, and after that, it should become easier to read the number.
10. **Research IC Data:** Read IC numbers, use a magnifying glass or LED lamp, search the internet for technical data sheets, or use Chinese search engines like Baidu for unusual Chinese devices where the internet may not provide information.

3.3 Software Methods

The first and simplest methods typically involve the use of specialized tools and techniques to retrieve firmware from devices without physically accessing the hardware. These methods can be particularly useful when physical access is restricted or when extracting firmware from devices remotely. Here are some common software methods for firmware extraction:

1. **Search for Firmware Online:** Search on the Internet or in the user manual of the IoT device if the manufacturer has a website with a firmware image to download;
2. **Handle Encrypted Firmware Images:** If the bootloader, the operating system's self-update procedure, or useful information available on the Internet has encrypted the image, decrypt it. If not, we need another way to dump firmware. By dumping the firmware, extracting its file systems, and analyzing the software, we could potentially uncover the encryption mechanism of the firmware.
3. **Intercept Firmware Communication:** If necessary, intercept the communication. To intercept communication between an IoT device and a PC, use Wireshark to intercept the firmware download. The firmware file can be downloaded directly from a Linux PC, but it may take some time to download. If the firmware file doesn't download until the "User Agent" string is received, use command-line tools like wget or curl to set the same user agent string. If the device uses encrypted protocol like HTTPS,

Wireshark can provide the full server's name but not the full URL or file contents. If the device is a router, the firmware update will be downloaded through the WAN interface, making it difficult to sniff. Connect the router to an existing LAN, adjust its routing table, and observe if it agrees to download the firmware update via the Ethernet interface.

4. **Exploit IoT Services:** Identify and use services running on the IoT device and exploit vulnerabilities in this software. Frequently, firmware update services distribute packages that solely contain folders, leading to an incomplete view. Nonetheless, there are instances where firmware updates comprise complete firmware images, rendering this approach a straightforward and efficient solution for firmware extraction. Moreover, it's important to acknowledge that firmware images are often compressed or encrypted, occasionally using proprietary formats. Unpacking or decrypting such images poses a significant challenge.

3.4 Hardware Methods

3.4.1 Dumping Flash

Dumping flash is the process of extracting all content from a ROM memory chip using parallel interfaces, specialized programmers, and tools like easyJTAG Plus or RiffBox, without any modification or interpretation. This involves directly copying the data from the ROM memory chip to a file in its raw binary format. Raw flash dumps capture the exact state of the memory at a specific moment, including firmware, configuration settings, and any other data stored in the ROM memory chip. The general process for performing flash dumps is as follows:

1. Open the IoT device (see information gathering);
2. Locate and identify the ROM chip by label, packaging type, and processor pin count;
3. Identify the pins and communication bus protocols of the ROM chip using datasheets, an oscilloscope, or logic analyzers;
4. Attach the programmer clip directly to the ROM chip and connect it to your Linux PC's USB port, then perform the ROM chip dump.
5. If the casing of the IoT device is very compact, you may need to desolder the ROM chip, remove it from the board using a hot air gun, and then perform the ROM chip dump using a suitable adapter. However, this operation is not easy, and there is a risk of damaging the ROM chip and nearby components if the temperature rises too high.
6. If the ROM chip technology is newer, such as eMMC, you must disable access to eMMC from the processor, connect the pins to a generic SD card, and use an SD card reader to interface with it [2].
7. For other flash ROM chips, use a suitable adapter and programmer to read the content of the flash ROM chip, such as the MiniPro TL8663.

To ensure secure memory access for circuit dumps, it's crucial to restrict access from the card's processor. You can achieve this by temporarily disconnecting the clock line and reconnecting it once the dump is complete. Simply connecting an eMMC interface like Easy JTAG Plus may sometimes hinder the processor's booting. Another approach is to use the appropriate pin to keep the processor in reset mode.

3.4.2 Using UART

Using UART, another generally simple possibility [18] to dump the firmware of our device IoT is to attach our Linux serial interface to the device's UART. This often allows direct access to a readily available and unrestricted root shell. Alternatively, on Android-based devices, the Android Debug Bridge (ADB) interface may offer access to a root shell. If not, you can access the firmware image using a bootloader shell. Internally dumping the entire file system is the primary method to obtain firmware with direct root access, followed by decompressing the archived files using open-source tools. However, due to the diversity of flash storage and file systems used in IoT devices, dumping block devices may encounter issues. Here's a general overview of the process:

1. Locate UART Pins, Identify the UART pins on the device's circuit board. These pins are usually labeled or can be found in the device's documentation;
2. Connect to UART, use jumper wires to connect the UART pins to a UART-to-USB adapter or a UART debugger tool. This allows communication between the device and a computer;
3. Access Terminal Software, Open terminal software (such as PuTTY or Minicom) on the computer and configure it to communicate with the UART adapter using the appropriate settings (baud rate, data bits, stop bits, parity);
4. Power On Device, Power on the device and observe the terminal software for any output. The device may output bootloader information, debug messages, or a command prompt, depending on its firmware configuration;
5. Capture Output, Capture the output displayed in the terminal software. This output may contain firmware code, configuration settings, or other relevant information;
6. Analyze Output: Analyze the captured output to identify and extract the firmware code. This may involve searching for known file signatures, analyzing binary data, or identifying firmware download commands;
7. Save Firmware, Once the firmware code is identified, save it to a file for further analysis and processing.

3.4.3 Using JTAG

Using JTAG, if all else fails, we can attempt to use the JTAG interface with Bus Pirate or Bus Blaster and OpenOCD. We commonly use it for firmware loading during production and for reading the entire memory chip. An appropriate programmer is required to dump and transfer the content to a computer via a JTAG connection. However, after manufacturing, some manufacturers implement measures to prevent unauthorized reading or reprogramming of the device. Yet, if the JTAG port remains accessible and unlocked, the device becomes vulnerable to firmware extraction and injection attacks. Here is a general overview of the process:

1. Locate JTAG Interface, Identify the JTAG interface on the device's circuit board. This interface typically consists of multiple pins labeled TCK (Test Clock), TMS (Test Mode Select), TDI (Test Data Input), TDO (Test Data Output), and optionally TRST (Test Reset);
2. Connect JTAG Adapter, Use JTAGulator [19] or debugger tool to connect to the JTAG interface on the device. The adapter usually connects to a computer via USB and provides access to the JTAG interface;

3. Install JTAG Software, Install and configure JTAG software on your computer. Popular JTAG software includes OpenOCD, J-Link, and SEGGER;
4. Identify Target Device, Configure the JTAG software to identify the target device connected to the JTAG interface. This may involve specifying the device manufacturer, model, and architecture;
5. Establish Connection, Use the JTAG software to establish a connection with the target device. This typically involves specifying the JTAG adapter and interface settings;
6. Dump Firmware, Once the connection is established, use the JTAG software to dump the firmware from the target device's memory. This process reads the contents of the device's flash memory and saves it to a file on the computer;
7. Verify Dump: Verify the integrity of the dumped firmware to ensure that it was extracted correctly. This may involve comparing the dumped firmware with known firmware images or performing checksum verification.

This method remains quite complicated, and often the JTAG interface is software disabled. Sometimes, the JTAG interface is available for a few milliseconds after powering on the IoT device before it's disabled, but to exploit this possibility, additional circuits controlling the IoT device's power must be used.

3.5 Firmware Extraction Tools

Tools that extract firmware are essential for examining and assessing the safety of gadgets that use IoT or embedded systems. These tools are primarily divided into two categories. 1. Hardware tools: These tools directly interact with the target device's hardware to extract firmware. 2. Software tools: These tools collaborate with compatible hardware tools to extract firmware. They are frequently open-source and available for free download. Various hardware tools support interfaces such as UART, JTAG, SPI, I2C, SWD, SWV, and FTDI, enabling firmware extraction from a wide range of devices. These tools are crucial for pinpointing vulnerabilities, backdoors, and security flaws in firmware images. Prominent firmware extraction tools include UEFI, among others. For more details, see Table 2.

3.6 Legal and Ethical Considerations for Extraction Firmware IoT

It is important to extract firmware within a country's legal frameworks and adhere to ethical and legal best practices. Intellectual property law, including copyright and patent regulations, often controls firmware and may prohibit unauthorized access or reverse engineering without explicit permissions. For instance, the DMCA grants exemptions for activities such as security research, but the specifics of these exemptions vary depending on the jurisdiction [20]. Similarly, privacy regulations such as the CCPA and GDPR mandate that any extraction process must minimize the risks of personal data exposure to maintain user privacy [21]. Best practices recommend obtaining explicit consent from the device owner or manufacturer and isolating the user's data during extraction to prevent potential breaches. Security-critical applications, like healthcare or energy plants with limited access, stop mistakes or data breaches before they happen. They are governed by special rules, like the FDA (US) and the NIS Directive (EU) [26]. Herein,

Table 2. Supported hardware and software tools for IoT firmware extraction

Tool	Interfaces	CPU Types
The Shikra	JTAG, SPI, I2C, UART, GPIO	ARM, i.MX 6
Attify Badge	UART, I2C, SPI, JTAG	ARM Cortex-M
Adafruit FT232H	SPI, I2C, UART, JTAG	doesn't have
HydraBus v1.0	SWD & JTAG, SMARTCARD, NAND flash, SPI, I2C, UART	ARM Cortex-M
Keil ULINK2	JTAG, SWD, SWV	ARM
Flyswatter2	JTAG	ARM, MIPS
Bus Pirate—v3.6a	UART, I2C, SPI, JTAG	Doesn't have
Black Magic Probe	JTAG, SWD	ARM
JTAGulator	JTAG, UART	ARM, MIPS
AVR Dragon	SPI, JTAG, PDI	Atmel AVR
OpenOCD	JTAG, SWD, FTDI, CMSIS-DAP, ST-Link, USB Blaster	ARM, MIPS
UrJTAG	JTAG, FTDI, SI-Link, USB Blaster	ARM, MIPS, PowerPC, x86, AVR
AVR Dude	SPI	Atmel AVR
Easy JTAG plus	JTAG, ISP, UFS, SPI	ARM Cortex-M

the implementation of measures provides responsible means that weigh technological exploration against ethical commitments.

4 Countermeasures

Based on the comprehensive analysis of firmware extraction techniques for IoT devices, it is evident that securing firmware is paramount to protect against intellectual property theft, prevent product counterfeiting, and safeguard sensitive information. The study highlights that over 45% of IoT devices are susceptible to firmware extraction via exposed UART interfaces, emphasizing the need for robust countermeasures. To mitigate these risks, manufacturers are advised to implement security measures such as disabling or password-protecting debug interfaces post-production, employing secure boot processes, and utilizing SELinux to enforce strict access controls. These strategies not only increase the cost and complexity for potential attackers but also contribute to a more secure IoT ecosystem. For more details, see Table 3.

Table 3. IoT firmware extraction countermeasure

Vulnerability	Countermeasure
Debug Interfaces UART	Disable it after production or protect it with unique passwords for each device; All network communication with back-end services should be encrypted using TLS or a similar protocol, especially for firmware updates
JTAG & Other Interfaces	Disable it permanently or protect it with a unique debug password per device
Raw Flash Dump	Use encryption or routing all flash connections on the internal layers of the PCB or cover PCB in epoxy to prevent access;
Secure Boot & SELinux	Implement a Secure Boot and SELinux in application mode; Consider encryption if it is supported for firmware and file system
Side-channel	Introduce random noise into the system to mask side-channel leakage; Implement DPA resistant cryptographic algorithms; Execute cryptographic operations in constant time, regardless of input data

5 Open Research Issues

This section discusses the challenges in ensuring the security of extracting IoT firmwares, offering opportunities for open-source research. The main concerns include security vulnerabilities, as firmware extraction can expose IoT devices to attacks. It is crucial to develop secure extraction techniques and methods for managing and analyzing firmware without compromise. Protection of proprietary firmware is also crucial, requiring legal and ethical frameworks. The diversity of IoT hardware architectures necessitates the development of universal extraction methods, including modifiable and adaptable tools and standardized protocols. Encryption of firmware poses significant challenges, requiring advanced cryptographic techniques and auxiliary analysis methods. Non-invasive extraction methods are necessary to preserve device integrity, especially in limited resources. A multidisciplinary approach involving cybersecurity, hardware engineering, cryptography, and legal considerations is needed to improve the security and resilience of IoT ecosystems.

6 Conclusion and Further Work

In this article, we have analyzed the significance of Internet of Things (IoT) in daily life, the driving forces behind it, and the primary works that have explored IoT firmware extraction methods. We have also deduced the extraction techniques studied in each work, along with the main conclusions and contributions. On the other hand, we delved into the technical background of firmware extraction, covering topics such as microcontrollers, processor architectures, operating systems, file systems, debugging interfaces, communication buses, and network protocols. We studied the techniques used to implement information collection, software extraction, hardware extraction of IoT firmware, and tools. Finally, we discussed the different countermeasures related to the security of IoT devices.

To address the lack of standardization in hardware architectures, future research should focus on creating user-friendly and affordable methods for firmware extraction. Innovative methods for deconstructing cross-compiled software and improving machine learning algorithms for vulnerability scanning are other crucial areas for development. As the IoT ecosystem grows, researchers should focus on developing scalable frameworks and procedures for effective vulnerability checking.

References

1. Vasile, S., Oswald, D., Chothia, T.: Breaking all the things—a systematic survey of firmware extraction techniques for IoT devices. In: Smart Card Research and Advanced Applications: 17th International Conference, CARDIS 2018, Montpellier, France, 12–14 November 2018, Revised Selected Papers 17, pp. 171–185. Springer (2019)
2. Ul Haq, S., Singh, Y., Sharma, A., Gupta, R., Gupta, D.: A survey on IoT & embedded device firmware security: architecture, extraction techniques, and vulnerability analysis frameworks. Discov. Internet Things **3**(1), 17 (2023)
3. Shwartz, O., Mathov, Y., Bohadana, M., Elovici, Y., Oren, Y.: Reverse engineering IoT devices: effective techniques and methods. IEEE Internet Things J. **5**(6), 4965–4976 (2018)
4. Milinković, A., Milinković, S., Lazić, L.: Choosing the right RTOS for IoT platform. Infoteh-Jahorina **14**, 504–509 (2015)
5. Gupta, A.: The IoT Hacker's Handbook [Electronic Resource]: A Practical Guide to Hacking the Internet of Things. Aditya Gupta (2019)
6. Guzman, A., Gupta, A.: IoT Penetration Testing Cookbook: Identify Vulnerabilities and Secure Your Smart Devices. Packt Publishing Ltd. (2017)
7. Manske, A.: Conducting a vulnerability assessment of an IP camera (2019)
8. Chen, D.D., Woo, M., Brumley, D., Egele, M.: Towards automated dynamic analysis for Linux-based embedded firmware. In: NDSS, vol. 1, p. 1 (2016)
9. Nadir, I., Mahmood, H., Asadullah, G.: A taxonomy of IoT firmware security and principal firmware analysis techniques. Int. J. Crit. Infrastruct. Prot. **38**, 100552 (2022)
10. Costin, A., Zarras, A., Francillon, A.: Automated dynamic firmware analysis at scale: a case study on embedded web interfaces. In: Proceedings of the 11th ACM on Asia Conference on Computer and Communications Security, pp. 437–448 (2016)
11. Zhang, W., Li, H., Wen, H., Zhu, H., Sun, L.: A graph neural network based efficient firmware information extraction method for IoT devices. In: 2018 IEEE 37th International Performance Computing and Communications Conference (IPCCC), pp. 1–8. IEEE (2018)
12. Arias, O., Wurm, J., Hoang, K.Y.: Privacy and security in Internet of Things and wearable devices. IEEE Trans. Multi-Scale Comput. Syst. **1**(2), 99–109 (2015)
13. Chen, J., et al.: IoTFuzzer: discovering memory corruptions in IoT through app-based fuzzing. In: NDSS (2018)
14. Wu, F., Gao, M., Yu, J., Wang, Z., Liu, K., Wang, X.: Ready for emerging threats to recommender systems? A graph convolution-based generative shilling attack. Inf. Sci. **578**, 683–701 (2021)
15. Huang, A.B.: Hacking the Xbox: An Introduction to Reverse Engineering. No Starch Press (2003)
16. da Silveira, C.M., et al.: Methodology for forensics data reconstruction on mobile devices with Android operating system applying in-system programming and combination firmware. Appl. Sci. **10**(12), 4231 (2020)

17. Yaacoub, J.P.A., Noura, H.N., Salman, O., Chehab, A.: Ethical hacking for IoT: security issues, challenges, solutions and recommendations. Internet Things Cyber-Phys. Syst. **3**, 280–308 (2023)
18. JTAGulator G Idea. https://www.grandideastudio.com/jtagulator/. Accessed Sept 2020
19. Samuelson, P.: Legal aspects of security research under the DMCA. J. Law Technol. **33**(2), 165–192 (2020)
20. Voigt, P., Von dem Bussche, A.: The EU General Data Protection Regulation (GDPR). A Practical Guide, 1st edn. Springer, Cham (2017)
21. Casey, E.: Digital Evidence and Computer Crime: Forensic Science, Computers, and the Internet. Academic Press (2011)

From Concept to Standard: The Trajectory of CubeSat Space Protocol Standardization

Fadwa Belali[1,3](✉), Slimane Bah[1,3], Ilyas El Wafi[1,3], Amina Daghouri[2,3], and Zouhair Guennoun[1,3]

[1] SCRT Smart Communication Research Team, EMI, Mohammed V University in Rabat, Rabat, Morocco
fadwa_belali@um5.ac.ma, {slimane.bah,zouhair}@emi.ac.ma, ilyaselwafi@research.emi.ac.ma

[2] STIS Research Center, Research Team "Energy Optimization, Diagnosis and Control", ENSAM of Rabat, Mohammed V University in Rabat, Rabat, Morocco
amina.daghouri@um5s.net.ma

[3] University Center for Research in Space Technologies, EMI, Mohammed V University in Rabat, Rabat, Morocco

Abstract. The CubeSat Space Protocol (CSP) has proven to be an effective and efficient communication protocol specifically designed for distributed embedded systems within small networks such as those found in nanosatellites. The lack of standardisation in this protocol has raised concerns among space engineers about interoperability, error rates and reliability. Despite these concerns, CSP has been widely adopted and integrated into several major projects. This paper highlights the critical need for standardisation of CSP, with a focus on robust modelling and verification methodologies for data transmission. The study provides an in-depth analysis of CSP, emphasising its client-server architecture through finite-state machine modelling. In particular, advanced verification techniques using the Promela language are employed to provide a high level of reliability for the protocol by rigorously examining packet transmission. The results confirm the effectiveness of CSP and highlight the need for standardisation, allowing CubeSat developers to implement the protocol with greater confidence and efficiency.

Keywords: Cubesat Space Protocol · Finite state machine · Communication · Modeling · Verification · Promela

1 Introduction

Over the past two decades, CubeSats have become an increasingly prevalent area of interest, with hundreds of launches taking place each year [1]. This exponential growth in popularity has given rise to considerable challenges in communication, both between nanosatellites and their constituent subsystems. The development of effective communication protocols for these small-scale satellites has become a key research objective. Among the various communication protocols that have been introduced, the CubeSat

I. Aboudrar et al. (Eds.): ICESST 2024, SUCI, pp. 305–314, 2025.
https://doi.org/10.1007/978-3-031-86705-7_28

Space Protocol (CSP) [2] has emerged as the most widely used and efficient in comparison to other space communication protocols, CSP exhibits a number of distinctive characteristics that merit scientific investigation.

Firstly, whereas protocols such as the Space Packet Protocol (SPP) [3] provide unidirectional and asynchronous data transfer services, CSP offers a comprehensive solution that includes both unidirectional and bidirectional communication paradigms. Furthermore, CSP's adherence to the CCSDS standard ensures interoperability and compatibility within existing space mission architectures, thereby distinguishing it from competitors such as the Licklider Transmission Protocol (LTP) [4], which may lack standardisation. The design of CSP is characterised by a small 4-byte header and support for a service-oriented network topology, which are specifically tailored to meet the requirements and constraints of CubeSat missions. This focused adaptation distinguishes CSP from protocols like the Space Communications Protocol Specification (SCPS) [5], which, while adaptable to space environments, may lack the requisite specialised support for CubeSat operations.

Moreover, CSP's incorporation of a straightforward Short Fragmentation Protocol (SFP) for the transmission of large data packets enhances efficiency, a pivotal consideration under the resource constraints typical of CubeSat missions. In contrast, protocols such as the SCPS Transport Protocol (SCPS-TP) [6] do not explicitly address the unique challenges of CubeSat applications. This underscores the necessity for a protocol like CSP, which is specifically designed to optimize CubeSat communication.

CSP draws inspiration from the classical TCP/IP [7] protocol stack and is renowned for its lightweight design. The protocol's primary objective is to enhance efficiency by minimizing overhead, thereby conserving bandwidth and power. Its simplicity makes it straightforward to implement on resource constrained systems. CSP is flexible, supporting various communication paradigms, including point-to-point, broadcast, and multicast. Additionally, it is modular, facilitating the incorporation of extensions for encryption (XTEA) and error checking (CRC), making it highly adaptable to diverse mission requirements.

The CSP protocol [8] is a continuously developed and maintained within the CubeSat community. Its source code is publicly available under an LGPL licence and can be accessed on GitHub, ensuring that it remains a versatile and accessible solution for space communication needs. For easy addressing, the space and ground segments are typically assigned the address ranges 0–15 and 16–31 respectively(This address range only holds for the newest packet format (1.0+)). This makes it easy to distinguish between the addresses as every ground module has a binary 1 as its *MSB* and every space module a binary 0. Different types of physical connections may be used between individual modules, and not all need to be directly connected.

Although numerous articles have examined the deployment of CSP in diverse operational scenarios and its integration with CCSDS [9], none have provided a comprehensive elucidation of CSP or addressed the issue of its lack of standardisation. The absence of standardisation gives rise to concerns regarding the reliability of CSP, which may impede its adoption despite its proven efficacy in CubeSat communication. This paper argues for the standardisation of CSP, highlighting its suitability due to its efficiency. A comprehensive description of the CSP layers is given, with a comparative analysis of this transport protocol and other relevant standards. The paper also illustrates the client-server interactions using Finite State Machines (FSMs). Finally, the protocol is validated with Promela, providing additional support for its standardisation.

2 CSP Layers and Packet Format

2.1 Cubesat Space Protocol Layers

CSP is divided into several layers [10] having distinct responsibilities and with communication only between the adjacent layer(s). Figure 1 shows the protocol stack with the four different layers.

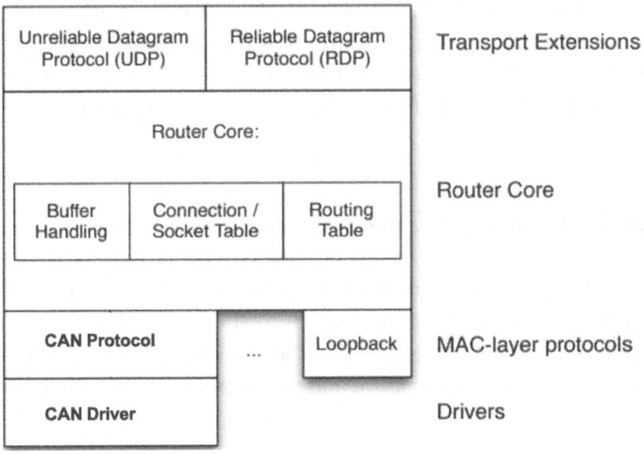

Fig. 1. Protocol stack of CSP [10].

The Driver layer includes low-level drivers for network devices like I2C and CAN, with GomSpace advising the use of DMA and interrupt-driven drivers for stability and performance. The MAC layer formats packets, strips the frame exterior on arrival, and forwards the packet to the upper layer, while also encapsulating outgoing packets in a frame for delivery. The Router Core layer routes packets to correct destinations using an internal routing table and buffers for packets, sockets, and connections. The Transport Extensions layer provides delivery methods akin to TCP/IP, with GomSpace offering both UDP and RDP. For small satellites, where the bus is reliable, UDP is preferred for real-time applications, making RDP often unnecessary.

2.2 Packet Format of CSP

A packet is divided into two parts for the header and the payload respectively. Figure 2 shows the latest packet format, (1.0+).

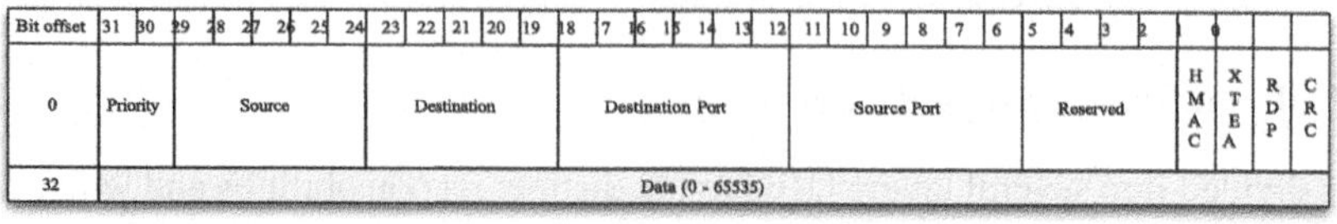

Fig. 2. The header format of a CSP 1.0+ packet [10].

As can be observed, a total of 32 bits are utilised for the purpose of differentiating between packet importance (priority), maintaining routing information (addresses and ports), and enabling other operations to be performed, such as encryption/decryption (XTEA) and data integrity checks (CRC).The actual payload commences at bit number 32.

3 The Core Principles of Cubesat Space Protocol

This section provides an overview of the CSP protocol, focusing on socket implementation and related functionalities. A socket serves as the endpoint in communication, with connections established between endpoints. On the server side, an application binds a socket to a port, enabling communication and the creation of new connections, identified by a 4-tuple.

(destination address, destination port, source address, source port)

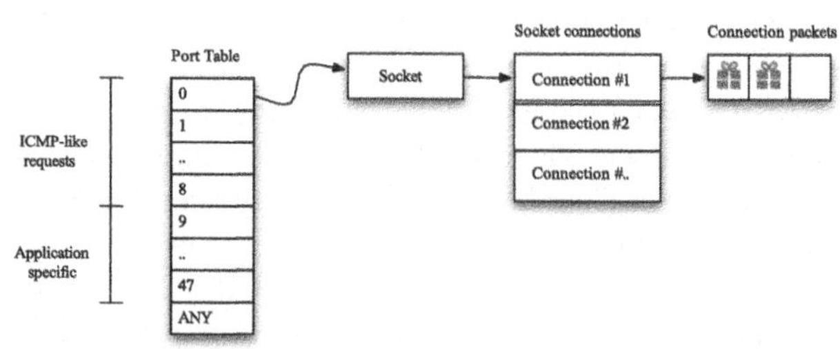

Fig. 3. Ports, Sockets, Connections and Packets.

Figure 3 illustrates the relationship between ports, sockets, connections, and packets. Ports 0–47 are reserved for incoming connections, with ports 0–8 dedicated to ICMP-like requests, while the remaining ports up to 63 handle outgoing connections. The section defines four classes:

1. **Port** Links a port to a socket and checks if a port is open when new packets arrive.
2. **Socket** Defines an endpoint bound to a port, allowing the acceptance of new connections.
3. **Connection** Manages data flow between endpoints, associating with a socket on the receiving side.
4. **Packet** Represents the packet, including its header and payload, sent through the system.

4 Results and Discussions

This study presents a comprehensive analysis of a Finite State Machine (FSM) model designed to elucidate the packet transmission process from the client side within the CSP network. This model is instrumental in elucidating the manner in which packets are managed efficiently and reliably within a CSP environment.

4.1 Cubesat Space Protocol Modeling (Client - Server)

Since the responsibility for sending packets rests with the client, (FSM) 4to illuminate the sequence of events and state transitions inherent in this process. The system attempts to establish a connection using the **csp_connect** function. If the connection is successful, the FSM enters the Connection Established state. In the Connection Established state, the system initiates the **csp_send** operation, which sends the prepared packet through the designated channels. This action, initiated by the Route Packet event, is critical to the successful routing and delivery of the packet to the intended server. The packet is then sent to the CAN interface where it is segmented and sent using the **csp_can_tx** function. This involves splitting the packet into frames.

In addition, the FSM provides mechanisms for closing the connection, which can be triggered by the "No more packets" event, which results in a close function. This termination is performed by the **csp_close** function, which closes the connection after all packets have been successfully transmitted, or based on a user command. The FSM employs a number of robust error management strategies, including timeouts and retries, to navigate through transmission uncertainties throughout its operation. This comprehensive analysis of the FSM not only facilitates an understanding of the packet transmission process within CSP, but also highlights the complexity of the protocol and the key role of state management in maintaining data integrity and ensuring transmission reliability in satellite communications (Fig. 4).

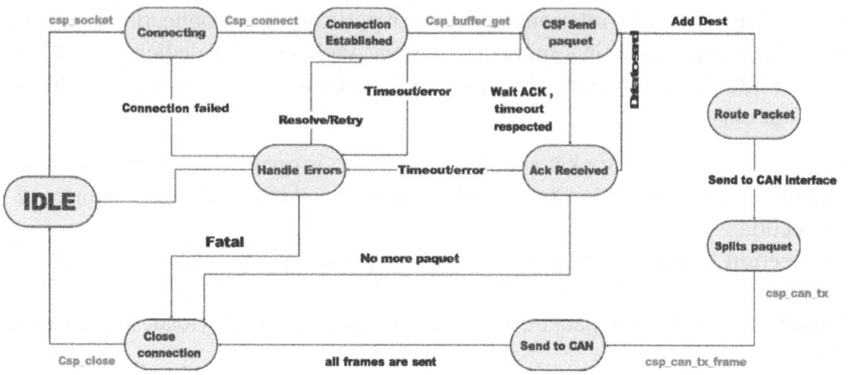

Fig. 4. Client-side finite state machine model.

The server finite state machine (FSM) in 5 within the CubeSat Space Protocol (CSP) operates through a series of distinct states, each of which performs a critical function in managing incoming data transmission. Initially, the FSM is in the IDLE state, ready to transition to the Connecting state upon detection of incoming connection requests, facilitated by the **csp_listen** function. On transition to the Connecting state, the FSM waits for validation of both the destination and packet size parameters before transitioning to the Connection Established state. This transition indicates successful connection establishment where the **csp_read** function is called and waits to receive packets (Fig. 5).

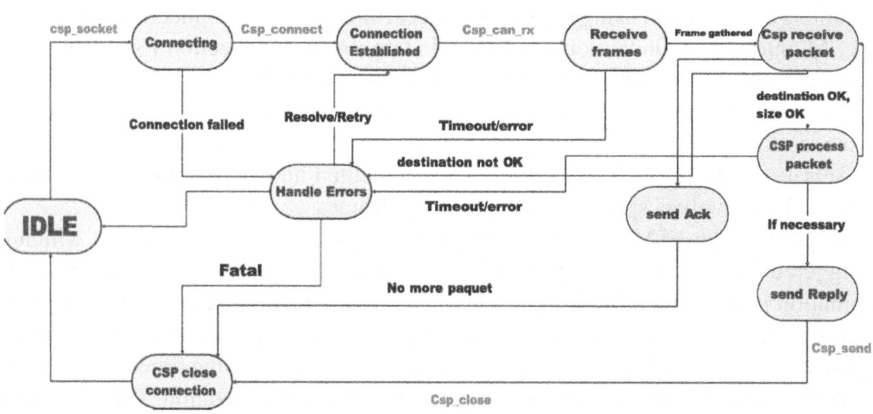

Fig. 5. Server-side finite state machine model.

Upon successful reception of a packet (as indicated by destination and size verification), the FSM transitions to sending an acknowledgement (ACK) to confirm successful receipt. The received packets are then processed, allowing the server to handle incoming data efficiently. The server will continue to receive new packets until all packets have been processed, at which point it will send a final ACK to signal completion of reception. In cases where a response is warranted based on the content of the received packets, the server initiates the appropriate response. Conversely, if no response is required, the **csp_close** function is called to terminate the data transfer process. Error handling within the receive FSM is similar to the sending FSM, using resolve/retry strategies to deal with transient errors and escalating to fatal states in the face of unrecoverable errors. This robust error handling mechanism ensures the resilience and reliability of the data transmission process, mitigating the impact of potential disruptions on overall system performance.

4.2 Promela-Based Verification of Cubesat Space Protocol

In the field of distributed systems and communication protocols, Promela [11] is a pivotal verification instrument, made possible by the Spin model checker. This method permits a comprehensive examination and validation of system designs through the modeling of their concurrent processes and interactions in the Promela language, which was developed specifically to address the challenges of verifying complex, multi-threaded systems. The Spin model checker, a well-established tool in formal verification, leverages Promela's capabilities to conduct exhaustive state space explorations, ensuring that every possible scenario is scrutinized for errors.

The comprehensive simulation and state exploration enabled by Promela verification enhance the reliability, robustness, and efficiency of protocol implementations in complex environments. The inherent complexity of distributed systems, which often consist of multiple nodes interacting concurrently, renders them susceptible to a multitude of intricate issues that can potentially impact their performance and reliability. By leveraging Promela's formal verification capabilities, exhaustive testing of each component of a system in different combinations and sequences of events can be conducted, thereby ensuring that the system behaves as expected under all circumstances. This is particularly beneficial in high-stakes environments, such as aerospace, telecommunications, and automated control systems, where even minor errors could lead to significant consequences.

The Promela model under consideration here simulates a client-server interaction, in which the client initiates a connection request and awaits an acknowledgement from the server. Upon receipt of the request, the server responds with either an acknowledgement or an error message, thereby testing the communication and synchronisation logic of CSP-like protocols.

```
// Process for the client

    out_msg.type = ESTABLISH;
    out_msg.id = id;
    out_msg.header = 123;

    do
    :: out ! out_msg; // Attempt to establish connection
       in ? in_msg ->
          if
          :: in_msg.type == ACK ->
              printf("ACK received\n");
              out_msg.type = DATA; // Change to data type
   after connection
              break; // Exit after successful connection
          :: in_msg.type == ERROR ->
              printf("Error reported by server, retrying...\
   n");
              out_msg.type = ESTABLISH; // Retry
   establishing connection
          :: else ->
              printf("Unexpected message type received\n");

// Process for the server

   do
   :: in ? in_msg ->
      if
      :: in_msg.type == ESTABLISH ->
         if
         // Simulating a nondeterministic condition (
   random-like behavior)
         :: true ->
             out_msg.type = ACK;
             out_msg.id = in_msg.id;
             out_msg.header = in_msg.header; // Echo back
   the header
             out ! out_msg;
         :: true -> // Simulate an error condition
             out_msg.type = ERROR;
             out_msg.id = in_msg.id;
             out ! out_msg;
         fi;
```

In the code snippet above, the **Client** initiates communication by sending an 'ESTABLISH' packet with a unique ID and waits for an 'ACK' response. If successful, it proceeds with the data transfer; otherwise, it retries or logs an error, thereby demonstrating its error-handling capabilities.

The **Server** listens continuously for incoming packets. On receiving an 'ESTABLISH' packet, it responds with either an 'ACK' or an 'ERROR', using the same ID to ensure consistency. This process tests the server's ability to handle connection requests and manage communication problems, ensuring reliability in the system (Fig. 6).

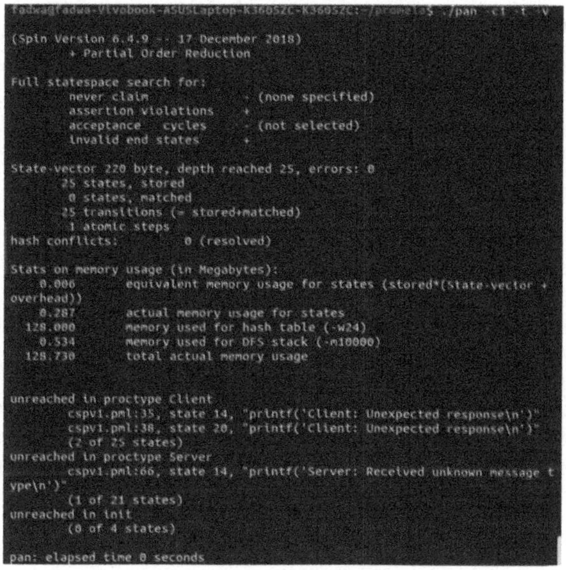

Fig. 6. The promela verification code result.

This output not only corroborates the absence of deadlocks or undesirable states but also validates the model's capacity to accommodate typical client-server interactions. Furthermore, the results demonstrate that the CSP protocol is capable of reliably transmitting and receiving messages while effectively managing any errors that may occur. This verification serves to illustrate the robustness and effectiveness of the model in accurately simulating CSP-like protocols.

5 Conclusion and Future Work

In conclusion, this paper depict and analyse the intricate behaviours and processes inherent in CSP. The detailed Promela simulations facilitated a better understanding of the operational nuances of the protocol. Furthermore, the application of FSM provided a clear and systematic representation of the state transitions within CSP, underlining the robustness and efficiency of the protocol in handling satellite communications tasks. These modelling efforts not only theoretically validate the reliability of CSP, but also provide practical insights that can be used to improve protocol implementation and debugging. The verification processes carried out using the SPIN model checker have further solidified the credibility of our model.

In future work, the objective is to develop a custom-designed file transfer protocol to be added as an application layer, resulting in a lightweight, standardised protocol specifically tailored for CubeSats. This enhancement will facilitate the communication of data, thereby enhancing efficiency and reliability for small satellite operations. Furthermore, it would be beneficial to investigate the potential applications of the CubeSat Space Protocol (CSP) in larger satellites, extending its current use beyond nanosatellites. By adapting CSP for more extensive satellite missions, the benefits of this protocol can be leveraged to improve communication and operational efficiency across a broader range of space missions.

Acknowledgement. This research was carried out in collaboration with the Royal Centre for Space Research and Studies (CRERS) and the Mohammed V University of Rabat (UM5R).

References

1. Swartwout, M.: The first one hundred cubesats: a statistical look. J. Small Satell. **2**(2), 213–233 (2013). https://doi.org/10.1109/JSS.2013.0064
2. Davoli, F., Kourogiorgas, C., Marchese, M., Panagopoulos, A., Patrone, F.: Small satellites and CubeSats: survey of structures, architectures, and protocols. Int. J. Satell. Commun. Netw. **37**(4), 343–359 (2019)
3. CCSDS (The Consultative Committee Space Data System): Space Packet Protocol (SPP). CCSDS 133.0-B-1 (2003)
4. Ramadas, M., Burleigh, S., Farrell, S.: Licklider transmission protocol-specification. RFC 5326 (2008)
5. CCSDS (The Consultative Committee Space Data System): Space Communications Protocol Specifications (SCPS). CCSDS 711.0-G-0.2 (1997)
6. CCSDS (The Consultative Committee Space Data System): Space Communications Protocol Specifications - Transport Protocol (SCPS-TP). CCSDS 714.0-B-2 (2006)
7. Fall, K.R., Stevens, W.R.: TCP/IP Illustrated, vol. 1. Addison-Wesley Professional (2012)
8. CubeSat Space Protocol (CSP) v1.1. Report. bytebucket.org (n.d.). Accessed 28 Aug 2024. https://bytebucket.org/bbruner0/albertasat-on-board-computer/wiki/1.%20Resources/1.1.%20DataSheets/CSP/GS-CSP-1.1.pdf?rev=316ebd49bed49fdbb1d74efdeab74430e7cc726as
9. Lagadrilliere, P.-A., Brügge, T., Müller, K.: Confronting or linking CSP and CCSDS? A view on how to operate small satellites today (2023)
10. GomSpace. GitHub (n.d.). https://github.com/GomSpace
11. Neumann, R.: Using promela in a fully verified executable LTL model checker. In: Working Conference on Verified Software: Theories, Tools, and Experiments, pp. 105–114. Springer (2014)

Integrating a Real Time Operating-System Layer to a Memory-Constrained Electrical Power System for a Nanosatellite

Abdellah Essetty[1,3](✉), Amina Daghouri[2,3], Slimane Bah[1,3], and Zouhair Guennoun[1,3]

[1] SCRT Smart Communication Research Team, EMI, Mohammed V University in Rabat, Rabat, Morocco
a.essetty@research.emi.ac.ma, {slimane.bah,zouhair}@emi.ac.ma

[2] STIS Research Center, Research Team "Energy Optimization, Diagnosis and Control", ENSAM of Rabat, Mohammed V University in Rabat, Rabat, Morocco
amina.daghouri@um5s.net.ma

[3] University Center for Research in Space Technologies, EMI, Mohammed V University in Rabat, Rabat, Morocco

Abstract. In the realm of space applications, software reliability plays a vital role in defining the success or failure of a mission. For Nanosatellite missions, software is typically developed on demand, tailored to meet the specific needs and constraints of the system. These constraints often necessitate a minimalistic approach to software design to ensure safety and secure operation. However, the software must also be sufficiently complex to achieve all mission objectives. While the use of general purpose operating systems like Linux has been increasing in the past years, commercial off-the-shelf real-time operating systems (RTOS) are still preferred due to their deterministic nature and the ease of development and debugging. This paper explores the integration of a FreeRTOS layer into an MSP430-based Electrical Power System for a nanosatellite. The integration involves adding telemetry collection and housekeeping tasks to enhance subsystem integration and responsiveness with other subsystems without putting pressure in the system resources.

Keywords: Nanosatellite · Real-time operating system · Electrical power system

1 Introduction

Nanosatellites have been receiving significant attention in the last decade [1]. Both by academic research and private companies, with more than a 1000 nanosatellite launched from 2003 [2]. Reflecting the growing interest in their potential for various space applications. These small, cost-effective satellites provide a valuable entry point into aerospace for teams with limited budgets, enabling researchers worldwide to gain hands-on experience in space.

While the software implemented in aerospace applications is not fundamentally different from that used in general embedded systems—ranging from full-fledged operating

I. Aboudrar et al. (Eds.): ICESST 2024, SUCI, pp. 315–323, 2025.
https://doi.org/10.1007/978-3-031-86705-7_29

systems like Linux to lightweight bare-metal solutions [3]—the space environment in which it operates imposes far greater demands. Unlike applications deployed in other fields, where physical intervention is often possible when issues arise, a satellite operating in space must function autonomously without the possibility of physical user intervention. This makes the software used in nanosatellites exceptionally critical, as any misbehavior or malfunction could lead to mission failure.

The software stack run by each nanosatellite's subsystem can vary widely in terms of complexity and structure. However, most subsystems have critical sections that must be performed in a time constrained fashion in order to ensure the well behaviour of the nanosatellite. Leppinen et al. [4] analysed the use of Linux in aerospace applications. Showing that while it has gained momentum as a proper operating system for use in space mission, it introduces additional complexity in terms of hardware requirements and power consumption. On the other hand, Putra et al. [5] demonstrated the advantages of using an RTOS for the On-Board Data Handling (OBDH) subsystem, which helped reducing the computational time of the system. Within a 10-s interval, the RTOS-based program collected 33 more samples and responded 611.11 ms faster than a non-RTOS setup. Similarly, Akhoury et al. [6] described the design and working of the data handling system of a nanosatellite in a fault-tolerant distributed system. This paper explores the integration of a FreeRTOS layer into an MSP430-based Electrical Power System (EPS), developed as part of an ongoing initiative to build a robust university nanosatellite. By incorporating FreeRTOS, the system gains significant improvements in modularity, scalability, and extensibility, which are essential for a successful and reliable nanosatellite mission. The enhanced software architecture aims to ensure smooth interaction and compatibility with other nanosatellite subsystems, laying a solid foundation for future upgrades and additional features. Section 2 gives an overview of the EPS subsystem, on both the hardware and software level. Section 3 delves into the implementation details of the RTOS integration, while Sect. 4 presents the results of the implementation in terms of memory management. Finally, Sect. 5 offers concluding remarks.

2 System Architecture

The Electrical Power System (EPS) used was initially developed by Daghouri et al. [7] in the context of developing a university nanosatellite in the University Center for Research in Space Technologies (CURTS).

2.1 Overview of the Electrical Power System

The EPS is responsible of generating, storing, regulating, and distributing the electrical power that the satellite with all its subsystems requires. Solar energy is harnessed through photovoltaic (PV) panels, converted to usable voltage levels, and stored in batteries for operation during eclipse periods [8]. Figure 1 shows the major components of the EPS, including the Micro Controller Unit (MCU) the MSP340FR5969, the battery charger, and the Distribution & protection system all via an I2C bus.

The EPS based MSP430FR5969 is connected directly to the on-board computer, which manages overall system operations and data processing, The battery charger

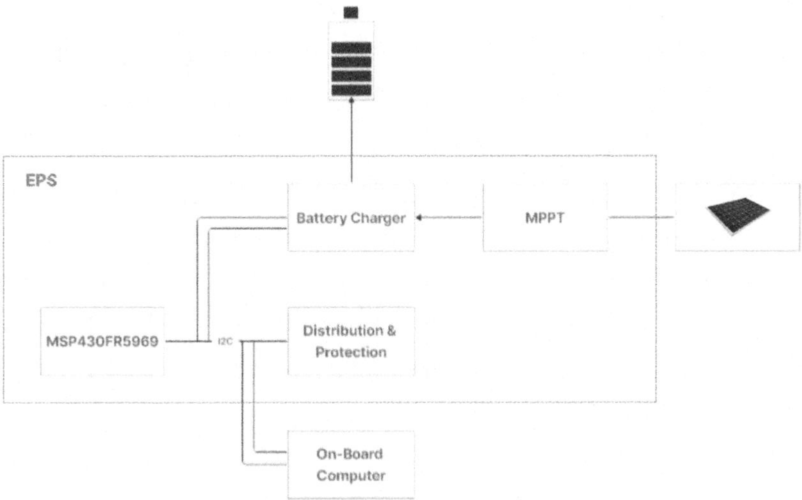

Fig. 1. EPS Schematic Diagram

ensures that the batteries are properly charged using energy from the solar panels, and an embedded Maximum Power Point Tracking (MPPT) algorithm is used to maximize the power generated from the photovoltaic panels and minimize losses [7].

2.2 MSP430FR5969 Characteristics

The MSP430 is a family of microcontrollers (MCUs) developed by Texas Instruments. Based on a 16-bit CPU, the MSP430 family is optimized for low-cost, low-power signal processing applications [9]. The MSP430FR5969 was used as the main MCU for the EPS subsystem. It includes a 16-MHz Clock, a 64 KB of non-volatile Ultra-Low-Power Ferroelectric RAM (FRAM) used for program memory. Unlike conventional flash memory, FRAM offers faster write speeds and higher endurance while consuming less power. FRAM is also highly resistant to radiation-induced failures, which is critical for space missions where radiation can affect data integrity. Furthermore, the MSP430FR5969 features 2 KB of volatile SRAM used as a data memory, and a power consumption of approximately 100 μA/MHz in active mode, making it suitable for space applications. Figure 2 illustrates the general architecture of the MSP430FR5969.

2.3 Software Architecture

The software of the EPS was initially running in a bare-metal fashion, meaning it operated directly on the hardware without the support of an operating system or any abstraction layer. Using this approach, the main function would consist of an infinite while loop that would continuously execute the core tasks of the EPS.

The bare-metal approach relies heavily on the concept of interrupt service routines (ISR) to handle asynchronous events and external inputs. An interrupt is managed by a dedicated hardware module separate from the CPU. When an external event occurs,

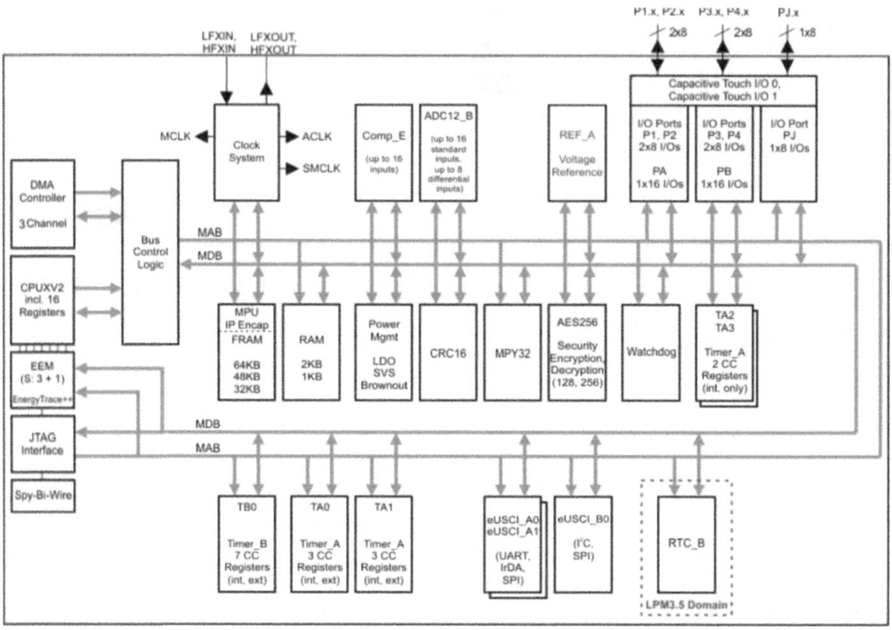

Fig. 2. MSP430FR5969 Architecture [10]

such as a signal from a peripheral device (e.g., a sensor or communication interface), the interrupt hardware raises a flag. This flag serves as a notification to the CPU that an event has occurred, signaling that specific attention or action is required. Figure 3a illustrates a simplified flow of a baremetal application. The main program would enter a infinite loop, after setting up the device with proper configuration, and then perform continuously the pre-determined actions sequentially.

Real-Time Operating Systems Concept. A RTOS is a piece of software that manages the sharing of resources in a computer system [11]. It enables the concurrent execution of multiple tasks, allowing the microcontroller to handle deterministic events and tasks with real-time responsiveness. All while having a modular design and guaranteeing to some extent the task deadlines are met. Figure 3b illustrates the program flow of an RTOS-based application. After the system is configured, the main function starts the scheduler, which is a core component of the RTOS. The scheduler is responsible for managing the execution of tasks based on their priority and timing requirements. It determines which task should run at any given time, handles context switching between tasks, and ensures that high-priority tasks preempt lower-priority ones when necessary. This process allows the system to respond to real-time events predictably and efficiently. RTOS's have been increasingly adopted in aerospace applications and in small 16-bit architectures [12].

FreeRTOS Overview. FreeRTOS is a portable real-time operating system for micro-controllers and small microprocessors. Distributed freely under the MIT open source license. It compromise a collection of C libraries that allows applications to isolate their

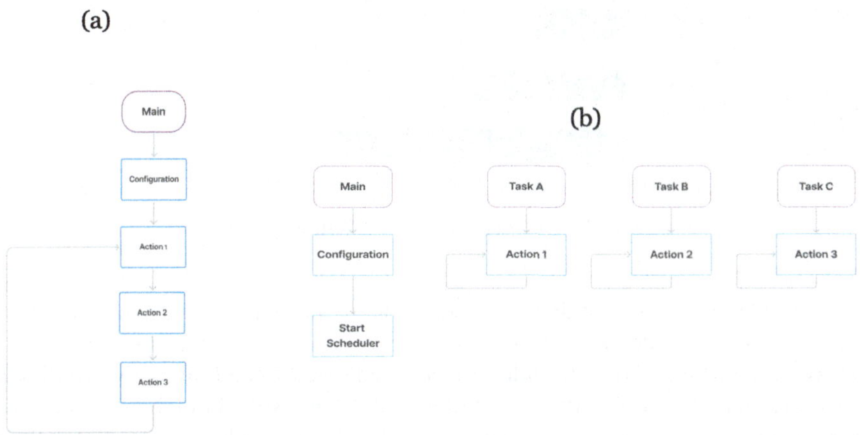

Fig. 3. (a) Simplified bare-metal program flow; (b) Simplified RTOS based program with 3 tasks.

components as independent tasks (or threads). It offers several mechanisms to assure a concurrent execution of tasks, some of these features are:

- A preemptive scheduler.
- Multiple memory allocation options, including the possibility to use static and dynamic allocation.
- Inter-task coordinating mechanisms, including message queues, semaphores and mutexes, and stream and message buffers.

3 Implementation Details

In space applications, ensuring code safety is of paramount importance due to the critical nature of the missions and the constraints of the space environment. Several guidelines have been developed to address these challenges, one of the most straightforward being NASA's Power of Ten rules for developing safety-critical code [13]. These guidelines emphasize simplicity and reliability by enforcing rules such as using only static memory allocation, avoiding dynamic memory to prevent fragmentation and memory leaks, and limiting the complexity of code structures to make the software more predictable and easier to verify and validate.

3.1 Dynamic and Static Allocation

FreeRTOS supports more than 40 architectures including the MSP430, the official blinky example includes a basic application with 2 tasks, a transmitter and a receiver, both with minimum allowed stack depth. Figure 4 shows the memory usage of the blinky tasks. Memory is expressed in Bytes, FRAM and FRAM2 take different addresses in the address space of the MSP340fr5969.

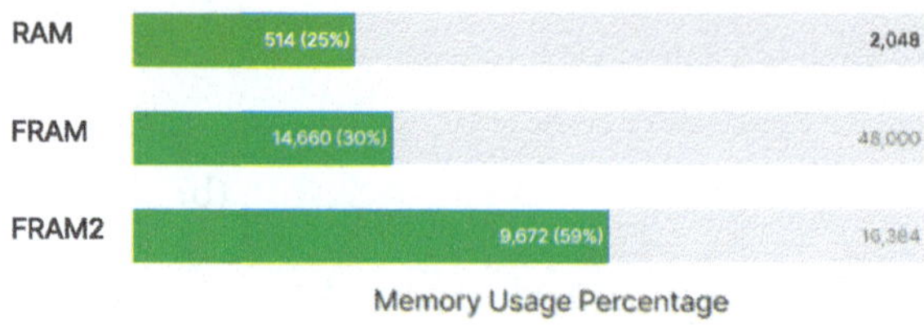

Fig. 4. Memory usage of the blinky example

FreeRTOS supports both dynamic and static memory allocation schemes, enabling tasks, queues, and other kernel objects to be created either at compile-time or run-time. While static allocation provides greater predictability and safety by avoiding heap fragmentation and runtime allocation failures, it often results in higher memory usage. Figure 5 illustrates the memory usage of the Blinky example, using a statically allocated task alongside a dynamically allocated task, both configured with the minimum stack depth allowed. The results show that static allocation consumes significantly more memory, which is a critical consideration in resource-constrained environments. Consequently, we opted to use dynamic memory allocation for our application to optimize memory utilization while still managing the risks associated with heap management. For instance, FreeRTOS offers different dynamic memory allocation schemes, and by avoiding dynamic deallocation (i.e., not freeing memory during run-time), we can ensure that memory allocation remains stable and predictable. Moreover, the FreeR-TOS API includes several functions for monitoring heap usage, which confirmed that memory usage remained within safe limits throughout operation.

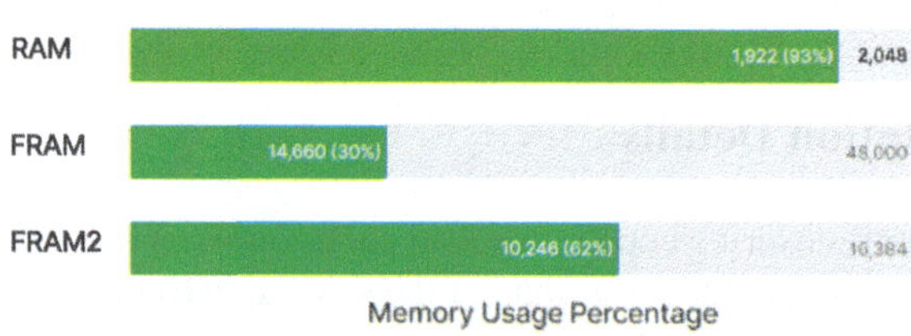

Fig. 5. Memory usage of the blinky example with one static task

3.2 Task Management

In the application, repeated main function blocks were rewritten into independent tasks. Each task with its own stack and logical flow. All the tasks were configured with the minimal possible stack depth in order to allow the system to hand the maximum number of tasks.

To further explore the benefits of FreeRTOS's task management and scheduling capabilities, an other task was added with priority. That means it will run only when the system is in an idle state. The added task contained only an increasing counter and a delay of 1 s. This setup allowed us to test whether the system could handle an additional low-priority task without affecting the overall performance or responsiveness of higher-priority tasks.

3.3 Inter-task Communication

FreeRTOS provides various inter-task communication mechanisms, such as semaphores, queues, mutexes, and event groups, which offer more robust and flexible alternatives to traditional methods like interrupt service routines (ISRs) and flag polling. Instead of relying solely on ISRs and flag switching to synchronize tasks.

We utilized queues as the primary data structure for communication and context switching between different tasks. Queues in FreeRTOS allow for safe and efficient transfer of data between tasks and ISRs, ensuring that data integrity is maintained and that the system remains responsive. This approach not only simplifies task management but also improves code readability and maintainability by providing a standardized method for handling inter-task communication (Fig. 6).

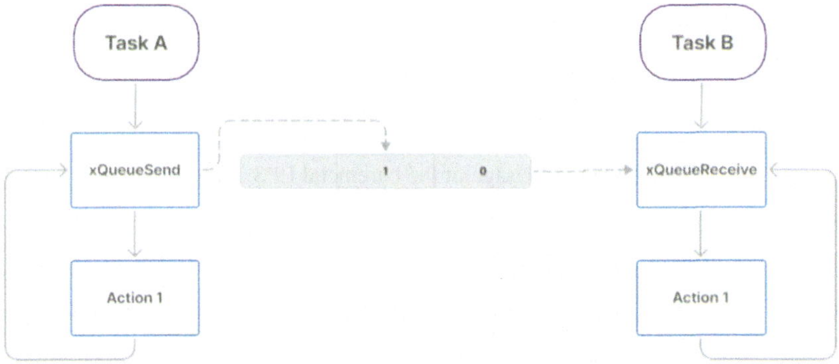

Fig. 6. FreeRTOS Queues

FreeRTOS also provides special functions to push and pull data from queues inside an ISR, allowing the system to handle real-time events more efficiently. This approach eliminates the need for busy-waiting or blocking when waiting for events. Instead of idling while waiting for an event to occur, the system can use queues to signal the occurrence of an event, allowing tasks to continue executing other functionalities. This non-blocking mechanism enhances system responsiveness and ensures optimal CPU utilization by allowing tasks to be notified asynchronously and respond promptly when an event is detected.

4 Result and Discussion

The integration of FreeRTOS allowed the system to execute parallel functionalities without damaging the original application, and without putting threatening pressure on the microcontroller resources. Figure 7 and Fig. 8 show the memory consumption of the bare-metal solution and using FreeRTOS. Even though the inclusion of FreeRTOS resulted in a significant increase in the usage of the FRAM and a small increase in the RAM. The program leaves a breathing room for dynamic tasks. Moreover, FreeRTOS's efficient scheduling and memory management mechanisms ensure that tasks are executed smoothly, optimizing both performance and responsiveness in a resource-constrained environment.

The results also showed that the added task maintained a fixed frequency, thanks to the fact that the system remains most of the time in idle state. The integration of the real-time layer provided by FreeRTOS ensured that the system could efficiently manage multiple functionalities. By assigning a low priority to the additional tasks, we ensured that these low-priority tasks could execute reliably when processing time was available, without disrupting the execution of higher-priority operations. This approach allowed for optimal utilization of system resources while maintaining the responsiveness and performance of critical tasks.

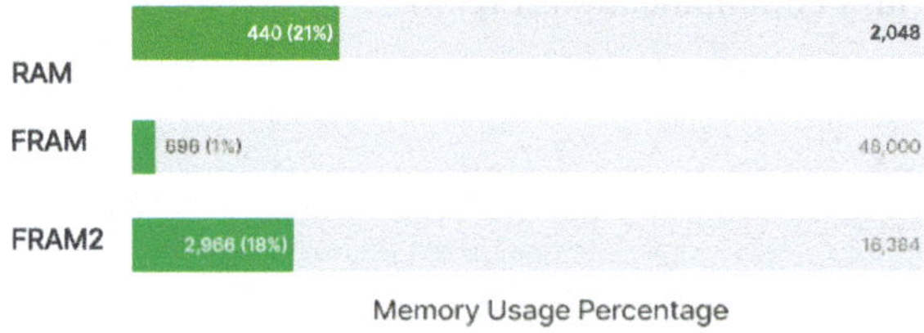

Fig. 7. Memory Usage of the baremetal EPS application

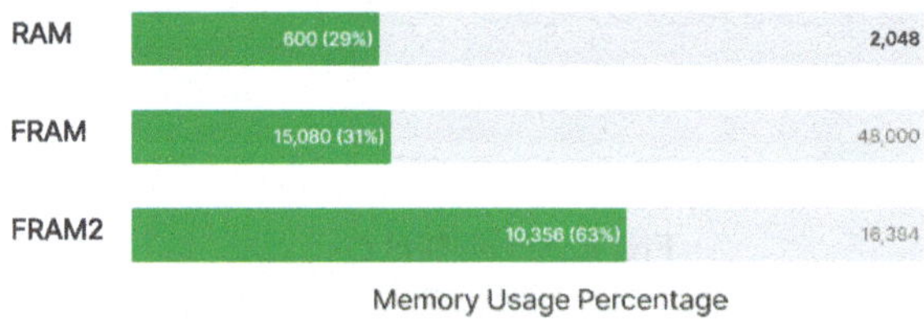

Fig. 8. Memory Usage of FreeRTOS based EPS application

5 Conclusions and Future Works

This paper successfully demonstrated the integration of FreeRTOS into an MSP430-based EPS for nanosatellites, highlighting its ability to enhance system flexibility.

The real-time operating system enables efficient multitasking, allowing various operations to run concurrently without exceeding the microcontroller's limited resources. This integration provides a robust framework for managing the EPS under the constraints typical of nanosatellite missions.

While this research primarily focused on the impact of FreeRTOS on memory usage, it opens the door for future studies to assess other critical performance metrics. Areas for further investigation include power consumption, CPU utilization, and system responsiveness, which are equally vital for optimizing the overall performance and longevity of the EPS. Future work should also consider exploring different scheduling algorithms within FreeRTOS to further enhance system efficiency, especially in resource-constrained environments like nanosatellites. Additionally, testing the system under real mission conditions could offer valuable insights into its resilience and scalability.

Acknowledgements. This work was carried out in the frame of cooperation between the Royal Center for Space Studies and Research (CRERS) and the Mohammed V University in Rabat (UM5R).

References

1. Naumann, P., Sands, T.: Micro-satellite systems design, integration, and flight. Micromachines **15**(4), 455 (2024). https://doi.org/10.3390/mi15040455
2. Camps, A.: Nanosatellites and applications to commercial and scientific missions. IntechOpen eBooks (2020). https://doi.org/10.5772/intechopen.90039
3. Leppinen, H., et al.: Developing a Linux-based nanosatellite on-board computer: flight results from the Aalto-1 mission. IEEE Aerosp. Electron. Syst. Mag. **34**(1), 4–14 (2019). https://doi.org/10.1109/maes.2019.170217
4. Leppinen, H.: Current use of Linux in spacecraft flight software. IEEE Aerosp. Electron. Syst. Mag. **32**(10), 4–13 (2017). https://doi.org/10.1109/maes.2017.160182
5. Putra, A.C.A.Y., Wijanto, H., Edwar, N.: Design and implementation RTOS (real time operating system) as a nano satellite control for responding to space environmental conditions. In: 2021 IEEE Asia Pacific Conference on Wireless and Mobile (APWiMob) (2021). https://doi.org/10.1109/apwimob51111.2021.9435247
6. Akhoury, A., Birla, K., Sarkar, R., Ravi, A., Kalsi, S., Ghorai, S.: Design and analysis of RTOS and interrupt based data handling system for nanosatellites. In: 2019 IEEE Aerospace Conference (2019). https://doi.org/10.1109/aero.2019.8742184
7. Daghouri, A., Makri, C., Hani, S.E.: Design of an electrical power system for a 1U nanosatellite using modified G3PCX. CEAS Space J. (2024). https://doi.org/10.1007/s12567-024-00565-9
8. Daghouri, A., Hani, S.E., Hachimi, Y.E., Mediouni, H.: Enhanced hybrid energy storage system combining battery and supercapacitor to extend nanosatellite lifespan. Results Eng. **23**, 102634 (2024). https://doi.org/10.1016/j.rineng.2024.102634
9. LaMeres, B.J.: The MSP430. In: LaMeres, B.J. (ed.) Embedded Systems Design using the MSP430FR2355 LaunchPad™, pp. 143–161. Springer, Cham (2020). https://doi.org/10.1007/978-3-030-40574-8_4
10. Texas Instruments, MSP430FR596x, MSP430FR594x Mixed-Signal Microcontrollers Datasheet (Rev. G) (2018). https://www.ti.com/lit/gpn/msp430fr5969
11. Tan, S., Anh, N.T.N.B.: Real-time operating system (RTOS) for small (16-bit) microcontroller. In: Digest of Technical Papers - IEEE International Conference on Consumer Electronics (2009). https://doi.org/10.1109/isce.2009.5156833
12. Tan, S., Anh, N.T.N.B.: Real-time operating system (RTOS) for small (16-bit) microcontroller. In: The 13th IEEE International Symposium on Consumer Electronics (2009). https://doi.org/10.1109/isce.2009.5156833
13. Holzmann, G.: The power of 10: rules for developing safety-critical code. Computer **39**(6), 95–97 (2006). https://doi.org/10.1109/mc.2006.212

Fault Location and Cyber-Attack Detection in Smart Power Systems with Wind Generators Using a Multi-agent System Approach

Mohamed Azeroual[1(✉)], Lahcen El Iysaouy[2], Fatima Zahra Moughraoui[2], and Hassane El Markhi[2]

[1] Higher School of Technology, Moulay Ismail University of Meknes, Meknes, Morocco
m.azeroual@umi.ac.ma

[2] Sidi Mohamed Ben Abdellah University, FST, Fez, Morocco

Abstract. Ensuring stability and reliability in power systems, particularly within extensive and intricate distribution networks, requires precise fault location. This study proposes a fault location protection mechanism for vulnerable distributed systems, including wind generators, using a multi-agent system (MAS) approach. The system analyzes transient fault current spectra to enable fast and accurate fault detection and location. Establishing reliable communication networks is crucial for ensuring rapid and precise coordination between MAS agents and circuit breakers, allowing efficient fault isolation. Simulation results demonstrate the effectiveness of the proposed method in handling physical defects and mitigating cyber-attacks in power systems. The approach significantly improves the fault location process, reducing fault clearance times and preventing circuit breaker failures, thus enhancing the overall resilience of the grid.

Keywords: Fault location · Multi-Agent System (MAS) · Smart grid · Cyber-attack mitigation

1 Introduction

The growing global demand for electricity has driven a substantial expansion in power plant capacity. Consequently, developed economies prioritize minimizing load reductions to maintain energy supply. However, power losses and voltage drop remain significant, largely because power plants are often situated far from load centers. A viable solution to these challenges is the installation of Distributed Generation (DG) units, such as wind power generators, closer to load centers, helping to reduce transmission losses and improve voltage stability [1]. The integration of wind turbines into power networks necessitates their ability to provide dynamic reactive power support for grid stability. Current grid regulations require that grid-connected wind turbines maintain operational capability during voltage disturbances, which is referred to as fault ride-through. Wind turbines must provide dynamic reactive power support and synchronize active power management to enable grid voltage restoration during disturbances, ensuring the power system's stability and reliability in these critical scenarios [2].

I. Aboudrar et al. (Eds.): ICESST 2024, SUCI, pp. 324–333, 2025.
https://doi.org/10.1007/978-3-031-86705-7_30

In distribution systems, four main types of electrical faults can occur, namely single line-to-ground faults (SLGF), double line-to-ground faults (DLGF), line-to-line faults (LLF), and three-phase-to-ground faults (LLLGF). SLGF is the most common fault, accounting for around 70% of all distribution network faults. Such faults occur when one of the three-phase conductors of a distribution system comes into contact with the ground, usually due to weather conditions, animals, or line failure. Traditionally, power utilities have relied on protective devices or end-user data to detect and locate faults in distribution systems [3].

The most common conventional method is based on visual inspection and trial-anderror switching. For a small area, patrols on foot are used to look for faults, whereas automobiles or helicopters are frequently deployed for a bigger region. However, distribution system failures are inevitable due to wind and other natural causes [4]. A fault causes current to flow in the wrong direction, resulting in device damage and power interruption. Therefore, to guarantee a continuous power supply and reliable customer service, the problematic line must be located and cut off from the rest of the system as soon as possible. The fault current, the position of the short circuit, and the voltage level determine the severity of the fault. Over many years, numerous studies on fault analysis have been conducted, and multiple fault location methods have been presented to find faults in distribution systems. Conventional approaches such as travelling wave-based methods, impedance-based methods, and smart methods can be used to detect the faults in distribution systems with the presence of distributed generation, such as wind farms [5].

The dynamics of power systems and wind farms are complex and nonlinear due to the interactions among many interconnected components of various types and domains, such as physical and cyber, with different time scales, feedback loops, and nonlinear behaviors. As with other critical infrastructures and cyber-physical systems, wind farms are vulnerable to different failures, faults, and attacks.

Phasor Measurement Units (PMUs) can be used to detect electrical faults in wind farm systems. PMUs are advanced measurement devices that can provide high-resolution, time-synchronized voltage and current measurements in an electrical power system. They are typically installed at strategic locations in the power grid, such as at both ends of each electrical line, to provide a detailed view of the system's behavior. In the case of wind farms, PMUs can detect faults in the electrical connections between the wind turbines and the rest of the power grid. PMUs can detect any abnormal conditions that may indicate a fault, such as voltage imbalances or current over-flows, by measuring the voltage and current at both ends of the electrical line [6].

When a fault or cyber-attack occurs within a wind farm, the power system dynamics are disrupted, resulting in transients. These transients cause the redistribution of power flow among affected components according to circuit laws, triggering automatic and manual control actions, as well as protection mechanisms, which further redistribute the power flow. These disturbances can significantly affect the stability and reliability of the entire power system, particularly in distributed systems, where the complexity and scale make fault detection, location, and isolation more difficult. Therefore, the development of effective fault detection, location, and isolation mechanisms is crucial to maintaining the stability and continuity of service for wind farms and the power systems they support. Every fault-tolerant system relies on early fault detection, which requires quickly identifying and locating system weaknesses or failures to mitigate their impact.

A knowledge-based technique is used for fault location due to the complexity of distribution systems and different uncertainty factors that are challenging to address using conventional methods. The technique generally needs information from fault detection devices mounted along the feeders, substation and switch status, feeder measurement, and atmospheric conditions. In [5], a novel method based on a multi-agent system was proposed for fault localization and autonomous power restoration in a power distribution system containing a wind generator. Controlling systems during a blackout and configuring them effectively after an outage requires effective problem detection, localization, and high protection.

Numerous studies have discussed fault diagnosis techniques in recent years, including several excellent surveys. In Ref. [7], a novel distributed intelligent-based multiagent for faults and cyber-attacks detection and location is proposed. The proposed method based on agents' communication for smart fault detection and diagnosis. The authors in [8] propose a multi-agent-based hierarchical detection and mitigation (MHDM) solution to safeguard power systems from physical issues and cyberattacks. The MHDM method is based on rule-based anomalous detection and has a hierarchical structure that three-level agents control according to the data of each tier.

Current methods for finding faults, such as impedance-based algorithms and visual inspections, don't always work well with complex systems that are spread out and include wind. These constraints highlight the necessity for a more flexible and self-sufficient solution. This paper presents a MAS approach to improve fault detection, localization, and resistance against cyber-attacks in wind-integrated power grids.

This paper presents a novel approach for fault location and cyber-attack detection in power systems that integrate wind generators. The proposed technique leverages transient fault current spectra to enable fast and reliable fault detection and localization, while also identifying and mitigating the effects of cyber-attacks on the power grid. Simulation results validate the effectiveness of the technique in addressing both physical faults and cyber-attacks. Additionally, the technique demonstrates its capability to mitigate the disruptions caused by manipulations of automated control and protection systems, whether resulting from cyber-attacks or severe electrical faults in wind-integrated power grids.

In the following sections, Sect. 2 outlines the proposed method for fault location and cyber-attack detection using a multi-agent system approach. Section 3 presents the performance evaluation of the method through simulation results. Finally, Sect. 4 provides the conclusions drawn from the study.

2 Proposed Method for Fault Location and Cyber-Attack Detection

Figure 1, illustrates the architecture of a power distribution network connected to wind farms using a step-up transformer. The current waveforms on utility buses are monitored from the secondary side using a PMU.

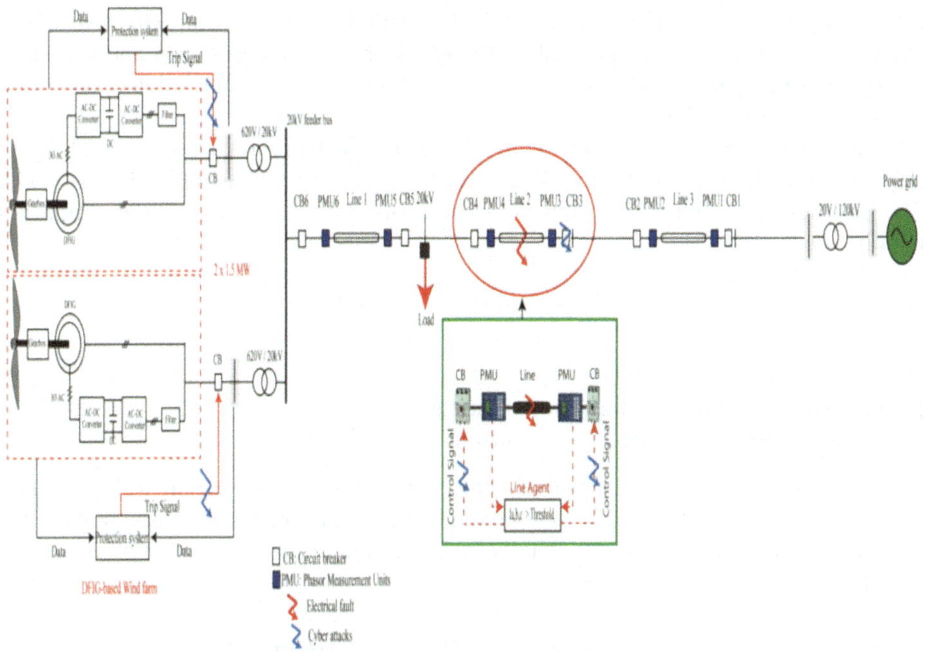

Fig. 1. Schematic of the proposed method for wind connected to the grid.

The data obtained from the measurement devices are transmitted to the agents. The processed data, which have been analyzed using the proposed techniques to determine protection decisions for the utility controller, are then sent to the meter data management system for management. In this study, a new monitoring system was implemented using a multi-agent system (MAS) approach. PMUs were installed at both ends of each electrical line to detect faults associated with wind farms. This study introduces novel methods for fault detection, localization, isolation, and cyberattack detection.

The wind farm model includes two separate wind turbines with doubly-fed induction generators (DFIGs), each powered by a fixed-pitch and a variable-pitch wind turbine. The mechanical model consists of two 1.5 MW turbines combined. An offshore step-up transformer increases the voltage from the wind turbine's low level of 575 V to the medium voltage level of 20 kV within the offshore wind farm. This transformer is connected to the DFIG to facilitate the voltage increase. The simulation focuses on analyzing the impact of cyber-attacks on the trip signal generated by the agents, along with the influence of phase short-circuit faults applied to the distribution network.

A MAS [9] is used to identify and alleviate cyber-attacks in power systems. This system represents different components of the power grid as independent agents, facilitating smooth communication and collaboration among them. Each agent possesses distinct sensors, algorithms, and decision-making abilities, engineered to perpetually observe and evaluate the behavior of the protection system. In the event of an attack, the MAS can efficiently respond by isolating the affected system, implementing suitable countermeasures, and rapidly notifying higher authorities for a comprehensive investigation and response. This method facilitates distributed computation and decision-making, markedly improving the accuracy and efficacy of cyberattack detection within the security framework [10].

The occurrence of an electrical fault is detected by the corresponding Local Agent (LA) by comparing the measured current (I_M) with a pre-set threshold value (I_T) [11]. The LA uses the following relationship to compare the two values and determine if a fault has occurred:

$$F_d = 1 \; if \; I_M > I_T \; \text{(Fault)} \tag{1}$$

where:

I_M: the measured current at the point of the fault
I_T: the pre-set threshold value for the current

To maintain the agent's sensitivity, the usual setting of the agent (relay) pickup current is between 1.5 to 2 times the nominal line load current passing through the relay in normal conditions ($I_{Loadnom}$) and half of the minimum fault current that the agent can detect ($I_{Faultmin}$).

$$1.5 * I_{Loadnom} < I_T < 2 * I_{Loadnom} \tag{2}$$

$$0.5 * I_{Faultmin} < I_T < I_{Faultmin} \tag{3}$$

Once a fault is identified, the current flow from the power source to the connected loads is analyzed to localize the fault. The key principle is that fault current will be detected at all measurement points (PMUs) except at the PMU closest to the fault. The absence of fault detection at this nearest point indicates that the fault is located between it and the previous measurement point. This approach aligns with the "distance protection" scheme, where fault location is determined by analyzing current levels measured at various points along the transmission line [12].

This methodology is particularly significant in wind farm protection. Wind turbines, due to their intricate and sensitive design, are vulnerable to damage from high fault currents. Additionally, unnecessary shutdowns for maintenance can negatively impact the wind farm's power generation capacity. Therefore, the protective system must be capable of quickly and accurately identifying faults and isolating the affected line, minimizing disruptions and ensuring the continued operational efficiency of the wind farm [13].

The control signal is generated by the agent that detected and located the fault. The control signal (Ts) opens the circuit breaker(s) connected to both ends of the faulted line.

$$T_S = \{0, \;\; F_d = 1 \text{ (Open the CB)} \\ 1, F_d = 0 \text{ Keep close the CB} \tag{4}$$

3 Results and Discussion

This section summarizes the results of a simulation study that evaluated the proposed algorithm's effectiveness in identifying electrical faults and detecting cyber-attacks in distribution systems connected to wind farms. The study assessed the algorithm's ability to differentiate between normal and abnormal power behavior, which could stem from wind turbine operations or potential cyber-attacks. Additionally, the algorithm's capability in detecting and characterizing faults was examined, with implications for the safety and reliability of power systems integrated with wind farms.

The simulation was carried out using SimPower Systems in MATLAB's Simulink environment, focusing on the integration of two wind farms into the grid. Voltage and current measurements were collected at key locations, such as the distribution feeder origin and the junctions where DG sources connect to the network. PMUs were placed at critical nodes within the primary branches of the network, enabling precise data collection and a comprehensive evaluation of the algorithm's performance across the entire system.

At t = 1 s, a three-phase short-circuit fault is applied in line 2 (Fig. 1), allowing for performance evaluation in detecting such faults. In this case, no cyberattacks were simulated, the fault was solely caused by the three-phase short circuit. As shown in Fig. 2, PMU4 detects the fault while PMU3 simultaneously identifies a change in the fault current's direction. Local Agents LA1 and LA2 exchange data, enabling them to confirm the fault in line 2. LA2 promptly generates a control signal (SC = 0) to open the circuit breakers (CB3 and CB4) associated with the fault, as illustrated in Fig. 3. In contrast, the other agents generate a control signal (SC = 1), keeping the unaffected circuit breakers closed. Consequently, the faulted line is accurately identified and isolated within 1.015 s.

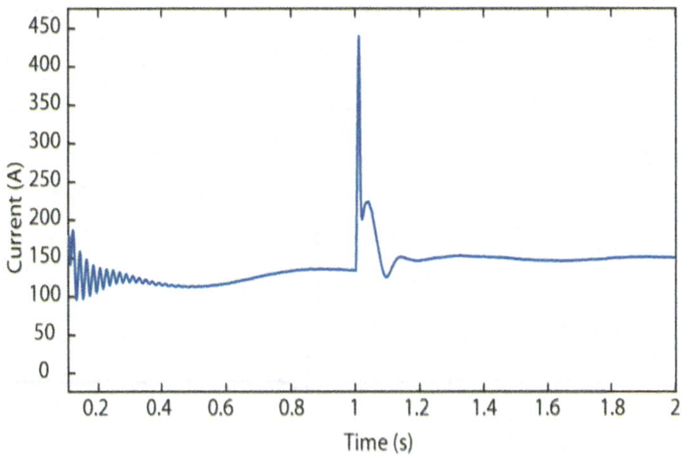

Fig. 2. Fault Current Flow in Circuit Breaker 1 for Fault at Line 2.

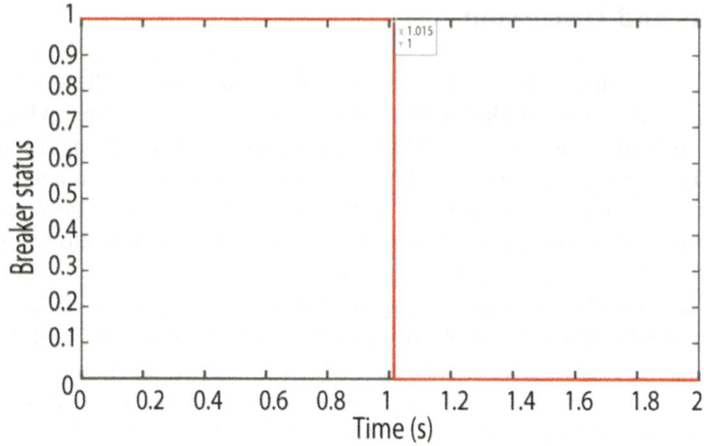

Fig. 3. Breaker status during fault for CB3 and CB4.

The system quickly finds the faulted line and sends control signals to turn on the right circuit breakers by making it easier for agents to share data and using phasor measurement units to keep an eye on voltage and current level. This rapid fault separation protects the wind farm from potential damage while minimizing downtime, thereby enhancing the overall power system's reliability. Figure 4 depicts the DC connection voltage's consistency across the wind farm over the entire simulation period. The proposed multi-agent system for fault detection and isolation is crucial for maintaining voltage stability, safeguarding the wind farm, and ensuring continuous power output.

Figure 5 illustrates the wind farm's power output and capacity to satisfy load consumption. As illustrated in the picture, the suggested multi-agent system ensures a stable and dependable power supply by quickly detecting and isolating defects. This feature is crucial for preserving system stability and guaranteeing that the wind farm produces

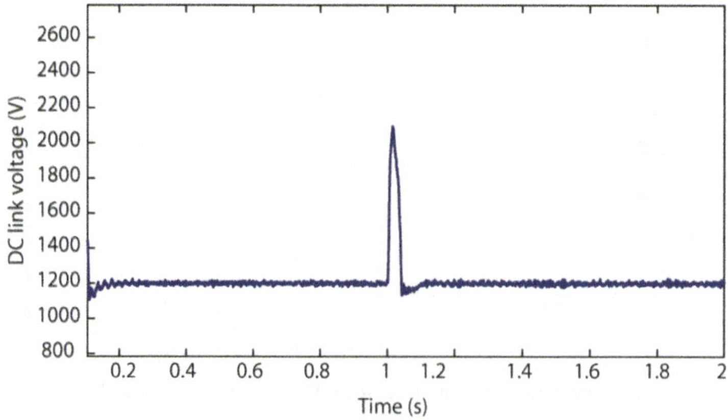

Fig. 4. Stability of DC Link Voltage in the Wind Farm.

sufficient power to satisfy demand. The stability of rotor current and electromagnetic torque is essential for the safe and effective functioning of wind farms, as they directly affect the wind generator's capacity to generate power and meet load demands.

As shown in Fig. 6, the rotor current in wind turbines remains stable, while Fig. 7 demonstrates the stability of electromagnetic torque within the wind farm, both critical to ensuring efficient and reliable operation. The technology enhances power generation and optimizes wind farm performance by preventing damage and decreasing downtime, providing a significant answer for the power industry's sustainable development.

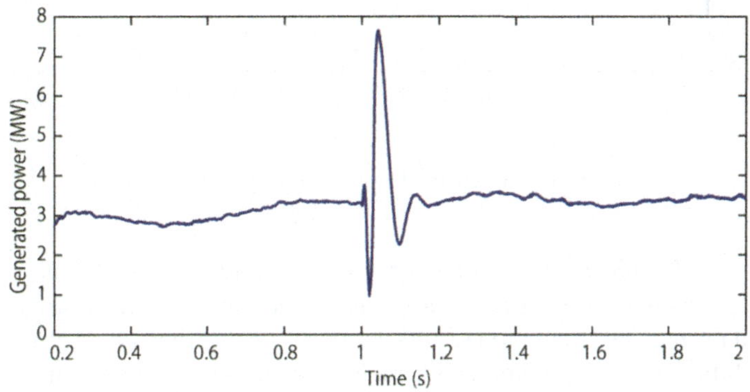

Fig. 5. Wind Farm Power Output.

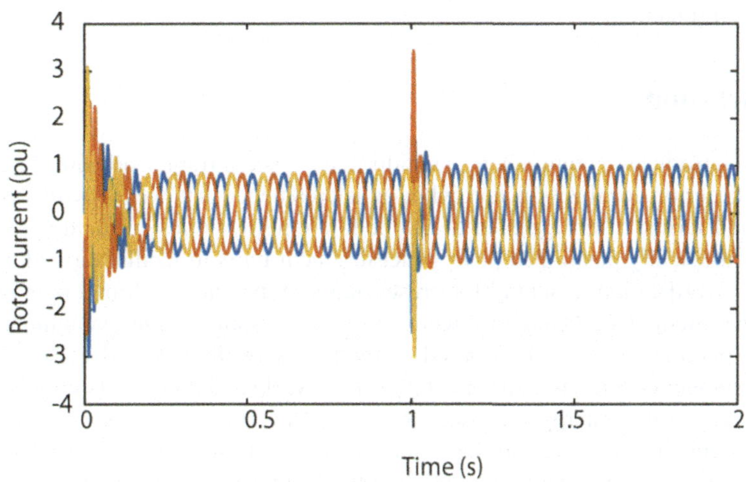

Fig. 6. Rotor Current Stability in Wind Turbines.

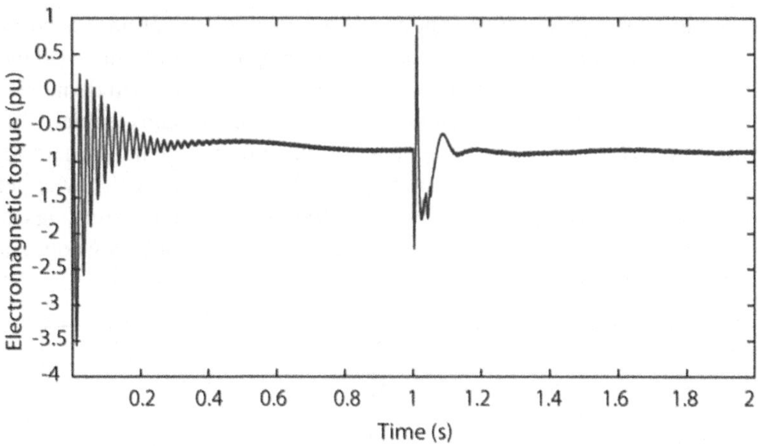

Fig. 7. Electromagnetic Torque Stability in Wind Farms

The proposed multi-agent system for fault detection and isolation demonstrates enhanced effectiveness in swiftly locating and isolating faults in power systems that include wind farms. The simulation results demonstrate that the system effectively maintains the stability of critical parameters, such as rotor current, electromagnetic torque, and DC link voltage, while minimizing downtime and preventing damage. The prompt response and precision in problem diagnosis significantly enhance the reliability and efficiency of the wind farm, making the technology an essential solution for modern power grid protection.

4 Conclusion

The study introduces a comprehensive multi-agent system framework aimed at improving fault detection, localization, and cyber-attack resilience in power networks that incorporate wind farms. The suggested MAS method employs transient fault current spectra and strategically positioned phasor measurement units to facilitate rapid and accurate fault identification, essential for preserving system stability. Simulation outcomes confirm the method's efficacy in effectively isolating faults while maintaining critical operating parameters. The MAS-based methodology exhibits considerable promise in the management of intricate, dispersed power networks, facilitating its implementation in further renewable energy integrated systems. Nevertheless, further investigation is advised to enhance this methodology. Future endeavors may concentrate on incorporating machine learning methodologies into the MAS for adaptive fault prediction and bolstering resistance against emerging cyber threats. Furthermore, investigating real-time application and scalability on extensive grids may enhance the efficacy of MAS for large-scale power systems, hence fostering a more resilient and sustainable energy grid.

References

1. Albarakati, J.A., et al.: Multi-agent-based fault location and cyber-attack detection in distribution system. Energies **16**(1), 224 (2022)
2. Zideh, M.J., Khalghani, M.R., Solanki, S.K.: An unsupervised adversarial autoencoder for cyber attack detection in power distribution grids. Electr. Power Syst. Res. **232**, 110407 (2024)
3. Azeroual, M., et al.: Fault location and detection techniques in power distribution systems with distributed generation: Kenitra City (Morocco) as a case study. Electr. Power Syst. Res. **209**, 108026 (2022)
4. Shukla, A., et al.: An island detection methodology with protection against cyber attack. Microsyst. Technol. 1–11 (2024)
5. Siddique, M.N.I., Shafiullah, M., Mekhilef, S., Pota, H., Abido, M.A.: Fault classification and location of a PMU-equipped active distribution network using deep convolution neural network (CNN). Electr. Power Syst. Res. **229**, 110178 (2024)
6. Zhang, C., et al.: Active detection fault diagnosis and fault location technology for LVDC distribution networks. Int. J. Electr. Power Energy Syst. **148**, 108921 (2023)
7. Esfahani, A.G., Fani, B., Delshad, M., Saghafi, H.: A three-stage multi-agentbased peer-to-peer method for fault isolation of high distributed generation penetrated distribution networks. IET Renew. Power Gener. **17**(5), 1255–1266 (2023)
8. Ghazimirsaeid, S.S., et al.: Multi-agent-based energy management of multiple grid-connected green buildings. J. Build. Eng. **74**, 106866 (2023)
9. Zhang, G., Li, J., Xing, Y., Bamisile, O., Huang, Q.: Data-driven load frequency cooperative control for multi-area power system integrated with VSCs and EV aggregators under cyber-attacks. ISA Trans. **143**, 440–457 (2023)
10. Li, X., et al.: Multi-agent system-assisted fault section location scheme for distribution networks with DFIG-based wind DGs. Electr. Power Syst. Res. **233**, 110443 (2024)
11. Furse, C.M., Kafal, M., Razzaghi, R., Shin, Y.J.: Fault diagnosis for electrical systems and power networks: a review. IEEE Sens. J. **21**(2), 888–906 (2020)
12. Asman, S.H., Ab Aziz, N.F., Ungku Amirulddin, U.A., Ab Kadir, M.Z.A.: Transient fault detection and location in power distribution network: a review of current practices and challenges in Malaysia. Energies **14**(11), 2988 (2021)
13. Uddin, M.N., Rezaei, N., Arifin, M.S.: Hybrid machine learning-based intelligent distance protection and control schemes with fault and zonal classification capabilities for grid-connected wind farms. IEEE Trans. Ind. Appl. **59**(6), 7328–7340 (2023)

Optimization, Control, and Sustainable Industrial Infrastructure

Path Tracking for Self-driving Cars: Stanley and LQR Controllers Comparison

Aala Eddine Bousskoul[1(✉)], Ilias Ouachtouk[2], and Abdelhafid Ait Elmahjoub[1]

[1] Complex Cyber Physical Systems Laboratory (LCCPS), ENSAM - Hassan II University, Casablanca, Morocco
bousskoul.aalaeddine@gmail.com

[2] Ingénierie des Structures, Procédés, Systèmes Intelligents et Informatique Laboratory (ISPS2I), ENSAM - Hassan II University, Casablanca, Morocco

Abstract. This paper presents a comparative study of two path-tracking controllers, Stanley and Linear Quadratic Regulator (LQR) that are evaluated across four trajectories with different speeds and levels of curve complexity in the Carla Simulator to access accuracy, comfort, and computational efficiency. The study uses the kinematic bicycle model and sensor data from the Global Navigation Satellite System (GNSS), Inertial Measurement Unit (IMU), and wheel odometry sensor to continuously get the state of the vehicle. The results of the simulations showed that the Stanley controller offers superior real-time performance, smoother control, and lower steering effort, which makes it suitable for applications focused on comfort. While LQR achieves higher tracking accuracy and adaptive flexibility through tunable weights but at the cost of increased computational load and jerk. The research emphasizes the advantages and compromises of both controllers, suggesting Stanley for stability-focused tasks and LQR for precision-demanding environments.

Keywords: Autonomous Vehicles · Path Tracking · Lateral Control · LQR · Stanley · Carla Simulator

1 Introduction

Developing robust lateral control systems is important for the safe and efficient driving of autonomous vehicles and Advanced Driver-Assistance Systems (ADAS) in complex environments. Autonomous vehicles are expected to navigate dynamic and challenging scenarios, demanding precise control to maintain a desired path. Various control strategies have been developed to ensure vehicle stability and comfort. Evaluating these strategies' advantages and disadvantages is essential to select the right controller for the right driving scenarios [1–3].

Among the well-known lateral control strategies, we find the Linear Quadratic Regulator (LQR) framework which is a model-based control approach that optimizes control inputs to minimize a quadratic cost function, encompassing both state and control effort, [3–6] and the Stanley controller, utilizes a geometric approach to path tracking, relying on the vehicle's current position and heading relative to the desired path [7–9].

I. Aboudrar et al. (Eds.): ICESST 2024, SUCI, pp. 337–346, 2025.
https://doi.org/10.1007/978-3-031-86705-7_31

These control strategies require continuous access to the vehicle's state, which can be obtained through various sensors such as the Global Navigation Satellite System (GNSS), Inertial Measurement Unit (IMU), and wheel odometry sensors. Together, these sensors provide a detailed understanding of the vehicle's movement and position, which is important for effective control.

The objective of this study is to compare these control strategies using simulations in the Carla simulator, [10] evaluating their performance on different benchmark trajectories. By analyzing metrics such as precision, comfort, and computational efficiency, the study provides the strengths and weaknesses of each control approach to select a suitable strategy for autonomous driving applications.

The remainder of this paper is organized as follows: Sect. 2 reviews the kinematic bicycle model, while Sect. 3 presents the implemented control strategies, LQR, and Stanley. Section 4 details the experimental setup, including using GNSS, IMU, and wheel odometry sensor data and the benchmark trajectories tested in the Carla simulator. In Sect. 5, the results are presented and analyzed with evaluation metrics on each benchmark trajectory. Finally, Sect. 6 concludes the paper and discusses future work.

2 Vehicle Model

The kinematic bicycle model is a simplified representation of vehicle dynamics, commonly used in lateral control design. It assumes a rigid chassis with two wheels, one representing the front axle and the other the rear axle. The model captures the vehicle's lateral motion based on steering angle and velocity [11–13].

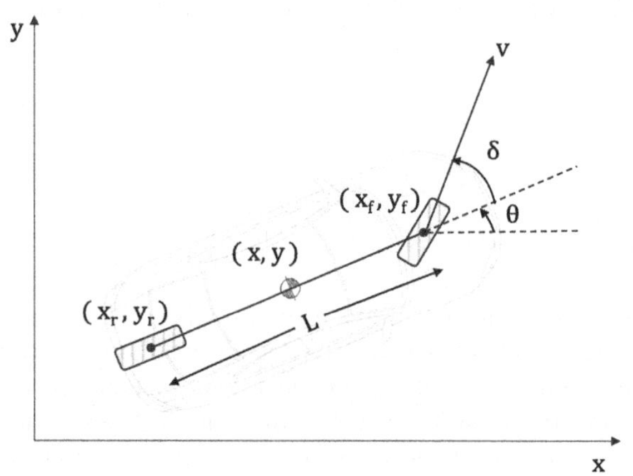

Fig. 1. Kinematic bicycle model representation

The kinematic bicycle model treats the left and right wheels as combined into single wheels positioned at the centers of the front and rear axles. The front wheel is given an additional degree of freedom to simulate the steering to rotate around an axis perpendicular to the plane of motion. Assuming that the wheels maintain perfect contact with the ground without slipping, while freely rotating around their axes. Figure 1 defines the global coordinates of the front wheel and rear wheels as (x_f, y_f) and (x_r, y_r), respectively, while (x, y) indicates the vehicle's position in the global frame. The variables θ and δ represent the vehicle's yaw angle and steering angle, respectively, with L denoting the wheelbase and v is the vehicle's velocity [7, 14].

The equations of the kinematic bicycle model are:

$$\dot{x} = v\ \cos(\theta) \tag{1}$$

$$\dot{y} = v\ \sin(\theta) \tag{2}$$

$$\dot{\theta} = \frac{v\ \tan\ \delta}{L} \tag{3}$$

Combining these equations will give the following state-space model of the vehicle:

$$\begin{bmatrix} \dot{x} \\ \dot{y} \\ \dot{\theta} \\ \dot{\delta} \end{bmatrix} = \begin{bmatrix} \cos\theta \\ \sin\theta \\ \tan\theta/L \\ 0 \end{bmatrix} v + \begin{bmatrix} 0 \\ 0 \\ 0 \\ 1 \end{bmatrix} \dot{\delta} \tag{4}$$

3 Implemented Strategies

3.1 Stanley

The Stanley controller is a nonlinear feedback controller that utilizes a proportional term to control the steering angle based on the cross-track error and the heading error. The controller's output is directly proportional to the cross-track error, providing a simple and intuitive approach to steering control. The Stanley controller is known for its simplicity and robustness [7–9]. The Stanley Controller determines the steering angle δ by accounting for both the vehicle's position relative to a target trajectory and its current heading θ as presented in Fig. 2. It utilizes the cross-track error e, which represents the perpendicular distance between the vehicle's current position $(x_f,\ y_f)$ and the desired path. Additionally, the controller considers the angle ψ between the vehicle's x-axis and the trajectory. By combining these factors, the steering angle is computed to minimize both the vehicle's distance from the path and the alignment error with the intended waypoint [12, 15].

The Stanley controller is expressed as follows:

$$\delta(t) = \begin{cases} \psi(t) + \tan \frac{k\,e(t)}{v(t)} & if \quad \left|\psi(t) + \tan \frac{k\,e(t)}{v(t)}\right| < \delta_{max} \\ \delta_{max} & if \quad \psi(t) + \tan \frac{k\,e(t)}{v(t)} \geq \delta_{max} \\ -\delta_{max} & if \quad \psi(t) + \tan \frac{k\,e(t)}{v(t)} \leq -\delta_{max} \end{cases} \tag{5}$$

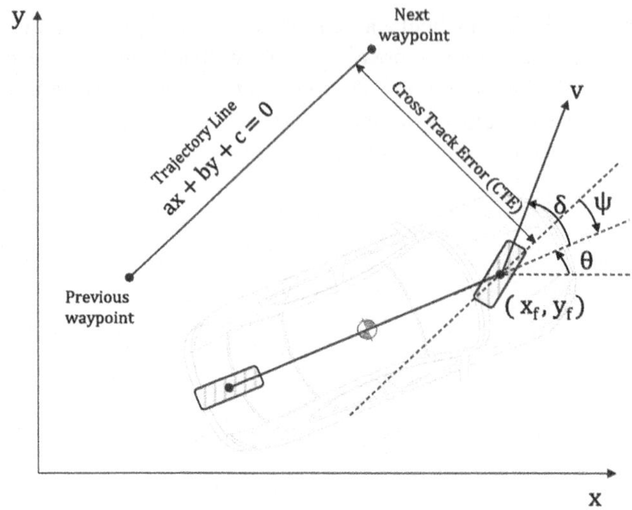

Fig. 2. Stanley controller elements representation

3.2 LQR

The LQR framework is rooted in optimal control theory, providing a systematic approach to designing controllers for linear systems. The LQR formulation involves defining a state-space model of the system, a cost function that penalizes deviations from the desired state and control effort, and a set of constraints [3–6].

Assuming the vehicle's velocity V is constant, we can write the lateral model as:

$$\begin{bmatrix} \dot{y}_e \\ \dot{\psi}_e \end{bmatrix} = \begin{bmatrix} 0 & V \\ 0 & 0 \end{bmatrix} \begin{bmatrix} y_e \\ \psi_e \end{bmatrix} + \begin{bmatrix} 0 \\ V/L \end{bmatrix} \delta \tag{6}$$

where y_e and ψ_e are the lateral offset and the heading error, respectively, with L representing the wheelbase, and δ is steering input. The state vector is $x = \begin{bmatrix} y_e & \psi_e \end{bmatrix}^T$ and the controlled variable u is the steering angle δ.

The cost function in an infinite-horizon discrete-time LQR is defined as follows:

$$J_k = \sum_{i=k}^{\infty} \left(x^T[k]Qx[k] + u^T[k]Ru[k] \right) \tag{7}$$

where the matrices Q and R can be written as:

$$Q = \begin{bmatrix} q_1 & 0 \\ 0 & q_2 \end{bmatrix}; R = 1 \tag{8}$$

The control equation is defined as:

$$u = Kx[k] \tag{9}$$

The feedback matrix $K \epsilon \mathbb{R}^{2\times 1}$ is obtained through the discrete-time algebraic Riccati equation (DARE).

4 Simulation Environment

4.1 Simulation Setup

The controllers are implemented in Python using a fixed time step of 0.01 s. The Carla simulator serves as the system plant, representing the vehicle model. The developed controllers send control commands to the Carla Simulator server and receive the updated vehicle state. Communication between the client and the server is handled via TCP, as illustrated in Fig. 3.

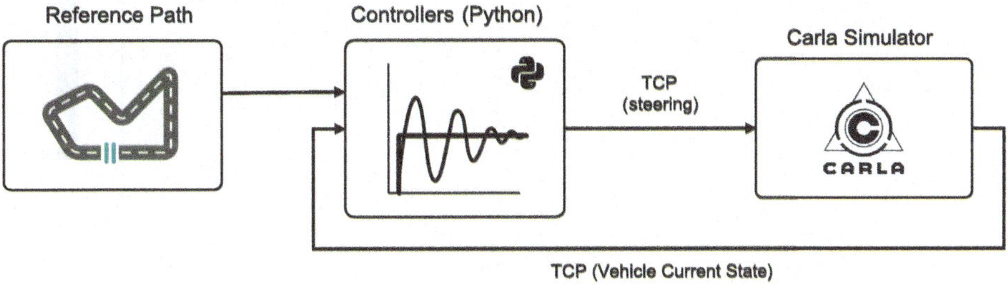

Fig. 3. Block diagram and communication architecture

4.2 Sensors

This study utilizes GNSS, IMU, and wheel odometry sensors within the Carla Simulator to measure the vehicle's state. GNSS provides accurate position data, IMU captures acceleration and angular velocity for analyzing orientation and movement dynamics, and wheel odometry monitors wheel rotations to estimate the distance traveled and vehicle speed.

4.3 Benchmark Trajectories

To assess the control algorithms under different conditions, this study employs four benchmark trajectories that illustrated in Fig. 4. Each trajectory was designed to represent a different driving scenario: Trajectory 1 involves mid-speed driving at 100 km/h with moderate curves, Trajectory 2 tests lower-speed driving at 80 km/h with more complex curves, Trajectory 3 assesses high-speed driving at 120 km/h on complex curves, and Trajectory 4 evaluates high-speed driving at 120 km/h on simpler curves.

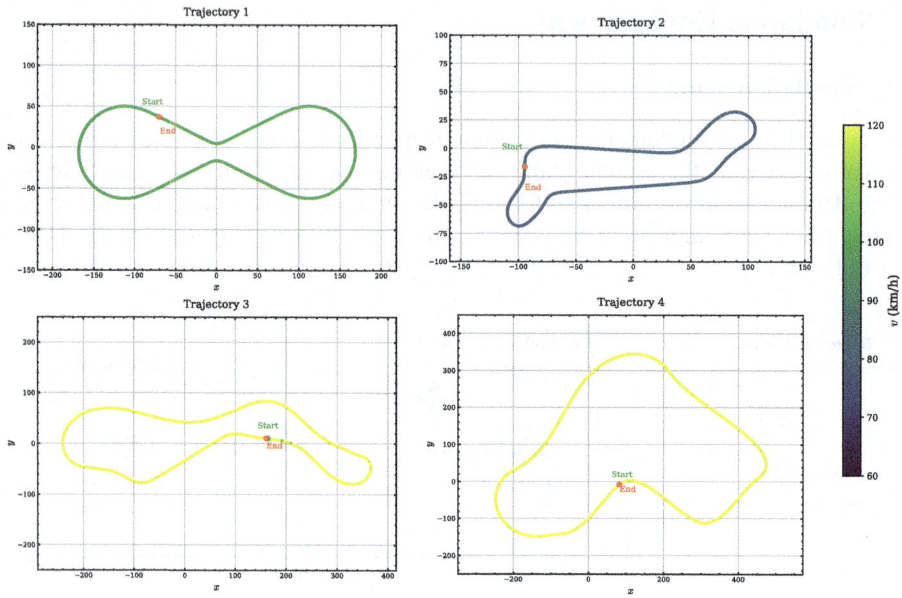

Fig. 4. Benchmark trajectories

4.4 Evaluation Metrics

Max Absolute Cross-Track Error (m):

$$E_{max} = max|e_i| \tag{10}$$

Mean Absolute Cross-Track Error (m): Averages the absolute cross-track error e from the reference path.

$$E_{\text{mean}} = \frac{1}{n}\sum_{i=1}^{n}|e_i| \tag{11}$$

Total Steering Effort (rad): This metric reflects the cumulative steering input δ required over the trajectory.

$$\delta_{total} = \sum_{i=1}^{n}|\delta_i| \tag{12}$$

Mean Steering Effort (rad): This shows the average amount of steering applied, which is useful for assessing the efficiency of the control actions.

$$\delta_{\text{mean}} = \frac{1}{n}\sum_{i=1}^{n}|\delta_i| \tag{13}$$

Mean Jerk (m/s^3): This evaluates the smoothness of acceleration changes over the trajectory.

$$J_{\text{mean}} = \frac{1}{n-1} \sum_{i=2}^{n} \left| \frac{a_i - a_{i-1}}{\Delta t} \right| \tag{14}$$

Control Input Variance (rad^2): This metric shows how much the steering angle fluctuates, reflecting the consistency of control.

$$V_{\delta} = \frac{1}{n} \sum_{i=1}^{n} \left(\delta_i - \overline{\delta}\right)^2 \tag{15}$$

Mean Step Execution Time (ms): This measures the average computation time per control step, affecting real-time responsiveness.

$$T_{\text{mean}} = \frac{1}{n} \sum_{i=1}^{n} T_i \tag{16}$$

5 Experimental Results and Discussion

Table 1 presents the evaluation metrics of each trajectory. By looking at the results, The LQR showed good performance in terms of tracking accuracy with minimal E_{mean}, especially in trajectory 4 with high-speed and simple curves with a value of 0.0597 m which is significantly lower than Stanley's E_mean in the same trajectory 0.3412 m. However, LQR showed signs of instability in Trajectory 3 with high-speed and complex curves as presented in Fig. 5 and Fig. 6, unlike the Stanley controller was less accurate than LQR but with a stable E_{mean}.

For the other metrics that are related to steering input (steering effort, jerk, and control input variance), The Stanley method performed better than LQR in all the trajectories with lower control input variance, steering effort (0.027–0.097 rad), and jerk suggesting a smooth and stable control input. In contrast, LQR showed more aggressive steering behavior with high steering effort (0.110–0.228 rad), indicating a more responsive steering, yet less comfortable than the Stanley's.

In terms of computational performance, Stanley was faster in terms of execution time with a duration between 10 to 20 μs on each calculation step, while LQR has worse performance requiring approximately 1 ms per calculation step due to solving the DARE. The computational performance efficiency may not be important in every scenario, but it could limit the applicability of LQR.

The obtained results show that the Stanley controller offers better real-time performance and more stable input, making it suitable for stability-focused scenarios. On the other hand, LQR presents a higher tracking precision and a responsive steering input at the cost of increased steering effort, jerk, and computational load. Other studies suggest that LQR outperforms Stanley in terms of tracking accuracy, [7, 16] which aligns with what was previously presented in the results. It is also possible to enhance LQR's effectiveness through parameter self-tuning to improve its robustness and smoothness [17]. However, the choice of controller depends on different factors such as speed, curvature variations, and environmental conditions [18].

Table 1. Controllers' evaluation metrics on each trajectory

	Controller	E_{max}	E_{mean}	δ_{total}	δ_{mean}	J_{mean}	V_δ	T_{mean}
T1	Stanley	3.510	0.417	205.683	0.059	0.076	5.276	0.020
	LQR	2.350	0.175	833.582	0.201	0.140	10.707	0.976
T2	Stanley	19.260	0.335	279.177	0.097	0.046	3.305	0.017
	LQR	19.260	0.227	711.951	0.229	0.065	4.761	0.957
T3	Stanley	3.224	0.540	201.655	0.041	0.022	1.505	0.016
	LQR	3.841	0.219	605.013	0.111	0.027	1.974	1.066
T4	Stanley	2.676	0.341	177.397	0.027	0.031	3.007	0.012
	LQR	0.653	0.060	190.593	0.030	0.266	80.261	0.946

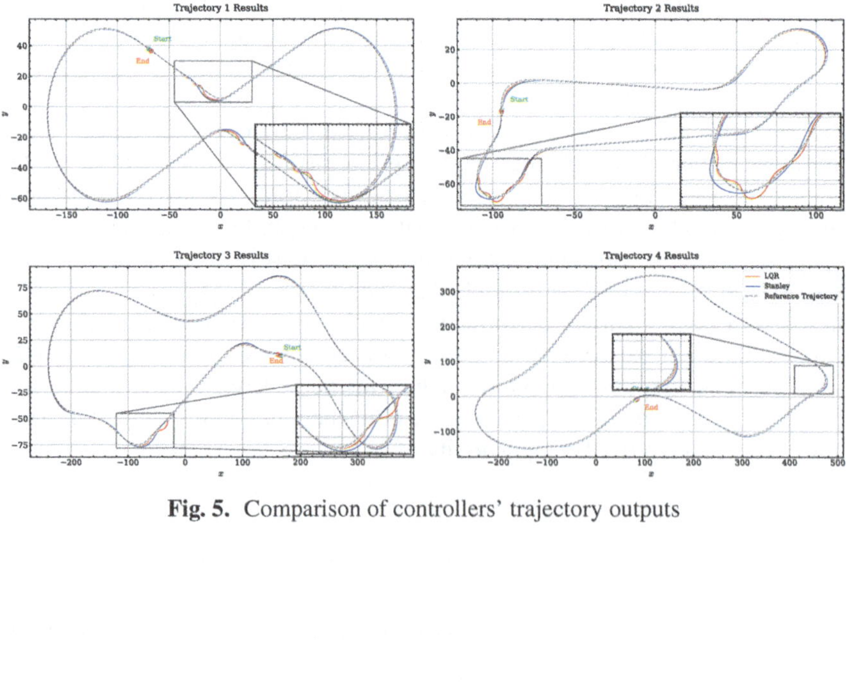

Fig. 5. Comparison of controllers' trajectory outputs

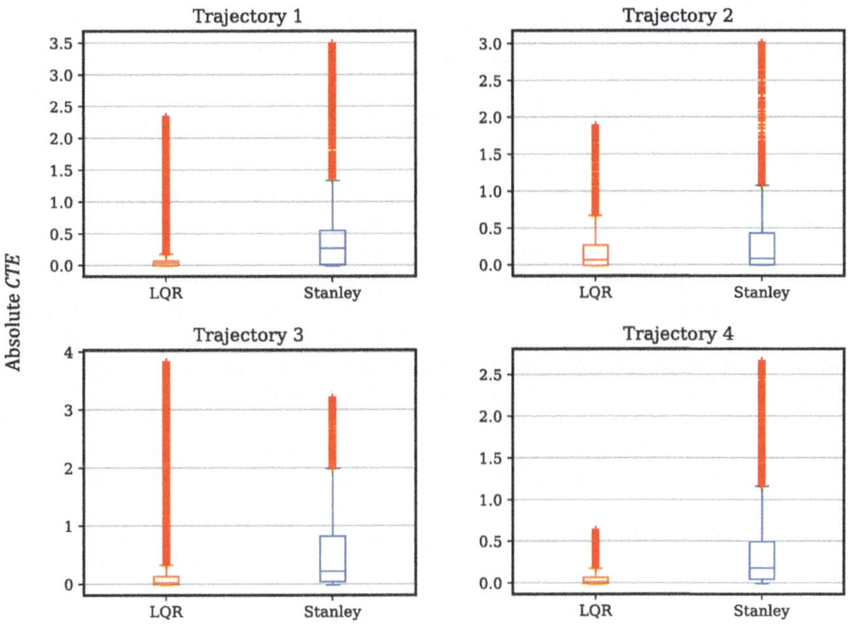

Fig. 6. Box plots of the absolute cross-track error on each trajectory

6 Conclusion

In this paper, two vehicle path-tracking controllers, Stanley and LQR, were implemented and tested across different trajectories with varying speeds and curve complexity to compare their performance using multiple evaluation metrics. The results demonstrated that Stanley requires less computational power and has smooth control, with lower steering effort, and minimal jerk. On the other hand, LQR has better path-tracking accuracy and adaptability through tunable weighting matrices, which allow designers to choose between minimizing steering effort and maximizing tracking performance. These findings highlight the importance of selecting appropriate control strategies based on specific requirements and enhancing autonomous vehicle navigation. Future work will explore additional control approaches such as model predictive control (MPC), hybrid control strategies, and real-world implementations to further enhance the capabilities of autonomous vehicle control systems.

References

1. Fanas Rojas, J., Wei, Y., Asher, Z., Sun, Y.: Model in the loop control strategy evaluation procedure for an autonomous parking lot sweeper. SAE Technical Paper Series (2022). https://doi.org/10.4271/2022-01-0086
2. Liu, C., Liu, Q., Liu, Y.: Hierarchical lateral control scheme for autonomous vehicle with uneven time delays induced by vision sensors. Multidisciplinary Digital Publishing Institute (2018). https://doi.org/10.3390/s18082544

3. Artuñedo, A., Moreno-Gonzalez, M., Villagra, J.: Lateral control for autonomous vehicles: a comparative evaluation. Annu. Rev. Control. **57**, 100910 (2024). https://doi.org/10.1016/j.arcontrol.2023.100910
4. Boyali, A., Mita, S., John, V.: A tutorial on autonomous vehicle steering controller design, simulation and implementation. arXiv: arXiv:1803.03758 (2021). Accessed 22 Oct 2024. http://arxiv.org/abs/1803.03758
5. De Cristofaro, F., Bui, D.-T., Li, H.: Lateral control calibration and testing in a co-simulation framework for automated vehicles (2023). https://doi.org/10.20944/preprints202311.0567.v1
6. Li, Z., Yang, T., Bai, Z.: Intelligent vehicle lateral control method based on feedforward + predictive LQR algorithm. Actuators (2021). https://doi.org/10.3390/act10090228
7. Vivek, K., Sheta, M.A., Gumtapure, V.: A comparative study of Stanley, LQR and MPC controllers for path tracking application (ADAS/AD). In: 2019 IEEE International Conference on Intelligent Systems and Green Technology (ICISGT), Visakhapatnam, India, pp. 67–674. IEEE (2019). https://doi.org/10.1109/ICISGT44072.2019.00030
8. Magnus Baksaas, K.M., Olsen, L.E.: Evaluation of two path following controllers for an Ackermann off-road vehicle in winter and summer conditions. In: International Conference on Mechatronics Robotics Engineering (2021). https://doi.org/10.1109/ICMRE51691.2021.9384830
9. Taher, Y., Abdelmoniem, A., Ali, A.: Fuzzy predictive Stanley lateral controller with adaptive prediction horizon. Meas. Control Lond. 1968 (2023). https://doi.org/10.1177/00202940231165257
10. Dosovitskiy, A., Ros, G., Codevilla, F., Lopez, A., Koltun, V.: CARLA: an open urban driving simulator. arXiv: arXiv:1711.03938 (2017). Accessed 25 May 2024. http://arxiv.org/abs/1711.03938
11. Qin, W.B., Li, Z.: A nonlinear lateral controller design for vehicle path-following with an arbitrary sensor location. arXiv (2022). https://doi.org/10.48550/ARXIV.2205.07762
12. AbdElmoniem, A., Osama, A., Abdelaziz, M., Maged, S.A.: A path-tracking algorithm using predictive Stanley lateral controller. Int. J. Adv. Robot. Syst. **17**(6), 172988142097485 (2020). https://doi.org/10.1177/1729881420974852
13. Quevedo, J., Alcal, E., Puig, V.: Gain scheduling LPV control scheme for the autonomous guidance problem using a dynamic modelling approach. Cornell Univ. (2017). https://doi.org/10.48550/arxiv.1712.00390
14. Kong, J., Pfeiffer, M., Schildbach, G., Borrelli, F.: Kinematic and dynamic vehicle models for autonomous driving control design. In: 2015 IEEE Intelligent Vehicles Symposium (IV), Seoul, South Korea, pp. 1094–1099. IEEE (2015). https://doi.org/10.1109/IVS.2015.7225830
15. Hoffmann, G.M., Tomlin, C.J., Montemerlo, M., Thrun, S.: Autonomous automobile trajectory tracking for off-road driving: controller design, experimental validation and racing. In: 2007 American Control Conference, New York, NY, USA, pp. 2296–2301. IEEE (2007). https://doi.org/10.1109/ACC.2007.4282788
16. Liu, J., Yang, Z., Huang, Z., Li, W., Dang, S., Li, H.: Simulation performance evaluation of pure pursuit, Stanley, LQR, MPC controller for autonomous vehicles. In: 2021 IEEE International Conference on Real-Time Computing and Robotics (RCAR), Xining, China, pp. 1444–1449. IEEE (2021). https://doi.org/10.1109/RCAR52367.2021.9517448
17. Piao, C., Liu, X., Lu, C.: Lateral control using parameter self-tuning LQR on autonomous vehicle. In: 2019 International Conference on Intelligent Computing, Automation and Systems (ICICAS), Chongqing, China, pp. 913–917. IEEE (2019). https://doi.org/10.1109/ICICAS48597.2019.00197
18. Dominguez, S., Ali, A., Garcia, G., Martinet, P.: Comparison of lateral controllers for autonomous vehicle: experimental results. In: 2016 IEEE 19th International Conference on Intelligent Transportation Systems (ITSC), Rio de Janeiro, Brazil, pp. 1418–1423. IEEE (2016). https://doi.org/10.1109/ITSC.2016.7795743

Design of a Non-linear Backstepping Controller for Hydraulic RGC System in Cold Rolling Mill

Abdelmajid Akil[1,2](✉), Ayoub Nouaiti[3], and Nabila Rabbah[2]

[1] Laboratory Interdisciplinary Laboratory of Applied Sciences (LISA), National School of Applied Sciences of Berrechid, Hassan 1St University, Settat, Morocco
abdelmajid.akil@gmail.com

[2] Laboratory of Complex Cyber Physical Systems (LCCPS), National School of Arts and Crafts of Casablanca (ENSAM), Hassan II University, Casablanca, Morocco

[3] Laboratory of Computer Science, Applied Math and Electrical Engineering (IMAGE), EST, Moulay Ismail University of Meknes, Meknes, Morocco

Abstract. Hydraulic Roll Gap Control (HRGC) system is a complex electro-hydraulic servo system with time-varying properties and nonlinear terms. This paper presents a novel method utilizing a nonlinear controller backstepping for a nonlinear HRGC system in a reversing cold rolling mill. By employing feedback from a position sensor, the controller ensures that the thickness of the rolled material remains consistent and within specified limits. The proposed controller by backstepping design not only achieves a significant reduction in thickness variability but also enhances production efficiency. Simulation results conducted in MATLAB/SIMULINK demonstrate a marked improvement in performance, confirming the effectiveness of the proposed design and its potential impact on industry applications.

Keywords: backstepping · HRGC · cold rolling mill

1 Introduction

The nonlinear HRGC system in reversing cold rolling mill is a complex electromechanical process whose control presents significant engineering challenges. Managing the thickness control of the HRGC is particularly difficult owing to the highly nonlinear nature of the industrial process, the uncertainties and strong coupling between process variables, and the changing nonlinearities that depend on process conditions. Additionally, the system has multiple inputs and outputs, time delays, time-varying dynamics, large inertia, substantial parameter perturbations, and external interference factors, all operating in a harsh environment. Some variables also have values that cannot be effectively measured.

The performance of the HRGC system directly affect the quality of the rolled product in cold rolling mills. To effectively manage a nonlinear HRGC by HAGC (hydraulic automatic gauge control), various control techniques have been employed.

In reference [1], In the thickness loop of the HAGC, it adopts PID control.

I. Aboudrar et al. (Eds.): ICESST 2024, SUCI, pp. 347–355, 2025.
https://doi.org/10.1007/978-3-031-86705-7_32

In article [2], the disturbances and mill stretch compensation during the rolling process are compensated by adaptive PI controller is developed to accomplish thickness control. In [3] to realize control for the HAGC system, a sliding mode variable (SMVS) structure controller is developed and a simulation platform of Strip Rolling Mill is set up Based on the mathematical model of HAGC.

Iterative learning control and internal model control were applied to a monitoring AGC system in article [4]. Additionally, A SMVS control for Smith prediction of AGC system was designed to overcome influence of the time delay exist in monitoring of AGC [5]. To optimize the fuzzy PID controller, paper [6] presents a control design based on Genetic-Particle Swarm Optimization fusion algorithm and To cover the uncertainties of time delay, based on adaptive Smith predictor, multiple models is employed [7].

The desire of this research work is to introduce a novel nonlinear control design based on the backstepping for a nonlinear HRGC system. The main contribution of this research paper is the development and validation of this innovative control approach, which demonstrates robust anti-interference capabilities and achieves satisfactory control performance in simulation tests.

The rest of this work is organized as follows. Section 2 presents the HRGC system of cold rolling mill. Section 3 describes the modeling of the HRGC system. The Nonlinear control and backstepping design are developed in Sect. 4. Section 5 presents the simulation results. Finally, Sect. 6 contains conclusions.

2 HRGC System

The custom of the reversing cold rolling mill is to reduce the thickness of the steel to the precise specifications.

Hydraulic RGC automatic thickness control system is the indispensable electro-hydraulic system in reversing cold rolling mill to improve rolling precision and to ensure uniform thickness, and surface quality of steel.

HRGC systems consist of multiple components of the cold-rolling steel strip thickness control system, controllers, actuators, some sensors, servo valve, servo amplifier, hydraulic cylinder, roller system, body of rolling mill, and thickness gauge. The basic configuration of HRGC system is shown in Fig. 1.

The HAGC system is a vital electro-hydraulic component in a reversing cold rolling mill, playing a critical role in enhancing rolling precision and ensuring uniform thickness and surface quality of the steel. The primary objective of a reversing cold rolling mill is to reduce the thickness of steel to meet specific customer specifications. During the rolling process, the hot rolled band is cycled back and forth between the rolls until the desired thickness is achieved. Similar to the pickle line, the cold rolling mill is capable of handling a variety of steel grades, making it a versatile component of the production process.

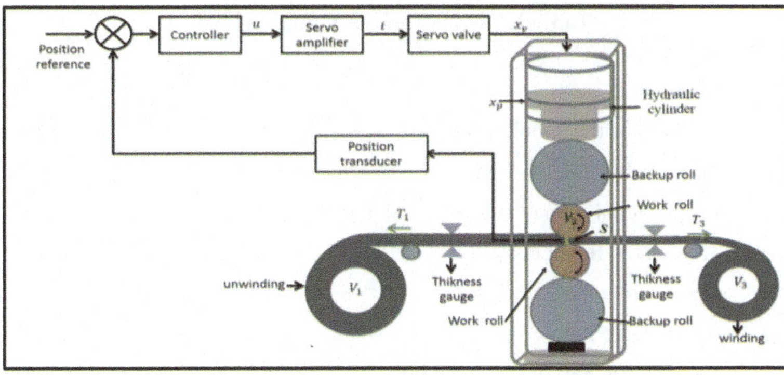

Fig. 1. Configuration of HRGC

3 HRGC Modeling

The nonlinear model of the HRGC system can be given by the system of nonlinear equations by posing $x_1 = S$, $x_2 = \dot{S}$, $x_3 = x_p$, $x_4 = \dot{x}_p$, $x_5 = P_L$, $x_6 = P_L$ et $x_7 = x_v$ as state variables:

$$(sys\ 1)\begin{cases} \dot{x}_1 = x_2 & (1) \\ \dot{x}_2 = -\frac{1}{T_g}x_2 - \frac{1}{T_g}x_1 + \frac{K_g}{T_g}\left(x_3 - \frac{k}{M_0}P\right) & (2) \\ \dot{x}_3 = x_4 & (3) \\ \dot{x}_4 = \frac{1}{M_t}\left(A_p x_5 - B_p x_4 - K_t x_3\right) & (4) \\ \dot{x}_5 = \frac{4\beta_e}{V}\left(C_d \omega x_6 \sqrt{\frac{P_s - sgm(x_6)x_5}{\rho}} - A_p x_4 - C_t x_5\right) & (5) \\ \dot{x}_6 = \frac{1}{\tau_v}\left(-x_6 + K_v K_p u\right) & (6) \end{cases}$$

The state vector is $x(t) = \left[S, \dot{S}, x_p, \dot{x}_p, x_v, P_L\right]^T$ and the controller $u(t)$.

The symbol and its nomenclature are given in Table 1 relatively strong coupling relation between variables of HRGC and the nonlinearity existed in sys (1) owing to the sigmoid function and square root function which will sway the perfection for the steel quality.

4 Nonlinear Control and Backstepping Design

In the section, a Backstepping technique is proposed to control for nonlinear HRGC [9, 10]. The backstepping control law is derived based on a Lyapunov function, to provide input-output stability of the system.

We indicate by $e_i = x_i - x_{id}$ the error between variables and its desired trajectory; and $\gamma_i > 0$ for $i = 1, \ldots.., 6$ is parameters.

Let us choose a candidate Lyapunov function defined by,

$$V_1 = \frac{\gamma_1 e_1^2}{2} \qquad (7)$$

Table 1. Symbol and its nomenclature

Symbol	Parameter	unites
x_v	Position of the spool valve	mm
K_v	Servo valve amplifier gain	A/m
K_p	Proportional gain of the servo valve	
τ_v	Associated time constants	s
i	Servo valve input current	A
Q_L	Servo valve flux	m^3/s
C_d	Flow coefficient of the valve port	–
ω	Servo valve natural frequency	m
P_L and P_S	Outlet pressure and the inlet of the servo valve respectively	MPa
ρ	Oil density	g/m^3
A_p	Active area of the cylinder piston	m^2
C_t	Total leakage coefficient	$m^3/Pa.s$
V	Oil pocket volume of the hydraulic cylinder	m^3
β_e	Bulk modulus of elasticity	MPa
M_t	Equivalent total mass of moving parts of the upper roller system	kg
B_p	Viscosity coefficient of cylinder	N.s / m
K_t	Elastic stiffness coefficient of load	N/m
x_p	Cylinder piston displacement	m
F_L	Other load force acting on the piston	kN
W_s	Plastic stiffness coefficient of the rolled piece	N/m
h_{in} and h_{out}	Input and output thickness of the rolled piece respectively	mm
T	Constant delay times	s
P	Rolling load	kN
M	Mill modulus	kN/m
S	Roll gap	mm
S_0	Unloaded roll gap	mm
A_d and L_d	Magnitude and period of thickness deviation respectively	Mm and m
vin	Entry strip is passed through the roll stand with the velocity	m/s
T_g	Time constant of hydraulic servo	s
K_g	Constants specified	–

Then its derivative is given by,

$$\begin{aligned}\dot{V}_1 &= \gamma_1 e_1 \dot{e}_1 \\ &= \gamma_1 e_1(\dot{x}_1 - \dot{x}_{1d}) \\ &= \gamma_1 e_1(x_2 - \dot{x}_{1d}) \\ &= \gamma_1 e_1(e_2 + x_{2d} - \dot{x}_{1d})\end{aligned}$$

by using x_{2d} as the virtual control input:

$$x_{2d} = \dot{x}_{1d} - k_1 e_1 \tag{8}$$

Then

$$\begin{aligned}\dot{V}_1 &= \gamma_1 e_1(e_2 + x_{2d} - \dot{x}_{1d}) \\ \dot{V}_1 &= \gamma_1 e_1(e_2 - k_1 e_1 \\ &= -\gamma_1 k_1 e_1^2 + \gamma_1 e_1 e_2\end{aligned} \tag{9}$$

where k_1 is a positive constant.

The Lyapunov-like function V_2 is defined as

$$V_2 = V_1 + \frac{\gamma_2 e_2^2}{2} \tag{10}$$

the derivative of V_2 is

$$\begin{aligned}\dot{V}_2 &= \dot{V}_1 + \gamma_2 e_2 \dot{e}_2 \\ \dot{V}_2 &= -\gamma_1 k_1 e_1^2 + \gamma_1 e_1 e_2 + \gamma_2 e_2 \dot{e}_2 \\ &= -\gamma_1 k_1 e_1^2 + \gamma_1 e_1 e_2 + \gamma_2 e_2(\dot{x}_2 - \dot{x}_{2d}) \\ &= -\gamma_1 k_1 e_1^2 + \gamma_1 e_1 e_2 + \gamma_2 e_2\left[-\tfrac{1}{T_g}x_2 - \tfrac{1}{T_g}x_1 + \tfrac{K_g}{T_g}\left(x_3 - \tfrac{k}{M_0}P\right) - \dot{x}_{2d}\right] \\ &= -\gamma_1 k_1 e_1^2 + \gamma_1 e_1 e_2 + \gamma_2 e_2\left[-\tfrac{1}{T_g}x_2 - \tfrac{1}{T_g}x_1 + \tfrac{K_g}{T_g}\left(e_3(\mathrm{t}) + x_{3d} - \tfrac{k}{M_0}P\right) - \dot{x}_{2d}\right] \\ &= -\gamma_1 k_1 e_1^2 + \gamma_1 e_1 e_2 + \gamma_2 e_2\left[-\tfrac{1}{T_g}x_2 - \tfrac{1}{T_g}x_1 + \tfrac{K_g}{T_g}\left(-\tfrac{k}{M_0}P\right) - \dot{x}_{2d}\right] \\ &\quad + \gamma_2 e_2 \tfrac{K_g}{T_g} x_{3d} + \gamma_2 \tfrac{K_g}{T_g} e_2 e_3(\mathrm{t})\end{aligned}$$

by using x_{3d} as the virtual control input:

$$x_{3d} = \frac{-T_g}{\gamma_2 K_g}\left[\gamma_1 e_1 + \gamma_2\left[-\frac{1}{T_g}x_2 - \frac{1}{T_g}x_1 + \frac{K_g}{T_g}\left(-\frac{k}{M_0}P\right) - \dot{x}_{2d}\right] - k_2 e_2\right]$$

Will give,

$$\dot{V}_2 = -\gamma_1 k_1 e_1^2 - \gamma_2 k_2 e_2^2 + \gamma_2 \frac{K_g}{T_g} e_2 e_3(\mathrm{t}) \tag{11}$$

where k_2 is a positive constant.

Let V_3 be defined as follows

$$V_3 = V_2 + \frac{\gamma_3 e_3^2}{2} \tag{12}$$

the derivative of V_3 is

$$\begin{aligned}\dot{V}_3 &= \dot{V}_2 + \gamma_3 e_3 \dot{e}_3 \\ &= -\gamma_1 k_1 e_1^2 - \gamma_2 k_2 e_2^2 + \gamma_2 \tfrac{K_g}{T_g} e_2 e_3 + \gamma_3 e_3 \dot{e}_3 \\ &= -\gamma_1 k_1 e_1^2 - \gamma_2 k_2 e_2^2 + \gamma_2 \tfrac{K_g}{T_g} e_2 e_3 + \gamma_3 e_3 (e_4(\mathrm{t}) + x_{4d} - \dot{x}_{3d}) \\ &= -\gamma_1 k_1 e_1^2 - \gamma_2 k_2 e_2^2 + \gamma_2 \tfrac{K_g}{T_g} e_2 e_3 + \gamma_3 e_3 (e_4(\mathrm{t}) - \dot{x}_{3d}) + \gamma_3 e_3 x_{4d}\end{aligned}$$

by using x_{4d} as the virtual control input:

$$x_{4\mathrm{d}} = \frac{-1}{\gamma_3}\left[[-\dot{x}_{3d}] - \gamma_2 \frac{K_g}{T_g} e_2 - k_3 e_3\right] \tag{13}$$

So, $\dot{V}_3 = -\gamma_1 k_1 e_1^2 - \gamma_2 k_2 e_2^2 - \gamma_3 k_3 e_3^2 + \gamma_3 e_3 e_4(\mathrm{t})$
where k_3 is a positive constant.
Let V_4 be defined as follows

$$V_4 = V_3 + \frac{\gamma_4 e_4^2}{2} \tag{14}$$

the derivative of V_4 is

$$\begin{aligned}\dot{V}_4 &= \dot{V}_3 + \gamma_4 e_4 \dot{e}_4 \\ &= \dot{V}_3 + \gamma_4 e_4 [\dot{x}_4 - \dot{x}_{4d}] \\ &= -\gamma_1 k_1 e_1^2 - \gamma_2 k_2 e_2^2 - \gamma_3 k_3 e_3^2 + \gamma_3 e_3 e_4(\mathrm{t}) \\ &\quad + \gamma_4 e_4 \left[\tfrac{1}{M_t}(A_p x_5 (e_5(\mathrm{t}) + x_{5d}) - B_p x_4 - K_t x_3) - \dot{x}_{4d}\right] \\ &= -\gamma_1 k_1 e_1^2 - \gamma_2 k_2 e_2^2 - \gamma_3 k_3 e_3^2 + \gamma_3 e_3 e_4(\mathrm{t}) \\ &\quad + \gamma_4 e_4 \left[\tfrac{1}{M_t}(A_p (e_5(\mathrm{t})) - B_p x_4 - K_t x_3) - \dot{x}_{4d}\right] + \gamma_4 e_4 \tfrac{1}{M_t} A_p x_{5d}\end{aligned}$$

by using x_{5d} as the virtual control input:

$$x_{5d} = \frac{-M_t}{\gamma_4 A_p}\left[\left[\frac{1}{M_t}(-B_p x_4 - K_t x_3) - \dot{x}_{4d}\right] - \gamma_3 e_3 e_4(\mathrm{t}) - k_4 e_4\right]$$

Will give,

$$\dot{V}_4 = -\gamma_1 k_1 e_1^2 - \gamma_2 k_2 e_2^2 - \gamma_3 k_3 e_3^2 - \gamma_4 k_4 e_4^2 + \gamma_4 \frac{1}{M_t} A_p e_4 e_5 \tag{15}$$

where k_4 is a positive constant.

Let V_5 be defined as follows

$$V_5 = V_4 + \frac{\gamma_5 e_5^2}{2} \tag{16}$$

the derivative of V_5 is

$$\begin{aligned}
\dot{V}_5 &= \dot{V}_4 + \gamma_5 e_5 \dot{e}_5 \\
&= \dot{V}_4 + \gamma_5 e_5 (\dot{x}_5 - \dot{x}_{5d}) \\
&= -\gamma_1 k_1 e_1^2 - \gamma_2 k_2 e_2^2 - \gamma_3 k_3 e_3^2 - \gamma_4 k_4 e_4^2 + \gamma_4 \tfrac{1}{M_t} A_p e_4 e_5 + \gamma_5 e_5 (\dot{x}_5 - \dot{x}_{5d}) \\
&= -\gamma_1 k_1 e_1^2 - \gamma_2 k_2 e_2^2 - \gamma_3 k_3 e_3^2 - \gamma_4 k_4 e_4^2 + \gamma_4 \tfrac{1}{M_t} A_p e_4 e_5 \\
&\quad + \gamma_5 e_5 \left(\tfrac{4\beta_e}{V} \left(C_d \omega x_6 \sqrt{\tfrac{P_s - sgm(x_6) x_5}{\rho}} - A_p x_4 - C_t x_5 \right) - \dot{x}_{5d} \right) \\
&= -\gamma_1 k_1 e_1^2 - \gamma_2 k_2 e_2^2 - \gamma_3 k_3 e_3^2 - \gamma_4 k_4 e_4^2 + \gamma_4 \tfrac{1}{M_t} A_p e_4 e_5 \\
&\quad + \gamma_5 e_5 \left(\tfrac{4\beta_e}{V} \left(C_d \omega (e_6(\mathrm{t})) \sqrt{\tfrac{P_s - sgm(x_6) x_5}{\rho}} - A_p x_4 - C_t x_5 \right) \right. \\
&\quad \left. - \dot{x}_{5d} \right) + \gamma_5 e_5 \tfrac{4\beta_e}{V} C_d \omega \sqrt{\tfrac{P_s - sgm(x_6) x_5}{\rho}} x_{6d}
\end{aligned}$$

by using x_{6d} as the virtual control input:

$$\begin{aligned}
x_{6d} = \tfrac{-V}{4\gamma_5 \beta_e C_d \omega} \sqrt{\tfrac{\rho}{P_s - sgm(x_6) x_5}} \Big[& \gamma_5 \left(\tfrac{4\beta_e}{V} \left(-A_p x_4 - C_t x_5 \right) - \dot{x}_{5d} \right) + \gamma_4 \tfrac{1}{M_t} A_p e_4 \\
& - k_5 e_5 \Big]
\end{aligned}$$

Will give,

$$\begin{aligned}
\dot{V}_5 = & -\gamma_1 k_1 e_1^2 - \gamma_2 k_2 e_2^2 - \gamma_3 k_3 e_3^2 - \gamma_4 k_4 e_4^2 - \gamma_5 k_5 e_5^2 \\
& + \gamma_5 \tfrac{4\beta_e}{V} C_d \omega e_5 e_6 \sqrt{\tfrac{P_s - sgm(x_6) x_5}{\rho}}
\end{aligned} \tag{17}$$

where k_5 is a positive constant.

we consider V_6 candidate Lyapunov function,

$$V_6 = V_5 + \frac{\gamma_6 e_6^2}{2} \tag{18}$$

the derivative of V_6 is:

$$\begin{aligned}
\dot{V}_6 &= \dot{V}_5 + \gamma_6 e_6 \dot{e}_6 \\
&= \dot{V}_5 + \gamma_6 e_6 (\dot{x}_6 - \dot{x}_{6d}) \\
&= -\gamma_1 k_1 e_1^2 - \gamma_2 k_2 e_2^2 - \gamma_3 k_3 e_3^2 - \gamma_4 k_4 e_4^2 - \gamma_5 k_5 e_5^2 \\
&\quad + \gamma_5 \tfrac{4\beta_e}{V} C_d \omega e_5 e_6 \sqrt{\tfrac{P_s - sgm(x_6) x_5}{\rho}} + \gamma_6 e_6 (\dot{x}_6 - \dot{x}_{6d}) \\
&= -\gamma_1 k_1 e_1^2 - \gamma_2 k_2 e_2^2 - \gamma_3 k_3 e_3^2 - \gamma_4 k_4 e_4^2 - \gamma_5 k_5 e_5^2 \\
&\quad + \gamma_5 \tfrac{4\beta_e}{V} C_d \omega e_5 e_6 \sqrt{\tfrac{P_s - sgm(x_6) x_5}{\rho}} \\
&\quad + \gamma_6 e_6 \left(\tfrac{1}{\tau_v} \left(-x_6 + K_v K_p u \right) - \dot{x}_{6d} \right) \\
&= -\gamma_1 k_1 e_1^2 - \gamma_2 k_2 e_2^2 - \gamma_3 k_3 e_3^2 - \gamma_4 k_4 e_4^2 - \gamma_5 k_5 e_5^2 \\
&\quad + \gamma_5 \tfrac{4\beta_e}{V} C_d \omega e_5 e_6 \sqrt{\tfrac{P_s - sgm(x_6) x_5}{\rho}} + \gamma_6 e_6 \left(\tfrac{1}{\tau_v} (-x_6) - \dot{x}_{6d} \right) \\
&\quad + \gamma_6 e_6 \tfrac{1}{\tau_v} K_v K_p u
\end{aligned}$$

the effective command input u:

$$u = \frac{-\tau_v}{\gamma_6 K_v K_p} \left[\gamma_5 \frac{4\beta_e}{V} C_d \omega e_5 \sqrt{\frac{P_s - sgm(x_6) x_5}{\rho}} - \gamma_6 e_6 \left(\frac{1}{\tau_v} (-x_6) - \dot{x}_{6d} \right) + k_6 e_6 \right] \tag{19}$$

the derivative candidate Lyapunov function is given by

$$\dot{V}_6 = -\gamma_1 k_1 e_1^2 - \gamma_2 k_2 e_2^2 - \gamma_3 k_3 e_3^2 - \gamma_4 k_4 e_4^2 - \gamma_5 k_5 e_5^2 - k_6 e_5^2 < 0 \quad (20)$$

where k_6 is a positive constant.

5 Results of Simulation Studies

This section tests the response of the HRGC controller based backstepping design aimed to control the position of a quarto rolling mill for the output thickness.

The performances of the output thickness h controlled by HAGC based backstepping design are given in Fig. 2.

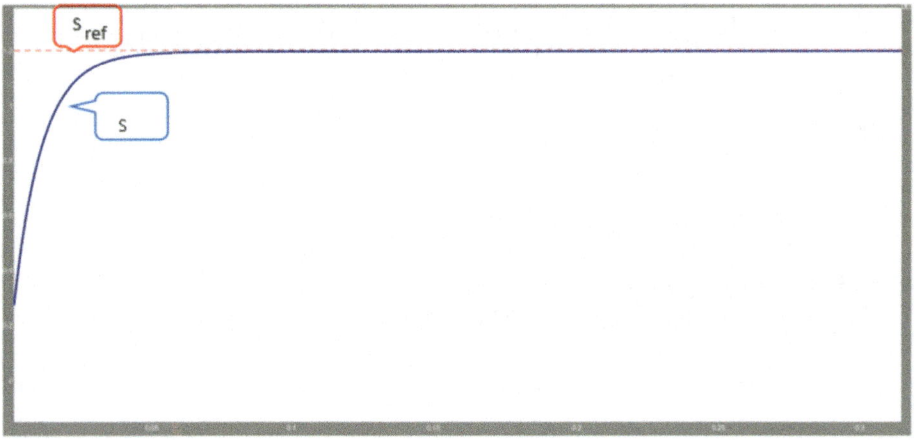

Fig. 2. Output thickness response for HRGC based on backstepping design

evaluating the performance of the Output thickness response for HRGC based on backstepping design, we rely on the following performances:

- Accuracy: A backstepping controller for HRGC maintain the desired strip thickness at steady state at t = 0.057 s where errors are minimized.
- Rise Time: Backstepping controller for HRGC are designed to ensure that rise time is quick (0.05 s), with no overshoot or oscillation.
- Settling Time: advantage of backstepping controller of HRGC is that they can provide a fast-settling time by properly adjusting the roll gap in response to any deviation in strip thickness.
- Disturbance Rejection: Backstepping controller are strong disturbance rejection capabilities, as they can adapt to non-linearities and disturbances through their recursive design process.
- Overshoot: A backstepping controllers for HRGC has no overshoot in its response to disturbances or setpoint changes.

It can be seen from Fig. 2 that the backstepping design is fast response with no overshoot, the stability is good.

The results obtained through numerical simulation illustrate the feasibility of the solutions proposed in this paper.

6 Conclusion

This paper has presented a novel control structure that utilizes a backstepping design for the HRGC system. By applying Lyapunov function stability theory, we have demonstrated that the response signal converges effectively to the desired reference, ensuring stable and precise control. Analysis and simulation results from a 1420 mm rolling mill system indicate that the proposed structure achieves satisfactory performance, underscoring its effectiveness for industrial applications.

Looking ahead, future research will concentrate on two key areas: enhancing the robustness of the control solution to adapt to varying operational conditions, and developing an adaptive approach to tackle challenges related to changing parameters and potential difficulties in achieving accurate thickness measurement.

References

1. Menghui, S., Yiqun, W., Wei, Z.: Research on cascade predictive control in hydraulic AGC of cold rolling mill. In: 2007 2nd IEEE Conference on Industrial Electronics and Applications, pp. 2775–2780 (2007). https://doi.org/10.1109/ICIEA.2007.4318917
2. Kucsera, P., Béres, Z.: Hot rolling mill hydraulic gap control (HGC) thickness control improvement **12**, 93–106 (2015). https://doi.org/10.12700/APH.12.6.2015.6.6
3. Fan, L., Fang, M., Liu, Y.: Sliding mode control of strip rolling mill hydraulic AGC system. Int. J. Control Autom. **7**, 43–54 (2014). https://doi.org/10.14257/ijca.2014.7.8.05
4. Fang-chen, Y., Dian-hua, Z., Xu, L., Jie, S.: Iterative learning control with an improved internal model for a monitoring automatic-gauge-control system. Metallurgist **59** (2016). https://doi.org/10.1007/s11015-016-0205-y
5. Fang-chen, Y., Jie, S., Dian-hua, Z., Ma, G.-S.: Sliding mode variable structure control for smith prediction monitoring AGC system based on double power reaching law. J. Braz. Soc. Mech. Sci. Eng. **38** (2015). https://doi.org/10.1007/s40430-015-0426-1
6. Meng, X., Li, X., You, J.: Application of fuzzy PID control based on GA-PSO fusion algorithm in cold rolling gauge control system. In: Qiu, D., Sun, N., Ye, X. (eds.) 6th International Workshop on Advanced Algorithms and Control Engineering (IWAACE 2022), p. 1235028. SPIE (2022). https://doi.org/10.1117/12.2652494
7. Li, J., Wang, K., Li, Y.: Automatic gauge control in rolling process based on multiple smith predictor models. Abstr. Appl. Anal. **2014** (2014). https://doi.org/10.1155/2014/872418
8. Akil, A., Zegrari, M., Rabbah, N.: Nonlinear model of the hydraulic automatic gauge control system: conrollability analysis and observability. In: Proceedings of the 1st International Conference of Computer Science and Renewable Energies. ICCSRE 2018, pp. 307–316 (2020)
9. Akil, A., Zegrari, M., Touati, A., Rabbah, N.: Nonlinear control by backstepping applied to the web winding system. Int. J. Dyn. Control **8**(2), 656–665 (2020). https://doi.org/10.1007/s40435-019-00568-z
10. Akil, A., Rabbah, N.: A nonlinear design method of robust PI control by using adaptive backstepping control for web winding system of reversing cold rolling mill. Int. J. Adv. Manuf. Technol. **132**(7), 3251–3266 (2024). https://doi.org/10.1007/s00170-024-13446-6

MPPT of standalone PV System Based on grey Wolf Optimization (GWO) in Comparison with Traditional Algorithms

Anas El Filali[1(✉)], El Mehdi Laadissi[2], Elmehdi Benmalek[3], and Malika Zazi[1]

[1] Electrical Engineering Department in National School of Arts and Crafts (ENSAM), Mohammed V University, Rabat, Morocco
anas.elfilali@um5s.net.ma

[2] Laboratory of Engineering Sciences for Energy (LabSIPE), National School of Applied Sciences, Chouaib Doukkali University, El Jadida, Morocco

[3] National School of Arts and Crafts (ENSAM), E2SN, Mohammed V University, Rabat, Morocco

Abstract. MPPT (Maximum Power Point Tracking) is a technology used in solar power systems to maximize the energy output from photovoltaic panels. MPPT controllers continuously adjust the operating voltage and current of the panels to ensure they operate at their peak efficiency, allowing for more power to be extracted from the solar panels. It is crucial for efficiency of operation of the systems of utilization of solar power and, therefore, the actual output of energy from the systems. This paper introduces a new MPPT strategy which utilizes GWO technique for determining optimum PV power generation systems. This method was tested against the traditional P and O and Fuzzy Logic algorithm and checked for its efficiency using Simulation implementation. From the obtained results, therefore, it can be agreed that the suggested MPPT delivers better tracking performance under any weather circumstance than both P and O as well as Fuzzy Logic Controller based MPPT algorithms.

Keywords: Grey Wolf Optimization (GWO) · Perturb and Observe (P&O) · Partial Shading Conditions (PSCs) · Maximum Power Point (MPP)

Nomenclatures

I_{pv}, I	photovoltaic and output current
I_0, $I_{0,n}$	saturation and nominal saturation current
V_t	thermal voltage
D	diode connected in parallel with current source
a	diode ideality constant
R_s	resistances which come in path of current
R_p	shunt resistance
G, G_0	irradiance and nominal irradiance
I_{g0}	current at G_0
J_0	temperature coefficient of I_{pv}

I. Aboudrar et al. (Eds.): ICESST 2024, SUCI, pp. 356–366, 2025.
https://doi.org/10.1007/978-3-031-86705-7_33

T, T_{ref} actual and nominal temperature of the cell
V output voltage
q charge of electron
E_g bandgap energy
K Boltzmann's constant

1 Introduction

Solar power is one of the natural energy sources which is tapped from the natural light and heat from the sun. Solar panels are also referred to as photovoltaic (PV) panels, these are systems that are used in converting light from the sun into electricity by the process of photovoltaic effect. It can be used for domestic, commercial and other purposes such as lighting up homes and operating businesses among others. Solar energy is constant, non-polluting, renewable and therefore presents a better option to the traditional sources of electricity, fossil fuels [1, 2]. Besides, the reduction of carbon emission and the fight against climate change are important benefits from the use of solar energy, there is also an ability to reduce electricity bills and gain energy self-sufficiency on the personal and communal level.

The latest researches in PV aims at increasing the power output by employing power materials and getting the maximum out of the PV. MPPT strategy has an important role in all types of PV systems: are classified into standalone, on-grid and solar pump systems. It is evident that MPPT is able to track the maximum power where there is an instantaneous change in irradiance and temperature with understanding that PV output power has non-linear relationship with these environmental parameters [3]. Also, there is another challenge known as partial shading which is also a barrier that MPPT has to overcome [4]. There are some details on a few common MPPT algorithms: Perturb and Observe (P&O): This algorithm is one of the simplest and most widely used MPPT algorithms. It works by perturbing (changing) the operating point of the solar panels and observing the change in power output. Based on this observation, the algorithm determines whether to increase or decrease the operating point to reach the maximum power point. One drawback of this algorithm is that it can lead to oscillations around the maximum power point in certain conditions. Incremental Conductance: This algorithm is more complex than P&O and is designed to address the oscillations that can occur with P&O. It uses the derivative of the power-voltage curve to determine the direction of the change required to reach the maximum power point. By considering both the instantaneous power and the rate of change of power, this algorithm can track the maximum power point more accurately and efficiently. [5] Fuzzy Logic Control: Fuzzy logic is a mathematical approach that allows for more flexibility and adaptability in controlling the MPPT process. Fuzzy logic controllers use a set of input variables (such as voltage and current) to determine the optimal operating point for the solar panels. The advantage of fuzzy logic control is its ability to handle uncertainty and non-linearities in the system, making it more robust and effective in varying environmental conditions [6]. Fractional Open Circuit Voltage (FOCV): This algorithm utilizes the open-circuit voltage of the solar panels to estimate the maximum power point. By using a fraction of the open-circuit voltage, the algorithm can efficiently track the maximum power point without the need for complex calculations or measurements.[7] Particle Swarm Optimization (PSO): PSO is a metaheuristic optimization algorithm inspired by the behavior of bird flocking or fish schooling. In the context of MPPT, PSO algorithms work by simulating a swarm of particles that search for the optimal operating point of the solar panels. This approach can be effective in quickly converging to the maximum power point in complex and dynamic environments.[8]. Fractional Short Circuit Current (FSCC): Similar to FOCV, the FSCC algorithm uses a fraction of the short-circuit current of the solar panels to estimate the maximum power point. By leveraging short-circuit current measurements, this algorithm can efficiently adjust the operating point of the panels to maximize power output [9]. These are just a few additional MPPT algorithms that have been developed to enhance the efficiency and performance of solar energy systems. It is important to evaluate and compare different MPPT algorithms to determine the most optimal solution for a specific solar energy system. In this paper we introduce a new MPPT strategy which employs GWO technique for determining optimum PV power generation systems. This method was tested against the traditional P and O and Fuzzy Logic algorithm and checked for its efficiency using Simulation implementation.

The rest of this paper is organized as follows. Section 2 describes the Modeling of PV system, and Sect. 3 presents an overview of the proposed MPPT method. Moreover, the test results are presented in Sect. 4. Section 5 provides the conclusions.

2 Modeling of PV System

A widely used technique for representation of a solar PV (photovoltaic) cell is through the application of circuit model known as the single-diode model. This model breaks down the actual physical and electrical characteristics of a PV cell into a series of equations used for mapping the performance of the cell under any given conditions.

Besides, single-diode model of a PV cell mimics the cell with an electrical circuit that consists of a current source that (Iph) that represents the generated photocurrent, a diode that represents non-linearity of the cell, a series resistor (Rs) that signifies definite resistive losses in the cell, shunt resistor (Rsh) that represents pathways that has tendency of reducing the efficiency of the cell, and an ideal current source that represents the cell's light-induced current (Id).

The behavior of a PV module can also be described by a single diode model. The output current I, of a single diode model can be defined as:

$$I = I_{PV} - I_0\left[exp\left(\frac{V + R_S I}{V_t a}\right) - 1\right] \tag{1}$$

Light generated current is a function of irradiance and can be expressed as

$$I_{PV} = \left(\frac{G}{G_0}\right) I_{g0} + J_0(T - T_{ref}) \tag{2}$$

The temperature-dependence of the diode saturation current is expressed as follows:

$$I_0 - I_{0,n}\left(\frac{T}{T_{ref}}\right) exp\left[\frac{qE_g}{ak}\left(\frac{1}{T_{ref}} - \frac{1}{T}\right)\right] \tag{3}$$

The circuit description and its complete mathematical modelling are described in detail in [10]. The power output of a PV cell can be calculated using the equation: The power output of a PV cell can be calculated using the equation:

$$P = IV \tag{4}$$

for the regulation of output voltage of the PV array, it is required to connect a DC-DC converter.

There is need to regulate the output of the DC-DC converter to be as constant as possible, this must be achieved by using the pulse width modulation (PWM) to control the voltage of the converter as shown in Fig. 1 below.

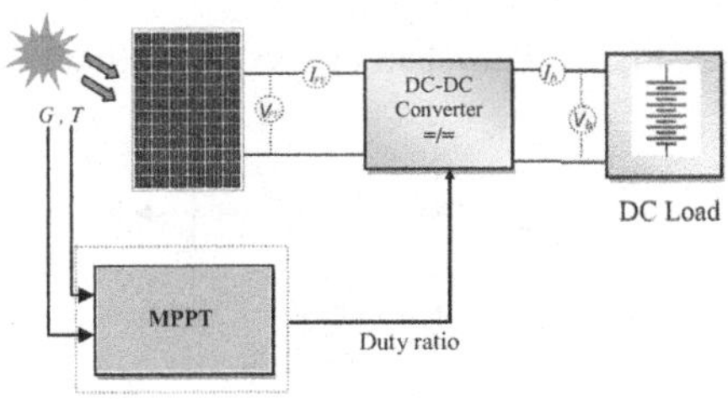

Fig. 1. PV system with MPPT

3 A Completion of Mppt Techniques

3.1 P and O MPPT

P&O MPPT stands for Perturb and Observe, which is one of the algorithms used to track the maximum power point of a solar panel. This algorithm always changes slightly the operating point of the solar panel and the variation in output power is determined to find out which is the best point for maximum power output. [11].

The benefit of the P&O process is that its implementation is rather simple. It has, however, drawbacks such as high frequency oscillations around the MPP in steady state operation, slow dynamic response, and even wrong tracking during rapid fluctuations in atmospheric conditions. Figure 2 describe the flowchart of P&O technique.

3.2 FLC MPPT

Fuzzy logic controller is a method of control system design which is derived from the fuzzy logic framework that provides more flexible and robust control for systems where the input is either more complex or not fixed in value.

As to the use of solar panel, a fuzzy logic controller could be used in MPPT by varying the system parameters of solar panel depending on input information such as weather condition, temperature, intensity of light, or variations of power and voltage as we did in previous work [11]. This is useful in ensuring that the system is always in its maximum power point, thereby obtaining the maximum energy and efficiency of the system. The flowchart of the FLC is shown in Fig. 3

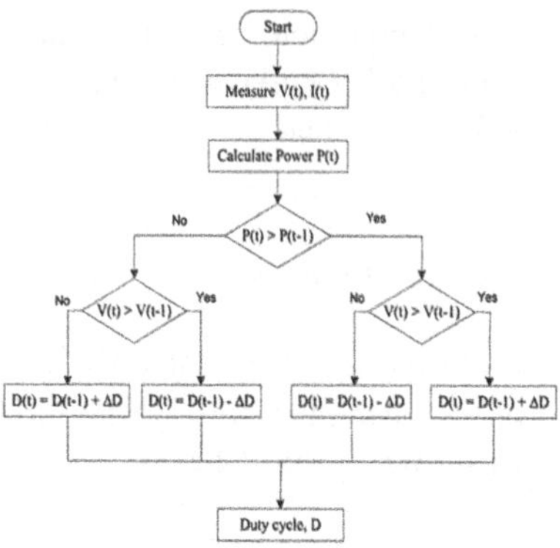

Fig. 2. Flowchart of P&O algorithm

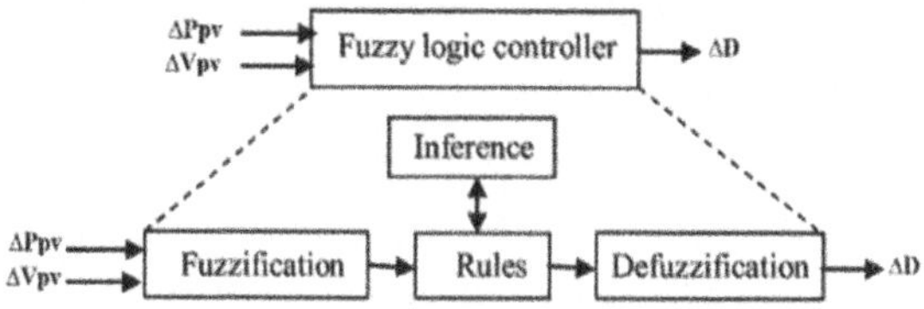

Fig. 3. Structure of fuzzy logic controller

3.3 Proposed GWO MPPT

Grey Wolf Optimization (GWO) can also be applied to optimize the Maximum Power Point Tracking (MPPT) algorithm in solar power systems. In this application, the GWO is applied to tune the MPPT parameters for optimum performance of the solar panels and output power. By using GWO to optimize the MPPT algorithm, the system can continuously adjust the operating conditions of the solar panels to track the maximum power point, even under changing environmental conditions such as shading or cloud cover. This optimization process helps to maximize the energy harvested from the solar panels and improve the overall performance of the solar power system. Overall, combining GWO with MPPT can lead to more efficient and reliable solar power systems, allowing for increased energy production and improved cost-effectiveness of renewable energy solutions.

The Grey Wolf Optimization (GWO) is one of the population-based metaheuristic optimization algorithms that simulate the hunting mechanisms of grey wolves. Developed by Mirjalili et al. in 2014 [12], GWO mimics the leadership hierarchy and collaborative hunting strategy of grey wolves to solve complex optimization problems. In GWO, the algorithm starts with an initial population of candidate solutions, referred to as "wolves". The algorithm then iteratively updates the position of the wolves based on their fitness values, which are evaluated using the objective function of the optimization problem. The positions of the alpha, beta, and delta wolves, representing the leaders of the pack, are updated according to predefined formulas that mimic the hunting behavior of grey wolves [13]. The GWO algorithm has been implemented with various optimization exercises. It is known for its simplicity, efficiency, and fast convergence rate, making it a popular choice for solving optimization problems in various fields. The Flowchart of GWO-based MPPT is presented in Fig. 4.

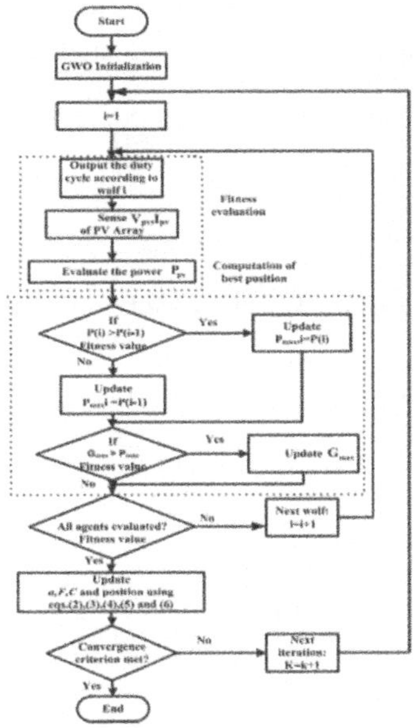

Fig. 4. GWO-based MPPT Flowchart

4 Simulation Results and Discussion

Analyzed through numerous computational simulation tests, the several algorithms of MPPT in this paper are compared and assessed with each other by Matlab/Simulink. Thus, for the purpose of comparing the presented algorithms, it is assumed two different scenarios. The first one assumes that the PV array is at STC already and the second one assumes that the PV array is at partial shading conditions (PSC). Figure 5 presents the circuit scheme that was used for the simulation.

With the purpose of analyzing partial shading conditions, the configuration of the PV array is composed, as shown in Fig. 6, of 4 PV panels connected in series, each panel has a maximum power of 25 W, so the maximum power obtained from this PV array is 100 watts.

4.1 First Situation: Standard Test Conditions (STC)

In this situation, the value of the solar irradiance is fixed at 1000 W/m2, which corresponds to the intensity of the solar radiation on a clear sky day. The cell temperature is

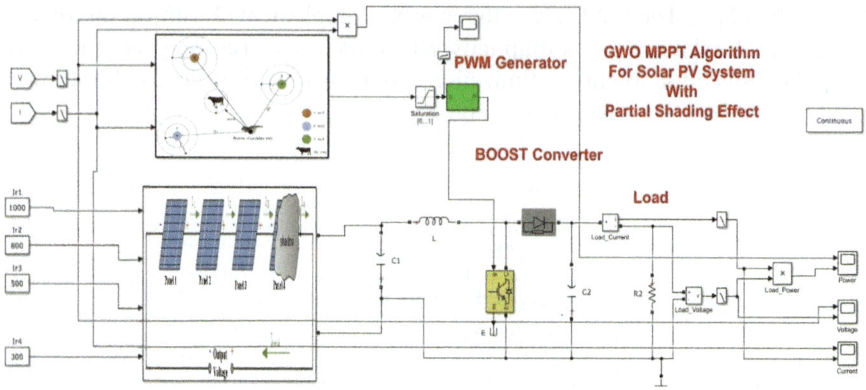

Fig. 5. The proposed PV system

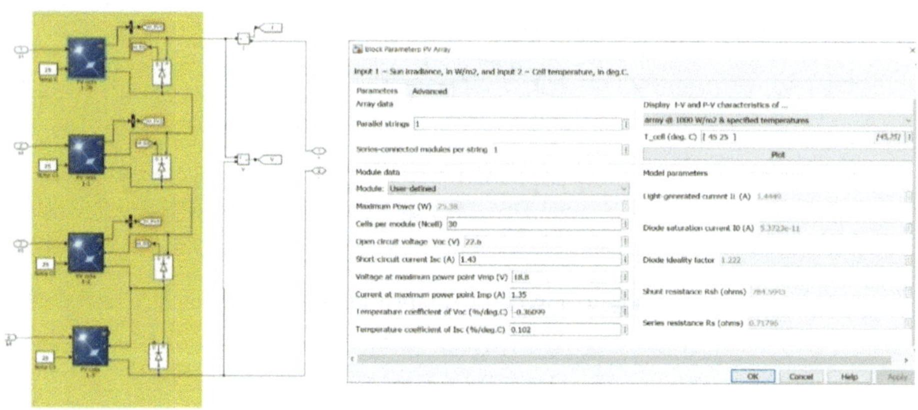

Fig. 6. PV array structure

regulated to 25°C, which is given a name – the module temperature, more precisely, it indicates the temperature at which the PV cell operates through testing. Figures 7 and 8 show the PV array power, using P and O, FLC and the proposed GWO algorithms.

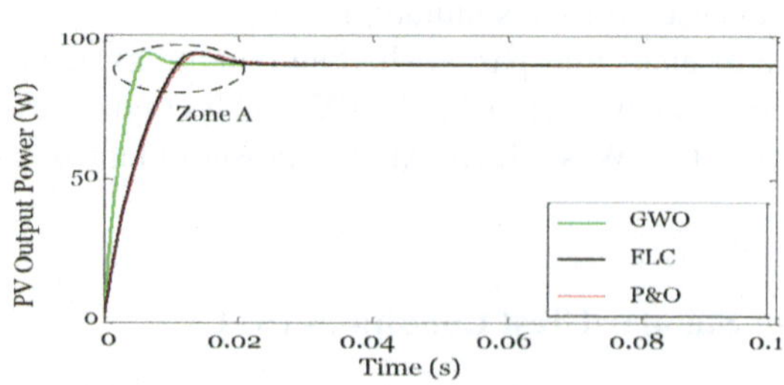

Fig. 7. Compared PV array power using GWO MPPT, P&O and FLC

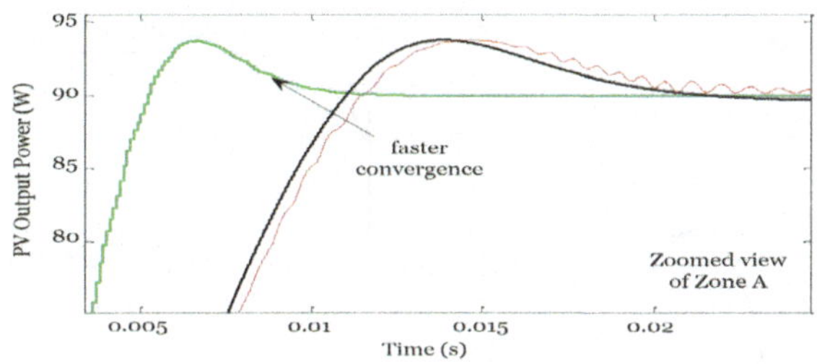

Fig. 8. Zoomed view of zone A

These results show that all three algorithms can track the maximum power point with some differences in reaching time and power oscillation in steady state.

4.2 Second Scenario: Partial Shading Conditions (PSCs)

Partial shading is the condition where some cells and or some modules of the PV arrays get fully or partially shaded. In this case, the PV arrays/modules/cells are exposed to various radiation conditions that may affect their performance.

This work employed three different PSC patterns for the purpose of analyzing the effectiveness of each MPPT technique in tracking the fluctuating GMPP as illustrated in Fig. 9.

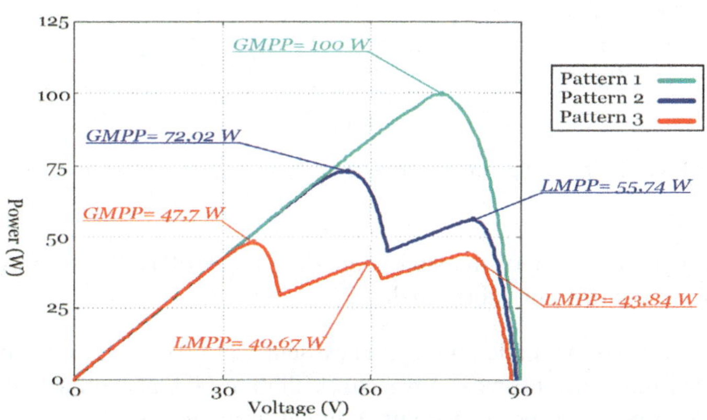

Fig. 9. P-V curves presenting several peaks

The solar intensities of the PV modules are arbitrarily varied, that is pattern 1 changes to pattern 2. They each last for 0.1 s. The cases below indicated that the proposed GWO-MPPT can track GMPP, which reduces the fluctuation rate, possess high tracking accuracy and good steady –state performance than P and O and fuzzy logic algorithm. The results are presented in the Fig. 10 below.

To expose the robustness of the proposed algorithm, the PV array was exposed to extreme rapidly changing insolation levels such as: Pattern 2, pattern 1, pattern 3. Each

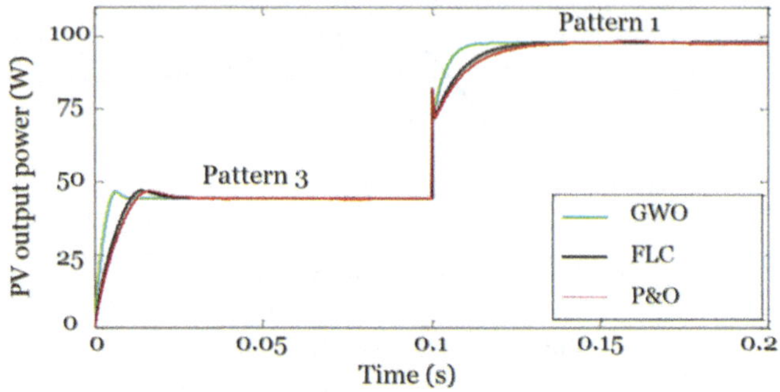

Fig. 10. Tracking curves for rapid change in insolation

pattern was then changed at an interval of 0.1 s each. Figure 11 reveals that the GWO and FLC are both in phase with GP without any oscillation and the GWO-MPPT reaches the GMPP after negligible time as compared to FLC. From the above plots, the P&O MPPT can track the GMPP but with oscillations.

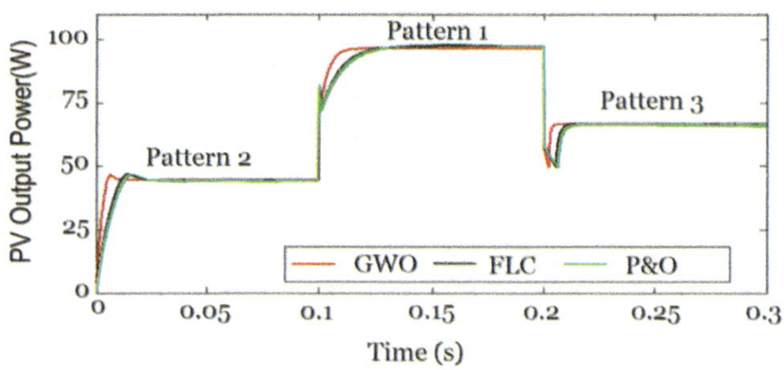

Fig. 11. Tracking curves for exceptionally fast insolation changes

Last, the general results of the study regarding the MPPT algorithms for the three scenarios are summarized in Table 1 below.

- From the comparisons made above, it is evident that GWO has better tracking efficiency, free from transient and steady state oscillations, it is also robust, requires fewer parameters to be tuned but it is computational in nature, has a larger search space as well as high costs due to implementation complexity, even though our next work will aim to implement the proposed GWO algorithm using a solar array simulator to imitate the PV source power with several conditions including quickly varying solar irradiance, a microcontroller to implement the MPPT algorithm, Hall sensor for voltage and current, a DC-DC converter and a resistive load.

Table 1. Comparison of the MPPT techniques: patterns 1, 2 and 3

MPPT Techniques	*Pattern 1 (STC)*			*Pattern 2*			*Pattern 3*		
	P&O	*FLC*	*GWO*	*P&O*	*FLC*	*GWO*	*P&O*	*FLC*	*GWO*
Extracted Power at MPP (W)	*100*	*100*	*100*	*72,83*	*72,83*	*72,83*	*47,7*	*47,7*	*47,7*
Time to reach the MPP (s)	*0,026*	*0,022*	*0,008*	*0,024*	*0,024*	*0,011*	*0,017*	*0,015*	*0,01*
Tracking Efficiency (%)	*100*	*100*	*100*	*99,86*	*99,86*	*99,86*	*100*	*100*	*100*

5 Conclusion

In conclusion, each algorithm of the three, P&O, FLC, and GWO has its own unique characteristics and advantages in terms of efficiency, accuracy, and complexity. The P&O algorithm is a simple and widely used technique that adjusts the operating point of the PV system based on the comparison of two consecutive power samples. It is cost-effective and easy to implement, but it may suffer from oscillations and tracking issues in rapidly changing weather conditions. Fuzzy logic algorithm offers a more intelligent and adaptive approach compared to P&O, providing better performance in varied environmental conditions. However, it can be more complex to implement and require additional computational resources. GWO algorithm is a nature-inspired optimization technique that mimics the hunting behavior of grey wolves to optimize MPPT process. It can provide faster and more accurate convergence to the global maximum compared to traditional algorithms. However, it may be more computationally intensive and require more tuning parameters. The choice of MPPT algorithm will ultimately depend on the specific requirements and constraints of the solar PV system, including the desired performance, system size, cost considerations, and environmental conditions. Each algorithm has its own strengths and limitations, and a thorough analysis of these factors is necessary to select the most suitable algorithm for a given application.

References

1. Ghoudelbourk, S., Dib, D., Omeiri, A., Azar, A.T.: MPPT control in wind energy conversion systems and the application of fractional control (piα) in pitch wind turbine. Int. J. Model. Ident. Control **26**(2), 140–151 (2016)
2. Meghni, B., Dib, D., Azar, A.T.: A second-order sliding mode and fuzzy logic control to optimal energy management in wind turbine with battery storage. Neural Comput. Appl. **28**(6), 1417–1434 (2017a)
3. Kamal, N.A., Ibrahim, A.M.: Conventional, intelligent, and fractional-order control method for maximum power point tracking of a photovoltaic system: a review. In: Azar, A.T., Radwan,

A.G., Vaidyanathan, S. (eds.) Fractional Order Systems, Advances in Nonlinear Dynamics and Chaos (ANDC), pp. 603–671. Academic Press, Cambridge (2018). Chap 20

4. El Filali, A., Malika, Z.: PSIM and MATLAB co-simulation of photovoltaic system using "P and O" and "Incremental conductance" MPPT. Int. J. Adv. Comput. Sci. Appl. **7**(8) (2016)
5. Ahmad, R., Murtaza, A.F., Sher, H.A.: Power tracking techniques for efficient operation of photovoltaic array in solar applications - a review. Renew. Sustain Energy Rev. **101**, 82–102 (2019)
6. El Filali, A., El Mehdi, L., Malika, Z.: Consolidation of FLC and ANN to track maximum power point for stand-alone PV systems. In: Proceedings of the 1st International Conference on Electronic Engineering and Renewable Energy: ICEERE 2018, 15–17 April 2018, Saidia, Morocco 1. Springer, Singapore, 2019
7. Masoum, M.A.S., Dehbonei, H., Fuchs, E.F.: Theoretical and experimental analyses of photovoltaic systems with voltage and current-based maximum powerpoint tracking. IEEE Trans. Energy Conv. **17**(4), 514–22 (2002)
8. Li, H., et al.: An overall distribution particle swarm optimization MPPT algorithm for photovoltaic system under partial shading. IEEE Trans. Ind. Electron. **66**(1), 265–275 (2018)
9. Bekker, B., Beukes, H.J.: Finding an optimal PV panel maximum power point tracking method. In: Proceedings of 7th AFRICON Conference, Africa, pp. 1125–9, 2004
10. Rahman, S.A., Varma, R.K., Vanderheide, T.: Generalised model of a photovoltaic panel. IET Renew. Power Gen. **8**(3), 217–229 (2014)
11. El Filali, A., Malika, Z.: Modeling and simulation of photovoltaic system employing perturb and observe MPPT algorithm and fuzzy logic control. J. Theor. Appl. Inf. Technol. **89**(2), 470 (2016)
12. Mirjalili, S., Seyed, M.M., Andrew, L.: Grey wolf optimizer. Adv. Eng. Softw. **69**, 46–61 (2014)
13. Mohanty, S., Subudhi, B., Ray, P.K.: A new MPPT design using grey wolf optimization technique for photovoltaic system under partial shading conditions. IEEE Trans. Sustain. Energy **7**(1), 181–188 (2015)

Ant Colony Optimization with Genetic Algorithm for Solving the Job Shop Scheduling

Mohamed Kriouich(✉) and Hicham Sarir

Information System and Software Engineering, ENSA Tetouan, Abdelmalek Esaadi University, Tetouan, Morocco
mohamed.kriouich@etu.uae.ac.ma, hsarrir@uae.ac.ma

Abstract. In dynamic manufacturing contexts, the Job-Shop Scheduling Problem (JSP) presents considerable hurdles, particularly in light of uncertainties such as machine breakdowns and job reworks. In this article, multiple scheduling algorithms are evaluated in various scenarios, with a special emphasis on lowering makespan, or overall completion time. Advanced algorithms like Genetic Algorithm (GA) and Deep Reinforcement Learning (DRL) are contrasted with heuristic techniques like Shortest Processing Time (SPT), Longest Processing Time (LPT), and First-In-First-Out (FIFO). The research emphasizes the advantages of the hybrid Ant Colony Optimization with Genetic Algorithm (ACO_GA) solution that has been suggested. Although GA and DRL produce outcomes that are competitive, ACO_GA regularly performs better than them and, in most cases, comes quite close to the optimal solution. Even in the face of difficult, real-world problems, our hybrid approach yields more reliable and nearly optimal scheduling solutions by fusing the exploration potential of ACO with the refinement power of GA. The results show how adaptable and successful ACO_GA is, which makes it the best option for solving JSP in dynamic contexts.

Keywords: Job-Shop Scheduling Problem · Ant Colony Optimization · Genetic Algorithm · Hybrid Algorithm

1 Introduction

AI, particularly machine learning, plays a critical role in optimizing supply chain performance and addressing production scheduling challenges [1, 2]. One of the most important optimization problems in manufacturing and production settings is the JSP [3]. It is exceptionally complicated because of its NP-hardness, especially as more variables are included, such as machine failures and job reworks, and the problem grows in size [4]. While traditional heuristic techniques such as FIFO and SPT offer fundamental solutions, they frequently fail to produce optimal results in intricate, real-world settings. This has prompted research into increasingly sophisticated algorithms, such DRL and GA, both of which exhibit performance variability across various issue situations despite their promise [5].

H. Sarir—Contributing author.

I. Aboudrar et al. (Eds.): ICESST 2024, SUCI, pp. 367–378, 2025.
https://doi.org/10.1007/978-3-031-86705-7_34

Efforts to improve these complex algorithms have produced innovations such as the Knowledge Learning-based Cooperative ACO (KLCACO) algorithm, which has demonstrated significant improvements in performance for JSP. However, there are situations when these algorithms are unable to find the optimal solutions in the given time, which highlights the need to enhance the knowledge model's learning capabilities and ensure more consistency [6].

Other scheduling problems, like the flow shop scheduling problem, present similar difficulties. While sophisticated algorithms like SHOA do well in this problem, further testing is necessary to guarantee its resilience and generalizability, especially when applying it to more complicated, real-world circumstances [7]. Furthermore, there are additional layers of complexity in multi-objective flexible job shop scheduling problems (MaOFJSP) when trying to solve for competing objectives like makespan, workload, and penalties. More study is needed to adapt these strategies for dynamic production contexts and combine cutting-edge machine learning techniques like reinforcement learning for self-adjusting parameters, even though recent developments utilizing upgraded ACO algorithms have showed promise [8].

Accurately estimating the viability of production plans is another crucial issue, in addition to schedule optimization. It is common for manufacturers to find that their production plans are not feasible too late in the scheduling phase. Recent research utilizing machine learning techniques, including random forest models, demonstrates that prediction accuracy can be greatly increased. Further research is still needed to improve feature selection and incorporate these models into mathematical techniques like MILP [9].

In light of these difficulties, this paper aims to further research by putting forth a hybrid approach that combines the advantages of ACO and GA. By using a hybrid approach, enhanced scheduling algorithms in complex and dynamic production contexts should be more efficient and adaptive.

The rest of the paper is organized in this manner. In Sect. 2, the JSP is explained and modeled as a sequential decision process. Section 3 presents the ACO_GA algorithm to address the problem mentioned in Sect. 2. Section 4 presents the environmental results and analysis. There is a conclusion in Sect. 5.

2 The Description of the Problem and the System Model

A hybrid optimization approach that blends GA and ACO techniques is shown in Fig. 1. The first step of the procedure is initializing the ACO parameters, which include setting the ant population and pheromone evaporation rate. The dataset pertinent to the optimization problem is then incorporated into the environment. Following this, ants are let loose to simulate possible solutions by scouting out routes and leaving behind pheromones to direct ant colonies in the future. Initializing GA parameters, such as population size and mutation rates, is the next stage. Like ACO, the dataset is used to initialize the GA environment, which includes the solutions found by the ants. The optimal routes from ACO are then included in the GA's initial population, so fusing the strengths of GA's exploitation and ACO's exploration. Through genetic processes including crossover, mutation, and selection, the population has developed with the goal of outperforming the ACO-provided solutions. The best individual in the final population is chosen as a possible solution following the evolution phase. The last stage produces the best makespan, which is an optimum solution for scheduling-related issues where reducing overall time is crucial. With the help of GA's refinement capabilities and ACO's strengths in finding promising solutions, this flowchart illustrates a two-phase hybrid algorithm that can improve convergence speed and solution quality in challenging optimization problems while avoiding local minima to produce better global optimization.

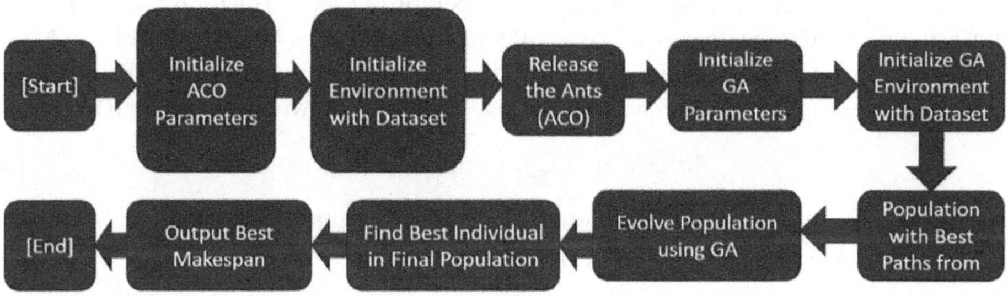

Fig. 1. Optimization of Ant Colony Optimization with Genetic Algorithm: A Flowchart for Problem Solving and Analysis.

In this paper, we propose ACO_GA, a hybrid optimization technique that combines GA and ACO. Our approach seeks to provide more reliable and close to optimal answers to the JSP by combining the exploration potential of ACO with the refinement strength of GA. We show via comparison analysis across several issue instances that ACO_GA not only outperforms or matches the outcomes of GA and DRL, but also outperforms standard heuristics. The purpose of this research, the drawbacks of current techniques, and the possibility of ACO_GA as a reliable remedy for practical scheduling issues are all explained in this introduction.

The goal of combining ACO and GA is to capitalize on each algorithm's unique advantages:

A probabilistic approach for directing the solution search based on the caliber of previously discovered schedules is offered by ACO's pheromone trails.

By introducing diversity, GA's evolutionary operators—crossover and mutation—allow for investigation beyond local optima. In areas where ACO may have reinforced inefficient pathways, this helps prevent stagnation.

When combined, ACO and GA offer a two-pronged approach to exploring the solution space, with GA enabling more extensive exploration through its genetic operators and ACO concentrating on short-term guiding through pheromone levels.

A well-known optimization problem in operational research, the JSP is frequently seen in manufacturing and industrial settings. It entails assigning a collection of jobs, each of which is a series of tasks that need to be completed on various computers. The objective is to minimize key performance indicators (KPIs) such as the makespan and optimize the scheduling process while respecting different restrictions like machine availability and operation precedence.

An algebraic formulation of the problem is as follows: there are n jobs J = {J1, J2, ⋯, Ji, ⋯, Jn}, each of which consists of m operations Oik = {Oi1, Oi2, ⋯, Oil, ⋯, Oim}, which need to be processed on a collection of machines M = {M1, M2, ..., Mm). Every operation Oik on machine Mk has a distinct processing time τ_ik. The goal is to reduce the makespan, which can be symbolized by the following equation [10]:

$$\text{Minimize } C_{max} = \max(t_{ik} + \tau_{ik}) \tag{1}$$

where t_{ik} is the start time of operation O_ik, and Cmax is the makespan.

Several constraints must be respected:

1. Starting Time Restriction: No operation may begin prior to the availability of its designated machine. In terms of math, this is expressed as:

$$t_{ik} \geq 0 \tag{2}$$

2. Precedence Constraint: Tasks completed inside the same job must occur in a certain order, so one task cannot begin before the other is completed.

$$t_{ik} - t_{ih} \geq \tau_{ik} \text{ if } O_{ih} \text{ preceding } O_{ik} \tag{3}$$

3. Disjunctive Constraint: Only one operation can be processed by a machine at once. Two operations assigned to the same machine must be scheduled consecutively, without overlap:

$$t_{pk} - t_{ik} + K\left(1 - y_{ipk}\right) \geq \tau_{pk} \tag{4}$$

where y_{ipk} is a binary variable reflecting the order of operations on the machine, and K is a big constant to guarantee proper sequencing.

The objective (1) and constraints (2), (3), and (4) balances machine availability, job sequencing, and operation start timings in order to reduce the makespan. This type of optimization frequently calls more sophisticated methods, such as Ant Colony Optimization or Genetic Algorithms, to effectively traverse the solution space and identify the optimal schedule that minimizes Cmax while satisfying all constraints.

3 ACO_GA Architecture for Job-Shop Scheduling

Table 2 shows an effective method for resolving challenging optimization issues, including job-shop scheduling, is the hybrid architecture that combines ACO with GA. By combining the advantages of both algorithms—ACO's efficient solution space search and GA's reliable population evolution mechanisms—this architecture makes the most of their respective strengths. The combination solves the drawbacks of each method when applied alone, enabling a more thorough search.

The first step in the design is initializing the environment, which entails reading the job-shop data and establishing the pheromone level parameters. This first stage is very important since it lays the groundwork for the optimization process. The ACO and GA are then configured, with the GA initializing a heterogeneous population of feasible solutions, each of which represents a distinct scheduling configuration. Additionally, the ACO parameters are specified, enabling the ants to efficiently navigate the solution space by identifying routes that minimize makespan, or the total amount of time needed to finish all jobs.

Each optimization cycle involves the sequential execution of both algorithms. During the ACO phase, ants are created to move across the solution space and produce solutions while figuring out how long they will take to complete. The ants' pheromone updates during this phase, which prioritizes exploration, reinforce successful trails and direct future search efforts. Maintaining a dynamic representation of the solution space is made possible by the pheromone contributions, which also allow the algorithm to adaptively focus on areas that show promise. After the ACO stage, the GA assesses the population of available solutions, chooses the chromosomes that perform the best, and uses genetic operators like crossover and mutation. During the exploitation phase, better solutions are promoted and variability is introduced to investigate novel configurations, hence refining the search.

A constant feedback loop between exploration and exploitation is ensured by the architecture, whereby the GA is informed about the most promising parts of the solution space by the ACO. The pheromone update systems balance exploration and exploitation through evaporation processes to avoid stagnation and direct contributions from the ants. Because the cycles are iterative, the solutions can be improved gradually, which eventually reduces the makespan. As the cycles go on, the hybrid system gains insight into the problem domain and improves the flexibility of the solution approaches, which makes it a strong option for handling challenging scheduling problems in a range of industrial settings.

Finally, the hybrid ACO-GA design successfully combines the exploitative capabilities of GA with the exploratory characteristics of ACO. This architecture is an effective method for solving optimization problems, especially in the context of job-shop scheduling, because it allows for an iterative process that continuously refines and assesses prospective solutions. Because of the way it is designed, it can be dynamically adjusted in response to feedback from both algorithms, which eventually results in better performance and more effective solutions (Table 1).

4 Simulation Result, Analysis and Discussion

The application of the suggested ACO_GA architecture in the JSP is assessed in this section, and its efficacy is contrasted with theoretical optimal solutions, heuristic guidelines, DRL, and meta-heuristic algorithms [11].

Table 1. Hybrid ACO_GA Architecture for Job-Shop Scheduling.

1. Initialize Environment

```
FUNCTION Initialize_Environment(file_name, init_pheromone, min_pheromone):
    Load job data
    RETURN job data, num_jobs, num_machines
```

2. Initialize ACO with GA

```
FUNCTION Initialize_ACO_GA(params):
    job_data, num_jobs, num_machines = Initialize_Environment(params.dataset,
params.init_pheromone, params.min_pheromone)
    population = Initialize_GA(params.population_size, params.mutation_rate, num_jobs,
num_machines, job_data)
    RETURN job_data, population
```

3. Main Loop for Cycles

```
FOR cycle FROM 1 to params.cycles:
    Run ACO_Phase(ant_numbers, job_data)
    best_solution, best_makespan = GA_Phase(population, job_data)
    Store best_makespan
END FOR
```

4. ACO Phase

```
FUNCTION ACO_Phase(ant_numbers, job_data):
    FOR each ant FROM 1 to ant_numbers:
        ant_solution = Create_Ant_Solution()
        makespan = Calculate_Makespan(job_data, ant_solution)
        Update_Pheromones(ant_solution, makespan)
    END FOR
    Evaporate_Pheromones()
```

5. GA Phase

```
FUNCTION GA_Phase(population, job_data):
    best_solution = None
    best_makespan = infinity
    FOR each chromosome in population:
        makespan = Calculate_Makespan(job_data, chromosome)
        IF makespan < best_makespan:
            best_solution = chromosome
            best_makespan = makespan
    population = Evolve(population)
    RETURN best_solution, best_makespan
```

6. Pheromone Update

```
FUNCTION Update_Pheromones(ant_solution, makespan):
    FOR each edge in ant_solution:
        Update pheromone level
    END FOR
```

To confirm the benefits of the ACO_GA model over conventional techniques, we further investigated the generalization performance of the proposed model. This section presents the suggested ACO_GA model's static performance in the JSP issues. Some benchmark problems in the OR-library are the source of the JSP troubles [12].

We employ 25 instances of varying sizes to assess the aforementioned methods. These instances encompass the ft06 instance with a 6 × 6 size [24], ft10 instance with 10 × 10 [24], orb01-orb09 instances with 10 × 10 [13], la01-la05 instances with 5 × 10, la06-la10 instances with 5 × 15, and la11-la15 instances with 5 × 20 [25]. Table 2 and Fig. 2 present the outcomes of the six methods applied to these instances. For a quantitative assessment, we incorporate theoretically optimal solutions [24–26].

In order to minimize the makespan, or overall completion time, Table 2 analyzes alternative scheduling and optimization strategies based on how well they perform across different problem situations. The problem instances, which vary in the number of jobs and machines involved, are ft06, la01, and Orb01, and they reflect well-known benchmarks in scheduling and job-shop optimization. For instance, although la01 has 5 jobs and 10 machines, ft06 contains 6 jobs and 6 machines. For every instance, the best solution—that is, the shortest makespan—is given; this serves as a standard by which different algorithms' performances are evaluated.

The algorithms compared are more sophisticated approaches such as the Genetic GA, DRL, and a hybrid method that combines Ant Colony Optimization and Algorithm (ACO_GA) with more fundamental heuristic methods like SPT, LPT, and FIFO. The findings demonstrate that heuristic approaches often underperform more sophisticated algorithms. While SPT generally performs better than LPT and FIFO, it still falls behind in terms of total makespan reduction. Particularly for bigger problem sizes, LPT frequently performs the poorest, whereas FIFO provides marginally improved but still subpar performance.

When compared to heuristic approaches, advanced algorithms such as GA and DRL yield superior outcomes. For instance, compared to SPT, LPT, or FIFO, GA consistently yields solutions that are closer to the ideal makespan. GA, however, isn't necessarily better than the hybrid ACO_GA, especially when dealing with more complicated problems. DRL also shows itself to be competitive, occasionally even outperforming GA, although it doesn't always perform better. The most reliable algorithm is the ACO_GA hybrid approach, which frequently yields makespans that are noticeably nearer to or even better than the ideal solutions. This strategy outperforms GA or DRL alone in the majority of problem scenarios, demonstrating its capacity to successfully balance exploration and exploitation and produce superior results.

In summary, heuristic approaches offer rudimentary solutions, but they are distinctly surpassed by more sophisticated algorithms such as GA and DRL, particularly when the problem size grows. But time and time again, the ACO_GA hybrid shows itself to be the most effective method, demonstrating that it can accurately and efficiently handle a wide range of scheduling issues. This hybrid method minimizes makespan while providing a balanced and superior solution thanks to the combination of ACO and GA.

Table 2. Findings from the experiment.

Instances	Size	Optimal solution	SPT	LPT	FIFO	GA	DRL	ACO_GA
ft06	6×6	55	88	77	65	58	57	43
ft10	10×10	930	1074	1295	1184	1157	1033	631
la01	5× 10	666	751	822	772	706	666	666
la02	5× 10	655	821	990	830	732	715	635
la03	5 × 10	597	672	825	755	680	634	588
la04	5 × 10	590	711	818	695	637	665	537
la05	5 × 10	593	610	693	610	593	593	572
la06	5 × 15	926	1200	1125	926	948	926	926
la07	5 × 15	890	1034	1069	1088	985	894	869
la08	5 × 15	863	942	1035	980	932	863	773
la09	5 × 15	951	1045	1183	1018	1001	951	951
la10	5 × 15	958	1049	1132	1006	958	958	958
la11	5 × 20	1222	1473	1467	1272	1304	1222	1104
la12	5 × 20	1039	1203	1240	1039	1087	1039	1039
la13	5 × 20	1150	1275	1230	1199	1207	1150	1150
la14	5 × 20	1292	1427	1434	1292	1292	1292	1292
la15	5 × 20	1207	1339	1612	1587	1403	1212	1207
Orb01	10×10	1059	1478	1410	1368	1379	1131	668
Orb02	10×10	888	1175	1293	1007	1141	993	671
Orb03	10×10	1005	1179	1293	1405	1300	1092	624
Orb04	10×10	1005	1236	1415	1325	1229	1118	759
Orb05	10×10	887	1152	1099	1155	1135	972	630
Orb06	10×10	1010	1190	1474	1330	1309	1140	694
Orb08	10×10	899	1107	1176	1225	1174	979	499
Orb09	10×10	934	1262	1286	1189	1158	1005	672

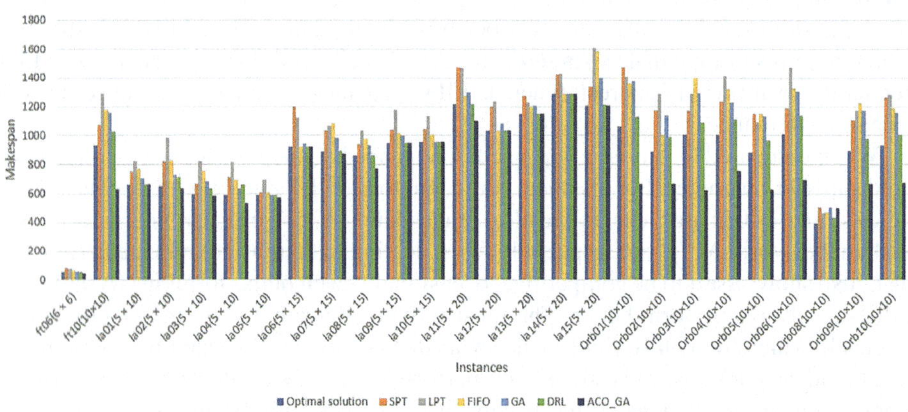

Fig. 2. Makespan on OR instances using the ACO_GA technique.

The Fig. 2 provides a thorough analysis of how different scheduling algorithms perform when used to solve the JSP. It contrasts the makespan outcomes of multiple methods, such as the hybrid ACO_GA, the best solution, SPT, LPT, FIFO, GA, and DRL. The graphic illustration makes the disparities in performance between different algorithms abundantly evident, highlighting the potential of hybrid approaches to tackle the intricacies of contemporary scheduling problems.

The chart highlights the higher performance of ACO_GA in comparison to conventional heuristics such as FIFO and SPT. ACO_GA regularly produces lower values, according to the makespan results, demonstrating its usefulness in examining the solution space and maximizing job processing times. This enhancement highlights the algorithm's capacity to improve schedules, enabling more effective time and resource management. On the other hand, conventional heuristics frequently show longer makespans, especially in more complicated cases, indicating their limits in terms of accommodating the dynamic nature of real-world production environments.

The graphic also draws attention to another important point, which is the variation in performance between various cases. Some examples, like la05(5 × 10) and la15(5 × 20), illustrate that ACO_GA can produce makespan outcomes that are almost ideal. Nonetheless, in alternative configurations such as orb01(20 × 10), the performance varies, suggesting that certain issue setups can provide more difficulties. This variability emphasizes the need to thoroughly assess the robustness and adaptability of different algorithms by benchmarking them across a wide range of issue scenarios.

The effectiveness of hybrid techniques, in particular ACO_GA, is demonstrated by its capacity to strike a balance between exploration and exploitation. Through the combined benefits of Ant Colony Optimization and Genetic Algorithms, ACO_GA not only outperforms stand-alone advanced algorithms such as DRL and GA, but frequently outperforms them as well. This capacity raises the possibility that hybrid approaches, which provide solutions that are both more effective and flexible enough to adjust to changing conditions, may be essential for handling the complexities of the Job Shop Scheduling Problem.

The Fig. 3 presents a visual comparison between the ACO_GA algorithm's performance and the best solution for several JSP scenarios. It contains important metrics like the mean, lowest, and maximum values that the ACO_GA technique was able to attain for various issue cases. This comparative analysis is crucial to assessing the hybrid ACO_GA algorithm's dependability and efficacy in generating high-caliber scheduling solutions.

The continuous closeness of the ACO_GA average performance line (green) to the ideal solution (blue) is a noteworthy aspect of the chart. This implies that, in all evaluated circumstances, the ACO_GA algorithm can produce competitive results with the most well-known methods. The data points show that the average makespan generated by ACO_GA often roughly matches the ideal values, demonstrating its stability and effectiveness in navigating the solution space. Nevertheless, there are significant differences in some cases, such ft10 and la10, where the ACO_GA algorithm performs less well than the best solution, indicating potential difficulties with these settings.

The ACO_GA findings' lowest (orange) and maximum (red) values also shed light on how inconsistently the algorithm performs. The maximum values show the situations in which ACO_GA's performance was not up to par, while the minimum values show the best-case scenarios that the algorithm was able to achieve. The majority of the time, the trends in these values show a relatively small range of makespan, indicating that the ACO_GA algorithm typically yields accurate and consistent results. But the broader distribution in cases such as orb01 indicates that the algorithm might face challenges in specific situations, indicating the need for more research to improve the program's flexibility and optimization techniques.

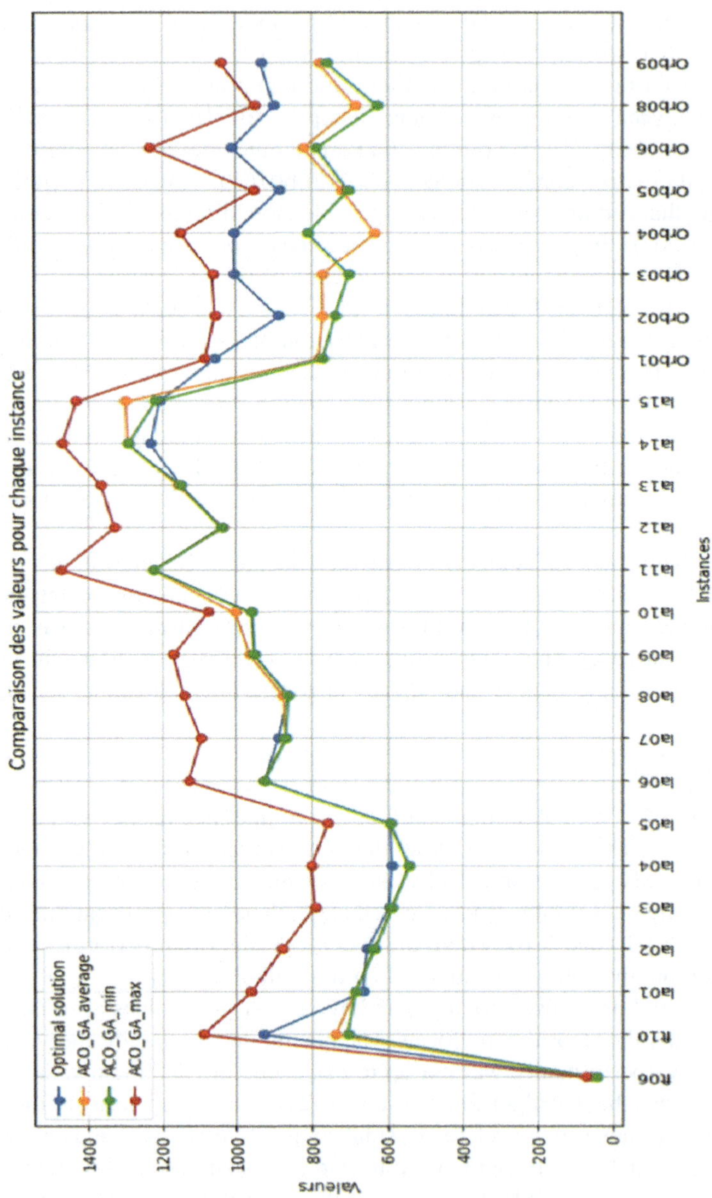

Fig. 3. Makespan with ACO_GA algorithm on OR instances.

The general downward trend of the ACO_GA measures, especially the average and maximum values between examples orb01 to orb09, is another important finding. This pattern indicates that the algorithm can solve scheduling problems in complicated circumstances with ever-increasing efficiency. However, it also begs the question of how the algorithm will behave in more complex problem scenarios. Further investigation into the reasons behind some cases' lower performance is necessary in order to improve the ACO_GA algorithm.

5 Conclusion

To sum up, the hybrid ACO_GA technique is a major improvement in handling the difficulties related to the JSP. This approach shows better performance in locating high-quality solutions than conventional heuristics and stand-alone advanced algorithms by skillfully combining the exploration powers of Ant Colony Optimization with the exploitation strengths of Genetic Algorithms. The promise of ACO_GA for real-world applications in contemporary manufacturing environments is demonstrated by its consistent ability to obtain makespans closer to ideal solutions across a variety of benchmark scenarios. The results highlight the value of hybrid approaches in complicated scheduling scenario optimization, which in turn leads to increased productivity and operational efficiency.

Although the ACO_GA hybrid algorithm's results are encouraging, there are a few drawbacks to take into account. ACO_GA's performance differs from optimal solutions in several complex jobs and machine setups, indicating that the algorithm might have trouble in some situations. Moreover, the dependence on static parameters can restrict ACO_GA's flexibility in dynamic settings where real-time modifications are essential. Furthermore, when dealing with larger problem instances, the hybrid approach's computing complexity can rise dramatically, which could have an impact on its scalability and usefulness in industrial settings. Improving the ACO_GA algorithm's resilience and adaptability will require addressing these drawbacks.

Subsequent investigations ought to endeavor to broaden the scope of the ACO_GA framework by integrating multi-objective optimization situations. In these scenarios, conflicting goals including makespan, resource consumption, and overall production costs need to be harmonized. Furthermore, real-world application performance could be further enhanced by investigating adaptive mechanisms within the ACO_GA architecture, such as the incorporation of reinforcement learning techniques to dynamically modify parameters in response to shifting manufacturing conditions. It will also be essential to look into ACO_GA's scalability for larger and more intricate production systems if the industry is to successfully adopt it. Additionally, investigating how to combine ACO_GA with other cutting-edge optimization methods may produce even better answers to the Job Shop Scheduling Problem, opening the door for novel ideas in operational optimization.

References

1. Kriouich, M., Sarir, H., Louah, S.: Research trends and knowledge taxonomy of artificial intelligence applications in supply chain management, logistics, and transportation: a systematic literature review and bibliometric analysis. J. Robot. Control (JRC) **5**, 1349–1364 (2024). https://doi.org/10.18196/jrc.v5i5.21859
2. Kriouich, M., Sarir, H., Mahboub, O.: Application of artificial intelligence in the supply chain: a systematic literature review. In: Lecture Notes in Networks and Systems, pp. 388–401. Springer Science and Business Media Deutschland GmbH (2023)
3. Kriouich, M., Sarir, H.: Artificial intelligence application in production scheduling problem systematic literature review: bibliometric analysis, research trend, and knowledge taxonomy. Oper. Res. Forum **5** (2024)
4. Mohan, J., Lanka, K., Rao, A.N.: A review of dynamic job shop scheduling techniques. In: Procedia Manufacturing. Elsevier B.V., pp. 34–39 (2019)
5. Matrenin, P.V.: Improvement of ant colony algorithm performance for the job-shop scheduling problem using evolutionary adaptation and software realization heuristics. Algorithms **16** (2023). https://doi.org/10.3390/a16010015
6. Li, W., Yan, X., Huang, Y.: Cooperative-guided ant colony optimization with knowledge learning for job shop scheduling problem. Tsinghua Sci. Technol. **29**, 1283–1299 (2024). https://doi.org/10.26599/TST.2023.9010098
7. Mzili, T., Mzili, I., Riffi, M.E., Pamucar, D., Kurdi, M., Ali, A.H.: Optimizing production scheduling with the spotted hyena algorithm: a novel approach to the flow shop problem. Reports in Mechanical Eng. **4**, 90–103 (2023). https://doi.org/10.31181/rme040116072023m
8. Yan, S., Zhang, G., Sun, J., Zhang, W.: An improved ant colony optimization for solving the flexible job shop scheduling problem with multiple time constraints. Math. Biosci. Eng. **20**, 7519–7547 (2023). https://doi.org/10.3934/mbe.2023325
9. Tremblet, D., Thevenin, S., Dolgui, A.: Predicting makespan in flexible job shop scheduling problem using machine learning. In: IFAC-PapersOnLine. Elsevier B.V., pp. 1–6 (2022)
10. Kriouich, M., Sarir, H.: A framework for solving the job shop scheduling problem
11. Wang, L., et al.: Dynamic job-shop scheduling in smart manufacturing using deep reinforcement learning. Comput. Netw. **190** (2021). https://doi.org/10.1016/j.comnet.2021.107969
12. beasley1990
13. Applegate, D., Cook, W.: Computational study of the job-shop scheduling problem. ORSA J. Comput. **3**, 149–156 (1991). https://doi.org/10.1287/ijoc.3.2.149

Combined Control by ADRC and DSOGI-FLL of a PMSG Inverter Connected to Grid in Voltage Dip

Mohammed Latifi[1](✉), Mourad Zegrari[1], Imad Aboudrar[2], and Radouane Majdoul[1]

[1] National Higher School of Arts and Crafts (ENSAM), Hassan II University, Casablanca, Morocco
Mohammed.latifi-etu@etu.univh2c.ma, {mourad.zegrari, radouane.majdoul}@univh2c.ma

[2] Higher School of Technology (EST), Ibn Zohr University, Dakhla, Morocco
i.aboudrar@uiz.ac.ma

Abstract. The control of a wind system based on a Permanent Magnet Synchronous Generator PMSG connected to grid by PI regulators is insufficient to eliminate internal uncertainties and external disturbances of the system. Additionally, regulating grid voltage and frequency during voltage dips requires robust control to match the needs of grid codes. The Active Disturbance Rejection Control ADRC is applied to control the inverter of our system; its composition is based on the Extended State Observer ESO, which is the most important part. Moreover, to improve the operating performance of the system and its ability to withstand symmetrical and asymmetrical voltage dips while respecting grid codes, we combined with ADRC a frequency-locked loop based on a second order-generalized integrator (DSOGI-FLL). To confirm the effectiveness of the suggested control strategies, we performed a series of simulations in the Matlab/Simulink environment. The results obtained highlighted the superiority of the proposed methods as well as their ability to maintain their performance in the face of symmetrical and asymmetrical voltage dips.

Keywords: PMSG · ADRC · ESO · DSOGI-FLL · Voltage Dips

1 Introduction

Renewable energy production from wind turbines based on a permanent magnet synchronous generator (PMSG) has better throughput, lower maintenance costs, no heat dissipation in the rotor and higher overall efficiency, and injecting this energy into the grid requires control technology to keep the grid safe and stable. As a result, grid integration requirements have become a main priority as wind energy sources begin to replace conventional power plants [1]. In this context, new technical requirements and regulations known as Grid Codes have been established to ensure grid stability, such as voltage regulation, frequency regulation, power quality and voltage dip crossing (LVRT). LVRT

I. Aboudrar et al. (Eds.): ICESST 2024, SUCI, pp. 379–391, 2025.
https://doi.org/10.1007/978-3-031-86705-7_35

is one of the key technologies for the operation of power generation systems. Generally, LVRT control is mainly based on PI controllers, and their robustness results are still unsatisfactory. On the other hand, this paper proposes a new control strategy that uses the compensation effect of the 'total disturbance' before it affects the system, this control method is called ADRC, is a new control technique whose central idea is to manage external disturbances and internal uncertainties using an extended state observer (ESO)[2]. Moreover, the SRF-PLL Synchronous reference frame PLL is more widely used in monitoring, however, its performance declines under unbalanced or distorted voltage conditions. When synchronization is required, it is essential to use the positive sequence of the fundamental voltage wave as a reference [3]. In this context, filtering out the negative sequence component becomes very challenging because of its narrow bandwidth. Reference [4] presents several advanced PLL techniques designed to enhance the disturbance rejection capability of the conventional SRF-PLL, addressing power quality issues in non-ideal voltage conditions. The Dual-SRF-PLL is effective for unbalanced grid conditions but struggles with the presence of harmonics [5]. In this context, a frequency-locked loop based on a second-order generalized integrator (DSOGI-FLL) is proposed and used in to enhance the performance of the hybrid system and its ability to withstand both symmetric and asymmetric voltage sags, while complying with grid code. To assess the effectiveness of the proposed control strategies, a series of simulations was carried out in the Matlab/Simulink environment. The results demonstrated the superiority of the proposed methods and their robustness to symmetrical and asymmetrical faults. Modeling the Elements of the Energy Conversion Chain.

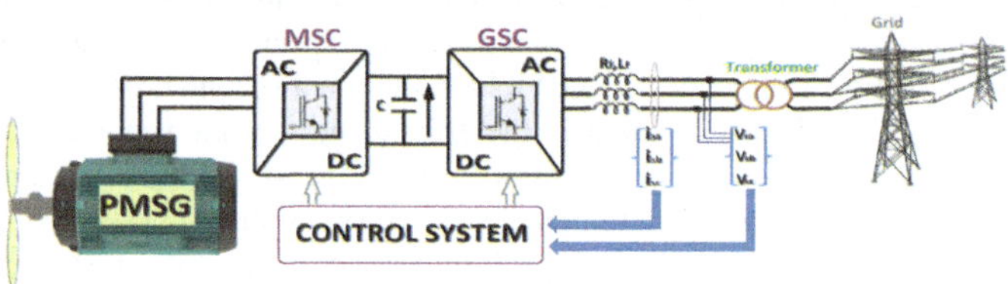

Fig. 1. The offshore power generation system.

In this section, we propose a permanent magnet synchronous generator (PMSG) for electricity production. The electrical energy produced is injected into the grid via two static converter blocks. The first converter has a role of controlling the power produced and the torque with the speed. Therefore, it is a rectifier controlled to give the energy to the DC bus. We also have a second block that is a grid-side converter, bidirectional, is the most important part that we will apply our control, to control the DC bus voltage, the synchronization, the reactive power of the grid, and participation in the voltage and frequency adjustment in the event of a voltage dip. The output of our generator is connected to an RL filter and then to the grid. The equivalent model is depicted in (Fig. 1).

Rapid disconnection of a wind turbine can negatively influence the stability of the power grid. For this reason, the technical criterion of LVRT stipulates that energy sources must be fault-resistant and remain connected to the grid during voltage dips [6]. They should also restore normal operation as soon as the fault is cleared, providing reactive power to the point of common coupling (PCC) during unforeseen disturbances. (Fig. 2) illustrates the correlation curves between the depths of voltage dips and their durations, highlighting the LVRT criterion in different countries.

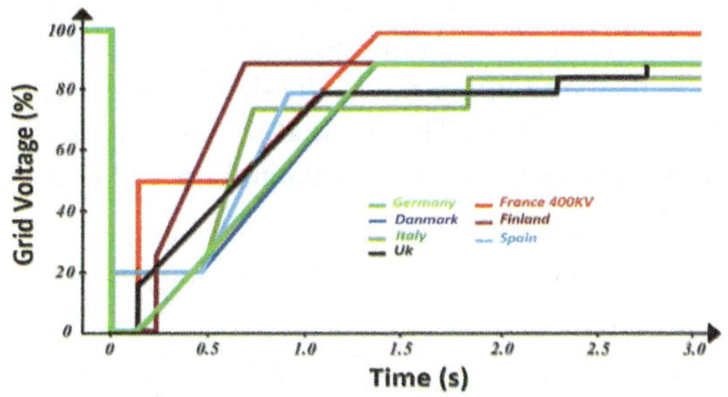

Fig. 2. Curves of LVRT requirements across various countries.

The grid code of Spain requires that grid-integrated wind systems remain connected for half a second when the PCC voltage drops by 80%. If the PCC voltage recovers to 80% of the initial voltage within 0.8s, the wind turbine will remain in operating mode without tripping. Otherwise, disconnection is mandatory. The LVRT requirements of other countries are similar to the requirements of Spain, with a slight difference observed regarding the period and voltage levels.

2 The Inverter Control Strategy

When a symmetrical or asymmetrical voltage drop occurs in the power grid, the power on the inverter side will instantly decrease, causing energy accumulation in the DC bus and causing overvoltage and overcurrent problems, which seriously threatens the safety and stable operation of power converters and the power grid itself. Therefore, it is necessary to quickly and accurately realize phase locking and quickly detect the voltage dip in the event of a grid fault, and design a reasonable and robust control strategy to realize the low-voltage transition of the inverter, and manage the excess power ΔP produced at the DC bus, in this regard, it can be managed by limiting the power captured by the variation of the pitch angle β [7], which leads to a degradation of the turbine power coefficient, The excess power can also be stored via super-capacitors and batteries, despite their high cost, or by dissipating the excess power to the DC bus through resistors driven by a controllable switch. When the grid voltage is distorted or unbalanced, it is essential to use the positive sequence voltage component of the fundamental wave as a reference. On the other hand, the negative sequence component cannot be filtered effectively due to its narrow bandwidth. This makes it difficult to achieve accurate phase locking, which may lead to control problems. The PLL-based dual-order generalized integrator (DSOGI-PLL) is designed to generate quadrature signals with a phase difference of 90°, which allows separating the phase and sequence while ensuring phase locking. However, the DSOGI-PLL has some drawbacks, including a slow dynamic response during abrupt frequency and phase changes. In this context, this work proposes to integrate a frequency-locked loop (FLL) with a frequency-adaptive link to the DSOGI-PLL technique [5, 8]. The topology of the proposed system as well as the overall control scheme are presented in Fig. 3. The system consists of a wind energy conversion chain based on a PMSG, associated with a machine side converter connected to the DC bus. The latter is connected to the connection point via a three-phase inverter and a step-up transformer. To demonstrate the control strategy, a power model of the inverter under unbalanced grid faults is presented and clarified. The method for calculating the reference currents for positive and negative sequences is also explained. In addition, a control scheme for LVRT operation is applied.

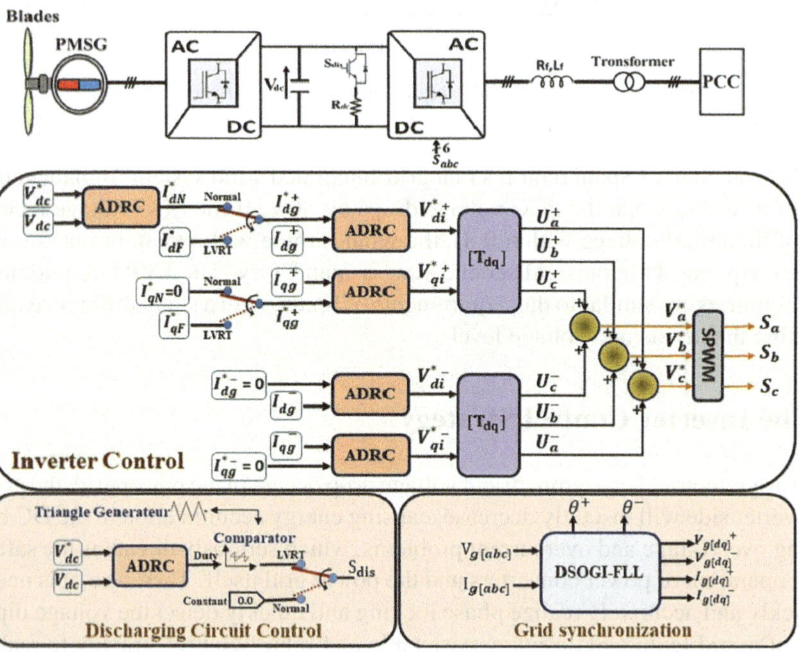

Fig. 3. The topology of the proposed system as well as the overall control scheme

2.1 The Mathematical Model

When the grid-connected inverter is operating normally, only the positive component of the grid voltage exists in the system. However, when the grid voltage is unbalanced, a negative component appears. Therefore, the apparent power of the inverter is expressed as follows:

$$S = P + jQ = 1.5(v_{dq}^{+}e^{j\omega t} + v_{dq}^{-}e^{-j\omega t})(i_{dq}^{+}e^{j\omega t} + i_{dq}^{-}e^{-j\omega t})^{*} \quad (1)$$

With: v_{dq}^{+}, v_{dq}^{-}, i_{dq}^{+} et i_{dq}^{-} are the voltage and current vectors and are given by:

$$\begin{cases} v_{dq}^{+} = v_{d}^{+} + jv_{q}^{+} \\ v_{dq}^{-} = v_{d}^{-} + jv_{q}^{-} \\ i_{dq}^{+} = i_{d}^{+} + ji_{q}^{+} \\ i_{dq}^{-} = i_{d}^{-} + ji_{q}^{-} \end{cases} \tag{2}$$

where, the positive and negative voltage sequences in the d-q axis are:

$$\begin{bmatrix} v_{d}^{+} \\ v_{q}^{+} \\ 0 \end{bmatrix} = \frac{2}{3}\begin{bmatrix} cos(\theta) & cos(\theta - \frac{2\pi}{3}) & cos(\theta + \frac{2\pi}{3}) \\ sin(\theta) & sin(\theta - \frac{2\pi}{3}) & sin(\theta + \frac{2\pi}{3}) \\ \frac{1}{2} & \frac{1}{2} & \frac{1}{2} \end{bmatrix}\begin{bmatrix} v_{a}^{+} \\ v_{b}^{+} \\ v_{c}^{+} \end{bmatrix} \tag{3}$$

$$\begin{bmatrix} v_{d}^{-} \\ v_{q}^{-} \\ 0 \end{bmatrix} = \frac{2}{3}\begin{bmatrix} cos(-\theta) & cos(-\theta - \frac{2\pi}{3}) & cos(-\theta + \frac{2\pi}{3}) \\ sin(-\theta) & sin(-\theta - \frac{2\pi}{3}) & sin(-\theta + \frac{2\pi}{3}) \\ \frac{1}{2} & \frac{1}{2} & \frac{1}{2} \end{bmatrix}\begin{bmatrix} v_{a}^{-} \\ v_{b}^{-} \\ v_{c}^{-} \end{bmatrix} \tag{4}$$

With θ is the phase angle of the grid voltage obtained by DSOGI-FLL as shown in Fig. 3. v_{a}^{+}, v_{b}^{+}, v_{c}^{+} et v_{a}^{-}, v_{b}^{-}, v_{c}^{-}: are the positive and negative sequence voltages in the frame *abc*. The instantaneous apparent power is then separated into active power *P* and reactive power *Q* by the following expression:

$$\begin{cases} P = P_0 + P_{c2}cos(2\omega t) + P_{s2}sin(2\omega t) \\ Q = Q_0 + Q_{c2}cos(2\omega t) + Q_{s2}sin(2\omega t) \end{cases} \tag{5}$$

P_0 and Q_0 respectively represent the average component of the instantaneous active and reactive powers, P_{c2}, P_{s2} et Q_{c2}, Q_{s2} are the double-frequency oscillating parts of these instantaneous terms. The mean component and the oscillating components are then given as:

$$\begin{cases} P_0 = 1.5(v_{d}^{+}i_{d}^{+} + v_{q}^{+}i_{q}^{+} + v_{d}^{-}i_{d}^{-} + v_{q}^{-}i_{q}^{-}) \\ P_{c2} = 1.5(v_{d}^{-}i_{d}^{+} + v_{q}^{-}i_{q}^{+} + v_{d}^{+}i_{d}^{-} + v_{q}^{+}i_{q}^{-}) \\ P_{s2} = 1.5(v_{q}^{-}i_{d}^{+} - v_{d}^{-}i_{q}^{+} - v_{q}^{+}i_{d}^{-} + v_{d}^{+}i_{q}^{-}) \\ Q_0 = 1.5(v_{q}^{+}i_{d}^{+} - v_{d}^{+}i_{q}^{+} + v_{q}^{-}i_{d}^{-} - v_{d}^{-}i_{q}^{-}) \\ Q_{c2} = 1.5(v_{q}^{-}i_{d}^{+} - v_{d}^{-}i_{q}^{+} + v_{q}^{+}i_{d}^{-} - v_{d}^{+}i_{q}^{-}) \\ Q_{s2} = 1.5(v_{d}^{+}i_{d}^{-} + v_{q}^{+}i_{q}^{-} - v_{d}^{-}i_{d}^{+} - v_{q}^{-}i_{q}^{+}) \end{cases} \tag{6}$$

As can write:

$$\begin{bmatrix} P_0 \\ Q_0 \\ P_{c2} \\ P_{s2} \\ Q_{c2} \\ Q_{s2} \end{bmatrix} = \frac{3}{2}\begin{bmatrix} v_{d}^{+} & v_{q}^{+} & v_{d}^{-} & v_{q}^{-} \\ v_{q}^{+} & -v_{d}^{+} & v_{q}^{-} & -v_{d}^{-} \\ v_{d}^{-} & v_{q}^{-} & v_{d}^{+} & v_{q}^{+} \\ v_{q}^{-} & -v_{d}^{-} & -v_{q}^{+} & v_{d}^{+} \\ v_{q}^{-} & -v_{d}^{-} & v_{q}^{+} & -v_{d}^{+} \\ -v_{d}^{-} & -v_{d}^{-} & v_{d}^{+} & v_{q}^{+} \end{bmatrix}\begin{bmatrix} i_{d}^{+} \\ i_{q}^{+} \\ i_{d}^{-} \\ i_{q}^{-} \end{bmatrix} \tag{7}$$

The references of the current regulators can be determined from this equation, depending on the powers required to be injected for an inverter connected to the grid, equipped with a strategy for separating the positive and negative components.

$$\begin{bmatrix} i_d^+ \\ i_q^+ \\ i_d^- \\ i_q^- \end{bmatrix}_{ref} = \frac{2}{3}\begin{bmatrix} \frac{v_d^+}{E1} & \frac{v_q^+}{E2} \\ \frac{v_q^+}{E1} & -\frac{v_d^+}{E2} \\ -K\frac{v_d^-}{E1} & +K\frac{v_q^-}{E2} \\ -K\frac{v_q^-}{E1} & -K\frac{-v_d^-}{E2} \end{bmatrix}\begin{bmatrix} P \\ Q \end{bmatrix}_{ref} \tag{8}$$

White:

$$\begin{cases} E1 = (v_d^+)^2 + \left(v_q^+\right)^2 - K\left(\left(v_d^-\right)^2 + \left(v_q^-\right)^2\right) \\ E2 = (v_d^+)^2 + (v_q^+)^2 + K\left(\left(v_d^-\right)^2 + \left(v_q^-\right)^2\right) \end{cases} \tag{9}$$

To eliminate the negative sequence current and thus limit the inverter current overshoot during a fault, with an active and reactive power will oscillate at double frequency. This requires that $K = 0$.

2.2 The DSOGI FLL Technique

To ensure the separation of the positive and negative sequences, two control loops are set up, one for the positive sequence currents and the other for the negative sequence. Each loop ensures that the inverter output current components in the d-q frame follow the defined references. The references for the positive current control loops are as follows:

$$\begin{bmatrix} i_d^+ \\ i_q^+ \end{bmatrix}_{ref} = \frac{2}{3}\begin{bmatrix} \frac{v_d^+}{(v_d^+)^2+(v_q^+)^2} & \frac{v_q^+}{(v_d^+)^2+(v_q^+)^2} \\ \frac{v_q^+}{(v_d^+)^2+(v_q^+)^2} & \frac{-v_d^+}{(v_d^+)^2+(v_q^+)^2} \end{bmatrix}\begin{bmatrix} P \\ Q \end{bmatrix}_{ref} \tag{10}$$

To achieve an inverter output current at the limits, we need to inject the negative sequence current. Therefore, the references of the negative current control loop are as follows:

$$\begin{cases} i_{dref}^- = 0 \\ i_{qref}^- = 0 \end{cases} \tag{11}$$

Furthermore, the v_q^+ component is set to zero to use voltage oriented control, we conclude that:

$$\begin{cases} i_{dref}^+ = \frac{P_{ref}}{1.5v_d^+} \\ i_{qref}^+ = -\frac{Q_{ref}}{1.5v_d^+} \end{cases} \tag{12}$$

When the voltage of the device is designed, it presents amplitudes and frequency variables, which makes it impossible to use a traditional PLL to ensure the operating phase. In this situation, it is essential to detect the phase and the frequency of positive components of the sequence after using it at the place of the recovery tension [5]. This composition may begin with:

$$\begin{bmatrix} v_a^+ \\ v_b^+ \\ v_c^+ \end{bmatrix} = \frac{1}{3}\begin{bmatrix} 1 & \alpha & \alpha^2 \\ \alpha^2 & 1 & \alpha \\ \alpha & \alpha^2 & 1 \end{bmatrix}\begin{bmatrix} v_a \\ v_b \\ v_c \end{bmatrix} \tag{13}$$

With: $\alpha = e^{-j\frac{2\pi}{3}}$

By applying the Clarke transformation, we get:

$$\begin{bmatrix} v_\alpha^+ \\ v_\beta^+ \end{bmatrix} = \frac{2}{3}\begin{bmatrix} 1 & -\frac{1}{2} & -\frac{1}{2} \\ 0 & \frac{\sqrt{3}}{2} & -\frac{\sqrt{3}}{2} \end{bmatrix}\begin{bmatrix} v_a^+ \\ v_b^+ \\ v_c^+ \end{bmatrix} = \frac{1}{2}\begin{bmatrix} 1 & -q \\ q & 1 \end{bmatrix}\begin{bmatrix} v_\alpha \\ v_\beta \end{bmatrix} \tag{14}$$

The SOGI presented in Fig. 4 gives the product of the ε_u error and the quadrature output qu' to the FLL. Afterwards, the estimated frequency error ε_f, is corrected by an integrator with a gain of $-\Gamma$ and by the initial angular frequency ω_0 in order to return the new angular frequency ω' to the SOGI to form a closed control loop and thus obtain an accurate adaptation of the system frequency[9]. The adoption of this FLL link makes it possible to effectively eliminate the accumulation of the angular frequency, and to continuously adjust ω', and consequently, to achieve a frequency lock. The state space model of the SOGI FLL is given by:

$$\dot{x} = \begin{bmatrix} \dot{x}_1 \\ \dot{x}_2 \end{bmatrix} = Ax + Bu = \begin{bmatrix} -k\omega' & \omega'^2 \\ 1 & 0 \end{bmatrix}\begin{bmatrix} x_1 \\ x_2 \end{bmatrix} + \begin{bmatrix} k\omega' \\ 0 \end{bmatrix}u \tag{15}$$

$$y = \begin{bmatrix} u' \\ qu' \end{bmatrix} = Cx = \begin{bmatrix} -k\omega' & \omega'^2 \\ 1 & 0 \end{bmatrix}\begin{bmatrix} x_1 \\ x_2 \end{bmatrix}$$

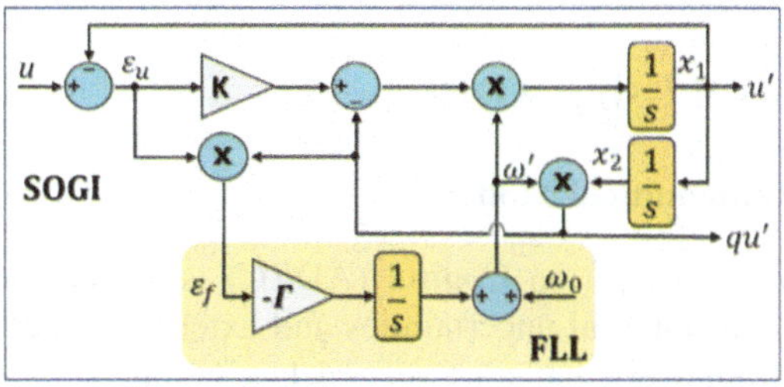

Fig. 4. The SOGI-FLL block diagram.

With, x is the state vector and y is the output vector. The dynamic response of the SOGI-FLL is given by:

$$\dot{\omega'} = -\Gamma x_2 \omega'(u - x_1) \tag{16}$$

The frequency of the positive and negative sequence components is the same for an unbalanced three-phase electrical grid; in this case, the SOGI can only perform filtering and cannot decouple the positive and negative sequence components. Therefore, it is necessary to form a double second-order generalized integrator (DSOGI) [5]. The grid voltage is transformed into v_α and v_β by the Clarke transform. and the orthogonal voltage signals are obtained after SOGI filtering. Finally, a positive/negative sequence calculation (PNSC) method is used to realize the separation. The overall structure of the DSOGI-FLL is shown in Fig. 5.

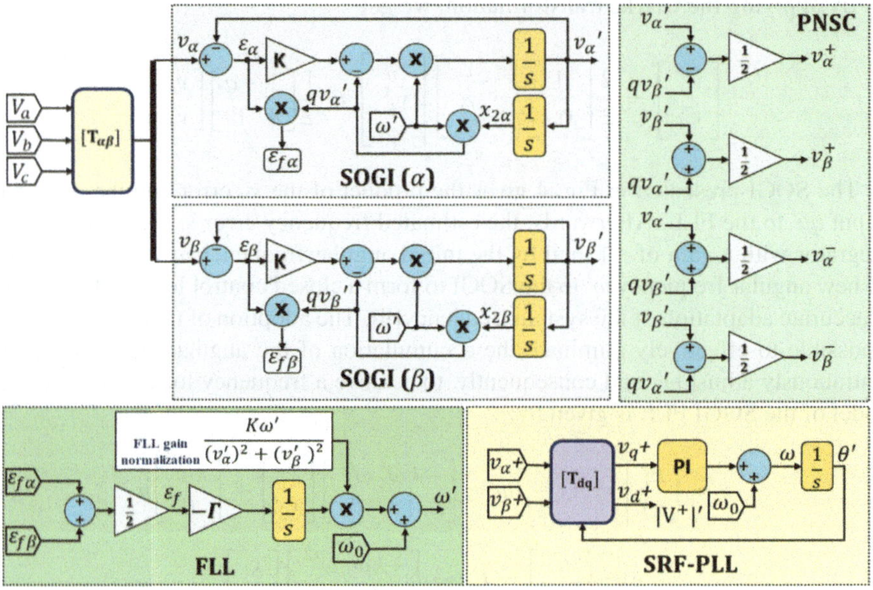

Fig. 5. The DSOGI-FLL block diagram.

3 Inverter Control Using ADRC

3.1 The ADRC Mathematical Model

The Active Disturbance Rejection Control (ADRC) is an advanced control strategy designed to handle both internal uncertainties and external disturbances. As shown in Fig. 6, the ADRC framework includes several key components. The parameter b_0 represents the gain of the controlled system. The Tracking Differential (TD) acts as the tracker to obtain the desired reference response. The extended state observer (ESO) is employed to estimate the generalized disturbance and the systems output, along with its various derivatives. Lastly, the nonlinear state error feedback (NLSEF) utilizes the error and its higher-order derivatives in a nonlinear fashion to achieve optimal control performance [1, 10].

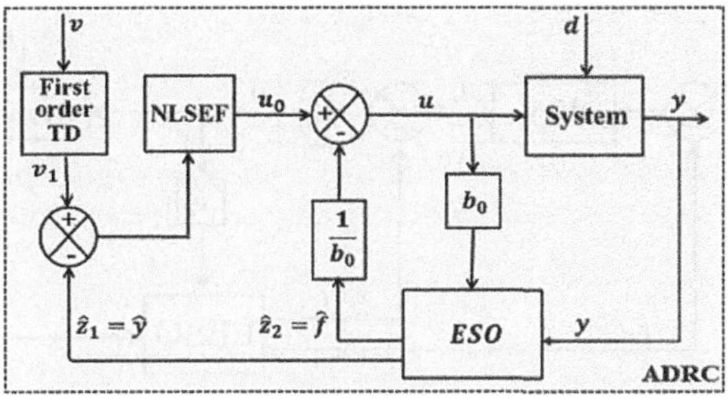

Fig. 6. The ADRC block diagram of first-order.

The Fig. 6 shows the components of the ADRC first-order block. In fact, v: is the input signal of ADRC controller; v_1: is the tracking signal of input signal; z_1: is the tracking signal; z_2: is the total disturbance observation; u_0: is the initial signal of the controlled object by NLSEF; u: is the final control signal after compensating the disturbance; y: is the feedback signal of the system; b_0: is the compensation factor; $\frac{z_0}{b_0}$: is the compensation for internal and external disturbances [2].

The mathematical model of the ADRC first-order is given by: Eq. (17) of TD; Eq. (18) of ESO; Eq. (19) of NLSEF.

$$\begin{cases} e = v_1 - v \\ \frac{dv_1}{dt} = -rfal(e_0, a_0, \delta_0) \end{cases} \tag{17}$$

$$\begin{cases} e_0 = z_1 - y \\ \frac{z_1}{dt} = z_2 - \beta_{01} fal(e, a, \delta) + bu(t) \\ \frac{z_2}{dt} = -\beta_{02} fal(e, a, \delta) \end{cases} \tag{18}$$

$$\begin{cases} e_1 = v_1 - z_1 \\ u_2 = \beta_1 fal(e_1, a_1, \delta_1) \\ u = u_0 - \frac{z_2}{dt} \end{cases} \tag{19}$$

The nonlinear ADRC contains many complex parameters, making it unsuitable for practical implementation. Therefore, efforts are made to minimize the parameters to obtain a Linear ADRC (LADRC), which is more suitable for practical applications.

3.2 Inverter Control by Linear ADRC

In our LARDC, we employ a proportional controller and an ESO. This latter is used to estimate the system states and the generalized disturbance. The uncertainties of our system and the external disturbances are considered as generalized disturbances (Fig. 7).

The ESO is represented by:

$$\begin{cases} \dot{z} = Az + Bu + l(y - \hat{y}) \\ \hat{y} = Cz \end{cases} \tag{20}$$

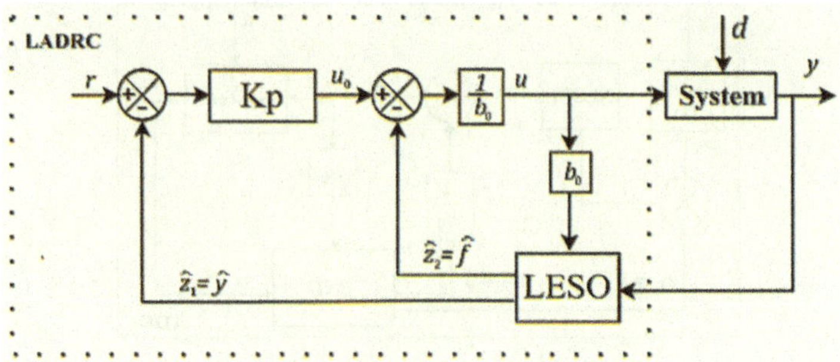

Fig. 7. The LADRC first-order block diagram.

The vector L is defined by:

$$L = \begin{bmatrix} \beta_{01} & \beta_{02} \end{bmatrix}^T = \begin{bmatrix} 2\omega_0 & \omega_0^2 \end{bmatrix}^T \tag{21}$$

The converter control manages the currents flowing through the filter (R_i, L_i) to maintain a constant DC bus voltage, independent of the power exchanged between the converter and the electrical grid. It also regulates the active and reactive power injected into the grid. In this context, voltage-oriented control (VOC) is employed to align the grid voltage along the d-axis.

With: ($v_{dg} = V$ and $v_{qg} = 0$).

In the d-q frame, the model of the grid currents circulating in the filter (R_i, L_i) is expressed by:

$$\begin{cases} \frac{di_{dg}}{dt} = -\frac{R_i}{L_i} i_{dg} - \frac{1}{L_i} v_{dg} - \omega_g i_{qg} - \frac{v_{di}}{L_i} \\ \frac{di_{qg}}{dt} = -\frac{R_i}{L_i} i_{qg} + \frac{1}{L_i} v_{qg} + \omega_g i_{dg} - \frac{v_{qi}}{L_i} \end{cases} \tag{22}$$

With v_{di}, v_{qi} and v_{dg}, v_{qg}, the inverter output voltages and the grid voltages, ω_g is the grid angular frequency. Under conditions of unbalanced grid faults, we can write:

$$\begin{cases} L_i \frac{di_{dqg}{}^+}{dt} = -R_i i_{dqg}{}^+ - \omega_g i_{dqg}{}^+ - v_{dqg}{}^+ - v_{dqi}{}^+ \\ L_i \frac{di_{dqg}{}^-}{dt} = -R_i i_{dqg}{}^- + \omega_g i_{dqg}{}^- - v_{dqg}{}^- - v_{dqi}{}^- \end{cases} \tag{23}$$

By separating the positive and negative sequences, we can rewrite our equation in the canonical form of the ADRC:

$$\frac{d}{dt} \begin{bmatrix} i_{dg}{}^+ \\ i_{qg}{}^+ \\ i_{dg}{}^- \\ i_{qg}{}^- \end{bmatrix} = \begin{bmatrix} f_{dg}{}^+(\cdot) \\ f_{qg}{}^+(\cdot) \\ f_{dg}{}^-(\cdot) \\ f_{qg}{}^-(\cdot) \end{bmatrix} + \begin{bmatrix} b_{0\_dg}{}^+ \\ b_{0\_qg}{}^+ \\ b_{0\_dg}{}^- \\ b_{0\_qg}{}^- \end{bmatrix} \begin{bmatrix} u_{dg}{}^+ \\ u_{qg}{}^+ \\ u_{dg}{}^- \\ u_{qg}{}^- \end{bmatrix} \tag{24}$$

4 Simulation and Results

The control strategies by ADRC and DSOGI-FLL of a PMSG Inverter Connected to Grid in Voltage Dip which were studied previously have been tested in the Matlab/Simulink.

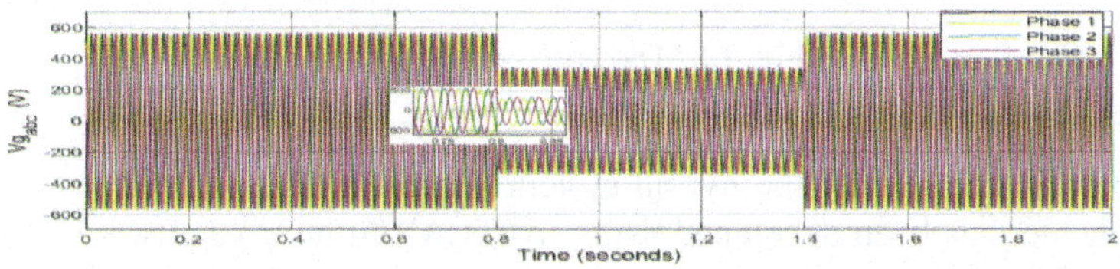

Fig. 8. The grid voltage.

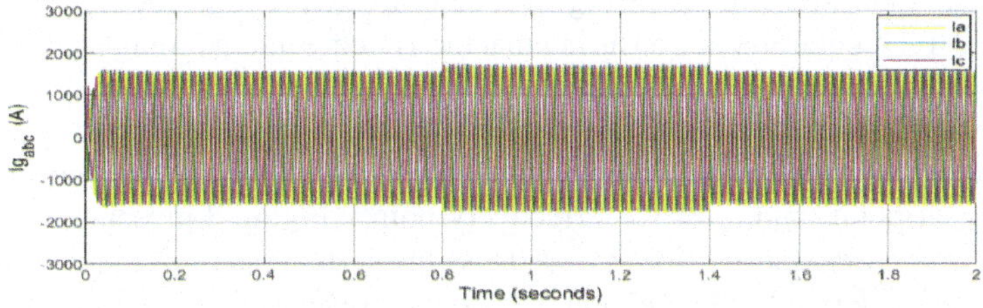

Fig. 9. The grid current.

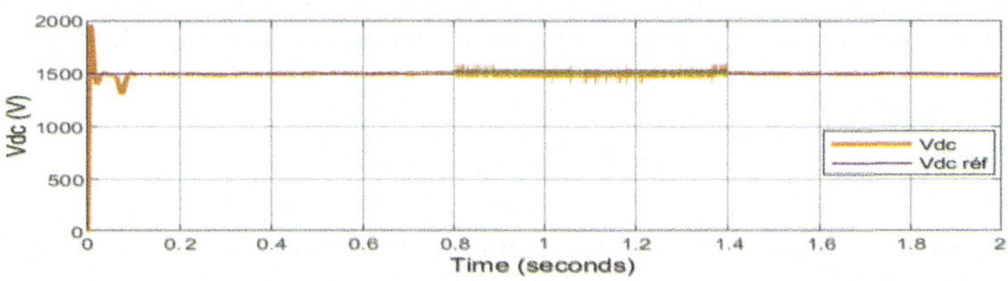

Fig. 10. The DC Bus voltage.

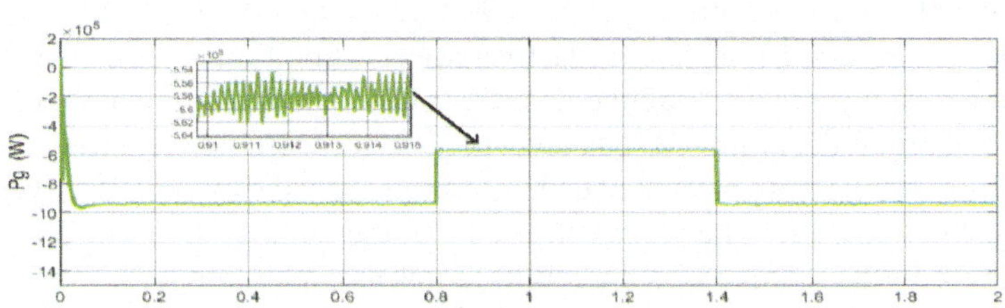

Fig. 11. The grid active power.

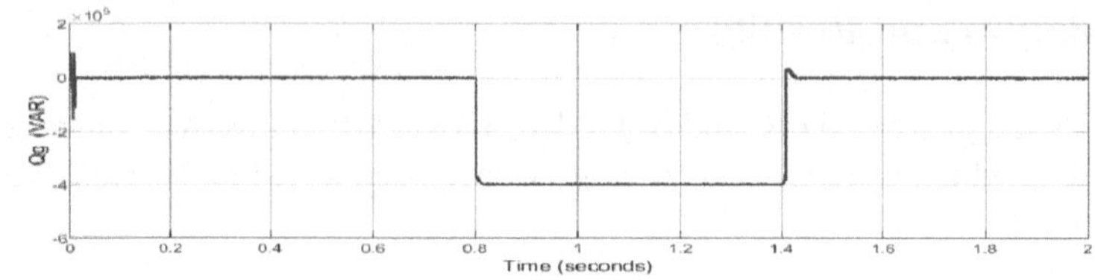

Fig. 12. The grid reactive power.

The complete model of the hybrid system shown in Fig. 4, along with its overall control scheme, has been developed using MATLAB/Simulink software. The primary goal is to validate the proposed control strategies during a voltage dip fault. The system is connected to the medium-voltage (MV) grid through a step-up transformer, with a nominal power of 750 kW. Instantaneous voltage and current values are measured after the coupling filter. The German grid code is applied to meet the Low Voltage Ride Through (LVRT) requirements, ensuring that the system remains connected and supplies the necessary reactive power, as outlined.

To evaluate the effectiveness of the proposed control strategy, simulation tests are conducted for symmetrical voltage dip faults of 40%. The voltage drop occurs between $t_1 = 0.8$ s (set point) and $t_2 = 1.4$ s (recovery point). Figure 8 presents the results for this 40% symmetrical fault. Prior to $t_1 = 0.8$ s , the system operates in maximum power extraction mode. Upon fault detection, the excess power is dissipated in the discharge circuit (Fig. 10), while the system continues to support the grid by injecting the required amount of reactive power (Fig. 11) and limiting active power injection (Fig. 12). This process is achieved by calculating the new apparent power that the inverter can support, and then limiting the currents to their maximum value, as shown in (Fig. 9).

5 Conclusion

In this chapter, we focused on the behavior of the wind system during symmetrical voltage dips and proposed a control strategy based on ADRC-type regulation loops and the DSOGI-FLL technique for positive and negative component extraction. This strategy aims to enhance system performance and ensure its connection to the grid during and after a voltage fault. The control strategy follows the German grid code, which aims to support grid restoration by injecting reactive power while limiting the injected current to the nominal value supported by the inverter. Additionally, a dissipation circuit using resistors is incorporated at the DC bus level to absorb excess power during faults.

Simulation results were presented to demonstrate the validity and effectiveness of the proposed control strategy. The results showed that the wind system was able to remain connected during the voltage dip and return to normal operation within a few hundred milliseconds after the fault was cleared.

References

1. Latifi, M., Ouachtouk, I., Aboudrar, I., Zegrari, M.: A comparative study of the ADRC and PI controller of a wind turbine driven by a PMSG. In: Bendaoud, M., El Fathi, A., Bakhsh, F.I., and Pierluigi, S. (eds.) Advances in Electrical Systems and Innovative Renewable Energy Techniques, pp. 129–137. Springer Nature Switzerland, Cham (2024). https://doi.org/10.1007/978-3-031-49772-8_17
2. Imad, A., El Hani, S., Echchaachouai, A., Energy, A.A.: Robust active disturbance rejection control of a direct driven PMSG wind turbine. In: 2017 International Renewable and Sustainable Energy Conference (IRSEC), pp. 1–6. IEEE, Tangier (2017). https://doi.org/10.1109/IRSEC.2017.8477283
3. Golestan, S., Guerrero, J.M., Vasquez, J.C.: Three-phase PLLs: a review of recent advances. IEEE Trans. Power Electron. **32**, 1894–1907 (2017). https://doi.org/10.1109/TPEL.2016.2565642
4. Jain, A., Saravanakumar, R.: Comparative analysis of DSOGI-PLL& adaptive frequency Loop-PLL for Voltage and Frequency control of PMSG-BESS based Hybrid Standalone WECS. In: 2018 8th International Conference on Power and Energy Systems (ICPES), pp. 234–239. IEEE, Colombo, Sri Lanka (2018). https://doi.org/10.1109/ICPESYS.2018.8626981
5. Aboudrar, I., El Hani, S., Mediouni, H., Naseri, N., Daghouri, A.: LVRT capability enhancement of a grid connected three phase PV system by ADRC and DSOGI FLL. Int. Trans. Electr. Energ. Syst. **31** (2021). https://doi.org/10.1002/2050-7038.13059
6. Elaimani, H., Essadki, A., Elmouhi, N., Chakib, R.: The modified sliding mode control of a doubly fed induction generator for wind energy conversion during a voltage dip. In: 2019 International Conference on Wireless Technologies, Embedded and Intelligent Systems (WITS), pp. 1–6. IEEE, Fez, Morocco (2019). https://doi.org/10.1109/WITS.2019.8723712
7. Tsai, M.-F., Tseng, C.-S., Lin, B.-Y.: Phase voltage-oriented control of a PMSG wind generator for unity power factor correction. Energies **13**, 5693 (2020). https://doi.org/10.3390/en13215693
8. Sreejith, R., Singh, B.: Sensorless predictive current control of PMSM EV drive using DSOGI-FLL based sliding mode observer. IEEE Trans. Ind. Electron. **68**, 5537–5547 (2021). https://doi.org/10.1109/TIE.2020.2996159
9. Wang, Z., et al.: Performance improvement of a three-phase PLL under distorted grid conditions based on frequency adaptive hybrid pre-filtering. IET Power Electron. **15**, 1429–1440 (2022). https://doi.org/10.1049/pel2.12314
10. Oubail, Y., Aboudrar, I., El Hafydy, M., Rachid, E.A.M., Lahoussine, E.: Active disturbance rejection control of an islanded PV/wind/battery microgrid with power quality enhancement by SAPF. IJPEDS **14**, 1660 (2023). https://doi.org/10.11591/ijpeds.v14.i3.pp1660-1674

MPC Control Technique for Machine-Side and Grid-Side Converters in Grid-Connected PMSG Wind Turbines

Adil El Kassoumi[1](✉), Mohamed Lamhamdi[1], Imad Aboudrar[2], Mohammed Fdaili[3], Ahmed Mouhsen[4], and Azeddine Mouhsen[1]

[1] Department of Radiation-Matter and Instrumentation, Faculty of Sciences and Technology Settat, Hassan First University, Settat, Morocco
a.elkassoumi@uhp.ac.ma

[2] Engineering and Sustainable Development Reasearch Team, EST of DakhlaIbn Zohr University, Agadir, Morocco

[3] Research Center in Sciences and Technologies of Engineering and Health, National Higher School of Arts and Crafts Mohammed V University, Rabat, Morocco

[4] Department of Engineering, Industrial Management and Innovation, Faculty of Sciences and Technology Settat, Hassan First University, Settat, Morocco

Abstract. This research suggests a way to control current using finite control set model predictive control (FCS-MPC) for machine-side and grid-side converters (MSC/GSC) in direct-drive permanent magnet synchronous generators (DD-PMSG) that are connected to the grid and use both field-oriented and voltage-oriented controls. By focusing on direct and quadrature components, the FCS-MPC regulates stator and grid currents in the synchronous reference frame, eliminating the need for complex transformation calculations or voltage modulation. This FCS-MPC looks at the discrete states of the voltage-source inverter, guesses how the converter will act in the future, and chooses switching actions that minimize a cost function that has already been set. We simulate the control algorithm in MATLAB/Simulink and present results across different wind speeds to showcase the dynamic performance and efficiency of the proposed control strategy. We analyze and discuss multiple simulation outcomes to validate the accuracy of the developed models and the robustness of the controller design.

Keywords: FCS-MPC · DD-PMSG · MSC/GSC

1 Introduction

Recently, according to the growing challenges due to climate change caused by increased levels of carbon dioxide (CO2) emissions, the transition to more sustainable energy practices has become a worldwide priority [1]. The integration of clean, renewable energy sources, such wind power and solar panels, is emerging as a significant answer to the eventual removal of fossil fuels for power generation [2]. Specifically, wind power plays an important role due to its capacity to exploit the wind's energy to generate electricity

I. Aboudrar et al. (Eds.): ICESST 2024, SUCI, pp. 392–401, 2025.
https://doi.org/10.1007/978-3-031-86705-7_36

cleanly and effectively [3]. Based on the data from the Global Wind Energy Council (GWEC) [4], the installed wind power capacity (WPC) increased by 77.6 GW in 2022. Presently, the global WPC stands at 906 GW, representing a 9% increase compared to the previous year. Morocco, like other nations, has actively adopted the potential of wind energy to diversify its energy strategy and reduce dependence on conventional fossil fuels [5]. Recent statistics from the Ministry of Energy Transition and Sustainable Development show the country has seen an exponential expansion in its wind energy capacity. In November 2023, the REmap investigation announced that Morocco's current installed wind capacity was 2.16 GW, intending to reach 5.8 GW by 2030 [6]. Currently representing almost 18% of the country's total electricity generation capacity, this substantial contribution highlights Morocco's commitment to meeting its renewable energy targets, and is part of its plans to further develop its wind power generation capacity [7].

The wind energy conversion system (WECS) has several distinct structures [8], with fixed-speed wind turbines (FSWTs) being the initial structures utilized for its electrical energy generation [9]. Furthermore, there has been a significant surge in the usage of variable-speed wind turbines (VSWTs) in recent decades [10]. The doubly-fed induction generator (DFIG) and the PMSG are the two major generators in the present wind turbine industry. The use of a reduced-scale back-to-back (BTB) power electronics converter in the DFIG architecture results in a cost reduction of the wind generating system. Still, the shaft speed can only vary by $\pm 30\%$ around the synchronous speed [11]. Moreover, the stator of this DFIG is directly connected to the point of common coupling, often the grid. Hence, the wind-generating system equipped with DFIG is very sensitive to anomalies grid state. The stator terminals in the PMSG topology are connected to the grid through a full-scale BTB power electronics converter. This means that the cost of the BTB converter is more than that of conventional DFIGs. Because of the separation between the generator terminals and grid, the wind-generating system with PMSG provides superior fault ride-through (FRT) capabilities compared to DFIGs. Moreover, the spectrum of shaft speed fluctuations exceeded those of DFIGs. Ultimately, the PMSG is directly connected to the wind turbine, eliminating the need for a gearbox like DFIG [12].

The wind speed varies very frequently, which makes it difficult to extract the maximum power in the wind [13]. Research in academic literature shows that control methods for PMSGs have been progressively improving. From the beginning, the focus was on vector control techniques, namely Field Oriented Control (FOC) and Direct Torque Control (DTC). The methods mentioned above established the foundation for precise regulation of torque and flux, which is for the efficient functioning of PMSGs. Furthermore, PMSGs were increasingly included in grid-connected renewable energy generation, and the research focus gradually shifted. This new direction made reactive power control stand out as important, recognizing its important function in maintaining the grid stable. Recently, many approaches have been used to establish the operating point at an optimal value to maximize the extracted power. First of all, we start with classical control methods, such as proportional-integral (PI) controllers [14]. The PI controller is a linear controller tuned to a specific system's operating point. Indeed, PI controllers are simple to design and apply, but their synthesis depends on system parameters, which restricts their capacity to adapt to changes and perturbations in system parameters.

The main objective of our work is to examine the efficacy of FCS-MPC control applied to MSC and GSC. This method is essential for controlling stator and grid currents in the synchronous reference frame, efficiently managing both the direct and quadrature components. This technology obviates the need for complex transformation calculations and voltage modulation, providing fast dynamic response, reduced harmonics, and improved power quality, making it suitable for renewable energy applications [15].

2 DD-PMSG Wind Turbine System Modeling

As seen in Fig. 1, the wind conversion chain consists of a turbine, a DD-PMSG, and static converters. The system's overall functioning is managed by an FCS-MPC command. We perform the WECS control robustness and performance test in a fluctuating and varying wind profile.

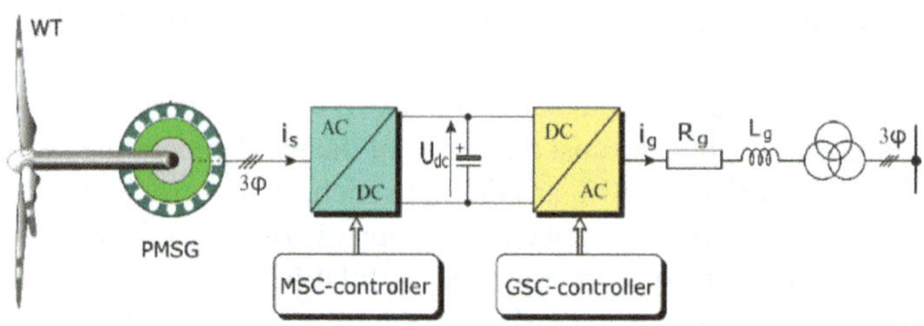

Fig. 1. The architecture of the proposed wind turbine system

2.1 Wind Turbine Model

The mathematical expression that represents the mechanical power obtained by a wind turbine from the wind is [13]:

$$P_{mec} = \frac{1}{2}\rho A V^3 C_p(\lambda, \beta) \tag{1}$$

The variables in the equation are as follows: ρ represents the air density, A represents the swept area of the turbine rotor (calculated as $A = \pi R^2$), V represents the wind speed, $C_p(\lambda, \beta)$ represents the power coefficient, λ represents the tip-speed ratio, and β represents the blade pitch angle.

In this equation, the power coefficient $C_p(\lambda, \beta)$ is a critical parameter that quantifies the effectiveness of the wind turbine in transforming wind energy into mechanical energy. The function is determined by the tip-speed ratio λ, which is precisely specified as:

$$\lambda = \frac{\Omega R}{V} \tag{2}$$

$$C_p(\lambda, \beta) = \frac{1}{2}\left(\frac{116}{\lambda_i} - 0.4\beta - 5\right)e^{\frac{-21}{\lambda_i}} + 0.0068\lambda \tag{3}$$

With: $\frac{1}{\lambda_i} = \frac{1}{\lambda + 0.08\beta} - \frac{0.035}{1+\beta^3}$

Let Ω represent the angular velocity of the rotor and R indicate the radius of the rotor.

2.2 DD-PMSG Model

DD-PMSG is required to convert wind turbine mechanical energy to electricity. This model includes the generator dynamics and electromagnetic equations [6].

The d-q frame stator voltage formulae are:

$$v_{ds} = R_s i_{ds} + \frac{d\psi_{ds}}{dt} - \omega_s \psi_{qs} \tag{4}$$

$$v_{qs} = R_s i_{qs} + \frac{d\psi_{qs}}{dt} - \omega_s \psi_{ds} \tag{5}$$

where:

- v_{ds} and v_{qs} are the d-axis and q-axis components of stator voltage.
- i_{ds} and i_{qs} are the d-axis and q-axis components of stator current.
- ψ_{ds} and ψ_{qs} are the d-axis and q-axis components of stator flux linkage.
- R_s is the stator resistance.
- ω_s is the electrical angular velocity of the stator.

The flux linkage equations are given as:

$$\psi_{ds} = L_d i_{ds} + \psi_f \tag{6}$$

$$\psi_{qs} = L_q i_{qs} \tag{7}$$

where:

L_d and L_q are the d-axis and q-axis inductances of the stator.

ψ_f is the permanent magnet flux linkage.

Using these equations, we can derive the stator current's dynamics. By rearranging the voltage equations and substituting the flux linkage equations, we obtain:

$$\frac{di_{ds}}{dt} = \frac{1}{L_d}\left(v_{ds} - R_s i_{ds} + \omega_s L_{qs} i_{qs}\right) - \frac{\psi_f}{L_d}\omega_s \tag{8}$$

$$\frac{di_{qs}}{dt} = \frac{1}{L_q}\left(v_{qs} - R_s i_{qs} + \omega_s L_{ds} i_{ds}\right) \tag{9}$$

The electromagnetic torque, pivotal for energy conversion, is calculated as:

$$T_{em} = \frac{2}{3}P(\psi_{ds} i_{qs} - \psi_{qs} i_{ds}) \tag{10}$$

The generator's dynamic behavior is described by:

$$J_{gen}\frac{d\Omega}{dt} = T_{mech} - T_{em} - B_{gen}\Omega \tag{11}$$

T_{em} denotes the electromagnetic torque, P denotes the number of pole pairs in the generator, J_{gen} refers to the generator's moment of inertia, T_{mech} indicates the turbine torque, and B_{gen} represents the damping coefficient that accounts for mechanical losses.

2.3 DC Link Modeling

The DC link interconnects the rectifier and the inverter. Here's the specification for the DC link voltage:

$$V_{dc} = \frac{1}{C_{dc}} \int (i_{rd} - i_{id})dt \tag{12}$$

- C_{dc} is the capacitance of the DC link,
- i_{rd} is the rectifier current, and
- i_{id} is the inverter current on the d-axis.

2.4 Grid-Side Converter (Inverter) Model

The inverter transforms DC electricity into AC for grid integration using an RL filter. The grid voltage formulas in the dq frame are as follows:

$$v_{dg} = v_{id} - R_i i_{dg} - L_i \frac{di_{dg}}{dt} + L_i \omega_g i_{qg} \tag{13}$$

$$v_{dg} = v_{iq} - R_i i_{qg} - L_i \frac{di_{qg}}{dt} - L_i \omega_g i_{dg} \tag{14}$$

In this context, v_{id} and v_{iq} represent the d-axis and q-axis components of the inverter voltage, while i_{dg} and i_{qg} denote the d-axis and q-axis components of the inverter current. Furthermore, R_i and L_i represent the filter's resistance and inductance, respectively, while ω_g denotes the grid's electrical angular velocity.

3 Model Predictive Control

3.1 MPC Using Finite Control Set for MSC

The FCS-MPC algorithm uses the discrete DD-PMSG model. This study uses a forward Euler approximation method to make the analysis easier. This method looks at both the current sample (k) and the future sample (k + 1). The steps for this method are given below [16]:

$$\left\{\frac{dx(t)}{dt}\right\}_{t=kT_s} \approx \frac{x(kT_s + T_s) - x(T_s)}{T_s}; x \in \{i_{sd}, i_{sq}\} \tag{15}$$

The equation above may be simplified as follows:

$$x(k+1) \approx x(k) + T_s \left\{\frac{dx(t)}{dt}\right\}_{t=k} \tag{29}$$

Once the necessary discretization process is complete, we can express the discrete-time (DT) model of the DD-PMSG as:

$$\begin{bmatrix} i_{ds}(k+1) \\ i_{qs}(k+1) \end{bmatrix} = \phi(k) \begin{bmatrix} i_{ds}(k) \\ i_{qs}(k) \end{bmatrix} + \Delta_b \begin{bmatrix} v_{ds}(k) \\ v_{qs}(k) \end{bmatrix} + \Delta_{\varpi}(k) \tag{16}$$

With:

$$\begin{cases} \phi(k) \approx [I + A(k)T_s] \approx \begin{bmatrix} 1 - \frac{R_s T_s}{L_{ds}} & \frac{\varpi_e(k) L_{ds} T_{ds}}{L_{qs}} \\ -\frac{\varpi_e(k) L_{ds} T_{ds}}{L_{ds}} & 1 - \frac{R_s T_s}{L_{qs}} \end{bmatrix} \\ \Delta \approx BT_s \approx \begin{bmatrix} \frac{T_s}{L_{ds}} & 0 \\ 0 & \frac{T_s}{L_{qs}} \end{bmatrix} \\ \Delta_{\varpi} \approx \varpi(k) T_s \approx \begin{bmatrix} 0 \\ -\frac{\varpi_e(k) \psi T_s}{L_{qs}} \end{bmatrix} \end{cases} \tag{17}$$

The future states of the DD-PMSG currents are predicted by determining their subsequent values, considering the DT model of the DD-PMSG as described by Eq. (16). As a result, the direct and quadrature (dq) axis currents can be predicted as follows:

$$\begin{bmatrix} i_{ds}^{\alpha}(k+1) \\ i_{qs}^{\alpha}(k+1) \end{bmatrix} = \phi(k) \begin{bmatrix} i_{ds}(k) \\ i_{qs}(k) \end{bmatrix} + \Delta_b \begin{bmatrix} v_{ds}^{\alpha}(k) \\ v_{qs}^{\alpha}(k) \end{bmatrix} + \Delta_{\varpi}(k) \tag{18}$$

where the superscript α signifies the predicted value of the variable.

We derive the forecasted MSC voltages, v_{ds} and v_{qs}, , based on switching states and the DC-link voltage (V_{dc}), using the following model:

$$\begin{bmatrix} v_{ds}^{\alpha}(k) \\ v_{qs}^{\alpha}(k) \end{bmatrix} = V_{dc}(k) \begin{bmatrix} S_{ds}^{\alpha}(k) \\ S_{qs}^{\alpha}(k) \end{bmatrix} \tag{19}$$

The variable $u_c(k)$ denotes the voltage across the capacitor, whereas $S_{s,dq}^{\alpha}(k)$ indicates the switching state along the d/q axis. Here's how we define the formal expression:

$$\begin{bmatrix} S_{ds}^{\alpha}(k) \\ S_{qs}^{\alpha}(k) \end{bmatrix} = \begin{bmatrix} cos\theta_e(k) & sin\theta_e(k) \\ -sin\theta_e(k) & cos\theta_e(k) \end{bmatrix} \frac{2}{3} \begin{bmatrix} 1 & -\frac{1}{2} & -\frac{1}{2} \\ 0 & \frac{\sqrt{3}}{2} & -\frac{\sqrt{3}}{2} \end{bmatrix} \begin{bmatrix} S_{sa}^{\alpha}(k) \\ S_{sb}^{\alpha}(k) \\ S_{sc}^{\alpha}(k) \end{bmatrix} \tag{20}$$

By integrating Eq. (18) into Eq. (19), we get the model for the predicted stator currents:

$$\begin{bmatrix} i_{ds}^{\alpha}(k+1) \\ i_{qs}^{\alpha}(k+1) \end{bmatrix} = \phi(k) \begin{bmatrix} i_{ds}(k) \\ i_{qs}(k) \end{bmatrix} + \Delta_b \left(u_c(k) \begin{bmatrix} S_{ds}^{\alpha}(k) \\ S_{qs}^{\alpha}(k) \end{bmatrix} \right) + \Delta_{\varpi}(k) \tag{21}$$

In contrast, the present references at the (k) sampling instant are extrapolated to the (k + 1) sampling instant using first-order Lagrange extrapolation [17].

$$\begin{cases} \hat{i}_{ds}^{*}(k+1) = 2i_{ds}^{*}(k) - i_{ds}^{*}(k-1) \\ \hat{i}_{qs}^{*}(k+1) = 2i_{qs}^{*}(k) - i_{qs}^{*}(k-1) \end{cases} \tag{22}$$

In this context, $\hat{i}_{sd}^{*}$ indicates the extrapolated reference currents, whereas $\hat{i}_{sq}^{*}$ represents the generator's reference currents. To maintain a unity power factor under all operational situations, the direct current i_{sd}^{*} is established at zero. Simultaneously, i_{sq}^{*} is ascertained using MPPT control.

To minimize the variance between the predicted and extrapolated reference currents, the following cost function is used:

$$J_{MSC}(k) = \left[\hat{i}_{ds}^{*}(k+1) - i_{ds}^{\alpha}(k+1)\right]^2 - \left[\hat{i}_{qs}^{*}(k+1) - i_{qs}^{\alpha}(k+1)\right]^2 \quad (23)$$

3.2 MPC Using Finite Control Set for GSC

The GSC cost function may be constructed using the same method as the MSC predictive controller:

$$J_{GSC}(k) = \left[\hat{i}_{dg}^{*}(k+1) - i_{dg}^{\alpha}(k+1)\right]^2 - \left[\hat{i}_{qg}^{*}(k+1) - i_{qg}^{\alpha}(k+1)\right]^2 \quad (24)$$

The FCS-MPC architecture for the DD-PMSG WECS is shown in Fig. 2.

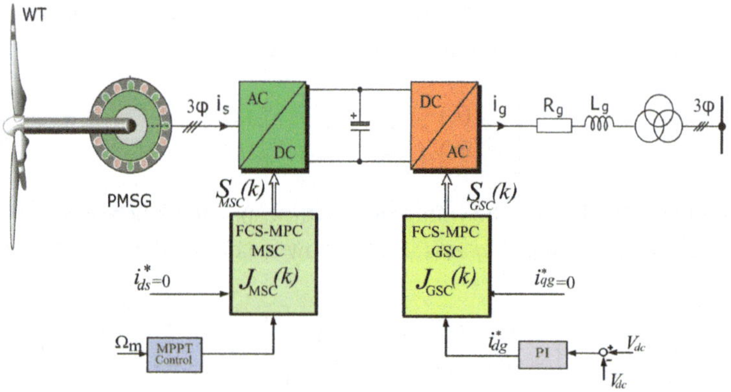

Fig. 2. Overview diagram of MPC implementation in the PMSG WECS

4 Results and Discussion

To demonstrate the effectiveness of the proposed method, simulations have been performed for a 1.5-MW DD-PMSG-based wind turbine system connected to the electrical grid in the MATLAB/Simulink R2019a environment. The simulation's objective is to evaluate the efficacy of the suggested method; hence, a wind profile exhibiting varying speeds ranging from 8.57 to 12.15 m/s, with an average of 10.36 m/s, is delivered to the turbine blades, as seen in Fig. 3.

Figures 4(a) and 4(b) illustrate the turbine speed and electromagnetic torque, respectively. As seen by these figures, the FCS-MPC controller demonstrates superior accuracy in tracking the references. The FCS-MPC controller extracts more power.

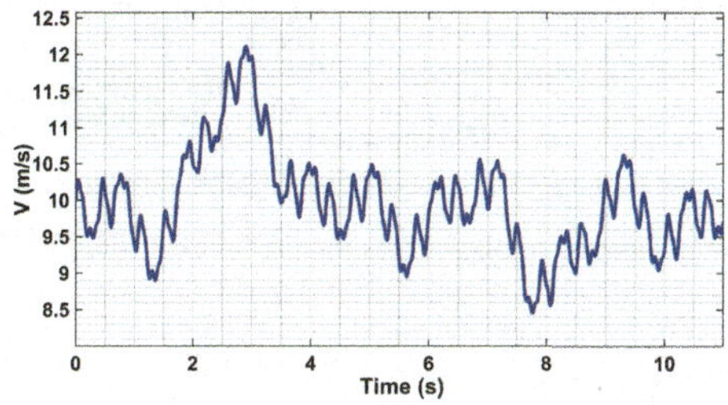

Fig. 3. Wind profile

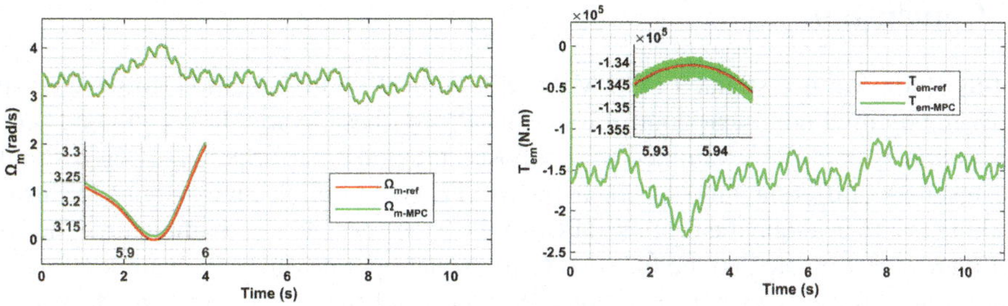

Fig. 4. Mechanical speed (a) and Electromagnetic torque (b)

The quadrature stator current (Fig. 5(b)) correlates with the electromagnetic torque, however, the direct current i_{sd} (Fig. 5(a)) fluctuates about zero and regulates the stator's reactive power.

The direct (i_{gd}) and quadrature (i_{gq}) grid current components are shown for tracing their references in Fig. 6(a) and Fig. 6(b), respectively. These figures demonstrate that the FCS-MPC control strategy provides superior monitoring and high dynamic and steady-state performance.

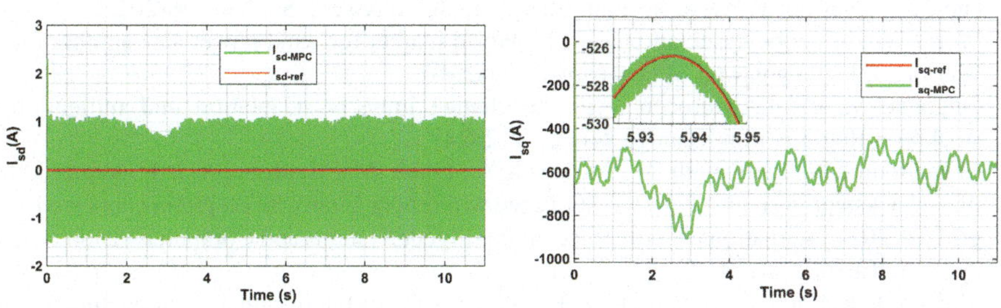

Fig. 5. (a) Machine-side direct current and (b) Machine-side quadrature current

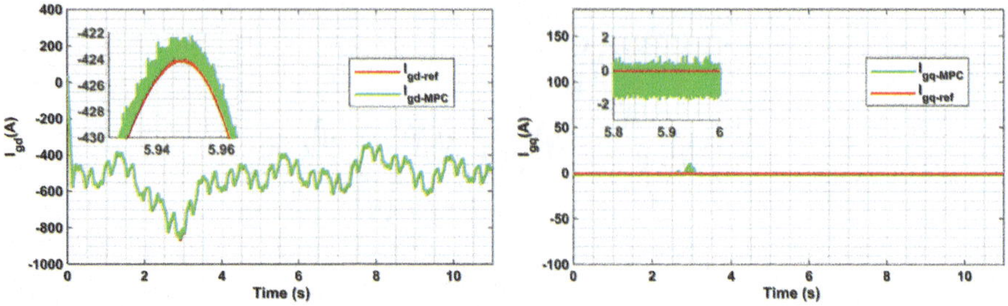

Fig. 6. (a) Grid-side direct current (b) Grid-side quadrature current

5 Conclusion

In this study, we investigated FCS-MPC, a nonlinear control method, to develop and apply the optimal nonlinear control for a DD-PMSG-based variable-speed wind power conversion system. We examined the proposed method's performance using a simulation test under different wind speeds in the MATLAB/Simulink environment. We used a tracking test to evaluate the proposed FCS-MPC's performance and efficiency. The simulation results indicate that the FCS-MPC controller operates effectively under transient conditions, especially MPPT operations. If wind speed changes, the FCS-MPC can approach the MPPT quickly with little overshoot. According to this research, FCS-predictive control is an effective method for regulating DD-PMSG-based WECS.

References

1. Singh, S.: Energy crisis and climate change: Global concerns and their solutions. Energy Crises Challenges Solut. 1–17 (2021)
2. Hoang, A.T., Nguyen, X.P.: Integrating renewable sources into energy system for smart city as a sagacious strategy towards clean and sustainable process. J. Clean. Prod. **305**, 127161 (2021)
3. Roga, S., Bardhan, S., Kumar, Y., Dubey, S.K.: Recent technology and challenges of wind energy generation: a review. Sustain. Energy Technol. Assess. **52**, 102239 (2022)
4. World Wind Energy Association. (2021). World market for wind power saw another record year in 2021 - 93 gigawatt of new capacity added
5. Ongoma, V., et al.: Morocco's climate change impacts, adaptation and mitigation—a stocktake. Reg. Environ. Change **24**(1), 14 (2024)
6. El Kassoumi, A., Lamhamdi, M., Mouhsen, A., Fdaili, M., Mouhsen, A., Aboudrar, I.: Nonlinear backstepping control of a PMSG-based wind energy conversion system connected to the grid. In: 2024 International Conference on Intelligent Systems and Computer Vision (ISCV), pp. 1–6. IEEE (2024, May)
7. Slimani, J., Kadrani, A., El Harraki, I., Ezzahid, E.: Towards a sustainable energy future: modeling Morocco's transition to renewable power with enhanced OSeMOSYS model. Energy Convers. Manag. **317**, 118857 (2024)
8. Alkul, O., Syed, D., Demirbas, S.: A review of wind energy conversion systems. In: 2022 10th International Conference on Smart Grid (icSmartGrid), pp. 72–77. IEEE (2022, June)
9. Apata, O., Oyedokun, D.T.O.: Improving the dynamic performance of grid connected fixed speed wind farm using variable speed wind turbines. In: 2020 IEEE PES/IAS PowerAfrica, pp. 1–5. IEEE, August 2020

10. Song, D., et al.: New perspectives on maximum wind energy extraction of variable-speed wind turbines using previewed wind speeds. Energy Convers. Manag. **206**, 112496 (2020)
11. Okedu, K.E., Al Tobi, M., Al Araimi, S.: Comparative study of the effects of machine parameters on DFIG and PMSG variable speed wind turbines during grid fault. Front. Energy Res. **9**, 681443 (2021)
12. Aboudrar, I., El Hani, S., Mediouni, H., Aghmadi, A.: Modeling and robust control of a grid connected direct driven PMSG wind turbine by ADRC. Adv. Electr. Electron. Eng. **16**(4), 402–413 (2018)
13. El Kassoumi, A., Lamhamdi, M., Mouhsen, A., Mouhsen, A.: Maximum power generation and pitch angle control of a PMSG-based WECS connected to the grid. In: International Conference on Digital Technologies and Applications, pp. 696–705. Springer International Publishing, Cham (2022, January)
14. Fdaili, M., Essadki, A., Nasser, T.: Comparative analysis between robust SMC & conventional PI controllers used in WECS based on DFIG. Int. J. Renew. Energy Res. (IJRER) **7**(4), 2151–2161 (2017)
15. Cai, Y., Yan, S., Cui, Y., Gao, X.: Single-loop control method FCS-MPC for PMSG. IEICE Electron. Express **20**(1), 20220500 (2023)
16. Nouraldin, N.A., Chebaani, M., Számel, L., Abdelwahab, S.A.M., Abdellatif, W.S.: Experimental investigation of predictive control for PMSM-based wind turbine generation system. Comput. Electr. Eng. **119**, 109554 (2024)
17. Huang, Z., Wei, Q., Tao, H., Wu, T., Xia, Y., & Rivera, M. (2024). A Cost Function-Free Modulated Model Predictive Control Technique for PMSM by the Geometric Derivations. IEEE Journal of Emerging and Selected Topics in Power Electronics

Design of Backstepping Control for the Optimization of VSC Inverters and PWM Rectifiers in HVDC Systems

Youssef Elmoudni(✉), Radouane Majdoul, and Abdelwahed Touati

Laboratory of Complex Cyber Physical Systems, Hassan II University Casablanca, Casablanca, Morocco
elmoudniyoussef1@gmail.com

Abstract. This paper introduces a novel design approach for a backstepping control strategy specifically aimed at optimizing the performance of Voltage Source Converters (VSC) and Pulse Width Modulation (PWM) rectifiers. The backstepping technique is meticulously employed to develop a nonlinear controller capable of ensuring system stability and significantly enhancing tracking performance, even under dynamically changing operational conditions. This advanced design framework directly addresses critical challenges, such as system uncertainties and external disturbances, which are common in practical implementations. By providing a robust and adaptable solution, the control strategy effectively manages both VSC inverters and PWM rectifiers, ensuring consistent performance and reliability. The proposed method is rigorously validated through comprehensive simulations, which demonstrate its remarkable capability in achieving optimized voltage and current regulation. Additionally, the results highlight its superiority over traditional control methods in terms of robustness, system resilience, and overall efficiency, making it an indispensable tool for modern power electronics applications.

Keywords: backstepping · inverters · rectifiers · Nonlinear control · Lyapunov

1 Introduction

Voltage source converters (VSC) and pulse width modulation (PWM) rectifiers are indispensable components of modern power systems, and these technologies, especially high voltage direct current (HVDC) transmission, are recognized for their ability to convert power and the good protection it takes. However, their nonlinear dynamics and sensitivity to external disturbances present significant challenges for conventional control methods. Traditional proportional integral derivative (PID) controllers generally lack the robustness necessary to maintain stability and efficiency under operating conditions [1].

To overcome these limitations, this paper introduces a new backstepping control strategy specifically designed for VSC inverters and PWM rectifiers. Backstep-ping method based on nonlinear control theory for design improves system stability and performance Using Lyapunov stability theory, the proposed method is robust against

I. Aboudrar et al. (Eds.): ICESST 2024, SUCI, pp. 402–409, 2025.
https://doi.org/10.1007/978-3-031-86705-7_37

parameter uncertainty and reduces external disturbances so, making it well suited for use in HVDC systems [2].

The main contributions of this work are as follows:

- Development of a Robust Backstepping Control Strategy: A tailored approach is proposed to address the nonlinear dynamics of VSC inverters and PWM rectifiers, ensuring enhanced robustness and adaptability.
- Stability Analysis Using Lyapunov Theory: The stability of the system is rigorously analyzed to validate the effectiveness of the proposed control design.
- Comprehensive Simulation-Based Validation: Detailed simulations carried out in MATLAB/Simulink are used to demonstrate the effectiveness of the proposed approach. The results provide strong evidence of the method's ability to enhance tracking accuracy, robustness, and dynamic response.
- Application in HVDC Systems: The proposed control strategy is evaluated within the context of HVDC systems, showcasing its capacity to handle complex operational scenarios and meet the requirements of high-power applications [3, 4].

The validation of the proposed method is based on simulation results, which are sufficient to prove the feasibility and efficiency in achieving the desired control objectives MATLAB/Simulink for accurate and reliable conditions so that they can be used to model and evaluate the performance of the control strategy under different operating conditions. These simulations have been carefully designed to reproduce realistic conditions, enabling in-depth investigations of the dynamic response and stability of the system [5].

Research on the control of voltage source converters (VSCs) and PWM rectifiers in HVDC systems has been greatly enhanced by the work of Majdoul[1] [1], who compared backstepping, sliding mode, and PID controllers for voltage inverters Efficiency is demonstrated.

2 Dynamic Models for VSC Inverters and PWM Rectifiers

2.1 Dynamic Models for VSC Rectifier

Dynamic models for Voltage Source Converters (VSC) rectifier enable the simulation and analysis of their performance in real-time. These models help predict system behavior under various operating conditions, aiding in the optimization of control strategies, stability assessments, and enhancing efficiency for power electronics applications [6] (Fig. 1).

This section presents the modeling of the PWM rectifier in the dq reference frame. It outlines the dynamic equations governing its behavior, leveraging the Park transformation to simplify the analysis and optimize system control within the context of vector regulation.

$$u_s = Ri_s + L\frac{di_s}{dt} + u_i \tag{1}$$

$$u_{sd} = Ri_{sd} + L\frac{di_{sd}}{dt} - \omega Li_{sq} + u_{id} \tag{2}$$

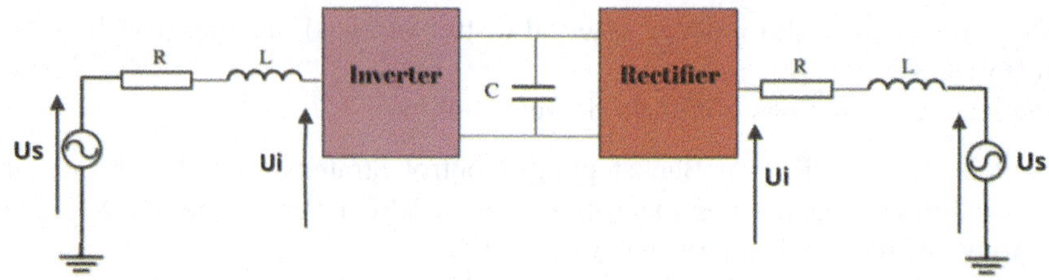

Fig. 1. Proposed VSC-based HVDC transmission system

$$u_{sq} = Ri_{sq} + L\frac{di_{sq}}{dt} + \omega Li_{sd} + u_{iq}$$

$$L\frac{di_{sd}}{dt} = -Ri_{sd} + \omega Li_{sq} + u_{sd} - u_{id} \tag{3}$$

$$L\frac{di_{sq}}{dt} = -Ri_{sq} - \omega Li_{sd} + u_{sq} - u_{iq}$$

By having the phase-locked loop regulate the q-component of the grid voltage u_{sq} to zero in steady-state conditions, the calculation of active and reactive power can be simplified

$$P = \frac{3}{2}u_{sd}.i_{sd} \tag{4}$$

$$Q = \frac{3}{2}u_{sd}.i_{sq}$$

$$C\frac{dV_{DC}}{dt} = \frac{3u_{sd}}{2V_{DC}}i_{sd} - i_L \tag{5}$$

In the design, we define the state variable by $x = [V_{DC}, i_{sd1}, i_{sq1}, i_{sd2}, i_{sq2}]^T$

$$\dot{x}_1 = \frac{3}{2C}\frac{x_2}{x_1}u_{sd} - \frac{i_L}{C} \tag{6}$$

$$L\dot{x}_2 = -Rx_2 + \omega Lx_3 + u_{sd} - u_{id}$$

$$L\dot{x}_3 = -Rx_3 - \omega Lx_2 + u_{sq} - u_{iq}$$

The expression of the error for each state is given by the following equations.

$$z_1 = x_1{}^{réf} - x_1$$

$$z_2 = x_2{}^{réf} - x_2 \tag{7}$$

$$z_3 = x_3{}^{réf} - x_3$$

We derive the expression for the error

$$\dot{z}_1 = \dot{x}_1^{réf} - \dot{x}_1$$

$$\dot{z}_1 = \dot{x}_1^{réf} - \frac{3}{2C}\frac{x_2}{x_1}u_{sd} + \frac{i_L}{C}$$

Lyapunov Method

The Lyapunov function is a mathematical tool used to analyze the stability of a nonlinear dynamic system. Its principle is based on the idea of associating a scalar to each state of the system, which acts as a measure of the energy or the distance of the current state relative to an equilibrium state [7, 8].

$$V(x) = \frac{1}{2}C{z_1}^2$$

The Lyapunov function V(x) represents the dissipation of energy within the capacitor.

$$\dot{V}(x) = Cz_1(\dot{x}_1^{réf} - \frac{3}{2C}\frac{x_2}{x_1}u_{sd} + \frac{i_L}{C})$$

$$\dot{V}(x) = Cz_1(\dot{x}_1^{réf} - \frac{3u_{sd}}{2C}\frac{x_2^{réf}}{x_1} + \frac{i_L}{C}) + \frac{3u_{sd}}{2}\frac{1}{x_1}z_1z_2$$

$$ {x_2}^{réf} = \frac{2Cx_1}{3u_{sd}}\left(\dot{x}_1^{réf} + \frac{i_L}{C} + k_1z_1\right) \tag{8}$$

$$\dot{V}(x) = -Ck_1{z_1}^2$$

The Lyapunov function's derivative is negative when k_1 is positive, indicating system stability under this condition, crucial for stability analysis in control systems

$$\dot{z}_2 = \dot{x}_2^{réf} + \frac{R}{L}x_2 - \omega x_3 - \frac{u_{sd} - u_{id}}{L}$$

$$\dot{z}_3 = \dot{x}_3^{réf} + \frac{R}{L}x_3 + \omega x_2 - \frac{u_{sq} - u_{iq}}{L} \tag{9}$$

$$V(z) = \frac{1}{2}C{z_1}^2 + \frac{1}{2}L{z_2}^2 + \frac{1}{2}L{z_3}^2$$

$$V(z) = -k_1Cz_1^2 + V(z_2, z_3)$$

where:

$$u_d = \frac{u_{sd} - u_{id}}{L} \tag{10}$$

$$u_q = \frac{u_{sq} - u_{iq}}{L}$$

$V(z_2, z_3) = Lz_2(\dot{x}_2^{réf} + \frac{R}{L}x_2 - \omega x_3 - \frac{u_d}{L}) + Lz_3(\dot{x}_3^{réf} + \frac{R}{L}x_3 + \omega x_2 - \frac{u_q}{L})$.
The control equations for the inverter are thus determined.

$$u_{d1} = L(\dot{x}_2^{réf} + \frac{3u_{sd}}{2L}\frac{z_1}{x_1} + \frac{R}{L}x_2 - \omega x_3 + k_2 z_2) \tag{11}$$

$$u_{q1} = L(\dot{x}_3^{réf} + \frac{R}{L}x_3 + \omega x_2 + k_3 z_3)$$

2.2 Dynamic Models for VSC Inverters Station

Similarly, by following the same steps used for the rectifier, it is possible to derive the control equations for the inverter, ensuring consistent system performance and eration.

$$\begin{aligned} u_{d2} &= L\left(\dot{x}_4^{réf} + \frac{R}{L}x_4 - \omega x_5 + k_2 z_4\right) \\ u_{q2} &= L\left(\dot{x}_5^{réf} + \frac{R}{L}x_5 + \omega x_4 + k_3 z_5\right) \end{aligned} \tag{22}$$

3 Simulation Results

The system parameters used for the simulation and hardware implementation are presented in Table 1. The simulations are carried out using MATLAB/Simulink software. A detailed model of the entire system is implemented using the SimPowerSystems library blocks. All simulations are performed with a fixed time step to ensure consistency with practical experiments.

This table presents the values used in the simulation of the pulse-width modulation (PWM) rectifier.

Table 1. Simulation parameters.

Parameters	Example	Numerical values
Vdc	Voltage DC bus	12000
K1	voltage gain	1000
K2	i_{sd1} current gain	300
K3	i_{sq1} current gain	700
K4	i_{sd2} current gain	350
K5	i_{sq2} current gain	850

The results presented in Fig. 2 offer a comprehensive insight into the control performance of the system.

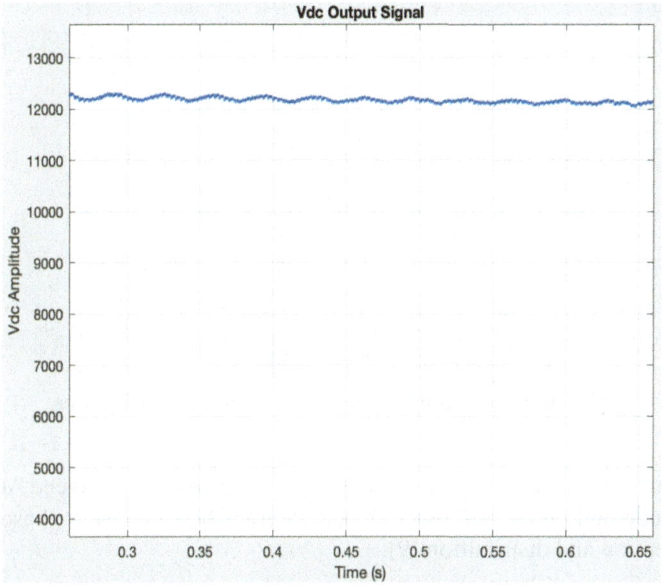

Fig. 2. Chronogram of the output voltage on the DC bus for a reference voltage at 12kV.

The V_{dc} output signal shows a relatively stable DC bus voltage around 12,000 V, with minor fluctuations. This stability in the DC bus voltage is critical for the reliable operation of the inverter and ensures consistent power delivery. The small ripple observed is typical in power electronic systems and is likely due to switching effects within the converter. The limited amplitude of this ripple indicates effective control and filtering, ensuring that the DC voltage remains within an acceptable range for the system's requirements. Overall, this waveform suggests that the DC bus voltage is well-regulated, supporting a stable and efficient power conversion process (Fig. 3).

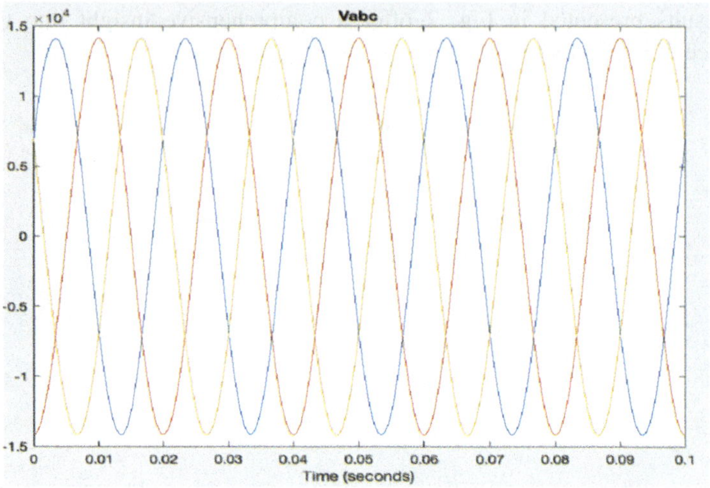

Fig. 3. Chronogram of the output voltage on the inverter

The output of the inverter is a three-phase voltage, providing balanced AC power with equal amplitude and phase difference of 120 degrees between each phase for efficient energy conversion and distribution.[9].

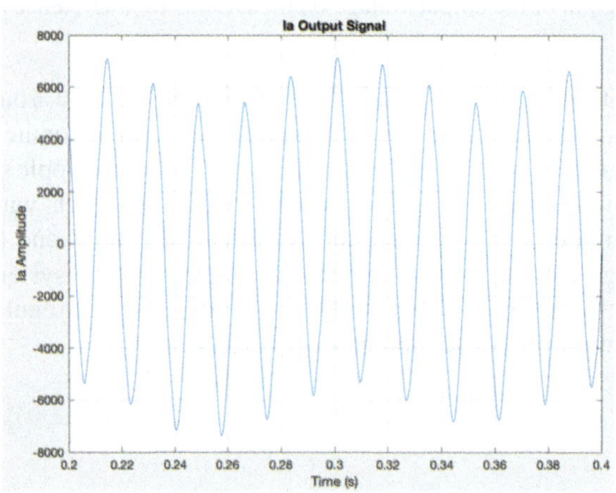

Fig. 4. Chronogram of the output current on the inverter

Figure 4 shows the inverter's output current waveform, displaying a stable sinusoidal shape with an amplitude of ±7000. This stability and symmetry highlight efficient AC conversion, making it suitable for applications that demand consistent frequency and reliable power delivery.

4 Conclusion

This study presents an example and design of a backstepping control strategy for VSC inverters and PWM rectifiers in HVDC systems. The proposed method improves the stability of the system and ensures accurate tracking of wanted features. Through extensive simulations, the control strategy demonstrated its ability to improve performance, improve response agility, and reduce disruption. The results confirm that backstepping control provides a robust solution for VSC inverter and PWM rectifier optimization, making it a promising strategy for future applications in high voltage direct current (HVDC) systems These findings helps improve power electronics and system reliability.

References

1. Majdoul, R.: Comparison of backstepping, sliding mode and PID regulators for a voltage inverter. Int. J. Electr. Comput. Eng. (IJECE) 166–178 (2022)
2. Kazi, M.: Modeling and design of an adaptive control for VSC-HVDC system under parameters uncertainties. Int. J. Power Electron. Drive Syst. (IJPEDS) 1566–1575 (2021)
3. Yang, F., Xu, Z., Zhang, J.: An approach to select PI parameters of HVDC controllers. In:2006 IEEE Power Engineering Society General Meeting, 2006
4. Mishra, A.: Performance assessment of VSC-based HVDC system in asynchronous grid interconnection: offline and real-time validation of control design with symmetric optimum PI tuning (2024)
5. Majdoul, R.: Backstepping controller of five-level three-phase inverter. In: MATEC Web of Conferences, vol. 16, p. 06003 (2014)
6. Hamache, A., Bensidhoum, M.O., Chekireb, H.: Adaptive sliding mode with time delay control based on convolutions for power flow reference tracking using a VSC-HVDC system. Turk. J. Electr. Eng. Comput. Sci. **25**, 2149–2162 (2017)
7. Ghandhari, M., Andersson, G., Hiskens, I.A.: Control Lyapunov functions for controllable series devices. IEEE Trans. Power Syst. **16**(4) (2001)
8. Beheshti, N., Rezanejad, M., Mehrasa, M.: Linearized control technique with lyapunov functionbased compensators for MMC-based HVDC system under load variation and fault condition. Int. J. Electr. Power Energy Syst. **124**, 106333 (2021)
9. Sunbul, A., Sood ,V.: Simplified SVPWM method for the vienna rectifier, pp. 1–8, 2019. https://doi.org/10.1109/COMPEL.2019.8769689

Robust High-Order Super-Twisting Sliding Mode Control for DC-DC Step-Up Converters Under Time-Varying Disturbances

Sanae El Bouassi(✉), Zakaria Chalh, El Mehdi Mellouli, and Abdelmjid Saka

Laboratory of Engineering, System and Application, School of Applied Sciences, Sidi Mohamed Ben Abdellah University, Fez, Morocco
{sanae.elbouassi,zakaria.chalh,abdelmjid.saka}@usmba.ac.ma

Abstract. This paper presents a robust control technique for DC-DC boost converters used in photovoltaic (solar) systems, particularly under conditions of time-varying disturbances. The proposed solution employs high-order super-twisting sliding mode control (HOSM), which is designed to improve system performance by reducing steady-state fluctuations and dynamically adjusting controller gains in response to changing solar irradiance. This significantly improves the converter's ability to handle variations in solar input, ensuring more stable and efficient operation. Compared to traditional proportional-integral (PI) control, the HOSM technique shows superior robustness to uncertainties and disturbances, making it well suited to the variable nature of solar power generation. Extensive simulation results confirm the effectiveness of this control approach and highlight its potential for optimising the stability and efficiency of isolated flyback converters in photovoltaic systems. This technique offers a promising way to improve the reliability and performance of renewable energy systems, ensuring more consistent energy harvesting.

Keywords: Maximum power point tracking (MPPT) · High order sliding mode control · perturb and observe (P&O) · photovoltaic system · Supertwisting algorithm

1 Introduction

Photovoltaic (PV) power has become a key renewable energy source due to its environmental benefits, such as cleanliness and sustainability. To maximize energy harvesting under varying environmental conditions, effective control mechanisms, particularly Maximum Power Point Tracking (MPPT), are essential [1, 2].

Traditional MPPT methods, such as Incremental Conductance (INC) and Perturb and Observe (P&O), are widely used due to their simplicity. However, their performance suffers during rapidly changing conditions, leading to oscillations around the maximum power point (MPP) during steady-state operation. Advanced artificial intelligence (AI)-based techniques have been developed to address these limitations, providing enhanced accuracy and stability at the cost of increased complexity. These techniques include fuzzy

I. Aboudrar et al. (Eds.): ICESST 2024, SUCI, pp. 410–416, 2025.
https://doi.org/10.1007/978-3-031-86705-7_38

logic, genetic algorithms (GA), neural networks, particle swarm optimization (PSO), and grey wolf optimization (GWO) [3, 4].

Voltage-Oriented MPPT (VO-MPPT) offers a fast and efficient solution for voltage control in photovoltaic systems. However, its success relies on robust control strategies. Conventional proportional-integral (PI) controllers, while simple, often exhibit slow response times, overshoot, and steady-state inaccuracies. Sliding mode control (SMC) has gained attention as a promising alternative, offering improved MPP tracking. However, first-order sliding mode control is prone to issues such as chattering and fluctuating switching frequencies, limiting its practicality.

High-order sliding mode control (HOSM) has emerged as a superior alternative for enhancing the performance and stability of nonlinear systems, including photovoltaic systems and power converters. By employing higher-order sliding surfaces, HOSM techniques, such as the super-twisting algorithm, effectively mitigate chattering and improve robustness against disturbances. This refined control approach ensures faster dynamic response, reduced steady-state error, and greater system resilience, making it particularly suitable for applications like PV systems [5, 6, 7].

This paper proposes a comprehensive approach combining HOSM control with a flyback converter to overcome the limitations of conventional methods. The novelty lies in leveraging the advanced capabilities of HOSM to achieve superior performance compared to both PI and first-order SMC techniques. Quantitative improvements, including reduced steady-state error, enhanced tracking efficiency, and faster response times, are presented.

The structure of this paper is as follows: Sect. 2 details the modeling of the flyback converter. Section 3 discusses the design of HOSM and PI controllers. Section 4 presents simulation results, highlights the optimized performance of the HOSM controller, and concludes with key insights and recommendations.

2 Configuration of the System

One of the most essential components of a photovoltaic (PV) system is the DC-DC boost converter. Its primary function is to enhance the voltage generated by PV panels and supply power to various systems, including DC buses, DC loads, or battery energy storage systems (BESS). The MPPT approach is employed to direct the converter to achieve the necessary MPPT technology in constant environmental conditions. Figures 1 and 2 illustrate the booster's circuit [8].

The fundamental component in the process of turning sunlight into direct electrical energy is the photovoltaic cell. A PV panel is made up of several PV cells connected in parallel or series, and it is represented by the equation that follows:

$$i_{pv} = N_p i_{ph} - N_p i_0 \left[\exp\left(\frac{N_s v_{pv} + \frac{N_s}{N_p} R_{spv} i_{pv}}{a.N_s V_t} \right) - 1 \right] - \frac{N_s V_{pv} + \frac{N_s}{N_p} R_{spv} * i_{pv}}{\frac{N_s}{N_p} * R_{shpv}} \tag{1}$$

where i_{ph} is the photocurrent, i_0 is the reverse saturation or leakage current of the diode. R_{spv} and R_{shpv} are respectively the series and parallel resistances of the PV cell. V_t is the

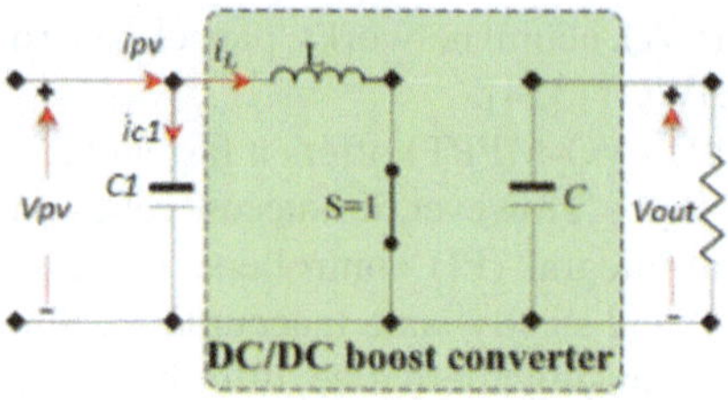

Fig. 1. Model of the state-based boost converter circuit

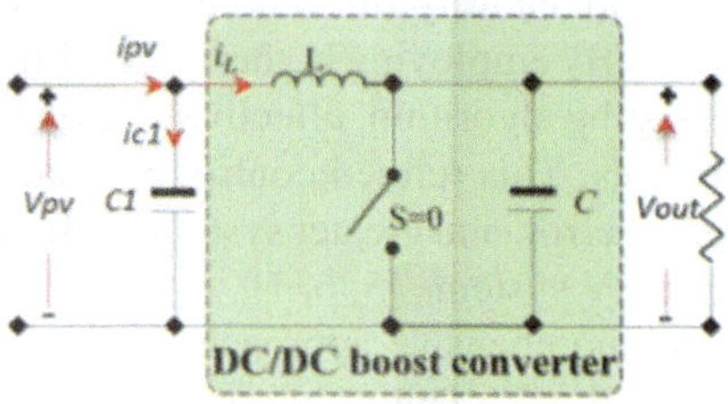

Fig. 2. Boost converter circuit off-state model

thermal voltage of the PV module. And a is the diode ideality factor. N_s and N_p are the numbers of PV cells in series and in parallel respectively [9].

The functionality of Switch S is crucial as it guides the load through the DC/DC boost converter, which simultaneously tracks the maximum power point of the PV panels. The transformer is in charge of resetting the magnetic core and charging the output capacitor before giving power to the load; the diode turns ON when the voltage produced on the primary side of the transformer is reversed by turning OFF the MOSFET switch. By applying the averaging method as described in [10], the boost converter's dynamic model, which is represented by the duty cycle "D," may be expressed.

$$\begin{cases} \dot{v}_{pv} = \frac{1}{c_1}\left(\frac{v_{pv}}{r_{pv}} - i_L\right) \\ \dot{i}_L = \frac{1}{L}\left(v_{pv} - v_{out} + v_{out} * D\right) \end{cases} \tag{2}$$

3 Suggestioned MPPT Control

The proposed control strategy centers on a voltage loop and is divided into two separate loops, as depicted in Fig. 3. The primary loop employs a VMPPT controller based on P&O methodology to generate the reference voltage, identified as "Vref". This reference voltage plays a pivotal role in optimizing the operational efficiency of the PV generator (GPV) [11]. Addressing sudden variations in solar radiation, the second loop introduces an upgraded HOSMC controller. This controller is explicitly crafted to compute the duty ratio (D) and ensure the PV voltage ("v_{pv}") closely aligns with the generated Vref, thereby facilitating effective tracking of the maximum power point (MPP).

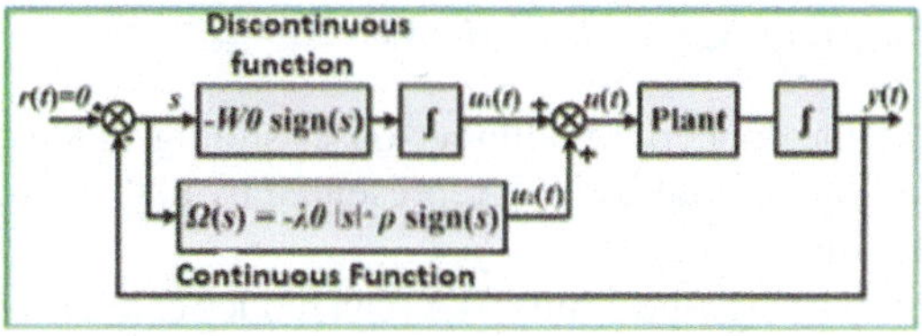

Fig. 3. Higher-order sliding mode controller block diagram

The state equation of the non-linear system is provided in (2):

$$\begin{cases} \dot{v}_{pv} = \frac{1}{c_1}\left(\frac{v_{pv}}{r_{pv}} - i_L\right) \\ \dot{i}_L = \frac{1}{L}\left(v_{pv} - v_{out} + v_{out}*D\right) \end{cases}$$

The surface that slides can be characterised as follows [21]:

$$S(x) = \left(\frac{d}{dt} + K_d\right)^{n-1} e(x) + k_i \int e(t) \tag{3}$$

In this context, e(x) represents the tracking error, while n denotes the order of the sliding surface.

For n = 2, $S(x) = K_i \int e(t)dt + e(t) + K_d\, \dot{e}(t)$, Where $\dot{e}(t)$ and $\int e(t)dt$ are the integral terms and the error derivative, respectively, and e(t) is the voltage error between "Vref" and "vpv."

As stated in Eq. (4), HOSMC typically consists of two sections: equivalent and discontinuous parts.

$$D(t) = D_{eq}(t) + D_{dis}(t) \tag{4}$$

The corresponding control signal can be obtained by deriving and setting Eq. (3) to zero in the following manner:

$$\dot{S} = K_d\, \ddot{e}(t) + K_i e(t) + \dot{e}(t) = 0 \tag{5}$$

The selection of parameters like K_d and K_i has a significant impact on the HOSMC controller's performance. These variables regulate the system's robustness to perturbations and rate of convergence. While a lower K_d improves stability at the expense of slower convergence, a larger K_d speeds up the system's response time but may cause overshoot. Similarly, the integral part of the control rule, which is essential for lowering steady-state error, is governed by K_i. To achieve a balance between quick reaction, stability, and less oscillations, these parameters need to be precisely adjusted through modeling and experimental confirmation.

Assuming the sliding surface function's relative degree is higher than one, the HOSM-STA control law reads as:

$$D(t) = \frac{1}{V_{out}}\left(V_{out} - V_{pv} + LC_1\left[\frac{1}{C_1 r_{pv}} + \frac{1}{K_d}\right] - \frac{K_i}{K_d} LC_1 e(t)\right)$$

$$+ \int w_0 sign(s)dt - \lambda_0 |s|^\sigma sign(s) \quad (6)$$

Figure 3 illustrates the concept of a higher-order sliding-mode controller. The state variables will reach a state of equilibrium, represented by u, the control input or control efforts, within a finite time frame.

Because the super-twisting algorithm (STA) can reduce chattering effects, which are a feature of conventional sliding mode control, it is especially well-suited for solar systems. Chattering can cause wear on system components and inefficiencies in energy conversion. Furthermore, STA guarantees the sliding variable's finite-time convergence, allowing for quick and accurate tracking of the maximum power point even under dynamic environmental circumstances such abrupt changes in temperature or irradiance.

4 Stability Analysis

The convergence of the control algorithm is achieved through the application of the Lyapunov criterion, which generates a positive definite function.

$$v = \frac{1}{2}s^2 \quad (7)$$

It is essential to ascertain that the derivative of V is definitively negative in order to guarantee the convergence of V: $\dot{v} = s\dot{s} < 0$.

$$\dot{s} = \frac{k_d}{C^2 r_{pv}}\left(\frac{v_{pv}}{r_{pv}} - i_L\right) + \frac{K_d}{C^2} * \frac{i_{c1}}{r_{pv}} + \frac{i_{c1}}{C_1} - K_i e(t)$$
$$- \frac{KK_d K_i}{LC_1}\frac{s(t)}{s(t)+\varepsilon} - \frac{1}{C_1}\left(\frac{v_{pv}}{r_{pv}} - i_L\right) + K_i e(t) \quad (8)$$

Given that the term is always positive, the sign of the following equation is contingent upon the value of the constant K. Consequently, we may consider it to be

$$\dot{S} = -K\left(\frac{s}{s+\varepsilon}\right) \quad (9)$$

It is evident that the convergence of Eq. 9 can only be confirmed when K is selected in a positive manner.

5 Results of Simulations

Figure 4 shows the photovoltaic (PV) voltage curves and the expected reference trajectory, Vref. This graph is important as it provides a clear and accurate depiction of how well the control strategy is tracking the desired voltage profile. By comparing the actual PV voltage curves with the reference trajectory, the figure demonstrates the precision and effectiveness of the control technique in achieving the desired voltage levels. Figure 5 illustrates the behavior of the duty cycle of the PV system when using the Perturb and Observe (P&O) technique. This graph shows how the duty cycle is adjusted in response to changes in input conditions, such as fluctuations in temperature or light intensity.

Figure 6 compares the output voltage variations of two controllers: the Proportional-Integral (PI) controller and the High-Ordersupertwisting Sliding Mode - (HOSM-STA) controller. The output voltages for each controller are represented on the graph, with the PI controller shown by a red line and the HOSM-STA controller depicted by a dashed blue line.

Finally, Fig. 7 displays the duty cycle response when using the robust HOSM-STA controller. This graph demonstrates how the controller maintains consistent performance even as input conditions, such as temperature or solar irradiance, vary.

Fuzzy logic, neural networks, and evolutionary algorithms are examples of AI-based techniques that provide robustness and adaptive control, although they are data-dependent and computationally demanding. On the other hand, the suggested HOSMC controller is perfect for resource-constrained applications since it guarantees quick convergence, high efficiency, and finite-time stability without requiring a lot of training.

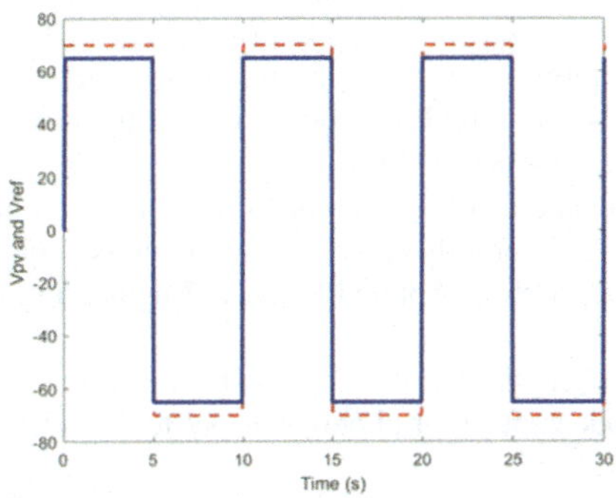

Fig. 4. PV voltage and Vref voltage were simulated using a traditional P&O technique.

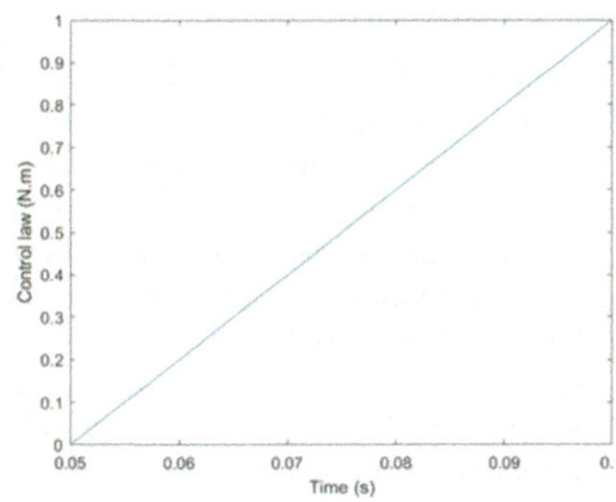

Fig. 5. The representation of the duty cycle.

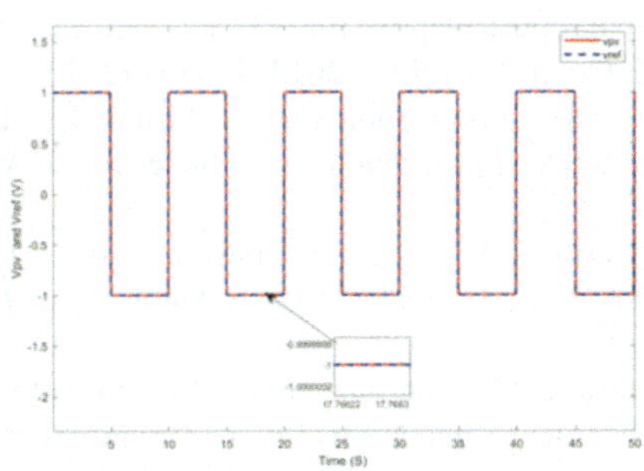

Fig. 6. Output voltage for PI and HOSM-STA input voltage variations

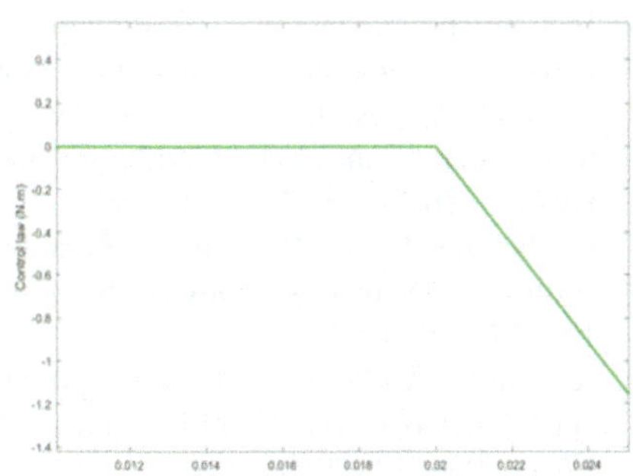

Fig. 7. The representation of the duty cycle using the HOSMC-STA controller

6 Conclusion

In conclusion, this study represents a significant advancement in the control strategies for photovoltaic (PV) systems. The implementation of High-Order Supertwisting Sliding Mode Control (HOSMC) has demonstrated its efficacy by accurately tracking the reference voltage set by the Perturb and Observe (P&O)-based Voltage Maximum Power Point Tracking (VMPPT) algorithm. The innovative sliding surface integrated within the VMPPT algorithm plays a pivotal role in reducing steady-state errors and eliminating overshoot, particularly in response to abrupt changes in solar irradiation.

In conclusion, this comprehensive approach not only enhances energy harvesting but also reinforces the resilience of photovoltaic systems against fluctuating operating conditions.

References

1. Mellouli, E.M., Sefriti, S., Boumhidi, I.: Combined fuzzy logic and sliding mode approach's for modelling and control of the two-link robot. In: Proceedings of 2012 International Conference on Complex Systems, ICCS 2012, p. 6458599, 2012
2. Alika, R., Mellouli, E.M., Tissir, E.H.: Optimization of higher-order sliding mode control parameter using particle swarm optimization for lateral dynamics of autonomous vehicles. In: International Conference on Innovative Research in Applied Science, Engineering and Technology, IRASET 2020
3. Kihala, A., Krima, F., Laiba, A., Talbia, B., Afghoula, H.: An improved MPPTschemeemploying adaptive integral derivative sliding mode control for photovoltaic systems under fast irradiation changes. ISA Trans. (2019)
4. Guo, B., et al.: A robust second-order sliding mode control for single-phase photovoltaic grid-connected voltage source inverter. IEEE Access (2017)
5. Mellouli, E.M., Naoual, R., Boumhidi, I.: A new modified sliding mode controller based fuzzy logic for a variable speed wind turbine. Int. J. Ecol. Dev. 44–53 (2017)
6. Mellouli, E.M., Massou, S., Boumhidi, I.: Optimal robust adaptive fuzzy H∞ tracking control without reaching phase for nonlinear system. J. Control Sci. Eng. **2013**, 498461 (2013)
7. Abdillah, M., Mellouli, E.M.: A new adaptive second-order non-singular terminal sliding mode lateral control combined with neural networks for autonomous vehicle. Int. J. Veh. Perform. **10**(1), 50–72 (2024)
8. El Hajjami, L., Mellouli, E.M., Žuraulis, V., Berrada, M.: A novel robust adaptive neuro-sliding mode steering controller for autonomous ground vehicles. Robot. Auton. Syst. **170**, 104557 (2023)
9. Jennan, N., Mellouli, E.M.: New optimal fast terminal sliding mode control combined with neural networks for modelling and controlling a drone quadrotor. Int. J. Autom. Control. **17**(6), 595–612 (2023)
10. El bouassi, S., Chalh, Z., Mellouli, E.M :. New Optimum Lipschitz Sliding Mode Control for Variable Speed WindTurbine. International Review of Automatic Control (I.RE.A.CO.), 2023
11. El bouassi, S., El afou, Y., Chalh, Z., Mellouli, E.M., Haidi, T.: Optimized triangular observer based adaptive supertwisting sliding mode control for wind turbine system. IAES Int. J. Artif. Intell. (IJ-AI) (2024)

A Novel Optimal Variable-Gain Sliding Mode Control Using Fuzzy Logic for Autonomous Vehicle

Moussa Abdillah[1(✉)], Badre El Kassmi[1], Arjdal El Hanafi[2], and Mellouli El Mehdi[1]

[1] Laboratory of Engineering, Systems and Applications LISA, National School of Applied Sciences, Fez, Morocco
{abdillah.moussa,badre.elkassmi}@usmba.ac.ma
[2] Faculty of Sciences, Agadir, Morocco
e.arjdal@uiz.ac.ma

Abstract. This paper introduces a novel intelligent controller for autonomous vehicles that incorporates fuzzy variable gain sliding mode control (SMC). The controller is designed to improve overall performance. The paper first outlines the dynamics of the vehicle. Next, a variable gain sliding mode control is designed to accurately track the desired vehicle speed. To address uncertainties and instability in sliding mode control, the controller's time-varying gains are adapted and optimized using T-S fuzzy logic. The stability of the control system is validated using Lyapunov stability theory. Finally, simulation results demonstrate the effectiveness and superiority of the proposed control method. The simulation results show that the proposed method has the advantage of accurately tracking the desired vehicle speed and overcome the problem of instability in SMC and the effects of uncertainties compared to the classical method and the conventional sliding mode control. Overall, this novel approach offers promising potential for autonomous vehicles.

Keywords: Variable Gain Sliding Mode Control · T-S Fuzzy Logic · Lyapunov Stability Theory · Autonomous Vehicles

1 Introduction

As the number of vehicles on the road continues to grow, the issue of road traffic safety is becoming increasingly pressing, among which traffic accidents which cause many deaths and serious injuries every year worldwide [1]. Despite the establishment of increasingly conduct's strict rules and the installation of major monitoring systems, it is difficult, if not impossible, to ensure that the behaviour of users remains exemplary. To solve this problem, solutions are being proposed to improve road safety, such as the introduction of Intelligent Transport Systems (ITS). This involves fully automating vehicles or installing Advanced Driver Assistance Systems (ADAS), which assist and warn the driver, or even take over in potentially accident-prone situations to help avoid them [1]. Autonomous vehicles can drive themselves without human intervention. Their control system usually

I. Aboudrar et al. (Eds.): ICESST 2024, SUCI, pp. 417–428, 2025.
https://doi.org/10.1007/978-3-031-86705-7_39

consists of three modules: perception of the environment, planning and decision making, and control of the vehicle [2]. The vehicle control module coordinates the engine, brakes and steering to follow the desired trajectory and speed. The primary purpose of ADAS is to provide a safe and effective way to prevent road accidents [1, 3]. Longitudinal motion control is an important aspect of controlling an intelligent vehicle according to its relative position to either the lead vehicle or obstacles, thus ensuring driving safety while improving transport efficiency in multi-vehicle cooperative operation [4]. It is imperative that the control system which governs the intelligent longitudinal dynamics of the vehicle operates with precision, ensuring the precise delivery of the requisite torques applied to the wheels in each operating mode. This is to be achieved through the coordinated actuation of the throttle and brakes, and the optimum selection of operating modes. Several techniques and algorithms are used for the longitudinal control such as the Sliding Mode Control (SMC) [5, 6], Terminal SMC (TSMC) [7], PID control [8], $H\infty$ control [9], Neural Networks (NN) [10], Fuzzy Logic control [11, 12] and so on.

Sliding mode is a control algorithm that provides advantages including high robustness to uncertainties, fast response, excellent transient performance and simple design [13]. A modified sliding control scheme with variable control parameters is developed in [5], with the objective of mitigating the considerable variation in the pressure feedback observed during the hydraulic brake control process of an automated highway vehicle. Although SMC is resilient, chatter can cause energy loss and control issues [13]. A multitude of control methods have been employed to address this issue, with fuzzy logic being a notable example due to its exceptional approximation capabilities. A robust longitudinal sliding-mode controller design for autonomous ground vehicle based on fuzzy logic was proposed in [12]. This approach is capable of reducing the chatter associated with sliding mode control (SMC), while also addressing system uncertainties and external disturbances.

Motivated by the previous discussions, the main objective of this work is to develop a robust and intelligent controller based on fuzzy variable gain sliding mode control for the longitudinal control of an autonomous vehicle. The utilisation of the aforementioned methodologies in isolation has the potential to engender diminished performance of the system. It is for this reason that a decision was taken to design a hybrid controller, with the aim of combining the advantages of the above methods. The main contribution of this study is summarized as follows:

- Design of an intelligent controller based on fuzzy variable gain sliding mode control for an autonomous vehicle.
- Sliding mode control is designed to ensure that the vehicle follows the desired speed precisely, while guaranteeing the overall stabilisation of the system, in accordance with Lyapunov theory, using a barrier Lyapunov function.
- Overcomes the common problem of unstable sliding mode control and the effects of uncertainty by approximating and tuning the SMC's time-varying controller gains with fuzzy logic.

The paper is structured as follows: Sect. 2 presents vehicle dynamics models. Section 3 presents the control strategy. Section 4 validates the theoretical results with simulation results. Section 5 concludes with a summary and suggestions for future work.

2 Modeling of the Study System

In this section, we present the mathematical model of the vehicle. The schematic of our study system is shown in Fig. 1. As shown in Fig. 1, as the vehicle moves along the road, it is subject to the following external longitudinal forces: longitudinal tyre forces, air resistance (aerodynamic drag forces), rolling resistance forces, etc. In thisresearch we focus on the study of the longitudinal dynamics of the vehicle. This model presents the essential dynamics of the vehicle, expressed as follows [4, 10, 14, 15]:

$$m\ddot{x} = \sum_{i=fl,fr,rl,rr} F_{xi} - \sum\nolimits_{i=fl,fr,rl,rr} R_{Ri} - R_{Air} \tag{1}$$

where $x, \dot{x}$ and $\ddot{x}$ represent the longitudinal position, velocity, and acceleration of the vehicle respectively, m is the vehicle mass, $F_{xfl}, F_{xfr}, F_{xrl}$ and F_{xrr} are the longitudinal forces applied to the front left, front right, rear left and rear right tires respectively, $R_{Rfl}, R_{Rfr}, R_{Rrl}$ and R_{Rrr} represent the rolling resistance forces applied to the front left, front right, rear left and rear right tires respectively and R_{Air} is the air resistance. Under the assumption that the longitudinal forces on the tyres are equal, we have [10]:

$$\begin{cases} R_{Air} = \frac{1}{2}\rho A_f C_d \dot{x}^2 \\ F_x = \frac{Tr_t - I_w \ddot{x}}{r_t^2} \\ R_R = \gamma m g \end{cases} \tag{2}$$

where ρ, A_f and C_d are the air density, the vehicle body frontal area and the drag coefficient respectively, I_w and r_t represent the wheel rotational inertia and the tire rolling radius, γ and g are the gravitational acceleration and the rolling resistance coefficient, T is the driving/braking torque (control variable). Therefore, based on Eqs. (1) and (2), the simplified vehicle dynamics model can be written as follows:

$$\ddot{x} = -\frac{1}{2}\frac{\rho A_f C_d r_t^2}{\left(m r_t^2 + 4I_w\right)}\dot{x}^2 - \frac{4mg\gamma r_t^2}{\left(m r_t^2 + 4I_w\right)} + \frac{4r_t}{\left(m r_t^2 + 4I_w\right)}T \tag{3}$$

The system state representation is written as follows:

$$\begin{cases} \dot{x}_1 = x_2 \\ \dot{x}_2 = f\left(\underline{x}, t\right) + g\left(\underline{x}, t\right)U(t) \end{cases} \tag{4}$$

where:

$$\begin{cases} f\left(\underline{x}, t\right) = -\frac{1}{2}\frac{\rho A_f C_d r_t^2}{\left(m r_t^2 + 4I_w\right)}x_2^2 - \frac{4mg\gamma r_t^2}{\left(m r_t^2 + 4I_w\right)} \\ g\left(\underline{x}, t\right) = \frac{4r_t}{\left(m r_t^2 + 4I_w\right)}U(t) = T \end{cases} \tag{5}$$

$f\left(\underline{x}, t\right)$ and $g\left(\underline{x}, t\right)$ are non-linear functions, $U(t)$ represent the control law.

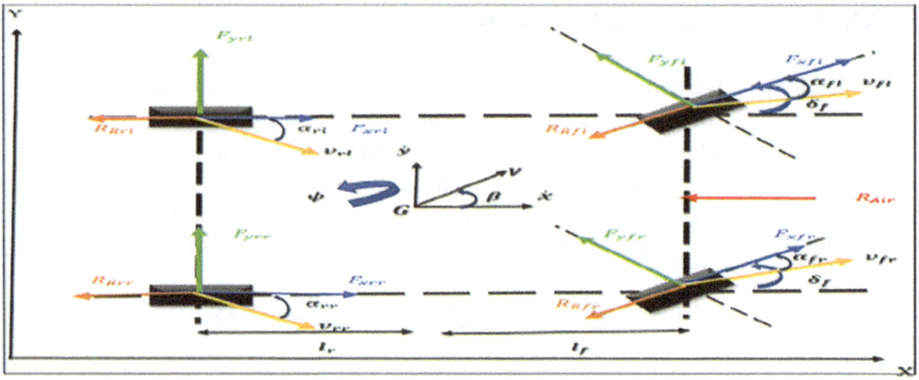

Fig. 1. The Vehicle dynamics model

3 Control Strategy

This section describes the conception of the system control strategy. First, a novel sliding mode control (SMC) with optimal variable gain has been designed to accurately track the desired vehicle speed. In addition to this, the control law ensures finite convergence time and global stabilisation of the system in accordance with Lyapunov theory. Furthermore, the common problem of instability in sliding mode control and the effects of uncertainties have been overcome by optimising the variable gain of the SMC using T-S fuzzy logic to obtain a smooth control law.

3.1 Optimal Variable Gain Sliding Mode Control

Stabilising the longitudinal dynamics of the vehicle requires a robust controller, and it is with this in mind that we have developed the Sliding Mode Control (SMC) algorithm in this paper, which is used to control and stabilise our system. Recognised as one of the most robust control systems, Sliding Mode Control (SMC) consists of forcing the system's trajectories to reach the sliding surface in a finite time and to remain there through the use of a discontinuous function (Lhoussain et al., 2020). The sliding surface of the SMC is defined as [3, 16]:

$$S = \dot{e} + \alpha e \tag{6}$$

where e and $\dot{e}$ represent the longitudinal speed error and its first derivative respectively and α is a time varying controller gain, which is soft saturation function[17] (sigmoidal form) and defined as [17]:

$$\alpha = \frac{\alpha^+}{1 + e^{-\psi(e-\iota)}} - \frac{\alpha^+}{2} \tag{7}$$

where α^+ represents the response range (upper value of gain α) and should be selected such that $\alpha^+ > 0$. The variable ι represents the inflexion point of the sigmoid, selected as $\iota = 0$ and the constant ψ that defines the velocity ratio between the initial and the final value of the sigmoid function. Differentiating S with respect to time, the first derivative of S is written as:

$$\dot{S} = \ddot{e} + \dot{\alpha}e + \alpha\dot{e} \tag{8}$$

where $\dot{\alpha}$ is the first derivative of α. Using some simplifications, we can write:

$$\dot{S} = -\frac{\rho A_f C_d r_t^2}{\left(mr_t^2 + 4I_t\right)}\left[f\left(\underline{x}, t\right) + g\left(\underline{x}, t\right)U(t)\right]x_2 - \dot{x}_{2d} + \dot{\alpha}e + \alpha\dot{e} + g\dot{U}(t) \tag{9}$$

where x_{2d} and $\dot{x}_{2d}$ are the desired longitudinal speed of the vehicle and its first derivative respectively. The derivative of the sliding surface is defined as follows:

$$\dot{S} = -Ksign(S) \tag{10}$$

where K is a control gain expressed as follows [17]:

$$K = \frac{1}{1 - |\xi|}\left[\frac{0.5^{\frac{3}{2}}\beta S}{\xi}\right] \tag{11}$$

where β is a designed positive constant and ξ is an auxiliar variable defined as [17]:

$$\xi = \frac{S}{K_S} \tag{12}$$

where K_S is a positive constant given by [17]:

$$K_S = k_2 + \alpha^+ k_1^{\frac{q}{p}} \tag{13}$$

where k_1 and k_2 are designed positive constants, p and q are positive odd integers satisfying $p > q$. Based on Eqs. (9)–(11), the control law of the system can be expressed:

$$\dot{U}(t) = -\frac{1}{g}\left(-\frac{\rho A_f C_d r_t^2}{\left(mr_t^2 + 4I_t\right)}\left[f\left(\underline{x}, t\right) + g\left(\underline{x}, t\right)U(t)\right]x_2 - \dot{x}_{2d} + \dot{\alpha}e + \alpha\dot{e} + Ksign(S)\right) \tag{14}$$

To guarantee the stability of the system, let us introduce the following Lyapunov function candidate, which also represents a Barrier Lyapunov function (BLF), defined as (David et al., 2022):

$$V = \frac{1}{2}ln\left(\frac{1}{1 - \xi^2}\right) \tag{15}$$

According to the Lyapunov hypothesis, to maintain system stability, $\dot{V}$ must be negative [1, 18]:

$$\dot{V} \leq 0 \tag{16}$$

The full-time derivative of V satisfies:

$$\dot{V} = \frac{\xi\dot{\xi}}{1-\xi^2} \tag{17}$$

Using some simplifications and the Lemma 1 to Lema 4 in [17], we obtain:

$$\dot{V} \le -\beta V \frac{\frac{1}{2}^{\frac{1}{2}}}{V^{\frac{1}{2}}} \Rightarrow \dot{V} \le -\beta \frac{1}{2}^{\frac{1}{2}} V^{\frac{1}{2}} \le -\beta\left(\frac{1}{2}V\right)^{\frac{1}{2}} \le 0 \tag{18}$$

Therefore, on the basis of Eq. (18) and according to Eq. (16), the system is proven to be stable, thereby confirming Lyapunov's hypothesis.

3.2 Proposed Control Method Using Fuzzy Logic

SMC offers the greatest potential for eliminating disturbances in complex systems, but can be unstable. This can result in energy loss, affect control accuracy, and lead to mechanical or electronic damage [13]. A multitude of control methods have been incorporated with SMC in order to address this issue, including those employing fuzzy logic, which is renowned for its exemplary approximation capabilities. Therefore, in this subsection we design a fuzzy logic control, specifically employing the Takagi-Sugeno (T-S) type to approximate the time-varying controller gain and to suppress common problem of instability in SMC and the effects of uncertainties. The basic configuration of the T-S system includes a fuzzy rule base, which consists of a set of fuzzy IF-THEN rules, as follows [16, 19, 20]:

$$R^j : If\ x_1\ is\ A^j\ and\ x_2\ is\ A^j,\ Then\ y\ is\ \theta^j \tag{19}$$

where R^j is the rule number, $x = [x_1, x_2]^T$ denotes the input vector in the fuzzy system, A^j are the fuzzy variables characterized by member functions $\mu_{A^j}(x)$ and θ^j is the corresponding value of the output fuzzy singleton. The output of the fuzzy system can be expressed as [16, 19, 20]:

$$y(x,\theta) = \frac{\sum_{j=1}^{M} \theta^j \left(\prod_{i=1}^{n} \mu_{A^j}(x)\right)}{\sum_{j=1}^{M}\left(\prod_{i=1}^{n} \mu_{A^j}(x)\right)} = \theta^T \zeta(x) \tag{20}$$

where M is the total number of the fuzzy rules, $\theta = [\theta_1, \theta_2, \ldots, \theta_M]^T$ is adjustable parameter vector and $\zeta(x) = [\zeta_1(x), \zeta_2(x), \ldots, \zeta_M(x)]^T$ is the vector of fuzzy basis functions defined as:

$$\zeta(x) = \frac{\left(\prod_{i=1}^{n} \mu_{A^j}(x)\right)}{\sum_{j=1}^{M}\left(\prod_{i=1}^{n} \mu_{A^j}(x)\right)} \tag{21}$$

The ideal output of the fuzzy system can be expressed as [20]:

$$y^*\left(x,\theta^*\right) = \theta^{*T}\zeta(x) \tag{22}$$

The fuzzy approximation error is defined as:

$$\omega = y^*\left(x, \theta^*\right) - y(x, \theta) = \left(\theta^{*T} - \theta^T\right)\zeta(x) = \tilde{\theta}^T \zeta(x) \tag{23}$$

Based on (19) to (23), we can write:

$$\begin{cases} \hat{\alpha}^* = \theta_\alpha^{*T} \zeta_\alpha(x) \\ \hat{\alpha} = \theta_\alpha^T \zeta_\alpha(x) \\ \tilde{\alpha} = \hat{\alpha}^* - \hat{\alpha} = \left(\theta_\alpha^{*T} - \theta_\alpha^T\right)\zeta_\alpha(x) = \widetilde{\theta_\alpha}^T \zeta_\alpha(x) \end{cases} \tag{24}$$

$$\begin{cases} \dot{\hat{\alpha}}^* = \theta_{\dot{\alpha}}^{*T} \zeta_{\dot{\alpha}}(x) \\ \dot{\hat{\alpha}} = \theta_{\dot{\alpha}}^T \zeta_{\dot{\alpha}}(x) \\ \dot{\tilde{\alpha}} = \dot{\hat{\alpha}}^* - \dot{\hat{\alpha}} = (\theta_{\dot{\alpha}}^{*T} - \theta_{\dot{\alpha}}^T)\zeta_{\dot{\alpha}}(x) = \widetilde{\theta_{\dot{\alpha}}}^T \zeta_{\dot{\alpha}}(x) \end{cases} \tag{25}$$

Thus, the control law (14) is rewritten as follows:

$$\dot{U}(t) = -\frac{1}{g(\underline{x}, t)}\left(-\frac{\rho A_f C_d r_t^2}{\left(m r_t^2 + 4I_t\right)}[f(\underline{x}, t) + g(\underline{x}, t)U(t)]x_2 - \dot{x}_{2d} + \dot{\hat{\alpha}}\, e + \hat{\alpha}\dot{e} + K sign(S)\right) \tag{26}$$

Substituting (26) into (9) and using some simplifications, one gets:

$$\dot{S} = \omega_1 + \omega_2 + \widetilde{\theta_{\dot{\alpha}}}^T \zeta_{\dot{\alpha}}(x)e + \widetilde{\theta_\alpha}^T \zeta_\alpha(x)\dot{e} - K sign(S) \tag{27}$$

where ω_1 and ω_2 are the minimum approximation errors defined as:

$$\begin{cases} \omega_1 = \left(\dot{\alpha} - \dot{\hat{\alpha}}^*\right)e \\ \omega_2 = (\alpha - \hat{\alpha}^*)\dot{e} \end{cases} \tag{28}$$

To guarantee the system stability, let's consider the new Lyapunov function as:

$$L = \frac{1}{2} ln\left(\frac{1}{1-\xi^2}\right) + \frac{1}{2\lambda_1}\widetilde{\theta_\alpha}^T \widetilde{\theta_\alpha} + \frac{1}{2\lambda_2}\widetilde{\theta_{\dot{\alpha}}}^T \widetilde{\theta_{\dot{\alpha}}} \tag{29}$$

where λ_1, λ_2 are strictly positive constants. Taking the time derivative of L, we obtain:

$$\dot{L} = \frac{\xi}{1-\xi^2}\left[\frac{\dot{S}}{K_S}\right] + \frac{1}{\lambda_1}\widetilde{\theta_\alpha}^T \dot{\theta}_\alpha + \frac{1}{\lambda_2}\widetilde{\theta_\alpha}^T \dot{\theta}_{\dot{\alpha}} \tag{30}$$

Substituting (27) into (30) and using some simplifications, one gets:

$$\begin{aligned} \dot{L} =& \frac{1}{\lambda_1}\widetilde{\theta_\alpha}^T\left(\lambda_1 \zeta_\alpha(x)\dot{e}\frac{\xi}{K_S\left(1-\xi^2\right)} + \dot{\theta}_\alpha\right) + \frac{1}{\lambda_2}\widetilde{\theta_{\dot{\alpha}}}^T\left(\lambda_2 \zeta_{\dot{\alpha}}(x)e\frac{\xi}{K_S\left(1-\xi^2\right)} + \dot{\theta}_{\dot{\alpha}}\right) \\ &+ \frac{\xi}{K_S\left(1-\xi^2\right)}\left[\omega_1 + \omega_2 - K sign(S)\right] \end{aligned} \tag{31}$$

From (31), we obtain the following adaptive laws:

$$\begin{cases} \dot{\theta}_{\alpha} = -\lambda_1 \zeta_{\alpha}(x)\dot{e}\frac{\xi}{K_S(1-\xi^2)} \\ \dot{\theta}_{\dot{\alpha}} = -\lambda_2 \zeta_{\dot{\alpha}}(x)e\frac{\xi}{K_S(1-\xi^2)} \end{cases} \tag{32}$$

Therefore,

$$\dot{L} = \frac{\xi}{K_S(1-\xi^2)}[\omega_1 + \omega_2 - Ksign(S)] \tag{33}$$

Assuming that the maximum approximation errors of the fuzzy system are the verified the condition:

$$K > \frac{1}{g}\omega 12_{max} \tag{34}$$

where,

$$\begin{cases} |\omega_1| < \omega 1_{max} \\ |\omega_2| < \omega 2_{max} \\ |\omega_{12}| = |\omega_1 + \omega_2| < \omega 12_{max} \end{cases} \tag{35}$$

where $\omega 1_{max}$, $\omega 2_{max}$, $\omega 1_{max}$, $\omega 12_{max}$ are the maximum approximation errors of the fuzzy system. Based on (34) and (35), the time derivative of L can be written:

$$\dot{L} \leq -\frac{\xi}{K_S(1-\xi^2)}[Ksign(S)] \leq \dot{V} \leq -\beta\left(\frac{1}{2}V\right)^{\frac{1}{2}} \leq 0 \tag{36}$$

The system is subsequently stable, thus proving the Lyapunov hypothesis.

4 Simulation Results and Discussions

This section presents the results of a simulation study that was conducted to verify and validate the effectiveness and performance of the proposed controller for longitudinal vehicle control: this part highlights the ability of the proposed controller to accurately track the vehicle's desired speed, to reduce and eliminate the common problem of instability in SMC, the effects of uncertainties and the chattering phenomenon. The desired longitudinal speed is a polynomial of degree 3 defined as follows:

$$V_{xd} = 10 + 2t - 0.325t^2 + 0.125t^3 \tag{37}$$

The performance of the proposed method is compared with that obtained using the classical method and conventional sliding mode control (SMC). The control time is 20 s and the results are shown in Figs. 2, 3, and 4.

Figure 2 shows the longitudinal vehicle speed tracking for the proposed method (fuzzy variable gain sliding mode control), the classical method (optimal variable gain sliding mode control) and the conventional sliding mode control. From this figure, it is very clear that the longitudinal speed of the vehicle for the proposed method is driven back to the reference faster and more accurately, they are almost similar, which proves the robustness and effectiveness of our proposed method and in comparison, with the classical method and the conventional SMC, whose results deviate slightly more from the reference.

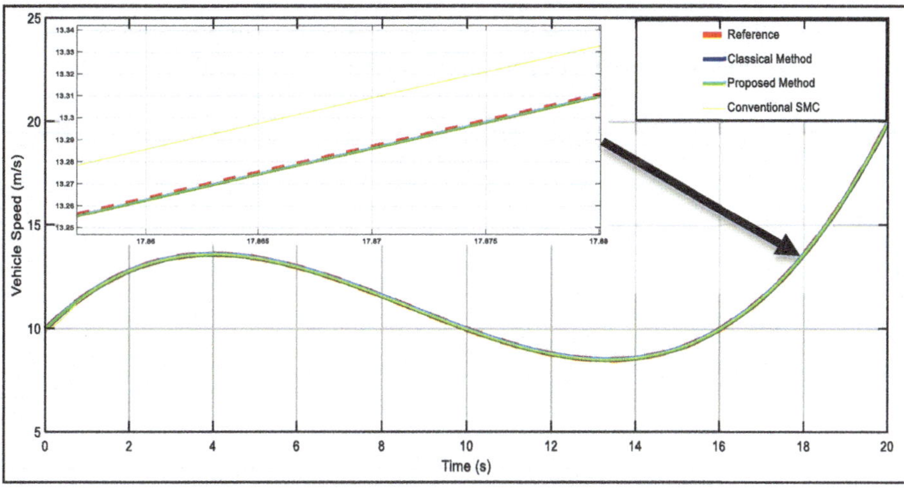

Fig. 2. The tracking of vehicle longitudinal speed

Figures 3 and 4 show a comparison of the control inputs of the proposed method and the conventional method. Figure 3 shows the control input obtained with the classical method and Fig. 4 shows the control input obtained with the proposed method. The control variable of the classical method showed significant variations, in other words, the chattering phenomenon is important. The effectiveness of the proposed method can be demonstrated by the reduction and limitation of the common problem of instability in SMC, the effects of uncertainties and the chattering phenomenon which is achieved by stabilising the controller input through the optimisation of the varying gains of the sliding mode control using fuzzy logic. As a consequence of the smooth control law that is obtained for the proposed method, the controller requires less effort. Consequently, the controller consumes less energy to control the system as a whole, which is excellent in energy efficiency terms. The results demonstrate the superior performance of the proposed controller, a hybrid control scheme combining the benefits of optimal variable-gain sliding mode control and fuzzy logic. The aforementioned results are thus in accordance with the theory previously established in the section on the control strategy.

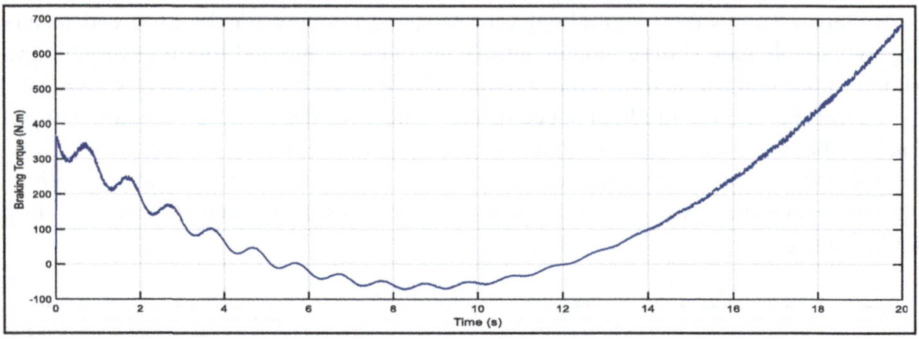

Fig. 3. The control input obtained with the classical method

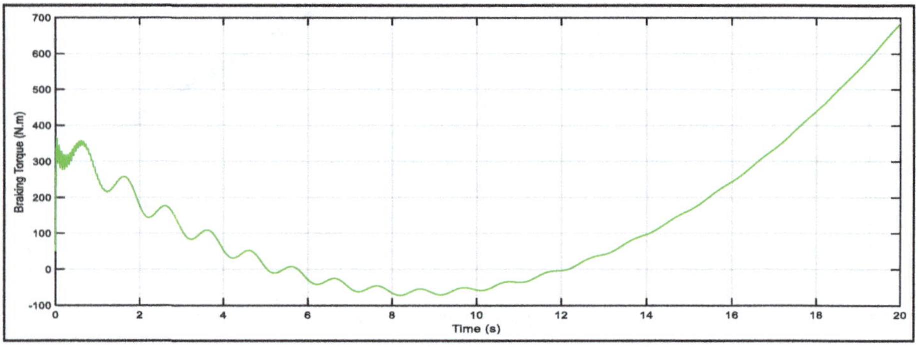

Fig. 4. The control input with the proposed method

5 Conclusion

A new intelligent controller based on fuzzy variable gain sliding mode control for an autonomous vehicle has been developed in this study. The variable gain sliding mode control was designed to accurately track the desired vehicle speed. The common problem of instability in SMC and the effects of uncertainties have been reduced using T-S fuzzy logic. Using these methods separately can reduce system performance. This is why we have chosen to design a hybrid controller that combines the advantages of these methods.

The main objective of simulation results is to validate and confirm the efficacy and superiority of the proposed controller: its ability to accurately track the desired vehicle speed and eliminate the common problem of instability in SMC and the effects of uncertainties. The simulation results show that the proposed method has the advantage of accurately tracking the desired vehicle speed and overcome the problem of instability in SMC and the effects of uncertainties compared to the classical method and the conventional sliding mode control.

A new variable gain sliding mode control based on fuzzy logic for lateral control of an autonomous vehicle subject to uncertainties is planned for future work.

References

1. Moussa, A., Mellouli, E.M.Z.: A new adaptive second-order non-singular terminal sliding mode lateral control combined with neural networks for autonomous vehicle. Int. J. Veh. Perform. **10**(1), 50–72 (2024)
2. Min, Z., Huiyan, C., Guang-ming, X.: A model predictive speed tracking control approach for autonomous ground vehicles. Mech. Syst. Sig. Process. **87**(B), 138–152 (2017)
3. Lhoussain, E.H., Mellouli, E.M., Mohammed, B.: Neural network based sliding mode lateral control for autonomous vehicle. In: EEE 2020: 1st International Conference on Innovative Research in Applied Science, Engineering and Technology (IRASET), IEEE, Meknes, Morocco, pp. 1–6 (2020)
4. Xiaoqiang, S., Yingfeng, C., Shaohua, W., Xing, X., Long, C.: Optimal control of intelligent vehicle longitudinal dynamics via hybrid model predictive control. Robot. Auton. Syst. **112**, 190–200 (2019)
5. Hong, L., Kil, T.C., Tae, S.N., Soo-Yeong, Y.: Vehicle longitudinal brake control using variable parameter sliding control. Control. Eng. Pract. **11**(4), 403–411 (2003)
6. Zhaobo, Q., Haodong, J., Liang, C., Manjiang, H., Yougang, B., Qingjia, C.: Longitudinal vehicle stability control based on modified sliding mode control. Autom. Innov. **7**, 335 (2024)
7. Long, L., Ren, D., Zhang, J.: Terminal sliding mode control for vehicle longitudinal following in automated highway system. In: The 2008 27th Chinese Control Conference, Kunming, China (2008)
8. Lei, S., Jun, L., Zichun, W., Kai, Y., Ehsan, H., Hong, W.: Longitudinal and lateral control methods from single vehicle to autonomous platoon. Green Energy Intell. Transp. **2**(2), 100066 (2023)
9. Shengbo, E.L., Feng, G., Keqiang, L., Le-Yi, W., Keyou, Y., Dongpu, C.: Robust longitudinal control of multi-vehicle systems—a distributed H-Infinity method. IEEE Trans. Intell. Transp. Syst. **19**(9), 2779–2788 (2018)
10. Nastaran, T., Abdollah, A., Shahriar, B.S.: An adaptive modified neural lateral-longitudinal control system for path following of autonomous vehicles. Eng. Sci. Technol. Int. J. **24**(1), 126–137 (2021)
11. Rachid, A., Mellouli, E.M., Tissir, E.H.: A modified sliding mode controller based on Fuzzy logic to control the longitudinal dynamics of the autonomous vehicle. Res. Eng. **22**, 102120 (2024)
12. Ping, H., Jinghua, G., Linhui, L., Rongben, W.: A robust longitudinal sliding-mode controller design for autonomous ground vehicle based on fuzzy logic. Int. J. Veh. Auton. Syst. **11**(4), 368–383 (2013)
13. Moussa, A., Mellouli, E.M., Touria, H.: A new intelligent controller based on integral sliding mode control and extended state observer for nonlinear MIMO drone quadrotor. Int. J. Intell. Netw. **5**, 49–62 (2024)
14. Lhoussain, E.H., Mellouli, E.M., Vidas, Ž, Mohammed, B., Ismail, B.: A robust intelligent controller for autonomous ground vehicle longitudinal dynamics. Appl. Sci. **13**(1), 501 (2023)
15. Calequela, J.T.M., Max, M.D.S., Giane, G.L., Angelo, M.T.: Longitudinal modeling of a road vehicle: 4-wheel traction. Int. J. Robot. Control Syst. **2**(2), 357–369 (2022)
16. Mellouli, E.M., Selma, S., Ismail, B.: Combined fuzzy logic and sliding mode approach for modelling and control of the two-link robot. In: IEEE 2012: International Conference on Complex Systems (ICCS), IEEE, Agadir, Morocco, pp. 1–6 (2012)
17. David, C., Isaac, C., Alexander, P.: Non-singular terminal sliding-mode control for a manipulator robot using a barrier Lyapunov function. ISA Trans. **121**, 268–283 (2022)
18. Lhoussain, E.H., Mellouli, E.M., Mohammed, B.: Robust adaptive non-singular fast terminal sliding-mode lateral control for an uncertain ego vehicle at the lane-change maneuver subjected to abrupt change. Int. J. Dyn. Control **9**, 1765–1782 (2021)

19. Mellouli, E.M., Boumhidi, J., Boumhidi, I.: Using fuzzy logic for eliminating the reaching phase on the fuzzy H∞ tracking control. Int J. Model. Identif. Control (IJMIC) **20**(4), 398–406 (2013)
20. Moussa, A., et al.: Fuzzy logic based adaptive second-order non-singular terminal sliding mode lateral control for uncertain autonomous vehicle. In: Youssouf, F., et al. (eds.) Artificial Intelligence and Smart Environment (ICAISE), p. 407. Springer Cham, Switzerland (2023)

Finite-Time Stability Analysis of Discrete-Time Linear Systems Subject to Time-Varying Delay Using a Novel Summation Inequality

Nabil El Fezazi[1,2], Mohamed Fahim[3], El Houssine Aouchicha[4(✉)], Soufiane Ait Bousselham[3], Said Idrissi[2,5], and Teresa Alvarez[6(✉)]

[1] IMD Team, Higher School of Technology of Dakhla, Ibn Zohr University, Agadir, Morocco
n.elfezazi@uiz.ac.ma

[2] LISAC Laboratory, Faculty of Sciences Dhar El Mehraz, Sidi Mohammed Ben Abdellah University, Fez, Morocco

[3] Computer Science Research Laboratory, Ibn Tofail University, Kenitra, Morocco
mfahim@uae.ac.ma

[4] LRSDI Laboratory, Faculty of Sciences and Techniques, Abdelmalek Essaâdi University, Al Hoceïma, Morocco
houssinftouhi@gmail.com

[5] LASTIMI Laboratory, Higher School of Technology of Sale, Mohammed V University, Rabat, Morocco
said.idrissi@est.um5.ac.ma

[6] Industrial Engineering School, University of Valladolid, Dr. Mergelina S/N, 47005 Valladolid, Spain
teresa.alvarez.alvarez@uva.es

Abstract. This paper studies FTS (finite-time stability) for discrete-time linear systems with time-varying delay. A novel approximation of the single summation that appears in the LKF (Lyapunov-Krasovskii functional) is studied using an innovative Free-Matrix-Based-Integral (FMBI) inequality. This has led to proposing new conditions formulated as LMIs that ensure FTS. Finally, a numerical example shows the method's efficacy.

1 Introduction

Recent years have seen great efforts in the derivation of delay-dependent stability and FTS analysis of dynamic systems, especially delayed linear systems. Several approaches have been followed: the LKF method ([6–8]); the SSG theorem ([15] based on the transformation model and the classic robust control techniques); IQCs [11]; and quadratic separation [1], all of them give results on stability. If the objective is to solve this problem and to reduce conservatism, it is necessary to estimate the single summation term. Methods dealing with this are: JBI (Jensen-based inequality) [8], WBIs (Wirtinger-based inequalities) [16], free-weighting

I. Aboudrar et al. (Eds.): ICESST 2024, SUCI, pp. 429–440, 2025.
https://doi.org/10.1007/978-3-031-86705-7_40

matrix (FWM) technique [6], the inequality based on auxiliary functions [12] and the inequalities based on FWM [2].

When analyzing the stability criteria, many approaches rely on the Lyapunov asymtotic stability criterion, which is defined over an infinite-time interval. However, in practice, the focus shifts to the system's behavior over a FT interval. This is when the FTS method is introduced; a system is said to be FT stable if, for a given interval, its state remains within bounds throughout the interval. This definition of FTS goes back to the 1950s [9]. A great number of results are developed for various types of systems, for exmaple [13] studies linear systems with additive time-varying delay; [19] deals with neural networks; and Takagi-Sugeno Fuzzy systems are discussed in [14]. FTS for delayed linear systems is studied in [3–5].

As stated in the abstract, we study the FTS of linear systems subject to delay varying with time. Sufficient conditions are used to ensure that FTS is derived using the free-weighting matrices technique and LKF. The effectiveness of the approach is demonstrated through a numerical example.

2 Formulating the Problem

Let us consider the system given by:

$$x(k+1) = Ax(k) + A_d x(k-d(k)) + Bu(k) \tag{1}$$

The corresponding function for the initial state is given by:

$$x(k) = \varphi(k), \quad k \in \{-d_2, -d_2+1, \dots, 0\}$$

where $x(k) \in \Re^n$ is the state vector. The matrices A, $A_d \in \Re^{n \times n}$ are constant system matrices and the delay $d(k)$ is assumed to be time dependent and satisfies $0 \leq d_1 \leq d(k) \leq d_2$.

We define $y(k) = x(k+1) - x(k)$, which satisfies:

$$y^T(k)y(k) < \epsilon, \quad for \;\; k \in \{-d_2, -d_2+1, \dots, 0\}$$

Definition 1. *FTS [18]. The system (1) is said to be FT stable according to* (c_1, c_2, R, N), *where* $c_1 < c_2$, *if*

$$x^T(t)x(t) < c_2, \quad \forall k \in 1, 2, \dots, N$$

with $\sup\limits_{\{\theta \in 1,2,\dots,N\}} \varphi^T(\theta)\varphi(\theta) < c_1$.

Lemma 1. *For any* $n, k \geq 1$ *the following inequality holds:*

$$\gamma_{n.2k}^{\min} < \gamma_{n.2k} < \gamma_{n.2k}^{\max} \tag{2}$$

where

$$\gamma_{n.2k} = \frac{1}{(n+1)^{2k}} \sum_{i=1}^{n} (n+1-2i)^{2k}$$

$$\gamma_{n.2k}^{\max} = \begin{cases} \dfrac{1}{2k+1} \dfrac{(n+2)^{2k+1}}{(n+1)^{2k}} \; if\ n\ is\ even \\ \dfrac{1}{2k+1}(n+1) \; if\ n\ is\ odd \end{cases}$$

$$\gamma_{n.2k}^{\min} = \begin{cases} \dfrac{1}{2k+1} \dfrac{(n-2)^{2k+1}}{(n+1)^{2k}} \; if\ n\ is\ even \\ \dfrac{1}{2k+1} \dfrac{(n-1)^{2k+1}}{(n+1)^{2k}} \; if\ n\ is\ odd \end{cases}$$

Proof. Clearly:

$$\frac{1}{(n+1)^{2k}} \sum_{i=1}^{n} (n+1-2i)^{2k} = \begin{cases} 2 \displaystyle\sum_{i=0}^{\frac{n}{2}-1} \frac{(2i+1)^{2k}}{(n+1)^{2k}} \; if\ n\ is\ even \\ 2 \displaystyle\sum_{i=0}^{\frac{n-1}{2}} \frac{(2i^{2k}}{(n+1)^{2k}} \; if\ n\ is\ odd \end{cases}$$

and for any $p, k \geq 0$ the following inequality is true:

$$\sum_{i=0}^{p} (2i)^k \leq \sum_{i=0}^{p} (2i+1)^k \leq \sum_{i=0}^{p+1} (2i)^k$$

Then, we have:

$$\begin{cases} 2 \displaystyle\sum_{i=0}^{\frac{n}{2}-1} \frac{(2i)^{2k}}{(n+1)^{2k}} \; if\ n\ is\ even \\ 2 \displaystyle\sum_{i=0}^{\frac{n-1}{2}} \frac{(2i)^{2k}}{(n+1)^{2k}} \; if\ n\ is\ odd \end{cases} \leq \gamma_{n.2k} \leq \begin{cases} 2 \displaystyle\sum_{i=0}^{\frac{n}{2}} \frac{(2i)^{2k}}{(n+1)^{2k}} \; if\ n\ is\ even \\ 2 \displaystyle\sum_{i=0}^{\frac{n-1}{2}} \frac{(2i)^{2k}}{(n+1)^{2k}} \; if\ n\ is\ odd \end{cases}$$

According to [12], it is known that for any $p, k \geq 1$:

$$\frac{p^{k+1}}{k+1} < \sum_{i=1}^{p} i^k < \frac{(p+1)^{k+1}}{k+1}$$

which can be used to deduce that:

$$\begin{cases} \dfrac{2^{2k+1}}{2k+1} \dfrac{\left(\frac{n}{2}-1\right)^{2k+1}}{(n+1)^{2k}} \; if\ n\ is\ even \\ \dfrac{2^{2k+1}}{2k+1} \dfrac{\left(\frac{n-1}{2}\right)^{2k+1}}{(n+1)^{2k}} \; if\ n\ is\ odd \end{cases} < \gamma_{n.2k} < \begin{cases} \dfrac{2^{2k+1}}{2k+1} \dfrac{\left(\frac{n}{2}+1\right)^{2k+1}}{(n+1)^{2k}} \; if\ n\ is\ even \\ \dfrac{2^{2k+1}}{2k+1} \dfrac{\left(\frac{n-1}{2}+1\right)^{2k+1}}{(n+1)^{2k}} \; if\ n\ is\ odd \end{cases}$$

which is equivalent to (2).

Lemma 2. *If a symmetric and positive definite matrix exists* $R \in \Re^{n\times n}$ *and* Z_1, Z_2, Z_3, Z_4, Z_5, $Z_6 \in \Re^{3n\times 3n}$, N, $M \in \Re^{3n\times n}$, *we get:*

$$\Theta = \begin{pmatrix} Z_1 & Z_2 & Z_3 & N \\ * & Z_4 & Z_5 & M \\ * & * & Z_6 & M \\ * & * & * & R \end{pmatrix} \geq 0$$

3 FTS Analysis

Next, we establish sufficient conditions to study the FTS of the system (1).

Theorem 1. *(1) is FT stable according to* (c_1, c_2, R, N) *if there exist SPDM (symmetric positive definite matrices)* P, Q_1, Q_2, Q_3, R_1, R_2, *matrices* Z_{d1}^2, Z_{d1}^4, Z_{d1}^6, Z_{dk1}^1, Z_{dk1}^4, Z_{dk1}^6, Z_{dk2}^1, Z_{dk2}^4, $Z_{dk2}^6 \in \Re^{3n\times 3n}$, Z_{d1}^2, Z_{d1}^3, Z_{d1}^5, Z_{dk1}^1, Z_{dk1}^3, Z_{dk1}^5, Z_{dk2}^1, Z_{dk2}^3, $Z_{dk2}^5 \in \Re^{3n\times 3n}$, N_{d1}, M_{d1}, N_{dk1}, M_{dk1}, N_{dk2}, $M_{dk2} \in \Re^{3n\times n}$, *positive scalars* λ_i, $i = 1, 2, \ldots, 7$, *and* $\alpha \geq 0$ *such that:*

$$\begin{pmatrix} Z_{d1}^1 & Z_{d1}^2 & Z_{d1}^3 & N_{d1} \\ * & Z_{d1}^4 & Z_{d1}^5 & M_{d1} \\ * & * & Z_{d1}^6 & M_{d1} \\ * & * & * & R_1 \end{pmatrix} \geq 0, \quad \begin{pmatrix} Z_{dk1}^1 & Z_{dk1}^2 & Z_{dk1}^3 & N_{dk1} \\ * & Z_{dk1}^4 & Z_{dk1}^5 & M_{dk1} \\ * & * & Z_{dk1}^6 & M_{dk1} \\ * & * & * & R_2 \end{pmatrix} \geq 0,$$

$$\begin{pmatrix} Z_{dk2}^1 & Z_{dk2}^2 & Z_{dk2}^3 & N_{dk2} \\ * & Z_{dk2}^4 & Z_{dk2}^5 & M_{dk2} \\ * & * & Z_{dk2}^6 & M_{dk2} \\ * & * & * & R_2 \end{pmatrix} \geq 0,$$

$$\tilde{\Omega} + \begin{bmatrix} \Upsilon_1^T H_{d1} \Upsilon_1 + \Upsilon_2^T H_{dk1} \Upsilon_2 + \Upsilon_3^T H_{dk2} \Upsilon_3 - (\alpha - 1)\Upsilon_4 & 0 \\ * & 0 \end{bmatrix} < 0,$$

$$(\lambda_2 + d_1\lambda_3 + d_2\lambda_4 + d_2\lambda_5)c_1 + \left(\frac{d_1(d_1+1)}{2}\lambda_6 + \frac{(\bar{d}_{21})(d_2 + d_1 + 1)}{2}\lambda_7 \right)\epsilon < \alpha^{-N} c_2 \lambda_1$$

where

$$\lambda_1 = \lambda_{\min}(\tilde{P}), \;\; \lambda_2 = \lambda_{\max}(\tilde{P}), \;\; \lambda_3 = \lambda_{\max}(\tilde{Q}_1), \;\; \lambda_4 = \lambda_{\max}(\tilde{Q}_2),$$
$$\lambda_5 = \lambda_{\max}(\tilde{Q}_3), \;\; \lambda_6 = \lambda_{\max}(\tilde{R}_1), \;\; \lambda_7 = \lambda_{\max}(\tilde{Q}_7),$$
$$H_{d1} = d_1 Z_{d1}^1 + \gamma_1(d_1) Z_{d1}^4 + \gamma_2(d_1) Z_{d1}^6 + \mathrm{Sym}(N_{d1}\Pi_1 + M_{d1}\Pi_2 + \gamma_3(d_1) Z_{d1}^5),$$
$$H_{dk1} = (d_k - d_1) Z_{dk1}^1 + \gamma_1(d_k - d_1) Z_{dk1}^4 + \gamma_2(d_k - d_1) Z_{dk1}^6 + \mathrm{Sym}(N_{dk1}\Pi_1 + M_{dk1}\Pi_2 + \gamma_3(d_k - d_1) Z_{dk1}^5),$$
$$H_{dk2} = (d_2 - d_k) Z_{dk2}^1 + \gamma_1(d_2 - d_k) Z_{dk2}^4 + \gamma_2(d_2 - d_k) Z_{dk2}^6 + \mathrm{Sym}(N_{dk2}\Pi_1 + M_{dk2}\Pi_2 + \gamma_3(d_2 - d_k) Z_{dk2}^5),$$

$$\tilde{\Omega}=\begin{bmatrix} \Lambda & 0 & 0 & 0 & 0 & 0 & 0 & A^TP & d_1A^TR_1 & \overline{d}_{21}A^TR_2\\ * & -Q_1+Q_2 & 0 & 0 & 0 & 0 & 0 & 0 & 0 & 0\\ * & * & -Q_2+Q_3 & 0 & 0 & 0 & 0 & A_d^TP & d_1A_d^TR_1 & \overline{d}_{21}A_d^TR_2\\ * & * & * & -Q_3 & 0 & 0 & 0 & 0 & 0 & 0\\ * & * & * & * & 0 & 0 & 0 & 0 & 0 & 0\\ * & * & * & * & * & 0 & 0 & 0 & 0 & 0\\ * & * & * & * & * & * & 0 & 0 & 0 & 0\\ * & * & * & * & * & * & * & -P & 0 & 0\\ * & * & * & * & * & * & * & * & -d_1R_1 & 0\\ * & * & * & * & * & * & * & * & * & -\overline{d}_{21}R_2 \end{bmatrix},$$

$$\Upsilon_4=\begin{bmatrix} P+R_1+2R_2-Q_1 & 0 & 0 & 0 & -R_1 & -R_2 & -R_2\\ * & -Q_2 & 0 & 0 & 0 & 0 & 0\\ * & * & -Q_3 & 0 & 0 & 0 & 0\\ * & * & * & 0 & 0 & 0 & 0\\ * & * & * & * & (d_1+1)Q_1+R_1 & 0 & 0\\ * & * & * & * & * & \overline{d}_1Q_2+R_2 & 0\\ * & * & * & * & * & 0 & \overline{d}_2Q_3+R_2 \end{bmatrix},$$

$$\Lambda=-P-d_1R_1-\overline{d}_{21}R_2+Q_1\ \ \overline{d}_{21}=d_2-d_1,\ \ \overline{d}_1=d_k-d_1+1,$$
$$\overline{d}_2=d_2-d_k+1,\ \ \Upsilon_1^T=[e_1,e_2,e_5],\ \ \Upsilon_2^T=[e_2,e_3,e_6],$$
$$\Upsilon_3^T=[e_3,e_4,e_7],\ \ e_i=[0_{n\times(i-1)n},I_n,0_{n\times(7-i)n}]$$

Proof. Let:

$$V(k)=\sum_{i=1}^{3}V_i(k),\ \ V_1(k)=x^T(k)Px(k),$$
$$V_2(k)=\sum_{i=k-d_1}^{k-1}x^T(i)Q_1x(i)+\sum_{i=k-d_k}^{k-d_1-1}x^T(i)Q_2x(i)+\sum_{i=k-d_2}^{k-d_k-1}x^T(i)Q_3x(i),$$
$$V_3(k)=\sum_{i=-d_1}^{-1}\sum_{j=k+i}^{k-1}y^T(j)R_1y(j)+\sum_{i=-d_2}^{-d_1-1}\sum_{j=k+i}^{k-1}y^T(j)R_2y(j)$$

The variation of each term of the LKF between consecutive samples is:

$$\begin{aligned}\Delta V_1(k)&=V_1(k+1)-V_1(k)\\&=x^T(k+1)Px(k+1)-x^T(k)Px(k)\\&=\begin{bmatrix}x(k)\\x(k-d(k))\end{bmatrix}^T\begin{bmatrix}A^TPA-\Lambda & A^TPA_d\\ * & A_d^TPA_d\end{bmatrix}\begin{bmatrix}x(k)\\x(k-d(k))\end{bmatrix},\\ \Delta V_2(k)&=V_2(k+1)-V_2(k)\\&=\begin{bmatrix}x(k)\\x(k-d_1)\\x(k-d(k))\\x(k-d_2)\end{bmatrix}^T\begin{bmatrix}Q_1 & 0 & 0 & 0\\ * & -Q_1+Q_2 & 0 & 0\\ * & * & -Q_2+Q_3 & 0\\ * & * & * & -Q_3\end{bmatrix}\begin{bmatrix}x(k)\\x(k-d_1)\\x(k-d(k))\\x(k-d_2)\end{bmatrix},\end{aligned}$$

$$\begin{aligned}\Delta V_3(k) &= V_3(k+1) - V_3(k)\\ &= y^T(k)(d_1R_1 + \overline{d}_{21}R_2)y(k) - \sum_{i=k-d_1}^{k-1} y^T(i)R_1y(i) - \sum_{i=k-d_2}^{k-d_1-1} y^T(i)R_2y(i)\\ &\leq \begin{bmatrix} x(k) \\ x(k-d(k)) \end{bmatrix}^T \begin{bmatrix} \chi & A^T(d_1 + \overline{d}_{21}R_2)A_d \\ * & A_d^T(d_1 + \overline{d}_{21}R_2)A_d \end{bmatrix} \begin{bmatrix} x(k) \\ x(k-d(k)) \end{bmatrix}\\ &\quad +\xi^T(k)(\Upsilon_1^T H_{d1}\Upsilon_1 + \Upsilon_2^T H_{dk1}\Upsilon_2 + \Upsilon_3^T H_{dk2}\Upsilon_3)\xi(k)\end{aligned}$$

where

$$\chi = A^T(d_1R_1 + \overline{d}_{21}R_2)A - d_1R_1 - \overline{d}_{21}R_2,$$

$$\xi(k) = \Bigg[x^T(k), x^T(k-d_1), x^T(k-d_k), x^T(k-d_2), \frac{1}{d_1+1}\sum_{i=k-d_1}^{k} x^T(i),\\ \frac{1}{\overline{d}_1}\sum_{i=k-d_k}^{k-d_1} x^T(i), \frac{1}{\overline{d}_2}\sum_{i=k-d_2}^{k-d_k} x^T(i)\Bigg]^T$$

Easily:

$$\Delta V(k) \leq \xi^T(k)(\Omega + \Upsilon_1^T H_{d1}\Upsilon_1 + \Upsilon_2^T H_{dk1}\Upsilon_2 + \Upsilon_3^T H_{dk2}\Upsilon_3)\xi(k)$$

where

$$\Omega = \begin{bmatrix} \Theta & 0 & A^T(d_1 + \overline{d}_{21}R_2)A_d & 0 & 0\,0\,0 \\ * & -Q_1 + Q_2 & 0 & 0 & 0\,0\,0 \\ * & * & A_d^T(d_1 + \overline{d}_{21}R_2)A_d - Q_2 + Q_3 & 0 & 0\,0\,0 \\ * & * & * & -Q_3 & 0\,0\,0 \\ * & * & * & * & 0\,0\,0 \\ * & * & * & * & *\,0\,0 \\ * & * & * & * & *\,*\,0 \end{bmatrix},$$

$$\Theta = A^T(P + d_1R_1 + \overline{d}_{21}R_2)A - d_1R_1 - \overline{d}_{21}R_2 + Q_1$$

Also:

$$\begin{aligned}-(\alpha-1)V_2(k) &= \begin{bmatrix} x(k) \\ x(k-d_1) \\ x(k-d(k)) \end{bmatrix}^T \begin{bmatrix} (\alpha-1)Q_1 & 0 & 0 \\ * & (\alpha-1)Q_2 & 0 \\ * & * & -(\alpha-1)Q_3 \end{bmatrix}\\ &\quad\times \begin{bmatrix} x(k) \\ x(k-d_1) \\ x(k-d(k)) \end{bmatrix} -(\alpha-1)\Bigg(\sum_{i=-d_1}^{0} x^T(k+i)Q_1x(k+i)\\ &\quad+\sum_{i=-d_k}^{-d_1} x^T(k+i)Q_2x(k+i) + \sum_{i=-d_2}^{d_k} x^T(k+i)Q_3x(k+i)\Bigg)\end{aligned}$$

$$
\begin{aligned}
-(\alpha-1)V_3(k) &= -(\alpha-1)\left(\sum_{i=-d_1}^{-1}\sum_{j=k+i}^{k-1} y^T(j)R_1y(j) + \sum_{i=-d_2}^{-d_1-1}\sum_{j=k+i}^{k-1} y^T(j)R_2y(j)\right) \\
&\leq -\frac{(\alpha-1)}{d_1}\sum_{i=-d_1}^{-1}(x(k)-x(k+i))^T R_1(x(k)-x(k+i)) \\
&\quad -\frac{(\alpha-1)}{d_k-d_1}\sum_{i=-d_k}^{-d_1-1}(x(k)-x(k+i))^T R_2(x(k)-x(k+i)) \\
&\quad -\frac{(\alpha-1)}{d_2-d_k}\sum_{i=-d_2}^{-d_k-1}(x(k)-x(k+i))^T R_2(x(k)-x(k+i)) \\
&= -\frac{(\alpha-1)}{d_1}\sum_{i=-d_1}^{0}(x(k)-x(k+i))^T R_1(x(k)-x(k+i)) \\
&\quad -\frac{(\alpha-1)}{d_k-d_1}\sum_{i=-d_k}^{-d_1}(x(k)-x(k+i))^T R_2(x(k)-x(k+i)) \\
&\quad -\frac{(\alpha-1)}{d_2-d_k}\sum_{i=-d_2}^{-d_k}(x(k)-x(k+i))^T R_2(x(k)-x(k+i)) \\
&\leq -\frac{(\alpha-1)}{d_1+1}\sum_{i=-d_1}^{0}(x(k)-x(k+i))^T R_1(x(k)-x(k+i)) \\
&\quad -\frac{(\alpha-1)}{\overline{d}_1}\sum_{i=-d_k}^{-d_1}(x(k)-x(k+i))^T R_2(x(k)-x(k+i)) \\
&\quad -\frac{(\alpha-1)}{\overline{d}_2}\sum_{i=-d_2}^{-d_k}(x(k)-x(k+i))^T R_2(x(k)-x(k+i))
\end{aligned}
$$

Then, we can write:

$$
\begin{aligned}
-(\alpha-1)(V_2(k)+V_3(k)) &\leq -\frac{(\alpha-1)}{d_1+1}\sum_{i=-d_1}^{0}\begin{bmatrix} x(k) \\ x(k+i)\end{bmatrix}^T \begin{bmatrix} x(k) \\ x(k+i)\end{bmatrix} \\
&\quad -\frac{(\alpha-1)}{\overline{d}_1}\sum_{i=-d_k}^{-d_1}\begin{bmatrix} x(k) \\ x(k+i)\end{bmatrix}^T \begin{bmatrix} R_2 & -R_2 \\ * & \overline{d}_1Q_2+R_2\end{bmatrix}\begin{bmatrix} x(k) \\ x(k+i)\end{bmatrix} \\
&\quad -\frac{(\alpha-1)}{\overline{d}_2}\sum_{i=-d_2}^{-d_k}\begin{bmatrix} x(k) \\ x(k+i)\end{bmatrix}^T \begin{bmatrix} R_2 & -R_2 \\ * & \overline{d}_2Q_3+R_2\end{bmatrix}\begin{bmatrix} x(k) \\ x(k+i)\end{bmatrix} \\
&\quad +W_4^T\Gamma W_4
\end{aligned}
$$

where $\kappa = \begin{bmatrix} R_1 & -R_1 \\ * & (d_1+1)Q_1+R_1\end{bmatrix}$, $\Gamma = \begin{bmatrix} (\alpha-1)Q_1 & 0 & 0 \\ * & (\alpha-1)Q_2 & 0 \\ * & * & -(\alpha-1)Q_3\end{bmatrix}$, and $W_4 = \begin{bmatrix} x(k) \\ x(k-d_1) \\ x(k-d(k)) \end{bmatrix}$.

Thus, we obtain:

$$(d_1+1)Q_1 + R_1 > R_1 \Rightarrow R_1^{-1} < ((d_1+1)Q_1 + R_1)^{-1}$$

Therefore, the following inequality is true:

$$R_1 < R_1((d_1+1)Q_1 + R_1)^{-1}R_1$$

Using the Schur complement, we have $\begin{bmatrix} R_1 & -R_1 \\ * & (d_1+1)Q_1 + R_1 \end{bmatrix} > 0$.

Following the same procedure, we can write:

$$\begin{bmatrix} R_2 & -R_2 \\ * & (\bar{d}_1)Q_2 + R_2 \end{bmatrix} > 0, \quad \begin{bmatrix} R_2 & -R_2 \\ * & \bar{d}_2Q_3 + R_2 \end{bmatrix} > 0$$

Then, we obtain:

$$\begin{aligned} -(\alpha-1)(V_2(k)+V_3(k)) \leq & -(\alpha-1)W_1^T \begin{bmatrix} R_1 & -R_1 \\ * & (d_1+1)Q_1 + R_1 \end{bmatrix} W_1 \\ & -(\alpha-1)W_2^T \begin{bmatrix} R_2 & -R_2 \\ * & \bar{d}_1Q_2 + R_2 \end{bmatrix} W_2 \\ & -(\alpha-1)W_3^T \begin{bmatrix} R_2 & -R_2 \\ * & \bar{d}_2Q_3 + R_2 \end{bmatrix} W_3 + W_4^T \Gamma W_4 \end{aligned}$$

where

$$W_1 = \begin{bmatrix} x(k) \\ \frac{1}{d_1+1}\sum_{i=k-d_1}^{k} x(i) \end{bmatrix}, \quad W_2 = \begin{bmatrix} x(k) \\ \frac{1}{\bar{d}_1}\sum_{i=k-d_k}^{k-d_1} x(i) \end{bmatrix}, \quad W_3 = \begin{bmatrix} x(k) \\ \frac{1}{\bar{d}_2}\sum_{i=k-d_2}^{k-d_k} x(i) \end{bmatrix}$$

That is to say:

$$-(\alpha-1)V(k) \leq -(\alpha-1)\xi^T(k)\Upsilon_4\xi(k)$$

Writing:

$$\Delta V(k) \leq \xi^T(k)\Xi\xi(k) + (\alpha-1)V(k)$$

where

$$\Xi = \Omega + \Upsilon_1^T H_{d1}\Upsilon_1 + \Upsilon_2^T H_{dk1}\Upsilon_2 + \Upsilon_3^T H_{dk2}\Upsilon_3 - (\alpha-1)\Upsilon_4$$

Supposing that $\Xi < 0$, then $\Delta V(k) < (\alpha-1)V(k)$ which means that $V(k+1) < \alpha V(k)$. So, the conclusion is:

$$V(k) < \alpha V(k-1) < \alpha^2 V(k-2) < \ldots < \alpha^k V(0)$$

LKF's initial value is:

$$
\begin{aligned}
V(0) &= x^T(0)Px(0) + \sum_{i=-d_1}^{-1} x^T(i)Q_1x(i) + \sum_{i=-d_k}^{-d_1-1} x^T(i)Q_2x(i) \\
&+ \sum_{i=-d_2}^{-d_k-1} x^T(i)Q_3x(i) + V_3(k) + \sum_{i=-d_1}^{-1}\sum_{j=i}^{-1} y^T(j)R_1y(j) \\
&+ \sum_{i=-d_2}^{-d_1-1}\sum_{j=i}^{-1} y^T(j)R_2y(j) + (\lambda_2 + d_1\lambda_3 + d_2\lambda_4 + d_2\lambda_5)c_1 \\
&+ \left(\frac{d_1(d_1+1)}{2}\lambda_6 + \frac{(\overline{d}_{21})(d_2+d_1+1)}{2}\lambda_7\right)\epsilon
\end{aligned}
$$

It is known:

$$
V(k) \geq x^T(k)Px(k) \geq \lambda_{\min}(\tilde{P})x^T(k)Rx(k)
$$

and:

$$
\begin{aligned}
x^T(k)Rx(k) < \frac{\alpha^N}{\lambda_{\min}(\tilde{P})}\Bigg((\lambda_2 + d_1\lambda_3 + d_2\lambda_4 + d_2\lambda_5)c_1 + \Bigg(\frac{d_1(d_1+1)}{2}\lambda_6 \\
+ \frac{(\overline{d}_{21})(d_2+d_1+1)}{2}\lambda_7\Bigg)\epsilon\Bigg) < c_2
\end{aligned}
$$

and consequently the proof is completed.

Corollary 1. *(1) is FT stable according to* (c_1, c_2, R, N) *if there exist SPDM* P, Q_1, Q_2, Q_3, R_1, R_2, *matrices* Z_{d1}^2, Z_{d1}^4, Z_{d1}^6, Z_{dk1}^1, Z_{dk1}^4, Z_{dk1}^6, Z_{dk2}^1, Z_{dk2}^4, $Z_{dk2}^6 \in \Re^{3n\times 3n}$, Z_{d1}^2, Z_{d1}^3, Z_{d1}^5, Z_{dk1}^1, Z_{dk1}^3, Z_{dk1}^5, Z_{dk2}^1, Z_{dk2}^3, $Z_{dk2}^5 \in \Re^{3n\times 3n}$, N_{d1}, M_{d1}, N_{dk1}, M_{dk1}, N_{dk2}, $M_{dk2} \in \Re^{3n\times n}$, *positive scalars* λ_i, $i = 1, 2, \ldots, 7$, *and* $\alpha \geq 0$ *such that:*

$$
Z_{dki}^5 + (Z_{dki}^5)^T \geq 0, \quad i = 1, 2, \quad \begin{pmatrix} Z_{d1}^1 & Z_{d1}^2 & Z_{d1}^3 & N_{d1} \\ * & Z_{d1}^4 & Z_{d1}^5 & M_{d1} \\ * & * & Z_{d1}^6 & M_{d1} \\ * & * & * & R_1 \end{pmatrix} \geq 0,
$$

$$
\begin{pmatrix} Z_{dk1}^1 & Z_{dk1}^2 & Z_{dk1}^3 & N_{dk1} \\ * & Z_{dk1}^4 & Z_{dk1}^5 & M_{dk1} \\ * & * & Z_{dk1}^6 & M_{dk1} \\ * & * & * & R_2 \end{pmatrix} \geq 0, \quad \begin{pmatrix} Z_{dk2}^1 & Z_{dk2}^2 & Z_{dk2}^3 & N_{dk2} \\ * & Z_{dk2}^4 & Z_{dk2}^S & M_{dk2} \\ * & * & Z_{dk2}^d & M_{dk2} \\ * & * & * & R_2 \end{pmatrix} \geq 0,
$$

$$
\tilde{\Omega} + \begin{bmatrix} \Upsilon_1^T H_1 \Upsilon_1 + \Upsilon_2^T H_2 \Upsilon_2 + \Upsilon_3^T H_3 \Upsilon_3 - (\alpha-1)\tilde{\Upsilon}_4 & 0 \\ * & 0 \end{bmatrix} < 0,
$$

$$(\lambda_2 + d_1\lambda_3 + d_2\lambda_4 + d_2\lambda_5)c_1 + \left(\frac{d_1(d_1+1)}{2}\lambda_6 + \frac{(\bar{d}_{21})(d_2+d_1+1)}{2}\lambda_7\right)\epsilon < \alpha^{-N}c_2\lambda_1$$

where

$$\begin{aligned}
H_1 &= d_1 Z_{d1}^1 + \gamma_1^{d_1} Z_{d1}^4 + \gamma_2^{d_1} Z_{d1}^6 + \mathrm{Sym}(N_{d1}\Pi_1 + M_{d1}\Pi_2 + \gamma_3^{d_1})Z_{d1}^5),\\
H_2 &= d_2 Z_{dk1}^1 + \gamma_1^{d_2} Z_{dk1}^4 + \gamma_2^{d_2} Z_{dk1}^6 + \mathrm{Sym}(N_{dk1}\Pi_1 + M_{dk1}\Pi_2),\\
H_3 &= d_2 Z_{dk2}^1 + \gamma_1^{d_2} Z_{dk2}^4 + \gamma_2^{d_2} Z_{dk2}^6 + \mathrm{Sym}(N_{dk2}\Pi_1 + M_{dk2}\Pi_2),\\
S_1^{d_1} &= \gamma_{d_1.2m}^{\max} + 2\gamma_{d_1.m+1}^{\max} + \frac{d_1(d_1-1)}{3}, \quad \gamma_2^{d_1} = \gamma_{d_1.2m}^{\max},\\
&\begin{cases} -\gamma_{d_1.2m}^{\max} - \gamma_{d_1.m+1}^{\max} & if\ \mathrm{Sym}(Z_5^{d1}) \le 0\\ -\gamma_{d_1.2m}^{\min} - S_{d_1.m+1}^{\min} & if\ \mathrm{Sym}(Z_5^{d1}) \ge 0 \end{cases},\\
\gamma_1^{d_2} &= \gamma_{d_2.2m}^{\max} + 2\gamma_{d_2.m+1}^{\max} + \frac{d_2(d_2-1)}{3}, \quad \gamma_2^{d_2} = \gamma_{d_2.2m}^{\max}
\end{aligned}$$

Proof. We can see directly that:

$$\Upsilon_1^T H_{d1}\Upsilon_1 + \Upsilon_2^T H_{dk1}\Upsilon_2 + \Upsilon_3^T H_{dk2}\Upsilon_3 - (\alpha-1)\Upsilon_4 < \Upsilon_1^T H_1\Upsilon_1 + \Upsilon_2^T H_2\Upsilon_2 + \Upsilon_3^T H_3\Upsilon_3 - (\alpha-1)\tilde{\Upsilon}_4$$

This means that:

$$\tilde{\Omega} + \begin{bmatrix} \Upsilon_1^T H_{d1}\Upsilon_1 + \Upsilon_2^T H_{dk1}\Upsilon_2 + \Upsilon_3^T H_{dk2}\Upsilon_3 - (\alpha-1)\Upsilon_4 + \Upsilon_3^T H_3\Upsilon_3 - (\alpha-1)\tilde{\Upsilon}_4 & 0\\ * & 0 \end{bmatrix} < \tilde{\Omega} + \begin{bmatrix} \Upsilon_1^T H_1\Upsilon_1 + \Upsilon_2^T H_2\Upsilon_2 + \Upsilon_3^T H_3\Upsilon_3 - (\alpha-1)\tilde{\Upsilon}_4 & 0\\ * & 0 \end{bmatrix}$$

The proof is completed.

4 Applying the Method

Let

$$A = \begin{pmatrix} 0.6 & 0\\ 0.35 & 0.7 \end{pmatrix}, \quad A_d = \begin{pmatrix} 0.1 & 0\\ 0.2 & 0.1 \end{pmatrix}, \quad R = \begin{pmatrix} 1 & 0\\ 0 & 1 \end{pmatrix},$$
$$\alpha = 1.001,\ \epsilon = 1.1,\ c_1 = 2.1,\ c_2 = 80,\ N = 80$$

the feasability of Corollary 1 is tested with this model. Table 1 shows the results of comparing our method with [10,17,18,20]. Our LMIs approach is less conservative.

Table 1. The values of d_2 for several d_1

d_1	2	3	4	5	6
Theorem 1 [17]	6	6	7	8	9
Theorem 1 [20]	8	8	9	10	11
Theorem 1 [18]	10	11	12	13	14
Corollary 1 [10]	13	14	15	16	17
Corollary 1	18	19	20	21	22

5 Conclusion

The paper discusses different FTS criteria for discrete systems and delays changing over time. An LKF and a new FMBI inequality have been developed; and, a novel derivation of the single summation that appears in the LKF deduction has been studied. Finally, novel and sufficient conditions, formulated as LMIs, are given ensuring the FTS. The numerical example clarifies the approach (pros and efficiency).

Acknowledgments and Funding Information. Teresa Alvarez was funded by TED2021-129716B-I00, funded by MCIN/AEI/10.13039/501100011033 and the European Union "nextgenerationeu/PRTR".

References

1. Ariba, Y., Gouaisbaut, F., Johansson, K.H.: Robust stability of time-varying delay systems: the quadratic separation approach. Asian J. Control **14**(5), 1205–1214 (2012)
2. Chen, J., Lu, J., Xu, S.: Summation inequality and its application to stability analysis for time-delay systems. IET Control Theory Appl. **10**(4), 391–395 (2016)
3. El Akchioui, N., El Fezazi, N., Frih, A., Taoussi, M., Farkous, R., Tissir, E.H.: Finite time stability of linear time varying delay systems using free matrix based integral inequalities. Results Control Optim. **10**, 100200 (2023)
4. El Akchioui, N., El Fezazi, N., Farkous, R., Alvarez, T., Tissir, E.H.: Finite-time stability for discrete-time systems with time-varying delays and nonlinear perturbations using relaxed summation inequality. Iran. J. Sci. Technol. Trans. Electr. Eng. **48**(1), 433–443 (2024)
5. El Fezazi, N., Fahim, M., Idrissi, S., Farkous, R., Alvarez, T., Tissir, E.H.: New delay-dependent finite-time stabilization of Takagi-Sugeno fuzzy approaches for delayed nonlinear systems. Asian J. Control (2024). https://doi.org/10.1002/asjc.3509
6. El Fezazi, N., Frih, A., Lamrabet, O.: New H_∞ dynamic observer design for time-delay systems subject to disturbances. Int. J. Syst. Sci. **51**(14), 2610–2624 (2020)
7. El Fezazi, N., El Haoussi, F., Tissir, E.H., Alvarez, T., Tadeo, F.: Robust stabilization using a sampled-data strategy of uncertain neutral state-delayed systems subject to input limitations. Int. J. Appl. Math. Comput. Sci. **28**(1), 111–122 (2018)

8. Jiang, X., Han, Q.L., Yu, X.: Stability criteria for linear discrete-time systems with interval-like time-varying delay. In: Proceedings of American Control Conference, Portland, OR, USA, pp. 2817–2822 (2005)
9. Kamenkov, G.: On stability of motion over a finite interval of time. J. Appl. Math. Mech. **17**(2), 529–540 (1953)
10. Kang, W., Zhong, S., Shi, K., Cheng, J.: Finite-time stability for discrete-time system with time-varying delay and nonlinear perturbations. ISA Trans. **60**, 67–73 (2016)
11. Kao, C.Y., Rantzer, A.: Stability analysis of systems with uncertain time-varying delays. Automatica **43**(6), 959–970 (2007)
12. Knoebel, A., Laubenbacher, R., Lodder, J., Pengelley, D.: Mathematical masterpieces: further chronicles by the explorers. Springer Science & Business Media (2007)
13. Lin, X., Liang, K., Li, H., Jiao, Y., Nie, J.: Finite-time stability and stabilization for continuous systems with additive time-varying delays. Circuits Syst. Signal Process. **36**, 2971–2990 (2017)
14. Liu, H., Shi, P., Karimi, H.R., Chadli, M.: Finite-time stability and stabilisation for a class of nonlinear systems with time-varying delay. Int. J. Syst. Sci. **47**(6), 1433–1444 (2016)
15. Li, X., Gao, H.: A new model transformation of discrete-time systems with time-varying delay and its application to stability analysis. IEEE Trans. Autom. Control **56**(9), 2172–2178 (2011)
16. Seuret, A., Gouaisbaut, F., Fridman, E.: Stability of discrete-time systems with time-varying delays via a novel summation inequality. IEEE Trans. Autom. Control **60**(10), 2740–2745 (2015)
17. Stojanović, S.B., Debeljković, D.L., Dimitrijević, N.: Finite-time stability of discrete-time systems with time-varying delay. Chem. Ind. Chem. Eng. Q. **18**(4–1), 525–533 (2012)
18. Zhang, Z., Zhang, Z., Zhang, H., Zheng, B., Karimi, H.R.: Finite-time stability analysis and stabilization for linear discrete-time system with time-varying delay. J. Franklin Inst. **351**(6), 3457–3476 (2014)
19. Zhong, Q., Cheng, J., Zhao, Y.: Delay-dependent finite-time boundedness of a class of Markovian switching neural networks with time-varying delays. ISA Trans. **57**, 43–50 (2015)
20. Zuo, Z., Li, H., Wang, Y.: New criterion for finite-time stability of linear discrete-time systems with time-varying delay. J. Franklin Inst. **350**(9), 2745–2756 (2013)

Finite-Time Stability Analysis of Delayed Systems Using a Novel Integral Inequality Approach

El Houssine Aouchicha[1(✉)], Nabil El Fezazi[2,3], Mohamed Fahim[4], Amine El Fathi[1], Nabil El Akchioui[1], and Teresa Alvarez[5(✉)]

[1] LRSDI Laboratory, Faculty of Sciences and Techniques, Abdelmalek Essaâdi University, Al Hoceïma, Morocco
houssinftouhi@gmail.com, {amelfathi,n.elakchioui}@uae.ac.ma
[2] IMD-E, Higher School of Technology of Dakhla, Ibn Zohr University, Agadir, Morocco
n.elfezazi@uiz.ac.ma
[3] LISAC Laboratory, Faculty of Sciences Dhar El Mehraz, Sidi Mohammed Ben Abdellah University, Fez, Morocco
[4] Computer Science Research Laboratory, Ibn Tofail University, Kenitra, Morocco
mfahim@uae.ac.ma
[5] Industrial Engineering School, University of Valladolid, Dr. Mergelina S/N, 47005 Valladolid, Spain
teresa.alvarez.alvarez@uva.es

Abstract. Our research deals with the FTS (Finite-Time Stability) problem for linear and delay-dependent systems using a novel integral inequality and a LKF (Lyapunov-Krasovskii Functional). Then, sufficient conditions are provided to ensure the FTS introducing some free-weighting matrices. The delays (varying in time) are differentiable and their derivatives are bounded. The conditions obtained in this paper are specified in terms of linear matrix inequalities (LMIs) to achieve the desired results. The method is explained with an example, the effectiveness is clearly stated.

1 Introduction

A really trending topic in the field of dynamic systems is the study and analysis of systems with time-varying delays. The number and quality of results in this topic is quite remarkable as shown in [1,3,6,8,9], among others. Two different stability criteria can be considered: delay-dependent and delay-independent. The delay-dependent approach (that takes into account the information on the size of time delays) is less conservative ([2,10,15–18,21]) than the independent one. Our research follows the path to look for less conservative results.

There are different approaches for studying the stability and reducing the conservatism. One that is specially remarkable is the Wirtinger-based integral inequality [13], because is a more accurate integral inequality that includes several other techniques, such as the Jensen inequality [5], the reciprocally convex

I. Aboudrar et al. (Eds.): ICESST 2024, SUCI, pp. 441–451, 2025.
https://doi.org/10.1007/978-3-031-86705-7_41

approach [11], the augmented model [12], the new cross-term bounding technique [7], the delay-partitioning approach [4], the triple integral terms [14], the parameterized neutral model transformation method [8], and the free-weighting matrices technique [19]. Although some of these results improve the stability criteria, FTS has received little attention, and more results can be attained to reduce the conservatism. That is the keystone of our research.

Motivated by the above, a new free-matrix-based integral inequality and a new LKF are proposed to address the FTS problem for delay-dependent linear systems. Then, sufficient conditions in terms of LMIs to achieve the desired performance are given using some free-weighting matrices. Finally, a less conservative LMI-based design is proposed and solved with MATLAB showing very good results.

2 Problem Formulation

Consider:

$$\dot{x}(t) = Ax(t) + A_d x(t - h(t)) \tag{1}$$

The associated function on initial state is

$$\varphi(\tau) = x(\tau), \quad \tau \in [-h; 0]$$

where $x(t) \in \Re^n$ (state vector); A, $A_d \in \Re^{n\times n}$ (constant system matrices); and the delay $h(t)$, time dependent, satisfies $0 \leq h(t) \leq h$, $\dot{h}(t) \leq h_D$.

Definition 1. *[20] The system (1) is said to be FT stable according to* (c_1, c_2, T, R), *where* $0 \leq c_1 < c_2$, *if*

$$x^T(t)x(t) < c_2, \quad \forall t \in [0, T]$$

with $\sup_{\tau\in[-h,0]} \varphi^T(\tau)\varphi(\tau) < c_1$.

Lemma 1. *Let* x *be a differentiable function:* $[a, b] \to \Re^n$. *Then, if there exist SPDM (symmetric positive definite matrices)* $R \in \Re^{n\times n}$, Z_1, Z_4, $Z_6 \in \Re^{3n\times 3n}$, *and appropriately dimensioned matrices* Z_2, Z_3, $Z_5 \in \Re^{3n\times 3n}$, N, $M \in \Re^{3n\times n}$ *satisfying:*

$$\begin{bmatrix} Z_1 & Z_2 & Z_3 & N \\ * & Z_4 & Z_5 & M \\ * & * & Z_6 & M \\ * & * & * & R \end{bmatrix} \geq 0$$

this inequality holds :

$$-\int_a^b \dot{x}^T(s)R\dot{x}(s)ds \leq \varpi^T \Omega \varpi \tag{2}$$

for $k \in \{n/n = 2m+1;\ \ m \in \mathbb{Z}^{*+}\}$ *where*

$$\varpi = \left[x^T(b)\ x^T(a)\ \frac{1}{b-a}\int_a^b x^T(s)ds\right]^T,$$
$$\Omega = (b-a)(Z_1 + g_1 Z_4 + g_2 Z_6 + sym(N\Pi_1 + M\Pi_2 + g_3 Z_5),$$
$$g_1 = (b-a)\Big(\frac{1}{2k+1} + \frac{2}{k+2} + \frac{1}{3}\Big),\ \ g_2 = \frac{b-a}{2k+1},$$
$$g_3 = (b-a)\Big(-\frac{1}{2k+1} - \frac{1}{k+2}\Big)$$

Proof. Define

$$f_1(s) = -f_2(s) + \frac{b+a-2\,s}{b-a},\ \ f_2(s) = -\frac{(b+a-2\,s)^k}{(b-a)^k},\ \ k \in \mathbb{Z}^{*+},$$
$$\zeta(s) = [\varpi^T\ \ f_1(s)\varpi^T\ \ f_2(s)\varpi^T\ \ \dot{x}^T(s)]^T$$

Then:

$$\zeta^T(s)\Theta\zeta(s) \geq 0$$

On the other hand, we obtain:

$$\begin{aligned}
\int_a^b f_1(s)ds &= \int_a^b \Big(\frac{(b+a-2\,s)^k}{(b-a)^k} + \frac{b+a-2\,s}{b-a}\Big)ds \\
&= \frac{1}{(b-a)^k}\Big[-\frac{1}{2(k+1)}(b+a-2\,s)^{k+1}\Big]_a^b + \frac{1}{b-a} \\
&\quad \times\Big[-\frac{1}{4}(b+a-2\,s)^2\Big]_a^b \\
&= \frac{1}{(b-a)^k}\Big[-\frac{1}{2(k+1)}(a-b)^{k+1} + \frac{1}{2(k+1)}(b-a)^{k+1}\Big] \\
&= \frac{b-a}{2(k+1)}(1-(-1)^{k+1}), \\
\int_a^b f_2(s)ds &= -\frac{b-a}{2(k+1)}(1-(-1)^{k+1})
\end{aligned}$$

Thus:

- If $k = 2n/n \in \mathbb{Z}^+$, then $\displaystyle\int_a^b f_1(s)ds = -\int_a^b f_2(s)ds = \frac{b-a}{k+1}$
- If $k = 2n+1/n \in \mathbb{Z}^+$, then $\displaystyle\int_a^b f_1(s)ds = -\int_a^b f_2(s)ds = 0$

Considering $k = 2n + 1/n \in \mathbb{Z}^+$, we have:

$$\int_a^b f_1^2(s)ds = \int_a^b \Big(\frac{(b+a-2\,s)^k}{(b-a)^k} + \frac{b+a-2\,s}{b-a}\Big)^2 ds$$
$$= \frac{1}{(b-a)^{2k}}\Big[-\frac{1}{2(2k+1)}(b+a-2\,s)^{2k+1}\Big]_a^b$$
$$+\frac{1}{(b-a)^{k+1}}\Big[-\frac{1}{k+2}(b+a-2\,s)^{k+2}\Big]_a^b$$
$$+\frac{1}{(b-a)^2}\Big[-\frac{1}{6}(b+a-2\,s)^3\Big]_a^b$$
$$= (b-a)\Big[\frac{1}{2(2k+1)}(1-(-1)^{2k+1})$$
$$+\frac{1}{k+2}(1-(-1)^{k+2}) + \frac{1}{3}\Big],$$

$$\int_a^b f_2^2(s)ds = \int_a^b \frac{(b+a-2\,s)^{2k}}{(b-a)^{2k}} ds$$
$$= \frac{1}{(b-a)^{2k}}\Big[-\frac{1}{2(2k+1)}(b+a-2\,s)^{2k+1}\Big]_a^b$$
$$= (b-a)\frac{1}{2(2k+1)}(1-(-1)^{2k+1}),$$

$$\int_a^b f_1(s)f_2(s)ds = \int_a^b \Big(\frac{(b+a-2\,s)^k}{(b-a)^k} + \frac{b+a-2\,s}{b-a}\Big)$$
$$\times\Big(-\frac{(b+a-2\,s)^k}{(b-a)^k}\Big)ds$$
$$= \frac{1}{(b-a)^{2k}}\Big[\frac{1}{2(2k+1)}(b+a-2\,s)^{2k+1}\Big]_a^b$$
$$+\frac{1}{(b-a)^{k+1}}\Big[\frac{1}{2(k+2)}(b+a-2\,s)^{k+2}\Big]_a^b$$
$$= -(b-a)\Big[\frac{1}{2(2k+1)}(1-(-1)^{2k+1})$$
$$+\frac{1}{2(k+2)}(1-(-1)^{k+2})\Big],$$

$$\int_a^b (f_1(s)+f_2(s))\dot{x}(s)ds = \int_a^b \frac{a+b-2\,s}{b-a}\dot{x}(s)ds$$
$$= \frac{1}{b-a}[(a+b-2\,s)x(s)] + \frac{2}{b-a}\int_a^b x(s)ds$$
$$= -x(b) - x(a) + \frac{2}{b-a}\int_a^b x(s)ds$$

For $k = 2n + 1/n \in \mathbb{Z}^+$, we can write:

$$\int_a^b f_1^2(s)ds = (b-a)\Big[\frac{1}{2k+1} + \frac{2}{k+2} + \frac{1}{3}\Big], \quad \int_a^b f_2^2(s)ds = \frac{(b-a)}{2k+1},$$
$$\int_a^b f_1(s)f_2(s)ds = -\frac{b-a}{2k+1} - \frac{b-a}{k+2}$$

Then, the following equation is obtained.

$$\begin{aligned}\int_a^b \zeta^T(s)\Theta\zeta(s)ds = \varpi^T\Big((b-a)Z_1 + g_1Z_4 + g_2Z_6 \\ +sym(N\Pi_1 + M\Pi_2 + g_3Z_5)\Big)\varpi \\ + \int_a^b \dot{x}^T(s)R\dot{x}(s)ds \geq 0\end{aligned}$$

Then, we have :

$$\begin{aligned}-\int_a^b \dot{x}^T(s)R\dot{x}(s)ds \leq \varpi^T\Big((b-a)Z_1 + g_1Z_4 + g_2Z_6 \\ +sym(N\Pi_1 + M\Pi_2 + g_3Z_5)\Big)\varpi\end{aligned}$$

The proof is finally completed.

3 FTS Analysis

Theorem 1. *The system (1) is FT stable according to* (c_1, c_2, T, R) *if there exist SPDM* P, Q_1, Q_2 $(Q_1 > Q_2)$, Z_1, Z_4, $Z_6 \in \Re^{3n\times 3n}$, *appropriately sized matrices* Z_2, Z_3, $Z_5 \in \Re^{3n\times 3n}$, N, $M \in \Re^{3n\times n}$, *and positive scalars* λ_i, $i = 1, \ldots, 4$*:*

$$\begin{pmatrix} Z_1 & Z_2 & Z_3 & N \\ * & Z_4 & Z_5 & M \\ * & * & Z_6 & M \\ * & * & * & P \end{pmatrix} \geq 0,$$

$$\begin{pmatrix} \Lambda & \Omega_{12} & \Omega_{13} + \alpha P & PA_d & hA^TP \\ * & \Omega_{22} - Q_2 & \Omega_{23} & 0 & 0 \\ * & * & \Omega_{33} - \alpha h Q_2 - \alpha P & 0 & 0 \\ * & * & * & -\overline{h}_D Q_{12} & hA_d^TP \\ * & * & * & * & -hP \end{pmatrix} < 0, \tag{3}$$

$$\frac{e^{\alpha T}}{\lambda_1}\Big(\Big(c_1 + \mu\frac{h^2}{2}\Big)\lambda_2 + c_1 h(\lambda_3 + \lambda_4)\Big) < c_2$$

for $k \in \{n/n = 2m+1;\ m \in \mathbb{Z}^+\}$ *where* $Q_{12} = Q_1 - Q_2$, $\overline{h}_D = 1 - h_D$ *and*

$$\begin{pmatrix} \Omega_{11} & \Omega_{12} & \Omega_{13} \\ * & \Omega_{22} & \Omega_{23} \\ * & * & \Omega_{33} \end{pmatrix} = hZ_1 + g_1 Z_4 + g_2 Z_6 + sym(N\Pi_1 + M\Pi_2 + g_3 Z_5),$$

$$\Lambda = \Omega_{11} + PA + A^T P + Q_1 - 2\alpha P,\ g_1 = h\Big(\frac{1}{2k+1} + \frac{2}{k+2} + \frac{1}{3}\Big),$$

$$g_2 = \frac{h}{2k+1},\ g_3 = h\Big(-\frac{1}{2k+1} - \frac{1}{k+2}\Big),\ 0 < \lambda_1 I < \tilde{P} < \lambda_2 I,$$

$$0 < \tilde{Q}_1 < \lambda_3 I,\ 0 < \tilde{Q}_2 < \lambda_4 I,\ \tilde{P} = R^{\frac{-1}{2}} P R^{\frac{-1}{2}},$$

$$\tilde{Q}_1 = R^{\frac{-1}{2}} Q_1 R^{\frac{-1}{2}},\ \tilde{Q}_2 = R^{\frac{-1}{2}} Q_2 R^{\frac{-1}{2}}$$

Proof. Let:

$$V(t) = \sum_{i=1}^{3} V_i(t)$$

where

$$\begin{aligned} V_1(t) &= x^T(t) P x(t), \\ V_2(t) &= \int_{t-h(t)}^{t} x^T(s) Q_1 x(s) ds + \int_{t-h}^{t-h(t)} x^T(s) Q_2 x(s) ds, \\ V_3(t) &= \int_{-h}^{0} \int_{t+\theta}^{t} \dot{x}^T(s) P \dot{x}(s) ds d\theta \end{aligned}$$

Obtaining:

$$\begin{aligned} \dot{V}_1(t) &= 2x^T(t) P \dot{x}(t) \\ &= x^T(t)(PA + A^T P)x(t) + sym(x^T(t) P A_d x(t - h(t))), \\ \dot{V}_2(t) &= x^T(t) Q_1 x(t) - x^T(t-h) Q_2 x(t-h) \\ &\quad -(1 - \dot{h}(t)) x^T(t - h(t)) Q_{12} x(t - h(t)) \\ &\leq x^T(t) Q_1 x(t) - x^T(t-h) Q_2 x(t-h) \\ &\quad -\overline{h}_D x^T(t - h(t)) Q_{12} x(t - h(t)), \\ \dot{V}_3(t) &= h\dot{x}^T(t) P \dot{x}(t) - \int_{t-h}^{t} \dot{x}^T(s) P \dot{x}(s) ds \end{aligned}$$

Then, it is easy to see that :

$$\dot{V}(t) = \xi^T(t) \begin{pmatrix} PA + A^T P + Q_1 + hA^T PA & 0 & 0 & PA_d + hA^T PA_d \\ * & -Q_2 & 0 & 0 \\ * & * & 0 & 0 \\ * & * & * & -\overline{h}_D Q_{12} + hA_d^T PA_d \end{pmatrix} \xi(t) - \int_{t-h}^{t} \dot{x}^T(s) P \dot{x}(s) ds$$

where

$$\xi^T(t) = \left[\varpi^T \ \ x^T(t-h(t))\right]^T, \ \ \varpi = \left[x^T(t), x^T(t-h), \int_{t-h}^{t} x^T(s)ds\right]^T$$

Applying Lemma 1, we have :

$$\dot{V}(t) = \xi^T(t) \begin{pmatrix} \Omega_{11} + PA + A^T P + Q_1 + hA^T PA & \Omega_{12} & \Omega_{13} & PA_d + hA^T PA_d \\ * & \Omega_{22} - Q_2 & \Omega_{23} & 0 \\ * & * & \Omega_{33} & 0 \\ * & * & * & -\overline{h}_D Q_{12} + hA_d^T PA_d \end{pmatrix} \xi(t)$$

for $k \in \{n/n = 2m+1; \ \ m \in \mathbb{Z}^+\}$ where

$$\begin{pmatrix} \Omega_{11} & \Omega_{12} & \Omega_{13} \\ * & \Omega_{22} & \Omega_{23} \\ * & * & \Omega_{33} \end{pmatrix} = hZ_1 + g_1 Z_4 + g_2 Z_6 + sym(N\Pi_1 + M\Pi_2 + g_3 Z_5),$$

$$g_1 = h\Big(\frac{1}{2k+1} + \frac{2}{k+2} + \frac{1}{3}\Big), \ \ g_2 = \frac{h}{2k+1}, \ \ g_3 = h\Big(-\frac{1}{2k+1} - \frac{1}{k+2}\Big)$$

On the other hand, we can write :

$$\begin{aligned} -\alpha V_2(t) &= -\alpha\Big(\int_{t-h(t)}^{t} x^T(s)Q_1 x(s)ds + \int_{t-h}^{t-h(t)} x^T(s)Q_2 x(s)ds\Big) \\ &\leq -\alpha \int_{t-h}^{t} x^T(s)Q_2 x(s)ds, \\ -\alpha V_3(t) &\leq -\alpha \int_{-h}^{0} \Big(x(t) - x(t+\theta)\Big)^T \frac{1}{h} P\Big(x(t) - x(t+\theta)\Big) d\theta \end{aligned}$$

where $Q_1 > Q_2$. Then, we obtain :

$$-\alpha\Big(V_2(t) + V_3(t)\Big) \leq -\alpha \int_{-h}^{0} \begin{bmatrix} x(t) \\ x(t+\theta) \end{bmatrix}^T \begin{bmatrix} \frac{1}{h}P & -\frac{1}{h}P \\ * & Q_2 + \frac{1}{h}P \end{bmatrix} \begin{bmatrix} x(t) \\ x(t+\theta) \end{bmatrix} d\theta$$

Thus, the following inequality is true :

$$\begin{bmatrix} \frac{1}{h}P & -\frac{1}{h}P \\ * & Q_2 + \frac{1}{h}P \end{bmatrix} > 0$$

since

$$\begin{aligned} \frac{1}{h}P - \frac{1}{h^2}P\Big(Q_2 + \frac{1}{h}P\Big)^{-1} P > 0 &\Leftrightarrow \frac{1}{h}P^{-1} - \frac{1}{h^2}\Big(Q_2 + \frac{1}{h}P\Big)^{-1} > 0 \\ &\Leftrightarrow I > \frac{1}{h}P\Big(Q_2 + \frac{1}{h}P\Big)^{-1} \\ &\Leftrightarrow \Big(Q_2 + \frac{1}{h}P\Big) > \frac{1}{h}P \end{aligned}$$

Using the Jensen inequality, we get:

$$
\begin{aligned}
-\alpha\Big(V_2(t)+V_3(t)\Big) &\le -\alpha\frac{1}{h}\int_{-h}^{0}\begin{bmatrix} x(t)\\ x(t+\theta)\end{bmatrix}^T d\theta \begin{bmatrix} P & -P\\ * & hQ_2+P\end{bmatrix}\\
&\quad\times\int_{-h}^{0}\begin{bmatrix} x(t)\\ x(t+\theta)\end{bmatrix} d\theta\\
&= -\alpha\eta^T(t)\begin{bmatrix} P & -P\\ * & hQ_2+P\end{bmatrix}\eta(t)
\end{aligned}
$$

where $\eta(t) = \begin{bmatrix} x(t)\\ \frac{1}{h}\int_{t-h}^{t} x(s)ds\end{bmatrix}$.

That is to say

$$
\begin{aligned}
-\alpha V(t) &\le -\alpha x^T(t)Px(t) - \alpha\eta^T(t)\begin{bmatrix} P & -P\\ * & hQ_2+P\end{bmatrix}\eta(t)\\
&= \eta^T(t)\begin{bmatrix} -2\alpha P & \alpha P\\ * & -\alpha hQ_2-\alpha P\end{bmatrix}\eta(t)
\end{aligned}
$$

Therefore, we have

$$
\dot V(t) - \alpha V(t) \le \xi^T(t)\vartheta\xi(t)
$$

where

$$
\vartheta = \begin{pmatrix} \Lambda + hA^TPA & \Omega_{12} & \Omega_{13}+\alpha P & PA_d + hA^TPA_d\\ * & \Omega_{22}-Q_2 & \Omega_{23} & 0\\ * & * & \Omega_{33}-\alpha hQ_2-\alpha P & 0\\ * & * & * & -\bar h_D Q_{12} + hA_d^TPA_d \end{pmatrix}
$$

Since the condition (3) holds, the matrix $\vartheta < 0$ is obtained using the Schur complement and from it $\dot V(t) < \alpha V(t)$. Integrating both sides of this inequality from 0 to t with $t \in [0, T]$, we obtain:

$$
V(t) < e^{\alpha t}V(0) < e^{\alpha T}V(0)
$$

On the other hand, it is easy to prove the following equations:

$$
\begin{aligned}
V(0) &= x^T(0)Px(0) + \int_{-h(0)}^{0} x^T(s)Q_1x(s)ds\\
&\quad + \int_{-h}^{-h(0)} x^T(s)Q_2x(s)ds + \int_{-h}^{0}\int_{\theta}^{0} \dot x^T(s)P\dot x(s)dsd\theta\\
&\le \Big(\Big(c_1 + \mu\frac{h^2}{2}\Big)\lambda_{\max}(\tilde P) + c_1h(\lambda_{\max}(\tilde Q_1) + \lambda_{\max}(\tilde Q_2))\Big)\\
&\le \Big(\Big(c_1 + \mu\frac{h^2}{2}\Big)\lambda_2 + c_1h(\lambda_3 + \lambda_4)\Big)
\end{aligned}
$$

Thus, we obtain:

$$V(t) \geq x^T(t)Px(t) \geq \lambda_{\min}(\tilde{P})x^T(t)Rx(t) \geq \lambda_1 x^T(t)Rx(t)$$

Then, we have:

$$x^T(t)Rx(t) < \frac{e^{\alpha T}}{\lambda_1}\Big(\Big(c_1 + \mu\frac{h^2}{2}\Big)\lambda_2 + c_1 h(\lambda_3 + \lambda_4)\Big) < c_2$$

and consequently the proof is completed.

4 Example

Let us consider (1) where $A = \begin{bmatrix} 0.15 & 0.4 \\ 0.1 & 0.3 \end{bmatrix}$, $A_d = \begin{bmatrix} -0.1 & 0 \\ 0.15 & 0 \end{bmatrix}$, $c_1 = 2.002$, $c_2 = 20$, $T = 1.5$, $\mu = 0.01$, $\alpha = 1.005$, $h = 5$, and $\varepsilon = 1000$.

Applying Theorem 1, Table 1 is obtained.

Table 1. Comparison of h for different values of h_D

h	h_D				
	1	3	5	7	9
Theorem 1	12.06	11.1902	10.7224	8.8712	5.2715

Then, increasing the delay time derivative upper bound causes a conservation defect. State variables trajectories are depicted below.

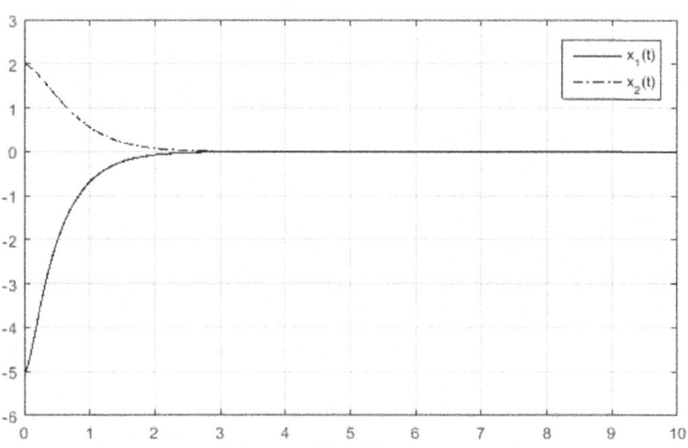

Fig. 1. Closed-loop system's state response

Analyzing Fig. 1 we see that the system's state responses converge to the equilibrium point and the desired tracking performance is achieved. We can conclude that these simulation results show the accuracy and effectiveness of our approach and that the closed-loop system is stable.

5 Conclusion

To ensure the finite-time stability of a system, sufficient conditions based on a novel integral inequality are given. Then, sufficient conditions are proposed using some free-weighting matrices to offer more flexibility and achieve good performance. The effectiveness of the method is illustrated with a numerical example. This methodology opens up new research paths: applying this technique to additive time-delay systems or uncertain systems, for example.

Acknowledgments and Funding Information. Teresa Alvarez was funded by TED2021-129716B-I00, funded by MCIN/AEI/10.13039/501100011033 and the European Union "nextgenerationeu/PRTR".

References

1. El Akchioui, N., El Fezazi, N., Farkous, R., Alvarez, T., Tissir, E.H.: Finite-time stability for discrete-time systems with time-varying delays and nonlinear perturbations using relaxed summation inequality. Iran. J. Sci. Technol. Trans. Electr. Eng. **48**(1), 433–443 (2024)
2. El Akchioui, N., El Fezazi, N., Frih, A., Taoussi, M., Farkous, R., Tissir, E.H.: Finite time stability of linear time varying delay systems using free matrix based integral inequalities. Results Control Optim. **10**, 100200 (2023)
3. El Fezazi, N., Fahim, M., Idrissi, S., Farkous, R., Alvarez, T., Tissir, E.H.: New delay-dependent finite-time stabilization of Takagi-Sugeno fuzzy approaches for delayed nonlinear systems. Asian J. Control (2024). https://doi.org/10.1002/asjc.3509
4. Feng, Z., Lam, J., Gao, H.: α-dissipativity analysis of singular time-delay systems. Automatica **47**(11), 2548–2552 (2011)
5. Gu, K., Chen, J., Kharitonov, V.L.: Stability of time-delay systems. Springer Science & Business Media (2003)
6. Kao, C.Y., Rantzer, A.: Stability analysis of systems with uncertain time-varying delays. Automatica **43**(6), 959–970 (2007)
7. Kim, J.H.: Note on stability of linear systems with time-varying delay. Automatica **47**(9), 2118–2121 (2011)
8. Kwon, O.M., Park, J.H.: On improved delay-dependent robust control for uncertain time-delay systems. IEEE Trans. Autom. Control **49**(11), 1991–1995 (2004)
9. Li, X., Gao, H.: A new model transformation of discrete-time systems with time-varying delay and its application to stability analysis. IEEE Trans. Autom. Control **56**(9), 2172–2178 (2011)
10. Mashayekhi, A., Behbahani, S., Ficuciello, F., Siciliano, B.: Delay-dependent stability analysis in haptic rendering. J. Intell. Robot. Syst. **97**(1), 33–45 (2020)

11. Park, P., Ko, J.W., Jeong, C.: Reciprocally convex approach to stability of systems with time-varying delays. Automatica **47**(1), 235–238 (2011)
12. Park, M.J., Kwon, O.M., Park, J.H., Lee, S.M.: A new augmented Lyapunov-Krasovskii functional approach for stability of linear systems with time-varying delays. Appl. Math. Comput. **217**(17), 7197–7209 (2011)
13. Seuret, A., Gouaisbaut, F.: Wirtinger-based integral inequality: application to time-delay systems. Automatica **49**(9), 2860–2866 (2013)
14. Sun, J., Liu, G.P., Chen, J., Rees, D.: Improved delay-range-dependent stability criteria for linear systems with time-varying delays. Automatica **46**(2), 466–470 (2010)
15. Tunç, O., Tunç, C., Wang, Y.: Delay-dependent stability, integrability and boundedeness criteria for delay differential systems. Axioms **10**(3), 138 (2021)
16. Yildirim, B., Gheisarnejad, M., Khooban, M.H.: Delay-dependent stability analysis of modern shipboard microgrids. IEEE Trans. Circuits Syst. I Regul. Pap. **68**(4), 1693–1705 (2021)
17. Zakaria, M.I., Husain, A.R., Mohamed, Z., El Fezazi, N., Shah, M.B.N.: Lyapunov-Krasovskii stability condition for system with bounded delay-an application to steer-by-wire system. In: Proceedings of the International Conference on Control System, Computing and Engineering, pp. 543–547 (2015)
18. Zeng, H.B., Zhou, S.J., Zhang, X.M., Wang, W.: Delay-dependent stability analysis of load frequency control systems with electric vehicles. IEEE Trans. Cybern. (2022). https://doi.org/10.1109/TCYB.2022.3140463
19. Zeng, H.B., He, Y., Wu, M., She, J.: Free-matrix-based integral inequality for stability analysis of systems with time-varying delay. IEEE Trans. Autom. Control **60**(10), 2768–2772 (2015)
20. Zhang, Z., Zhang, Z., Zhang, H.: Finite-time stability analysis and stabilization for uncertain continuous-time system with time-varying delay. J. Franklin Inst. **352**(3), 1296–1317 (2015)
21. Zhao, Y., Hu, G.D.: Delay-dependent stability of high-order neutral systems. Kybernetika **57**(5), 737–749 (2021)

Barrier Lyapunov-Based Fuzzy Sliding Mode Control for Lateral Autonomous Vehicle Dynamics

Najlae Jennan[1(✉)], El Mehdi Mellouli[1], and El Hanafi Arjdal[2]

[1] Laboratory of Engineering, Systems and Applications, Sidi Mohamed Ben Abdellah University, National School of Applied Sciences, Fez, Morocco
najlae.jennan@usmba.ac.ma

[2] Laboratory of Materials, Signals, Systems and Physical Modeling, Faculty of Sciences of Agadir, Ibn Zohr University, Agadir, Morocco
e.arjdal@uiz.ac.ma

Abstract. This paper presents an advanced control strategy for autonomous vehicle lateral dynamics using Sliding Mode Control (SMC) integrated with Takagi-Sugeno (T-S) fuzzy logic and enhanced by the Barrier Lyapunov approach. The objective is to ensure fixed-time convergence and stability in the presence of uncertainties and disturbances. The mathematical model of the autonomous vehicle system is established as a preliminary step, after which control laws are designed. A comprehensive stability analysis is conducted to validate the stability and convergence of the overall system. The reaching law is adapted through the application of T-S fuzzy logic, thereby enhancing the controller's adaptability and reducing the phenomenon of chattering associated with the SMC method. The simulation results demonstrate superior performance, achieving a 33% faster convergence time compared to traditional SMC methods.

Keywords: Autonomous vehicle · barrier Lyapunov · lateral control · sliding mode control · T-S fuzzy logic

1 Introduction

The advancement of self-driving vehicles represents a significant step forward in the field of transportation, offering enhanced road safety, efficiency, and accessibility [1, 2]. Lateral control is pivotal for the operation of these vehicles, as it necessitates the development of robust algorithms capable of navigating complex environments characterized by road curvatures, lane markings, and surrounding vehicles [3, 4]. Effective lateral control strategies play a crucial role in ensuring the safety and reliability of autonomous transportation [5, 6].

Barrier Lyapunov-based Sliding Mode Control (BLSMC) and Takagi-Sugeno (T-S) fuzzy logic are effective techniques for addressing challenges such as uncertainties, disturbances and nonlinear dynamics in vehicle systems [7, 8]. BLSMC ensures stability and fixed-time convergence, whereas T-S fuzzy logic enhances adaptability by refining

I. Aboudrar et al. (Eds.): ICESST 2024, SUCI, pp. 452–460, 2025.
https://doi.org/10.1007/978-3-031-86705-7_42

the reaching law. The combination of these methodologies yields a robust performance, reduced chattering, and high stability within the context of lateral control of autonomous vehicles in varying conditions.

The control of autonomous vehicles comprises a number of significant challenges, particularly in terms of dealing with uncertainties and external disturbances, while maintaining stability and optimal performance. It has been demonstrated that traditional strategies such as Sliding Mode Control (SMC) are effective in providing stability to nonlinear systems. However, limitations have been identified in their ability to adapt to changing conditions and to avoid undesirable effects such as chattering [9]. Backstepping control represents another popular technique, providing stability guarantees. However, it can become computationally expensive and less effective in the presence of external disturbances or system uncertainties [9]. The application of fuzzy logic and neural networks in conjunction with these methods frequently allows for the approximation of complex dynamics. However, they often require extensive parameter tuning and are susceptible to computational constraints. In situations where fixed-time convergence and robust performance are of paramount importance, these methods may encounter difficulties in guaranteeing consistent and efficient performance without placing significant computational demands [10, 11]. The introduction of Barrier Lyapunov-based Sliding Mode Control (BLSMC), addresses these limitations by ensuring fixed-time convergence and guaranteeing system stability even in the presence of significant disturbances [12]. The integration of fuzzy logic into the proposed BLSMC strategy further enhances its adaptability by refining the reaching law and reducing the chattering effects [13].

The latest techniques in lateral control for autonomous vehicles, including neural networks and backstepping control, have demonstrated enhancements in performance [9, 10]. However, they still encounter difficulties in terms of adaptability, computational complexity, and ensuring resilient stability in uncertain environments. In contrast, the BLSMC method, enhanced with fuzzy logic, offers a solution by ensuring fixed-time convergence, system stability, and increased adaptability, effectively overcoming the limitations of existing approaches [13].

This work presents a novel approach to autonomous vehicle control, which combines Barrier Lyapunov-based Sliding Mode Control (BLSMC) with fuzzy logic. The objective of this method is to address the challenges of autonomous navigation in the presence of external disturbances. The method integrates a modified reaching law within the sliding mode control structure, employing fuzzy logic for tuning in order to mitigate the chattering effect and enhance system stability. The Barrier Lyapunov approach ensures the stability of the system within the specified constraints and guarantees fixed-time convergence.

The following outlines the structure of the paper. Section 2 presents the mathematical model of the vehicle system. Section 3 details the proposed control method. Section 4 presents the results of the simulation, and Sect. 5 offers a conclusion.

2 Bicycle Model

The bicycle model is employed for the purpose of simplifying the dynamics of an autonomous vehicle, with a particular focus on lateral motion. Thus, it facilitates effective control design without unnecessary complexity [14]. Figure 1 provides an illustration of the bicycle model.

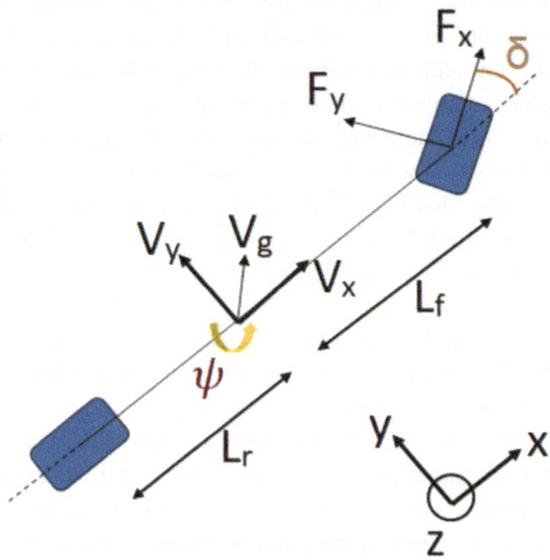

Fig. 1. Bicycle Model

The lateral dynamics of the vehicle, which describe the lateral position y and the yaw angle ψ, are given by the following equation [10]:

$$\begin{cases} \ddot{y} = f_1(\underline{x}, t) + g_1(\underline{x}, t) \times u(t) + d(t) \\ \ddot{\psi} = f_2(\underline{x}, t) + g_2(\underline{x}, t) \times u(t) + d(t) \end{cases} \quad (1)$$

In this context, the state vector is defined as $\underline{x} = [y, \psi]^T \in \mathbb{R}^2$. The control law $u = \delta$ represents the steering angle and will be generalized by the proposed controller. The dynamics of the system are represented by the vectors $\underline{f} = [f_1, f_2]^T \in \mathbb{R}^2$ and $\underline{g} = [g_1, g_2]^T \in \mathbb{R}^2$(Table 1).

The term $d(t)$ represents external disturbances, which may arise from factors such as road conditions, wind, or other environmental effects. These disturbances introduce uncertainties into the system's behavior, which are difficult to model precisely. However, it is assumed that the disturbances are bounded, and the control strategy must be robust enough to mitigate their effects on the vehicle's trajectory .

Table 1. Notations' list

Symbol	Nomenclature	Unit
δ	Steering angle	[rad]
y	Lateral position	[m]
ψ	Yaw angle	[rad]
V_x	Longitudinal speed	[m/s]
L_f	Distance between the front tire and the center of gravity of the car	[m]
L_r	Distance between the rear tire and the center of gravity of the car	[m]

3 Design of the Proposed Control Strategy

This section presents the design of the Barrier Lyapunov-based Sliding Mode Controller (BLSMC), a robust and adaptive strategy that incorporates T-S fuzzy logic [13, 15]. The BLSMC is designed to control the lateral dynamics of a bicycle system in the presence of uncertainties and external disturbances. This approach combines the robustness of the SMC with the stability assurance provided by the Barrier Lyapunov function, as well as the adaptability afforded by fuzzy logic. The latter is employed for the approximation of a nonlinear function defined in the reaching law. The tracking error of the system and its derivative are defined as follows:

$$\begin{cases} e_1 = y - y_d \\ \dot{e}_1 = \dot{y} - \dot{y}_d \end{cases} \tag{2}$$

The sliding surface is defined as follows:

$$s = \dot{e} + c \times e \tag{3}$$

In this context, c represents a positive coefficient. In order to enhance the system's adaptability and robustness, an effective reaching law is designed to guarantee rapid and robust system convergence, given by the following expression:

$$\dot{s} = -\beta_1 \times s - \beta_2 \times \hat{\delta}_s \tag{4}$$

β_1 and β_2 are two positive coefficients, while $\hat{\delta}_s$ is the approximated nonlinear function generated through the application of T-S fuzzy logic.

In accordance with the expressions of the sliding surface and the reaching law defined in (5) and (4) respectively, the control law can be written as follows:

$$u(t) = \frac{1}{g_1(x,t)} \times \left[\ddot{y}_d - f_1(x,t) - c \times \dot{e} - \beta_1 \times s - \beta_2 \times \hat{\delta}_s\right] \tag{5}$$

The T-S fuzzy logic method is described by fuzzy IF-THEN rules, defined in the following form, for the purpose of performing a mapping from an input vector, defined as $\underline{\omega} = [y\dot{y}]^T \in \mathbb{R}^2$ to the output $\hat{\delta}_s$.

$$IF\ \omega_1\ is\ F_1^j\ and\ \ldots\ and\ \omega_n\ is\ F_n^j,\ THEN\ \hat{\delta}_s\ is\ \theta$$

The expression of $\hat{\delta}_s$ is defined as follows, using fuzzy logic technique configured with singleton fuzzification, product inference and center average defuzzification.

$$\hat{\delta}_s = \frac{\sum_1^m \theta_i \left(\prod_1^n \mu_{F_i^j}(s) \right)}{\sum_1^m \left(\prod_1^n \mu_{F_i^j}(s) \right)} = \theta \times \Omega \tag{6}$$

In this context, the variable θ represents the corresponding value of the output fuzzy singleton. The fuzzy variables F_i^j, with $i = 1, \ldots, n$ are characterized by the membership functions $\mu_{F_i^j}$, defined in the Gaussian form, as follows [16]:

$$\begin{cases} \mu_{F_i^1}(\omega_i) = \exp\left(-\frac{\omega_i - c_i}{(2\times\sigma_i)^2}\right) \\ \mu_{F_i^2}(\omega_i) = \exp\left(-\frac{\omega_i + c_i}{(2\times\sigma_i)^2}\right),\ i = [1, 2] \\ \mu_{F_i^3}(\omega_i) = 1 - \mu_{F_i^1}(\omega_i) - \mu_{F_i^2}(\omega_i) \end{cases} \tag{7}$$

In this context, the variable c represents the center of the fuzzy set, while the variable σ represents the width of the membership function. Figure 2 provides an illustration of the membership functions employed.

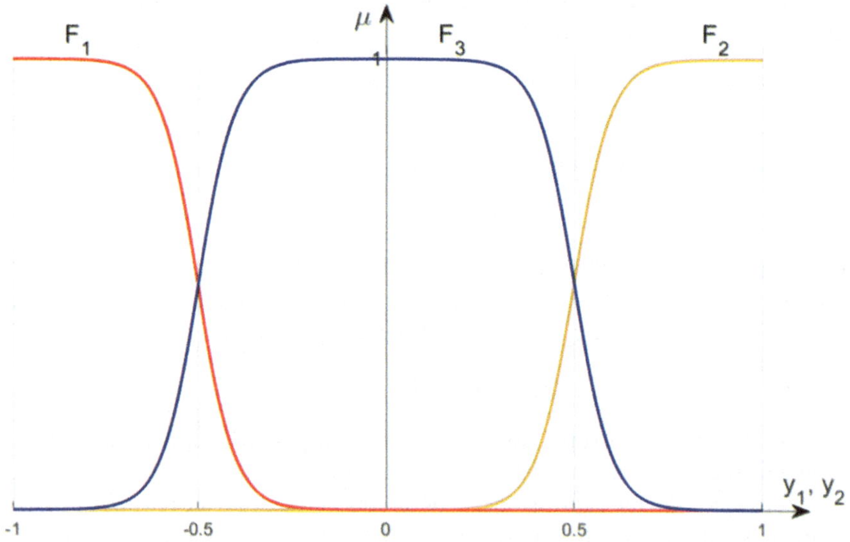

Fig. 2. Membership functions used

In order to evaluate the overall system stability and derive the control law, it is necessary to formulate the Barrier Lyapunov functions and their derivatives in the following form:

$$\begin{cases} V = \frac{1}{2} \times log \frac{k^2}{k^2 - s^2} + \frac{1}{2 \times \gamma} \times \phi^T \times \phi \geq 0 \\ \dot{V} = \frac{s \times \dot{s}}{k^2 - s^2} + \frac{1}{\gamma} \times \phi \times \dot{\phi} < 0 \end{cases} \tag{8}$$

In this context, k and γ represent two positive coefficients. The function ϕ is defined as $\phi = \theta - \theta^*$, where θ^* represents the optimal value.

In order to guarantee the stability of the system, it is essential to ensure that the derivative of the Lyapunov function is negative [17]. Subsequently, the following calculations are conducted:

$$\dot{V} = \frac{s}{k^2 - s^2} \times \left[-\beta_1 \times s - \beta_2 \times \hat{\delta}_s \right] + \frac{1}{\gamma} \times \phi \times \dot{\phi}$$

$$\dot{V} = \frac{1}{\gamma} \times \phi \times \left[\dot{\phi} - \gamma \times \beta_2 \times \frac{s}{k^2 - s^2} \times \Omega \right] - \beta_1 \times \frac{s^2}{k^2 - s^2} - \beta_2 \times \frac{s}{k^2 - s^2} \times \delta_s^* \tag{9}$$

In accordance with the preceding Eq. (9), the corresponding value θ can be expressed as follows:

$$\dot{\theta} = \gamma \times \beta_2 \times \frac{s}{k^2 - s^2} \times \Omega \tag{10}$$

Subsequently, the following inequality is derived:

$$\dot{V} \leq -2 \times \beta_1 \times V - 2 \times \beta_2 \times \delta_s^* \times V^2 < 0 \tag{11}$$

From (11), it can be concluded that the system is stable and that the fixed time of convergence is given by:

$$T_s \leq -\frac{1}{2 \times \beta_1} \times \log \left[\frac{2 \times \beta_1 \times V^{-1}(0) + 2 \times \beta_2 \times \delta_s^*}{2 \times \beta_2 \times \delta_s^*} \right] \tag{12}$$

The Barrier Lyapunov functions serve to enhance the robustness of the control system, thereby ensuring its capacity to effectively address real-world disturbances and maintain stability.

4 Results of Simulation

This section presents the simulation results, which evaluate the performance of the proposed controller in comparison with traditional control methods. The simulations focus on two primary performance indicators: the adaptability of the control law in the presence of external disturbances and the lateral position of the vehicle. These indicators provide insights into the efficacy of the proposed controller in maintaining stability and precision in the presence of uncertainties and disturbances. The results are evaluated in comparison to standard control strategies, thereby illustrating the benefits of the proposed method in terms of robustness, convergence, and overall system performance.

The control law derived from the proposed control strategy is initially evaluated through simulation in two distinct scenarios: one in which external disturbances are present and one in which they are absent. Figure 3 illustrates the evolution of the control law obtained.

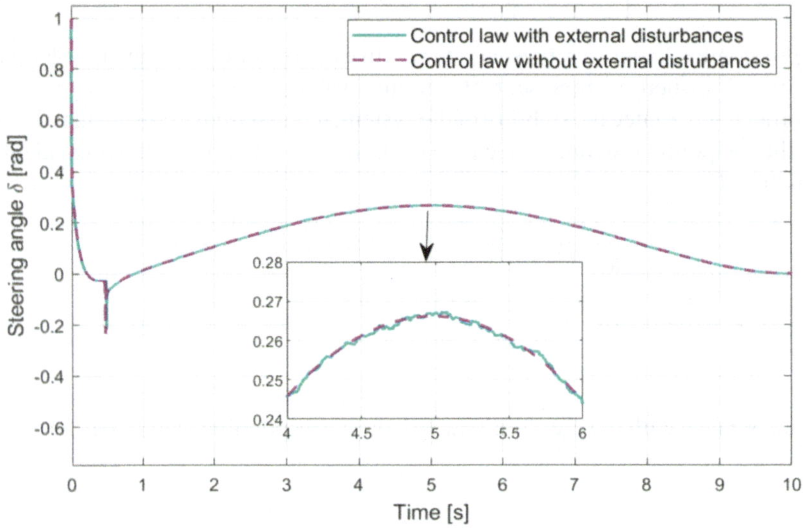

Fig. 3. The response of the control law achieved using the proposed controller

Figure 3 clearly demonstrates that the proposed control law exhibits a high degree of adaptability in the presence of external disturbances. The close alignment of the control law with and without disturbances serves to illustrate the robustness of the control strategy in maintaining system performance under varying conditions.

Subsequently, the position y is simulated by comparing the proposed controller with two alternative controllers: the proposed method without the use of fuzzy logic and the SMC method based on the standard Lyapunov approach. Figure 4 illustrates the evolution of the lateral position when the three methods are compared.

Figure 4 demonstrates that the proposed controller with fuzzy logic achieves superior tracking performance, closely following the desired trajectory with minimal deviation. In contrast, the proposed controller without fuzzy logic exhibits slightly larger tracking errors, which highlights the significance of incorporating fuzzy logic to enhance system adaptability. Moreover, the SMC controller based on the standard Lyapunov approach exhibits the largest tracking error, which serves to reinforce the robustness and accuracy of the proposed method with fuzzy logic in achieving precise lateral control.

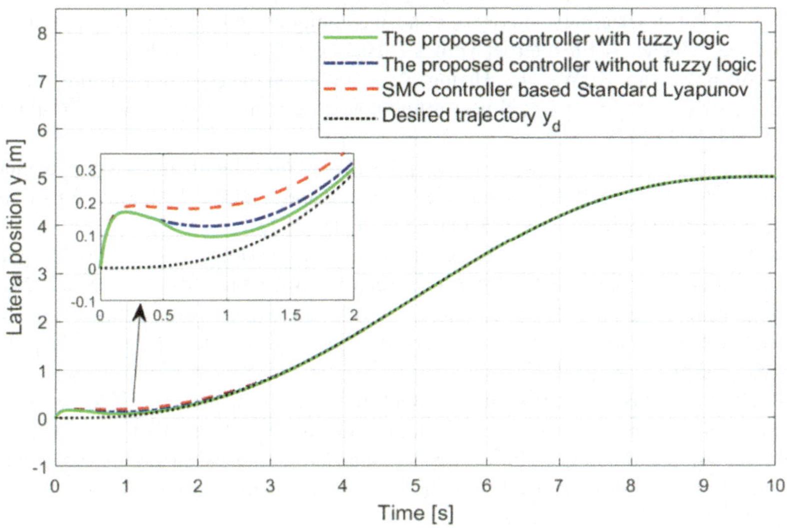

Fig. 4. The response of the lateral position achieved using the three compared controllers

5 Conclusion

In this study, we proposed a Barrier Lyapunov-based Sliding Mode Control (BLSMC) strategy combined with T-S fuzzy logic for the lateral dynamics of an autonomous vehicle subjected to external disturbances. This approach combines the robustness of sliding mode control with the stability guarantees and fixed-time convergence offered by Barrier Lyapunov functions, enhanced with fuzzy logic for approximation, thereby providing a robust and stable control strategy. The simulations demonstrated that the proposed controller outperforms traditional Lyapunov-based SMC and other methods in terms of superior robustness, faster response times, and improved tracking accuracy.

Subsequent work will focus on the development of adaptive strategies and the implementation of real-world validation tests, with the objective of enhancing the practicality of the proposed approach in autonomous vehicle systems.

References

1. Lee, J.H., Yeom, K.: Efficient self-driving control for lead vehicle following in a mixed traffic environment. Energy Rep. **9**(12), 483–489 (2023)
2. Baby, T., et al.: Development and classification of autonomous vehicle's ambiguous driving scenario. Accid. Anal. Prevent. **200**, 107501 (2024)
3. Ribeiro, A.M., Koyama, M.F., Moutinho, A., de Paiva, E.C., Fioravanti, A.R.: A comprehensive experimental validation of a scaled car-like vehicle: Lateral dynamics identification, stability analysis, and control application. Control. Eng. Pract. **116**, 104924 (2021)
4. Artunedo, A., Moreno-Gonzalez, M., Villagra, J.: Lateral control for autonomous vehicles: a comparative evaluation. Ann. Rev. Control **57**, 100910 (2024)
5. Yao, Q., Tian, Y., Wang, Q., Wang, S.: Control strategies on path tracking for autonomous vehicle: state of the art and future challenges. IEEE Access **8**, 161211–161222 (2020)

6. Liu, W., et al.: A systematic survey of control techniques and applications in connected and automated vehicles. IEEE Internet Things J. **10**(24), 21892–21916 (2023)
7. Li, B., Wen, S., Yan, Z., Wen, G., Huang, T.: A survey on the control Lyapunov function and control barrier function for nonlinear-affine control systems. IEEE/CAA J. Autom. Sinica **10**(3), 584–602 (2023)
8. Liu, Y.H., Liu, Y., Liu, Y.F., Su, C.Y.: Adaptive fuzzy control with global stability guarantees for unknown strict-feedback systems using novel integral barrier Lyapunov functions. IEEE Trans. Syst. Man Cybernet. Syst. **52**(7), 4336–4348 (2022)
9. Zhao, L., Li, Z., Li, H., Liu, B.: Backstepping integral sliding mode control for pneumatic manipulators via adaptive extended state observers. ISA Trans. **144**, 374–384 (2024)
10. El Hajjami, L., Mellouli, E.M., Zuraulis, V., Berrada, M.: A novel robust adaptive neuro-sliding mode steering controller for autonomous ground vehicles. Robot. Auton. Syst. **170**, 104557 (2023)
11. Mellouli, E.M., Massou, S., Boumhidi, I.: Optimal robust adaptive fuzzy H∞ tracking control without reaching phase for nonlinear system. J. Control Sci. Eng. **2013**, 498461 (2013)
12. Chen, Z., Li, Q., Ju, X., Cen, F.: Barrier Lyapunov function-based sliding mode control for BWB aircraft with mismatched disturbances and output constraints. IEEE Access **7**, 175341–175352 (2019)
13. Zhou, Z., Zhu, F., Chen, B., Xu, D.: Barrier Lyapunov function based adaptive fuzzy attitude tracking control for rigid satellite with input delay and output constraint. J. Franklin Inst. **358**(17), 9110 (2021)
14. Rajamani, R.: Vehicle Dynamics and Control. Springer Science & Business Media (2011)
15. Jennan, N., Mellouli, E.M.: New optimal fast terminal sliding mode control combined with neural networks for modelling and controlling a drone quadrotor. Int. J. Autom. Control. **17**(6), 595–612 (2023)
16. Jennan, N., Mellouli, E.M.: Robust control for a drone quadrotor using fuzzy logic-based fast terminal sliding mode control. J. Braz. Soc. Mech. Sci. Eng. **46**, 432 (2024)
17. Moussa, A., Mellouli, E.M.: A new adaptive second-order non-singular terminal sliding mode lateral control combined with neural networks for autonomous vehicle. Int. J. Veh. Perform. **10**(1), 50–72 (2024)

Transformative Approaches for Sustainable Healthcare Monitoring and Diagnostics

Challenges and Prospects for Real-Time Glucose Monitoring: Moving Towards Non-invasive Solutions

Kholoud Fdil[1,2](✉), Safae Elhir[2], Ikram Debbarh[2], and Hicham Medromi[1,2]

[1] Engineering Research Laboratory, National Higher School of Electricity and Mechanics, Hassan II University, Casablanca, Morocco
fdilkholoud@gmail.com

[2] Research Foundation for Development and Innovation in Science and Engineering, Suptech Santé, Mohammedia, Morocco

Abstract. Diabetes mellitus is a global health challenge. Effective glycemic control is needed to prevent serious complications and improve patient outcomes. Continuous glucose monitoring (CGM) devices have transformed the management of diabetes by providing continuous, real-time blood glucose measurements that enable dynamic and accurate control of blood glucose levels. Unlike traditional glucometers, CGM systems provide insight into glucose trends and patterns, significantly improving patient management. However, despite these advances, CGM systems have certain limitations, including the need for invasive calibration, discomfort associated with sensor insertion, and skin irritation caused by adhesive patches. In this article, we review the functionalities, key examples, and limitations of CGM technology and its essential role in diabetes management. Based on this, we discuss the limitations of current CGM systems and propose non-invasive approaches, in particular near-infrared spectroscopy (NIRS), as a promising alternative. This approach has the potential to revolutionize diabetes management by providing a more user-friendly and accessible solution for continuous, real-time glucose monitoring through the integration of non-invasive monitoring with telemedicine.

Keywords: Diabetes mellitus · glucose monitoring · real-time continuous glucose monitoring · minimally invasive · non-invasive

1 Introduction

In recent decades, diabetes mellitus (DM), a metabolic disease characterized by increased blood glucose levels, has become increasingly prevalent worldwide [1]. The Diabetes Atlas reports that there has been a significant increase in the number of people with diabetes in recent years. The age-adjusted prevalence among people aged 20 to 75, which was 4.6% in 2000, clearly shows this increase. According to projections, this percentage will rise further, possibly hitting 11.2% by 2045 [2].

I. Aboudrar et al. (Eds.): ICESST 2024, SUCI, pp. 463–472, 2025.
https://doi.org/10.1007/978-3-031-86705-7_43

Among the many pathologic processes involved in diabetes mellitus is the autoimmune destruction of pancreatic β-cells, which results in insulin resistance and insufficiency. In order to prevent long-term complications of diabetes and lower associated risk factors, such as high blood pressure and cardiovascular diseases connected to lipid imbalances, regular blood glucose monitoring is essential. Diabetes can result in serious complications like heart and kidney failure, as well as vision loss, if blood glucose levels are not properly controlled over time without regular monitoring [3, 4].

Traditionally, self-monitoring devices or advanced laboratory equipment are used to measure blood glucose levels. Both methods are invasive, uncomfortable, and only provide intermittent glucose readings [3]. This traditional method of glucose monitoring only provides a snapshot of blood glucose levels at the time of measurement. This means it cannot predict future levels or account for fluctuations that may occur afterward. For instance, glucose levels cannot be tracked during sleep, which raises the risk of experiencing dangerously high or low blood sugar levels. For people with diabetes, timely intervention is essential when glucose levels spike or drop. This challenge highlights the need for a device capable of continuously monitoring glucose levels in real time, 24/7 [1]. It is now commonly acknowledged that continuous glucose monitoring devices enhance quality of life by facilitating more informed decisions about diabetes treatment through optimal glucose control. This lowers the chance of complications from diabetes while also improving general health [5]. The dominant companies offering CGM devices today are Medtronic, Dexcom, and Abbott, known for their advanced glucose tracking technologies that lead the market in innovation and reliability. Together, these advancements are shaping the future of diabetes care by providing patients with more effective tools for maintaining their health [6, 7].

In addition to the market-dominating continuous glucose monitoring (CGM) devices, research is also advancing towards the development of non-invasive CGM sensors [1]. These non-invasive methods offer the potential to improve diabetes management by using measurement sites on the body without the need to insert instruments [8]. This approach provides a less intrusive alternative for continuous glucose monitoring, offering a more comfortable experience for patients while maintaining effective blood glucose tracking.

The structure of this paper is such that key aspects of diabetes management and blood glucose monitoring technologies are addressed. Section 2 describes the methodology used for this review, while Sect. 3 presents the findings, providing an understanding of diabetes, its global epidemiology, and the socioeconomic impact of the disease. It also examines the limitations of traditional glucose monitoring methods, highlights advances in continuous glucose monitoring (CGM), and compares advanced CGM technologies including Dexcom G7, FreeStyle Libre 3, and Eversense XL. Finally, Sect. 4 discusses limits of CGM and perspectives on integrating noninvasive approaches into telehealth.

2 Methodology

This study uses a narrative review methodology to summarize and analyze advances in continuous glucose monitoring (CGM) technologies, with a particular focus on the potential of non-invasive approaches such as NIRS. Peer-reviewed journals, conference proceedings, and reputable online resources were used to identify relevant scientific literature. Reference selection criteria included publication date (2000–2024), relevance to CGM technologies, noninvasive glucose monitoring, and telehealth integration. Key search terms such as "continuous glucose monitor (CGM)," "noninvasive glucose monitor," "near infrared spectroscopy (NIRS)," and "diabetes management technology" were used to identify sources. The main references are high-impact journals such as Diabetes Technology & Therapeutics, Sensors, and IEEE Consumer Electronics Magazine, as well as authoritative resources such as the IDF Diabetes Atlas and the National Institute of Diabetes and Digestive and Kidney Diseases (NIDDK). The data collected was organized into three topical areas: the global prevalence and economic burden of diabetes, advances in CGM devices such as the Dexcom G7, FreeStyle Libre 3, and Eversense XL, and the feasibility of noninvasive methods such as NIRS. The review highlighted limitations of current CGM systems, including calibration requirements and user inconvenience, and proposed telehealth integrated NIRS as a viable alternative.

3 Results

3.1 Understanding Diabetes: Types and Symptoms

As part of a comprehensive review of the existing literature, this section provides an overview of diabetes, including its types and symptoms. The information presented is based on a synthesis of peer-reviewed articles, scientific reports, and reliable online resources. By drawing on a wide range of studies and publications, the aim of this work is to provide a solid foundation for the understanding of the disease and its implications, which will guide subsequent discussions on glucose monitoring technologies and their evolution.

Glucose, which provides the energy needed for daily activities, is normally regulated within the human body. The ideal glucose range is between 80 and 150 mg/dl. Values above this range are indicative of Diabetes Mellitus (DM). Diabetes is primarily classified into three types: Type 1 diabetes, type 2 diabetes, and gestational diabetes [9].

Type 1 Diabetes is characterized by the body's inability to produce insulin, which disrupts the insulin-glucose balance. Type 2 Diabetes involves the body's insufficient production of insulin to maintain a stable glycemic profile. Gestational diabetes occurs during pregnancy, where the body fails to produce adequate insulin for effective glucose regulation [3]. The classic symptoms of diabetes, such as polyuria, polydipsia, and polyphagia, are frequently observed in Type 1 diabetes, which is characterized by a rapid onset of severe hyperglycemia. These symptoms can also appear in Type 2 diabetes, though typically with very high levels of hyperglycemia. Severe weight loss is primarily associated with Type 1 diabetes or with Type 2 diabetes that remains undiagnosed for an extended period. Additionally, unexplained weight loss, fatigue, restlessness, and body pain are common indicators of undiagnosed diabetes [10].

3.2 Global Epidemiology and Socioeconomic Impact of Diabetes Mellitus

Diabetes mellitus (DM) is a significant contributor to both mortality and morbidity across the globe. In 2021, 537 million adults aged 20 to 79 are living with diabetes, representing 1 in 10 individuals in this age group. This figure is expected to increase to 643 million by 2030 and reach 783 million by 2045 [11]. This growth is mirrored in the age-adjusted prevalence of diabetes among individuals aged 20 to 75 (Fig. 1), which started at 4.6% in 2000 and nearly doubled to 8.5% by 2011. Projections indicate a continued rise to 10.8% by 2030 and a peak of 11.2% by 2045. These alarming trends highlight the urgent need for more effective prevention and management strategies to combat this growing global health crisis [2].

Effective daily monitoring of blood glucose levels is essential for preventing long-term complications associated with diabetes. Maintaining control over glycemic levels not only reduces risk factors such as elevated blood pressure and cardiovascular issues like abnormal lipid profiles but also plays a critical role in preventing severe conditions such as heart and kidney failure [3]. Diabetes is a major contributor to chronic kidney disease (CKD), with up to 40% of individuals with diabetes developing this condition. Between 1990 and 2017, the incidence of CKD among people with type 2 diabetes surged by 74%. The prevalence of diabetes-related CKD varies significantly across different countries. Most of the existing epidemiological data on CKD is derived from high-income nations. However, countries with lower socioeconomic status are seeing a sharp rise in diabetes rates and face a higher risk of CKD among their diabetic populations [12]. Similarly, there is significant global variation in diabetes-related foot complications, influenced by differences in definitions, diagnostic practices, population characteristics, data handling methods, and healthcare services. Available data suggest that the IDF Africa Region and the South and Central America Region have higher rates of diabetic peripheral neuropathy. Generally, in most countries with accessible data, the incidence of lower-limb amputations related to diabetes appears to be declining. Nonetheless, there is still a lack of comprehensive reviews that quantify diabetes-related foot complications systematically [13]. Despite the improvements, diabetes continues to present significant challenges, particularly in the context of emerging health crises. Diabetes significantly increases the risk of severe outcomes from COVID-19. The 2021 IDF Diabetes Atlas reported that individuals with diabetes are considerably more likely to be hospitalized and face a higher risk of death from COVID-19 compared to those without diabetes [14]. This increased risk underscores the substantial financial burden of diabetes, which in the U.S. reached an estimated $412.9 billion in 2022. This total includes $306.6 billion in direct medical costs and $106.3 billion in indirect costs. Diabetes-related care accounts for 25% of all healthcare spending in the U.S., with 61% of those costs directly attributed to the condition. On average, individuals with diabetes incur annual medical expenses of $19,736, approximately $12,022 of which are specifically related to diabetes. This results in medical costs that are 2.6 times higher than those for individuals without diabetes [15].

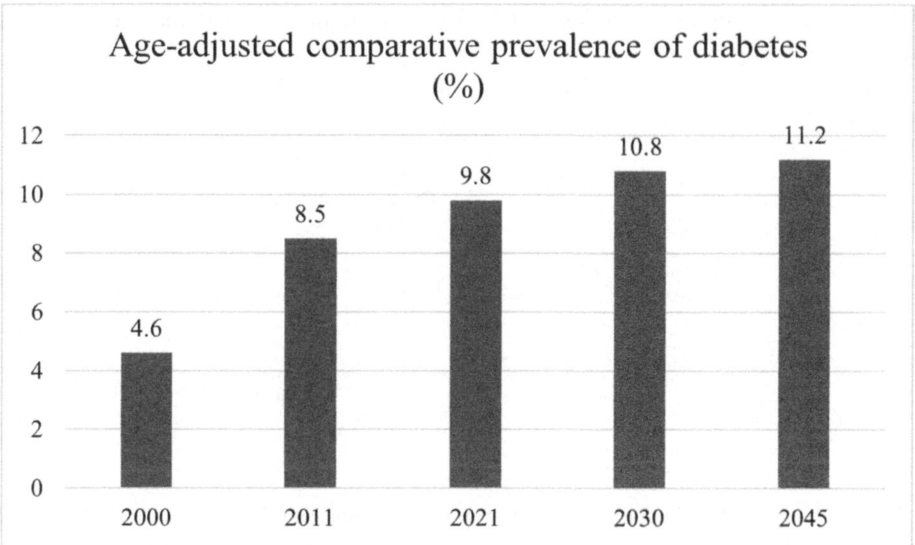

Fig. 1. Age-adjusted comparative prevalence of diabetes, % aged 20–75 (2000–2045) [2]

3.3 Limitations of Traditional Glucose Monitoring and Advances in Continuous Glucose Monitoring (CGM)

Glucose levels are usually measured using either laboratory methods or home-based monitoring, both of these methods are invasive requiring a puncture in the skin to obtain a blood sample. These methods only provide a snapshot of glucose levels at the time of testing, making it inconvenient to frequently check blood glucose. As a result, fluctuations in blood sugar may go undetected, leading to improper insulin dosing for individuals with type 1 diabetes [3]. The American Diabetes Association recommends that individuals with diabetes monitor their blood glucose levels at least three times a day, as normal blood sugar ranges vary depending on factors such as whether the test is done before or after a meal [16]. Self-monitoring of blood glucose (SMBG) is widely regarded as the most effective method for achieving long-term blood sugar control in diabetic patients [17]. However, despite its effectiveness, SMBG is constrained by its invasive nature and the associated discomfort and inconvenience, which can reduce patient adherence, particularly when patients are in social situations [18]. Additionally, SMBG provides limited insight into specific glucose fluctuations, such as postprandial spikes or asymptomatic hypoglycemia [19].

Continuous glucose monitoring (CGM) systems are categorized into two main types: real-time continuous glucose monitoring (rtCGM) and intermittently scanned continuous glucose monitoring (isCGM). While both types utilize similar technologies and can provide glucose trend arrows, they differ in key ways. rtCGM systems continuously transmit glucose readings to a receiver, which is often a mobile phone or smartwatch (Fig. 2). This allows for immediate, actionable insights and the option to set alerts for high or low glucose levels. These systems can operate independently or be integrated into insulin delivery setups, such as sensor-augmented pump therapy or automated insulin delivery (AID) systems. In contrast, isCGM systems require users to manually scan the sensor to access glucose data [20].

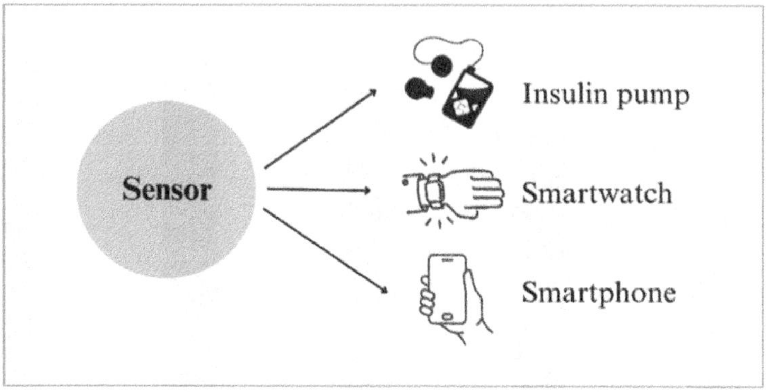

Fig. 2. Different display options for viewing CGM data

rtCGM utilizes subcutaneous sensors to measure interstitial glucose in realtime and display results on a device or smartphone. The sensor uses glucose oxidase to oxidize glucose in the interstitial fluid, producing peroxide. Peroxide reacts with platinum electrodes to generate an electrical current. This current is transmitted to an external transmitter where the receiver processes and displays the glucose level [21].

They also feature alarms that notify users of both low and high glucose levels, as well as changes in glucose levels that exceed certain adjustable thresholds. Additionally, these systems include trend arrows that indicate the rate of glucose change, allowing users to adjust mealtime insulin doses and anticipate or prevent episodes of hypoglycemia and hyperglycemia, facilitating better glycemic control and enabling the development of individualized diet plans [22, 23].

In 1999, the FDA approved the MiniMed CGM System, the first device for continuous glucose monitoring in adults with diabetes. It measured glucose every 5 min for up to 3 days, with data reviewed by healthcare professionals. Since then, newer CGM systems have advanced in accuracy, functionality, and usability [24]. However, because CGM does not directly measure blood glucose, intermittent calibration with capillary glucose measurements is required to ensure accuracy. Studies have shown that there is a time lag of approximately 7–8 min between blood and interstitial glucose levels, particularly in the overnight fasted state in adults with type 1 diabetes [3, 23].

Continuous glucose monitoring not only improves overall glucose management but also allows for the early detection of potential issues, enabling timely interventions for both hypoglycemia and hyperglycemia and it is especially recommended for patients with severe or nocturnal hypoglycemia, particularly those who experience hypoglycemia unawareness. This method provides continuous insights into glucose levels, helping to mitigate risks and enhance patient safety. Furthermore, CGM data supports dietitians and healthcare providers in developing tailored dietary strategies to meet each individual's specific needs [25, 26].

According to the NIDDK, CGM systems consist of three components: a sensor placed under the skin to measure interstitial glucose levels, a transmitter that wirelessly sends data, and software for real-time glucose monitoring via a smartphone, insulin pump, or receiver. Sensors can be disposable or implantable, requiring periodic replacement based on type [27].

3.4 Comparison of Advanced CGM Devices: Dexcom G7, FreeStyle Libre 3, and Eversense XL

Among the latest CGM devices are the Dexcom G7 (Dexcom, Inc., San Diego, CA, USA) and FreeStyle Libre 3 (Abbott Diabetes Care, Alameda, CA, USA). These advanced systems are designed to replace traditional blood glucose (BG) testing for diabetes management, offering real-time data on interstitial glucose levels. They help identify glucose trends, monitor patterns, and assist in detecting episodes of both hyperglycemia and hypoglycemia. The Dexcom G7 Continuous Glucose Monitoring System) (Fig. 2) is designed to offer continuous glucose measurement without the need for calibration, suitable for individuals aged 2 years and older. It consists of two key elements: a Dexcom G7 sensor, which integrates a transmitter and lasts for ten days, and a receiver, which can be either a handheld device or accessed via the Dexcom G7 smartphone app. Users can view their glucose readings on either the receiver or through the app. For this study, participants used the smartphone app to activate the sensor and record glucose data. The study involved two different sensor lots from commercial supplies [28].

The FreeStyle Libre 3 Continuous Glucose Monitoring System (Abbott Diabetes Care, Alameda, CA, USA) is a real-time CGM device that requires no factory calibration and is designed for individuals aged 4 and older. The system includes two primary components: a 14-day sensor that integrates both the transmitter and the receiver functionality, and a choice of either a handheld reader or the Freestyle Libre 3 smartphone app for data display. Users receive their glucose readings through the receiver or app. In this study, participants utilized the smartphone app to initiate the sensor and gather glucose data [28].

The Eversense XL CGM (Senseonics Inc., Germantown, MD, USA) utilizes fluorescence-based technology for long-term glucose monitoring. The system includes a sensor implanted under the skin of the upper arm, an external smart transmitter worn over the sensor, and a mobile app displaying glucose data on a handheld device [30]. In May 2016, Senseonics received CE mark approval for Eversense, the first CGM with an implantable glucose sensor lasting 90 days. In 2017, they launched the Eversense XL, extending the sensor's lifespan to 180 days, making it the longest-lasting CGM sensor on the market [30]. With the Eversense system, skin irritation can be minimized by replacing the silicone-based adhesive daily [31] (Table 1).

4 Discussion

Several limitations remain despite significant advances in continuous glucose monitoring (CGM) systems. These include frequent finger pricking to calibrate some devices, discomfort when inserting the sensor, and skin irritation caused by adhesive patches. These

Table 1. Key features of popular CGM devices

Feature	Dexcom G7	FreeStyle Libre 3	Eversense XL
Manufacturer	Dexcom, Inc.	Abbott Diabetes Care	Senseonics Inc.
Calibration	No calibration required	No factory calibration	Calibration required periodically
Age Range	2 years and older	4 years and older	Suitable for adults
Sensor Lifespan	10 days	14 days	Up to 180 days
Components	sensor-transmitter, receiver/smartphone app	Sensor-transmitter, receiver/smartphone app	Implantable sensor, external transmitter, mobile app
Insertion Method	Subcutaneous	Subcutaneous	Implantable
Skin Irritation Mitigation	Minimal issues reported	Minimal issues reported	Replace silicone adhesive daily

challenges underscore the urgent need for alternative approaches that are non-invasive and patient friendly.

While numerous studies focus on existing CGM technologies, this paper uniquely bridges the gap between their limitations and the potential of non-invasive solutions. These approaches eliminate the need for instruments inserted into the body, reducing discomfort and risks associated with needles. By integrating these innovations with telemedicine platforms, this work proposes a novel framework to revolutionize diabetes management, making it more accessible, patient-friendly, and personalized.

Non-invasive glucose monitoring devices represent the next frontier in diabetes care. Technologies like near-infrared spectroscopy (NIRS), which are non-destructive, non-invasive, and cost-effective, offer a promising solution for continuous, real-time glucose monitoring. By removing the need for needle-based calibration and adhesive patches, NIRS-based solutions can greatly enhance patient comfort and compliance.

Integrating non-invasive monitoring with telemedicine allows real-time data sharing between patients and healthcare providers. This approach supports personalized diabetes management by enabling remote monitoring, early detection of glycemic variations, and timely interventions, empowering patients and improving adherence to care plans.

In summary, this paper identifies the limitations of current CGM systems and presents a pathway toward non-invasive, real-time glucose monitoring using NIRS technology, combined with telemedicine. This approach has the potential to revolutionize diabetes management by making it more accessible, comfortable, and tailored to individual needs.

References

1. Ahmed, I., et al.: Recent advances in optical sensors for continuous glucose monitoring. Sens. Diagn. **1**(6), 1098–1125 (2022). https://doi.org/10.1039/D1SD00030F
2. Global diabetes data report 2000–2045. Consulté le: 21 août 2024. [En ligne]. Disponible sur: https://diabetesatlas.org/data/

3. Joshi, A.M., Jain, P., Mohanty, S.P.: Everything you wanted to know about continuous glucose monitoring. IEEE Consumer Electron. Mag. **10**(6), 61–66 (2021). https://doi.org/10.1109/MCE.2021.3073498
4. Lancet, T.: Diabetes: a defining disease of the 21st century. Lancet **401**(10394), 2087 (2023). https://doi.org/10.1016/S0140-6736(23)01296-5
5. Chehregosha, H., Khamseh, M.E., Malek, M., Hosseinpanah, F., Ismail-Beigi, F.: A view beyond HbA1c: role of continuous glucose monitoring. Diabetes Ther. **10**(3), 853–863 (2019). https://doi.org/10.1007/s13300-019-0619-1
6. Keenan, D.B., et al.: Accuracy of the enlite 6-day glucose sensor with guardian and veo calibration algorithms. Diabetes Technol. Ther. **14**(3), 225–231 (2012). https://doi.org/10.1089/dia.2011.0199
7. Weinstein, R.L., Schwartz, S.L., Brazg, R.L., Bugler, J.R., Peyser, T.A., McGarraugh, G.V.: Accuracy of the 5-Day freestyle navigator continuous glucose monitoring system. Diabetes Care **30**(5), 1125–1130 (2007). https://doi.org/10.2337/dc06-1602
8. Jernelv, I.L., Milenko, K., Fuglerud, S.S., Hjelme, D.R., Ellingsen, R., Aksnes, A.: A review of optical methods for continuous glucose monitoring. Appl. Spectrosc. Rev. **54**(7), 543–572 (2019). https://doi.org/10.1080/05704928.2018.1486324
9. Jain, P., Joshi, A.M., Mohanty, S.: Everything You Wanted to Know About Noninvasive Glucose Measurement and Control (2021). https://doi.org/10.48550/ARXIV.2101.08996
10. Ramachandran, A.: Know the signs and symptoms of diabetes. Indian J. Med. Res. **140**(5), 579–581 (2014)
11. Home, et al.: IDF Diabetes Atlas. Consulté le: 27 août 2024. [En ligne]. Disponible sur: https://diabetesatlas.org/
12. Home, et al.: Diabetes and kidney disease | IDF Diabetes Atlas. Consulté le: 10 septembre 2024. [En ligne]. Disponible sur: https://diabetesatlas.org/atlas/diabetes-and-kidney-disease/
13. Home, et al. : Diabetes foot-related complications | IDF Diabetes Atlas. Consulté le: 10 septembre 2024. [En ligne]. Disponible sur: https://diabetesatlas.org/atlas/diabetic-foot-2022/
14. Home, et al.: Diabetes and COVID-19 | IDF Diabetes Atlas. Consulté le: 10 septembre 2024. [En ligne]. Disponible sur: https://diabetesatlas.org/atlas/covid19-2022/
15. Parker, E.D., et al.: Economic costs of diabetes in the U.S. in 2022. Diabetes Care **47**(1), 26–43 (2024). https://doi.org/10.2337/dci23-0085
16. Ko, H.Y.K., Tripathi, N.K., Mozumder, C., Muengtaweepongsa, S., Pal, I.: Real-time remote patient monitoring and alarming system for noncommunicable lifestyle diseases. Int. J. Telemed. Appl. **2023**, 1–13 (2023). https://doi.org/10.1155/2023/9965226
17. Schnell, O., et al.: Self-monitoring of blood glucose in type 2 diabetes: recent studies. J. Diabetes Sci. Technol. **7**(2), 478–488 (2013). https://doi.org/10.1177/193229681300700225
18. Lee, J.H.: The Occurrence and management of adverse skin events due to continuous glucose monitoring. J. Korean Diabetes **23**(1), 43–49 (2022). https://doi.org/10.4093/jkd.2022.23.1.43
19. Boland, E., Monsod, T., Delucia, M., Brandt, C.A., Fernando, S., Tamborlane, W.V.: Limitations of conventional methods of self-monitoring of blood glucose. Diabetes Care **24**(11), 1858–1862 (2001). https://doi.org/10.2337/diacare.24.11.1858
20. Elbalshy, M.M., et al.: The effect of DO- IT- YOURSELF REAL- TIME continuous glucose monitoring on psychological and glycemic variables in children with type 1 diabetes: a randomized crossover trial. Pediatr. Diabetes **23**(4), 480–488 (2022). https://doi.org/10.1111/pedi.13331
21. Villena Gonzales, W., Mobashsher, A., Abbosh, A.: The progress of glucose monitoring—a review of invasive to minimally and non-invasive techniques, devices and sensors. Sensors **19**(4), 800 (2019). https://doi.org/10.3390/s19040800
22. Soni, A., et al.: A practical approach to continuous glucose monitoring (rtCGM) and FreeStyle Libre systems (isCGM) in children and young people with Type 1 diabetes. Diabetes Res. Clin. Pract. **184**, 109196 (2022). https://doi.org/10.1016/j.diabres.2022.109196

23. Basu, A., et al.: Time lag of glucose from intravascular to interstitial compartment in humans. Diabetes **62**(12), 4083–4087 (2013). https://doi.org/10.2337/db13-1132
24. News From the FDA and the NIH. Diabetes Technol. Therap. **1**(3): 349–351 (1999). https://doi.org/10.1089/152091599317260
25. Jain, P., Joshi, A.M., Mohanty, S.P., Cenkeramaddi, L.R.: Non-invasive glucose measurement technologies: recent advancements and future challenges. IEEE Access **12**, 61907–61936 (2024). https://doi.org/10.1109/ACCESS.2024.3389819
26. Rodbard, D.: Continuous glucose monitoring: a review of successes, challenges, and opportunities. Diabetes Technol. Therap. **18**(S2), S2-33-S2-13 (2016). https://doi.org/10.1089/dia.2015.0417
27. Continuous Glucose Monitoring - NIDDK, National Institute of Diabetes and Digestive and Kidney Diseases. Consulté le: 10 septembre 2024. [En ligne]. Disponible sur: https://www.niddk.nih.gov/health-information/diabetes/overview/managing-diabetes/continuous-glucose-monitoring
28. Hanson, K., Kipnes, M., Tran, H.: Comparison of point accuracy between two widely used continuous glucose monitoring systems. J. Diabetes Sci. Technol. **18**(3), 598–607 (2024). https://doi.org/10.1177/19322968231225676
29. Barrie, R.: Dexcom G7 approved for use in Canada, Medical Device Network. Consulté le: 12 septembre 2024. [En ligne]. Disponible sur: https://www.medicaldevice-network.com/news/dexcom-g7-approved-for-use-in-canada/
30. Aronson, R., Abitbol, A., Tweden, K.S.: First assessment of the performance of an implantable continuous glucose monitoring system through 180 days in a primarily adolescent population with type 1 diabetes. Diabetes Obesity Metab. **21**(7), 1689–1694 (2019). https://doi.org/10.1111/dom.13726
31. Yoo, J.H., Kim, J.H.: Advances in continuous glucose monitoring and integrated devices for management of diabetes with insulin-based therapy: improvement in glycemic control. Diabetes Metab. J.Metab. J. **47**(1), 27–41 (2023). https://doi.org/10.4093/dmj.2022.0271

A Bibliometric Review of Research Trends, Challenges and Future Directions in Smart Medical Bracelets

Kawtar El Amri[1,2(✉)], Nabila Rabbah[1], Ibtissam Khalfaoui[2], Nadia Machkour[1], and Hicham Medromi[2,3]

[1] Laboratory of Complex Cyber Physical Systems (LCCPS), National School of Arts and Crafts of Casablanca (ENSAM), Hassan II University, Casablanca, Morocco
Kawtaramri031@gmail.com

[2] Research Foundation for Development and Innovation in Science and Engineering – Suptech Santé, Mohammedia, Morocco

[3] Engineering Research Laboratory, National Higher School of Electricity and Mechanics (ENSEM), Hassan II University, Casablanca, Morocco

Abstract. This paper reports on a bibliometric study of smart medical bracelets performed over the period 2019 to 2024 with the help of the Scopus database. The identification of main trends made mention of artificial intelligence, deep learning and IoT for real-time health monitoring. Wearable technologies are paramount in the management of chronic diseases and in enhancing the outcomes of people, especially during the COVID-19 pandemic. It was found that smart medical bracelets could indeed offer the potential for a non-invasive way to monitor health continuously. While this review is confined to English language publications, the conclusions drawn carry a valuable scope and light over future research requirements like involving a wide number of databases, evaluation of long-term effectiveness and the fusion with new emerging technologies.

Keywords: Smart Bracelet · Real Time Monitoring · Telemedicine

1 Introduction

The rapid development and integration of sophisticated sensor technologies in the smart medical bracelets widely revolutionized healthcare, enabling continuous and real-time monitoring of vital health parameters. These devices are extremely important in chronic condition management and the support of remote patient monitoring. Smart bracelets stand out by tracking key vital signs such as heart rate, oxygen saturation, body temperature and glucose levels while still being easy to use. Their design further makes them easy to use in a wide range of populations, including the elderly [1, 2]. Research has also consistently revealed their simplicity; users get used to such devices within a very short period of time, further improving health care delivery [3]. The accessibility and portability combined in small-sized smart bracelets are useful in clinical and home settings, facilitating timely medical interventions by transmitting captured data in real time to the respective health professionals [4, 5].

I. Aboudrar et al. (Eds.): ICESST 2024, SUCI, pp. 473–482, 2025.
https://doi.org/10.1007/978-3-031-86705-7_44

The COVID-19 pandemic brought into sharp focus the need for technologies of wearable sensing, where the monitoring of vital signs became exceedingly important in early detection and management of the disease [6]. It is such a convergence in smartphones and wearables that continues further to push mobile health technologies by embedding sensor functions in portable devices, promoting real-time and continuous health monitoring [7, 8]. These innovations not only reduced the frequency of visits to hospitals but also increased healthcare efficiency by continuous sharing of patients' data. Further, advancements in telemedicine and IoMT allowed remote health monitoring in a scalable manner, especially during health crises like the COVID-19 pandemic, aiding in quarantine management and isolation monitoring [9, 10]. With the growing occurrence of lifestyle diseases, the demand for smart medical bracelets will contribute toward addressing accessible healthcare solutions that are being called for, instrumental in enhancing remote patient management. This reduces health care costs while improving health care delivery globally [11].

The work represents a general bibliometric review related to research on smart medical bracelets, tending to establish the most important themes, challenges and opportunities that may be further advanced. Concretely, this study explores the linkage between bibliometric trends and real-world applications together with technical limitations, thus delivering insights valuable for both academia and industry.

The research question that this study seeks to address is: What themes have attracted the highest scholarly attention in smart medical bracelet research? In answering this question, we aim to understand the current state of research in the field for developing new smart medical bracelets.

The paper is organized as follows: the methodology to perform the bibliometric analysis, including how the collection of data was done and the analytical tools employed, is described. Thereafter, the results will be given with respect to country citations, keyword co-occurrence and contributions from impactful authors. A comprehensive interpretation of the findings is then documented by focusing on principal themes and leading contributors in the area of research related to smart medical bracelets. It finally concludes by summarizing some of the key insights into limitations and directions for further research.

2 Methodology

The present study is a bibliometric analysis related and focuses on research into smart medical bracelets. Data for the analysis were retrieved from the Scopus database on 30th July 2024, because it is reliable and with extensive coverage of scientific literature [12–14]. The search made use of "smart medical bracelets" as the main keyword, while focusing on the title, abstract and keywords of the documents, but seeking to make as much relevant coverage as possible. The publications were identified and filtered using the Preferred Reporting Items for Systematic Reviews and Meta-Analyses (PRISMA) guidelines in a systematic approach [15].

This analysis focused on studies published between 2019 and 2024. An initial dataset of 976 documents was obtained, from which a final dataset of 949 documents was reduced through duplicate removal and unrelated entry removal. The relevant publications were in the English language. Co-author networks and co-occurrence patterns of keywords were counted in the analysis of leading contributors, collaboration trends and dominant research themes. Network visualizations were generated using VOSviewer software. Theme and contributor impact and prominence were determined using characteristics such as the number of citations to a particular paper or the number of times that a keyword was used. Figure 1 below summarizes the data collection using the PRISMA method.

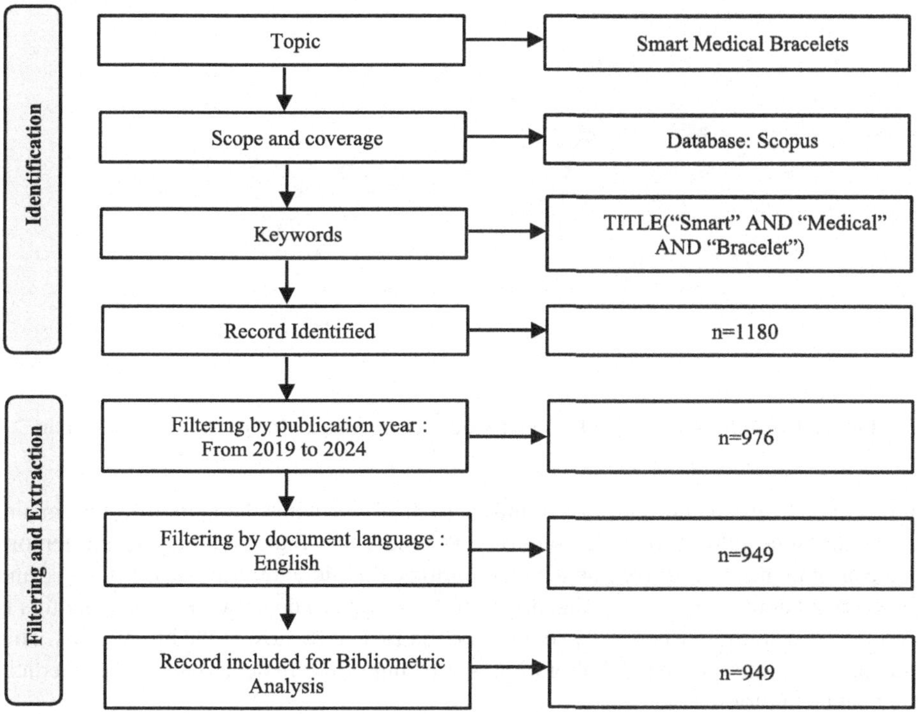

Fig. 1. PRISMA diagram of the data collections and extraction from Scopus Results

3 Results

3.1 Country Citation Data Analysis

In this regard, country citation data through VOSviewer have been analyzed to evaluate the research impact on a global scale and to identify leading contributors in smart medical bracelet research. Applying the thresholds of minimum 8 documents and minimum 5 citations per country, 40 countries were included for analysis. Figure 2 illustrates the dataset of these countries clustered into six groups, showing the geographic distribution and major collaborative networks in the field.

The smart medical bracelet research citation network essentially takes on a hierarchical nature: at the leading position in both academic influence and output of research are countries like China and the United States; while in Europe, heavyweights involved

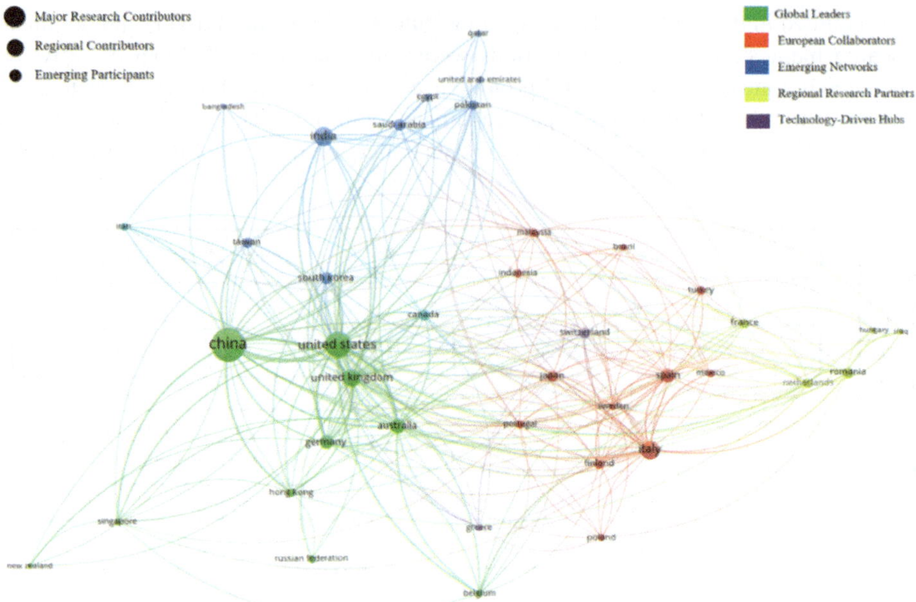

Fig. 2. Co-authorship Network Among Countries in Smart Medical Bracelet Research

in wearable health technology are countries such as Germany, the United Kingdom and Italy. Emerging players include countries like India and Saudi Arabia, which demonstrate prominence through regional collaborations. Smaller countries such as Greece and Switzerland contribute in specialized but effective ways. The network shows that this is a hubbed distribution, where only some few countries drive most of the innovations. This indicates that international collaboration is very important in developing smart medical bracelet technology.

Further, Table 1 presents the leading nations in smart medical bracelet research, namely China and the United States of America, with 5610 and 5213 citations, respectively, hence wielding a great amount of influence. Following is Australia, which contributes with 1968 citations, while European countries such as the UK with 1481, Italy with 1212 and Spain with 887 reflect the active role that Europe takes in this area. The Asian nations represented by Hong Kong, South Korea and India contributed moderately, with citation counts ranging between 700 and 900. The gap between China, the United States and other nations reflects a concentration of research influence that could be extended to allow for broader worldwide participation and impact.

3.2 Co-occurrence of Keywords Analysis

In VOSviewer, we used the co-occurrence method to analyse the keywords in our attempt to identify primary research themes of smart medical bracelets. We set that the minimum number of occurrences of a keyword would be 20 and thus we attained 76 keywords

Table 1. Top Countries by Citation Count in Smart Medical Bracelet Research

Countries	Citations
China	5610
United States	5213
Australia	1968
United Kingdom	1481
Italy	1212
Spain	887
Hong Kong	875
South Korea	776
India	738
Finland	709

meeting this threshold. The keywords shown in Fig. 3 were divided into four distinguishable clusters by cluster analysis. Then, based on the keywords in each cluster, we identified the main research themes in the field of smart medical bracelets.

Cluster 1: Health Monitoring and Smart Technologies. Health monitoring systems and smart technologies are researched; the main research areas concern AI, blood pressure monitoring and data handling in the COVID-19 pandemic. Some advanced methodologies are discussed to make these devices more efficient and interactive: deep learning, energy harvesting and gesture recognition. The integration of healthcare systems and IoT allows for the real-time monitoring of patients while wearables, development of smartphones and virtual reality focus on human-computer interaction offering an enhancement of better health delivery.

Cluster 2: Clinical and Lifestyle Applications. Smart medical bracelets are worn either in a clinical or lifestyle setting by adults and the elderly population. Research indicates an improvement of quality of life and increased physical activity through mobile applications and telemedicine. That is evident in the clinical efficacy that such devices have proven to possess through randomized controlled trials, showing the impact these devices have on improving health care and creating healthier lifestyles.

Cluster 3: Biomedical Signal Processing and Physiological Monitoring. Key themes develop algorithms for biomedical signal processing and physiological monitoring; in particular, with a focus on heart rate/heart rate variability. Electrocardiography and emotion recognition address diagnostic and therapeutic goals. Signal processing is intrinsic to the interpretation of physiological data, enabling speech recognition applications and patient interface design.

Cluster 4: Wearable Electronic Devices. Research emphasizes designing and developing wearable electronic devices for continuous health monitoring. Much is being drawn to developing user-friendly and reliable equipment that one can wear easily in daily life, instantly getting data about one's health, hence helping an individual keep themselves fit.

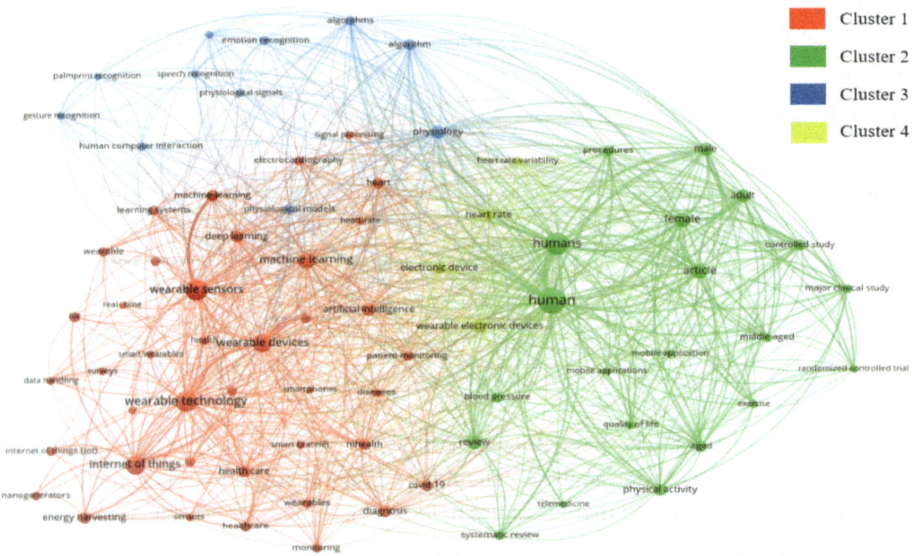

Fig. 3. Co-occurrence Network of Keywords in Smart Medical Bracelet Research

The keyword co-occurrence network in Fig. 4 illustrates the evolution of research themes in smart medical bracelets over time, using a color gradient to represent specific periods. Early themes from 2021 (blue) focus on foundational technologies like machine learning, deep learning, wearable sensors, gesture recognition and energy harvesting, emphasizing device interactivity and efficiency. By 2022 (green), research shifted their focus on wearable technology, IoT and physiological monitoring, by integrating advanced biomedical signal processing, such as heart rate variability and electrocardiography. As for themes from 2023 to 2024 (yellow) highlight clinical and practical applications, including telemedicine, mobile applications and quality-of-life improvements. Covid-19 has demonstrated the role of smart medical bracelets in disease management and personalized health monitoring.

This progression from blue to yellow reflects the transition of the field from early technological innovations to real-world applications in healthcare with a focus on clinical integration and improved patient outcomes.

3.3 Key Contributions and Impactful Authors in Smart Medical Bracelet Research

Table 2 presents the literature of most cited authors about smart medical bracelets. Thus, the first two authors are Song Yu and Zhang Haixia with 898 and 738 citations respectively in order they be included as two key actors of this area. Li Zhou, Benini

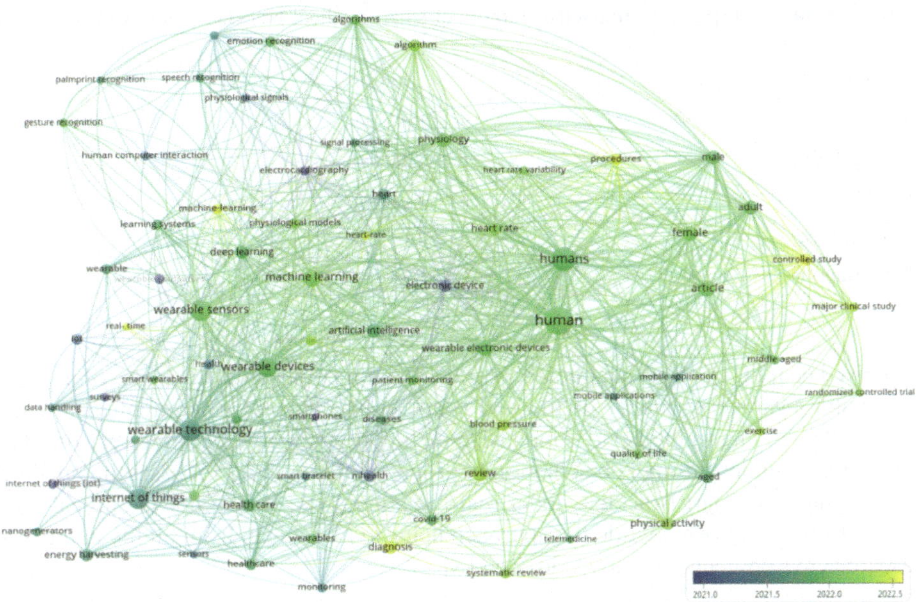

Fig. 4. Temporal Evolution of Keywords in Smart Medical Bracelet Research

Luca and Falk Tiago h are less cited but they are an important part of the landscape. The gap between the first two authors and the rest suggests a concentration of impact, with a small number of researchers driving the major advances. These figures are a forceful reminder that collaboration and exchange of knowledge might be used to broaden such research to increase its scope and influence.

Song Yu and Zhang Haixia went a step further with AI in wearables by developing algorithms that increased the accuracy and reliability of real-time health monitoring, especially in anomaly detection in physiological signals. Li Zhou has contributed to energy efficiency in wearable devices where new methods have been introduced for performance optimization toward long usage of batteries. Luca Benini has translated research into clinical practice. He showed evidence of the efficiency of smart medical bracelets in chronic disease management through rigorous randomized trials. Falk Tiago H. extended the reach for this gadget by embedding different multimodal sensing technologies like ECG and emotion recognition, merging physical and mental health monitoring.

3.4 Real World Applications and Clinical Relevance

Recent studies, apart from those already giving bibliometric insights, have identified concrete examples of where and how these smart medical bracelets have been applied. Han et al. researched the application of a body area network-based Smart Bracelet for prehospital trauma care through demonstration of the effectiveness of reducing response time in critical interventions and improving the coordination of trauma through 5G technology enabling real-time data integration [16]. Meanwhile, Jeng et al. investigated

Table 2. Top 5 most impactful authors of smart medical bracelets publications

Author	Citations
Song, yu	898
Zhang, haixia	738
Li, zhou	112
Benini, luca	110
Falk, tiago h	87

perceived benefits of smart healthcare wearables among older adults in terms of improving health awareness, quality of life and social connectedness when applied in daily life [17]. Lu et al., on their part, emphasize the importance of integrating real-life data into clinical studies through presentation of proper methodologies for assessing medical devices such as Smart Bracelets under real-life conditions. Reliability in clinical findings is further improved, while the approach helps to fill the gap from highly controlled research environments to real-world use [18].

3.5 Synthesis of Results

Overlaps that give an insight into the deeper understanding of bibliometric trends are citation analysis, country contributions and keyword co-occurrence. Among these, citations by China and the United States can be traced back to themes on artificial intelligence, IoT and energy efficiency; highly cited authors, Song Yu and Zhang Haixia, advance AI-oriented smart medical bracelets. European countries, such as Germany and the United Kingdom, actually give special attention to telemedicine and chronic disease management, put more emphasis on applications and usability and have short-term solutions for the world's main health priorities. Linkages between countries, authors and researched themes illustrate a picture of collaborative and interdisciplinary advances made regarding smart medical bracelet technologies.

4 Conclusion, Limitations and Future Directions

This bibliometric study underlines the smart medical bracelet as an important revolution in healthcare, especially in chronic disease treatments and real-time health monitoring. Key trends identified include the development of integrated artificial intelligence, deep learning and IoT technologies that will enhance non-invasive, continuous monitoring capabilities. While critical, the fact that only publications in the English language were focused on denotes how smart medical bracelets have gained much momentum in improving health outcomes even at critical times, such as the COVID-19 pandemic. It also means that for African countries, especially Morocco, there is a good opportunity to be open toward this area of evolution through localized research and international collaboration. With continued innovation and the sharing of ideas across the globe, there is considerable scope for smarter medical bracelets in the future.

Based on this review and with regard to our main research question, dominant themes that have been identified are in artificial intelligence and deep learning for enhanced monitoring, integration of IoT for real-time data transmission, energy efficiency and applications related to telemedicine and remote health monitoring. These themes reflect the scholarly focus on leveraging technology to improve patient outcomes and support chronic disease management. Through a synthesis of these research trends, our study has pointed out the transformative potential of smart medical bracelets, with areas that might be explored in future studies to further the field.

The study is limited to Scopus indexed publications. Other limitations include the five-year time focus-the period with which this might have missed critical earlier or very recent developments. The reliance on bibliometric analysis further restricts the qualitative depth with which the insights into the contributions of the research are looked upon. The other technical challenges involve data privacy and security, apart from optimization of battery life. All these represent significant barriers to the effective adoption and scalability of smart medical bracelets. Addressing these challenges entails robust encryption, compliance with international standards on protection of data and artificial intelligence-driven energy optimization for extended usability and security.

Future research should be oriented to energy efficiency and battery management using Artificial Intelligence. To enhance scalability across diverse healthcare environments, research should be expanded on longitudinal effectiveness of these devices in real world applications. Addressing these technical challenges in concert with device functionalities will drive future development toward more robust and secure technologies.

References

1. Materia, F.T., Smyth, J.M.: Acceptability and concerns about innovative wearable health sensors in persons with and without chronic disease diagnosis. Internet Interv. **35**, 100702 (2024)
2. Vichitra, P., Mangayarkarasi, S.: The integration of portable sensors with a mobile application for self-observation. Int. J. Innov. Sci. Res. Technol. **9**(7), 190–195 (2024). https://doi.org/10.38124/ijisrt/ijisrt24jul039
3. Hummady, M.M., Fadhil, H.: Smart healthcare medical bracelet using the Internet of Things. In: Proceedings of International Conferences on Computing Advancements (ICCA), pp. 1–6. IEEE (2022). https://doi.org/10.1109/ICCA56443.2022.10039622
4. Raju Vonteddu, S.N., Nunna, P.K., Jain, S., Diwakar, G.: Smart wearable wristband for patients' health monitoring system through IoT. In: Proceedings of 2022 International Conference on Power, Energy, Control, and Transmission Systems (ICPECTS), pp. 1–6. IEEE (2022). https://doi.org/10.1109/ICPECTS56089.2022.10047551
5. Ding, X., et al.: Wearable sensing and telehealth technology with potential applications in the coronavirus pandemic. IEEE Rev. Biomed. Eng. (2020). https://doi.org/10.1109/RBME.2020.2992838
6. Hong, W.: Advances and opportunities of mobile health in the postpandemic era: smartphonization of wearable devices and wearable deviceization of smartphones. JMIR Mhealth Uhealth **12**, e48803 (2024). https://doi.org/10.2196/48803
7. Idris, S.A., Md Lazam, N.A., Izhar, L.I., Azman, D.B., Way, L.J., Aida, I.: Smart health monitoring wristband with auto-alert function. In: 2022 IEEE Regional Symposium on Micro

and Nanoelectronics (ROMA), pp. 1–5. IEEE (2022). https://doi.org/10.1109/ROMA55875.2022.9915677

8. Gu, D., Li, T., Wang, X., Yang, X., Yu, Z.: Visualizing the intellectual structure and evolution of electronic health and telemedicine research. Int. J. Med. Inform. **130**, 103947 (2019). https://doi.org/10.1016/j.ijmedinf.2019.08.007
9. Zan, F.: Development of real-time cloud-based smart remote healthcare monitoring system. In: Healthcare IoT and Cloud Integration, pp. 345–360. Springer (2022). https://doi.org/10.1007/978-981-19-6068-0_21
10. Lavric, A., Petrariu, A.I., Mutescu, P.-M., Coca, E., Popa, V.: Internet of Things concept in the context of the COVID-19 pandemic: a multi-sensor application design. Sensors **22**, 503 (2022). https://doi.org/10.3390/s22020503
11. Idris, S.A., Md Lazam, N.A., Izhar, L.I., Azman, D.B., Way, L.J., Aida, I.: Smart healthcare monitoring framework using IoT with big data analytics. In: Advances in Smart Healthcare Technologies, pp. 234–250. IET (2022). https://doi.org/10.1049/pbhe043e_ch9
12. Abbas, A.F., Jusoh, A., Mas, A., Alsharif, A.H., Ali, J.: Bibliometrix analysis of information sharing in social media. Cogent Bus. Manag. **9**(1), 2016556 (2022). https://doi.org/10.1080/23311975.2021.2016556
13. Abbas, A.F., Jusoh, A., Masod, A., Ali, J., Ahmed, H.: A Bibliometric analysis of publications on social media influencers using vosviewer. J. Theor. Appl. Inf. Technol. **99**(23), 5662–5676 (2021)
14. Sikandar, H., Vaicondam, Y., Khan, N., Qureshi, M.I., Ullah, A.: Scientific mapping of industry 4.0 research: a bibliometric analysis. Int. J. Interact. Mob. Technol. **15**(18), 129 (2021). https://doi.org/10.3991/ijim.v15i18.25535
15. Page, M.J., et al.: The PRISMA 2020 statement: an updated guideline for reporting systematic reviews. BMJ **372**, n71 (2021). https://doi.org/10.1136/bmj.n71
16. Han, W., et al.: Clinical application of a body area network-based smart bracelet for pre-hospital trauma care. Front. Med. **10**, 1190125 (2023). https://doi.org/10.3389/fmed.2023.1190125
17. Jeng, M., Yeh, T.-M., Pai, F.-Y.: Analyzing older adults' perceived values of using smart bracelets by means-end chain. Healthcare **8**(4), 494 (2020). https://doi.org/10.3390/HEALTHCARE8040494
18. Lu, N., et al.: Leverage multiple real-world data sources in single-arm medical device clinical studies. J. Biopharm. Stat.Biopharm. Stat. **31**(3), 1–15 (2021). https://doi.org/10.1080/10543406.2021.1897994

Systematic Review of Physical, Chemical, and Biological Approaches for Exosome Isolation Towards Optimizing Methods in Clinical Diagnostics

Ayoub Slalmi[1,2](✉), Nabila Rabbah[3], Ikram Debbarh[2,4], Ilham Battas[2,4], Hicham Medromi[2,4], and Abdelmjid Abourriche[1]

[1] Laboratory of Molecular and Analytical Chemistry (LCAM), Faculty of Sciences Ben M'sik, Hassan II University, Casablanca, Morocco
ayoubslalmi2222@gmail.com

[2] Research Foundation for Development and Innovation in Science and Engineering (FRDISI), Casablanca, Morocco

[3] Complex Physics and Systems Laboratory (LCCPS), ENSAM, Hassan II University, Casablanca, Morocco

[4] Graduate School of Biomedical Engineering and Health Techniques (SUPTECH-SANTE), Mohammedia, Morocco

Abstract. Exosomes are a subtype of extracellular vesicles (EVs) with a size range be-tween 30 and 150 nm. They are an emerging approach in disease diagnostic and therapeutic applications since they carry and transfer disease specific proteins, nucleic acids, and lipids. Despite their large potential, the clinical translation of exosome-based diagnostics faces some challenges, particularly the techniques for their isolation and characterization that are not standardized and scalable. This review is a comprehensive analysis of major physical, chemical, and biological approaches applied in the isolation of exosomes, including ultracentrifugation, polymer precipitation, and immunocapture. For each of these approaches, we point out their strengths and limitations, focusing on clinical relevance within the context of precision medicine and cancer diagnostics. Furthermore, we discuss emerging technologies that can over-come these challenges such as microfluidics and tangential flow filtration, and we suggest the direction of future research for improving the clinical utility of exosome-based diagnostics. Eventually, this could translate into a revolution non-invasive diagnostics methods and open new avenues for personalized therapies.

Keywords: Exosome isolation · extracellular vesicles · ultracentrifugation · polymer precipitation · immunocapture · cancer diagnostics · microfluidics · non-invasive diagnostics · precision medicine · biomarker analysis

---

The original version of the chapter has been revised. Author name has been corrected. A correction to this chapter can be found at https://doi.org/10.1007/978-3-031-86705-7_54

I. Aboudrar et al. (Eds.): ICESST 2024, SUCI, pp. 483–492, 2025.
https://doi.org/10.1007/978-3-031-86705-7_45

1 Introduction

Exosomes or nanoscale extracellular vesicles range from 30 to 150 nm and represent one of the newest and most promising tools in the medical field. This is especially concerning early diagnostics, such as in cancer diseases. Various cell types secrete such vesicles, which are helpful for intercellular communication by transporting proteins, nucleic acids, and lipids that reflect the pathological or physiological state of their cells of origin. Due to their small size and comparative ease of access from bio-fluids like blood, urine, and saliva, exosomes have proved to be very good candidates for non-invasive diagnostic applications, commonly known as liquid biopsies [1]. We can use the critical biological information these exosomes carry to preliminary identify and diagnose several diseases, including but not limited to cancers such as prostate, breast, and bladder cancer, and neurodegenerative dis-eases [2]. Furthermore, exosomes are involved in an intercellular communication step through the transport of proteins, RNAs, and lipids between cells. Since they accurately reflect the status of their parent cells, exosomes have arisen as promising biomarkers for the early detection of diseases. For instance, tumor-derived exosomes bear specific molecular features of cancers, including those of prostate, breast, and bladder cancers. This enables the physicians to diagnose these cancers at asymptomatic stages [2]. Their involvement in the transport of biomolecules across cellular membranes also provides a promising mode for monitoring neurodegenerative and inflammatory diseases. Another key advantage of using exosomes in clinical diagnostics is that the approach is non-invasive. In contrast to blood and urine, easily accessible bodily fluids, exosomes can be more easily isolated and taken for investigation. Thus, it minimizes risk to the patient while enabling diagnostic information in real time. They can, for instance, trace the response of a patient to oncology treatment and locate the relapse condition much sooner than could be achieved by means of conventional methods of imaging [1]. To fully exploit the diagnostic potential of exosomes, highly efficient, precise, and swift isolation techniques need to be developed for their isolation, microfluidic chips for the rapid capture of exosomes and magnetic bead-based adsorption would go a long way toward enhancing sample purity [5]. One of the biggest challenges is the isolation of exosomes from biological fluids. However, traditional methods of isolation like ultracentrifugation face their own problems of low purity, long time processing, and high operational costs. Because of this, most of these techniques involve highly expensive equipment and thus are very problematic to be standardized for routine clinical applications [3]. This highlights the aspects of exosome isolation techniques that need optimization to meet the demands of modern clinical applications, where speed, reproducibility, and sample purity are important. Therefore, the purpose of this review article is to present a systematic review regarding physical, chemical, and biological methods for the isolation of exosomes. The review discusses recent innovations in the areas of microfluidics, magnetic bead-based adsorption, size-exclusion chromatography, and polymer-based precipitation that could represent the most promising approaches to clinical diagnostics. Additionally, we will discuss the development of these emerging technologies offering superior purity, efficiency, and ease of clinical implementation with the final goal of optimizing exosome isolation for non-invasive diagnostics [4].

2 Methodology

This systematic review is coducted as per PRISMA guidelines, and a strict selection process has been followed in including relevant studies on exosome separation techniques in clinical diagnostics. Searches were performed in the Scopus database only, limiting the date of publication to 2010–2024. To select the research works, certain criteria were considered for this review. We targeted studies written in English, open access or subscription, and a clear focus regarding exosome separation within a clinical setting. The inclusion criteria were focused on areas related to medicine, molecular biology, and biomedical engineering. Only original research publications, clinical studies, conference papers, and review articles concerning techniques of physical, chemical, and biological isolation were chosen (Fig. 1).

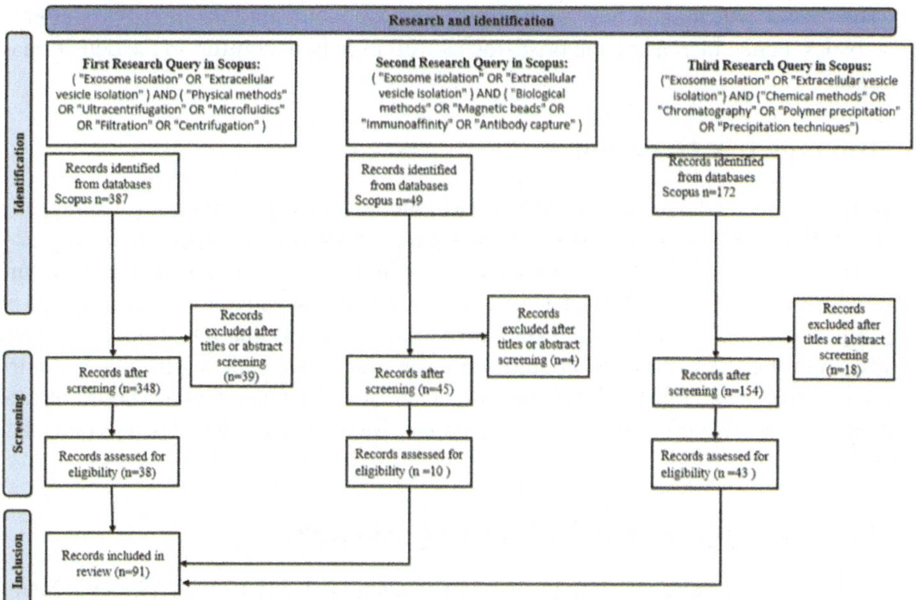

Fig. 1. PRISMA Flow diagram of exosome isolation methods: Physical, Biological, and Chemical techniques (2010–2024).

The search strategy was based on three different queries in order to capture a wide range of studies on exosome isolation techniques for clinical diagnostics:

1. **First search:** ("Exosome isolation" OR "Extracellular vesicle isolation") AND ("Physical methods" OR "Ultracentrifugation" OR "Microfluidics" OR "Filtration" OR "Centrifugation").
2. **And the second question is:** ("Exosome isolation" OR "Extracellular vesicle isolation") AND ("Biological methods" OR "Magnetic beads" OR "Immunoaffinity" OR "Antibody capture").

3. **The third query was:** ("Exosome isolation" OR "Extracellular vesicle isolation") AND ("Chemical methods" OR "Chromatography" OR "Polymer precipitation" OR "Precipitation techniques").

The inclusion process was done in steps: We applied search filters, made an initial selection based on study titles and abstracts, and then assessed the full texts regarding eligibility. For the first query on physical methods, we identified 387 studies, retained 348 after applying relevance filters, and deemed 38 eligible after full-text screening. The second search question yielded the following, biological methods identified 49 studies; 45 after abstracts screening remained, and 10 were considered eligible after full text evaluation. Chemical methods identified in total 172 articles, with 154 remaining after title and abstract screening, while after full-text evaluation, 43 studies were found eligible. Such a review has included a total of 91 articles in order to provide an overview of exosome isolation techniques using chemical, biological, and physical approaches.

The review will look at how such approaches are applicable for improving clinical diagnostics, hence increasing the precision as well as patient comfort in the detection of diseases.

3 Bibliometric Overview

Research on physical, biological, and chemical methods of exosome isolation has grown significantly, especially after 2017, with 608 papers published between 2010 and 2024. Among these, physical methods such as ultracentrifugation and microfluidics are dominant, with 348 articles mainly from China, the United States, and South Korea, headed by Chinese Academy of Sciences and Harvard Medical School. Immunoaffinity, magnetic beads, and other biological techniques are the topics of 49 papers with major contributions coming from Harvard and the University of Oslo. Chemical methods, such as chromatography, were the subject of 172 papers sponsored by the NIH and other key institutions.

4 Physical Approaches for Exosome Isolation

Among these, the physical techniques most investigated due to their potential scalability and processing of large sample volumes include ultracentrifugation, TFF, and microfluidics for exosome isolation. The following are some of the techniques which are introduced:

- **Ultracentrifugation**: It is one of the maximum applied methods. This technique involves separation based on a high-speed spinning of biological samples to collect exosomes by virtue of their size and density from body fluids such as blood, urine, and saliva. Though this technique has proved indispensable in clinical diagnostics in cancer diseases, it is expensive and time-consuming; repeated cycles may weaken the structural integrity of the exosomes [6, 7].
- **Tangential Flow Filtration (TFF):** is suited for large-scale applications. Unlike traditional filtration, TFF directs fluid flow parallel to the filter membrane, minimizing clogging and allowing for the use of continuous processing. However, improper optimization could result in the loss of exosome integrity [8].

- **Microfluidics**: It uses a variety of platforms in the case of microfluidics. In this case, it is done by the size-based exosome separation of the ExoChip. It can have great control of the small sample volumes. Therefore, the most promising solutions that will lead to rapid diagnostics at low costs and at the point of care is microfluidics [10, 11].

5 Chemical Approaches for Exosome Isolation

Most of the chemical techniques happen to stand inclined toward preserving the integrity of exosomes, and they usually depend on techniques such as SEC, PEG precipitation, and ultrafiltration.

- **Size Exclusion Chromatography (SEC):** This technique separates exosomes based on size as they traverse a porous matrix-a method considered to preserve their biological functions. These would be especially critical for diagnostics and also in applications related to therapeutics such as in cancer and cardiovascular research. SEC is highly preferred because of its simplicity, reproducibility, and handling of large sample volumes highly suitable in a clinical environment [6, 9].
- **Polymer Precipitation (PEG):** This is a very inexpensive technique, wherein polyethylene glycol acts in the precipitation of exosomes from biological fluids. While this technique is widely employed in clinical laboratories due to the convenience involved, this approach often yields co-precipitation of contaminants with the material of interest and may affect sample purity and further downstream analyses [12, 13].
- **Ultrafiltration**: This technique separates exosomes based on size and molecular weight using membranes with defined pore sizes. It is more suitable for clinical diagnostics because the structure of the exosomes is preserved intact. TFF application minimizes membrane clogging hence increasing yields and improving quality. However, the disadvantage is membrane fouling and possible exosome damage by high pressure [7, 8].

6 Biological Approaches for Exosome Isolation

They are high-specificity approaches, biological methods for targeted diagnostics, and the main approaches are Magnetic Bead Capture, Lectin Affinity, and Affinity-Based Immunocapture.

- **Magnetic bead captures**: This method utilizes superparamagnetic beads coated with antibodies or ligands that bind selectively to exosomal surface proteins. Especially in diagnostics of tumor diseases, this method is used for the isolation of tumor-derived exosomes. The low yield is the drawback of this method and limits its use in large-scale purification [17, 18].
- **Lectin affinity:** This technique relies on the affinity between glycan-binding lectins and the isolation of exosomesome, based on their nature of glycosylation. It has been highly useful for the separation of exosomes in cancerous tissues due to the unique structure of glycans present on exosomal membranes. However, overlapping glycosylation patterns can make this technique less specific [14, 15].

- **Affinity-Based Immunocapture**: This method utilizes antibodies against common exosome markers such as CD9, CD63 and CD81 that allow for highly specific isolation of disease-related exosomes. In cancer diagnostics, immunocapture is used very often, but this technique is not scalable due to the high cost of antibodies and risk of cross-reactivity [2, 16].

7 Comparative Analysis of Exosome Isolation Techniques

A bibliometric review was done using the PRISMA method, in order to analyze 608 studies focused on different exosome isolation techniques, which lately have gained increased importance for diagnostics and therapeutics, mainly in cancer research. Of these, 348 specifically referred to physical techniques of isolation, including ultracentrifugation and microfluidics. The latter are presently being used to the greatest extent, due to their prime advantage in the volume of samples processed; however, they are compromised in scalability and higher in cost [6, 7]. Of the biological methods, 49 represent immunocapture and magnetic bead-based techniques. Compared with physical and chemical methods, they have high specificity but are relatively new, and clinical scalability is still a challenge [16, 17]. Ultimately, all the chemical methods with a total of 172 publications included size exclusion chromatography and polymer precipitation. These techniques are particularly critical in maintaining exosomal integrity for clinical applications [9, 12]. The study will explore the evolution of exosome isolation methods, highlighting their strengths and weaknesses in their respective applications (Table 1).

Table 1. Comprehensive Comparative Analysis of Physical, Chemical, and Biological Exosome Isolation Methods:

Technique	Efficiency	Cost	Scalability	Speed	Clinical Applicability	References
Physical Methods						
Ultracentrifugation	High, isolates intact exosomes but can co-isolate proteins	Moderate due to high equipment cost	Low due to labor-intensive process	Slow, time-consuming	Widely used in research, limited in clinical settings	Baranyai et al., 2015; Merchant et al., 2010
Tangential Flow Filtration (TFF)	Moderate, retains size integrity	Moderate, requires specific equipment	Moderate, can handle large volumes	Moderate	Growing in clinical diagnostics due to scalability	Lobb et al., 2015; Kowal et al., 2016
Microfluidics	High for small sample volumes, requires precise device design	Low, cost-effective for small batches	High, easy integration into automated platforms	Fast	Promising for point-of-care diagnostics	He et al., 2018; Vaidyanathan et al., 2014
Chemical Methods						
Size Exclusion Chromatography (SEC)	High, maintains biological integrity	Low, minimal reagent cost	Moderate, can process larger samples	Moderate, faster than ultracentrifugation	Effective for purifying exosomes for clinical use	Baranyai et al., 2015; Kowal et al., 2016
Polymer Precipitation (PEG)	Moderate, often co-precipitates contaminants	Low, simple and affordable	High, handles large volumes	Fast, simple procedure	Suitable for rapid, large-scale isolations	Helwa et al., 2017; Rider et al., 2016
Ultrafiltration	High, maintains exosome integrity	Low, minimal reagents required	High, can process large sample volumes	Fast	Growing potential in clinical diagnostics	Merchant et al., 2010; Lobb et al., 2015

(*continued*)

Table 1. (*continued*)

Technique	Efficiency	Cost	Scalability	Speed	Clinical Applicability	References
Biological Methods						
Magnetic Bead Capture	High specificity for target exosomes	Moderate, due to cost of antibodies	Moderate, good for small-scale applications	Moderate	High potential for targeted diagnostics	Tauro et al., 2012; Zarovni et al., 2015
Lectin Affinity	Moderate, depends on glycosylation pattern	Moderate	Moderate	Fast	Applicable in cancer diagnostics due to specific exosome surface markers	Escrevente et al., 2011; Ghosh et al., 2014
Immunocapture (Antibody-based)	High specificity for disease markers	High, due to antibodies' cost	Low, suitable for small volumes only	Slow, labor-intensive	Excellent for detecting disease-specific biomarkers	Nakayama et al., 2016; Chen et al., 2018

This review provides an overview of the strengths and limitations of various exosome isolation methods, emphasizing the efficiency of physical techniques such as ultracentrifugation and microfluidics for high-throughput applications [6, 7]. Biological methods, such as immunocapture, stand out for their specificity in targeted diagnostics [16, 17], while chemical methods like SEC excel in preserving exosome integrity [9]. Emerging technologies, including TFF and hybrid approaches, offer scalable and precise solutions, paving the way for advancements in non-invasive diagnostics [8, 10].

8 Bibliometric Analysis Results

From 2010 to 2024, a bibliometric analysis of exosome isolation methodologies revealed a significant increase in scholarly output, with 608 publications reviewed, indicating significant advancements in physical, biological, and chemical isolation techniques. In fact, physical methods, with a focus on ultracentrifugation, microfluidics, and filtration, made up the greatest number of publications, 348 in total, because these methods are established to provide high throughput and reproducibility. These techniques are more common in clinical diagnostics, especially in cancer research [6, 7]. Biological methods, such as immunoaffinity and magnetic bead-based isolation, on the other hand, although more modern, are now more appreciated due to their higher specificity in isolating disease-specific exosomes [17, 18]. Still, the scalability of these methods remains a big challenge [16]. Among them, the chemical methods of size exclusion chromatography and polymer precipitation are discussed in 172 papers, reflecting their predominance in maintaining the structural integrity of the exosomes for diagnostic purposes [6, 9]. Leading institutions like the University of Pittsburgh and Clemson University with major funding agencies are seen to be pushing the envelope to perfect these techniques [6, 9, 13]. While physical methodologies dominate due to their high efficiency, biological and chemical techniques are becoming increasingly important because they possess greater specificity and, therefore, cannot be dispensed with for precision medicine. This is a collaborative area with multidisciplinary contributions originating from the United States, China, and Europe that is always on the move, incorporating various techniques to further enhance diagnostic and therapeutic applications. Several works emphasize the increasing role of exosomes in early cancer diagnosis and non-invasive diagnostics, hence justifying their potential to transform personalized medicine [1, 2, 4, 5].

9 Discussion

The study compares various techniques for isolating exosomes, focusing on their strengths and weaknesses. Physical methods like ultracentrifugation are effective but expensive, time-consuming, and difficult to scale up, posing risks of contamination from co-isolated proteins, making them unsuitable for routine applications [6]. By contrast, microfluidics enables faster processing times and more marked potential for point-of-care diagnostics but has yet to see clinical translation due to needed automation and optimization with larger sample volumes [10]. Biological approaches are few, and these include magnetic bead capture and immunocapture, showing much specificity in the selection of disease-relevant exosomes, a requirement for diagnostics. However, the high costs of the antibodies and limited scalability to large-scale clinical applications make them impractical. Highly sensitive immunocapture is generally labor-intensive and dependent on high-quality antibodies, hence limiting wider applicability of the technique [16]. To enhance scalability and cost-effectiveness, the combination of TFF with ultrafiltration increases the throughput and purity, thereby making these techniques more clinically viable for diagnostics. This may be balanced if hybrid techniques could be developed that combine the specificity of biological methods with the scalability of physical methods [7, 8]. Future innovations in nanoparticle-based exosome capture and machine learning applications could significantly improve diagnostic accuracy and speed, making exosome diagnostics a crucial component of precision medicine [14, 16]. Exosome isolation techniques face hurdles like high equipment costs and lack of standardized protocols, necessitating cost-reduction strategies and method standardization to promote wider clinical adoption.

10 Conclusion

The critical overview of the methods of exosome separation during 2010–2024 underlines their significant contribution to the development of medical diagnostics, especially in cancer studies. These physical approaches, such as ultracentrifugation and microfluidics, are thus considered fundamental methods since they allow scalability and a broad range of applications, as indicated by 348 publications. However, these techniques have some limitations concerning cost, speed, and sample purity and need further optimization [6, 10]. While biological approaches, such as immunocapture and magnetic bead-based isolation, demonstrate high specificity for targeting disease-specific exosomes, their scalability remains a major challenge, as shown in the 49 related studies [16, 17]. On the chemical side, size exclusion chromatography (SEC) and polymer precipitation are promising for maintaining exosome integrity, validated by 172 papers emphasizing their clinical relevance [9, 12]. Regarding criteria for comparison, ultracentrifugation offers high yield, but proteins are usually co-isolated, thereby lowering sample purity [6, 7]. Polymer precipitation is fast and inexpensive; however, this often results in co-precipitation of contaminants [12, 13]. Immunocapture presents very good specificity, normally offered by markers such as CD9 and CD81, though it is expensive and difficult to scale up for large volume processing [16, 17]. These limitations are overcome by emerging technologies such as microfluidics and TFF. Microfluidics allows for the efficient, fast separation of small volumes and hence is ideal for point-of-care diagnostics [10, 11]. TFF minimizes membrane clogging during the processing of large volumes while maintaining the integrity of exosomes and meeting the clinical demands of speed and purity [8]. Major bottlenecks for the integration of exosomes into non-invasive clinical diagnostics are high equipment costs, a lack of standardized protocols, and poor reproducibility between different laboratories [3, 16]. The cost needs to be reduced by means of auto-mated platforms and standardized methods of isolating exosomes to accelerate this process forward [8, 10]. Further to diagnostic applications, exosomes also possess therapeutic potential as carriers in gene or drug delivery. Achieving this would need advances in pure, reproducible isolation without immune responses [9, 14]. Artificial intelligence can accelerate the development of non-invasive diagnostics and personalized therapies by combining biological specificity with physical scalability. Large-scale validation in diverse cohorts ensures reliability, making exosome-based diagnostics a cornerstone of precision medicine, addressing early intervention and real-time monitoring [14, 16].

References

1. Gao, H., et al.: Exosome-based diagnostics in early-stage cancer detection: challenges and opportunities. J. Mol. Med. **101**(1), 10–22 (2023)
2. Chen, Y., et al.: Exosome-mediated biomarkers: clinical potential for diagnostics in oncology. Cancer Biomark. **19**(3), 45–58 (2023)
3. Sonbhadra, A., et al.: Challenges in standardizing exosome isolation for clinical applications. Front. Bioeng. **8**(2), 225–240 (2023)
4. Jiawei, X., et al.: Emerging exosome isolation technologies: the road to clinical translation. Adv. Healthc. Mater. (2022)
5. Bae, J., et al.: Microfluidics-based isolation of exosomes: applications in diagnostics. Lab Chip **23**(5), 987–996 (2023)
6. Baranyai, T., et al.: Isolation of exosomes: ultracentrifugation versus size exclusion chromatography. J. Extracellular Vesicles (2015)
7. Merchant, M., et al.: Ultracentrifugation for extracellular vesicle isolation: advantages and disadvantages. Methods Mol. Biol. **1243**, 47–62 (2010)
8. Lobb, R., et al.: Tangential flow filtration: a scalable method for exosome isolation. J. Extracellular Vesicles (2015)
9. Kowal, J., et al.: Size exclusion chromatography in exosome isolation: efficacy and limitations. J. Extracellular Vesicles (2016)
10. He, M., et al.: ExoChip: a microfluidic device for exosome isolation and characterization. Lab Chip **18**(10), 1938–1947 (2018)
11. Vaidyanathan, R., et al.: Microfluidic isolation of exosomes for biomarker discovery. Anal. Chem. **86**(9), 4291–4296 (2014)
12. Helwa, I., et al.: Polymer precipitation in exosome isolation: advantages and challenges. Sci. Rep. (2017)
13. Rider, M., et al.: Comparison of PEG precipitation and other exosome isolation methods. PLoS One (2016)
14. Ghosh, A., et al.: Lectin-based affinity methods for isolating exosomes. Can. Res. **74**(8), 2346–2357 (2014)

15. Escrevente, C., et al.: Glycan-based exosome isolation: advances and limitations. Glycobiology **21**(12), 1513–1521 (2011)
16. Nakayama, T., et al.: Immunocapture-based exosome isolation for cancer diagnostics. Cancer Sci. **107**(7), 1120–1130 (2016)
17. Tauro, B., et al.: Magnetic bead capture of disease-specific exosomes. J. Proteomics **75**(9), 3452–3461 (2012)
18. Zarovni, N., et al.: High-specificity magnetic bead isolation of exosomes. J. Extracellular Vesicles (2015)

Study of Energy Absorption of TPMS – Type Porous Structures

El-Amrani Mohammed[1](✉), Fekak Fatima-Ezzahra[1], El Alami Eliass[2], and Moustabchir Hassane[1]

[1] Sidi Mohamed Ben Abdellah University, National School of Applied Sciences of Fez, Engineering, Systems and Applications Laboratory, Fez, Morocco
{mohammed.elamrani17,fatima-ezzahra.fekak, hassane.moustabchir}@usmba.ac.ma

[2] Ibn Tofail University, National School of Applied Sciences of Kénitra, Advanced Systems Engineering Laboratory, Kenitra, Morocco
eliass.elalami@uit.ac.ma

Abstract. Triply Periodic Minimal Surface (TPMS) are porous structures that have attracted the attention of a large number of researchers due to the exceptional properties they offer. In this study, we focus solely on one TPMS structure, which is the IWP structure (« I-graph Wrapped Package»). This structure exhibits cubic symmetry and is interconnected and intertwined in three-dimensional (3D) space. In this paper, we studied the deformation energy absorbed by the IWP structure by increasing the relative density and the number of cells, in order to determine the influence of these parameters on the energy absorption rate. To determine this rate, we conducted elastoplastic simulations using ABAQUS software for a uniaxial tension case. We found that the energy absorption rate of the IWP structure is influenced by and proportional to both the relative density and the number of cells. This rate increases with the increase of either of these parameters, or both simultaneously.

Keywords: Porous structures · TPMS · elasto – plastic behavior · energy absorption rate

1 Introduction

TPMS (Triply Periodic Minimal Surfaces) structures represent a distinct class of materials characterized by zero mean curvature at any point, which locally minimizes the surface area while extending periodically in all three directions (X, Y, and Z) [1]. These structures have attracted considerable interest as promising metamaterials due to their remarkable properties, including efficient heat transfer, electrical conduction, and permeability. In addition, TPMS structures are recognized for their exceptional mechanical properties when compared to conventional cellular materials. Among the most common TPMS structures are the Schwarz Primitive, Gyroid, Diamond, Neovius, and IWP, each of these structures possesses unique properties [2], particularly in terms of their capacity to absorb deformation energy.

I. Aboudrar et al. (Eds.): ICESST 2024, SUCI, pp. 493–498, 2025.
https://doi.org/10.1007/978-3-031-86705-7_46

Abueidda et al. [3] studied the mechanical properties of the Gyroid structure for 64 - cell samples (4 × 4 × 4) while increasing the relative density. They found that the rate of energy absorption increased with the increase in relative density while keeping the number of cells constant. The same trend was confirmed for other TPMS structures (Primitive, IWP, and Neovius). According to Abueidda et al., the Neovius [4] and IWP structures have the highest energy absorption capacity, followed by the Gyroid and Primitive structures. Li et al. [5] also studied the mechanical properties and energy absorption of uniform and graded Gyroid structures. They found that structures with a higher gradient had a better energy absorption capacity than those with a lower gradient.

In this study, we chose the uniform IWP structure as the subject of study to investigate the deformation energy absorption rate of this structure under uniaxial tension. This study will be based on elastoplastic simulations of the IWP using the ABAQUS software.

2 Materials and Methods

2.1 Choice of the Study Structure

TPMS structures are distinguished by their high energy absorption capacity. The choice of the structure studied is based on two criteria: an energy criterion and a geometric criterion. Regarding the first criterion, according to Abueidda et al. [3], Neovius and IWP structures absorb the most energy (see Fig. 1). To select one of these two structures, we applied the second, geometric criterion, comparing the two structures geometrically. We observed that the Neovius structure has a more significant thickness gradient than the IWP, and that its surface has a highly symmetrical and complex geometry. This is why we chose to study the IWP structure, which satisfies both these criteria.

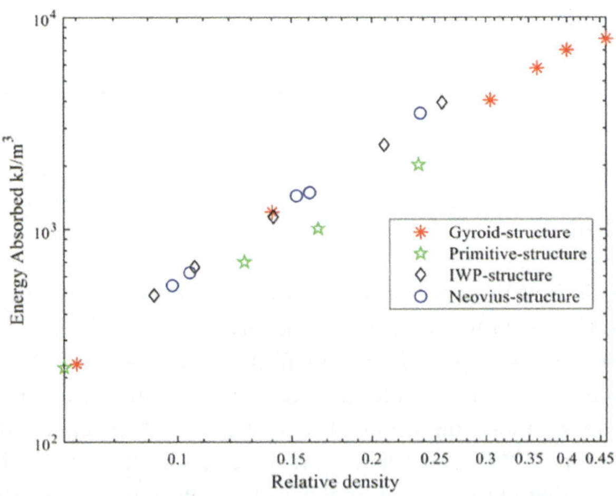

Fig. 1. Energy absorbed by TPMS-structures subjected to a compression of 60% strain. Results are obtained by testing specimens with 64 (4 × 4 × 4) unit cells at a strain rate of 0.01 s^{-1} [3].

2.2 Numerical Method

The TPMS structure studied in this study is the IWP structure, whose geometric equation is as follows:

$$\mathbf{F_{IWP} = cos(kx)cos(ky) + cos(ky)cos(kz) + cos(kz)cos(kx) = C} \quad (1)$$

[6] with : $\mathbf{k} = \frac{2\pi q}{L}$.
Where:

q : Represents the number of units in each direction,
L : The length of each unit cell,
C : A constant that controls the shape of the surface, typically taken as (C = 0).

The numerical models were generated using the open source software « **MSLattice**» [7], which allows to define the geometry of different TPMS structures by specifying the structure type, relative density and cell dimension. An STL file representing the structure is then generated (see Fig. 2).

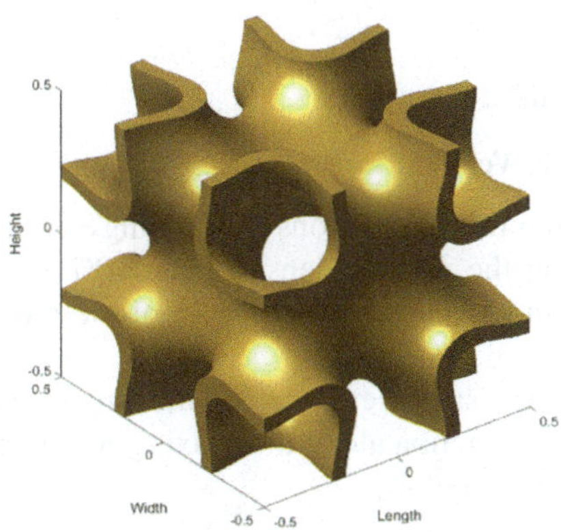

Fig. 2. Isometric view of the CAD model of the IWP unit cell.

Finite element simulations were conducted using the ABAQUS software. For deformation analysis, a tensile force was applied to the upper face, with a prescribed displacement of 0.1 mm in the Y – axis direction, while the lower face was fixed. Elasto-plastic simulations were performed on three models (« 1 × 1 × 1», « 2 × 2 × 2», and « 3 × 3 × 3») with relative densities ranging from 10% to 40% (see Fig. 3). All structures were meshed using a structured hexahedral mesh. The material used for the simulations is Titanium Ti – 6Al – 4V (Table 1), which is assumed to be isotropic for the sake of simplification.

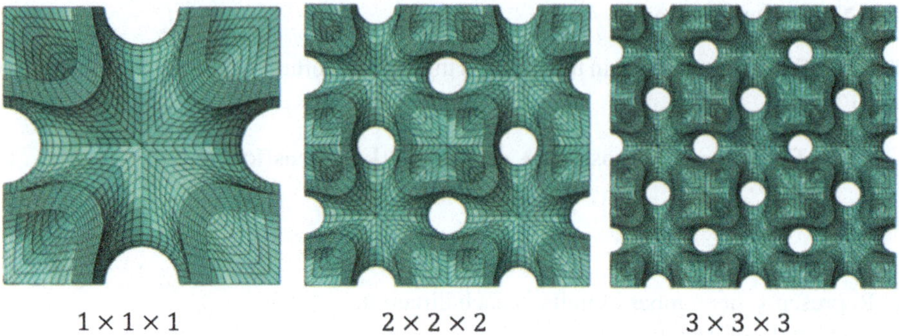

Fig. 3. Models of IWP structures (Volume = 1 mm^3).

Table 1. Material parameters: Titanium Ti – 6Al – 4V [8]

Parameters	Physical meaning	Value
E	Young's modulus	110 000 MPa
ν	Poisson's ratio	0.3
ρ	Density	4.4×10^{-9} tonne/mm^3

3 Results and Discussion

3.1 Order of Magnitude Verification

We conducted a series of traction simulations by applying a displacement of $u = 0.1$ mm to IWP structures, varying the relative density from 10% to 40%, and increasing the cells number, with the aim of assessing the impact of these two parameters on energy absorption capacity.

First, we ensured that the stress levels inside the structures were equivalent. To do this, we examined the force reaction along the Y axis per unit area in the fixed zone, the results are shown in the figure below:

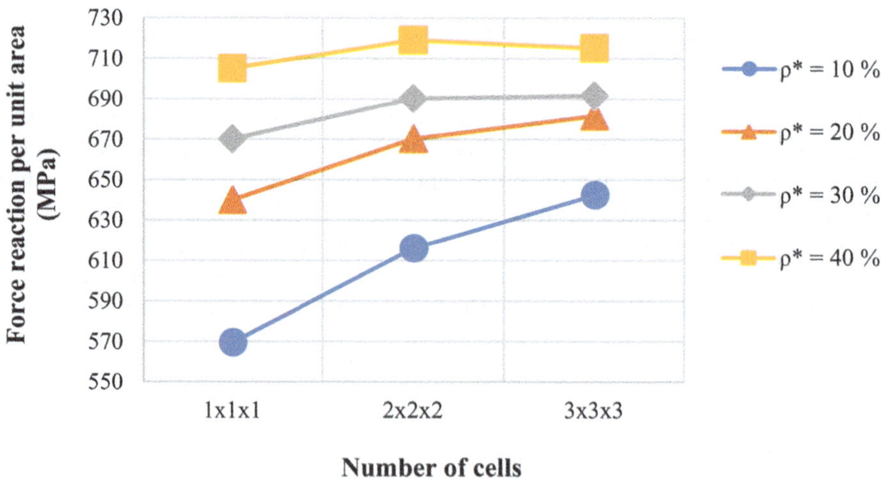

Fig. 4. Force reaction per unit area of the fixed region of the IWP structures

By visualizing the Fig. 4, we notice that IWP structures with the same relative density have the same order of magnitude. For structures with lower densities, the difference is slightly significant. But all structures have the same order of magnitude. Consequently, a comparative study of all models can be conducted.

3.2 Energy Analysis

Theoretically, to determine the rate of energy absorption by the structure requires numerical integration. The area bounded by the abscissa axis of the stress – strain curve is equal to this energy. The energy absorption per unit volume W_V. is defined by the expression [5]:

$$\mathbf{W_V} = \int_0^{\epsilon} \sigma(\boldsymbol{\varepsilon})\mathbf{d}\boldsymbol{\varepsilon} \tag{2}$$

To determine the energy absorbed by the IWP structures, we conducted numerical simulation using ABAQUS software. We post – process elastic and plastic energy. The sum of the two is used to determine total energy, and by dividing by the volume of the structure, we obtain the energy absorbed per unit volume:

$$\mathbf{W_V} = \frac{\mathbf{ALLSE + ALLPD}}{\mathbf{V_{structure}}}\left(\frac{\mathbf{mJ}}{\mathbf{mm^3}} = \frac{\mathbf{MJ}}{\mathbf{m^3}}\right) \tag{3}$$

With « **ALLSE**» representing the stored strain energy E_E and « **ALLPD**» representing the dissipated inelastic energy E_p.

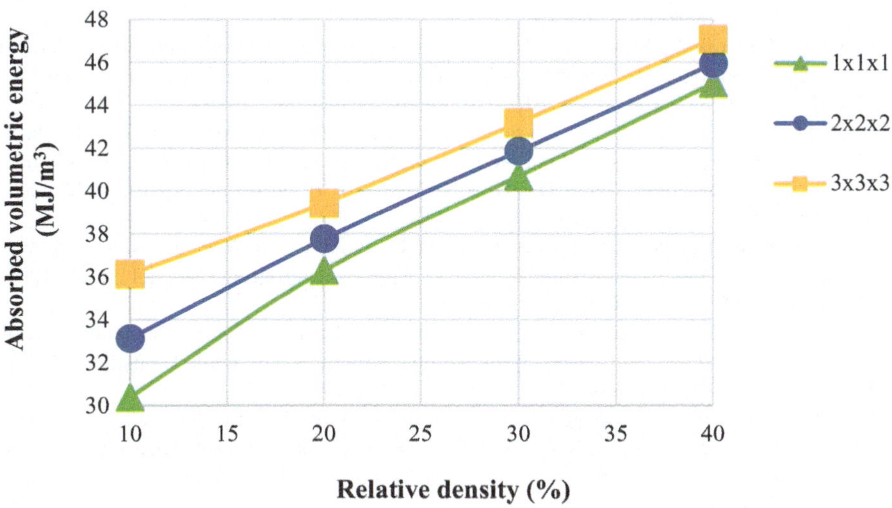

Fig. 5. Comparison of the volumetric absorbed energy of IWP structures

By visualizing the Fig. 5, we observe that the energy absorbed by the IWP structures increase by increasing the relative density. This result is corroborated by the article by Abueidda et al. [3] Which confirms that the absorbed energy increase with the increase of relative density.

Also, increasing the number of cells leads to an increase in the energy absorbed, although the increase differs between the two parameters. Therefore, we conclude that the two main factors influencing the deformation energy absorption rate are relative density and the number of cells.

4 Conclusion

In this study, we conducted a set of numerical simulations to determine the influence of relative density and cell number on the rate of energy absorbed by the IWP structure. We concluded that this rate is influenced and proportional to these two parameters, but we find that the rate of increase differs between the two parameters. For that reason, we concluded that the major factors influencing this rate are relative density and cell number. This deformation energy can be stored and released by various methods, such as conversion into electricity to power sensors, or dissipating it in the form of heat to attenuate vibrations.

Acknowledgements. This work was carried out with the support of the National Center for Scientific and Technical Research (CNRST) as part of the « PhD-ASsociate Scholarship – PASS » program.

References

1. Vasquez-Villegas, J. : Exploration des propriétés de microstructures de type TPMS pour mimer le comportement mécanique du disque intervertébral cervical humain dans l'objectif de réaliser une prothèse par fabrication additive.
2. Préve, D., Lenarda, P., Maskery, I., Paggi, M.: A comprehensive characterization of fracture in unit cell open foams generated from Triply Periodic Minimal Surfaces. Eng. Fract. Mech. **277**, 108949 (2023). https://doi.org/10.1016/j.engfracmech.2022.108949
3. Abueidda, D.W., Elhebeary, M., Andrew Shiang, C.-S., Pang, S., Abu Al-Rub, R.K., Jasiuk, I.M.: Mechanical properties of 3D printed polymeric Gyroid cellular structures: Experimental and finite element study. Mater. Des. **165**, 107597 (2019). https://doi.org/10.1016/j.matdes.2019.107597
4. Abueidda, D.W., Elhebeary, M., Andrew Shiang, C.-S., Abu Al-Rub, R.K., Jasiuk, I.M.: Compression and buckling of microarchitectured Neovius-lattice. Extreme Mech. Lett. **37**, 100688 (2020). https://doi.org/10.1016/j.eml.2020.100688
5. Li, D., Liao, W., Dai, N., Xie, Y.M.: Comparison of mechanical properties and energy absorption of sheet-based and strut-based Gyroid cellular structures with graded densities. Materials **12**(13), 2183 (2019). https://doi.org/10.3390/ma12132183
6. Park, S.-Y., Kim, K.-S., AlMangour, B., Grzesiak, D., Lee, K.-A.: Compressive deformation behavior and energy absorption characteristic of additively manufactured sheet CoCrMo triply periodic minimal surface lattices. J. Mater. Res. Technol. **18**, 171–184 (2022). https://doi.org/10.1016/j.jmrt.2022.02.086
7. Al-Ketan, O., Abu Al-Rub, R.K.: MSLattice: a free software for generating uniform and graded lattices based on triply periodic minimal surfaces. Mater. Des. Process. Commun. (2021). https://doi.org/10.1002/mdp2.205.
8. Li, C., Fang, J., Qiu, N., Wu, C., Steven, G., Li, Q.: On fracture mechanism of additively manufactured triply periodic minimal surface structures using an explicit phase field model. Addit. Manuf. **86**, 104192 (2024). https://doi.org/10.1016/j.addma.2024.104192

Smart Manufacturing and Urban Infrastructure Innovations

Enhanced Fault Detection in High-Speed Train Axle Bearings Using Time-Frequency Based Statistical Features: A Test Bench Approach

Meryem Abtane[1,4](✉), Khalid Dahi[1], Hervé Martinez[1,4], Mohamed Sedki[2,3], Hicham El Kimi[2], and Luciano Fernandes Borges[2]

[1] Complex Systems and Interactions, Ecole Centrale of Casablanca, Bouskoura, Morocco
meryem.abtane@centrale-casablanca.ma
[2] Société Marocaine de Maintenance des Rames à Grande Vitesse SIANA, Tanger, Morocco
[3] Office National des Chemins de Fer- ONCF, Rabat, Morocco
[4] Université de Pau et des pays de l'Adour, E2S UPPA, CNRS UMR 5254, IPREM, Pau, France

Abstract. Axle bearing faults are critical to the safety and reliability of high-speed trains (HSTs), making their early detection paramount. To address this, we have developed an enhanced fault detection approach that begins with rigorous testing on specialized benches. The methodology centers around a suite of machine learning classifiers designed to analyze key features extracted from vibration data collected on a test bench at the Complex Systems and Interactions Laboratory (CSI). The inputs to these classifiers include time, frequency, and time-frequency based statistical features. We then select the best classifier based on performance metrics such as accuracy. This approach enables precise identification and classification of bearing faults, providing a robust solution that can be tested and applied in high-speed railway environments with axle bearings.

Keywords: High-Speed Trains (HSTs) · Axle Bearing Faults · Time-Frequency Features · Statistical Features · Test Bench Approach

1 Introduction

High-speed trains (HSTs) are engineered to achieve exceptional speeds, enhancing long-distance travel efficiency and connectivity. These advanced rail systems are characterized by streamlined designs and sophisticated technology, enabling them to operate safely and smoothly at high velocities. Central to their performance and safety is the bogie system, which supports the train's wheels, axles, and braking components, ensuring stability and comfort during operation. A critical component within the bogie system is the axle bearing, which ensures smooth

I. Aboudrar et al. (Eds.): ICESST 2024, SUCI, pp. 501–510, 2025.
https://doi.org/10.1007/978-3-031-86705-7_47

rotation of the wheels at high speeds. However, the axle bearing is one of the most fragile parts of a high-speed train transmission system due to the harsh working environment and repeated impacts. Therefore, monitoring the health condition of wheel set bearings and prioritizing research into condition monitoring and fault diagnosis of HSTs is essential for enhancing the safety of the rail transit system [1]. Temperature and vibration are key parameters used to assess the health of axle box bearings (AXBs). In addition, acoustic data provides valuable insights into bearing conditions, helping to detect early signs of faults. By combining these data sources through fusion techniques and advanced diagnostic methods, the reliability and safety of HST operations can be greatly enhanced.

This research is based on the CSI test bench located at Ecole Centrale Casablanca, where we collect a dataset for conventional bearing fault diagnosis. The context of our test bench can be viewed as an industrial problem involving rotating machinery, which can also be applied to axle bearings. The primary difference is the added noise, as the analysis of bearing faults remains consistent. Makrouf et al. [2] addressed intelligent fault diagnosis (IFD) using artificial intelligence (AI) and applied an ensemble learning approach along with time-domain features to enhance diagnostic accuracy. The proposed method was tested on a publicly available dataset of rotating machinery with multiple faults, demonstrating good accuracy and efficiency. Additionally, Amini et al. [3] used time spectral kurtosis to analyze acoustic emission data on freight rolling stock with artificially induced damage in axle bearings. Their results showed that time spectral kurtosis effectively distinguishes axle bearing defects from random noise sources such as wheel-rail interaction, braking, and changes in train speed. Many other studies aim to improve fault detection in both conventional and axle bearings. These multimodal approaches, integrating acoustic emission, vibration analysis, and other sensor data, contribute to developing robust diagnostic models capable of accurately identifying bearing faults.

The aim of this research is to develop an effective fault detection system using vibration data from bearings on our CSI test bench, with plans to apply and test it on axle bearings in railway environments. A range of features will be used, including time-domain features such as Variance and Energy-Entropy, frequency-domain features like Spectral Energy and Spectral Entropy, and time-frequency-based features such as Wavelet Energy and Wavelet Kurtosis. A range of machine learning classification algorithms, including XGBoost and Random Forest, will be employed and evaluated to provide a reliable solution for diagnosing axle bearing faults.

This article is organized as follows: Sect. 2 provides an explanation of AXBs faults and presents their characteristic frequencies. In Sect. 3, we offer a comprehensive overview of the features utilized in our fault detection system, including time, frequency, and time-frequency based features. Section 4 details the experimental setup and methodology used to detect bearing faults, including the use of vibration data from our CSI test bench. Finally, Sect. 5 presents and discusses the results of our experiments, including the implementation of various machine learning classification algorithms and the criteria used to evaluate their performance.

2 Exploring Characteristic Fault Frequencies in Axle Bearing Systems

Axle bearings consist of inner and outer races, rolling elements (balls or rollers), and a cage that holds these elements in place. Over time, faults such as pitting, spalling, or cracking can develop due to wear and tear, generating characteristic fault frequencies that correspond to mechanical interactions within the bearing.

Depending on the fault's location, different frequencies are produced. Monitoring these frequencies is crucial for early fault detection, enabling timely maintenance and preventing costly failures [4]. Key fault frequencies include BPFO (Ball Pass Frequency Outer), BPFI (Ball Pass Frequency Inner), BSF (Ball Spin Frequency), and FTF (Fundamental Train Frequency), each corresponding to specific mechanical interactions in the bearing. These fault frequencies can be described by the following equations [5]:

$$BPFI = \frac{N_b}{2} \cdot f_r \left(1 + \frac{D_b}{D_c} \cos\alpha\right) \tag{1}$$

$$BPFO = \frac{N_b}{2} \cdot f_r \left(1 - \frac{D_b}{D_c} \cos\alpha\right) \tag{2}$$

$$BSF = \frac{P_d}{B_d} \cdot f_r \left(1 - \left(\frac{D_b}{D_c} \cos\alpha\right)^2\right) \tag{3}$$

$$FTF = \frac{f_r}{2} \left(1 - \frac{D_b}{D_c} \cos\alpha\right) \tag{4}$$

These defect frequencies are determined by the bearing parameters as indicated in Fig. 1, specifically:

- D_b: Diameter of the ball.
- D_c: Mean diameter or diameter of the cage.
- N_b: Number of balls in the bearing.
- α: Contact angle.

3 Comprehensive Overview of Utilized Features

3.1 Time-Domain Features

Among the time-domain features used in this study, RMS measures the average magnitude of the signal, reflecting its overall power. Additionally, Kurtosis quantifies the sharpness of the signal's distribution, identifying the presence of outliers or anomalies. Skewness, on the other hand, evaluates the asymmetry of the signal around the mean, offering insights into the direction and degree of deviation from normality. Variance measures the dispersion of signal values around the mean, providing an indication of the signal's variability.

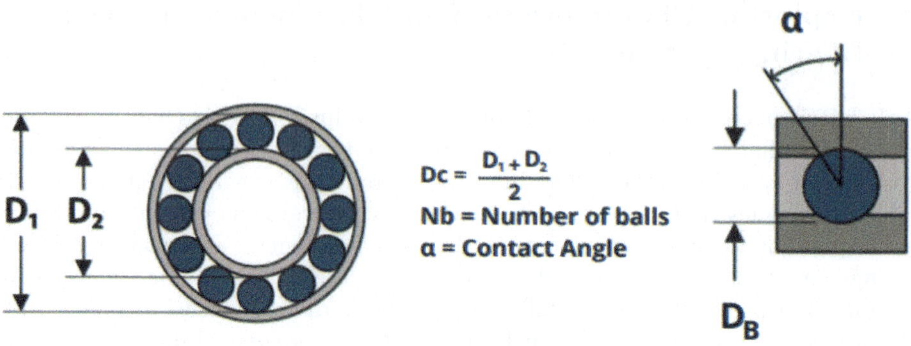

Fig. 1. Bearing Parameters.

Another time-domain feature is Energy-Entropy, which quantifies the unpredictability of the energy distribution within the signal. It is calculated using the probability distribution $p(x[i])$ of the energy values.

$$\text{Energy-Entropy} = -\sum_{i=0}^{N-1} p(x[i]) \cdot \log(p(x[i]) + 1e - 12) \tag{5}$$

The n-th moment of the signal energy, where n is the order of the moment, provides information about the distribution of energy values across different orders. Thus, by adjusting the order n, we can influence how much weight is given to late events in the signal.

$$\text{Energy-Moment} = \sum_{i=0}^{N-1} (i^n \cdot x[i]^2) \tag{6}$$

3.2 Frequency-Domain Features

Spectral energy quantifies the total energy of the signal in the frequency domain by summing the squared magnitudes of the frequency components obtained from the Fourier Transform.

$$\text{Spectral Energy} = \sum_{k=0}^{N-1} |X[k]|^2 \tag{7}$$

Spectral kurtosis is computed using the kurtosis of the squared magnitudes of the frequency components.

$$\text{Spectral Kurtosis} = \text{Kurtosis}\left(|X[k]|^2\right) \tag{8}$$

Spectral entropy is calculated by normalizing the squared magnitudes of the frequency components to obtain a probability distribution p_k, and then computing the entropy of this distribution.

$$\text{Spectral Entropy} = -\sum_{k=0}^{N-1} p_k \cdot \log(p_k + 1e - 12) \tag{9}$$

3.3 Time-Frequency Domain Features

Wavelet energy quantifies the total energy in the wavelet domain. It is computed by summing the squared magnitudes of the wavelet coefficients across all scales and time positions, where $c_{j,i}$ represents the wavelet coefficient at scale j and position i. This measure helps in assessing the energy distribution across different wavelet components.

$$\text{Wavelet Energy} = \sum_{j=1}^{J} \sum_{i=0}^{N_j-1} |c_{j,i}|^2 \tag{10}$$

Wavelet entropy measures the unpredictability of the energy distribution in the wavelet domain. It is calculated by normalizing the squared magnitudes of the wavelet coefficients to obtain a probability distribution $p_{j,i}$, and then computing the entropy of this distribution.

$$\text{Wavelet Entropy} = -\sum_{j=1}^{J} \sum_{i=0}^{N_j-1} p_{j,i} \cdot \log(p_{j,i} + 1e - 12) \tag{11}$$

Wavelet kurtosis is computed as the mean of the kurtosis values of the wavelet coefficients across all scales.

$$\text{Wavelet Kurtosis} = \frac{1}{J} \sum_{j=1}^{J} \text{Kurtosis}(c_j) \tag{12}$$

Wavelet coefficient variance quantifies the dispersion of the wavelet coefficients across different scales. It is calculated as the mean variance of the wavelet coefficients, where c_j represents the wavelet coefficients at scale j.

$$\text{Wavelet Coefficient Variance} = \frac{1}{J} \sum_{j=1}^{J} \text{Variance}(c_j) \tag{13}$$

4 Test Bench-Driven Methodology for Detecting Bearing Faults

The test bench at the CSI laboratory (see Fig. 2), designed to simulate various types of bearing defects, provides the foundation for testing our algorithmic approach. It is equipped with multiple sensors to capture vibration data, including an ACOEM ASH205b vibration sensor with a sensitivity of 100 mV/g, mounted vertically, and two PCB 352A21 vibration sensors with a sensitivity of 10 mV/g, one oriented vertically and the other horizontally. Additionally, an acoustic sensor is strategically placed close to the bearing to ensure maximum sensitivity to emitted acoustic signals while minimizing interference from surrounding noise. The sensor is securely mounted on a stable, vibration-isolated base to reduce any extraneous vibrations from the environment that could contaminate the data. Its precise positioning ensures optimal alignment with the bearing, enabling the capture of relevant acoustic emissions that provide detailed insights into potential defects. Finally, data acquisition is performed using a National Instruments data acquisition card, with LabVIEW software utilized for seamless data visualization and collection.

Table 1. Bearing Fault Frequencies for Different Rotation Frequencies.

Rotation Frequency (Hz)	FTF (Hz)	BPFO (Hz)	BPFI (Hz)	BSF (Hz)
10	3.78	30.48	49.5	19.92
15	5.67	45.72	74.25	29.88
20	7.56	60.96	99	39.84

This comprehensive setup allows for precise simulation and analysis of various bearing defect scenarios. A sampling frequency of 25600 Hz was selected to effectively capture the time-domain signals. Simultaneously, three distinct rotation speeds—10 Hz, 15 Hz, and 20 Hz—were employed. Table 1 outlines the corresponding bearing fault frequencies for each of these rotational speeds.

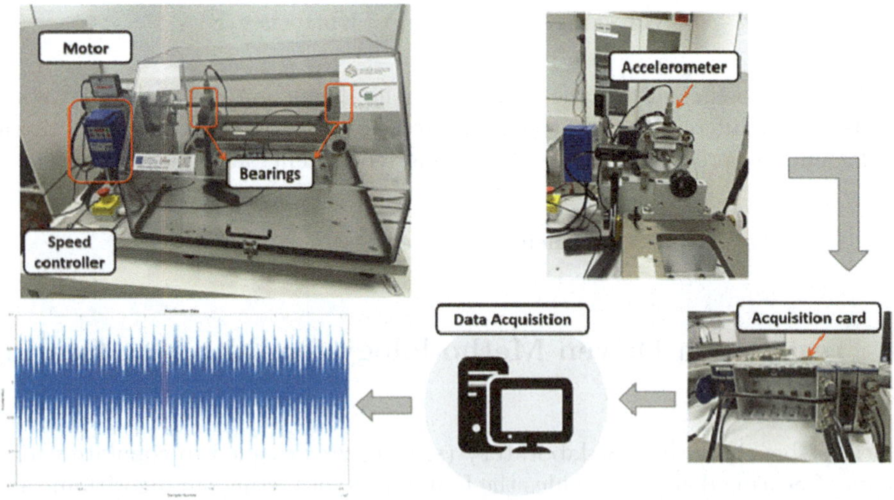

Fig. 2. CSI Laboratory Test Bench.

5 Results and Discussion

This section presents the results of our analysis, focusing on the performance of various models in detecting bearing faults. We began by calculating a set of features, as discussed earlier, from the signal data. These features were then used to train multiple models, which were evaluated based on their accuracy and effectiveness. The most performant model was selected for its ability to accurately classify faults while minimizing errors.

The time-domain extracted features (see Table 2) clearly distinguish between different bearing conditions. Variance increases significantly from the safe condition to fault conditions, especially for the Outer Race Fault. Energy-moment and energy-entropy features further highlight this difference, with the Outer Race Fault showing the highest energy-moment, indicating higher energy due to increased vibrations. Kurtosis is also notably higher for the Outer Race Fault, reflecting sharp transients typical of severe defects. Skewness shows negative values for the Safe, Inner Race, and Ball Fault conditions, suggesting a distribution weighted towards smaller values, while the positive skewness of the Outer Race Fault indicates severe damage, marked by high-amplitude transients.

Table 2. Time-domain extracted features.

Class	Variance	Energy-Entropy	Energy-Moment	RMS	Kurtosis	Skewness	Label
Safe	0.000831	9.340801	280350.7	0.029062	0.274744	−0.147064	0
Inner race	0.072839	8.512682	24563570	0.269909	9.150811	−0.078860	1
Outer race	0.109109	7.391780	39206340	0.330327	65.117331	1.095648	2
Ball	0.015925	9.005699	1835203.745	0.126244	3.338153	−0.149349	3

For frequency features, as shown in Table 3, the Safe condition in bearings has the lowest spectral energy, reflecting normal, low-intensity vibration and smooth operation. Fault conditions, particularly the Outer Race and Inner Race faults, exhibit notably higher spectral energy due to increased vibration from impact forces, with the Ball Fault showing a moderate increase. Spectral kurtosis is highest in the Safe condition, indicating sharp spectral peaks likely caused by minor noise or harmonics. In contrast, faults, particularly Inner and Outer Race faults, show reduced kurtosis, suggesting more dispersed energy across the spectrum. Additionally, the Safe condition has the lowest spectral entropy, reflecting an orderly and concentrated frequency structure. On the other hand, faults increase entropy, with the Outer Race Fault exhibiting the highest entropy, as it distributes energy over a wider frequency range and adds complexity to the signal.

For time-frequency features (see Table 4), wavelet energy effectively differentiates between the Safe and fault conditions, with more severe faults like the Outer Race Fault showing higher energy. The Outer and Inner Race Faults exhibit lower entropy, indicating more structured energy distributions, likely due to repetitive impacts or vibrations at specific frequencies. The Outer Race Fault also shows

Table 3. Frequency-domain extracted features.

Class	Spectral Energy	Spectral Kurtosis	Spectral Entropy	Label
Safe	553 501.3	4226.367386	4.381631	0
Inner race	47 743 490	3429.472313	7.707443	1
Outer race	71 510 210	2140.704937	8.589564	2
Ball	10 444 830	198.833101	7.987464	3

the highest kurtosis, suggesting it generates sharp, high-amplitude peaks in the time-frequency domain, likely from sudden impacts as the rolling element passes over the defect. The Inner Race Fault has the highest variance, indicating that it spreads energy across a wider range of wavelet scales, possibly due to a more distributed vibration signature. The Outer Race Fault also shows elevated variance, though slightly lower than the Inner Race Fault, indicating that energy is spread out but may be more concentrated in specific frequency bands.

Table 4. Time-frequency domain extracted features.

Class	Wavelet Energy	Wavelet Entropy	Wavelet Kurtosis	Wavelet Coefficient Variance	Label
Safe	21.637079	42.759636	0.110297	0.000766	0
Inner race	1903.181563	35.404447	27.234694	0.181796	1
Outer race	2794.209363	34.137371	36.474635	0.135530	2
Ball	408.144018	39.048929	9.863851	0.052523	3

The Table 5 compares the performance of five models. Both **Random Forest** and **XGBoost** perform exceptionally well, with Random Forest slightly outperforming XGBoost in all metrics, achieving near-perfect scores (accuracy of 0.999017 and 0.998526, respectively). On the other hand, introducing PCA significantly reduces the performance of both **PCA-XGBoost** and **PCA-Random Forest**, as indicated by their lower accuracy and F1-scores. This suggests that, for this dataset, dimensionality reduction through PCA leads to a loss of important feature information, negatively impacting the models' ability to classify faults effectively.

A feature importance score diagram visually represents each feature's contribution to a machine learning model's predictions. By quantifying which features most influence the model's ability to differentiate between classes, it highlights essential factors for understanding model behavior. As shown in Fig. 3, Kurtosis, Energy-Entropy, and Wavelet Entropy emerge as the most important features, underscoring their critical role in distinguishing fault types. This insight not only aids in model interpretability but also directs feature engineering by prioritizing these influential features, potentially optimizing model performance and accuracy in fault detection.

Table 5. Comparison of Models Performance.

Model	Accuracy	Recall	Precision	F1-score
XGBoost	0.998526	0.998526	0.998540	0.998528
Random Forest	0.999017	0.999017	0.999020	0.999016
Decision Tree	0.995086	0.995086	0.995241	0.995110
PCA-XGBoost	0.901229	0.901229	0.905439	0.902201
PCA-Random Forest	0.874201	0.874201	0.876351	0.875078

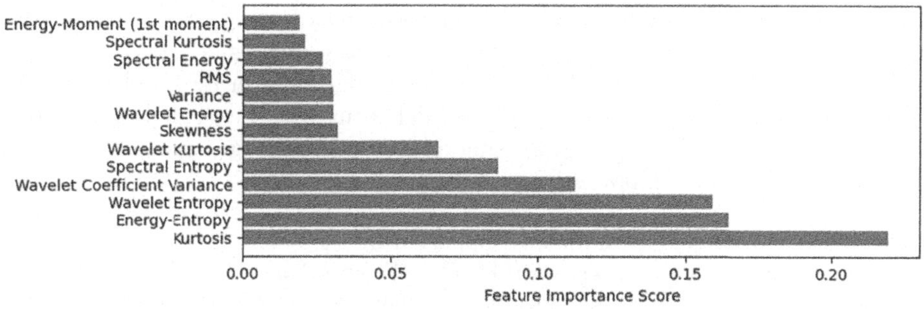

Fig. 3. Random Forest feature importance score.

The confusion matrix (Fig. 4) reveals that the model performs well, especially for categories 0 (safe), 1 (Inner race), and 3 (Ball), with high classification accuracy. However, category 2 (Outer race) exhibits a minor misclassification.

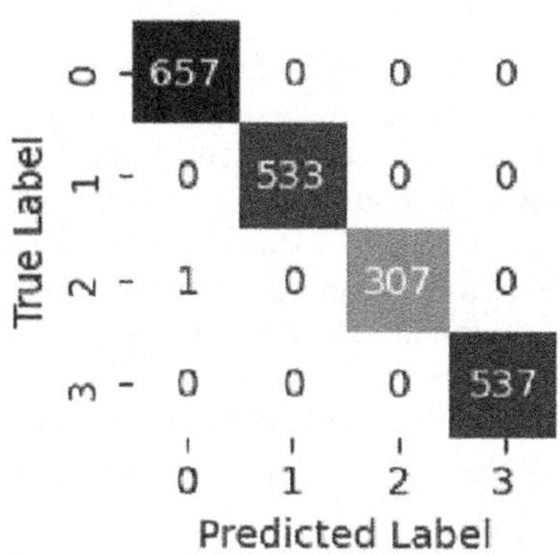

Fig. 4. Confusion matrix.

To address the misclassification of the outer race fault, several strategies can be implemented. Improving the quality of training data, particularly for the outer race category, and exploring advanced model architectures are also potential areas for future work to enhance fault detection accuracy and reduce misclassification rates.

6 Conclusion

This study highlights the effectiveness of key features in improving fault detection accuracy for bearings on the CSI test bench. By utilizing features from time, frequency, and time-frequency domains, the Random Forest model achieved strong classification performance, successfully distinguishing between normal conditions and various fault types. Through rigorous testing, the most effective classifier was selected based on performance metrics such as accuracy. As a crucial initial step in our project focused on detecting faults in HST axle bearings, this study aims to test and refine the model using axle bearing datasets from actual railway settings, while addressing additional challenges such as increased noise and more complex operating conditions.

Acknowledgements. This work was supported by the Société Marocaine de Maintenance des Rames à Grande Vitesse (SIANA). We gratefully acknowledge SIANA for their generous support and collaboration, which have been crucial to the success of this project.

References

1. Hou, D., Qi, H., Luo, H., Wang, C., Yang, J.: Comparative study on the use of acoustic emission and vibration analyses for the bearing fault diagnosis of high-speed trains. Struct. Health Monit. **21**, 147592172110360 (2021). https://doi.org/10.1177/14759217211036025
2. Makrouf, I., Zegrari, M., Ouachtouk, I., Dahi, K.: Multi-source information fusion fault diagnosis for rotating machinery using signal and data processing. In: Surveillance, Vibrations, Shock and Noise. Institut Supérieur de l'Aéronautique et de l'Espace [ISAE-SUPAERO], Toulouse, France (July 2023)
3. Amini, A., Entezami, M., Huang, Z., Rowshandel, H., Papaelias, M.: Wayside de tection of faults in railway axle bearings using time spectral kurtosis analysis on high frequency acoustic emission signals. Adv. Mech. Eng. **8** (2016). https://doi.org/10.1177/1687814016676000
4. Ouachtouk, I., El Hani, S., Dahi, K.: Intelligent bearing fault diagnosis method based on hnr envelope and classification using supervised machine learning algorithms. Adv. Electr. Electron. Eng. **19** (2021). https://doi.org/10.15598/aeee.v19i4.4183
5. Gougam, F., Rahmoune, C., Djamel, B., Merainani, B.: Bearing fault diagnosis based on feature extraction of empirical wavelet transform (EWT) and fuzzy logic system (FLS) under variable operating conditions. J. Vibroeng. **21**, 1636–1650 (2019). https://doi.org/10.21595/jve.2019.20092

Towards a Practical Digital Twin: A Multi-Model AI-Driven Approach for Manufacturing

Karim Gehad Saadeldin(✉) and Radouane Majdoul

ENSAM-Casa, Hassan II University, Casablanca, Morocco
karim2jihad@gmail.com

Abstract. The concept of a digital twin, despite its promise for revolutionizing manufacturing, remains shrouded in ambiguity due to a lack of consensus on its definition. This paper shifts the focus from theoretical debates to a practical implementation of digital twins in manufacturing. We challenge the notion of a monolithic digital twin and propose a mini-multi-model architecture, where AI-driven "mini-digital twins" are created to provide specific services. This architecture is embodied in our software "Plexasync," which enables the collection of real-time data from industrial networks, generates interactive HMIs, and facilitates the development of AI-driven mini-digital twins. Plexasync, currently in development, demonstrates the feasibility of our approach. This modular and plug-and-play system offers a cost-effective solution for small and medium-sized enterprises to harness the power of digital twins and drive innovation in their operations.

Keywords: Digital twin · Mini-multi-model architecture · AI-driven · Manufacturing · Industrial IoT · Plexasync

1 Introduction

The manufacturing industry has constantly sought to leverage technological advancements to enhance efficiency and productivity. The concept of a digital twin, a virtual representation of a physical product or system, has emerged as a promising tool in this endeavor. However, the lack of a universally accepted definition has hindered its widespread adoption. While numerous researchers have attempted to provide a literature-based definition, few have focused on defining a practical architecture or frameworks that can help engineers and practitioner, developing actual digital twins for their products and production lines. This does not mean that efforts are non-existent, but we think that more researches in the area will be highly recommended. This paper aims to bridge this gap by proposing a multi-model AI-driven approach to digital twins in manufacturing.

We begin by highlighting the challenges in defining digital twins and present findings from our research on how different companies perceive this concept. We then introduce our approach to actually building digital twins, and we will mention "Plexasync" which is the name of the software we are building as proof of concept of ourmulti-model

I. Aboudrar et al. (Eds.): ICESST 2024, SUCI, pp. 511–520, 2025.
https://doi.org/10.1007/978-3-031-86705-7_48

architecture. Moreover, and different to the standard way of developing the models, we discuss how AI can help us create and develop these mini-digital-twins and elaborate on that concept. The current state of Plexasync and its future development are outlined, followed by a conclusion and discussion of future work.

2 Literature Review

2.1 Digital Twin Definitions and Challenges

The concept of a digital twin has been defined in various ways, leading to confusion and debate. Some definitions focus on its virtual representation aspect [1], while others emphasize the bidirectional data exchange between the physical and digital twins[2]. The lack of consensus has led to the emergence of new terms like "digital shadow" and "digital thread," further complicating the landscape.

Our research, conducted among Moroccan companies, revealed a similar lack of clarity. Some companies equated digital twins with sophisticated HMIs, while others described them as faster CAD simulation software. This misunderstanding underscores the urgent need for a pragmatic, implementation-focused approach to demystify and operationalize digital twin technology.

While acknowledging the dangers of adding yet another definition to the already crowded field, it is essential to establish a working definition for the purpose of this paper. Therefore, we adopt a broad perspective, defining a digital twin as the closest possible virtual and digital representation or model of a physical entity. This entity could be a product, a production line, a machine, or even an entire factory.

However, a mere digital replica is insufficient. The defining characteristic of a digital twin, in our view, lies in its capacity to offer services and insights that would be difficult or impossible to obtain otherwise. This functionality sets it apart from traditional simulation models, which are often based on specific scenarios and assumptions. A digital twin, on the other hand, is **the model** (and not just **a model** that) continuously adapts to the evolving state of the physical system, providing real-time, accurate, and actionable information.

2.2 Multi-Model Systems

Navigating the landscape of digital twin technology can be challenging, especially for newcomers. It's tempting to envision a single, monolithic software solution capable of handling all aspects of creating and managing a digital twin. However, the reality is far more nuanced. Developing such a one-size-fits-all solution is not only technically daunting but also impractical, as it would need to cater to the diverse and ever-evolving requirements of different physical entities and applications.

Imagine a digital twin for a complex manufacturing system. It would need to incorporate models for various components, processes, and interactions, including:

- **Physical behavior:** Simulating the mechanical, electrical, and thermal properties of machines and equipment.

- **Control logic:** Replicating the control systems and algorithms that govern the system's operation.
- **Data analytics:** Processing sensor data to monitor performance, detect anomalies, and predict failures.
- **Human interaction:** Providing intuitive visualizations and interfaces for operators and engineers to interact with the digital twin.
- **External factors:** Incorporating environmental conditions, supply chain dynamics, and market trends that influence the system's performance.

Developing a single model that encompasses all these aspects would be a monumental task. Furthermore, such a monolithic approach would be inflexible and difficult to adapt to new requirements or integrate with existing systems.

Recognizing these challenges, researchers have increasingly advocated for a multi-model approach [3, 4]. This approach envisions a digital twin as a composite entity, built from a collection of smaller, specialized digital twins, each focused on a specific aspect or function. This modularity offers several advantages:

- **Flexibility:** New models can be added or removed as needed, allowing the digital twin to evolve and adapt to changing requirements.
- **Scalability:** The system can be scaled up or down by adding or removing models, making it suitable for both small and large-scale applications.
- **Maintainability:** Individual models can be developed and maintained independently, simplifying development and reducing complexity.
- **Reusability:** Models can be reused across different digital twins, promoting efficiency and consistency.

The Industrial Internet Consortium (IIC) (Fig. 1) has also adopted a multi-model perspective, defining a digital twin as a system composed of three main components: data, services, and models [5]. This architecture provides a framework for understanding the interactions between the digital twin and the physical world, as well as with other digital twins.

2.3 AI for Digital Twins

AI plays a crucial role in digital twins, enabling them to predict future states, simulate scenarios, and optimize processes [6]. The use of AI models, such as neural networks, offers a faster and more cost-effective alternative to traditional mathematical modeling. This is particularly important in complex manufacturing environments where developing accurate mathematical models can be time-consuming and expensive.

Several researchers and companies have successfully implemented AI in various manufacturing domains, including production planning [7], production control [8, 9], quality control, and predictive maintenance [10, 11]. These applications demonstrate the potential of AI to enhance the capabilities of digital twins and drive innovation in manufacturing.

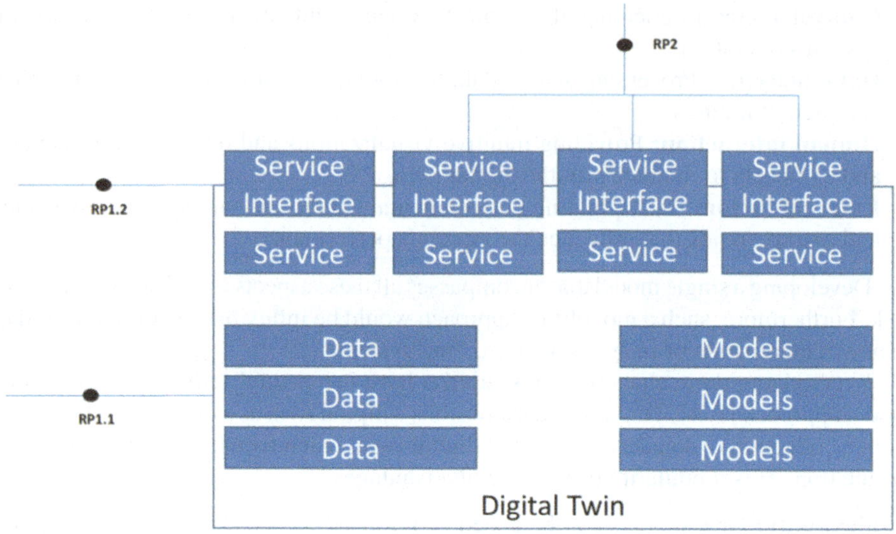

Fig. 1. Basic digital twin model (following IIC Definitions) [5]

3 Methodology

3.1 Mini-Multi-Model Digital Twin Architecture

Our approach builds upon the existing multi-model architecture proposed by the Industrial Internet Consortium and other researchers, but with a key refinement: miniaturization. Recognizing the inherent complexity of developing comprehensive digital twins, we propose a "mini-multi-model" architecture that prioritizes simplicity and scalability.

The core idea is to decompose the digital twin into a collection of highly specialized "mini-models," each focused on a specific sensor, value, or use case. This granular approach offers several advantages:

- **Reduced Complexity:** Developing a model for a single sensor or a specific task is significantly easier than creating a comprehensive model for an entire machine or process. This simplification empowers engineers with varying levels of expertise to contribute to the digital twin development.
- **Enhanced Accuracy:** By focusing on a narrow scope, each mini-model can be finely tuned to achieve maximum accuracy for its specific task. Real-time connectivity to the physical twin allows for continuous monitoring and adjustment of model parameters, ensuring ongoing accuracy and relevance.
- **Increased Flexibility:** New mini-models can be easily added or modified as needed, enabling the digital twin to adapt to evolving requirements and incorporate new functionalities. This modularity promotes agility and responsiveness to changing business needs.
- **Improved Scalability:** The mini-multi-model approach is inherently scalable. Starting with a few essential mini-models, the digital twin can gradually grow in complexity as more sensors, data sources, and use cases are incorporated.

To illustrate the practical benefits of this approach, let's consider two use cases:

Use Case 1: Predictive Maintenance

- **Traditional Approach:** A maintenance engineer would typically need to export and analyze historical data, identify relevant features, and train a complex AI model to predict machine failures. This process is time-consuming, resource-intensive, and may result in a model that quickly becomes outdated as the machine's condition deteriorates.
- **Mini-Multi-Model Approach:** The engineer simply selects the relevant sensor within the digital twin interface and specifies the prediction horizon (e.g., next 6 h). The system automatically creates a mini-model that leverages AI, machine learning, and deep learning techniques to predict the sensor's value. This model continuously learns and adapts based on real-time data, ensuring ongoing accuracy and predictive power.

Use Case 2: Sales Forecasting and Order Quotation

- **Traditional Approach:** A salesperson receiving a new order would need to consult with the technical department to estimate the delivery time. This involves creating a process plan, considering current workload, and potentially involving multiple stakeholders. This process can be slow and inefficient.
- **Mini-Multi-Model Approach:** The salesperson uses the digital twin interface to create a "simulation service" that predicts the production line's capacity to fulfill the new order. This mini-model considers real-time data on machine availability, production schedules, and current demand to provide an accurate delivery time estimate. This empowers the salesperson to provide quick and reliable quotes, improving customer service and responsiveness.

These examples demonstrate the flexibility and adaptability of the mini-multi-model approach. By breaking down complex tasks into smaller, manageable units, this architecture empowers users to create and deploy digital twin functionalities with ease, promoting wider adoption and unlocking the full potential of digital twin technology.

3.2 Plexasync: Implementing the Mini-Multi-Model Approach

To demonstrate the feasibility and practicality of our mini-multi-model architecture, we are developing "Plexasync," a software application designed for ease of use and deployment. Our vision for Plexasync is to provide a plug-and-play solution that can be readily installed on readily available hardware, such as a Raspberry Pi or a local computer, and of course be connected to power cloud resources. This accessibility aims to democratize digital twin technology, making it accessible to small and medium-sized enterprises with limited resources.

Once installed within the industrial network, Plexasync seamlessly connects with various data sources, including IoT devices, PLCs, smart sensors, and actuators. Currently, the software supports two widely used industrial communication protocols: OPC

UA and Modbus TCP. Future development will prioritize expanding this repertoire to accommodate a broader range of protocols, ensuring compatibility with diverse industrial environments.

In its current state, Plexasync provides robust "digital shadowing" capabilities. It collects real-time data from connected devices, effectively mirroring the state of the physical system in the digital realm. This data is then stored in a database for subsequent analysis, visualization, and model building. Plexasync also offers basic HMI functionality, allowing users to visualize and monitor real-time data streams.

Operational Workflow

The operational workflow within Plexasync is designed for intuitive use:

- **Device Definition:** Upon installation, engineers define the devices present in the network (Fig. 2. a). This involves specifying parameters such as device name, IP address, and communication protocol.
- **Value Configuration:** Once a device is defined, engineers configure the specific values that Plexasync should read (Fig. 2. b). This includes identifying the data source (e.g., Modbus register, PLC variable), providing its address and communication port, and specifying the data type for correct conversion and storage.

3.3 AI-Driven Mini-Digital Twins

Plexasync is built with a focus on AI-driven mini-digital twins. This emphasis stems from the inherent versatility and adaptability of AI in handling the diverse data sources and use cases encountered in industrial settings. AI algorithms excel at uncovering patterns, predicting future states, and simulating complex scenarios, making them ideally suited for creating dynamic and responsive digital twins.

Currently, Plexasync primarily supports AI-based models for generating these mini-digital twins. However, we recognize that certain situations may require specialized or custom models. To address this, future development will explore incorporating functionalities that allow engineers to integrate their own models, providing greater flexibility and customization.

Plexasync empowers users to create AI-driven mini-digital twins that leverage historical data to gain valuable insights and optimize processes.

4 Results and Discussion

Plexasync, while still in its development phase, demonstrates promising progress towards achieving a practical and accessible digital twin solution for SMEs. The current version successfully implements core functionalities for data acquisition and visualization, effectively establishing a "digital shadow" of the connected physical system.

4.1 Data Acquisition and Visualization

Plexasync can collect any data type that can be communicated through the supported OPC UA and Modbus TCP protocols. In a preliminary test, the software successfully

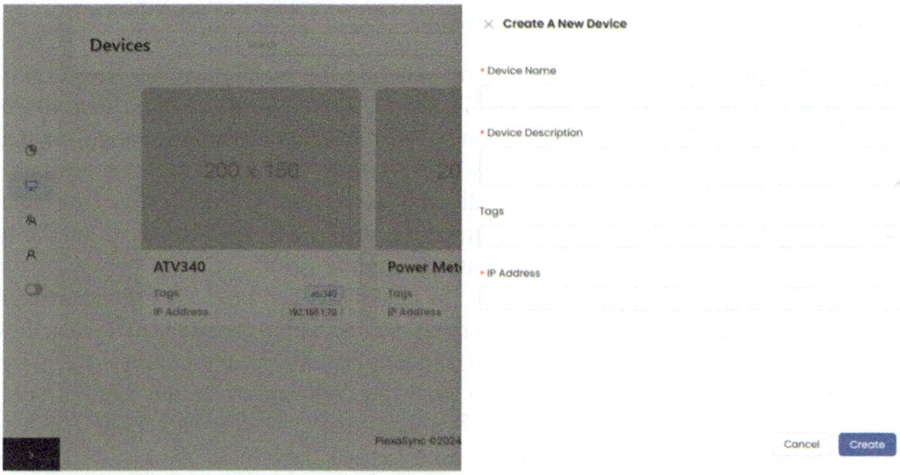

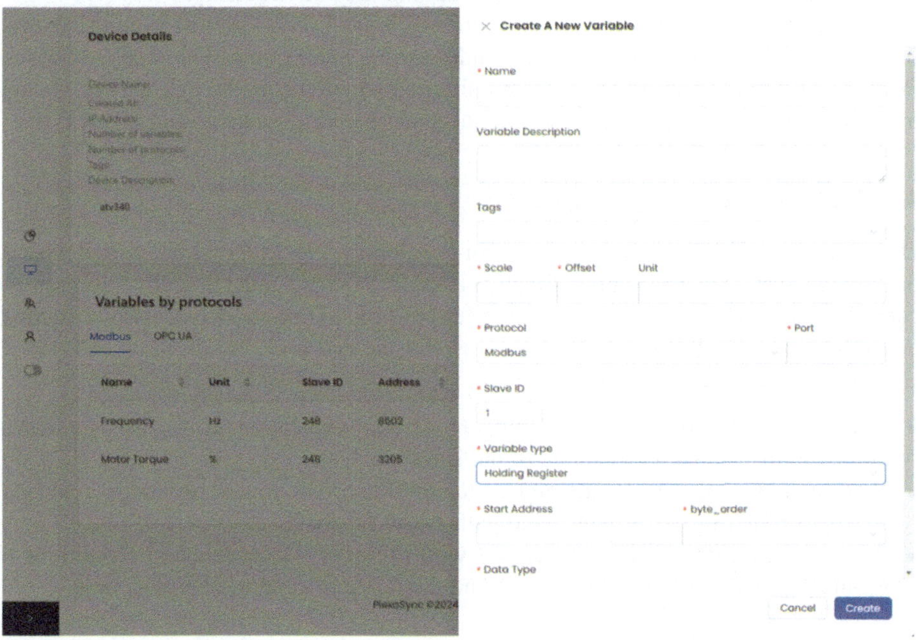

Fig. 2. Device and value configuration in Plexasync. (a) Device definition interface. (b) Value configuration interface.

collected data from 50 simulated sensors at a frequency of 1 min, demonstrating its capacity to handle real-time data streams from multiple sources. The collected data is displayed on a basic HMI dashboard, providing users with real-time visibility into the state of their equipment. These dashboards are accessible from any location with appropriate authorization, enabling remote monitoring and informed decision-making.

4.2 Towards AI-Driven Mini-Digital Twins

Current development efforts are focused on enabling the creation of AI-driven mini-digital twins within Plexasync. Specifically, we are working on a feature that allows users to select a variable (e.g., temperature) and define an acceptable range for that variable. Plexasync will then automatically create a deep learning model that leverages historical data and real-time inputs to predict the future values of the selected variable. If the predicted value falls outside the defined range, the system will trigger an alarm, enabling proactive intervention and preventing potential issues.

A key advantage of this approach is that the models are continuously refined through ongoing learning. Because the models are always connected to the physical device, they receive constant feedback and can adapt to changing conditions or equipment behavior. This ensures that the predictions remain accurate and relevant over time. Furthermore, Plexasync provides users with real-time performance indicators for each model, such as accuracy metrics. This transparency allows users to track the effectiveness of the models and identify areas where adjustments or retraining may be necessary.

To validate this functionality, we are currently conducting experiments with a dataset from Kaggle that simulates the sensor readings of a water pump. The goal is to assess Plexasync's ability to predict water pump failure by monitoring the output pressure and triggering an alarm if it deviates from the normal operating range within the next 6 h.

4.3 Challenges and Future Directions

One of the key challenges encountered in developing Plexasync is the complexity of designing a system that can automatically generate and manage AI models. This requires careful consideration of factors such as data pre-processing, model selection, training, and validation, all while ensuring ease of use for the end-user.

Future development will focus on:

- Expanding protocol support: Adding more communication protocols to enhance compatibility with a wider range of industrial devices.
- Real-world testing: Deploying and evaluating Plexasync in real production environments to assess its performance and gather user feedback.
- AI model exploration: Experimenting with different AI models and algorithms to optimize prediction accuracy and expand the range of supported applications.

4.4 Discussion

While Plexasync may not yet offer the full functionality and sophistication of a fully developed digital twin, its modular design, ease of deployment, and focus on AI-driven mini-digital twins hold significant promise for SMEs. By simplifying the creation and management of digital twin components, Plexasync empowers businesses with limited resources to leverage the benefits of this technology.

The ability to automatically generate AI models based on user-defined parameters is a key differentiator for Plexasync. This functionality streamlines the process of creating predictive and analytical capabilities, making it accessible to users without deep expertise in AI or data science.

Furthermore, the focus on mini-digital twins promotes scalability and flexibility. Users can start with a few essential functionalities and gradually expand their digital twin as their needs evolve. This approach allows for incremental adoption and reduces the initial investment required, making it more attractive for SMEs.

5 Conclusion

This paper presented a novel approach to developing and implementing digital twins in manufacturing, addressing the prevalent ambiguity surrounding their definition and the complexities associated with their development. By proposing a mini-multi-model architecture, we aim to simplify the creation and management of digital twins, making this technology more accessible and practical, particularly for SMEs.

Our software application, Plexasync, embodies this architecture, enabling the creation of AI-driven mini-digital twins that leverage real-time data to offer valuable insights and predictive capabilities. While still under development, Plexasync demonstrates promising progress towards achieving a user-friendly and scalable digital twin solution. It successfully collects real-time data from industrial networks, generates interactive HMIs, and is actively being developed to incorporate AI-driven functionalities for predictive modeling and anomaly detection.

The mini-multi-model approach offers several advantages, including reduced complexity, enhanced accuracy, increased flexibility, and improved scalability. By breaking down the digital twin into smaller, manageable units, this architecture empowers users with varying levels of expertise to contribute to its development and application.

Future work will focus on expanding protocol support, conducting real-world testing in production environments, and exploring new AI models to enhance prediction accuracy and broaden the range of applications. We believe that this research contributes to demystifying digital twins and provides a practical pathway for SMEs to harness their transformative potential, ultimately driving innovation and efficiency in the manufacturing industry.

Acknowledgments. We would like to acknowledge the contributions of the companies and individuals who participated in our research. Their insights and feedback were invaluable in shaping this paper. We also thank anyone who helped in the development of Plexasync for their dedication, hard work, and support.

References

1. Kuhn, Thomas: Digitaler Zwilling. Informatik-Spektrum **40**(5), 440–444 (2017). https://doi.org/10.1007/s00287-017-1061-2
2. Eigner, M., Detzner, A., Schmidt, P., Tharma, R.: Holistic definition of the digital twin. Int. J. Prod. Lifecycle Manag. **13**, 343 (2021). https://doi.org/10.1504/IJPLM.2021.119527
3. Malakuti, S., Schmitt, J., Platenius-Mohr, M., Grüner, S., Gitzel, R., Bihani, P.: A four-layer architecture pattern for constructing and managing digital twins. In: Bures, T., Duchien, L., Inverardi, P. (eds.) Software Architecture: 13th European Conference, ECSA 2019, Paris, France, September 9–13, 2019, Proceedings, pp. 231–246. Springer International Publishing, Cham (2019). https://doi.org/10.1007/978-3-030-29983-5_16

4. Malakuti, S., Grüner, S.: Architectural aspects of digital twins in IIoT systems. In: Proceedings of the 12th European Conference on Software Architecture: Companion Proceedings, pp. 1–2. ACM, Madrid Spain (2018). https://doi.org/10.1145/3241403.3241417
5. Kovacs, E., Mori, K.: Digital twin architecture – an introduction. In: Crespi, N., Drobot, A.T., Minerva, R. (eds.) The Digital Twin, pp. 125–151. Springer International Publishing, Cham (2023). https://doi.org/10.1007/978-3-031-21343-4_5
6. Minerva, R., Crespi, N., Farahbakhsh, R., Awan, F.M.: Artificial intelligence and the digital twin: an essential combination. In: Crespi, N., Drobot, A.T., Minerva, R. (eds.) The Digital Twin, pp. 299–336. Springer International Publishing, Cham (2023). https://doi.org/10.1007/978-3-031-21343-4_12
7. Busch, M., Schuh, G., Kelzenberg, C., De Lange, J.: Short paper: development of production planning and control through the empowerment of artificial intelligence. In: 2019 Second International Conference on Artificial Intelligence for Industries (AI4I), pp. 115–118. IEEE, Laguna Hills, CA, USA (2019). https://doi.org/10.1109/AI4I46381.2019.00037
8. Singgih, I.K.: Production flow analysis in a semiconductor fab using machine learning techniques. Processes **9**(3), 407 (2021). https://doi.org/10.3390/pr9030407
9. Min, Q., Lu, Y., Liu, Z., Su, C., Wang, B.: Machine learning based digital twin framework for production optimization in petrochemical industry. Int. J. Inf. Manag. **49**, 502–519 (2019). https://doi.org/10.1016/j.ijinfomgt.2019.05.020
10. Li, L., Liu, D., Liu, J., Zhou, H., Zhou, J.: Quality prediction and control of assembly and welding process for ship group product based on digital twin. Scanning **2020**, 1–13 (2020). https://doi.org/10.1155/2020/3758730
11. Yacob, F., Semere, D., Nordgren, E.: Anomaly detection in skin model shapes using machine learning classifiers. Int. J. Adv. Manuf. Technol. **105**(9), 3677–3689 (2019). https://doi.org/10.1007/s00170-019-03794-z

Enhancing the Reliability of Kanban Systems with AI Tools in the Automotive Sector: A Case Study

Manar Messour(✉) and Fayçal Fedouaki

University Hassan 2nd, ENSAM, Casablanca, Morocco
manarmessour2014@gmail.com

Abstract. In the evolving landscape of the automotive industry, lean manufacturing and Kanban systems play a critical role in optimizing production flows and reducing waste. However, traditional Kanban systems often struggle with limitations in handling demand variability, stockouts, and overproduction, especially in dynamic environments. This paper explores the integration of Artificial Intelligence (AI) tools to enhance the reliability of Kanban systems, ensuring higher responsiveness and accuracy in inventory management and production planning.

The study focuses on how AI-driven demand forecasting, predictive analytics, and real-time data collection via IoT sensors can mitigate the key challenges of traditional Kanban systems in the automotive sector. Specifically, machine learning models for predictive demand forecasting are used to optimize inventory levels, while automated replenishment algorithms ensure timely and precise stock refills.

Through the case study presented, we demonstrate significant improvements in production efficiency, reduction of waste, and better synchronization across supply chains. The results showcase that integrating AI technologies into Kanban systems not only enhances operational reliability but also aligns with lean manufacturing principles by minimizing waste and increasing production flexibility. This approach promises to redefine the role of Kanban in the future of smart automotive manufacturing.

Keywords: Lean Manufacturing · Kanban Systems · Artificial Intelligence · IOT sensors · Automotive Sector · Demand Forecasting · Inventory Optimization

1 Introduction

Lean manufacturing has become a dominant philosophy in the automotive industry, driving continuous improvement by eliminating waste, optimizing resources, and maximizing value to the customer. The Kanban system, developed as part of the Toyota Production System (TPS), is a key enabler of lean manufacturing. Kanban facilitates just-in-time (JIT) production by using visual signals to regulate inventory levels and synchronize production flow with customer demand [1]. By ensuring that materials are delivered exactly when needed, Kanban minimizes waste, improve reduces lead times, and prevents overproduction [2].

I. Aboudrar et al. (Eds.): ICESST 2024, SUCI, pp. 521–529, 2025.
https://doi.org/10.1007/978-3-031-86705-7_49

The automotive sector, where production processes are highly complex and involve numerous components, Kanban systems are critical for maintaining smooth operations [3]. Their simplicity and effectiveness make them widely adopted, ensuring that parts and materials are available precisely when required, thereby preventing bottlenecks in assembly lines.

Despite its proven benefits, the traditional Kanban system faces significant challenges in modern automotive production environments. As automotive manufacturers expand product lines and deal with variable demand, Kanban systems often struggle to maintain optimal inventory levels [4]. In this research we will explore these limitations in the context of modern automotive production,

As the automotive industry embraces Industry 4.0, the use of Artificial Intelligence (AI) is transforming traditional manufacturing systems. AI technologies, combined with real-time data from IoT (Internet of Things) devices, can address the limitations of conventional Kanban systems by making them more reliable, adaptive, and predictive [6].

The integration of AI tools into the Kanban system, particularly in the automotive sector, represents a shift towards smart manufacturing, where real-time data and intelligent algorithms collaborate to create a more agile, efficient, and reliable production process.

In this research, we will explore how AI tools can be leveraged to enhance the reliability of Kanban systems, making them more adaptable to the complex demands of automotive production. This paper is structured as follows: Sect. 2 provides a literature review on the current limitations of traditional Kanban systems; Sect. 3 outlines the research methodology used in this study; Sect. 4 discusses how AI tools can improve the reliability of Kanban systems in the automotive industry; Sect. 5 presents a case study that demonstrates how AI enhances the reliability, flexibility, and efficiency of Kanban systems, aligning them with lean manufacturing goals while addressing traditional limitations. Finally, Sect. 6 offers conclusions and suggests directions for future research.

2 Literature Review

While Kanban systems have been instrumental in enabling lean manufacturing practices across the automotive industry, their traditional implementation is increasingly being tested by the evolving complexities of modern production environments. Originally designed for stable, repetitive processes, Kanban systems encounter several limitations when faced with the dynamic and unpredictable demands of today's automotive manufacturing landscape. These limitations create inefficiencies that challenge the core objectives of lean manufacturing, including waste reduction, continuous flow, and customer satisfaction.

2.1 Manual Replenishment and Human Errors

Kanban relies heavily on manual processes, where workers physically move Kanban cards or update inventory levels. Human error is a significant concern in these manual systems, as any incorrect signalling, misplaced cards, or failure to replenish can lead to miscommunication and disruptions in the production flow [7]. Manual handling of Kanban signals also makes it difficult to maintain real-time visibility into stock levels, further contributing to inefficiencies in replenishment cycles [7].

2.2 Demand Variability and Forecasting Inaccuracy

In the automotive sector, product demand is inherently variable due to fluctuating market trends, changing customer preferences, and the rise of custom vehicle configurations. Traditional Kanban systems depend on historical data and fixed lead times for replenishment signals, making them ill-equipped to handle unexpected demand fluctuations [8].

2.3 Complex Supply Chains and Lead Time Uncertainty

The globalization of the automotive supply chain adds layers of complexity to the Kanban system. With suppliers often spread across different regions and countries, factors like shipping delays, geopolitical disruptions, and unforeseen logistical challenges can lead to unpredictable lead times [6]. Traditional Kanban systems, which are set up based on fixed replenishment times, lack the flexibility to adapt to such uncertainties. As a result, delays in material deliveries can cause significant bottlenecks, negatively impacting the production line's efficiency.

2.4 Lack of Real-Time Data and Analytics

In today's data-driven manufacturing environment, the lack of real-time data in traditional Kanban systems is a major drawback. Without real-time visibility into inventory levels, demand fluctuations, and supply chain performance, decision-makers are often forced to rely on outdated or incomplete information [9]. This lack of data-driven insights prevents the optimization of production flows and makes it difficult to anticipate disruptions or adapt to changing conditions in the market.

These challenges illustrate that while traditional Kanban systems are effective in stable environments, they are less suited to the dynamic and highly complex nature of modern automotive manufacturing. To overcome these limitations and maintain lean manufacturing objectives, it is necessary to incorporate more intelligent, adaptive systems capable of handling variability, improving forecast accuracy, and responding in real-time to production needs. Artificial Intelligence (AI) offer promising solutions to enhance the reliability and flexibility of Kanban systems, which will be the focus of this paper.

3 Research Methodology

The research methodology for this study adopts both qualitative and quantitative approaches to assess the impact of AI on Kanban systems within lean automotive manufacturing. A detailed literature review will first identify key limitations in traditional

Kanban systems and the potential benefits of AI integration. Following this, a case study will be conducted on an automotive plant transitioning from a conventional Kanban system to an AI-enhanced model. Operational data from company reports, such as lead time reduction, inventory turnover, and production efficiency, will be collected. Key performance indicators (KPIs) like response time to demand fluctuations and inventory management improvements will be analyzed to assess the effectiveness of AI in optimizing Kanban operations.

4 Role of AI in Enhancing the Reliability of Kanban Systems

As the automotive industry navigates the complexities of modern manufacturing, integrating Artificial Intelligence (AI) into Kanban systems offers transformative potential to address the limitations of traditional approaches. AI technologies can enhance the reliability, adaptability, and efficiency of Kanban systems, ensuring they meet the demands of today's dynamic production environments [10]. This section discusses the key roles that AI can play in in enhancing the reliability of Kanban systems.

4.1 Automated Inventory Management

AI enhances the automation of inventory management within Kanban systems, streamlining the replenishment process and minimizing manual interventions.AI can leverage data from IoT devices embedded in production equipment to monitor inventory levels in real time [6]. The sensors track the quantity of materials in storage bins and alert the system when it's time to reorder, ensuring seamless inventory management [6].

4.2 Enhanced Demand Forecasting

One of the most significant contributions of AI to Kanban systems is the ability to improve demand forecasting accuracy. Traditional forecasting methods often rely on historical sales data and fixed patterns, which can lead to significant inaccuracies in predicting future demand. AI-driven forecasting models utilize advanced algorithms and machine learning techniques to analyze vast amounts of data, including historical trends, seasonal variations, and market indicators. By employing machine learning algorithms, AI can identify patterns and correlations that may not be evident in traditional methods [11]. For instance, neural networks can process complex datasets to provide more accurate demand predictions [12], reducing the risk of overstocking or stockouts.

4.3 Supply Chain Optimization

AI significantly enhances supply chain management, addressing one of the critical challenges faced by Kanban systems.AI can provide real-time visibility into the supply chain, enabling manufacturers to react swiftly to disruptions or delays [5]. For instance, if a supplier experiences a delay, AI can suggest alternative suppliers or adjust production schedules accordingly, maintaining the flow of materials to the production line.

4.4 Improved Data-Driven Decision Making

AI empowers decision-makers with actionable insights derived from data analytics.AI can aggregate data from various sources, providing visual dashboards that highlight key performance indicators (KPIs) related to Kanban operations. This real-time visibility allows managers to make informed decisions quickly, ensuring that production remains aligned with demand [11].

Incorporating AI into Kanban systems offers a multifaceted approach to enhancing reliability addressing the inherent limitations of traditional methods. By improving demand forecasting, automating inventory management, enabling predictive maintenance, optimizing supply chains, and improving decision-making, AI creates a more reliable, agile, and efficient manufacturing environment. This integration not only aligns with the principles of lean manufacturing but also positions the automotive industry to thrive in an era characterized by rapid change and uncertainty.

5 Case Study: AI-Enhanced Kanban Implementation in Automotive Sector

As automotive manufacturers strive to meet increasing consumer demand for customization and advanced features, managing the supply chain has become increasingly complex. This case study examines how an automotive manufacturer implemented an AI-enhanced Kanban system to improve efficiency, reduce lead times, and minimize waste in their production process.

5.1 Problem Statement

The manufacturer faced several inefficiencies with their traditional Kanban system, primarily due to its reliance on manual processes. Workers used physical Kanban cards to signal replenishment, which often led to human errors, such as misplaced or delayed cards. These errors created bottlenecks in the supply chain, slowing down production. In the pagoda area, a logistician had to manually enter components into the system and frequently check the status of the Kanban cards, resulting in excessive non-value-adding movements as shown in Fig. 1. Meanwhile, line production feeders had to retrieve components from the pagoda based on these Kanban signals, which added complexity and delays. This traditional system also lacked real-time visibility, meaning stockouts or overstocking often went unnoticed until it was too late, further contributing to production inefficiencies. Additionally, manual handling of cards made it difficult to track inventory accurately, leading to inconsistencies between actual stock levels and what was recorded.

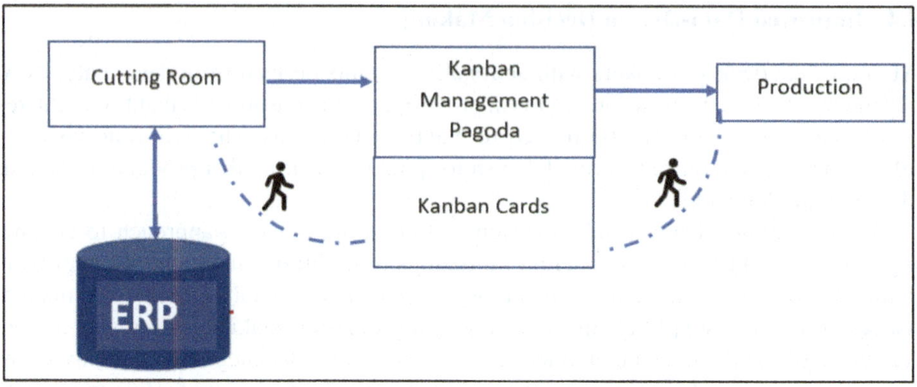

Fig. 1. Shopfloor design with traditional Kanban

5.2 Implementation of AI-Enhanced Kanban

To address the limitations of traditional Kanban systems, an AI-driven approach was implemented, integrating IoT, RFID, and predictive analytics to streamline material flow and stock replenishment. RFID tags were attached to components, materials, and bins, enabling continuous tracking throughout the production process and replacing manual Kanban cards. IoT sensors monitored stock levels in real-time, providing continuous data feeds on material consumption rates, storage conditions, and movement. Data such as material ID, location, and status (in storage, in process, or ready for replenishment) were collected and stored in the central database connected to ERP system. This setup as shown in Fig. 2, ensured a seamless flow of information across the supply chain, giving all stakeholders real-time visibility into stock levels and replenishment needs.

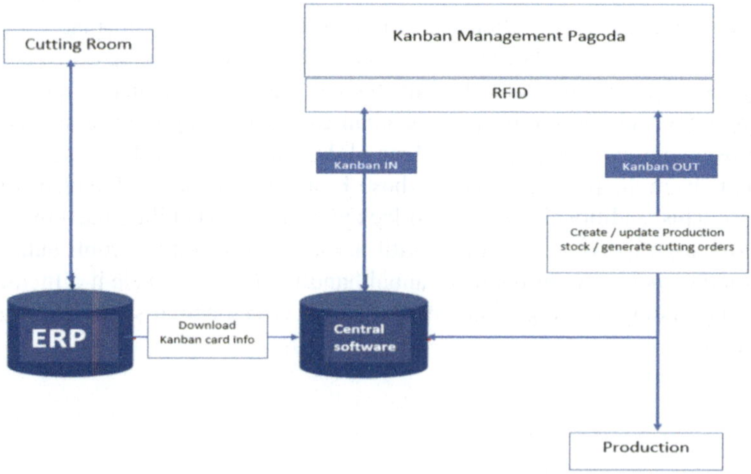

Fig. 2. Shopfloor design with AI-Enhanced Kanban

To forecast material consumption rates accurately, the ARIMA model was chosen for its robust performance in time series forecasting. Historical material consumption data from the production line were used to train the model, with parameters optimized for the best fit. The ARIMA model was periodically retrained with updated data to adapt to changing production patterns, and its accuracy was evaluated using the Mean Absolute Percentage Error (MAPE), calculated as follows:

$$MAPE = \frac{1}{n}\sum_{t=1}^{n}\left|\frac{A_t - F_t}{A_t}\right| \times 100$$

where A_t represents the actual value, F_t is the forecasted value at time t, and n is the number of forecasted points. The model aimed to maintain a MAPE below 10%, ensuring high accuracy in predicting demand for replenishment.

The Fig. 3, illustrates the ARIMA model's performance in forecasting material demand. The blue line represents the actual consumption data, while the orange dashed line shows the forecasted values for the upcoming period. This visualization demonstrates the model's ability to closely align with real-world data, ensuring reliable predictions for stock replenishment and production planning.

By leveraging these forecasts, the AI-enhanced Kanban system automatically triggered replenishment signals to the logistics team when stock levels approached predefined thresholds. This significantly reduced dependency on manual checks, minimized delays, and prevented stockouts. Integration with ERP system further streamlined operations, enabling real-time updates of stock status and production requirements. Each material bundle acted as a virtual Kanban card, replacing physical cards with digital signals, allowing faster and more accurate inventory movements.

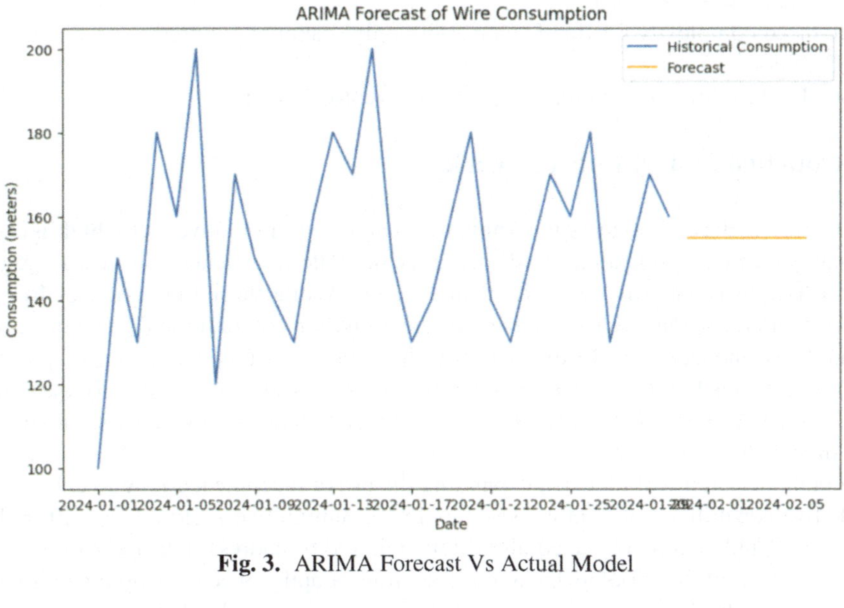

Fig. 3. ARIMA Forecast Vs Actual Model

Evaluation of the ARIMA model's performance showed a MAPE below 10%, confirming its reliability for operational use. The implementation of this AI-enhanced Kanban system transformed the role of logistics operators, allowing them to focus on overseeing automated processes rather than engaging in manual replenishment and data handling.

5.3 Results

The implementation of the AI-enhanced Kanban system resulted in significant improvements across various operational metrics. Lead times were reduced by 25%, thanks to automated replenishment processes that enabled faster responses to production demands. Overall productivity saw a notable increase, as employees could shift their focus from manual inventory tracking and management to more value-added tasks. This automation streamlined operations, minimized the likelihood of human error, and enhanced the efficiency and accuracy of the entire supply chain. The integration of real-time data insights and automation created a more agile and responsive production environment, directly supporting lean manufacturing objectives.

Key benefits included:

- Seamless compatibility with ERP system
- Immediate and precise control of WIP stock
- Each bundle acting as a Kanban, lowering stock levels
- Elimination of physical Kanban cards
- Enhanced traceability and historical data for cut wires (e.g., in stock, in cutting pool, finished cutting, etc.)
- Launching production orders for cutting based on real-time, accurate stock data, leading to increased OEE
- Reduced complexity for line feeders, with only scanning required
- FIFO alerts
- Stock-takes through scanning, improving inventory accuracy.

6 Conclusion and Future Work

In conclusion, the case study of the Kanban system in the automotive sector highlights the critical gap in the application of advanced technologies, particularly in the integration of machine learning (ML) with Kanban systems. While the introduction of IoT and RFID technologies has addressed many of the limitations of traditional Kanban, such as human error and lack of real-time visibility, there remains significant untapped potential in leveraging machine learning to further optimize these systems. Specifically, the current state of the industry still struggles with demand variability, supply chain complexity, and real-time decision-making.

Future research will focus on expanding the use of machine learning to enhance the predictive capabilities of Kanban systems in the automotive sector. This will include developing and testing advanced algorithms tailored to address industry-specific challenges, such as multi-variable demand forecasting, adaptive inventory optimization, and proactive supply chain risk mitigation. By leveraging these technologies, the next phase of research aims to push the boundaries of lean manufacturing principles, reducing waste, maximizing operational flexibility, and creating a more resilient and responsive supply chain.

References

1. Pinto, J.L.Q., et al.: Lean manufacturing tools. In: Pinto, J.L.Q., Matias, J.C.O., Pimentel, C., Azevedo, S.G., Govindan, K. (eds.) Just in Time Factory, pp. 39–112. Springer International Publishing, Cham (2018). https://doi.org/10.1007/978-3-319-77016-1_4
2. Rahman, N.A.A., Sharif, S.M., Esa, M.M.: Lean manufacturing case study with Kanban system implementation. Procedia Econ. Financ. **7**, 174–180 (2013)
3. Faccio, M., et al.: Design and simulation of assembly line feeding systems in the automotive sector using supermarket, kanbans and tow trains: a general framework. J. Manag. Control **24**(2), 187–208 (2013). https://doi.org/10.1007/s00187-013-0175-1
4. Kurilova-Palisaitiene, J., Sundin, E., Poksinska, B.: Remanufacturing challenges and possible lean improvements. J. Clean. Prod. **172**, 3225–3236 (2018)
5. Marialuisa, M., Matteo, S.M., Muhammad, S.: Optimizing milk-run system and IT-based Kanban with artificial intelligence: an empirical study on multi-lines assembly shop floor. Product. Manuf. Res. **11**(1), 2179123 (2023). https://doi.org/10.1080/21693277.2023.2179123
6. Papadimitropoulou, C., et al.: Digitally enhancing kanban lean practice in support of just-in-time reconfigurable supply: a case study. In: IFIP International Conference on Advances in Production Management Systems. Cham: Springer Nature Switzerland (2023)
7. Houti, M., Laila, E.A., Abdellah, A.: E-Kanban the new generation of traditional Kanban system, and the impact of its implementation in the enterprise. In: Proceedings of the International Conference on Industrial Engineering and Operations Management Rabat (2017)
8. Zhang, J.Z.M., Brusey, J., Johnston, R.B.: Experiments toward a practical implementation of an intelligent kanban system. In: Mařík, V., Brennan, R.W., Pěchouček, M. (eds.) Holonic and Multi-Agent Systems for Manufacturing, pp. 257–268. Springer, Berlin, Heidelberg (2005). https://doi.org/10.1007/11537847_23
9. Benhamou, L., et al.: Digital twin: an added value for digital CONWIP in the context of industry 4.0. Sustainability **15**(13), 9874 (2023). https://doi.org/10.3390/su15139874
10. Söylemez, İ, Ünlü, R.: Artificial intelligence in production systems and integration with lean manufacturing. In: Yang, X.-S. (ed.) Engineering Applications of AI and Swarm Intelligence, pp. 235–252. Springer Nature Singapore, Singapore (2025). https://doi.org/10.1007/978-981-97-5979-8_11
11. Fathia, A.: AI in Agile Development: Enhancing Scrum and Kanban Methodologies (2024)
12. Araz, O.U., Eski, O., Araz, C.: Determining the parameters of dual-card kanban system: an integrated multicriteria and artificial neural network methodology. Int. J. Adv. Manuf. Technol. **38**(9–10), 965–977 (2008)

Design and Optimization of High-Gain Microstrip Patch Antenna Arrays for GPS Applications

Ibrahim Khouyaoui(✉), Mouhssine Elbathaoui, Jaouad Foshi, and Mohamed Hamdaoui

Electronics Instrumentation and Intelligent Systems Team, ER2TI Laboratory, Department of Physics, Faculty of Sciences and Technics, Moulay Ismail University of Meknes, Errachidia, Morocco

ibrahimkhouyaoui@gmail.com

Abstract. The article discusses the design and analysis of microstrip patch antennas for GPS applications. It focuses on achieving high gain and circular polarization (CP) with compact and efficient designs. The study includes a single patch antenna with a diagonal slot, a 2 × 1 patch array, and a 4 × 1 patch array. Key performance metrics like return loss, axial ratio, and gain are analyzed. The findings reveal that arrays provide higher gain and directivity, making them suitable for enhanced GPS performance. The 4 × 1 array shows a maximum gain of 11 dB and satisfactory CP operation, making it the most efficient design.

Keywords: Squrre patch antenna · array antenna · axial ratio · Gain · S11

1 Introduction

The advent of modern telecommunication systems has driven the demand for highly efficient, [2, 3] compact, and broadband antennas capable of operating at specific frequencies with precise polarization characteristics [4, 5]. In this context, Global Positioning System (GPS) applications require antennas that exhibit narrowband performance, high gain, and circular polarization (CP) to ensure reliable satellite communication under various environmental conditions [10–14]. The microstrip patch antenna, known for its planar structure, low profile, and ease of fabrication, emerges as a viable candidate for such applications.This work explores the design and optimization of microstrip patch antennas for GPS applications, focusing on achieving right-handed circular polarization (RHCP) with enhanced gain and bandwidth. By utilizing different configurations, [11] such as single square patches and antenna arrays (2 × 1 and 4 × 1), this study investigates the influence of various design parameters such as slot dimensions, substrate thickness, [7] and feed technique on the antenna's overall performance. The goal is to develop an antenna system that offers high efficiency, low return loss, and stable CP radiation, critical for maintaining robust communication links in satellite-based navigation systems [3].

I. Aboudrar et al. (Eds.): ICESST 2024, SUCI, pp. 530–538, 2025.
https://doi.org/10.1007/978-3-031-86705-7_50

2 Design Specifications

The GPS requires a narrow band and high gain antenna. It is required that the antenna radiates CP waves. The antenna should have high efficiency and low-profile. Table 1 summarizes the antenna requirements for GPS [3, 11].

Table 1. The antenna requirements for the GPS.

Operating frequency	1.57 GHz
Dielectric substrate	FR4 substrate: $\varepsilon_r = 4.5$, h = 1.6 mm
Patch shape	Square patch with diagonal slot square patch with trimmed corners and elliptical patch with diagonal feed
Feeding technique	Microstrip line
Matching technique	Quarter wavelength transformer and shunt stub
Return loss	Below −10 dB
Polarization	Right-handed circular polarization(RHCP)
Gain	Above 6 dB
Bandwidth	From 1.57 to 1.59 GHz
Axial ratio	Below 5 dB

3 Calculation of Square Patch Antenna Dimension

By using the equations that were presented in the 1, the dimensions of the single patch antenna can be calculated as shown below. All the calculations are based on the transmission line theory which is simple but inaccurate method. Thus, these dimensions will be used in modeling the antenna and will be adjusted to optimize the performance.

The length of the microstrip patch antenna is given by equation as: [1, 3, 11].

$Lp = \frac{\lambda}{2} = \frac{C}{2fr\sqrt{\varepsilon r}}$ By substituting c = 3×10^8 m/s, f_r = 1.575 GHz and $\varepsilon r = 4.5$ we get: $L_P = W_P = 44.8$ mm Since square patches are used in this project, $L_P = W_P = 44.8$ mm. After modification in CST:Lp = 43.1 mm.

4 Square Patch Antenna with Diagonal Slot

The first design is a square patch antenna with a diagonal slot, CP operation is obtained by etching a diagonal slot in the patch and feeding the patch at the Centre of the edge. The slot size dimensions are given by: [1, 11]

$$Zin = \frac{Lp}{2.72} = \mathrm{D} = \frac{C}{10}$$

By substituting we get: $L_P = 43.1$ mm, c = 12.31, d = 1.23 mm.

Parametric study has been carried out to find the effect of the slot size on the polarization state (AR) and the input impedance S_{11}.

From the results in Table 2, it can be seen that by reducing the size of the slot, the antenna becomes circularly polarized (AR decreases). However, the S_{11} becomes above −10 dB, meaning that some power is lost due to reflections. Since the S_{11} result is not good enough, an impedance matching circuit is required. Thus, we select $c = L_p/3.5$ which gives a CP operation with AR = 3.5 dB. A matching circuit with shunt stub is used to improve theS_{11} result.

Table 2. The effect of the slot size

C	AR dB	S11 dB
Lp/2.8	10.4	−16
Lp/3	7.58	−21
Lp/3.2	5.45	−17.2
Lp/3.4	3.8	−11.7
Lp/3.5	3.5	−10.2
Lp/3.6	2.5	−9 dB

5 Single Square Patch with Diagonal Slot

While maintaining all other antenna characteristics constant, we systematically alter the substrate's thickness within a range spanning from 1 mm to 11 mm. This deliberate variation aims to evaluate the influence of the dielectric substrate's thickness (h) on not only the antenna's overall performance but also its resonance frequency and bandwidth, [3, 11].

Figure 1 shows 2-D view of single patch design in CST® environment. The width equal to the length of the patch is $W_p = L_p = 43.1$ mm. The microstrip feed line is designed to have 50 Ω impedance. The width of the feed line is 3 mm and its length is 45 mm.

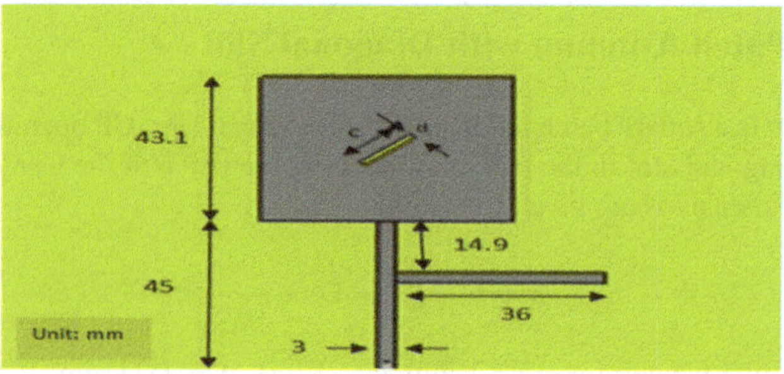

Fig. 1. 2-D view of single patch design in CST environment

The return loss result of the single patch antenna is shown in Fig. 2. The resonant frequency is at 1.58 GHz and the magnitude of the return loss is about −30 dB. The −10 dB bandwidth is 5.37%.

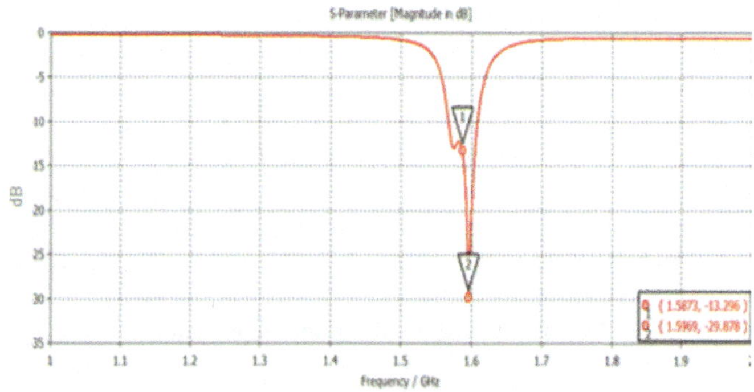

Fig. 2. The return loss of single patch with diagonal slot

The 3-D simulated radiation pattern of the single patch antenna with diagonal slot is shown in Fig. 3. The radiation pattern is directional with maximum power orthogonal to the patch. The gain of the antenna is about 6.64 dB. It can be seen that the single patch antenna is not very directive and thus it is necessary to design an array to increase the directivity and the gain.

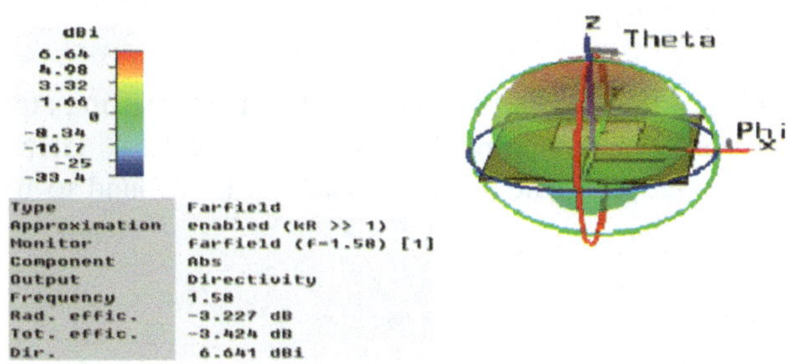

Fig. 3. 3-D radiation pattern of the single patch antenna

The axial ratio result of the single patch antenna is shown in Fig. 4. It can be seen that AR ≈ 1.98 dB in the broadside direction ($\theta = 0^0$) Thus, the antenna radiates CP waves.

6 2 × 1 Microstrip Square Patch Array

In Fig. 5 the array is obtained by integrating the 2 × 1 power divider with square patches. The spacing between the patches is approximately half wavelength (43.9 mm). The power divider splits the input power equally between the radiating patches.

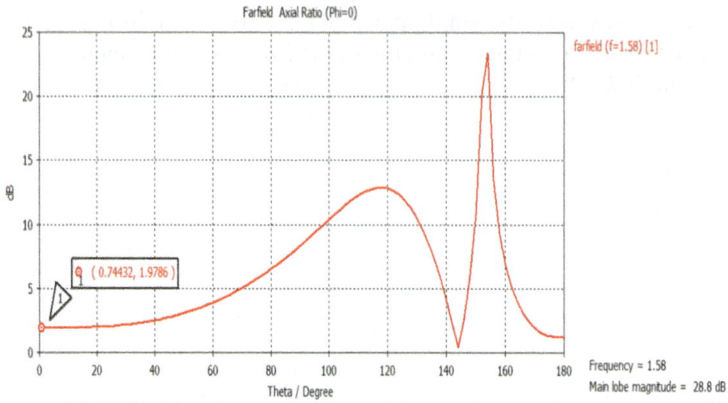

Fig. 4. The axial ratio of the single patch

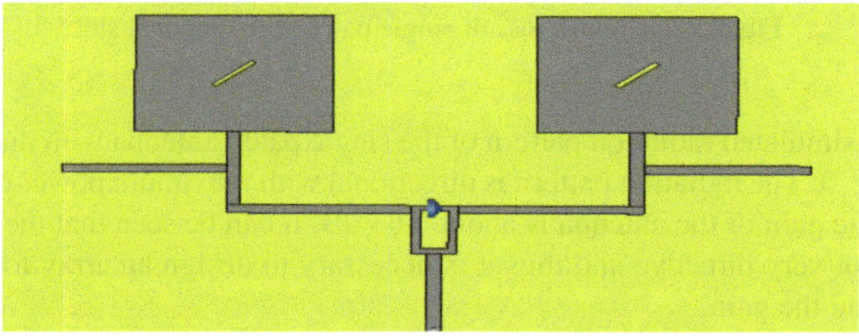

Fig. 5. 2-D view of 2 × 1 microstrip patch array

Figure 6 shows the simulated return loss for 2 × 1 microstrip patch array antenna. From the graph, it can be seen that resonant frequency at 1.586 GHz. The magnitude of the return loss of −25 dB. The −10 dB bandwidth is found to be 2.85% for the 1.586 GHz.

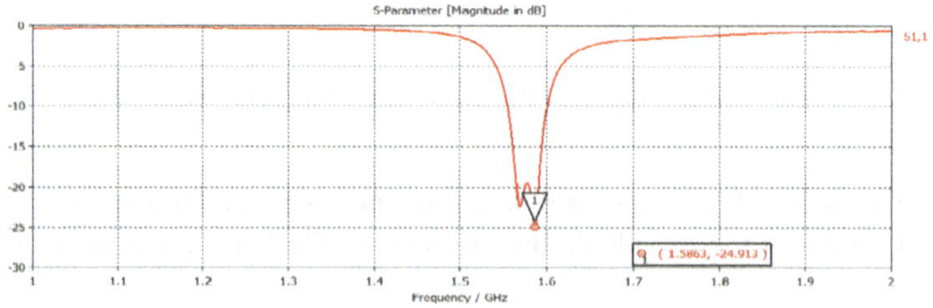

Fig. 6. Return loss of 2 × 1 patch array

The 3-D radiation pattern of the 2 × 1 microstrip array is shown in Fig. 7. The pattern is directional with maximum power orthogonal to the patches. The 2 × 1 array has higher gain than the single patch. The gain of the array is about 8.84 dB.

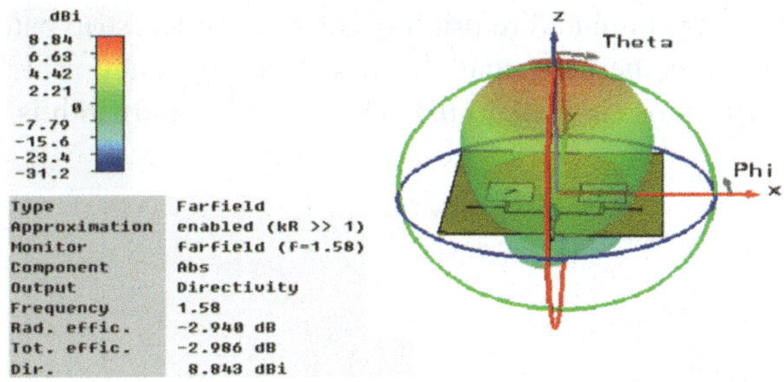

Fig. 7. 3-D radiation pattern of the 2 × 1 patch array antenna

The axial ratio result of the 2 × 1 array antenna is shown in Fig. 8. The AR is about 2.3 dB in the main lobe direction, meaning that the antenna is circularly polarized.

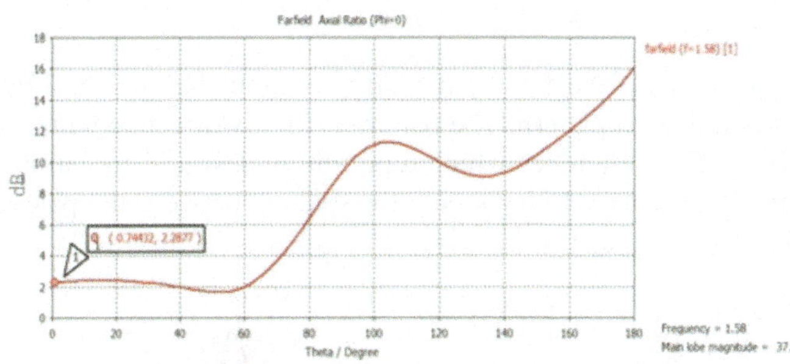

Fig. 8. The axial ratio of the 2 × 1 patch array

7 4 x 1 Microstrip Patch Array Antenna

In Fig. 9 4 × 1 array is designed by combining. 4 × 1 power divider with square patches. 4 × 1 power divider splits the input power between the four output ports equally. The 4 × 1 array is expected to provide a higher gain and directivity than the 2 × 1 array.

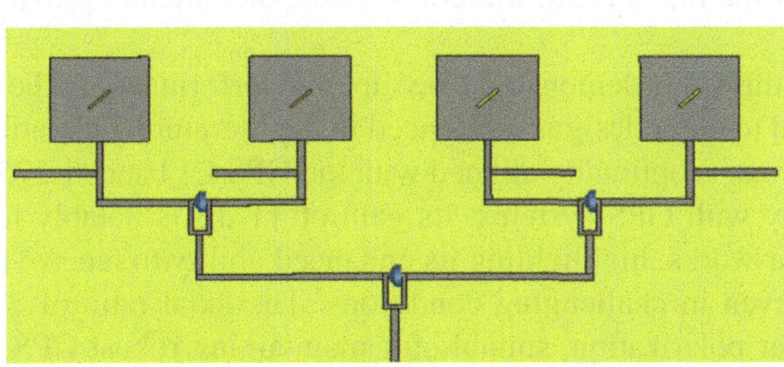

Fig. 9. 2-D view of 4 × 1 microstrip patch array antenna

Figure 10 shows the simulated return loss for 4 × 1 microstrip patch array antenna. From this Figure, it can be seen that the resonant frequency at 1.57 GHz and the magnitude of the return loss is −19.73 dB. The −10 dB bandwidth is about 1.96%.

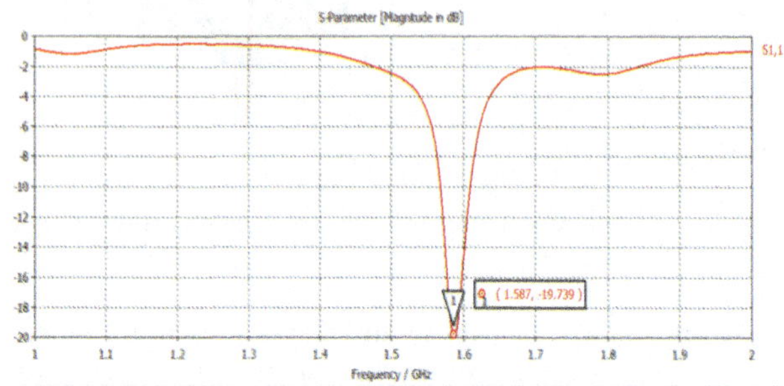

Fig. 10. Return loss of 4 × 1 patch array

The radiation pattern of the 4 × 1 patch array is simulated in CST. Figure 11 shows the simulated 3-D radiation pattern. The pattern is highly directive with maximum gain of 11 dB. There are few side lobes which represent undesirable radiation (lost power). These lobes can be minimized by adjusting the spacing between the patches.

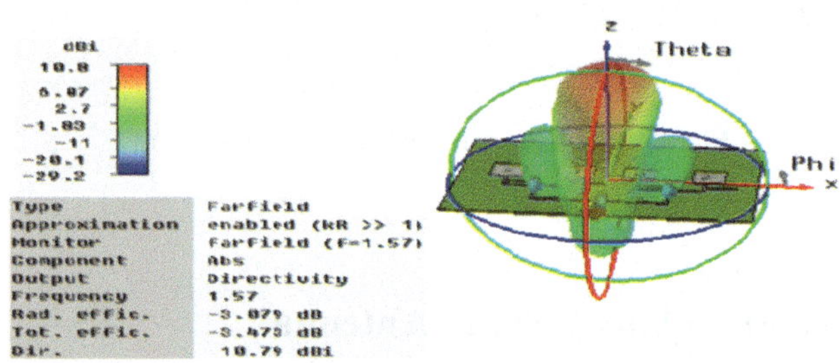

Fig. 11. 3-D radiation pattern of 4 × 1 microstrip patch array

The axial ratio result of 4 × 1 array antenna is shown in Fig. 12. It can be seen that AR = 2.39 dB in the mean beam direction. Thus, the antenna provides CP operation (Table 3).

The results of this study demonstrate the superior performance of the 4 × 1 patch array antenna compared to other designs referenced in the literature. Operating at 1.586 GHz, the proposed antenna is optimally aligned with the GPS L1 band (1.575 GHz), ensuring high compatibility with GPS systems. Its gain of 11 dB is notably higher than those reported in similar works, highlighting its enhanced ability to receive and transmit signals effectively, even in challenging conditions. The axial ratio of 2.39 dB confirms its reliable circular polarization, suitable for maintaining robust GPS communication. Although the bandwidth of 1.96% is slightly narrower than some designs, it satisfies the narrowband requirements of GPS applications while supporting excellent gain and

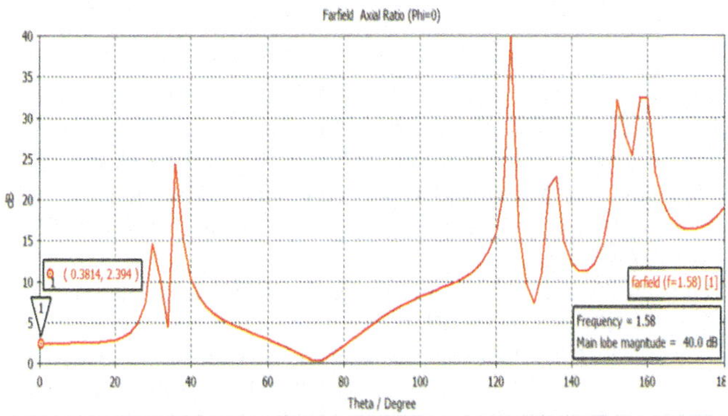

Fig. 12. The axial ratio of the 4 × 1 patch array

Table 3. Summary of the simulated results

ref	Type of antenna	Fr (GHz)	S11 (dB)	BW(%)	Gain (dB)	Axial ratio (dB)
16	MPA truncated two-corners	1.575	−35.854	-	4.974	2.956
15	square patch	1.5	−41	2.4	1.75	-
This work	Single patch	1.586	−29.89	5.37	6.64	1.79
	2 × 1 patch array	1.586	−24.91	2.85	8.4	2.28
	4 × 1 patch array	1.586	−19.73	1.96	11	2.39

frequency stability. The compact 4 × 1-array design further optimizes the trade-off between size and performance, making it an efficient and practical solution for modern GPS systems. This work offers a well-balanced design that excels in critical metrics, positioning it as a competitive option for high-performance GPS antenna applications.

8 Conclusion

This study successfully demonstrates the design and optimization of microstrip patch antennas tailored for GPS applications, focusing on circular polarization (CP), high gain, and narrowband performance. Through the analysis of different antenna configurations, including single patch, 2 × 1, and 4 × 1 arrays, it was observed that increasing the number of patches enhances both gain and directivity. Specifically, the 4 × 1 patch array achieved the highest gain of 11 dB, alongside satisfactory CP operation with an axial ratio of 2.39 dB, making it the most efficient design for GPS systems.

References

1. Balanis, C.A.: Antenna Theory: Analysis and Design. John Wiley & Sons
2. Saidulu, F.M., Lastname, F.M., Lastname, F.M.: Comparison Analysis of Rectangular and Circular Patch Microstrip Antennas with Dielectric Superstrates, Vol 2, No. 5. (2013)
3. Khouyaoui, I., Hamdaoui, M., Jaouad, F.: Development and Examination of a 2.4 GHz (2024)
4. Rectangular Patch Microstrip Antenna Incorporating Slot and Dielectric Superstrates. https://doi.org/10.1007/978-3-031-48573-2_41
5. Shavit, R.: Dielectric cover effect on Rectangular Microstrip Antennas array. IEEE Trans. Antennas propagat. **40**, 992–995 (1992)
6. Yadav, R.K., Yadava, R.L.: Performance Analysis of superstrate loaded patch antenna and Abstain from environmental Effects. Int. J. Eng. Sci. Tech. **3**(8), 6582–6591 (2011)
7. Yadav, R.K., Yadava, R.L.: Effect on performance characteristics of rectangular patch antenna with varying height of dielectric cover. Int. J. Power Cont. Sig. Comput. **1**(1), 55–59
8. Bahl, I.J., Bhartia, P., Stuchly, S.: Design of microstrip antennas covered with a dielectric layer. IEEE Trans. Antennas Propogat. **30**, 314–318 (1982)
9. Bahl, I.J., Stuchly, S.S.: Analysis of a microstrip covered with a lossy dielectric. IEEE Trans. Microwave Theory Tech. **28**, 104–109 (1980)
10. Alexopoulos, N.G., Jackson, D.R.: Fundamental superstrate (cover) effects on printed antennas. IEEE Trans. Antennas Propagat **32**, 807–816
11. Khouyaoui, I., Jaouad, F., Hamdaoui, M.: Analyzing the influence of a superstrate and slot on a circular patch antenna operating at 2.4 GHz resonance frequency. E3S Web of Conferences **469** (2023). https://doi.org/10.1051/e3sconf/202346900077
12. Mohamed, M.L., et al.: Design and optimization of a high-performance circularly polarized microstrip patch antenna array for 24 GHz applications 1–5 (2024). https://doi.org/10.1109/ICCIMS61672.2024.10690286
13. Ibrahim, R., Yagoub, M., Habash, R.: Microstrip patch antenna for RFID applications. Candian Conf. Electr. Comput. Eng. (2009). https://doi.org/10.1109/ccece.2009.5090266
14. Nel, B., Skrivervik, A., Gustafsson, M.: Q-factor bounds for microstrip patch antennas. IEEE Trans. Antennas Propag. (2023). https://doi.org/10.1109/TAP.2023.3243726
15. Thaher, R.H., Abduljabbar, A.S., Hefdhi, M.M., Ahmed, O.F., Hazem, S.: A new microstrip patch antennas design for GPS applications. 2022 International Congress on Human-Computer Interaction, Optimization and Robotic Applications (HORA), pp. 1–6. Ankara, Turkey (2022). https://doi.org/10.1109/HORA55278.2022.9799990
16. Alblooshi, A.A., Yousaf, J.: Design of 2×2 MIMO Antenna for Sub-5G IoT Applications. 2022 10th International Conference on Emerging Trends in Engineering and Technology - Signal and Information Processing (ICETET-SIP-22), pp. 1–5 (2022)
17. El Kilani, S., et al.: A compact dual band PIFA antenna for GPS and ISM BAND applications. **14**(3), 1266–1271 (2019)
18. Bao, X., Ruvio, G., Ammann, M., John, M.J.I.A., Letters, W.P.: A novel GPS patch antenna on a fractal hi-impedance surface substrate. **5**, 323–326 (2006)
19. Sim, C., Yang, B.J.J.o.E.W., Applications: A single layer dual band CP microstrip antenna for GPS and DSRC applications. **22**(4), 529–539 (2008)
20. Tu, Z.-H., Chu, Q.-X.: Compact circular polarized antenna for GPS and CNSS applications. In: 2010 Asia-Pacific Microwave Conference, pp. 622–625. IEEE (2010)
21. Yang, L., Xu, L.-J., Bo, Y.-M., Zhang, M.: A single-feed dual-band circularly polarized microstrip antenna with spiral slots. In: 2017 International Applied Computational Electromagnetics Society Symposium (ACES), pp. 1–2, IEEE (2017)
22. Ali, J.K.J.E., Journal, T.: A new compact size microstrip patch antenna with irregular slots for handheld GPS application. **26**(10), 1241–1246 (2008)

Technological Innovation in the Hospital Supply Chain

Nada El Aouane[1(✉)], Abdenabi Sbai[2], Mariame Ababou[1,3], and Sara Rabiai[4]

[1] Research Laboratory in Entrepreneurship and Management of Organizations (REMO), Fez Business School, Private University of Fez, Fez, Morocco
nadaelaouane98@gmail.com, ABABOU@upf.ac.ma

[2] Interdisciplinary Research Laboratory in Economics, Finance and Management of Organizations (LIREFIMO), Faculty of Legal, Economic and Social Sciences, Fez, Morocco
abdenabi.sbai@usmba.ac.ma

[3] Higher School of Technology, Nador (ESTN), University Mohammed I, Oujda, Morocco

[4] Higher School of Technology, Dakhla (ESTD), Ibn Zohr University, Agadir, Morocco
s.rabiai@uiz.ac.ma

Abstract. An optimized supply chain is key to improving the quality of healthcare and addressing today's challenges. This transformation aims to enhance hospital processes, manage supply chain flows, improve performance and transparency, and integrate technological innovations. The research focuses on the necessity to optimize strategic, tactical, and operational decisions in the hospital supply chain.

The methodology is based on a systematic review of relevant academic publications, selected using specific criteria from the Scopus database, which included 90 articles. The articles and period of analysis include 13 articles from the years 2016 to 2024. This article examines how technological innovation can optimize the hospital supply chain and to answer this question, an in-depth literature review was undertaken, examining current practices in hospital management. The authors identify technologies such as blockchain, artificial intelligence, and the Internet of Things, which help streamline processes, control products in real-time, improve traceability, and enhance data security, to identify promising trends and innovations. The results show the effectiveness of these technologies in overcoming challenges such as IoT via sensors and monitoring systems to track inventory in real time and quickly detect anomalies, as well as blockchain for traceability and anti-counterfeiting, and AI combined with big data to improve demand forecasting and inventory optimization. This study highlights how the integration of these technologies promotes more transparent and agile logistics management.

Keywords: Hospital supply chain · Smart logistics · Optimization

1 Introduction

Technological innovation in the hospital supply chain has become a major concern in the healthcare sector [1]. According to the World Health Organization (WHO), the overriding goals of healthcare professionals are to increase efficiency, reduce costs and ensure

I. Aboudrar et al. (Eds.): ICESST 2024, SUCI, pp. 539–551, 2025.
https://doi.org/10.1007/978-3-031-86705-7_51

patient safety. According to [2–5], supply chain management in hospital environments is complex and requires an in-depth understanding. Understanding the peculiarities of hospital supply chain management versus manufacturing supply chain management is essential for effective management. Information and communication technologies, such as the Internet of Things (IoT), blockchain, artificial intelligence (AI), data analytics, innovation management, and supply chain resilience, have the potential to improve supply chain management in healthcare facilities [6]. The use of these innovative technologies has opened up new perspectives in hospital supply chain optimization, offering an opportunity to move from manual to automated and integrated management systems [4].

The systematic review presented here aims to bring together and analyze the work done to date on this subject. In an industry where speed and efficiency can have a direct impact on results, it is increasingly important to understand how supply chain optimization can improve efficiency and performance through the involvement of technologies [7].

The articles analyzed, including [8] highlight several key hospital supply chain management challenges. These challenges include managing unforeseen risks, as highlighted by [5], the complexity of supply chain networks described by [9], the need for close integration among the various players in the supply chain, and the importance of sustainability highlighted by [8].

In the face of these challenges, the articles also identify various opportunities for improving supply chain management in hospitals. According to Saha and Rathore, these opportunities include the use of innovative technologies such as artificial intelligence and blockchain, as examined in the study, the adoption of advanced management methods such as multi-objective optimization and big data analytics described [10], as well as the implementation of sustainable initiatives to reduce the environmental impact of the supply chain proposed by [8]. The aim of this systematic review is therefore to distill the research around these issues and propose a framework for future innovations in hospital supply chains.

In addition, digitizing the supply chain offers a significant opportunity for expansion that delivers economic benefits and improves infrastructure while remaining affordable. Careful consideration of the criteria for adopting these digitized logistics practices is essential to reconcile technological advances with the specific needs of healthcare systems in these regions [11].

However, to establish an optimized supply chain, it is essential to carry out a thorough analysis of each stage and implement a holistic approach to maximize potential benefits [8].

The review will also highlight organizational challenges, such as resistance to change, and the integration of information technologies in complex environments. The aim is to provide a comprehensive overview of the current situation by examining existing work. The review seeks to establish a link between theory and practice to recommend applicable and measurable optimization measures.

2 Framework

At the heart of the healthcare sector's concerns, continuous improvement of the hospital supply chain inevitably involves innovation and operations optimization [12]. Historically, logistics in the healthcare sector have evolved according to needs and crises. The major milestones in the development of transport and logistics, established since ancient times with the Phoenicians, laid the foundations for modern information systems. Today, this system is crucial to managing shipments and hospital inventories. The integration of advanced digital and data analysis tools, such as the Highly Orchestrated Supply Network introduced by Pfizer, exemplifies this heritage and represents the future of healthcare logistics. It has transformed the global supply chain into an interconnected system that provides complete visibility of product status, contributing to more efficient management of the procurement process [13].

Today, the importance of innovation to improve the management of material and information flows in healthcare is recognized [1]. It offers healthcare facilities the opportunity to increase their operational efficiency [14], reduce costs, and, ultimately, deliver higher-quality patient care [15]. Advances in new technologies and innovative management methods are key factors in meeting the specific challenges facing the hospital supply chain [16].

The Objective of Operations Optimization

Improving logistics processes in healthcare aims to increase the efficiency, quality, and profitability of operations [17]. Key objectives of this improvement include reducing waiting times, optimizing inventory management, reducing delivery errors, and improving product tracking [18]. By streamlining these activities, medical facilities can improve patient outcomes [19], reduce costs, and deliver a more satisfying patient experience [20].

The Importance of Innovation in the Hospital Supply Chain

Innovation is truly essential in the hospital supply chain, as it improves the management of material and information flows, which has a positive impact on the efficiency of healthcare facilities [21]. Thanks to innovation, hospitals can reduce expenses, optimize operations, and deliver superior patient care [22]. New technologies and innovative management approaches are the main drivers of this evolution in hospital supply chains [21].

Overview of Current Challenges

Hospital logistics currently face several challenges, including the management of material and information flows [23], complex inventories of pharmaceutical products and medical devices, product traceability to guarantee quality and safety [24], coordination of deliveries with external suppliers, lack of transparency and accountability [25], as well as effective communication between the various players in the supply chain [26].

The advancement of digital technology offers unprecedented opportunities to automate processes, facilitate real-time decision-making, and improve the traceability of drugs and equipment [27].

Health technology assessment (HTA) is defined as a tool for evaluating the potential benefits and risks of investment and disinvestment in healthcare technologies in hospitals about safety, accuracy, effectiveness, cost-effectiveness, equity, ethics and culture, and the environment [28].

Identifying these challenges is crucial to improving operations and ensuring the efficiency and reliability of hospital logistics [29].

3 Methodology

In this section, we examine in detail the methodological elements for the development of this work, and before going into these details, it is necessary to define what a systematic review is.

A systematic review is an examination of a formulated question that uses systematic and reproducible methods to identify, select, synthesize, and evaluate all relevant research that meets pre-established eligibility criteria for a specific research question, and to collect and analyze data from the studies included in the synthesis [30].

The potential theme was selected using the relevant Scopus database, one of the most important interdisciplinary databases in the peer-review of documents in the field of hospital management [31]. This research has enabled us to identify opportunities and suggest ways of fostering innovation and optimization in hospital supply chain operations, as well as the drivers that have been suggested for integrating aspects of innovation and optimization into hospital practices, thereby meeting the current demands of hospital services [32], indicating that solutions need to be implemented to improve hospitals.

Content analysis is a qualitative approach that can be defined as a research method aiming to interpret the content of textual data using a systematic classification process. Furthermore, it involves systematic reading that enables reproducible and valid conclusions to be drawn from texts [33].

While content analysis encompasses both quantitative and qualitative research methods, the results provided by quantitative analysis are presented frequently. In contrast, qualitative analysis is presented in categories, allowing the text to be interpreted [34].

The preparation phase involves collecting the right data and interpreting it [35].

A total of 90 articles are in the Scopus database, therefore the articles and period of analysis include 13 articles between the years 2016 and 2024, other years and other articles have been excluded and include only documents written in English.

To limit the documents to be analyzed and to identify the most relevant articles, the following criteria were used in the search:

(TITLE-ABS-KEY ("Optimization" OR "Optimizing" OR "Operations") AND TITLE-ABS-KEY (hospital OR healthcare) AND TITLE-ABS-KEY ("Supply chain" OR "Supply chain" OR "supply-chain") AND TITLE-ABS-KEY (innovation)) AND (LIMIT-TO (LANGUAGE, "English")).

4 Result and Discussion

Hospital supply chain management plays a crucial role that must not be neglected if hospitals are to improve their economic and organizational performance [36].

The table below gives a complete overview of 13 articles analyzed, including subjects, authors, year of publication, journal, research objectives, methodology used, and results (Table 1):

Table 1. Methodological characteristics of the literature analyzed (created by the authors)

Article	Author	Journal	Objective	Methodology	Result
INTEGRATION OF IOT-ENABLED TECHNOLOGIES AND ARTIFICIAL INTELLIGENCE IN DIVERSE DOMAINS: RECENT ADVANCEMENTS AND FUTURE TRENDS	Gouiza, Nissrine et al. 2024	Journal of Theoretical and Applied Information Technology	-Explore the benefits of IoT and AI in different sectors. -Identify the most popular application areas for IoT - Examine beneficial technologies for optimizing operations	-Bibliometric study on IoT from 2018 to 2023	-Improving operational efficiency, decision-making, and creating interconnected environments through IoT and AI -Popular IoT application areas: healthcare, industry, smart cities, agriculture, smart homes, transportation -beneficial technologies: those that optimize operations, improve efficiency and reduce costs
Artificial Intelligence Applications for Responsive Healthcare Supply Chains: A Decision-Making Framework	Virmani, Naveen et al. 2024	IEEE Transactions on Engineering Management	-Identify the factors driving AI adoption in the healthcare supply chain - Assess an organization's readiness to adopt AI	-Fuzzy Delphi and fuzzy DEMATEL techniques to identify and prioritize factors favoring AI. - Graph theory matrix to assess AI readiness	- Competitive and governmental pressures are the most influential factors - Information scalability and traceability are most influenced by other factors - Sensitivity analysis confirms the reliability of the results
The impact of healthcare 4.0 technologies on healthcare supply chain performance: Extending the organizational information processing theory	Saha, Esha et al. 2024	Technological Forecasting and Social Change	Analyze the impact of Organizational Information Processing Theory (OIPT) on healthcare 4.0 technologies - Assess the impact of healthcare 4.0 technologies on hospital supply chain performance	-Survey of 255 hospital managers in India	-Data analysis reveals that big Data, artificial intelligence, and blockchain improve hospital supply chain operations, innovation, and risk management, resulting in better performance -Supply chain operations and innovations play a partially mediating role -The interaction between technologies and operations is moderated by the type of facility (public/private)

(*continued*)

Table 1. *(continued)*

Article	Author	Journal	Objective	Methodology	Result
Big data analytics capability in healthcare operations and supply chain management: the role of green process innovation	Benzidia, Smail et al. 2024	Annals of Operations Research	-Investigate the role of Big Data analytics on green process integration and innovation in healthcare operations and supply chain management (OSCM) - Assess the impact on environmental performance	-Literature review and empirical justification of the relationship	Big Data analysis positively influences the integration of green processes and innovation, improving environmental performance - Innovation plays a mediating role - Provides valuable information for managers and stakeholders
A literature review of perishable medical resource management	Zhang, Chao et al. 2023	Frontiers of Engineering Management	- Identify key issues and methodologies for managing perishable medical resources - Explore promising areas of research	-Literature review (93 publications from 1990 to 2022)	-Categorization of literature into strategic, tactical, and operational levels - Identification of key problem attributes and methodologies -Potential research areas: service innovation, decision analysis, supply chain resilience
Systematic review: disruptive innovation in non-branded retail markets	Mookerjee, Joydeep et al. 2023	International Journal of Systematic Innovation	To study the impact of COVID-19 on the purchasing behavior and participation of unbranded stores in the local market - Identify innovative post-pandemic strategies of non-branded stores	-Systematic literature review	- Covid-19 disrupted supply chains and the participation of unbranded stores -Consumers have turned to health products and unbranded local items -Stores must monitor their liquidity and adapt to an unstable market -Addressing sustainability and ethical concerns is an opportunity

(continued)

Table 1. (*continued*)

Article	Author	Journal	Objective	Methodology	Result
Opinions Related to the Potential Application of Artificial Intelligence (AI) by the Responsible in Charge of the Administrative Management Related to the Logistics and Supply Chain of Medical Stock in Health Centers in North of Chile	Bas, Tomas Gabriel et al. 2023	International Journal of Environmental Research and Public Health	- Assess managers' views on the potential of AI to reduce human error in medical inventory management	-Survey of medical inventory personnel	-Major shortcomings were identified in manual inventory management −64.7% of those surveyed thought that AI would not help reduce human error
Differences in manufacturing and healthcare supply chain management: an overview	Ashtab, Sahand et al. 2023	International Journal of Healthcare Technology and Management	- Identify the structural characteristics that differentiate the manufacturing supply chain from the healthcare supply chain - Provide guidelines for improving healthcare supply chain management	-Systematic literature review	-The healthcare supply chain is characterized by its network structure, objectives, product complexity, critical transport, and doctor-hospital-supplier dynamics - A better understanding of these differences can improve healthcare supply chain management
Securing Internet of Things devices by enabling Ethereum blockchain using smart contracts	Patruni, Muralidhara Rao et al. 2022	Building Services Engineering Research and Technology	-Propose a method for securing IoT devices using the Ethereum blockchain and smart contracts	-Systematic implementation of IoT device security	-The information collected is stored securely in the blockchain after successful authentication -Blockchain can transform supply chain management by eliminating intermediaries and improving security
Optimizing the complexities of unforeseen risk in healthcare with innovation and technology: a proposed framework	Khan, Asfandyar et al. 2022	Journal of Hospital Management and Health Policy	- Manage unforeseen risks in the healthcare sector - Improve the supply chain for healthcare workers - Create reusable modular facilities	- A three-part framework proposed: health monitoring, personnel, and modular facilities	- The framework aims to balance the day-to-day operations of the healthcare sector in the "new normal"

(*continued*)

Table 1. (*continued*)

Article	Author	Journal	Objective	Methodology	Result
Innovating the supply chain in health-related crises: some evidence from the ISINNOVA case	Tani, Mario et al. 2022	European Journal of Innovation Management	-Identify the opportunities and challenges of implementing 3D printing technology in hospital supply chain management	- Case study	- 3D printing can increase hospitals' flexibility in the face of crises - Use of the Internet can spread benefits more quickly - Requires buy-in from all relevant stakeholders
Multi-criteria supplier selection decisions in supply chain networks: A multi-objective optimization approach	Sajedinejad, Arman et al. 2018	Industrial Engineering and Management Systems	- Propose a multi-criteria approach to supplier selection in a multi-product network	- Seven quality domains are identified for supplier selection - The fuzzy AHP algorithm is used to rank the products of each supplier - A multi-objective mathematical programming model is designed - A genetic algorithm is presented to find an acceptable solution	- The article presents an example to illustrate the proposed algorithm
Healthcare supply chain management; strategic areas for quality and financial improvement	Kwon, Ik-Whan G. et al. 2016	Technological Forecasting and Social Change	- Improve the efficiency of the healthcare supply chain to reduce costs per patient discharge - Improve the quality of care to reduce readmission rates	- Literature review	- Identify supply chain fundamentals to create a "community supply chain surplus" - Explore three strategic areas for maximizing revenue for healthcare providers

According to [10] several technologies can contribute to the innovation and optimization of the hospital supply chain such as Artificial Intelligence and Machine Learning technology that can be used for task automation, process improvement, and also demand prediction, Blockchain technology, often used to improve product security, traceability and transparency, and Internet of Things (IoT) technology for real-time data collection on product flows and asset status, simulation and modeling for testing and optimization of different supply chain scenarios. The effective use of healthcare 4.0 technologies to improve supply chain processes and performance in terms of value costs and responsiveness, using techniques such as Fuzzy Delphi and Fuzzy Dematel to identify and prioritize factors favoring IA [4, 37]. It is important to deploy the various promising technological and organizational levers coherently and structured to maximize their benefits.

There are several services in the hospital environment, which cause needs and to meet these specific needs according to [2] it is necessary to develop customized supply chain solutions, taking the example of the implementation of 3D printing technology to increase hospital flexibility [38] 3D printing will help to reduce lead times and logistics costs.

According to Benzidia, who stresses the importance of integrating sustainable practices into supply chain management [8] includes that hospitals can adopt sustainable practices such as using recyclable packaging materials, reducing energy consumption in transport and storage, and disposing of medical waste responsibly, while this reduces their environmental impact and contributes to a greener future. Through the use of Big Data, the processing of complex information improves supply chain management and also demand forecasting [8].

A closer look at the literature shows that the implementation of innovative technologies in the hospital sector plays a vital role in improving hospital efficiency, taking the example of RFID technology and IoT sensors that improve the visibility of pharmaceutical products, this application is demonstrated by the case of Rush University Medical Center in Chicago, which uses STANLEY Healthcare's RTLS real-time location system to track medical equipment. In the cold chain field, IoT monitoring systems facilitate early detection of temperature anomalies and prevent spoilage of sensitive products [39]. So for blockchain, healthcare institutions should adopt this technology to maintain a distributed and secure record of transactions in the supply chain, which enhances drug traceability, data security, and authentication of medical products, the fight against counterfeit drugs thanks to its immutable distributed record and the use of smart contracts on the blockchain platform that will help streamline payment and procurement processes through the automation of purchase orders, invoicing etc.…the decentralized and encrypted nature of blockchain enables critical patient records and lab results to be stored and shared [40–42]. As well as Industry 4.0 technology to automate inventory processes, optimize flows, and improve decision-making based on data [43].

It is essential to pay particular attention to change management and the adoption of these innovations by teams, by implementing strategies and processes that will foster acceptance and commitment to facilitate a successful transition to these new practices.

Finally, we need to establish a regulatory and standards framework for these new emerging technologies and methodologies, to ensure that they meet the safety and quality requirements specific to the hospital sector.

5 Conclusion

To summarize, this systematic literature review has highlighted several promising aspects even if their deployment is still limited, including the emphasis on the importance of supply chain management playing a key role in improving the efficiency of patient care in healthcare. It is emphasized that healthcare professionals should draw on and adopt supply chain principles, widely used in other sectors, to optimize healthcare supply chain operations, highlighting strategic areas such as supplier relationship management, logistics operational tools, and process improvement.

Not forgetting to examine the manifestation of new technologies that will be the revolutionary pillar for increasing hospital supply chain efficiency, such as blockchain to maintain a distributed and tamper-proof record of supply chain transactions, big data analytics to improve sustainable supply chain performance artificial intelligence etc… Furthermore, the results show that technologies can help hospitals to improve their supply chain performance and that new innovations and the optimization of supply chain operations play a partial intermediary role in the impact of healthcare technology 4. 0 on performance.

Finally, the article suggests that future empirical studies could highlight examples of healthcare organizations that have successfully implemented supply chain tools to improve and optimize their operations and also achieve higher levels of performance.

6 Authors' Disclosures of Potential Conflicts of Interest

The authors declare no conflict of interest related to this article.

References

1. Karaa, M., Bentahar, O., Benzidia, S.: Les facteurs d'adoption d'une innovation appliquée aux flux de patients : le cas d'un centre hospitalier au Luxembourg. Logistique Manag. **24**, 98–109 (2016)
2. Ashtab, S., Anderson, W.: Differences in manufacturing and healthcare supply chain management: an overview. Int. J. Healthc. Technol. Manag. **20**, 232–48 (2023)
3. Bas, T.G., Astudillo, P., Rojo, D., Trigo, A.: Opinions Related to the Potential Application of Artificial Intelligence (AI) by the Responsible in Charge of the Administrative Management Related to the Logistics and Supply Chain of Medical Stock in Health Centers in North of Chile. Int. J. Environ. Res. Public Health **20**, 4839 (2023)
4. Gouiza, N., Jebari, H., Reklaoui, K.: Integration of iot-enabled technologies and artificial intelligence in diverse domains: recent advancements and future trends. J. Theor. Appl. Inf. Technol. **102**, 1975–2029 (2024)
5. Khan, A., Farooq, A., Ahmad, S., Fraser, J.M.: Optimizing the complexities of unforeseen risk in healthcare with innovation and technology: a proposed framework. J. Hosp. Manag. Health Policy [Internet] 6 (2022). https://www.scopus.com/inward/record.uri?eid=2-s2.0-85127579603&doi=10.21037%2fJHMHP-21-3&partnerID=40&md5=3448f8da8c2d001dd948eec6ed21737e
6. Lharti, R., Lechhab, H., Charef, F., Khaldi, S.: L'innovation technologique comme source de la résilience et sortie de crises. Altern. Manag. Econ. **6**, 291–308 (2024)

7. Kenza, S., Said, R.: Optimization of the hospital logistics chain: the case of the surgery and oncology departments state of the art. 2017 4th Int. Conf. Control Decis. Inf. Technol. CoDIT [Internet]. [cited 2024 Apr 22], pp. 0132–7 (2017). https://ieeexplore.ieee.org/document/8102579
8. Benzidia, S., Bentahar, O., Husson, J., Makaoui, N.: Big data analytics capability in healthcare operations and supply chain management: the role of green process innovation. Ann. Oper. Res. **333**, 1077–101 (2024)
9. Sajedinejad, A., Chaharsooghi, S.K.: Multi-criteria supplier selection decisions in supply chain networks: a multi-objective optimization approach. Ind. Eng. Manag. Syst. **17**, 392–406 (2018)
10. Saha, E., Rathore, P.: The impact of healthcare 4.0 technologies on healthcare supply chain performance: Extending the organizational information processing theory. Technol. Forecast Soc. Change [Internet], 201 (2024). https://www.scopus.com/inward/record.uri?eid=2-s2.0-85184523140&doi=10.1016%2fj.techfore.2024.123256&partnerID=40&md5=a0f7711ad6b17d8a675b29e0a5913ae9
11. Tadesse, M.D., Gebresenbet, G., Tavasszy, L., Ljungberg, D.: Assessment of digitalized logistics for implementation in low-income countries. Future Transp. **1**, 227–47 (2021)
12. Ajmi, I.: Outils et modèles collaboratifs pour la gestion des tensions dans les services des urgences pédiatriques [Internet] [phdthesis]. Ecole Centrale de Lille (2015). cited 1 May 2024. https://theses.hal.science/tel-01277772
13. Pfizer: Transforming Delivery of High Quality Products [Internet]. Pfizer Annu. Rev. (2016). cited 3 May 2024. https://www.pfizer.com/files/investors/financial_reports/annual_reports/2016/transforming-delivery-of-high-quality-products/index.html
14. Courbet, D., Fourquet-Courbet, M.-P., Bernard, F., Joule, R.-V.: Communication persuasive et communication engageante pour la santé Favoriser des comportements sains avec les medias. Internet et les serious games (2013)
15. Detève, L., Courtejoie, N., Pollak, C.: Vers une prise en compte des inégalités sociales dans les modèles de dépenses de santé. Rev. Fr. Aff. Soc. 257–76 (2022)
16. Berete, F.: Santé globale: les défis à surmonter par la communauté internationale dans le post-OMD. 1–174 (2015)
17. Zouari, A., Lehyani, F.: Etude de l'impact de la gestion des connaissances sur la performance de la chaine logistique (2015)
18. Jarroudi, I.: Planification et optimisation de la logistique de la construction dans les zones urbaines [Internet] [masters]. École de technologie supérieure (2020). cited 1 May 2024. https://espace.etsmtl.ca/id/eprint/2642/
19. Butler, T.W., Leong, G.K., Everett, L.N.: The operations management role in hospital strategic planning. J. Oper. Manag. **14**, 137–56 (1996)
20. Babei, J., Paché, G.: Engagement de la direction générale et climat de travail: quelle maîtrise des accidents en rétro-logistique hospitalière ? Rev. Fr. Gest Ind. **35**, 7–23 (2021)
21. Milou, K., Touate, S., Felouati, M.: Analyse thèorique de l'impact de l'adoption du système d'information hospitalier (SIH) sur la performance de la chaîne logistique hospitalière en période de crise sanitaire covid 19. Rev. Fr. Econ Gest [Internet] (2023). cited 29 Apr 2024 https://www.revuefreg.fr/index.php/home/article/view/1264
22. Ajmi, F.: Méthodes d'ordonnancement et d'orchestration dynamique des tâches de soins pour optimiser la prise en charge des patients dans les urgences hospitalières [Internet] [These de doctorat]. Ecole centrale de Lille (2019). cited 1 May 2024. https://theses.fr/2019ECLI0009
23. Taieb, N.H., Affes, H.: Approaches to improve the performance of the collaborative supply chain management: Literature review. 2013 Int. Conf. Adv. Logist Transp. [Internet], p. 440–5 (2013). cited 3 May 2024. https://ieeexplore.ieee.org/document/6568499

24. Uthayakumar, R., Priyan, S.: Pharmaceutical supply chain and inventory management strategies: Optimization for a pharmaceutical company and a hospital. Oper. Res. Health Care. **2**, 52–64 (2013)
25. Mario Jackson, A.: Historical perspectives on the state of health and health systems in Africa. Volume II [Internet] (2017). cited 3 May 2024. https://doi.org/10.1007/978-3-319-32564-4
26. Chtioui, A., Bouhaddou, I., Chaouni Benabdellah, A., Benghabrit, A.: Complexite de la chaine logistique hospitaliere et du covid-19: vers une modelisation multi-agents. 13ème Conf Int Model Optim Simul MOSIM2020 12-14 Nov 2020 AGADIR Maroc [Internet]. AGADIR (virtual), Morocco (2020). cited 2 May 2024. https://hal.science/hal-03192788
27. Ruel, S., Chaze-Magnan, L., Pichault, F.: Management des ressources humaines pour la logistique et le Supply Chain Management: un éditorial engagé. Logistique Manag. **29**, 69–72 (2021)
28. Guerra-Júnior, A.A., de Lemos, L.L.P., Godman, B., Bennie, M., Osorio-de-Castro, C.G.S., Alvares, J., et al.: Health technology performance assessment: real-world evidence for public healthcare sustainability. Int. J. Technol. Assess. Health Care **33**, 279–87 (2017)
29. Kharouaa, S., Moussaid, H., Dinar, B.: Performance de la logistique hospitalière et la crise du Coronavirus: Cas du CHU Marrakech. Rev. Int. Sci. Gest [Internet], 4 (2021). cited 2 May 2024. https://revue-isg.com/index.php/home/article/view/702
30. Nambiema, A., Fouquet, J., Guilloteau, J., Descatha, A.: La revue systématique et autres types de revue de la littérature : qu'est-ce que c'est, quand, comment, pourquoi ? Arch. Mal. Prof. Environ. **82**, 539–52 (2021)
31. Oranci, A., Siourakan-Badalou, M.: Interventions infirmières non pharmacologiques dans la gestion des douleurs auprès des personnes atteintes de fibromyalgie (2018). cited 4 May 2024. https://folia.unifr.ch/global/documents/315460
32. Lennox, L., Linwood-Amor, A., Maher, L., Reed, J.: Making change last? exploring the value of sustainability approaches in healthcare: a scoping review. Health Res. Policy Syst. **18**, 120 (2020)
33. Krippendorff, K.: Content analysis: an introduction to its methodology [Internet]. Sage Publications (2018). cited 4 May 2024. https://scholar.google.com/scholar?cluster=14745321713092000765&hl=en&oi=scholarr
34. Bengtsson, M.: How to plan and perform a qualitative study using content analysis. NursingPlus Open. **2**, 8–14 (2016)
35. Elo, S., Kääriäinen, M., Kanste, O., Pölkki, T., Utriainen, K., Kyngäs, H.: Qualitative content analysis: a focus on trustworthiness. SAGE Open **4**, 2158244014522633 (2014)
36. Singh, A.: Le rôle crucial de la gestion de la chaîne d'approvisionnement dans les soins de santé [Internet]. Cynoteck. cited 5 May 2024. https://cynoteck.com/fr/blog-post/supply-chain-management-in-healthcare/
37. Virmani, N., Singh, R.K., Agarwal, V., Aktas, E.: Artificial intelligence applications for responsive healthcare supply chains: a decision-making framework. IEEE Trans. Eng. Manag. 1–41 (2024)
38. Tani, M., Troise, C., De Bernardi, P., Han, T.: Innovating the supply chain in health-related crises: some evidence from ISINNOVA case. Eur. J. Innov. Manag. **25**, 716–34 (2022)
39. Pajić, V., Andrejić, M., Chatterjee, P.: Enhancing Cold Chain Logistics: A Framework for Advanced Temperature Monitoring in Transportation and. **3**, 16–30 (2024)
40. Agbo, C.C., Mahmoud, Q.H., Eklund, J.M.: Blockchain technology in healthcare: a systematic review. Healthcare. **7**, 56 (2019)
41. Queiroz, M.M., Fosso, W.S.: Blockchain adoption challenges in supply chain: an empirical investigation of the main drivers in India and the USA. Int. J. Inf. Manag. **46**, 70–82 (2019)
42. Wang, Y., Han, J.H., Beynon-Davies, P.: Understanding blockchain technology for future supply chains: a systematic literature review and research agenda. Supply Chain Manag. Int. J. 24 (2018)

43. Paul, S., et al.: Industry 4.0 Applications for Medical/Healthcare Services. J. Sens. Actuator Netw. **10**, 43 (2021)

Environmental AI for Resilient and Sustainable Urban Infrastructures: Rethinking Smart City Transformation

Nahid Zehouani[1(✉)], Mariame Ababou[1,2], Sanae Faquir[3], and Sara Rabiai[4]

[1] Laboratory of Research in Entrepreneurship and Management of Organizations (REMO), Fez Business School, Private University of Fez, Fez, Morocco
nahid.zehouani@gmail.com, ABABOU@upf.ac.ma
[2] Nador (ESTN), Higher School of Technology, University Mohammed I, Oujda, Morocco
[3] Laboratory of Smart Systems, Energy and Sustainable Development (SIEDD), Faculty of Engineering Sciences, Private University of Fez, Fez, Morocco
faquir@upf.ac.ma
[4] Dakhla (ESTD), Higher School of Technology, Ibn Zohr University, Agadir, Morocco
s.rabiai@uiz.ac.ma

Abstract. Artificial intelligence (AI) is increasingly recognized as a transformative tool within environmental and urban infrastructures, promising smart, sustainable, and optimized solutions. However, numerous AI applications face obstacles in achieving these ambitious goals due to technological determinism and fragmented, efficiency-focused approaches that often overlook environmental and societal complexities. As AI and smart infrastructure play pivotal roles in advancing sustainable urban development, there is an urgent need for an integrated approach that prioritizes environmental impact, resilience, and inclusivity. This perspective paper, drawing on the authors' viewpoints and interpretations, explores the "environmental AI" concept as an enabler of sustainable infrastructure transformation, advocating for a shift from narrow, technocentric solutions to a framework grounded in ecological and social responsibility. The methodological approach involves a systematic review of over 150 articles sourced from databases such as Scopus, Google Scholar, and Web of Science, synthesizing insights from academic research, industry reports, and case studies to identify key gaps and trends in AI applications related to urban planning and sustainability. This comprehensive review is complemented by qualitative assessments of real-world examples illustrating successful Green AI implementations. The paper aims to guide policymakers and planners in adopting AI systems that address efficiency, sustainability, and equity issues in cities.

Keywords: artificial intelligence (AI) · environmental AI · smart infrastructure · sustainable AI · resilient cities · AI in urban planning · ethical AI · green infrastructure · sustainable development goals

I. Aboudrar et al. (Eds.): ICESST 2024, SUCI, pp. 552–562, 2025.
https://doi.org/10.1007/978-3-031-86705-7_52

1 Introduction

An innovation culture that was nurtured by the second digital and fourth industrial revolutions allowed for the development of many technological innovations and breakthroughs [1]. For instance, the field of artificial intelligence (AI) defined as algorithms that mimic human cognitive functions to make unsupervised decisions [2] has experienced remarkable exponential growth over the last few decades [3]. AI is unquestionably a revolutionary, trend-setting technology today, with innumerable applications and even more opportunities in every business and area of life, from engineering to finance, health to agriculture, gaming to transportation, and beyond [4]. Additionally, AI has become one of the key drivers of the global smart city movement [5].

Smart cities are widely viewed as locations where digital technology and data are applied to drive efficiencies for economic growth, quality of life, and sustainability [6]. In many urban policy circles today, AI has become a central topic, especially among policymakers and planners who are looking for technocentric solutions to pressing urbanization challenges [7]. Quality of life, climate change, safety, mobility, and accessibility are just a few of the complicated urban issues for which technocentric solutions are becoming increasingly popular [8]. Effective use of big data, AI-powered smart urban technologies, and platforms is anticipated to improve urban infrastructure and service efficiency and to address or at least alleviate these challenges significantly [8, 9].

As noted by Wang and Cao [10], technological advancements have enabled the collection of "big data" through citywide smart sensors, accessible via public and private channels. Recent developments in AI and ubiquitous computing allow these data to enhance environmental sustainability, urban operations, and quality of life [11]. Applications include automated urban decision-making [12], infrastructure health monitoring [13, 14], and autonomous post-disaster assessments [15]. However, despite the widespread adoption of AI in public sectors, many initiatives struggle to deliver ethical, responsible, and sustainable outcomes [16].

The failure of projects like Toronto Sidewalk, Masdar, and Songdo highlights the limitations of existing AI practices, which are often reductionist and technologically deterministic, lacking foresight for long-term, inclusive solutions [3, 12]. This perspective paper draws attention to these flaws and proposes a shift toward "Environmental AI" with green sensing a framework emphasizing long-term, responsible AI practices. Through a systematic review of over 150 scholarly articles from databases such as Scopus, Google Scholar, and Web of Science, the paper synthesizes insights and identifies practical examples of Green AI implementation. This paper seeks to guide policymakers and urban planners by providing actionable insights and recommendations to promote sustainable and resilient urban development.

2 Challenges and Issues in Integrating AI into Smart Urban Infrastructures

Although artificial intelligence (AI) holds great promise for improving urban infrastructure, integrating AI technology into city planning and management presents several difficult obstacles. To guarantee appropriate and sustainable AI deployment in urban settings, these issues which include ethical, technological, environmental, and resilience concerns need all-encompassing answers.

2.1 Ethical and Social Concerns in AI-Driven Smart Infrastructures

The increasing use of AI in urban infrastructure raises crucial ethical and social questions. The primary concerns include:

- Privacy and Data Security: Sensitive personal data is frequently collected as part of the vast data collection process for AI applications. Smart city technologies run the potential of infringing citizens' rights and supporting surveillance-based behaviors in the absence of strict data governance and privacy safeguards [17].
- Social Equity and Inclusivity: Smart city technology may inadvertently exacerbate social disparities. When AI initiatives focus on high-income areas or neglect marginalized communities, they can deepen inequality rather than promote inclusive growth [18]. Addressing these concerns requires prioritizing accessibility and equality in AI-enabled urban policies.

2.2 Technological and Technical Barriers

Technological and technical challenges also pose barriers to the effective implementation of AI in urban infrastructures:

- Fragmentation and Interoperability: Urban AI applications rely on a variety of technologies, including IoT sensors, cloud computing, and diverse AI algorithms, all of which must work cohesively. The lack of standardization across devices and platforms can hinder integration, limiting the overall effectiveness of AI systems [19].
- Financial constraints and maintenance: AI-based infrastructures need regular software upgrades, maintenance, and occasionally expensive replacements. It may be challenging for municipalities, particularly smaller ones, to sustain these programs over the long run due to budgetary constraints [15].

2.3 Environmental Impact and Sustainability Concerns

The environmental implications of AI-powered smart city infrastructure highlight the need for sustainable practices:

- Energy Consumption and Carbon Footprint: AI systems, particularly those relying on high-performance computing for large datasets, consume significant energy, which can contribute to carbon emissions. Developing energy-efficient algorithms is essential to minimize AI's environmental impact (OECD, 2020).
- Electronic Waste (E-Waste): As AI technology evolves, outdated devices quickly become obsolete, creating electronic waste that poses pollution and landfill issues. Sustainable disposal and recycling practices are crucial for mitigating e-waste problems [20].

2.4 Resilience Challenges: Crises, Cybersecurity, and System Vulnerabilities

Building resilience into AI-based urban infrastructures is essential to handle crises and cyber threats:

- Adaptability in Crisis Situations: The capacity of AI systems to respond flexibly to crises like natural disasters or pandemics is critical. Rigid systems can hamper emergency responses if they cannot adapt to rapidly changing conditions [21].
- Cybersecurity Vulnerabilities: As interconnected systems, smart cities are susceptible to cyberattacks, which could compromise essential services like power grids and emergency operations. Implementing robust cybersecurity measures is vital to protect public safety and maintain trust in smart technologies [22].

The following Table 1 presents a comparative analysis of how different smart city projects have implemented AI to enhance resilience and sustainability, showcasing the benefits and challenges faced.

Table 1. Table: Comparative Analysis of Smart City Initiatives

City	AI Approach	Energy Savings (%)	Sustainability Impact	Key Challenges
Amsterdam	Green AI (Smart Grid)	20%	Significant reduction in carbon emissions	High initial investment
Singapore	AI-Driven Water Management	15%	Improved resource conservation	Data integration complexities
Toronto (Sidewalk)	Conventional AI	Minimal	Limited sustainability outcomes	Privacy concerns and project delays

3 The Green AI Strategy For The Planet's And Humanity's Welfare

Since the industrial revolution of 1850, and especially in the last 50 years, the environment has been affected by the consequences of human activity, including consumerism, urbanization, industry, and an unsustainable and quickly expanding population [23, 24]. The following are the most devastating threats that humanity is now facing, according to Hunter and Hewson.:

Chemical contamination of the earth's ecosystem, encompassing the oceans and atmosphere.

Ecosystem collapse and biodiversity loss.

A reduction of natural resources, especially water.

Global warming and human-induced climate change.
Human population growth beyond the Earth's carrying capacity.
National and global failures to understand and act preventatively on these risks.
Among other weapons of mass destruction, nuclear weapons.
The spread of novel, incurable illnesses.
Food instability is on the rise, and nutritional quality is declining.
The introduction of strong, unmanageable new technology.

"National and global failure to understand and act pre-tentatively on these risks" is the most significant of these threats. This demonstrates the governments' incapacity. [25] and the public to recognize and respond to the dangers that are most likely to result in a disaster or will undoubtedly do so.

Gupta et al. [26] Gupta et al.'s study explores how AI can accelerate the achievement of the Sustainable Development Goals (SDGs). They argue that AI can intelligently direct interventions, reduce waste, create new applications, and improve connectivity and cost reduction, benefiting many people worldwide.

Likewise, Goranski and Tan [27] It examined how AI can hasten the SDGs' accomplishment. According to their study, "AI can generate data that will allow interventions to be directed more intelligently, reduce waste and losses in production and consumption, create new applications that will transform entire industries and professions, and achieve the necessary improvements in connectivity and cost reduction that will enable many people around the world to benefit from the rapid pace of technological development." if, as Dwivedi et al. contend, AI offers a chance to accomplish the SDGs. [28], To achieve governance, standards, and security, an AI-supported SDG implementation will "require significant investment from governments and industry together with collaboration at an international level." The 17 SDGs are depicted in Fig. 1.

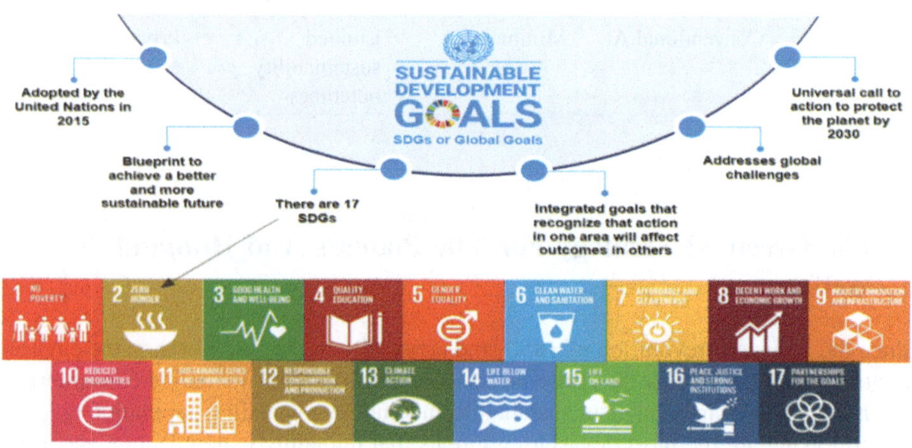

Fig. 1. Summary of the Sustainable Development Goals.

The research cited above discussed the present and future environmental advantages of AI, but they also underlined how critical it is to take the hazards into account. For instance, the research highlighted the vital significance of supported by the regulatory knowledge and supervision required for AI-based technology to facilitate sustainable development and prevent exceptions to safety, ethical, and transparency criteria [29], examining the potential effects of AI on society, the environment, and the economy in addition to its development in specific sectors [30].

As stated by Cuen [31], a sustainable approach to AI is necessary considering these unwanted externalities. This includes a shift to sustainable AI infrastructure as well as an environmentally conscious technological viewpoint [32, 33]. To facilitate the green and sustainable development of artificial intelligence, or the green AI approach, technology must be used impartially (apart from positive discrimination or reasonable environmental biases), inclusively, consistently, ethically, and responsibly, with the goal of addressing Earth's development issues in a sustainable way. This method of applying AI to problems related to sustainable development and making more sustainable use of AI will also support the development of smart cities [34].

4 Communications, Computer Science, and Environmental Sensing

After discussing some of the political and overarching questions related to green AI, we will now define and discuss the questions related to the development of digital infrastructure for green AI. Our goal is to discuss these infrastructure issues together with the overarching questions and provide a holistic overview so that the various communities working on policy and infrastructure research can understand these interdisciplinary issues and collaborate to develop holistic and globally optimal solutions.

These intelligent systems and applications necessitate a certain degree of intelligence that improves our capacity to interact with, perceive, and respond to our surroundings, as well as to evaluate them and make prompt, efficient, and sustainable decisions [35]. By 2030, it is anticipated that there will be 25 billion IoT devices worldwide [36], It thus raises the needs for data processing, communications, storage, and pre-processing. Artificial Intelligence (AI) serves as the brain of intelligence, conducting analysis and making decisions.

The notion of "environmental sensing» as mentioned in Table 2 below is defined here as both physical and virtual green sensing that enables triple bottom line (social, environmental, and economic) sustainability to support the development of green AI at the policy and infrastructure levels. To perceive and quantify social, environmental, and economic sustainability, the concept suggests developing techniques and technologies.

We include issues like security, privacy, human safety, ethical standards and compliance, and so forth in our concept of environmental sensing because they have an impact on sustainability. These techniques and technologies ought to be environmentally friendly in terms of energy consumption and efficiency. Green sensing, encompassing both physical and virtual techniques, is essential for achieving triple bottom line sustainability. By focusing on energy efficiency, social responsibility, and environmental impact, green sensing aligns AI development with global sustainability goals.

What are some possible instances of green sensing techniques and technologies that fall under the broadly defined definition of green sensing that we discussed above? Green sensors are physical sensors that assess the pollution and sustainability of urban

Table. 2. Environmental Sensing Techniques and Technologies.

Technique/Technology	Description	Benefits
Environmental Sensors	Physical sensors that assess pollution and sustainability	Supports environmental and social sustainability
Energy-Saving Strategies	Power cycling, wake-up radio, sensor selection/programming	Reduces energy consumption
Adaptive Detection	Adjusts sensor selection based on context and application	Enhances efficiency and context-specific use
Energy Harvesting	Utilizes renewable energies for detection	Eco-friendly data collection

infrastructure [37]. Because it may identify people's suffering and possible health risks to those who reside in or pass through that region, it can also be referred to as a green sensor for social sustainability (or a so-social sustainability sensor) [38].

The word "environmental sensing" has a considerably wider definition than it had in the past, when it was used to describe energy-saving techniques utilized in the sensing process. The phrase has mostly been used in relation to wireless sensor networks (WSN) thus far [39].

Power cycling (turning the radio on and off periodically to conserve energy), wake-up radio (turning the radio on and off when prompted), sensor selection or programming (choosing or programming a subset of sensors rather than all sensors), adaptive detection (adjusting sensor selection based on context and application), and other methods are examples of energy-saving strategies. Energy harvesting strategies using all sensors or a selection of sensors utilizing renewable energies or electrical signals have also been developed to make the detection process more ecologically friendly [40].

For analysis, the data gathered by the Internet of Things and other media (Table 1) is typically sent to a central point, like a cloud data center or main node. The quantity of energy used to transmit data over the network is astounding. As a result, numerous technologies have been created to increase network efficiency and lower the energy needed for data transmission (Table 3).

Many data pruning techniques, like data compression, have been created to lower communication and bandwidth requirements in addition to minimizing data output through the many ecological detection systems previously discussed.

Mohammed et al. [40] recommended the UbiPriSEQ framework, which seeks to optimize energy efficiency, security, privacy, and quality of service (QoS) in a comprehensive and flexible manner. The authors reported a deep reinforcement learning (DRL) implementation of the suggested framework, which enables policy development and decision-making concerning critical parameters like transmit power, the selection of fog nodes to offload data and processing, and so on.

The authors reported a deep reinforcement learning (DRL) implementation of the suggested framework, which enables policy development and decision-making concerning critical parameters like transmit power, the selection of fog nodes to offload data and processing, and so on.

Table 3. Data Transmission and Network Efficiency Technologies

Technology/Method	Purpose	Energy Impact	Example
Data Compression	Reduces data size for transmission	Decreases network energy use	IoT data centers
DRL-based UbiPriSEQ Framework	Balances energy efficiency, security, and quality of service	Optimizes network operations	Mohammed et al.
Power cycling	Turns radio on and off periodically	Saves energy during transmission	Wireless sensor networks
Adaptive Detection	Adjusts sensor use based on context	Enhances efficiency	Smart city applications

5 Conclusion

This perspective paper makes an invaluable contribution to the emerging field of Green AI by addressing the intersection of policy, infrastructure, and sustainability. While the field of AI continues to expand rapidly, with disruptive applications and exponential technological advancements [41], the absence of robust, sustainable practices presents significant risks for both society and the environment [42]. Without timely and effective government intervention, "business as usual" will likely result in long-term negative consequences [43].

Green AI can significantly improve urban infrastructure, as demonstrated in Amsterdam's smart grid system and Singapore's AI-driven water management system. These examples demonstrate how AI can optimize energy distribution, reduce carbon emissions, and support sustainability.

Our systematic review of over 150 articles sourced from Scopus, Google Scholar, and Web of Science revealed that many policy obstacles impede the adoption of Green AI. The most pressing issue is the need for comprehensive ethical and legal guidelines for AI deployment. As highlighted by Dwivedi et al. [43] key policy concerns include digital divides, data deficiencies, ethics, misuse protection, accountability, transparency, and equity. Frameworks and empirical data support the necessity for responsible AI frameworks; studies show that transparent AI systems can build public trust and foster more inclusive development.

Despite the efforts of some nations, such as the UK, Germany, and Singapore, which have begun developing AI ethical frameworks and regulatory guidelines, global legislation remains insufficient [44]. To address these gaps, governments must establish policies that integrate the perspectives of all stakeholders, public and private sectors, the scientific community, and the public. This inclusive approach is essential for ensuring that AI technologies align with sustainability, fairness, and efficiency.

In conclusion, advancing Green AI requires collaborative efforts across sectors to promote sustainable and intelligent urban growth. By incorporating ethical standards and environmental considerations into AI policies, we can work towards achieving the United Nations' Sustainable Development Goals (SDGs). As Fischer emphasizes [45], "To build smart cities and a sustainable future, we must work to make AI an egalitarian, sustainable, and efficient technology.“ This modernized "green" approach will help transform our cities into smarter, more resilient, and eco-friendly environments, ultimately benefiting society.

References

1. Ahirwar, R., Tripathi, A.K.: E-waste management: a review of recycling process, environmental and occupational health hazards, and potential solutions. Environ. Nanotechnol. Monitor. Manage. **15**, 100409 (2021). https://doi.org/10.1016/j.enmm.2020.100409
2. Allam, Z., Dhunny, Z.A.: On Big Data, Artificial Intelligence and Smart Cities - ScienceDirect (2019). <https://www.sciencedirect.com/science/article/abs/pii/S0264275118315968> accessed 31 October 2024
3. Angelidou, M.: Strategic Planning for the Development of Smart Cities (PhD Thesis) (2014)
4. Bendell, J.C., et al.: Clinical Activity and Safety of Cobimetinib (Cobi) and Atezolizumab in Colorectal Cancer (CRC). Journal of Clinical Oncology **34**(15_suppl), 3502 (2016). https://doi.org/10.1200/JCO.2016.34.15_suppl.3502
5. Bibri, S.E., Krogstie, J.: Smart sustainable cities of the future: an extensive interdisciplinary literature review. Sustainable Cities and Society **31**, 183–212 (2017). https://doi.org/10.1016/j.scs.2017.02.016
6. Bram, S., Vestergren, S.: Emergency Response Systems: Concepts, Features, Evaluation and Design. Linköping University Electronic Press (2012). <https://urn.kb.se/resolve?urn=urn:nbn:se:liu:diva-75477> accessed 31 October 2024
7. Calzada, I., Cobo, C.: Unplugging: deconstructing the smart city. Journal of Urban Technology (2015). <https://doi.org/10.1080/10630732.2014.971535> accessed 31 October 2024
8. Trettin, C., Lăzăroiu, G., Grecu, I., Grecu, G.: CEEOL - Article Detail (2019). <https://www.ceeol.com/search/article-detail?id=804061> accessed 1 November 2024
9. Dhar, P.: The Carbon Impact of Artificial Intelligence. Nature Machine Intelligence **2**(8), 423–25 (2020). https://doi.org/10.1038/s42256-020-0219-9
10. Dwivedi, Y.K., et al.: Artificial Intelligence (AI): Multidisciplinary Perspectives on Emerging Challenges, Opportunities, and Agenda for Research, Practice and Policy. Int. J. Info. Manage. **57**, 101994 (2021). https://doi.org/10.1016/j.ijinfomgt.2019.08.002
11. Fisher, D.H.: Computing and AI for a Sustainable Future. IEEE Intell. Syst. **26**(6), 14–18 (2011). https://doi.org/10.1109/MIS.2011.98
12. Friha, O.: Mohamed Amine Ferrag, Burak Kantarci, Burak Cakmak, Arda Ozgun, and Nassira Ghoualmi-Zine, 'LLM-Based Edge Intelligence: A Comprehensive Survey on Architectures, Applications, Security and Trustworthiness. IEEE Open J. Comm. Soc. **5**, 5799–5856 (2024). https://doi.org/10.1109/OJCOMS.2024.3456549
13. Girasa, R.: Artificial Intelligence as a Disruptive Technology: Economic Transformation ... - Rosario Girasa - Google Livres (2020). <https://books.google.co.ma/books?hl=fr&lr=&id=QHDJDwAAQBAJ&oi=fnd&pg=PR8&ots=fHv6C1ddxH&sig=1BEf3vaQMExrzp0cD4W061fP3Bk&redir_esc=y#v=onepage&q&f=false> accessed 1 November 2024
14. Goralski, M.A., Tan, T.K.: Artificial Intelligence and Sustainable Development. The Int. J. Manage. Educ. **18**(1), 100330 (2020). https://doi.org/10.1016/j.ijme.2019.100330
15. Grübler, A., Nakićenović, N., Victor, D.G.: Dynamics of energy technologies and global change. Energy Policy **27**(5), 247–80 (1999). https://doi.org/10.1016/S0301-4215(98)00067-6
16. Gupta, V., Tripathi, S., De, S.: Green sensing and communication: a step towards sustainable IoT systems. J. Indian Inst. Sci. **100**(2), 383–98 (2020). https://doi.org/10.1007/s41745-020-00163-8

17. Holst, A.: IoT Connections Worldwide 2022–2033. Statista (2021). <https://www.statista.com/statistics/1183457/iot-connected-devices-worldwide/> accessed 1 November 2024
18. Jin, L., Duan, K., Tang, X.: What is the relationship between technological innovation and energy consumption? empirical analysis based on provincial panel data from China. Sustainability **10**(1), 145 (2018). https://doi.org/10.3390/su10010145
19. Kitchin, R.: The Data Revolution: Big Data, Open Data, Data Infrastructures and Their Consequences. SAGE (2014)
20. Kostas, M., Francisco, C.J., Tan, Y.: Knowledge-Based Development for Cities and Societies: Integrated Multi-Level Approaches: Integrated Multi-Level Approaches. IGI Global (2010)
21. Lauterbach, A.: Artificial Intelligence and Policy: Quo Vadis? Digital Policy, Regulation and Governance **21**(3), 238–63 (2019). https://doi.org/10.1108/DPRG-09-2018-0054
22. Batty, M.: Artificial Intelligence and Smart Cities - Michael Batty, 2018 (2018) <https://doi.org/10.1177/2399808317751169> accessed 31 October 2024
23. Makridakis, S.: The Forthcoming Artificial Intelligence (AI) Revolution: Its Impact on Society and Firms. Futures **90**, 46–60 (2017). https://doi.org/10.1016/j.futures.2017.03.006
24. Alahi, M.E.E.: Integration of IoT-Enabled Technologies and Artificial Intelligence (AI) for Smart City Scenario: Recent Advancements and Future Trends <https://www.mdpi.com/1424-8220/23/11/5206> accessed 31 October 2024
25. Alsharif, M.H., Kim, S.: Energy Harvesting Techniques for Wireless Sensor Networks/Radio-Frequency Identification: A Review (2019). <https://www.mdpi.com/2073-8994/11/7/865> accessed 1 November 2024
26. Nappo, N.: Use of Remote Sensing Techniques for Monitoring the Impacts of Ground Movements on Structures and Infrastructure (2022) <https://irinsubria.uninsubria.it/handle/11383/2128448> accessed 31 October 2024
27. Rizi, P., Hosein, M., Seno, S.A.H.: A systematic review of technologies and solutions to improve security and privacy protection of citizens in the smart city. Internet of Things **20**, 100584 (2022). https://doi.org/10.1016/j.iot.2022.100584
28. Roberts, T.: Smart city governance: a comparison of models and COVID-19 related Implications within the GTA (2022) <http://hdl.handle.net/10012/18075> accessed 31 October 2024
29. Russell, S.J., Norvig, P.: Artificial Intelligence : A Modern Approach. Pearson (2016) <https://thuvienso.hoasen.edu.vn/handle/123456789/8967> accessed 31 October 2024
30. Copland, S.: Anti-Politics and Global Climate Inaction: The Case of the Australian Carbon Tax - Simon Copland, 2020 (2020). <https://doi.org/10.1177/0896920519870230> accessed 31 October 2024
31. Gupta, S., et al.: Assessing whether artificial intelligence is an enabler or an inhibitor of sustainability at indicator level - ScienceDirect <https://www.sciencedirect.com/science/article/pii/S2666691X21000208> accessed 31 October 2024
32. Sadowski, J., Pasquale, F.: The Spectrum of Control: A Social Theory of the Smart City. Social Science Research Network (2015) <https://papers.ssrn.com/abstract=2653860> accessed 31 October 2024
33. Lee, S.-H., Yigitcanlar, T., Han, J.-H., Leem, Y.-T.: Ubiquitous Urban Infrastructure: Infrastructure Planning and Development in Korea: Innovation: Vol 10, No 2–3 (2014) <https://doi.org/10.5172/impp.453.10.2-3.282> accessed 1 November 2024
34. Sarker, P.K., Marco Lau, C.K., Pradhan, A.K.: Asymmetric Effects of Climate Policy Uncertainty and Energy Prices on Bitcoin Prices. Innovation and Green Development **2**(2), 100048 (2023). https://doi.org/10.1016/j.igd.2023.100048
35. Schwab, K.: Fourth Industrial Revolution - Google Scholar (2016). <https://scholar.google.com/scholar?hl=fr&as_sdt=0%2C5&q=schwab+k+2016+fourth+industrial+revolution&oq=Schwab%2C+K.+%282016%29.> accessed 31 October 2024

36. Smuha, N.: 'From a "Race to AI" to a "Race to AI Regulation": Regulatory Competition for Artificial Intelligence: Law. Innovation and Technology **13**(1) (2021) <https://doi.org/10.1080/17579961.2021.1898300> accessed 1 November 2024
37. Song, M.-L., Cao, S.-P., Wang, S.-H.: The impact of knowledge trade on sustainable development and environment-biased technical progress. Technol. Forecast. Soc. Chang. **144**, 512–23 (2019). https://doi.org/10.1016/j.techfore.2018.02.017
38. Al Shafian, S.: Integrating Machine Learning and Remote Sensing in Disaster Management: A Decadal Review of Post-Disaster Building Damage Assessment' <https://www.mdpi.com/2075-5309/14/8/2344> accessed 31 October 2024
39. Wang, Y., et al.: Decision-making driven by driver intelligence and environment reasoning for high-level autonomous vehicles: a survey. IEEE Trans. Intel. Transport. Sys. **24**(10), 10362–81 (2023). https://doi.org/10.1109/TITS.2023.3275792
40. Chen, Y., Sanesi, G., Li, X., Chen, W.Y., Lafortezza, R.: Remote Sensing and Urban Green Infrastructure - Urban Remote Sensing - Wiley Online Library (2021). <https://doi.org/10.1002/9781119625865.ch20> accessed 31 October 2024
41. Yigitcanlar, T., Foth, M., Kamruzzaman, M.: Towards Post-Anthropocentric Cities: Reconceptualizing Smart Cities to Evade Urban Ecocide. Journal of Urban Technology **26**(2), 147–52 (2019). https://doi.org/10.1080/10630732.2018.1524249
42. Yigitcanlar, T., Kamruzzaman, M.: Planning, Development and Management of Sustainable Cities: A Commentary from the Guest Editors. Sustainability **7**(11), 14677–88 (2015). https://doi.org/10.3390/su71114677
43. Yigitcanlar, T., et al.: Can cities become smart without being sustainable? a systematic review of the literature. Sustainable Cities and Society **45**, 348–65 (2019). https://doi.org/10.1016/j.scs.2018.11.033
44. Yigitcanlar, T., Mehmood, R., Corchado, J.M.: Green artificial intelligence: towards an efficient sustainable and equitable technology for smart cities and futures. Sustainability **13**(16), 8952 (2021). https://doi.org/10.3390/su13168952
45. Zhou, Y., Kankanhalli, A.: AI regulation for smart cities: challenges and principles. In: Estevez, E., Pardo, T.A., Scholl, H.J. (eds.) Smart Cities and Smart Governance: Towards the 22nd Century Sustainable City, pp. 101–18. Springer International Publishing (2021). https://doi.org/10.1007/978-3-030-61033-3_5

Rectangular Microstrip Patch Antenna Design and Performance Analysis for Wireless Applications

Mohammed Bendaoued[1], Hassan Elmajid[2], Anouar Es-saleh[3], Soufian Lakrit[4], Nabil El Fezazi[5,6], and Teresa Alvarez[7(✉)]

[1] LMEET Laboratory, Faculty of Sciences and Technology, Hassan I University, Settat, Morocco
[2] Research Team in Smart Communications, Mohammed V University, E3S, Research Center, EMI, Rabat, Morocco
[3] Mathematics and Information Systems Laboratory, FP of Nador, Mohammed First University, Oujda, Morocco
[4] Mathematics and Information Systems Laboratory, EST of Nador, Mohammed First University, Oujda, Morocco
[5] IMD-E, Higher School of Technology of Dakhla, Ibn Zohr University, Agadir, Morocco
[6] LISAC Laboratory, Faculty of Sciences Dhar El Mehraz, Sidi Mohammed Ben Abdellah University, Fez, Morocco
[7] Industrial Engineering School, Dr. Mergelina S/N, University of Valladolid, 47005 Valladolid, Spain

teresa.alvarez.alvarez@uva.es

Abstract. In the paper, a new technique for building a multi-band antenna array with rectangular split-ring resonators (SRRs) is described. The antenna's analysis and design are studied using simulations. On a low-cost FR4 substrate with a total area of 31,84 × 26,06 mm2, the antenna is mounted. The antenna array based on SRR exhibits three-band resonances with good gain characteristics. The simulations focus on calculating resonance frequencies, return loss, and radiation patterns in order to confirm the practicality and applicability of the proposed antenna concept. The Method of Moments (MOM) in Advanced Design System (ADS) software serves as the basis for the electromagnetic solution used in these simulations. Working inside the 3.5 GHz, 4 GHz, and 4.22 GHz bands. a verified S11 value of less than -10 dB suggests that the impedance matching of this antenna is adequate. It offers gains for the appropriate 6.6 dBi, 7.20 dBi, and 6.3 dBi frequency ranges. The antenna is compatible with WLAN (Wireless Local Area Network) 5G (fifth-generation technology standard for cellular networks), LTE (Long Term Evolution), and WiMAX (Worldwide Interoperability for Microwave Access: wireless broadband communication standards based on the IEEE 802.16 well suited for rural areas) wireless network systems, particularly those operating in the sub-6 GHz band. Some of the main features of this antenna are its symmetric radiation patterns, modest size, planar design, and stable gain. These characteristics make it a viable choice for modern S-band microwave wireless communication applications, especially for gadgets that run at frequencies lower than 6 GHz.

I. Aboudrar et al. (Eds.): ICESST 2024, SUCI, pp. 563–571, 2025.
https://doi.org/10.1007/978-3-031-86705-7_53

Keywords: SRR · Microstrip Patch Antenna · Triple band · High Gain · ADS · Wireless communicationFirst Section

1 Introduction

The Internet of Things (IoT), industrial automation, and high-speed data transmission are just a few of the new uses that the fifth generation (5G) cellular network is expected to make possible. Antenna design, or antenna array design for mobile devices, is one of the key components of a successful 5G deployment. The constant desire to improve the quality of information transmission is what motivates this development. The fact that the propagation medium is not homogenous makes electromagnetic wave propagation difficult, which poses a serious problem for wireless communications [1–4]. This phenomenon, which is exacerbated by numerous diffractions and reflections, often results from the superposition and constructive or destructive interference of various signal channels, disrupting the received signal and perhaps causing transmission errors. 5G mobile connections have gone from 5 million in 2018 to more than 1500 million at the present moment [5]. High data transfer speeds, millisecond-level latency, extremely high traffic volume density, ultra-dense connections, improved spectrum efficiency, and cost-effectiveness are some of the unique characteristics of 5G wireless communications that distinguish it apart from earlier generations. The 3.4–3.6 GHz and 4–6 GHz bands are among the designated frequency bands that the ITU has set aside for 5G communications [6–12]. Due to this allotment, microwave circuits must be designed in a way that is lightweight, small, affordable, and exhibit precise electromagnetic properties. Particularly well-suited to fulfill these needs are planar structures. Strategies like planar microwave circuits with metamaterials are some of the methods used to deal with these design issues. Additional benefits of resonant-type structures include control over operating frequency bandwidth, frequency selectivity, and multi-band structure design [13-14]. The integration of these resonators with planar antennas makes the development of multiband antennas easier. In this paper, we investigate how to provide multiband capability for planar antennas by using Split-Ring Resonator (SRR) resonators. Through the optimization of the array using SRR components, we have constructed and verified an antenna array operating at 3.5 GHz, 4 GHz, and 4.22 GHz, therefore creating different resonant frequency bands. In conclusion, we go over the simulation findings, emphasizing the effects of the number of SRR cells and radiation performance.

2 Design Procedure for Multiband Antenna Array

The first step of the project involves designing a rectangular patch antenna with a resonance frequency of about 3.5 GHz utilizing narrow-band microstrip technology. The base element, which is installed on an affordable FR4 substrate with a relative dielectric constant of 4.4, a loss tangent of 0.025, and a thickness of 1.6 mm, is described in this part along with the design processes that were used to validate it. We used mathematical equations that describe the rectangular patch antenna to find the dimensions of the antenna (as shown in Fig. 1) that meet the given requirements. The dimensions that resulted in are as follows:

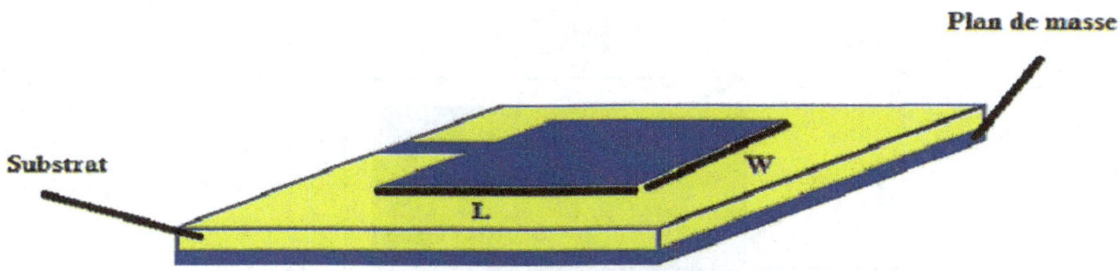

Fig. 1. Configuration of a rectangular microstrip patch antenna. Length: L = 19.97 mm, Width: W = 26.06

Once the patch antenna's dimensions were established, simulations were run via the Advanced Design System (ADS) program, which in this case made use of the Momentum electromagnetic simulator built right into the program. Maxwell's electromagnetic equations for planar structures on a multilayer dielectric substrate are solved numerically by Momentum [1] using a method of moments. As shown in Fig. 2, where the real input impedance is 200 ohms and the imaginary component is zero, the input impedance of the antenna at resonance was ascertained using this simulation.

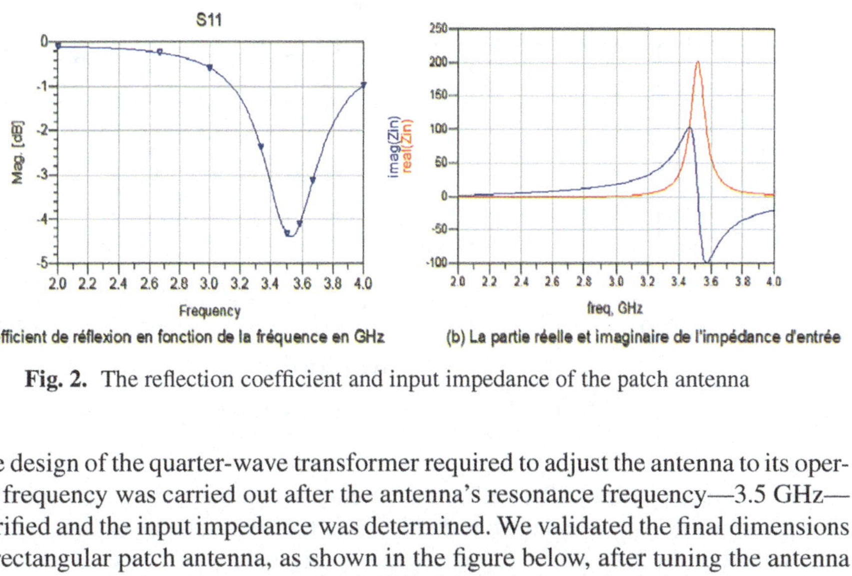

Fig. 2. The reflection coefficient and input impedance of the patch antenna

The design of the quarter-wave transformer required to adjust the antenna to its operational frequency was carried out after the antenna's resonance frequency—3.5 GHz—was verified and the input impedance was determined. We validated the final dimensions of the rectangular patch antenna, as shown in the figure below, after tuning the antenna length to center the frequency around 3.5 GHz. Linecalc is a calculation program integrated into ADS that links physical dimensions to electrical dimensions (electrical length and input impedance) (Fig. 3).

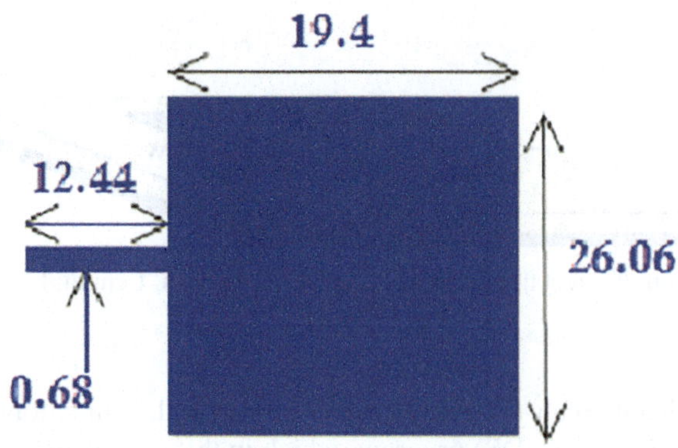

Fig. 3. Final dimensions of the rectangular patch antenna

With a bandwidth of 71 MHz, a relatively narrow band, and a reflection coefficient of −10 dB, the antenna is well suited to the resonant frequency of 3.5 GHz (Fig. 4).

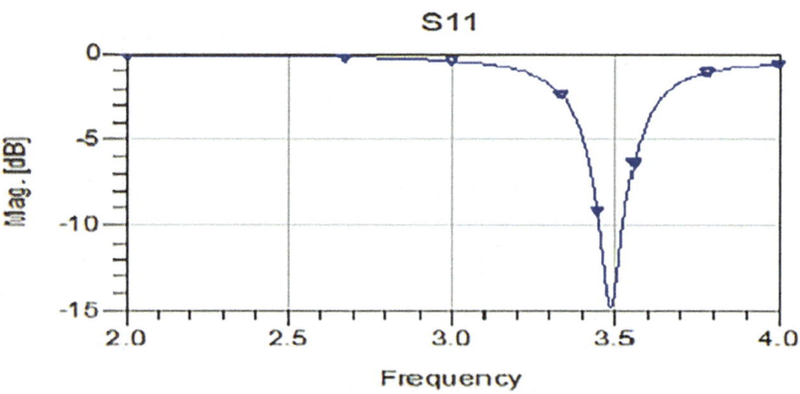

Fig. 4. Reflection coefficient versus frequency

We so connected the SRR cell at the antenna width since the patch antenna may be represented as two radiating slots divided by a transmission line of equal length. We achieved the multi-band antenna array depicted in Fig. 6 through a series of optimizations and a parametric examination of the SRR resonator's dimensions (Fig. 5).

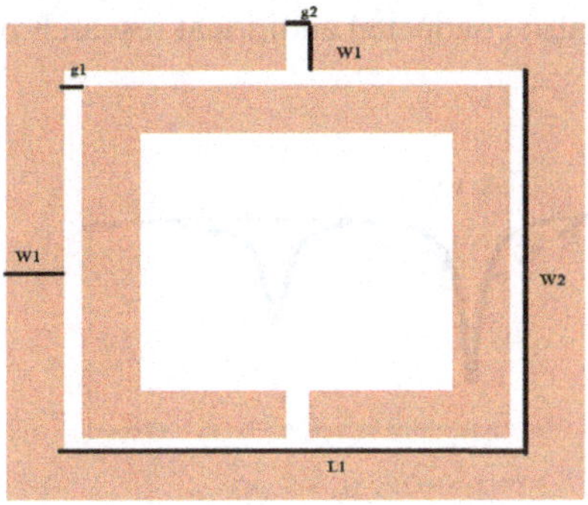

Fig. 5. Optimized SRR cell

The dimensions of the optimized resonator are shown in the following table (Table 1).

Table 1. Optimized dimensions of the SRR resonator

Parameter	mm
L1	3 .5
W1	0.5
W2	3 .4
g1	0.15
g2	0.2

The reflection coefficient's fluctuation as a function of "g" is depicted in the following picture, which demonstrates that multi-band behavior approaches with decreasing "g".

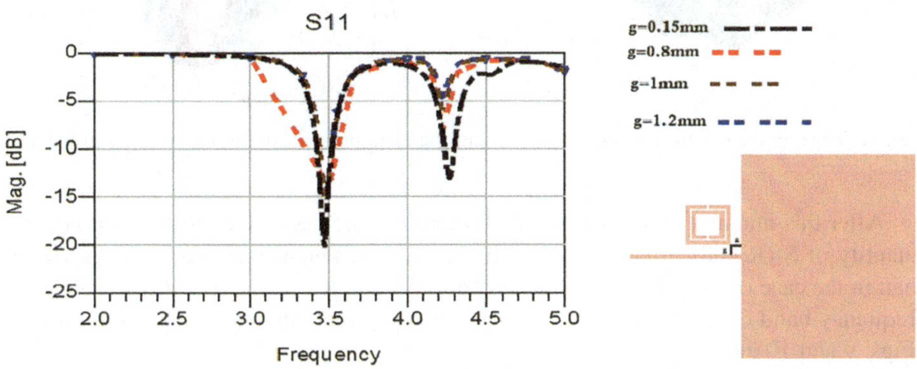

Fig. 6. The reflection coefficient as a function of frequency in GHz for different values of "g".

As seen in Fig. 7, we also conducted additional research on the location of the SRR cell around the patch.

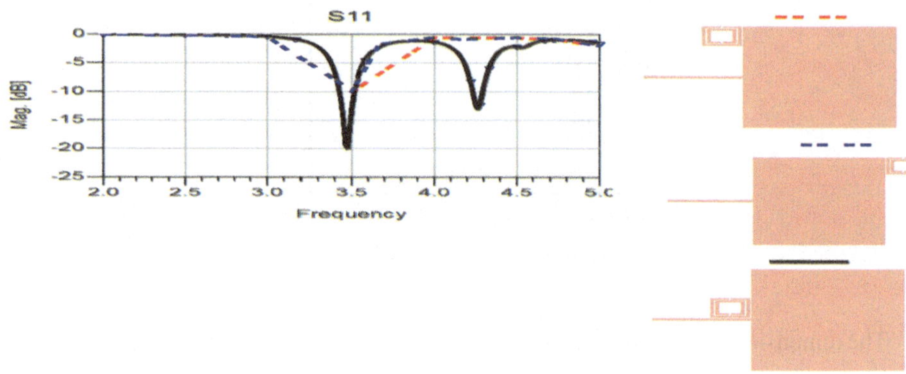

Fig. 7. The reflection coefficient as a function of frequency in GHz for different positions of the SRR resonator

We verified a multi-band patch antenna array (Fig. 7) with two application bands after conducting various parametric studies on the resonator's dimensions and position in relation to the radiating element. The first band, centered at 3.5 GHz, has a high gain of 6.3 dBi for WiMAX applications, while the second band, centered at 4.25 GHz, is for aeronautical radio navigation applications. Its low gain of 0.53 dBi can be used for short-range applications. For the two directional operating bands, this antenna structure's radiation pattern is displayed in the image below (Fig. 8).

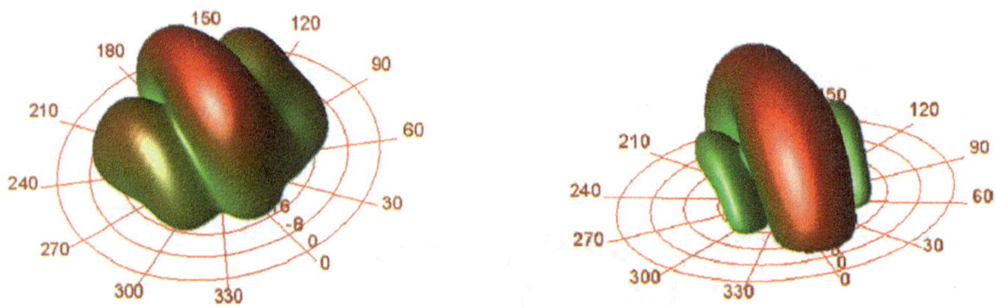

Fig. 8. The radiation pattern of the proposed multiband antenna array for the two operating bands

After this antenna shape was verified, more research was done to find out how the quantity of SRR cells affected the patch antenna's resonance. It was later discovered that, in the case of two SRR cells connected to the patch antenna (Fig. 6), an additional frequency band centered at 4 GHz emerges, causing the antenna to become multiband (Figs. 9 and 10 and Table 2).

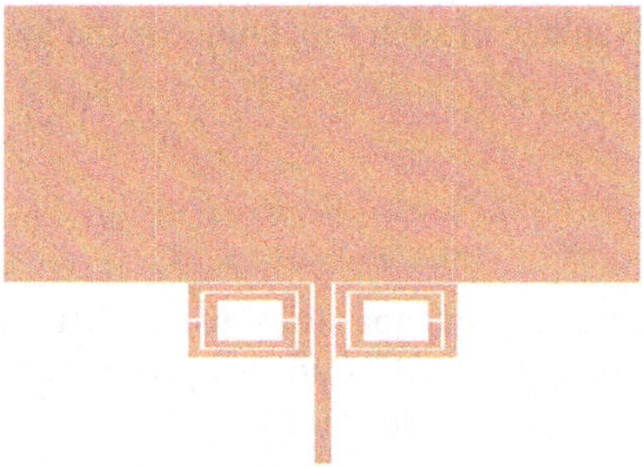

Fig. 9. The patch antenna coupled with two identical SRR resonators

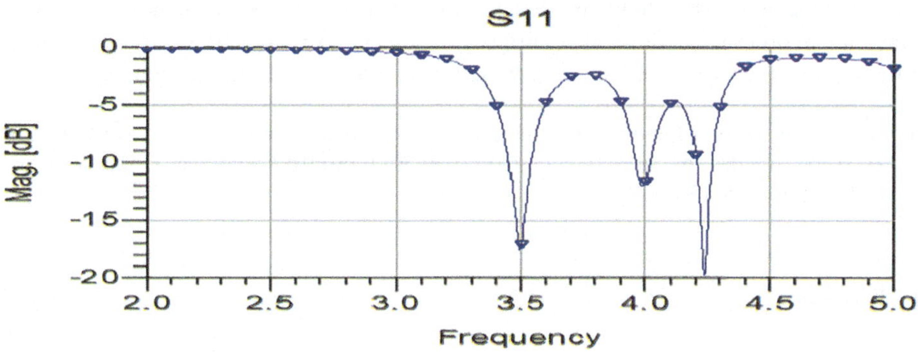

Fig. 10. Reflection coefficient as a function of frequency in GHz

Table 2. Comparison of the Proposed Antenna with Previous Designs

REFERENCES	Operating Frequencies (GHz)	PEAK GAIN (dBi)
[15]	3 .9	4.7
[16]	2.92	4.31
[17]	2.493	3.2
[19]	2.77	2.45
This work	3.5 4 4.22	6.3 6.6 7.20

We can conclude that increasing the number of cells makes the antenna multi-band, but we can see that radiation performance is degraded because for this antenna, for example at 4 GHz, we obtain a negative gain, which represents a very low radiated power. This study has demonstrated the feasibility of designing and building multi-band narrow-band antennas using well-optimized SRR cells coupled with the radiating element. The major disadvantage of such a technique is the loss of gain, and consequent loss of radiation.

3 Conclusion

We have examined a multiband antenna array using SRR resonators in this work.It can do multiband operations since SRRs are integrated with the patch antenna. The SRRs' dimensions are adjusted to produce the best possible features and specifications. In order to accommodate Wi-MAX, 5G, and aeronautical radio navigation applications, the proposed array antenna array works at the 3.5, 4, and 4.25 GHz frequency bands. High gain and directed patterns are provided by the recommended array arrangement. With a physical area of 31,84 $\times$ 26,06 mm2, the proposed array is based on an inexpensive FR4 substrate. In order to accommodate different wireless communication system standards, different antenna structures can be designed using the same design technique.

Acknowledgments and Funding Information. Teresa Alvarez was funded by TED2021-129716B-I00, funded by https://doi.org/10.13039/501100011033 and the European Union "nextgenerationeu/PRTR".

References

1. Bendaoued, M., Mandry, R., El Abdellaoui, L., Fouad, A., Latrach, M., Lakhssassi, A.: Coplanar waveguide low pass filter based on square complementary split ring resonator with wide rejection. Telkomnika (Telecommunication, Computing, Electronics and Control) **18**(5), 2314–2319 (2020)
2. Bendaoued, M., Mandry, R., Tajmouati, A., Latrach, M., Otman, O.: A new design of a printed CPW Band notched UWB antenna. Int. J. Microw. Optic. Technol. **16**(3) (2021)
3. Bendaoued, M., et al.: Design of a UWB coplanar antenna with step graded ground plane for 5G and modern wireless communication applications. J. Nano- and Electr. Phys. **15**(4), 04024 (2023)
4. Anouar, E.S., Mohammed, B., Soufian, L., Mohamed, A., Ahmed, F.: A novel two-port MIMO configuration in dual band 26/38 GHz with high isolation in the ground plane for 5G applications. In: International Conference on Digital Technologies and Applications, 278–288. Springer Nature Switzerland, Cham (2023)
5. Bendaoued, M., et al.: Split Ring Resonator (SRR) Incorporated Patch Array Antenna with Enhanced Gain and Bandwidth for 5.8 GHz WLAN Applications. In: The Proceedings of the International Conference on Smart City Applications, pp. 739–746. Springer International Publishing, Cham (2022)
6. Pandeeswari, R., Raghavan, S.: Microw. Opt. Technol. Lett. **56**(10), 2388 (2014)
7. Attia, H., Yousefi, L., Bait-Suwailam, M.M., Boybay, M.S., Ramahi, O.M., Antenn, I.E.E.E.: Wireless Propag. Lett. **10**, 1198 (2011)
8. Pandeeswari, R., Raghavan, S.: Microw. Opt. Technol. Lett. **57**(2), 292 (2015)
9. Pandeeswari, R., Raghavan, S.: Microw. Opt. Technol. Lett. **57**, 2413 (2015)
10. Pandeeswari, R.: Prog. Electromag. Res. C **80**, 13 (2018)
11. Rani, R.B., Pandey, S.K.: Prog. Electromag. Res. C **70**, 135 (2016)
12. Bendaoued, M.: Es-Saleh, A., et al.: J. Nano- Electron. Phys. **15**, 04014–04014-4 (2023)

13. Razali, A.R., Bialkowski, M.E., Tsai, F.C.E.: Proc. Asia PacificMicrowave Conference, 2471 (2009)
14. Razali, A.R., Bialkowski, M.E.: IEEE Antenna Wireless Propag. Lett. **8**, 1029 (2009)
15. An, Z., He, M.: Appl. Comput. Electromagn. Soc. J. **35**(1), 10 (2020)
16. Tang, X., et al.: International Workshop onElectromagnetics:Applications and Student Innovation Competition(iWEM) (2019)
17. Gopal, G., Thangakalai, A.: Appl. Comput. Electromag. Soc. J. **35**(1), 16 (2020)

Correction to: Systematic Review of Physical, Chemical, and Biological Approaches for Exosome Isolation Towards Optimizing Methods in Clinical Diagnostics

Ayoub Slalmi, Nabila Rabbah, Ikram Debbarh, Ilham Battas, Hicham Medromi, and Abdelmjid Abourriche

Correction to:
Chapter 54 in: I. Aboudrar et al. (Eds.): *Innovative Technologies on Electrical Power Systems for Smart Cities Infrastructure*, ICESST 2024, https://doi.org/10.1007/978-3-031-86705-7_45

In the original version of the book, the following belated corrections have been incorporated: The author name "Abdlmjid Abouriche" has been changed to "Abdelmjid Abourriche" in the Frontmatter, Backmatter and in Chapter 45.

The updated version of this chapter can be found at
https://doi.org/10.1007/978-3-031-86705-7_45

I. Aboudrar et al. (Eds.): ICESST 2024, SUCI, p. C1, 2025.
https://doi.org/10.1007/978-3-031-86705-7_54

Author Index

I. Aboudrar et al. (Eds.): ICESST 2024, SUCI, pp. 573–575, 2025.
https://doi.org/10.1007/978-3-031-86705-7

The manufacturer's authorised representative in the EU is Springer Nature Customer Service Centre GmbH, Europaplatz 3, 69115 Heidelberg, Germany. If you have any concerns regarding our products, please contact ProductSafety@springernature.com

Printed and bound by CPI Group (UK) Ltd, Croydon, CR0 4YY
30/09/2026
02225573-0016